Return Date

D0432299

5

CONSUMER BEHAVIOR
Theory and practice

Consumer behavior

Theory and practice

C. GLENN WALTERS, Ph.D
Southern Illinois University

1978 Third Edition

RICHARD D. IRWIN, INC. Homewood, Illinois 60430
Irwin-Dorsey Limited Georgetown, Ontario L7G 4B3

Third Edition

2 3 4 5 6 7 8 9 0 MP 5 4 3 2 1 0 9 8

ISBN 0-256-01999-1
Library of Congress Catalog Card No. 77–089788

Printed in the United States of America

Dedicated to
Michael, David, Gregory, and Julie

Preface

Consumer behavior has come a long way since the mid-1960s when it was being introduced into the marketing program. There is no need to justify consumer topics today since the subject is now an integral part of most marketing curriculums. It is recognized that every student, both business and nonbusiness, can benefit from a knowledge of consumer behavior.

This book is written for advanced undergraduate students. Every aspect of its design keeps this point in mind. Several points of this design are worth mentioning. First, the book is developed around consumer theory, concept interrelationships, and decision processes. Consumer theory furnishes the student with information for decision making. Concept interrelationships provide depth and substance to the total entity we call a consumer. The decision process brings into focus the functioning of consumers in practical situations. It is felt this approach provides the most comprehensive presentation of consumer behavior.

Second, a basic knowledge of marketing and the social sciences is assumed. However, it is not assumed that the student remembers every detail of that background. Explanation is provided where it is deemed helpful.

Third, concepts have been selected because of their importance in providing a comprehensive framework of consumer knowledge to undergraduate students. Although these concepts are often difficult, a conscious effort has been made to relate to students, rather than talk down to them. The previous editions of this book have been praised for their tightness of organization and clarity of presentation. I have also attempted to make it interesting.

Fourth, the book offers a balanced approach to consumer research. Experimentation in the field has reached explosive proportions in recent years. Many of the findings are unproven and contradictory. Any attempt to provide every divergent point of view for every concept presented is confusing to the undergraduate and counterproductive to learning. The attempt is made to demonstrate the accepted or reasonable position on various topics, while providing sufficient experimental research to indicate the controversy over as well as the excitement of consumer behavior. The footnotes augment this purpose. Some footnotes refer to specific research findings quoted in the text. Others are used to direct the interested student to important studies that either: (1) provide more in-depth knowledge of the subject under discussion, or (2) demonstrate positions contrary to those taken in the text.

The third edition of *Consumer Behavior* differs in several respects from the earlier editions. The decision section was moved to the front of the book and streamlined. Consumer decisions are just too important to be put off. The assortment and market-related decisions of the earlier editions were integrated into a single decision process. This integration allows for a clear discussion of consumer decisions and reduces student confusion concerning types of decisions. The writing has been tightened and more research findings have been incorporated into the discussion. The entire book has been updated.

ACKNOWLEDGMENTS

Many persons have provided both encouragement for and inputs into this book. The author is indebted to all of them, but especially to the professors who helped mold his perspective, and to his friends and colleagues all over the country. Most specifically he expresses appreciation to Edward J. Laurie, San Jose State University; William H. Brannen, Creighton University; Amin F. El-Drighami, University of Wisconsin-Oshkosh; Bruce Gunn, Florida State University; William Ingram, Memphis State University, Norm Govoni, Babson College; Sidney Bennett, St. Louis University. Their constructive criticism of the second edition as well as their insights and suggestions greatly influenced the direction of the revision. Finally, I express appreciation to my family for their patience and understanding, and a special thanks to Pat who is still the best copy editor and a constant challenge.

December 1977 C. GLENN WALTERS

Contents

PART ONE

The foundation for consumer behavior

This first part of the book is introductory. It contains three chapters:

1. The nature of consumer behavior.
2. Sources of consumer knowledge.
3. Consumer behavior models.

The information underlies the material presented in the remainder of the book. Chapter 1 is a presentation of what constitutes a consumer and contains the rationale, in the form of a model, upon which the book is built. Chapter 2 has a discussion of the sources of consumer information. Chapter 3 contains a presentation of the current status of theoretical development in consumer behavior. It is particularly important that the reader grasp the model presented at the end of Chapter 1. This model provides a frame of reference not only for tying the parts of the book together but also for relating the concepts presented in the individual chapters.

1

The nature of consumer behavior

It is 11:30 on Saturday morning as Mr. Smith wheels his shopping cart through the grocery store. It's a beautiful day for fishing, but Mr. Smith's mind is not on the weather. His mind isn't altogether on grocery shopping either. Mary is tired and fretful in the cart, and Bill has disappeared behind the meat counter. Mr. Smith wishes his wife could have passed up the overtime and run the errands. He has a million things to do—make a bank deposit, pick up the kid's shoes. . . . He wonders, looking at the grocery list, where the tomato paste is located. Absently, Mr. Smith picks up a box of cookies opens it, and hands one to Mary as a pacifier. Mr. Smith moves down the aisle still looking for tomato paste.

This is a completely familiar scene to most Americans. Examples similar to the one described are taking place across the country every day. The buying process is so familiar that we tend to accept it as a casual, uncomplicated act requiring little thought. Seldom do we consider the complex business decisions that make merchandise available when and where we want to purchase it. Even less attention is devoted to the consumer. What types of inner and external forces are at work that cause the individual to want certain products, why are specific brands and stores preferred over others, and what decision processes led to the final choices? In spite of the experience of every American as a consumer, these and similar questions are not fully understood. Such questions go to the very roots of human behavior and must be answered before the marketing executive can develop sound products and effective sales methods to appeal to consumers.

This book is about consumers, and how a better understanding of people, in the process of consuming, can lead to more efficient marketing operations.[1] The book is a marketing text because consumers are a basic ingredient in marketing. The emphasis is on the interrelationships between consumers and marketing organizations, but the perspective is from the consumer's side of the market. This book is a practical book. It deals with generally accepted concepts that can serve both to specify types of consumer information useful to marketers and to provide insights for interpreting these facts. It is aimed at high-level economies such as that of the United States. It is recognized that some points made have little significance for underdeveloped nations.

WHY STUDY CONSUMER BEHAVIOR?

The question often arises in the minds of students, "Why study this or that subject?" The obvious answer to this question is that knowing is always better than not knowing. One never really appreciates how useful any information can be until it is acquired.

The question of why one should study consumer behavior needs a more specific answer. We are all consumers, but the art of consuming is an inexact activity. The direct benefit from a clear understanding of the consumption process is that it can make us all better and more prudent consumers. The improvement can result from:

1. Obtaining greater appreciation of the complexity of decisions facing consumers.
2. A better understanding of our own motives and decision processes as consumers.
3. Sounder choices of products and stores.

A marketing student should be interested in consumers because consumption is one half of the marketing process. In its elemental form, marketing consists of an interaction between a buyer and a seller for the purpose of exchanging goods for money to the mutual benefit of both parties to the transaction. One cannot appreciate this marketing process by observing only the seller. Therefore, a student of marketing has to have a depth of understanding of demand as well as supply. Specifically, knowledge about the consumer provides the only sound basis for making marketing decisions. Markets are selected on the basis of consumer wants, as well as their location, numbers, characteristics, and expenditure patterns.[2] The basis for all sales appeal comes from information about the consumer. To ignore the consumer can lead to disaster in a modern economy.

WHO IS THE CONSUMER?

The consumer lies at the heart of consumer behavior. When we understand individual consumers—their requirements, thought processes, pressures, problems, and actions—we understand consumer behavior. So much emphasis, demands that we specify how the term consumer is used in this book. One of the facts that has made the study of consumer behavior difficult is that few writers define the term "consumer" carefully. We cannot conduct meaningful research designed to explain or convey to others the significance of consumer actions unless we come to grips with, "Who is the consumer?" As we shall see, the answer to this question is not as obvious as one might suspect.

Consumer defined

Observe a man working in the yard. He is using a lawnmower purchased by himself, drinking a soft drink purchased and brought home by his son, and wearing coveralls his wife picked out at his request. Who is the consumer? Well, obviously there are three different situations. The man bought the lawnmower and is using it. The son bought the drink, but the man is using it. The wife bought the coveralls, but the man determined need and is using them. So, is the consumer the one who determined need? The purchaser? The user? The answer to these questions is definitional, and for our purpose, a consumer is defined as:

> *the individual(s) who exercise the right of acquisition and use over goods and services (products) offered for sale by marketing institutions.*

Obviously, by this definition everyone is a consumer, although not everyone is necessarily a consumer of the same products. Consumers may, in some vague way, want products not offered for sale by firms, but these wishes can ordinarily be satisfied only if firms recognize the need and make the necessary goods available. The consumer may purchase to satisfy a personal want or to meet the collective requirements of a family or some similar community.

Consumer identification as a process

The problem with defining a consumer is that we attribute to one individual what is essentially a total process. The *consumption process* involves three interrelated activities:

1. Determine personal or group wants.
2. Seek out and purchase products.
3. Employ products to derive benefits.

As we have pointed out, this process can, and often is, engaged in by several different persons simultaneously.

Table 1–1 illustrates how the consumption process is related to different types of individuals. Specific terms have developed that apply in those cases where more than one person engages in consumption.[3] A *demander*, following the lead of economics, is one who has personal wants. A woman deciding on her particular hair style at the beauty shop is a demander. *Purchaser*, *shopper*, or *customer* are used

Table 1–1
Consumer terms and the consumption process

Terms for those engaged in consumption		*Consumption process*
Consumer or buyer	1. Demander	Determines wants
	2. Purchaser or shopper	Purchases products
	3. User	Employs products

synonymously to indicate one actively engaged in buying. A grocery shopper purchasing for the family fits this description. The *user* is a person who derives satisfaction or benefit from products bought. As you read this book, you are a user.

Consumption may involve any combination of these persons. A couple of examples can make the point. A man (purchaser) buys perfume for his girlfriend (user, demander), at her suggestion. A husband (demander) asks his wife (purchaser) to pick up a six pack of beer for his pals (users) to drink at the weekly poker party.

Consumer, or buyer, are the inclusive terms used when one individual determines personal wants, buys products, and uses those products. Throughout this book, consumer refers to (1) several persons each performing a part of the consumption process or (2) one person who engages in all three activities of consumption. There are places throughout the text where the specialized activities of consumption are pointed out.

Consumer versus influencer

Several people may be involved in a particular purchase decision, but we do not designate them all as consumers. Consider a young woman who has just taken a job to help support her family. She needs a new wardrobe consistent with her changed responsibility. As she shops for her requirements, she may consider her manager's dress preferences, ask a friend about a particular retailer's prices, check several newspaper and radio advertisements for available styles, and consult her husband on looks and fit. What is the status of the manager, the friend, the retailer's promotion, and the husband in this purchase?

Based on our earlier definition, only those persons having the right to purchase or use products are consumers.[4] All other persons who exercise a direct or indirect effect on the consumer are said to have influenced the decision. *Influencers* are persons or things, external to the consumer, that provide advise, information, or pressure to consume in a specific manner.[5] In the above example, the wife is the consumer. The manager, friend, and the advertisements are external influences that may or may not affect the consumer's decision.

Even the husband, in this instance, is an influencer since he did not perform any activity associated with the consumption process. Rather, he acted as an advisor. The difference between a consumer and an influencer is based on participation in consumption and not on marriage or even how much the consumer was affected by the information. Thus the husband may share responsibility as a consumer in one instance and be an influencer in another instance. The same is true for other members of the family.

CONSUMER BEHAVIOR: A PART OF HUMAN BEHAVIOR

Consumer behavior is a subdivision of human behavior, and the understanding of the one depends on clarification of the other.[6] *Human behavior* refers to:

> *the total process whereby the individual interacts with the environment.*

Every thought, feeling or action we have as individuals is a part of human behavior. Our motives for getting out of bed in the morning, our frame of mind toward others upon rising, the sensations we obtain while eating breakfast, and the activities we undertake that guide us through the day are all human behavior.

Consumer behavior is more narrowly conceived. It concerns specific types of human behavior that are market related. The definition can be derived from our earlier understanding of a consumer. In this book, *consumer behavior* is used to mean:

> *those decisions and related activities of persons involved specifically in buying and using economic goods and services (products).*

Consumer behavior includes both mental decisions and physical actions that result from these decisions.[7] Although some social scientists limit the use of "behavior" to observable actions, it is apparent that the reasons and decisions behind the actions involved in both human and consumer behavior are as important to understanding the fields as are the actions themselves.

Clearly, it is not always possible to separate consumer behavior from human behavior. For example, a person may be gossiping about a neighbor while selecting lawn furniture in a retail store. Both activities are human behavior, but only the selection of the lawn furniture is consumer behavior. Separation of the two may be even more difficult for a man or woman working at the office and mulling over the merits of purchasing an outboard versus an inboard motorboat. Perhaps human and consumer behavior occur simultaneously in this case. In spite of the problem of identification, this book is limited to consumer behavior. No attempt is made to generalize about the broader questions of human behavior. Human behavior is considered, but only to the extent that it aids the understanding of the consumption process.

TYPES OF CONSUMERS

Buyers of merchandise can be divided into several types. Some buyers are included in consumer behavior and some are not. Furthermore, knowledge of different consumer types can be used in different ways. At this point, we want to identify these consumer types and relate their importance to marketers.

Potential and realized consumers

One important method of classifying consumers is according to whether they are potential or realized. A given person may, or may not be in the act of buying a particular product or brand. It is important to business to recognize which state the consumer is in. We can identify three possibilities: (1) nonconsumers, (2) potential consumers, and (3) realized consumers. A *nonconsumer* is an individual who has no need for a given product and is not likely to have a need in the foreseeable future. For example, a person living in the tropics, who does not travel, is a nonconsumer of winter sports equipment. A ghetto dweller is a nonconsumer of fur coats and expensive jewelery.

An individual, not currently purchasing, but who may be influenced at some future time to buy is referred to as a *potential consumer*. A large number of potential consumers make a potential market which is available for some business to tap. A person may be a potential for some generic product such as crawfish. The product is excellent, grown almost everywhere, and easily within the means of most Americans. People could be induced to buy if their attitude toward this Louisiana delicacy could be changed. A person may be a potential for a particular product brand or a particular store. A purchaser of Folger's coffee or a customer of Sears is a potential buyer for all other competitors.

Potential consumers are explained by: (1) unawareness of need: (2) low intensity of present need; (3) lack of information concerning available products; (4) purchase from competing firms; or (5) lack of current means to purchase. Potential consumers are important to businesses because these individuals represent a means of increasing sales and extending the company's market.

Realized consumers generally conform to our earlier definition of purchasers or shoppers, since they are engaged in buying. When a business executive says, "She is one of our regular customers," it means that the designated woman is currently negotiating for the firm's products, or that she purchases regularly from the store. The manager means the same thing when instructing a salesperson to "Go wait on that customer." The major task of the business, where current customers are concerned, is keeping them satisfied in order to build repeat sales.

Household and industrial consumers

Any person engaged in the consumption process is a consumer, but these buyers can be identified by the type of market to which they belong. The two major types of markets are household and industrial. The *household market* consists of consumers who buy for personal consumption or to meet the collective needs of the family, or household, unit. Such persons are called household, or final, consumers. The household consumer removes products from the channel of distribution in the sense that there is no further sale by marketing organizations. The final consumer buys for the sole purpose of using up the product in order to obtain satisfaction.

Industrial markets consists of business firms that purchase for resale. Either the product bought by industrial consumers is resold as is; it becomes a part of some finished product that is sold; or it is consumed in the production of finished products. Industrial consumers include: business firms (manufacturers, wholesalers, retailers, business agents, retailers); government (federal, state, and local); and nonprofit organizations (universities, hospitals, churches, etc.). It is common to use the term consumer when referring to households and buyer when referring to either final or business consumers. We adhere to this practice, but this book is concerned only with household consumers. Unless otherwise specified, the term consumer or buyer refers to final consumers.

THE WORLD OF CONSUMERS

The author is a firm believer that any discussion proceeds more smoothly if there is some unifying device upon which all the participants agree. This unifying device, sometimes referred to as a model, stands for the thing or concept under discussion. Any model is basically a device for experimentation or a device for communication. Since this text is student, rather than research, oriented, we need a model to facilitate communications rather than to advance theory. The remainder of the chapter is devoted to such a model.

It is our intent to develop a simple but reasonably accurate model of consumer behavior. Such a model can facilitate discussion in three ways: (1) by specifying components it creates common parameters for discussion, (2) by pointing out relationships among parts it sets the stage for different points of view, and (3) by providing definitions for components everyone converses from a common vantage point. In this section, the broad components of consumer behavior are identified. In later sections the specific variables are identified and related in detail.

Consumer behavior is a complex subject, and there are many disagreements among scholars concerning specific points of the subject. Most serious students of the subject do agree that consumer behavior, in the broadest sense, involves interaction between an individual and his environment as demonstrated in Figure 1–1.[8] There are two types of components in the environment. They are social units, made up of individuals and groups, and business firms.

Figure 1–1

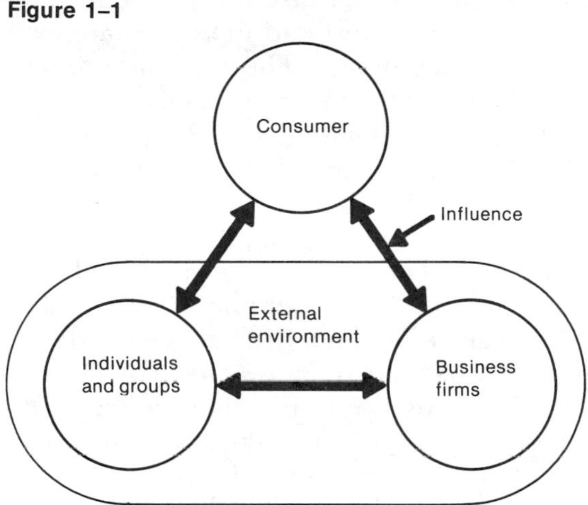

The consumer interacts both with such units as family, a friend, co-workers, etc. and with different types of businesses. The individual groups and business also interact. These interactions involve communications about wants, attitudes, feelings, biases, etc. When we say that there is an interaction among the three mentioned factors, we mean that the influence operates in both directions. The consumer affects and is affected by business and other groups. Furthermore, the effect in any case may be direct or indirect. A firm affects the consumer directly by means of advertisements. A business may also affect a consumer indirectly when a sales job is accomplished on a consumer's coworker, who, in turn, recommends the product to the consumer. Different groups influence each other and then may influence the individual. Individual consumers and groups also affect business. For example, if consumers do not purchase in sufficient quantity, the business may have to adjust its offering of goods and services.

Even businesses influence each other because of competition, and the results filter down to affect both other groups and individual consumers.

PURCHASE DECISION: GOAL OF CONSUMER BEHAVIOR

It has been established that people enter into activities for many purposes other than consumption, but when acting as a buyer, individuals have just one goal in mind. That goal is the satisfaction of their desires by obtaining goods and services.[9] The problems associated with acquiring the products to sustain life and to provide for some comforts face all consumers. Because the solutions to these problems are vital to the existence of most and the economic well-being of all, they are usually not taken lightly. The consumer must make specific types of decisions in order to obtain necessary products.

A list of all the considerations involved with consumer purchase decisions would be too complex to set down at this time, but the basic decision areas can be identified. The consumer must decide whether, what, when, where, and how to purchase. The basic decision is whether to purchase at all or not. This decision can be made before or after entering the market. A consumer may know intuitively that he or she does not want a given product. In this case the decision is simple, and no direct market activity is necessary. On the other hand, the decision may be made after entering the market. It may involve a careful or a superficial search and evaluation of the market.

The decision on what to purchase is directly related to product choices. Consumers seek satisfaction, or benefits, but satisfaction can only be achieved through owning goods and services. Furthermore, the accumulation of products allows consumers to store some satisfaction until needed. Thus, it is typically some perceived deficiency of products that is the stimulus causing consumers to enter the market. The individual may have a deficiency in a particular product normally stocked or may want to expand the total number of products presently held.

When to buy is a basic consumer decision involving product acquisition timing. The individual must decide on a convenient hour of the day, day of the week, and season in which to act. Of course, timing differs for different products. Some purchases lend themselves to habitual timing, but others do not. For example, a person may always grocery shop on Thursday morning, but may purchase hairspray only when the need arises. One consumer may buy early in the season, while another may wait for late season bargains.

Where to purchase can involve much more than the choice of a store. Persons in a small town may buy at home or travel to nearby larger cities. Within a city, choices must be made between downtown and shopping centers, between different shopping centers, and between specific stores. Because consumers often make several purchases, more than one store or trade area may be visited. Furthermore, the trade area and store selected condition the availability of specific product brands, prices, and services that are available to choose from. Obviously, the choice of a store or trade area is an extremely important consumer decision.

The decision on how to purchase is directly related to the others. It concerns, among other decisions, the amount of time and effort to be spent shopping, number of items to seek, whether to charge or pay cash, mode of transportation to use, the route and sequence of store visitation, and whether to shop alone or with others. It should be clear that when the buyer has satisfactorily answered all five questions he or she has made a purchase. How well the consumer answers these questions greatly affects one's standard of living. It is for this reason that the purchase decision is the central issue of consumer behavior.

DETERMINANTS OF CONSUMER BEHAVIOR

It is not enough to know how the consumer decides in a market situation. Our primary interest is in *why* the consumer decides in a certain manner. Thus, since we have established the importance of consumer decision making, we are prepared to discuss the major variables of consumer behavior that caused the consumer to select a particular product. In short, we need a general framework around which to relate the elements of consumer behavior.

The key to consumer behavior lies with the individual. The decision to buy or not to buy is an individual decision. One may accept advice, or even yield to outside pressure, but the purchase decision rests with the individual. Even if a mugger places her gun in your stomach and announces, "Your honor or your life," the decision is still yours. What happens is that information from the environment is taken in by the consumer and integrated into his or her own frame of reference. Such external information may then become the deciding influence on a purchase, but the consumer still makes the decisions on using the information or not, as well as on how to use it.

The marketing manager is interested in both the individual's internal decision process and the environmental influences on the individual. Therefore, we can identify two broad types of consumer behavior variables. They are: (1) variables that are internal to the individual and (2) variables that are external to the individual.[10] We shall call the internal variables *basic determinants,* and the external variables *environmental determinants* or *influences.*

Basic determinants of consumer behavior

It was established that the individual consumer is the ultimate decider of all purchase problems. This importance prompts us to call the variables internal to the individual basic determinants of consumer behavior. These internal variables are also often referred to as *endogeneous variables.*[11] Only these basic variables enter directly into the consumer's decision. Any external factor, often called *exogenous variables,* must operate indirectly by first influencing the basic determinants which, in turn, affect the consumer.

Types of basic determinants. There are four basic consumer variables that control all internal thought processes of the individual consumer: the consumer's needs, motives, personality, and awareness. These basic determinants can be arranged around a wheel as in Figure 1–2. Consumer purchase decisions are placed in the center of the wheel because this variable is the focal point of consumer behavior. The object of consumer behavior is to make sound decisions to the satisfaction of the individual's wants.

Figure 1–2
Basic determinants (internal to the individual)

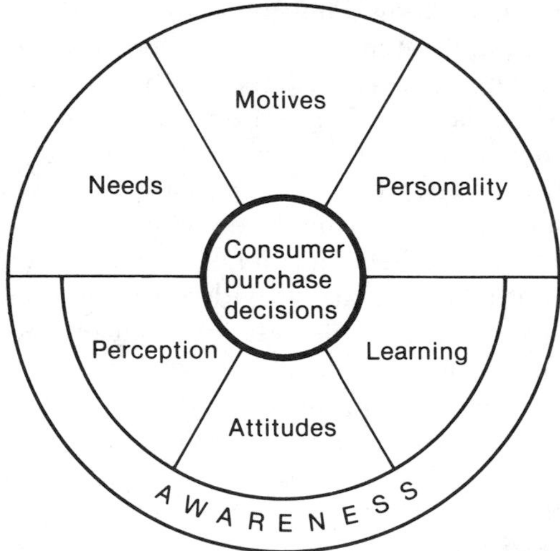

A *need* is defined as any physical or emotional body requirement. In a sense, it is a lack of something useful, required, or desired for any reason. In other words, a need is a condition requiring relief. A *motive* is an impulse or feeling that causes one to do something or act in a certain way. Motives make us aware of our needs and give us a reason for acting on these needs. *Personality* is defined as the human characteristics or traits built into a person that makes each person different from every other person. Motives cause the individual to act on their needs, but it is personality which makes an individual act in a specific manner. *Awareness* is a broad term. It is defined as having knowledge of something through the senses. It is awareness that most directly relates the individual to his external environment. Whereas personality is inward looking at the consumer's being, awareness is outward looking to interpret what that consumer sees, hears, feels, etc.

Consumer awareness is subdivided into three variables. They are perception, attitudes, and learning.[12] All three of these internal variables concern the consumer's external environment. *Perception* is defined as the particular interpretation one gives to objects or ideas observed or otherwise brought to the consumer's attention through the senses. What is referred to as *learning* means any change in the consumer's thoughts, responses, or behavior as a result of practice, experience, or intuition. In a sense it is knowing what was unknown before. *Attitude* is used to mean a broad group of innate human feelings or points of view that pattern behavior.

Relationship between basic determinants. There can be no question, based on the above set of definitions, that there is a direct relationship between the basic determinants of consumer behavior. As a matter of fact, the relationship is so close sometimes that it is difficult to tell where one variable leaves off and another begins. For example, many scholars treat needs and motives as essentially the same thing.[13] The fact is that there is a simultaneous interaction between the basic determinants. An example can aid in clarifying the differences. Such an example is shown below.

Basic determinant	*Example*
Need	Food
Motive	Hunger
Personality	Inclined toward direct action
Awareness	Knowledge that an observed steak will taste good
Consumer decision: Purchase and eat steak	

A person has a basic body requirement for food, but only becomes willing to act when sufficiently motivated by the physical discomfort of hunger. Awareness convinces the consumer that a preferred solution exists in the form of a steak, and since the consumer's personality indicates direct action, the consumer buys and enjoys the steak. However, notice that awareness in the above example involved the three variables under that heading. Knowledge that the steak tastes good was learned, perhaps by experience. Perception brought the steak to the consumer's attention and interpreted its meaning relative to the consumer's need. Attitude was brought into play in the sense that the other factors acting together had already created a favorable predisposition toward eating steak on the part of the consumer. All these variables are interacting simultaneously on the consumer, and it should be apparent that no one is more important than another. Each plays a part, and all four interact to condition the specific action taken by the consumer.

Basic determinants and the purchase decision. A person's needs, motives, personality, and awareness are not controllable at any given point in time. The basic determinants pertain to unconscious, as well as conscious, thought processes, established patterns of thought, innate points of view held, and attitudes and biases already formed in the mind. A person's basic determinants are constantly changing, but the changes are subtle. We seldom plan to change our basic nature; rather, our nature changes as we expand and develop as persons. These changes are slow and evolutionary. What a person is must be distinguished from what a person does. One does not decide how to feel or perceive; just the opposite is true. One decides what action to take according to how one feels or perceives. The basic determinants control consumer decision making but are not themselves controllable by the individual in the short run. A person does not plan to be introverted, but one who is introverted acts differently in the marketplace from one who is extroverted. Consumer decisions are the controllable aspect of consumer behavior. Thus, we can see the rationale for the wheel presented in Figure 1–2. Purchase decisions are placed in the center because the consumer's decision is dependent on the basic determinants.

Suppose one decides that a car is required in their product holdings because a car is compatible with their needs. The same consumer selects a Chevrolet over a Ford because the Chevrolet suits his or her attitudes and awareness of the two cars. The consumer's market activity may be to visit all available Chevrolet dealers in order to compare color, price, trade-in, and accessories, with the aim of taking the lowest price for comparable cars. Here the individual's motives play a large part in the market-related decision.[14]

The synthesis of basic determinants is a mental process. This mental process is still not fully understood, but we do know how the four determinants interact with one another. The totality of water would have no taste to the owner of a well in the desert, but the traveler dying of thirst would be willing to pay dearly for a drink.

Environmental influences

Consumers do not function in a vacuum. The individual is continually influenced by the environment. There are five broad environmental determinants of consumer behavior: (1) family influences, (2) social influences, (3) business influences, (4) cultural influences, and (5) economic influences. These important variables of consumer behavior are considered at this point.

The meaning of environmental influences. We can now complete the model of consumer behavior introduced earlier by placing the environmental influences around the outer circle of the wheel (Figure 1–3). At this point we must give meaning to each of the environmental variables before demonstrating their relationship to the individual and his or her decision processes.

Figure 1–3
Complete model of consumer behavior

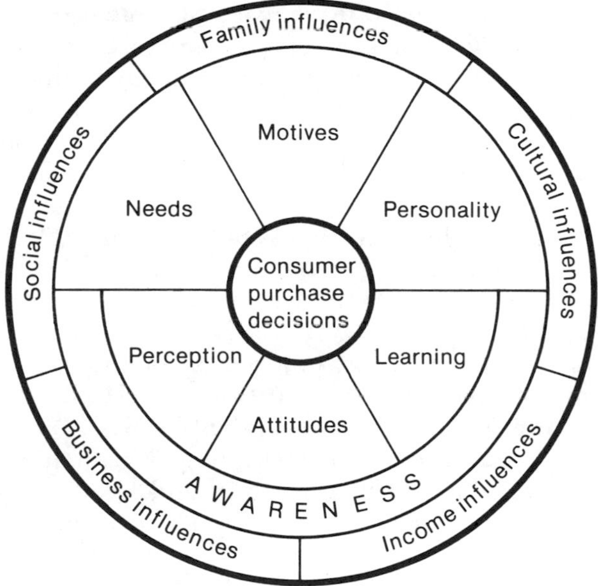

Family influences come from household members. *Social influences* result from all personal contacts other than family or business. Social influences arise, for example, from place of work, church, neighborhood, and school. *Business influences* refer to the direct contact, either at the store or through personal selling and advertising, the consumer has with business firms. *Cultural influences* are the innate beliefs and sanctions developed over time by the social system. *Income influences* are the constraints placed on the consumer by money and related factors.

The environmental factors are no more controllable by the individual consumer than was found earlier for the basic determinants. The individual cannot prescribe patterns of behavior for family members, social groups, culture, etc. Although the individual has some impact on the environment, it is typically not great in the short run. Thus the individual consumer must take the environment as he or she finds it. The environment does exert a strong influence on the individual that operates through the basic determinants. This influence has its most direct effect on perception because it is through perception that the individual comes to observe and understand the environment. Once the person has perceived, the information is synthesized into the other basic determinants: needs, motives, and attitudes.

Effect of the environment. The family has the greatest total influence on a consumer, although this fact may not be true for a given consumer. Social and business influences do not rate far behind the family in total impact. These three external influences comprise the individual's contact with other people. Ultimately, of course, all consumer activity results in interaction with businesses either in the form of shopping or actual purchasing. The cultural, ethnic, and religious variables, taken together, constitute a system of sanctions, biases, mores, and life styles that become a part of the person, but these variables are manifested through human contact.

It is not proper to leave a discussion of the model of consumer behavior without mentioning communications. It is through communications that the individual develops over time. This is true because individuals learn about themselves and their environment through communications. Thus, in a sense, communications connect the individual and the environment. Communications, the unifying factor in the entire model, pervade all the blocks.

Everything one does communicates information in the form of data. The consumer takes in the data, sorts it, and relates it to personal needs, motives, perception, and attitudes. The consumer can react in several ways to external data.

1. The consumer can consciously synthesize the data into his or her frame of reference.
2. The consumer can consciously reject the data.
3. The consumer can unconsciously synthesize the data.
4. The consumer can unconsciously forget the data.

None of these reactions leaves the consumer quite the same, but the conscious reactions have the most direct effect on the individual's overt behavior.

Interaction of environment and individual. In actuality, the external environment cannot be separated from the individual. The environment influences every decision the individual makes. It is not a case of the consumers making up their minds on a product and then having the environment influence this decision, because the environment also influences the initial decision. The two sets of determinants interact simultaneously and continuously. Furthermore, there is interaction between the individual's needs, motives, perception, and attitudes. Each influences the other, and every individual decision is influenced by all four factors.

DYNAMIC MODEL OF CONSUMER BEHAVIOR

We have, so far, discussed consumer behavior as a static concept. This view was necessary in order to become acquainted with the major variables of consumer behavior and to present a logical framework for analysis. However, consumer behavior is not static. It is a dynamic decision process as the term behavior implies.[15] Figure 1–4 shows a simplified schematic model of consumer behavior. It is based on the same major variables introduced in the static model. Because it is a simple model there is no attempt to show exact relationships between variables, rather broad interactions are illustrated.

Figure 1–4
Dynamic model of consumer behavior

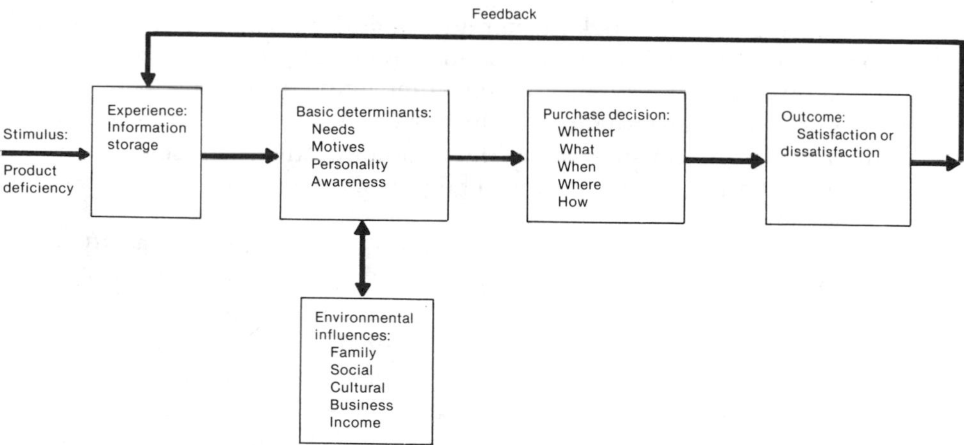

Consumer behavior begins when the individual is made aware of some product deficiency. This stimulus is then filtered through that individual's experience to determine if any stored information bears on the problem. Experience always enters into consumer behavior because one tests current situations against past knowledge. Experience may indicate that the consumer already has the product; that the product is not wanted; that the product is desirable but a routine purchase; or that the product is desirable but unknown. If the decision is routine, the consumer may purchase directly without much consideration of the basic or environmental determinants. If, however, the decision is uncertain then the consumer's basic determinants begin to act on the individual.

It is through the basic determinants that the consumer relates the perceived product deficiency to specific needs. If the product is relevant then the consumer becomes aware of a real need. This awareness is due to the combined action of the individual's perceptions, attitudes, and learning. As a result, the consumer is motivated to take some action. Whatever action the consumer decides to be appropriate must be consistent with personality. Even the manner in which the problem is understood is conditioned by the consumer's personality. Thus the consumer begins to develop purchase intentions based on internal determinants. These basic determinants have already been influenced by the environment. The environment is constantly at work on consumers even when they are not aware of a specific problem. In this manner the environment helps to form attitudes, establish patterns of perception, foster needs, and shape motivation even in advance of a stimulus. The environment may also be brought directly into a particular product decision.

The consumer may seek further advice and guidance from people who make up the environment. One may, for example, ask the family's opinion, and at some point the consumer may consult his or her finances or solicit the opinion of a salesperson. At some point during the deliberation, the consumer has the problem sufficiently clearly in mind to begin purchase decision. The person decides on the product and the manner of acquiring it.

The outcome of the purchase decision is that the consumer is either satisfied or dissatisfied with the selection. This outcome may or may not become immediately apparent. It is normal for the consumer to determine the consequence of purchase decisions over time as the product is used. Whether the consumer is satisfied or dissatisfied, this information becomes feedback to experience. If the consumer is satisfied, no further behavior is required, and the newly stored outcome is available to affect the individual the next time a similar purchase decision is encountered. If the outcome is dissatisfaction, then the consumer has not solved the problem, and this fact becomes a new stimulus to begin the entire process of consumer behavior over again. The alternative is to accept the dissatisfaction. In either case, dissatisfaction is also stored in the experience to affect future decisions. Remember, it is as important to know what did not provide benefit as what did when buying. In a real sense, consumer behavior by the individual never ends, because most consumers are always in some state of product deficiency or dissatisfaction which requires activity.

NOTES

1. Betsy D. Gelb, Gabriel M. Gelb, and Ricky W. Griffin, "Managing with the Consumer's Help," *Business Horizons* (April 1976), pp. 69–74.
2. Scott Ward, Thomas S. Robertson, and William Capitman, "What Will be Different About Tomorrow's Consumer?" *Relevance in Marketing: Problems, Research, Action*, ed. Fred C. Allvine (Chicago: American Marketing Assn., 1971), pp. 371–74.
3. Yoram Wind, "Preference of Relevant Others and Individual Choice Models," *Journal of Consumer Research*, vol. 3 (June 1976), pp. 50–57.
4. Ibid., pp. 50–51.
5. Russell W. Belk, "Situational Variables and Consumer Behavior," *Journal of Consumer Research*, vol. 2 (December 1975), pp. 157–64.
6. John Douglas, George A. Field, and Lawrence X. Tarpey, *Human Behavior in Marketing* (Columbus, Ohio: Charles E. Merrill, Inc., 1967); Rom J. Markin, Jr., *Consumer Behavior: A Cognitive Orientation* (New York: Macmillan Publishing Co., Inc., 1974), pp. 55–56.
7. Scott Ward and Thomas S. Robertson, *Consumer Behavior: Theoretical Sources* (Englewood Cliffs, N.J.: Prentice-Hall, Inc., 1973), pp. 6–7.
8. William J. McGuire, "Some Internal Psychological Factors Influencing Consumer Choice," *Journal of Consumer Research*, vol. 2 (March 1976), pp. 302–19; Francesco M. Nicosia, and Robert N. Mayer, "Toward a Sociology of Consumption," *Journal of Consumer Research*, vol. 3 (September 1976), pp. 65–75; Walter A. Henry, "Cultural Values Do Correlate with Consumer Behavior," *Journal of Marketing Research*, vol. 13 (May 1976), pp. 121–27; Edward M. Tauber, "Why Do People Shop?" *Journal of Marketing*, vol. 36 (October 1972), pp. 46–54.
9. Chester R. Wasson, Frederick D. Sturdivant, and David H. McConaughy, *Competition and Human Behavior* (New York: Appleton-Century-Crofts, 1968), pp. 6–8.
10. Francesco M. Nicosia, *Consumer Decision Processes* (Englewood Cliffs, N.J.: Prentice-Hall, Inc., 1966); James F. Engel, David T. Kollat, and Roger D. Blackwell, *Consumer Behavior*, 2d ed. (New York: Holt, Rinehart and Winston, Inc., 1973); John A. Howard and Jagdish N. Sheth, *The Theory of Buyer Behavior* (New York: John Wiley & Sons, Inc., 1969).
11. Ibid., p. 58.
12. Robert J. Holloway, Robert A. Mittelstaedt, and M. Venkatesan, eds., *Consumer Behavior: Contemporary Research in Action* (Boston: Houghton Mifflin Co., 1971), Part II–A.
13. See: Glenn M. Vernon, *Human Interaction*, 2d ed. (New York: The Ronald Press Co., 1972), pp. 139–41.
14. For a review of environmental effects on consumers see: David T. Kollat, Roger D. Blackwell, and James F. Engel, eds. *Research in Consumer Behavior* (New York: Holt, Rinehart and Winston, Inc., 1970); Steuart Henderson Britt, *Psychological Experiments in Consumer Behavior* (New York: John Wiley & Sons, Inc., 1970).

15. Jacob Jacoby, George J. Szybillo, and Carol Kohn Berning, "Time and Consumer Behavior: An Interdisciplinary Overview," *Journal of Consumer Research,* vol. 2 (March 1976), pp. 320–39.

QUESTIONS

1. Define consumer. Distinguish consumer and buyer. Distinguish consumer and user.
2. Does the fact that we are all so familiar with consumer behavior have anything to do with our lack of knowledge on the subject?
3. Discuss the relationship between consumer behavior and human behavior. Give examples of each.
4. Explain why the study of consumer behavior is important.
5. What is the central issue of consumer behavior? Explain. List and explain each of the five decisions involved in the consumer's purchase decision.
6. What is meant by basic determinants? Why are they called basic? Define each of the basic determinants.
7. Discuss the relationship between the basic determinants of consumer behavior. Are these determinants controllable? Explain.
8. What are environmental influences? Explain. Define the five types of environmental influences.
9. Discuss the relationship between the basic determinants of consumer behavior and the environmental influences.
10. Place the major consumer variables into a dynamic model of consumer behavior and explain this model.

2

Sources of consumer knowledge

Consumers receive through the economic system the products and services so necessary to their well-being. Marketing is a vital part of that system. The relationships among consumers, marketing, and the economic system are basic to our understanding of consumer behavior, so we must turn our attention to these points. Three subjects are discussed in this chapter: first, the consumer's place in the economic system; next, the important areas of study upon which marketers draw in explaining consumer behavior; and finally, the overall interaction between marketing and consumers. The discussion serves to point out the consumer's place in the system and to demonstrate the breadth and complexity of the problems associated with understanding consumer behavior.

THE SOCIOECONOMIC SYSTEM EXISTS FOR CONSUMERS

The purpose of any economic system is to satisfy human wants. Said another way, the rationale for any economic system is founded on the consumers served by that system. Marketing is a part of our economic system, and as such, it has essentially the same goal and purpose as the system as a whole. Economic systems have two characteristics in common. The people who comprise the system are social by nature, and people as consumers participate in the system because of the expected rewards to be gained from cooperative effort. Social interaction occurs between consumers, and between the firm on the one hand and the individual consumer on the other. The expected reward may be profit for the firm or the level of living enjoyed by the consumer, but the reward always results from joint efforts.

A modern economic system can be divided into three parts: production, distribution, and consumption.[1] Production is responsible for the manufacture of goods and services wanted by consumers in the system. Distribution, or marketing, is responsible for the buying, physical movement, and ultimate sale of goods and services necessary to place the goods in the hands of consumers. One important function of consumers is to destroy products and services. The term *consumers* is derived from "consume," meaning to destroy or use up. It is this continual destruction of goods and services, by consumers, that keeps the wheels of industry well oiled turning out replacements.

How the system satisfies consumers

The economic system fulfills its purpose by creating utility or satisfaction.[2] *Utility* is the ability of a thing, or an idea, to satisfy human wants. Consumer satisfaction can be viewed as form, time, place, and possession utility. Production creates form utility through physical change in the product. Marketing creates time, place, and possession utility. *Time utility* is defined as having the goods available when the consumer wants to purchase. *Place utility* is having the goods where the consumer wants them, and *possession utility* is everything necessary to transfer ownership of goods. Although four types of utility can be identified, they are not separable. The consumer cannot obtain the physical goods without marketing, and marketing serves no purpose without a product or service to distribute. Thus, both marketing and production are necessary to serve the consumers' requirements.

Areas of understanding necessary

The preceding discussion suggests that consumer behavior is a very complex subject. In order to understand consumers fully, it is necessary to understand our entire economic and social system.[3] This point cannot be overemphasized. Consumer behavior is a broad subject, impressive in the amount of detailed knowledge encompassed within its area. Obviously, a book such as this one cannot hope to deal with all ramifications of consumer behavior. Fortunately, the subject can be simplified in order to deal with the more meaningful concepts.

We pointed out previously that our system is social and economic. Thus, the major topics of consumer behavior can be grouped around economic influences and social influences. The major economic topics besides marketing are economic theory and management. The major social contributions to consumer behavior are found in psychology, sociology, and anthropology. Although we realize we are oversimplifying the problem, it is necessary to establish the contributions of each of these areas to consumer behavior before proceeding further with our discussion.

CONSUMER BEHAVIOR TRADITIONAL IN ECONOMICS

Consumers (in the sense of demanders), as distinguished from consumer behavior (mental processes whereby individuals decide), have traditionally been a part of economic theory. In this sense, consumer analysis is as old as economic analysis. It is a reasonable statement to say that the study of consumers developed out of the study of economics. However, dissatisfaction with the traditional economic treatment of consumers began to develop in the 1950s.

It was inevitable that the study of consumers break away from economics, and it was natural for marketers with their need to affect demand to undertake the development of the field. The break with economics was inevitable because the understanding of *consumer behavior* was never a central issue of economics. Economics was always preoccupied with understanding the *behavior of the system*, specifically the economic system. The economist was only interested in consumers to the extent that they contribute to explaining the allocation of resources or the interaction of supply and demand for the system. Under these circumstances, the treatment of consumers was bound to be limited in scope.

Nature of economic analysis

In spite of the overall thrust of economics being in another direction, the consumer was not completely ignored. However, to understand the contribution of economics, one must understand the nature of economic analysis. Economics is the most exact of all the areas of business study. This fact is true: (1) because, as the oldest business profession, economics has had time to perfect its concepts, and (2) because economics has gained in exactness of principles by restricting the nature and scope of its analysis. This latter statement is particularly true in the case of consumers.

The economic analysis of consumers is a general, limited, and specialized explanation. It is a general explanation because economics deals with the average consumer. There is no attempt to distinguish among consumers or to delve into the physical and emotional attributes of consumers. It is a limited explanation because economics operates at a high level of abstraction. The assumptions of perfect knowledge, complete rationality, large numbers of both buyers and sellers, homogeneous products, constant technology, and limited resources are well known. It is most particularly the existence of these assumptions that provides a basis for economic precision. It is a specialized explanation because only economic variables are considered. There is no consideration of emotions, external influences, etc. Consumers in economics react only to price, income, quantities, and competition. As the reader can observe, what economics gains in precision concerning consumers, it gives up in reality.

Contributions of economics to consumer behavior

Within the constraints of its nature, economics has made some significant contributions to consumer behavior.[4] First, it explains product choices under ideal conditions. Both marginal analysis and indifference analysis are used for this purpose. Second, economics has been instrumental in emphasizing the importance of income on the ability of consumers to buy. The consumption function, which is central to macroeconomic analysis, makes all consumption a result of income. Third, economics, by means of demand analysis, stresses the importance of price on the quantity of any product purchased. It has always been a basic part of economic analysis that the higher the price the less demanded, and the lower the price the more demanded. Fourth, economics has focused attention on the competition that goes on among consumers. It is this competition among consumers, along with the competition among suppliers, that causes the price of products to fluctuate until an equilibrium of supply and demand is reached.

Although over simplified and restricted in their presentation, the economics of consumer behavior aids in understanding the fundamentals of how consumers act in the market place. It also serves a practical purpose for the marketer. Potential and realized demand are used by business for forecasting and evaluating the results of operations. Market demand is also used for estimating expenditures, planning output, hiring, scheduling deliveries, planning stock size, ordering, etc. Furthermore, basic price movement has always entered into business decisions.

Economics: A beginning, not the end

The restrictions placed on economic analysis make it too narrowly conceived for present-day development of consumer behavior.[5] Economics provides a takeoff point for the analysis of consumer behavior by shedding light on *how* consumers act in the marketplace. This analysis of how consumers act naturally leads to questions of *why* they act that way. Unfortunately, answers to the why of consumer behavior cannot be fully found in either economics or traditional marketing. Until recently, about all we knew about consumers either came from very abstract theory or from what we observed in the marketplace. It has become increasingly clear that in order to satisfy consumers, a deeper understanding of their needs, motives, personality, and awareness is needed.

Economics lays the foundation and provides the basic explanation, but marketers have found its narrowly conceived analysis unsuited for their purposes. For this reason, marketers have in recent years turned to management, psychology, social psychology, sociology, social anthropology, and even history to gain understanding of consumers. It follows that, in the process, marketing has become a far broader field of study than it was ten or fifteen years ago.

CONTRIBUTIONS FROM ALLIED SOCIAL SCIENCE FIELDS

Consumer behavior has today outgrown its earlier economic foundation. The separation of economics and marketing around the turn of the century released consumer analysis from the many restrictions imposed by the parent field. Scholars began to perceive that consumer behavior was a far broader subject than ever conceived in economics. In order to answer the question, "why consumers buy," marketers had to delve inside the individual and also come to grips with the interaction between the individual and social groups. Thus the study of consumer behavior began to push out beyond the business college and take in aspects of all the social sciences. Concepts taken from psychology, sociology, and anthropology were found to be particularly important.[6] This broadening has caused an explosion of consumer knowledge, but it has also made the problem of understanding more complex. It is now time to bring into focus some important contributions of the social sciences to consumer behavior.

Psychology and consumer behavior

General psychology deals with relationships between the individual and the physical and socioeconomic environment. Often psychology is considered to be primarily related to motivation, but this is not true in practice. Learning, remembering, perception, attitudes, emotions, and opinions are but a few of the subjects with consumer behavior applications. Although, at first glance, there appears to be almost a complete transference of material from psychology to consumer behavior, this is not the case. Much psychological investigation is related to physiological psychology, animal psychology, therapy, abnormal psychology, and educational psychology. While these explorations may eventually make a contribution to consumer behavior, they do not do so at the present time. Psychology could contribute much to consumer behavior by providing a theory of normal behavior rather than focusing on abnormal or specialized types of behavior. Nevertheless, important inferences about consumers have come from psychology.

Psychological contributions to consumer behavior. A wide variety of psychological concepts is available to aid in explaining consumer behavior. Among the most useful pertain to motivation and learning. Motivation studies have shed light on the "why" of consumer behavior, and these studies aid business in selecting advertising appeals, meeting objections to buying, arousing interest, and stimulating action. Learning theory has been applied in developing advertising campaigns, branding, and pricing. Other psychological constituents, such as drives, cues, and rewards, render valuable insights into consumer behavior. For example, some anticipated reward lies behind all consumer behavior.

Perception, and the ways in which consumers perceive, are basic to explaining the individual's purchase actions. The individual's needs, attitudes, and personality influence the manner in which the person perceives, as well as the manner of motivation and learning. The number and importance of the subjects covered in psychology makes the contributions of the field to individual consumer actions clear.

Importance of social psychology. Social psychology is the scientific study of the experiences and behavior of individuals in relation to other individuals, groups, and cultures.[7] However, the basic unit of analysis, as in all psychology, remains the individual. Social psychology has contributed much toward understanding the individual's reaction to others. It has provided insights relating to changes in motives, learned responses, social perception, social cues, and social rewards and sanctions. Much of what is known of how people influence each other comes from social psychology. The subject is particularly useful to businessmen for discovering ways to influence consumers.

Sociology and consumer behavior

The task of defining sociology may be better accomplished by describing what a *sociologist* is. Sociologists are behavioral scientists who seek to define and describe human behavior in groups and social settings. Human nature, social interaction, social organization, and culture are all subjects of study for the sociologist.[8] Sociologists have developed materials significant for marketing as a product of their study of Man* and mankind's social and cultural environment.[9] They view the marketing processes as one type of example of the activities of groups. These groups consist of buyers and sellers, and these individuals act because of both group pressures and individual preferences. Although many of the same subjects dealt with by psychologists are also subjects for sociologists, the emphasis of the sociologist is on the group rather than on the individual. Human behavior is viewed in the context of mankind and social groups with all their social values and pressures.

General contributions. The individual who is a member of society has social needs such as the need to be accepted, to be loved, to participate, to achieve, to excell, etc.[10] Of course, there is an interaction here because society, as a whole, also has social needs such as group protection, group conformity, establishment of value systems, administering rewards and sanctions, etc. Sociology is concerned with both types of group interaction. Although the sociologist, like the psychologist, does not normally deal with consumers, per se, marketers are able to adapt many of their findings. For example, advertising finds consumer appeals and objections in the needs of individuals cited above. The needs of society as a whole provide clues as to what is

---

* Man (capitalized) denotes collectively all members of the human race.

socially acceptable in promotion and personal selling. Once marketers learn how individuals react in groups generally, this information can be applied to group interaction in retail stores and other marketing situations.

One of the major contributions sociologists have made to marketing has been in methodology. Measurement, scaling, sampling, and research design are but a few of the many technical aspects contributed toward consumer research. In addition, three other sociological areas of knowledge with direct relevance to consumer behavior are population, consumer motivation, and ecology.

Population studies. Population studies have long been an important branch of sociology. As we have already seen, knowledge about population factors goes far toward explaining purchasing behavior. Numbers and location of people are useful for pinpointing markets. Population characteristics, such as sex, age, education, employment, and marital status, aid in determining the type and quality of markets.

Human motivation. Studies of sociologists have often focused upon social needs as the basis of purchasing motivation. Social class, status, leisure, and recreation are all subjects of inquiry. What we have learned about opinion leaders and the acceptance of innovative products and services and life style concepts has been the end result of sociological inquiry.

Ecology. Our knowledge of the processes involved in the spatial and temporal distribution of consumers and market institutions is a direct outgrowth of sociologists' studies of human ecology. In our understanding of consumers, this becomes an important variable for consideration. The analysis of the changes occurring in both urban and rural markets takes on particular significance today, especially in view of the magnitude of some of these changes.

Contribution of anthropology to consumer behavior

Although marketers have employed many of the techniques and findings of the behavioral sciences, the use of anthropological insights and approaches have found somewhat less favor than those from some of the other disciplines. Because of the complex nature of modern anthropology, it is highly probable that many anthropological insights and techniques are used in studying and analyzing consumer behavior but are attributed to other disciplines. This fact occurs because the field of anthropology overlaps into the physical sciences, biological sciences, social sciences, and humanities. Certainly, anthropology plays a central role in the integration of studies of human behavior.

One of the classical descriptions of *anthropology* shows that it consists of the study of human beings as creatures of society.[11] A feature distinguishing anthropology from sociology is that anthropology includes serious study of societies other than our own. Anthropology also focuses attention on Man's past patterns of behavior that influence behavior today. Comparative marketing studies into cross-cultural purchasing behavior use many of the traditional anthropological techniques. Although anthropology has been described as the scientific study of the origin and development of Man, it cannot pretend to be the whole study of Man, even though it does play a central role. It is possible that this discipline may come *closer* to the complete study of Man than any other branch of science, but a comprehensive science of human behavior must encompass other skills and knowledge.

The field of anthropology is usually divided into two major subdivisions: physical and cultural. *Physical anthropology* is mainly concerned with the comparative study of human evolution, variation, and classification, largely through techniques of measurement and observation. *Cultural anthropology,* on the other hand, encompasses culture in all its aspects. It includes archaeology, the study of extinct cultures; ethnology, the study of the habits and customs of living or recent cultures; and linguistics, the scientific study of language. The three most important ways in which anthropology contributes to our understanding of consumer behavior are by providing specific knowledge, exploring cultural themes, and identifying taboos.[12]

Folklore. Folklore concerns deeply imbedded feelings handed down from generation to generation. Consumer resistance or acceptances of major innovations may be explained by this folklore and symbolism present within the culture. Deeply imbedded feelings toward products and services by consumers can often be discovered by anthropological insights and used to advantage in appealing to consumers.

Contributions of specific knowledge. Consumer resistance or acceptance of major innovations may be explained by the folklore and symbolism present within the culture in which the introduction takes place. Deeply imbedded feelings toward products and services by consumers can often be discovered and adapted to by anthropological insights. In this regard, specific knowledge about the fashion cycle of women's clothing was first used for predictive purposes by anthropologists.

The study of the buying behavior of subcultures is another way in which anthropology contributes to a better understanding of purchasing behavior. Specific knowledge of ethnic subcultures, provided by the cultural anthropologist, is very important in the individual's environment.

Cultural roles. Anthropologists contribute toward our understanding of the roles of various family members in a society. They remind us that things we often take for granted in our society are not necessarily true of all societies. The male and female roles in any society are complex and can be better understood with the help of anthropological insights. The meaning attached to the giving and receiving of gifts has been systematically studied by anthropologists.

Cultural standards. In each society there are certain cultural, religious, or political "do's" and "don'ts." The anthropologist, through investigation, can contribute knowledge about a particular society's don'ts or taboos. Such taboos are often involved in colors and symbols. For instance, the color white may be perfectly acceptable to us as a color for an automobile, but in Japan, white is considered to be a color of mourning and would be undesirable as an automobile color. On the other hand, purple is associated with death and grief in most Latin-American markets. An understanding of such attitudes toward colors and symbols is important for marketing at home as well as abroad. The purchase or rejection of certain products in the American market may often be directly attributable to color or package symbolism.

OTHER CONTRIBUTIONS TO CONSUMER BEHAVIOR

Contributions to consumer behavior are not limited to the behavioral sciences but come from all the social sciences, including economics, history, and political science. We have already discussed the contributions of economic theory to consumer actions, but the so-called branches of economics, marketing, management, and finance, also make contributions.

Management has been an important source of concepts dealing with consumer decision making. Concepts that relate to how consumers make decisions and to the processes and factors involved in decision making have been borrowed from management. Personal finance helps explain how consumers handle their money and how their expenditures are allocated.

THE ROLE OF MARKETING TO CONSUMER SATISFACTION

We pointed out earlier that in the economic system, production and marketing are entered into in order to satisfy consumer wants. Marketing is uniquely placed in this system between production and consumption. The placement of marketing brings it into constant contact with both producers and consumers, and marketing acts to bring these two groups together so that consumer needs are met.

Marketing is defined, for our purposes, as the performance of business activities related to the flow of goods and services from producer to consumer in order to satisfy consumers and achieve the firm's objectives.[13] The marketing system meets its responsibilities to consumers by means of physical distribution and communications. Marketing communication is of three types: communication back to the producer, communication forward to consumers, and horizontal communication. Such information from consumers as product choices, order quantities, service requirements, and market changes are communicated to the manufacturer so that production can be adjusted to consumer desires. Information on new products, prices, model features, brands, and services rendered are forwarded from seller to consumer. Horizontal information, about competitive conditions, is needed by consumers in order to buy effectively.

Marketing must be an active agent

To fulfill their consumer responsibility, marketing managers must be active, rather than passive, agents. It is not enough to react to the wants of consumers; rather, marketers must actively aid consumers by anticipating wants, shaping desires, and pointing the way to possible solutions.[14] For example, it is inefficient and costly for salespeople to "push" poorly designed or unwanted products. Instead, marketers should collect and employ consumer knowledge to aid engineers in designing customer satisfaction into the product or to develop entirely new products. In this way the tasks of selling and engineering are made easier, and profits are more likely to result.

The most difficult job is getting advance information on customer reaction to innovative product changes. If consumers had been asked to specify their lighting needs prior to Edison's invention of the incandescent lamp in 1879, they would probably have asked for better candles or more efficient oil lamps. Since they could not conceive of the electric light, it would have been difficult to obtain data on their reaction to such an invention.

Consumers had to be sold on the advantages of bathtubs, margarine, frozen foods, automobiles, and cologne for men. The attitudes of large numbers of people had to be changed before most of these products were accepted. The change may take generations, as in the case of men's cologne, or it may be that the product image can never be completely changed. The brewing industry has not been able to get beer fully accepted as a sociable drink by middle- and upper-income groups, although an intensive effort to do so has been made over a long period of time.

Consumer orientation: The marketing philosophy

The attitude of American business has changed significantly since 1950. There is a greater appreciation of the complexity of enterprise and of the consumer's importance to business success. This consumer orientation did not occur by accident. It was a result of the continuing maturity of the economic system that made methods of operation based on strict scarcity obsolete. The new orientation is called the marketing philosophy.[15]

A statement of philosophy. The fact that consumers are a force in the marketplace has been recognized for a long time.[16] However, the degree of consumer influence varies with market conditions. Consumers do not possess absolute power in the market, but they do have a veto over product, price, and service decisions made by firms. When goods are plentiful, consumers have greater freedom of choice and greater influence over businesses that must cater to their wishes.

> *Briefly stated, the marketing philosophy is that every act, operation, or policy undertaken by the firm has at its roots consumer satisfaction at a profit.*

No one forces consumers to buy the products and services offered by particular businesses. Everyone needs meat in his diet, but no person needs ham, and certainly no one needs any particular brand of canned ham. The decision on whether to buy or not resides with the individual. Literally, the authority for business operations, in a modern society, is vested in consumers. A fundamental task of marketing is to identify the firm's product so successfully with the consumer's own desires that the consumer not only wants to purchase the product but shopping for it actually becomes a pleasure.[17] This identification is never easy, but the difficulty is greater in a buyer's market than in a seller's market.

Consumer influence in seller's markets. In subsistence economies, where productivity is low, the output of goods is typically restricted. Not only is the quantity of particular goods produced relatively small, but fewer generic types of goods are produced. Low productivity is associated with low incomes, and consumer purchases are geared to the basic necessities of food, clothing, and shelter. Subsistence economies tend to have seller's markets.[18] The seller dominates trade, and the market is production oriented. Consumers have relatively little influence in these markets.

Seller's markets can be characterized in the following manner:

1. Preoccupation with the problems of production efficiency, and too little consideration to the problems of marketing efficiency.
2. Top executives from production or finance.
3. Preoccupation with sales volume as the only marketing strategy.
4. Marketing centered on the hard sell.
5. Little emphasis on research, particularly market and product research.

Problems in production-oriented economies center around increasing the output of goods. Little attention is paid to consumers, since, generally, all the goods that can be produced can be sold. The needs of consumers are greater than the output of manufacturing. Thus, individual purchase behavior becomes patterned around available goods, and individual influence in the market is limited.

Marketing, in seller's markets, is relatively simple. The major problem is pushing goods through the channel. The marketer shows little concern with adjusting to consumer tastes, because the consumer cannot afford more than the necessities of life. Both the producer and the consumer are preoccupied with how to increase productivity rather than with problems of product choice in the market. The typical attitude of the business is that the consumer has to purchase what the firm can make.

Consumer influence in buyer's markets. In modern, high-level economies, the marketing task is more complex. Increased productivity brings forth a greater variety of products, and the number of firms offering differential assortments of services and prices in combination with these products also multiply. Consumer income rises with productivity, so that individuals have the means to choose from among improved offerings of business. Not only can consumers buy more but they may exercise greater discretion over how they spend their income. As income increases, a smaller proportion of it is required for necessities, leaving some income that can be spent for improved living conditions. One consumer may improve diet, but another may decide to purchase new clothing or put a down payment on an automobile. Consumer influence in the market increases with this freedom of choice, and businesses increasingly must cater to the consumer's wants. When power passes from the producer to the consumer, a buyer's market exists, and this type of market is compatible with consumer orientation.[19]

The characteristics of buyer's markets are as follows:

1. The business becomes consumer oriented.
2. Top executives increasingly come from marketing.
3. Market research increases in importance.
4. The soft sell tends to replace the hard sell.
5. Marketing strategy replaces rule-of-thumb sales techniques.

The task of marketing managers is difficult in buyer's markets because the consumer must be provided sound reasons for patronizing a given business. Competing firms are continually attempting to draw customers away by giving them greater satisfaction. Thus, the firm's problems shift, relatively, from how to produce more to how to do a better job of marketing; the development of sound marketing strategy becomes one of the paramount problems of the business. Most modern Western economic systems tend to be buyer's markets, and consumer influence is relatively great.

Why satisfy consumers

Marketers undertake the satisfaction of consumers for a reward. It is useless to even consider a marketing philosophy without relating it to reward. No business can long serve the public unless it replenishes the means to serve. The reward may be profit, survival, market share, or some other benefit expected for effort expended, but it must exist.

There are two sides to every transaction, the firm and the customer, and each side must be satisfied before trade can occur.[20] The meaning of the marketing philosophy cannot be confused on this point. Consumer orientation does not imply that business is benevolent or that consumer satisfaction is placed ahead of profit to the firm. Consumer orientation means that the firm recognizes that the surest route to profit, in a buyer's market, is through service to consumers.

Effects of consumer orientation on business

Consumer orientation has increased among business leaders, yet all too few managers have grasped the full impact of the concept.[21] Too many executives feel that the implementation of the marketing philosophy is accomplished simply by changing the title of the sales manager to that of marketing manager. Some executives go one step further and instruct the marketing manager to coordinate the activities of personal selling and advertising.

The fact is that customer orientation is not, per se, an organizational problem. It is a mental problem. A firm is consumer oriented when every employee, from the top executive to the lowest sales person, believes in it and wants to help customers find satisfactory solutions to their problems. Organizational changes may be necessary to develop strategy, but the real crux of the problem is the attitude of the personnel.[22]

Consumer orientation affects business attitudes

First, market-oriented managers are not as likely to define the business as narrowly as managers who see their purpose as selling products simply because the firm produces these products. Progressive managers ask themselves, What are we presently doing that benefits the market, and what should we be doing? This attitude is more apt to lead to survival and growth. A business that devotes all its energies to promoting vested-interest products will find its market disappearing over time as competitors, both in and out of the industry, find better ways to cater to the customer's ever changing needs. The railroad industry is a good example of a vested-interest industry. The railroads have been in deep trouble for over 40 years because they have always defined their industry as railroading. If the industry had recognized the consumer's differing needs for transportation there is no reason why the railroads could not have been in the trucking and airline businesses today.

Second, consumer orientation leads a company to seek innovation and change.[23] The marketing philosophy requires that the management view its product as customer satisfaction rather than physical goods. Marketing must keep satisfying its customers. When a product ceases to satisfy, there is no hesitation in dropping it from the line. However, a company cannot long drop products without providing for new products. The result is that the customer-oriented company places greater emphasis on research and innovation. Product research, as well as market research, is given high priority in the company so that products can be more nearly fitted to changing consumer needs. Consumer-oriented management considers innovation as an opportunity rather than a disruptive force and actively seeks ways and means to improve. There is no waiting for competitors to jeopardize the firm's position.

A firm with the marketing philosophy is willing to put itself out of its traditional business and move forward to new business. Du Pont is a good example. The products that Du Pont depends on for its revenue today were not in existence 15 or 20 years ago. Du Pont, at the time a nontextile manufacturer, caused a tremendous readjustment in the textile industry with the development of synthetic fibers. It would have been better for the textile industry to have made these innovations, but the whole concept of the textile industry was too narrowly based to recognize the opportunity.

Third, consumer orientation leads to more emphasis on planning. It is vital that management plot the future, as well as the present, course of the company. The marketing philosophy, with its emphasis on ever changing markets, brings this fact home to management in no uncertain terms. The organization cannot become preoccupied with how well it is meeting today's demand requirements to the detriment of tomorrow's objectives.

NOTES

1. For a good explanation of the place and importance of marketing see: U.S. Chamber of Commerce, "The Value Added by Distribution," *Marketing*

in Progress, Pattern, and Potentials, ed. Hiram C. Barksdale (New York: Holt, Rinehart & Winston, Inc., 1964), pp. 34–46.

2. James U. McNeal, "Consumer Satisfaction: The Measure of Marketing Effectiveness," *MSU Business Topics* (Summer 1969), pp. 31–36.
3. Francesco M. Nicosia, "Consumer Behavior: Can Economics and Behavioral Science Converge?" *California Management Review,* vol. 16 (Winter 1973), pp. 71–78.
4. Brain T. Ratchford, "The New Economic Theory of Consumer Behavior: An Interpretive Essay," *Journal of Consumer Research,* vol. 2 (September 1975), pp. 65–75.
5. Rom J. Markin, Jr., *Consumer Behavior: A Cognitive Orientation* (New York: Macmillan Publishing Co., Inc., 1974), pp. 60–61.
6. Marguerite C. Burk, "Survey of Interpretations of Consumer Behavior by Social Scientists in the Postwar Period," *Journal of Farm Economics,* vol. 49 (February 1967), pp. 1–31.
7. Floyd H. Allport, *Social Psychology* (Boston: Houghton Mifflin Co., 1924), p. 13.
8. Christen T. Jonassen, "Contributions of Sociology to Marketing," *Journal of Marketing,* vol. 24 (October 1959), pp. 29–35.
9. Francesco M. Nicosia and Robert N. Mayer, "Toward A Sociology of Consumption," *Journal of Consumer Research,* vol. 3 (September 1976), pp. 65–75.
10. Joseph E. Bachelder, "How the Sociologists Can Help the Marketing Practicioner," *Successful Marketing at Home and Abroad,* ed. David Robbins, (Chicago: American Marketing Assn., 1958), pp. 287–93.
11. Ruth Benedict, *Patterns of Culture* (New York: Mentor Books, 1934), p. 1.
12. Adapted from Charles Winick, "Anthropology's Contribution to Marketing," *Journal of Marketing,* vol. 26 (July 1961), pp. 53–60.
13. Committee on Definitions of the American Marketing Association, *Marketing Definitions* (Chicago: American Marketing Association, 1960), p. 15.
14. Theodore Levitt, "Marketing Myopia," Reported in, *Readings in Basic Marketing,* eds. E. Jerome McCarthy, John F. Grashof, and Andrew A. Brogowicz (Homewood, Ill.: Richard D. Irwin, Inc., 1975), pp. 16–32.
15. Fred J. Borch, *The Marketing Philosophy as a Way of Business Life,* Marketing Series No. 99 (New York: American Management Assn., Inc., 1957).
16. E. Jerome McCarthy, *Basic Marketing: A Managerial Approach,* 5th ed. (Homewood, Ill.: Richard D. Irwin, Inc., 1975), Chap. 2; Richard R. Weeks and William J. Marks, "The Marketing Concept in Historical Perspective," *Business and Society,* vol. 9 (Spring 1969), pp. 24–32.
17. David W. Cravens, "Marketing Strategy Positioning," *Business Horizons* (December 1975).
18. James L. Heskett, *Marketing* (New York: Macmillan Publishing Co., Inc., 1976), p. 596.

19. Ibid.
20. Some marketers agree with the position that consumer satisfaction is the object of marketing and profit the incentive. Others argue that profit is the object and consumer satisfaction a requirement for achieving profit. The argument appears immaterial since satisfaction is simultaneous.
21. Martin L. Bell and C. William Emory, "The Faltering Marketing Concept," *Journal of Marketing,* vol. 35 (October 1971), pp. 37–42; Leslie M. Dawson, "The Human Concept: New Philosophy for Business," *Business Horizons,* vol. 12 (December 1969), pp. 29–38.
22. John B. Matthews, Jr., et al., *Marketing: An Introductory Analysis* (New York: McGraw-Hill Book Co., 1964), p. 492.
23. See: McCarthy, *Basic Marketing: A Managerial Approach,* Chap. 1, for an evaluation of the position of marketing in the American economy.

QUESTIONS

1. What is meant by socioeconomic system? What part does marketing play in this system? Consumers?
2. Discuss the contributions of economics to consumer behavior. Were these contributions significant?
3. What is psychology? How is it related to consumer behavior?
4. Discuss the major contributions of psychology to consumer behavior.
5. Relate sociology to the model of consumer behavior presented in Chapter 1. Discuss the general contributions of sociology to consumer behavior.
6. Define anthropology. How is it related to psychology and sociology? Does it have any relevance for consumer behavior? Explain.
7. What is marketing? How does consumer behavior relate to marketing?
8. What does the statement that marketing must be an active agent in the market mean? Discuss the pros and cons of this position.
9. What is the effect of consumers in a seller's market? In a buyer's market?
10. Discuss how consumer orientation affects business attitudes.

3

Consumer behavior models

Fundamentals of consumer models
Definition of consumer models
Purpose of consumer models
Types of consumer models
Model-building process
Points about the use of models

Human behavior models useful in consumer analysis
Allport socio-psychoanalytic model
Freudian psychoanalytic model
Pavlov learning model
Lewin topological model

Economic and behavioral models of consumer choice
Microeconomic model of consumer choice
Macroeconomic model of consumption
Kotler's behavioral choice model

Current status of experimental consumer models
Nicosia's model
Andreasen's model
Engel, Kollat, and Blackwell model
Howard-Sheth model
General comments on the four models

Chapter 3 is a continuation of the foundation material already begun. In Chapter 2 we gained some insight into the antecedents of knowledge about consumers. The present chapter deals with the types of theoretical constructs that have been developed, based on these antecedents. In other words, having knowledge and using that knowledge in a particular way are two different things. Scholars do not all agree as to how data from psychology, sociology, anthropology, marketing, management, economics, etc. fit together for the explanation of consumer behavior. Thus there is, at present, no consensus of how or why consumers behave in a certain way. However, a great deal of important work in the direction of integrating concepts has been accomplished, and some consensus is beginning to develop.

This chapter deals with the types of models that have evolved over time as conceptual explanations for consumer behavior. The study of these models can aid the reader in understanding the present status of the development of the field, point up differences of opinion, and indicate subject complexity. Of course, it is impossible to discuss every consumer model in every variation, but the discussion centers on some of the more representative types.

FUNDAMENTALS OF CONSUMER MODELS

Consumer behavior, as a separate course of study in colleges and universities, has developed only within the past ten years or so, compared to approximately 80 years for marketing in general. This fact has provided the study of consumers with some definite shortcuts in development not available to the analysis of such marketing areas as advertising, salesmanship, marketing research, retailing, etc. The basic theory in each of these latter areas was constructed piecemeal, often as the result of painstaking trial and error. There were no comprehensive theories available to guide and provide direction to the research. Recently, efforts to develop general theories of advertising, salesmanship, retailing, etc. are beginning to bear fruit. However, even now, there have been few concrete results in integrating the separate areas.

Consumer behavior has grown up in the era of the computer. It has also benefited from the results of earlier trial-and-error processes. Examples are the present availability of accumulated knowledge in areas affecting consumer behavior, development of modeling techniques, and the use of general systems theory.[1] As a result, consumer analysis has developed relatively rapidly, and with a somewhat different emphasis. Specific and comprehensive models were made available while the subject was still in its relative infancy. Thus some of the trial and error was avoided. These models are already undergoing empirical testing.[2] Of course, these comprehensive models have given consumer behavior development a distinct advantage over earlier marketing concepts, and the models, no doubt, have been a significant factor in the rapid development of consumer concepts. It is worthwhile reviewing some of the fundamentals of consumer models at this time.

Definition of consumer models

There exists in the whole world not one single thing that can be fully and completely comprehended by the combined senses of humans. Even the period at the end of the previous sentence has dimensions that cannot be fully understood, because it has to be filtered through the subjective mind. Therefore, we have to employ devices to stand for the things brought to the attention of our senses. These devices are what we refer to as models. Most scholars agree that a model represents something else, but there are differences as to the precision which must apply to the representation. Thus one author defines a *model* as "simply a representation of some or all of the properties of a larger system."[3] A more strict definition considers a model a hypothetical representation of some phenomenon which consists of one equation or a system of equations. Mathematical models are sometimes presented as flow charts.

The author prefers the first definition because of its greater breadth of application.

Based on the above definition of models, it is not difficult to specify what is meant by a *consumer model:*

> *anything used to represent all or a part of the variables of consumer behavior.*

The key word in the definition is represent. The reader must be aware that every model is an oversimplification. To some degree, the reader must supply the missing parts or processes that tie together or complete the representation. Any criticism of specific models must be accepted in this light.[4] The difference between models lies primarily in the emphasis given particular variables and the manner of presentation.

Purpose of consumer models

It can be stated that consumer models exist either for the purpose of: (1) identifying hypothesis and developing new consumer behavior theory or (2) explaining the present status of consumer behavior theory. The former is experimental and research oriented, and the latter integrative and teaching oriented. No matter which broad result is desired, the sophistication of the model depends on its scope and its purpose.[5] Both theory development and theory explanation models of consumer behavior run the gambit all the way from very limited purposes to very comprehensive purposes as demonstrated by the ranks below.[6]

1. Identify all or a part of consumer variables.
2. Explain fundamental relationships between the variables identified.
3. Demonstrate steps or flows in the decision or operational relationships among variables.
4. Specify exact cause and effect between variables and relationships.

The simplest consumer models have the limited purpose of variable identification. This is the first purpose of experimental models and a major responsibility of teaching models. Much work has been done at this level, but a lot of it informally. It is an important modeling step since all further steps depend on an effective identification of factors. More complex consumer models deal with fundamental relationships between variables or decision steps. These models attempt either to develop the relationships or to explain them. The model used as the basis for this book falls in the second rank. Its purpose is to explain rather than to create consumer theory, and it is designed to identify the major variables and interpret fundamental relationships. It does not reach as far as the third rank.

The most complex models attempt to specify exact cause and effect that relate to consumer behavior. These models are nearly always of the theory development kind. Present models fall short of this latter objective, but several are reaching toward it.[7] The emphasis of this book is explanation, but it is important to demonstrate the experimental work being undertaken in consumer behavior. Thus the models presented in this chapter generally concern theory development, and most are fairly advanced. They fall in the two or three rank where their purpose is concerned.

Mittelstaedt has provided five criteria for the development of consumer behavior theory.[8] These criteria are:

1. A theory must be able to incorporate known regularities.
2. A theory must be able to suggest new regularities to be observed.
3. To test hypotheses, operational definitions must exist for the terms of the theory.
4. A single, unified theory is preferred to eclectic borrowing.
5. Borrowed theories should come from the "mainstream" of one of the behavioral sciences.[9]

These criteria serve both to provide a basis for advancing theory, and as a means of evaluating the theories developed. The reader may wish to keep them in mind as the different models of consumer behavior are developed in this chapter.

Types of consumer models

Any model can be classified in several ways, and consumer models are no exception. Consumer models are generally classified according to their manner of presentation or their purpose as already discussed. Based on this criterion, there are five important methods of model classification that have a bearing on consumer behavior. They are: (1) physical or behavioral, (2) quantitative or verbal, (3) descriptive or analytical, (4) static or dynamic, and (5) partial or wholistic.

First, a model can be physical or behavioral. A physical model is a small, exact, or functional replica of some larger thing. A doll, model airplane, or wind tunnel are physical models. A behavioral model concerns performance duplication rather than physical duplication. Behavioral models concern why a thing, a person, or a group acts in a specified manner. Most consumer models are of the behavioral type.

Second, consumer models can be classified as quantitative or verbal. Quantitative models are expressed either in numeric or alphabetic symbolism. These models tend to emphasize cause-effect relationships. Verbal models employ language as their means of expression, and they tend to emphasize nonquantitative relationships. Very often, the same model can be expressed in either terms. For example, the quantitative model:

$$P = fI, G, S$$

can also be expressed verbally as purchases are a function of consumer desire to spend total income after payments to government and allowances for savings.

Third, consumer models can be classified as descriptive or analytical. A descriptive model is designed to explain some aspect of consumer behavior. It does not attempt to break new ground or extend knowledge. An analytical model is designed to compare, interpret, or challenge concepts. Each type of model is important to clarifying the field of consumer knowledge.

Fourth, static and dynamic describe the perspective of consumer models. A static model considers a slice of time. Such a model does not allow for change. Static models may show a type of change by indicating the difference in two static situations at different points in time, but the model does not indicate how you get from the one situation to the other. A dynamic model emphasizes the processes by which the change occurs. It is like a moving picture. The dynamic model focuses on steps or flows in the process of moving from one state to another. Both types of models are popular in consumer behavior.

Fifth, consumer models are partial or wholistic. A partial model is one that takes into account either one or a few of the variables of consumer behavior, but develops these variables in detail. A wholistic model is one that attempts to identify and relate, at least in some superficial manner, most or all the variables of consumer behavior. One problem with the wholistic view is to make sure that one understands what all the variables are.

Model-building process

Lazer identifies two model-building processes which he calls *abstraction* and *realization.*[10] Abstraction is an approach, based on inductive reasoning, whereby the researcher begins with a specific real world situation, abstracts it to a general model, and tests the model for soundness. Realization is an approach, based on deductive reasoning, whereby the researcher begins with a general abstract model, seeks real world situations, and tests the model against these specific real world situations.

Figure 3–1 below shows the steps in consumer model building based on abstraction. It begins with the perception of a real consumer

Figure 3–1
Consumer model building by abstraction

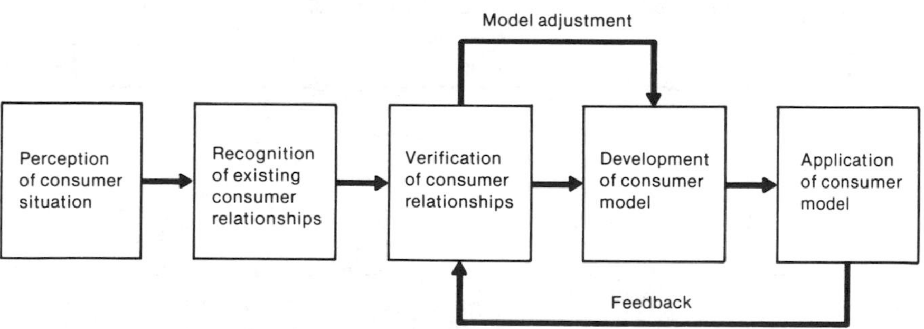

Source: Adapted from William Lazer, "The Role of Models in Marketing," *Journal of Marketing*, vol. 26, no. 2 (April 1962), p. 9. Published by the American Marketing Association.

situation such as a retail store visitation. The researcher seeks the relationships in the situation between the consumer, the environment, the store, and the purchase. The researcher attempts to verify the relationship by repeated research. When sufficient evidence is available of specific situations, the researcher develops a general consumer model to explain all similar store visitations. Finally, the researcher applies the model to check its accuracy for explanation. If problems develop, feedback allows for adjustment in the model.

Figure 3–2 demonstrates consumer model building by means of realization. Based on logical, deductive thought processes, the researcher develops a theoretical statement of consumer retail store visitations. This theory, by definition, must be a set of propositions that are internally consistent with each other. The researcher expresses the theory as a model. Next, empirical evidence of store visitations is collected which lead to the establishment of relationships. The abstract model is applied to the existing situation and comparisons made. As a result, the model is verified or problems are identified. This information provides feedback to the theoretical statement which provides a basis for modifying the model. Under either abstraction or realization, the modification of the model is continual until it is perfected.

Figure 3–2
Consumer model building by realization

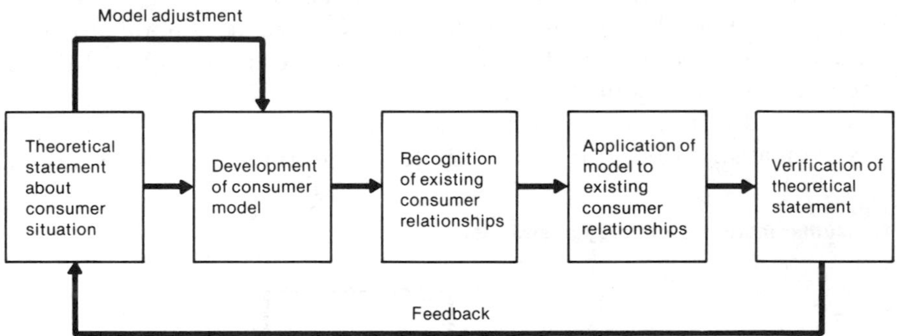

Source: Adapted from William Lazer, "The Role of Models in Marketing," *Journal of Marketing*, vol. 26, no. 2 (April 1962), p. 12. Published by the American Marketing Association.

Points about the use of models

There are both advantages and disadvantages associated with the use of consumer models. Let us consider some of the more important advantages. First, models incorporate a measure of logic to consumer investigations. If nothing else, a model is a logical construct. It forces one to consider the contribution of each part to the total picture. Second, models identify major consumer variables. The variables are necessary for model building. Thus, model building forces one to consider carefully which variables to include and which to exclude. Third, models provide a frame of reference for solving consumer problems. Consumer models help demonstrate basic relationships between variables, and they point the way for lines of new inquiry. The existence of a model also tends to emphasize nonfitting parts which in turn focuses attention on this factor. Fourth, models point the way for hypotheses needed for theory development. Fifth, models are useful as simple predictors of consumer behavior.

Some of the more important disadvantages of consumer models include the following. First, models tend to oversimplify complex situations. This fact can result in inadequate analysis, poor comprehension, and misunderstandings about the real world of the consumer. Second, models are sometimes substituted for reality in people's minds. There is a tendency for some people to take the model as a statement of the real world. No model is fully capable of expressing the complexity of consumer behavior. Third, models tend to reduce or retard discussion. There is a certain awe sometimes associated with the presence of models, particularly mathematical models. The idea exists that, if it can be expressed so precisely, then it must be fact. With this type of thinking, there may be little tendency to improve on the model. Furthermore, models become identified with specific persons, and this fact retards development. A scholar would often rather develop a new model than be accused of tampering with someone else's work. In turn, too many models just become confusing. This fact, in itself, retards work. Fourth, models lack flexibility. Most models are constructed under either explicit or implicit assumptions, and these assumptions become restrictive. In spite of these disadvantages, and they can be serious, it is generally felt that the advantages of model building are significant to the development of consumer behavior.

HUMAN BEHAVIOR MODELS USEFUL IN CONSUMER ANALYSIS

Up to this point, we have been discussing consumer models in general. It is now time to turn our attention to specific types of consumer models. A great many models of human behavior have a bearing on consumer analysis, and these models constitute an excellent point of departure for the more specific types of consumer models to come later.[11] It is, of course, not possible to deal with all the types of human behavior models here, but it is possible to consider some of the more representative types. Four models have been selected for presentation: (1) Allport's socio-psychoanalytic model, (2) Freudian psychoanalytic model, (3) Pavlov learning model, and (4) Lewin topological model.

Allport socio-psychoanalytic model

Allport, in *The Nature of Prejudice*, was not seeking a theory of consumer behavior.[12] However, he defines prejudice very close to what is referred to today as attitude. Allport says prejudice is, "a feeling, favorable or unfavorable, toward a person or thing, prior to, or not based on actual experience."[13] In his chapter entitled "Theories of Prejudice," Allport does an excellent job of identifying most of the major exogeneous and endogeneous variables that affect human decisions toward an object stimulus such as a product.

The variables of Allport have been adapted to consumer behavior as shown on Figure 3–3. While the model is a static representation, it begins with the broadest exogeneous variable, culture, and works down to the endogeneous variables of personality and motivation. The purchase decision is seen as the result of an interaction between the individual, who has been influenced by his environment, and the product. Of course, one could determine that the product is representative of the entire business sphere. Thus there are many similarities between Allport's model and that of the author.

Figure 3–3
Modified version of Allport's model

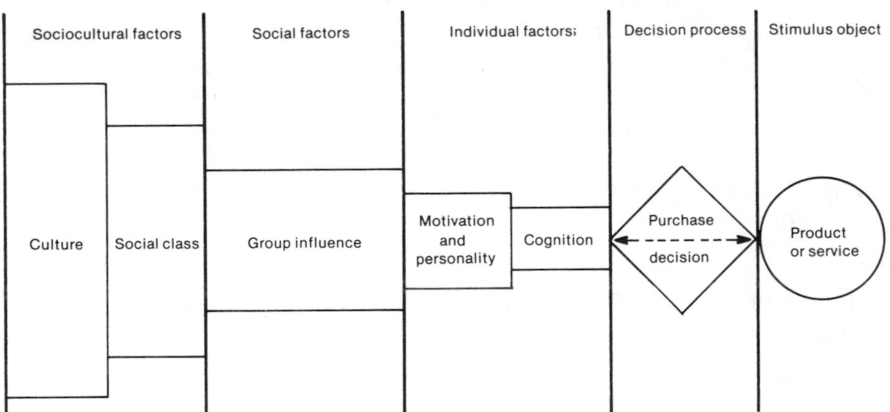

Source: Harold H. Kassarjian and Thomas S. Robertson, *Perspectives in Consumer Behavior* (Glenview, Ill.: Scott, Foresman & Co., 1968), p. 4. Reprinted by permission.

The principal contribution of Allport lies in identifying the major areas of external and internal human influence that can be applied to consumer behavior. Allport does little to connect these variables directly to consumer processes since his principal interest lies in another direction.

Freudian psychoanalytic model

There is no question but that Sigmund Freud has had a significant effect on people's awareness of themselves. His model of how the human mind operates is classic even today. "Copernicus destroyed the idea that man stood at the center of the universe; Darwin tried to refute the idea that man was a special creation; and Freud attacked the idea that man even reigned over his own psyche."[14] The Freudian model is primarily a word model, and it consists of four elements: the *psyche* or mind; the *id* or unconscious part of the mind related to strong drives or needs; the *ego* or conscious part of the mind; and the *superego* or unconscious part of the mind dealing with moral law.

Freud's basic idea is that, at birth, the child is practically all id. Needs lead the child into contact with others in order to satisfy these needs. At first the child is clumsy and attempts to use intimidation and force. Frustration leads the child through experience to use ego to plan more complex means of obtaining desires. In the process the person's superego acts as a brake on how far the person can go to reach desired ends. Freud believed that people could never have their psyches completely under control because of the unconscious elements involved. In effect, the people can never fully understand either their urges or means of satisfaction. The problem for every person is to reach a balance between the id, the ego, and the superego.

The Freudian model is no longer accepted as completely factual, and it has been continually modified and refined. Nevertheless, it has meant much to the understanding of consumer behavior. Its most important contributions include the following: first, it provides a basic explanation of the functioning of the conscious and unconscious mind; second, it emphasizes that consumers are influenced as much by product symbolism as by economic factors; and third, the presence of the unconscious indicates that consumers can be appealed to subtly and at several levels rather than by simple, logical explanation. These were great advances.

Pavlov learning model

Pavlov was a Russian psychologist whose contribution to human behavior was largely based on experiments with animals. Freud, and many other psychologists, believe that man arrives at conclusions by reasoning (cognition) processes. Pavlov's experiments indicated that Man can learn by a process of conditioning.[15] As a matter of fact, this learning technique has been given the name of *classical conditioning.* In experiments with dogs, Pavlov rang a bell each time before feeding the dog. It was discovered, over time, that the dog began to salivate and prepare for eating anytime the bell was rung. In short, through a repetitive, or reinforcement, process the dog began to associate the bell with food. Dogs were even taught how to obtain their own food by pressing a lever when the bell was rung. Thus Pavlov concluded that people can also be taught by association. The basic idea is that any two things presented together are associated together. Reinforcement tends to make the association stronger.

Obviously, Pavlov's classical conditioning provides an alternative to cognition as a means of learning. It has application to consumer behavior in any situation where a product can be associated with pleasure, happiness, or a desire to act. Furthermore, much repetitive promotion, personal selling, and branding are based on the concept of reinforcement.

Lewin topological model

The figure below demonstrates a summary model of Kurt Lewin's concept of human behavior.[16] Lewin conceived a person as to topolog-

Figure 3–4
Modified Lewin model

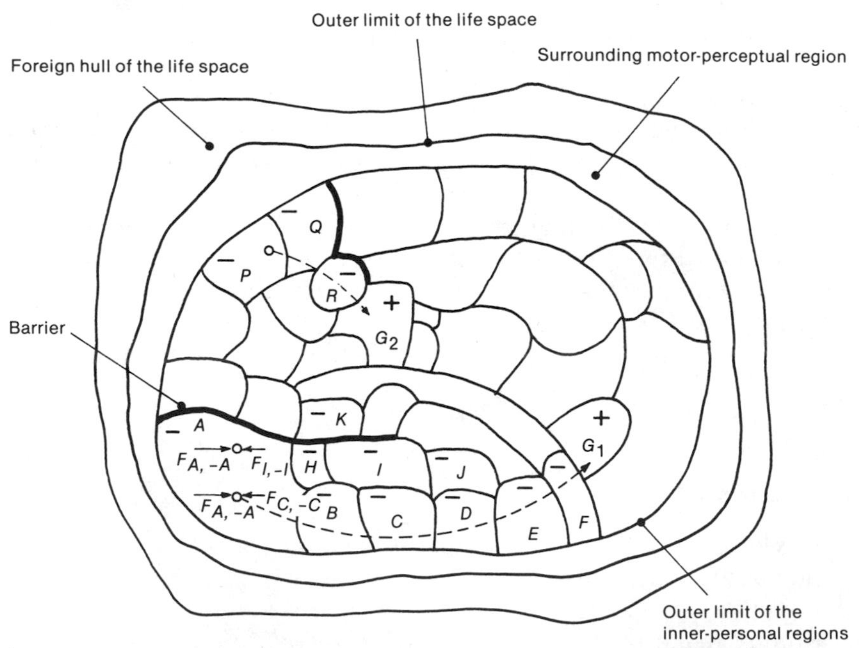

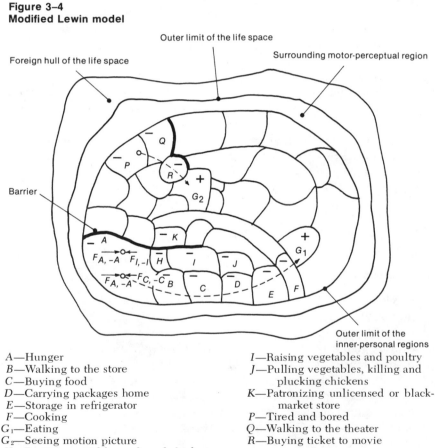

A—Hunger
B—Walking to the store
C—Buying food
D—Carrying packages home
E—Storage in refrigerator
F—Cooking
G_1—Eating
G_2—Seeing motion picture
H—Buying vegetable seeds and chicks
I—Raising vegetables and poultry
J—Pulling vegetables, killing and plucking chickens
K—Patronizing unlicensed or black-market store
P—Tired and bored
Q—Walking to the theater
R—Buying ticket to movie

Source: Joseph Clawson, "Lewin's Psychology and Motives in Marketing," *Theory in Marketing*, ed. Reavis Cox and Wroe Alderson (Homewood, Ill.: Richard D. Irwin, Inc., 1950).

ical area but with no significance given to its precise size or shape. The topological area is divided into three major areas: (1) inner-personal region, (2) motor-perceptual region, and (3) foreign hull of the life space.

First, the *inner-personal region* constitutes a person's wants or desires. Each want has a specific place as indicated in the model. Some are peripheral and less important, and some are central to the person's personality and very important. Each want can typically be reached by several paths. This fact indicates that the want can normally be satisfied in more than one direction. Each region has a boundary of resistance, and if sufficiently strong, it may limit the manner of satisfying a want by region. The motor-perceptual region is internal to the person but is the restricting path to the want.

Second, the *motor-perceptual region* surrounds the inner-personal region. The motor-perceptual region is internal to the person but is the mechanism that relates that person to the environment by means of sound, sight, taste, movement, speech, etc. What is understood in the inner-personal region must be filtered through these perceptions.

Third, Lewin calls the person's surrounding environment the *foreign hull of the life space*. What the person experiences in the environment is continually changing and modifying perceptions. Thus the person's inner-personal region is affected. The environment is real, whereas the person's perceptions are symbolic. The person continually attempts to make the two compatible.

Lewin sees the person as operating within a total situation. He expands on the more narrow views of Freud or Pavlov. Lewin's model does have applications to consumer behavior. First, by emphasizing the hierarchy of wants, we gain insight into, not only why different consumers behave differently, but also why some products are more important than others to the same consumer. Second, the model emphasizes that the consumer has more than one route for satisfying a particular need. Third, Lewin gives emphasis to the interaction between the individual and the environment. The effect of the environment on the individual is shown to be important.

ECONOMIC AND BEHAVIORAL MODELS OF CONSUMER CHOICE

Besides the general behavioral models presented in the previous section, the traditional concept of consumer behavior was incorporated into economic theory. Consumer concepts have been a part of economics almost from the inception of the subject. However, consumers have generally been treated in a partial rather than wholistic sense in economics. References to consumers can be found in both microeconomic theory (theory of the firm) and macroeconomic theory (national income analysis). Lately, some marketers have begun reworking the economic concepts of consumer choice to include more behavioral material.[17] In this section, we discuss the contributions and limitations of traditional economic analysis of consumers, and show how behavioral material may be related to economics.

Microeconomic model of consumer choice

When consumer behavior is isolated in microeconomic theory, we find that the primary focus is on how consumers make choices between products, given that these consumers have limited income. This consumer choice is founded on the concept of utility, or satisfaction, and diminishing returns. *Diminishing returns* refers to the fact that a consumer places more value on products held in short supply. The basic theory is referred to as far back as Adam Smith (1776), but Alfred Marshall, who worked about 1890, is given credit for its most serious construct.

When consumers must select between two products, they add more of the product held in short supply, until the *marginal utility* (additional satisfaction from one more unit) is equal between the two products. This statement can be illustrated as the mathematical model:

$$\frac{MU_x}{P_x} = \frac{MU_y}{P_y} = \frac{MU_n}{P_n}$$

where *MU* equals marginal utility; *P* equals price; *x* and *y* equal specific products; and *n* equals any other product.[18] The basic idea is that each consumer purchases those products in sufficient quantity so that the marginal utility per dollar of any product equals the marginal utility per dollar of any other product. In short, consumers equate marginal satisfaction between all products.

The individual choices of consumers can be summed into a single, and usually downsloping, demand curve. The basic question under demand analysis is how much consumers, in general, will purchase at a given series of prices. The economist assumes that individual differences average out when consumers' aggregates are considered. If the supply is known, then the quantity and price are set at the point where supply equals demand.

Consumer choice behavior is based on the assumptions that (1) perfect knowledge of individual wants and sources of supply exist, (2) preferences are perfectly ordered, and (3) utility is maximized. The assumption of maximization is particularly important since it depicts a completely rational consumer devoid of any emotions.[19] This person, known as economic man in the literature, is coldly calculating and never swayed by love, beauty, feelings, etc. His only motive for buying is to maximize product usefulness. All in all, a totally disgusting person. Thank goodness he is not found in real life.

The microeconomic model of consumer behavior has advanced the knowledge of consumer behavior. The marginal utility concept provides logic to fundamental choice tendencies. Although it can be attacked on its assumptions, no superior explanation of these *basic* tendencies, even including maximization, has yet been advanced. Of course, we know that consumers do not have perfect knowledge, often make mistakes, and do allow emotions to color their decisions. Still, so long as the model is not confused with reality, its contributions can be recognized. Demand analysis demonstrates the tendency of masses to adjust quantity purchased to price. Both models fall far short of explaining consumer behavior on two counts. First, while maximization of satisfaction may be a goal of consumers, it is certainly not the only goal. Furthermore, it is a mistake to assume maximization to be the desirable goal. Second, the models are restrictive since they deal only with choice behavior. Consumer behavior is much more complex. Actually, microeconomic analysis deals with "what" consumers buy. The important question left unanswered is "why" do they buy that way.

Macroeconomic model of consumption

Macroeconomic theory is highly complex, and any attempt to reduce it to a couple of paragraphs is bound to result in considerable over simplification. The subject is not only complex, but there is not always agreement even among economists on the variables involved and their interrelationships. This fact makes the importance of consumers even less definite in macroeconomic theory. The theory tends to abstract the consumer into a nonentity commonly known as the consumption function. The principal thrust of the model, including a statement of the consumption function, is shown below:

$$Y = C + S$$
$$C = f(Y)$$

where Y equals disposable personal income; C equals consumption; and S equals savings. It is obvious from the formula that savings can be determined by substracting consumption from income.

The consumption function certainly emphasizes the importance of income to consumer purchasing, and it has proved a useful analytical tool. It is a known fact that consumers spend nearly all their disposable personal income and the remainder is saved. The major questions left unanswered here are "how" is the consumer's income spent, and "why" is it distributed that way. As with microeconomic analysis, the theory does not address itself to these questions. It is for these reasons that economics is viewed as the beginning of consumer analysis instead of the end. Of course, it has been stated that the main impetus of this book is on the "why" of consumer behavior.

Kotler's behavioral choice model

Not all economists agree with the classical presentation of consumer choice. Thorstein Veblen struck off in a different direction by asserting that consumers choices are largely conditioned by the groups to which they belong and the groups to which they aspire.[20] Veblen felt that while satisfaction was a strong motivator of personal consumption, it was greatly influenced by prestige seeking and emulation of others.

Philip Kotler, following the lead of Veblen and other psychologists and sociologists, has devised a simple model of consumer choice behavior that emphasizes both economic and social factors. This model is illustrated in Figure 3–5. The buying influences of specific product features are communicated through channels composed of business and environmental factors to the individual (processor). The buyer's psyche is viewed as a "black box" into which the reader may plug any of the previously mentioned theories of human behavior to explain how the actual choices are made. Kotler does not actually address

Figure 3–5
Kotler's behavioral choice model

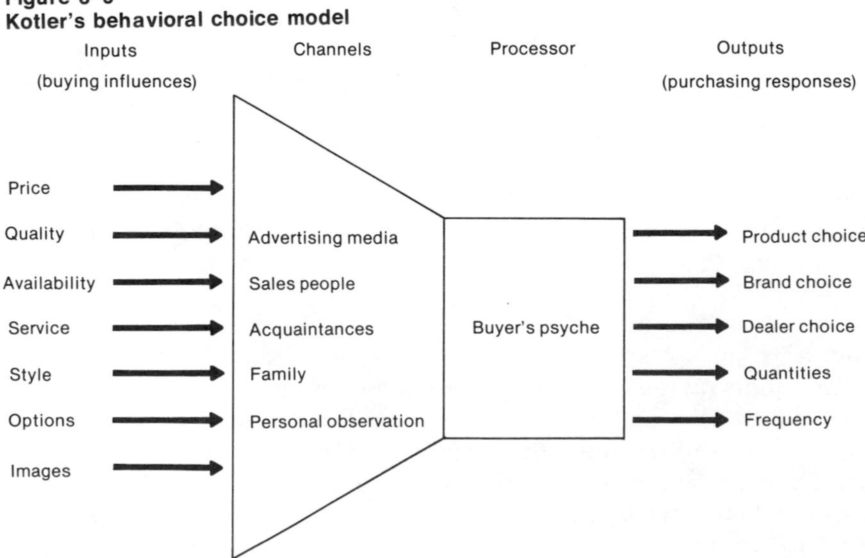

Source: Philip Kotler, "Behavioral Models for Analyzing Buyers," *Journal of Marketing*, vol. 29 (October 1965), pp. 37–45. Published by the American Marketing Association.

himself to this problem. He does indicate that the output is various types of buyer responses.

The primary virtue of Kotler's model is its simplicity and the fact that it does bring social and cultural considerations into the rather sterile economic models. Like any simple model, it can be criticized for not saying enough. It does not explain the buyer's psyche and it does not demonstrate the processes by which the various communications operate.

CURRENT STATUS OF EXPERIMENTAL CONSUMER MODELS

Scholars in marketing have learned much, not only from the human behavior models, but also from the economic models that directly involve consumers. In the past ten years, marketers, drawing on the foundations already established, have begun to develop consumer models of their own. Four current consumer models are selected to demonstrate the direction that experimental work is taking. These models are (1) Nicosia model, (2) Andreasen model, (3) Engel, Kollat, and Blackwell model, and (4) Howard-Sheth model.

These models are presented in simplified form on the following pages. It is recognized, in advance, that to discuss the models out of context is insufficient. What each developer has been careful to construct logically by the use of many words and detailed explanation, we can only summarize at this time. Therefore, the analysis related to each model presented is based on the model itself and not the full discussion of related material that in several cases includes entire books. The reader must recognize that such a brief summary cannot help but do an injustice to the concepts actually in the developer's mind.

Nicosia's model

One of the earlier, comprehensive consumer behavior models is that developed by Nicosia.[21] A simplified version of the Nicosia model is shown in Figure 3–6. It presents consumer behavior as a flow chart of decision sequences. The model is divided into four major fields. Field one, "From the Source of a Message to a Consumer's Attitude," contains two important subfields: the firm's attributes and the consumer's attributes. In field one, some form of promotion is presented by the firm and received by the consumer about a product previously unknown to the consumer. The message input is filtered through the consumer's predispositions and emerges as some attitude about the product. In field two, the consumer begins search and evaluation of the product and/or input from the firm, and the output of this field is some consumer motivation. In field three, the consumer, now effec-

Figure 3–6
Nicosia's consumer decision model

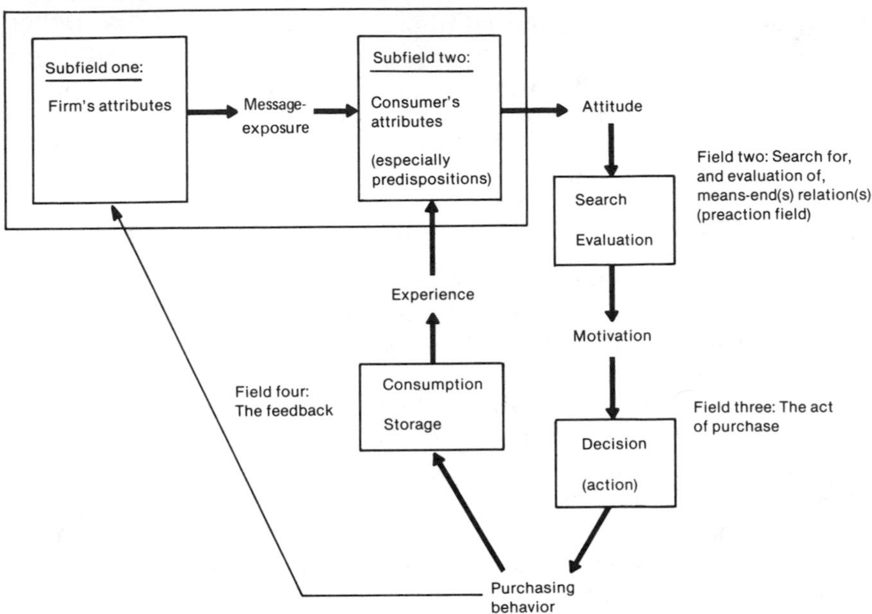

Source: Francesco M. Nicosia, *Consumer Decision Processes* (Englewood Cliffs, N.J.: Prentice-Hall, Inc., 1966), p. 156. Reprinted by permission.

tively motivated, purchases. The results are either stored for future reference or fed back to the firms as purchase behavior. Either of these two actions occurs in field four.

The model is generally good, but, as with all models, it does not depict the real world. Specific problems include the following. First, the assumption that the consumer has not previously known of the product, is limiting. Second, attitudes, motivation, and experience do not actually occur in precise sequence. In other words, the interaction of personal factors can be misleading. Third, the effects of the environment, other than the business, are not clearly spelled out in the model. One important factor in Nicosia's favor is that the model is reasonably complete, and yet it is not so complex as to be confusing. In terms of explaining basic tendencies it does a good job.

Andreasen's model

Although not precisely identified, the Andreasen model (Figure 3–7) contains the social, cultural, and business environments plus

Figure 3–7
Andreasen's consumer decision model

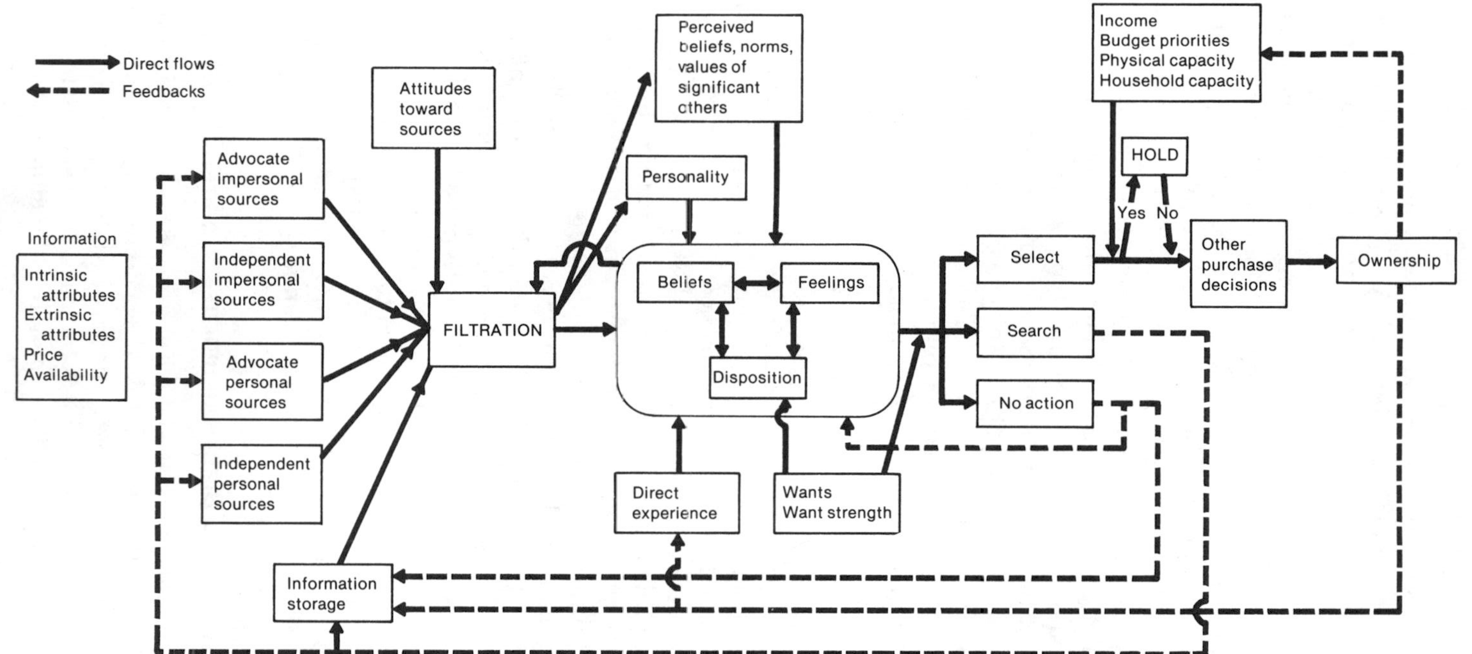

Source: Alan R. Andreasen, "Attitudes and Customer Behavior: A Decision Model," *New Research in Marketing*, ed. Preston E. Lee (Berkeley: University of California, Institute of Business and Economic Research, 1965), p. 8.

communications, decision processes, and constraints. The central variable in the model is the individual. Andreasen's model, like Nicosia's, assumes no prior knowledge of the product on the part of the consumer. Inputs about products reach the consumer through any of the five senses. Inputs to the individual may be either personal or impersonal. The information is filtered through the individual's perceptual processes. This filtration is largely determined by preexisting attitudes. The filtered information, whether distorted or not, has some effect on the individual's attitudes, beliefs, and feelings. Cultural values, personality, experience, and wants are also fed into the individual along with the new product information. The internalization process may lead to three possible types of decisions. The consumer may select the product, begin a search process, or take no action. The latter two decisions are put into the consumer's storage to affect future stimulus or filtration processes. The select decision has to take into account constraints and other purchases.

The Andreasen model offers more explicit variables and relationships than the Nicosia model. The model is reasonably comprehensive, and it does provide a measure of explanation for environmental and individual variables of consumer behavior. Furthermore, it particularly emphasizes the strong influence of emotions on consumer behavior. Therefore, it is a reasonable statement of the major relationships involved in consumer behavior.

There are several problems with the model, as is generally the case with comprehensive models. To a much greater extent than Nicosia's, the model tends to depict the consumer as a mechanical thing much like a computer. You put in certain inputs, press the correct button, and the consumer cranks out the answers. Unfortunately, this is not the case with real people. Second, some of the variables offer difficulties. For example, the positioning of personality, attitudes, and experience as either internal or external to the individual cannot be clearly determined from the model. Third, it appears that constraints enter into the consumer's decision process much too late. Fourth, the interaction of the consumer and the business firm is not too well established in the model. In spite of the problem, the Andreasen model does offer a sound basis for further experimentation.

Engel, Kollat, and Blackwell model

This model, illustrated in Figure 3–8, is referred to here as the Engel model. It is an improved version of an earlier presentation.[22] The Engel model is the best known of all the experimental approaches to consumer behavior, and it is the basis for a successful graduate text on consumer behavior. The model is developed around four major

Figure 3–8
Engel, Kollat, and Blackwell consumer behavior model

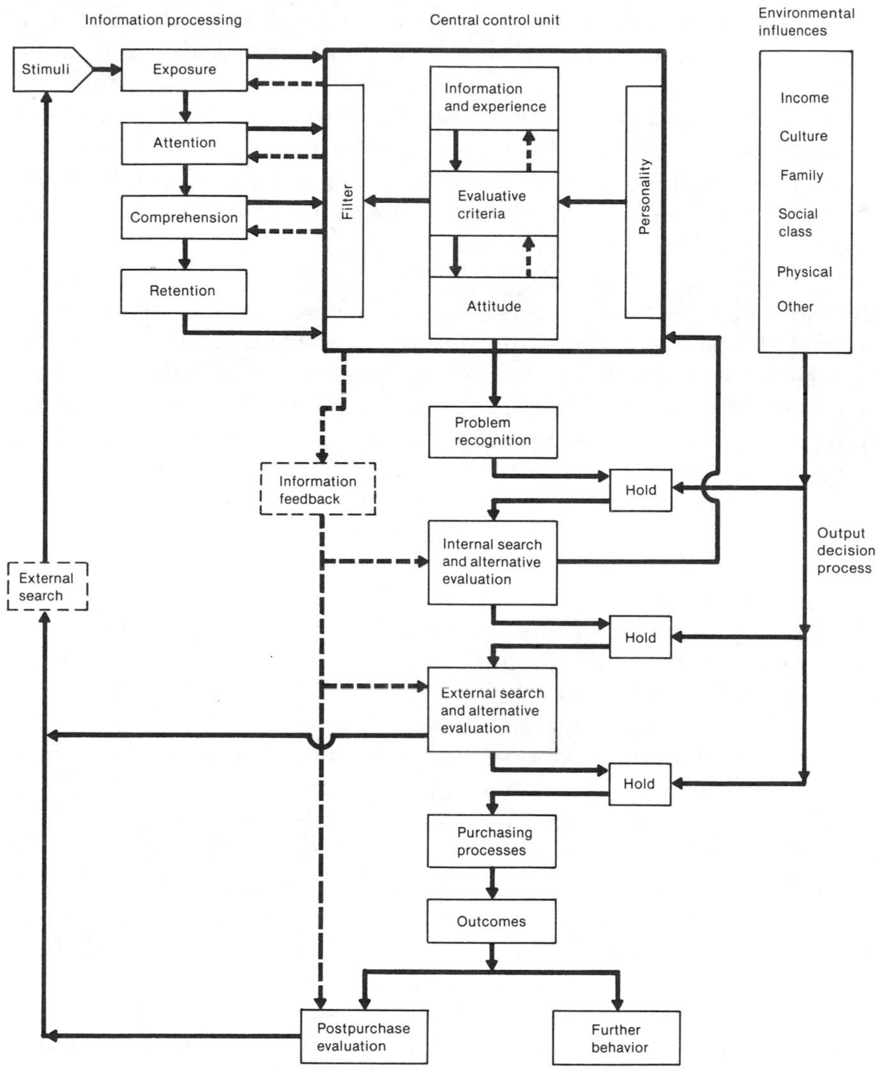

Source: James F. Engel, David T. Kollat, and Roger D. Blackwell, *Consumer Behavior*, 2d ed. (New York: Holt, Rinehart, & Winston, Inc., 1973), p. 58. Reprinted by permission.

concepts. They are: (1) the central control unit, (2) information processing, (3) the decision process, and (4) the environment.

The *central control unit* is essentially the individual consumer's mind. Here experience, attitudes, and personality are coordinated through evaluative criteria (specifications used to compare) in response to information filtered in from external sources. The individual's mind has two basic relationships: (1) it reacts to external stimuli and (2) it initiates the decision process. In short, the individual controls his or her interaction with the surrounding world. *Information processing* is the means by which external stimuli pass through the filter to become a part of the central control unit. Four phases are involved which are called exposure (physical and social stimuli), attention (becoming a part of the mind), comprehension (understanding), and retention (stored for future use). In this way the individual gains knowledge and experience.

Based on the manner in which stimuli are received and stored in the mind, the consumer enters into a decision process to decide what action to take in response to the stimuli. This decision process is fairly standard decision making. It consists of problem recognition, internal search and evaluation of data, external search and evaluation of data, purchasing, and postpurchase evaluation. Environmental influences enter into the decision process between each of the steps and can affect either or both the information or the evaluation. Postpurchase evaluation may become a part of any new stimuli.

The Engel model is preferred over the other theoretical approaches to consumer behavior. It has several advantages for experimentation. First, and perhaps most important, is that it combines relative completeness with a logical ordering of information. Second, it emphasizes decision making more than the other theoretical models. Third, of the models based on flows, the Engel model is the easiest to follow in its revised form. Fourth, the model does a better job of emphasizing how relationships occur.

As one expects with any experimental model, the Engel model has its deficiencies. First, important internal variables such as needs and motivation are not specified, although they are contained in discussion. Second, it is the most mechanical of all the experimental models. It reads as if it were written by an excellent computer programer. Third, it is unclear how the environment is related to the central control unit and to the stimuli. Fourth, business is assumed to be a part of the stimuli but is not specified. Fifth, although the authors state that stimuli pass through the filter, this does not appear to be the case entirely with exposure and retention as shown on the model.[23]

Howard-Sheth model

The Howard-Sheth model is perhaps the most sophisticated theoretical construct of consumer behavior yet developed.[24] The model is built on inputs, perceptual constructs, learning constructs,

Figure 3–9
Howard-Sheth model of consumer behavior

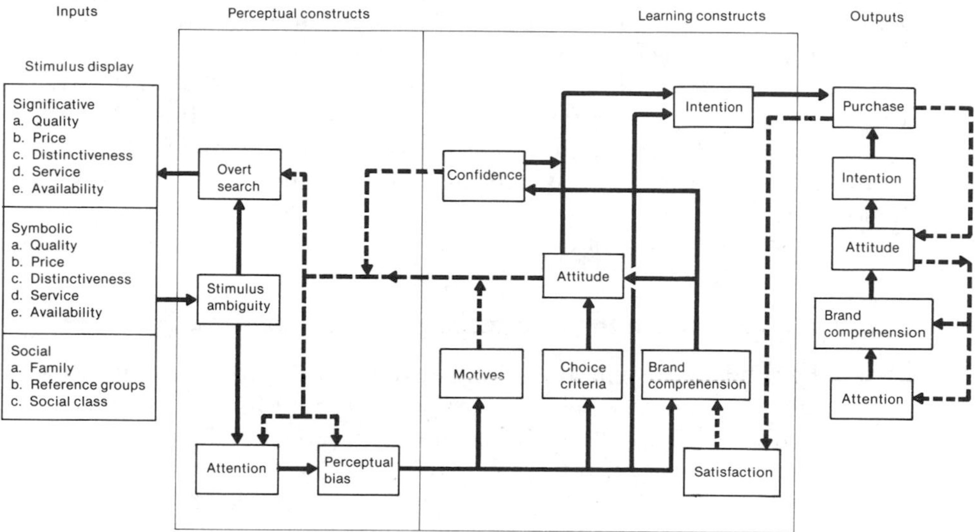

Note: Solid lines indicate flow of information; dashed lines, feedback effects.
Source: John A. Howard and Jagdish N. Sheth, *The Theory of Buyer Behavior* (New York: John Wiley & Sons, 1969), p. 30.

and outputs as shown in Figure 3–9. The inputs—designated significative, symbolic, and social—include both business and environmental factors. When the senses pick up any of these inputs, stimulus ambiguity results. This ambiguity concurrently leads to overt search for more information and perceptual bias brought about by attitudes, confidence, search, and motives—some of which are already stored in the consumer's memory. In turn, the new information may cause changes in motives, choice criteria, intentions, and brand comprehension. These factors, in turn, affect confidence, intention, and purchase. Once a purchase is decided, this information becomes data feedback in several directions. It may feed back as satisfaction to affect brand comprehension. Feedback also directly affects attitudes and indirectly affects intention, brand comprehension, and attention.

The Howard-Sheth model is a very precise construct with the variables clearly connected in their major interactions. It points emphatically to the great variety of inputs that affect consumer behavior. In the construction of the theory, the authors have done an excellent job of drawing from business, psychology, sociology, management, etc. and of bringing these areas into the concept of consumer behavior. To this extent, the model is not only precise, it is very comprehensive.

The more important problems with the Howard-Sheth model can be stated as follows. The very complexity of the model causes problems with quantification. In the model as presented, there is no allowance for product rejection or product postponement, and there is no real connection between purchase and the inputs that started the entire process. The interaction of the inputs, stimulus ambiguity, and perceptual bias are inadequately explained. Another problem is the redundancy in learning constructs and outputs which can lead to confusion. Furthermore such variables as needs, communications, and decision processes are not emphasized in the model.

General comments on the four models

All the models presented in this section have similarities and dissimilarities which can be summarized at this time. First, each model is similar in that consumer behavior is viewed as a type of flow process or computer program. Second, each model contains, directly or indirectly, the same three broad variables. These variables are the individual, the firm, and the environment. Third, each model is similar in its tendency to consider the individual as the central component of the model and the basic decider of consumer problems. Environmental variables are generally treated either as constraints or influences. Fourth, each model similarly demonstrates that consumer behavior is a highly complex subject on which we, as yet, have no consensus. The major dissimilarities between models revolve around the particular manner of treating the major variables. These differences can be summarized as the emphasis given to each variable in specific models, the factors included under each major variable, and the relationships that exist between the major variables and the specific factors.

There are also a group of problems common to all four models. First, it has not been as popular with marketers, as with economists, to spell out clearly the assumptions under which the models are constructed. Second, none of the models has yet stood the test of time and empirical investigation. Third, all the models are primarily experimental tools designed to aid in the identification of hypotheses and the development of theory. This is both their virtue and their principal problem. Experimental models must display completeness. This completeness is a virtue because it leads to testing, verification, and refinement of consumer concepts. Completeness is a problem because no model can depict the real world completely, thus the developers leave themselves open to criticism on every turn. This fact also may be a virtue.

NOTES

1. Gerald Zaltman, Christian R. A. Pinson, and Reinhard Angelmar, *Metatheory and Consumer Research* (New York: Holt, Rinehart, and Winston, Inc., 1973).
2. Luis V. Dominguez and Philip C. Burger, "An Empirical Analysis of the Process of Buyer Behavior," *Relevance in Marketing: Problems, Research, Action,* ed. Fred C. Allvine (Chicago: American Marketing Assn., 1971), pp. 391–96; Tanniru R. Rao, "A Pseudo-Heuristic Model of Consumer Purchase Behavior," *Marketing Education and the Real World,* ed. Boris W. Becker and Helmut Becker (Chicago: American Marketing Assn., 1972), pp. 360–65.
3. David B. Montgomery and Glenn L. Urban, *Management Science in Marketing* (Englewood Cliffs, N.J.: Prentice-Hall, Inc., 1969), p. 9.
4. J. Scott Armstrong and Alan C. Shapiro, "Analyzing Quantitative Models," *Journal of Marketing,* vol. 38 (April 1974), pp. 61–66.
5. Montrose S. Sommers, "Problems and Opportunities in the Development of Consumer Behavior Theory," *Consumer Behavior: Contemporary Research in Action,* eds. Robert J. Holloway, Robert A. Mittelstaedt, and M. Venkatesan, (Boston: Houghton Mifflin Co., 1971), pp. 14–22.
6. Zaltman, Pinson, and Angelmar, *Metatheory and Consumer Research,* pp. 129–31.
7. Donald R. Lehmann, Terrence V. O'Brien, John U. Farley and John A. Howard, "Some Empirical Contributions to Buyer Behavior Theory," *Journal of Consumer Research,* vol. 1 (December 1974), pp. 43–55.
8. Robert A. Mittelstaedt, "Criteria for a Theory of Consumer Behavior," *Consumer Behavior: Contemporary Research in Action,* eds. Robert J. Holloway, Robert A. Mittelstaedt, and M. Venkatesan (Boston: Houghton Mifflin Co., 1971), pp. 8–13.
9. Ibid.
10. William Lazer, "The Role of Models in Marketing," *Journal of Marketing,* vol. 26 (April 1962), pp. 9–14.
11. Flemming Hansen, "Psychological Theories of Consumer Choice," *Journal of Consumer Research,* vol. 3 (December 1976), pp. 117–42.
12. Gordon W. Allport, *The Nature of Prejudice,* (Cambridge, Mass.: Addison-Wesley Publishing Co., Inc., 1954).
13. Ibid., p. 6.
14. Philip Kotler, "Behavioral Models for Analyzing Buyers," *Journal of Marketing,* vol. 29 (October 1965), pp. 37–45.
15. James A. Schellenberg, *Social Psychology* (New York: Random House, Inc., 1970), pp. 108–11.
16. Joseph Clawson, "Lewin's Psychology and Motives in Marketing," *Theory in Marketing,* eds. Reavis Cox and Wroe Alderson (Homewood, Ill.: Richard D. Irwin, Inc., 1950).

17. Brian T. Ratchford, "The New Economic Theory of Consumer Behavior: An Interpretive Essay," *Journal of Consumer Research,* vol. 2 (September 1975), pp. 65–75.
18. Harold H. Kassarjian and Thomas S. Robertson, *Perspectives in Consumer Behavior,* rev. ed. (Glenview, Ill.: Scott, Foresman and Company, 1973), pp. xii–xiii.
19. George Katona, "Rational Behavior and Economic Behavior," *Psychological Review* (September 1953), pp. 307–18.
20. Kotler, "Behavioral Models for Analyzing Buyers."
21. Francesco M. Nicosia, *Consumer Decision Processes* (Englewood, Cliffs, N.J.: Prentice-Hall, Inc., 1966), p. 156.
22. James F. Engel, David T. Kollat, and Roger D. Blackwell, *Consumer Behavior* 2d ed. (New York: Holt, Rinehart & Winston, Inc., 1973), p. 58.
23. Ibid., p. 58.
24. John U. Farley and L. Winston Ring, "An Empirical Test of the Howard-Sheth Model of Buyer Behavior," *Journal of Marketing Research,* vol. 7 (November 1970), pp. 427–38; John U. Farley and L. Winston Ring, "Empirical Specification of a Buyer Behavior Model," *Journal of Marketing* Research, Vol. 11 (February 1974), pp. 89–96; Shelby D. Hunt and James L. Pappas, "A Crucial Test for the Howard-Sheth Model of Buyer Behavior," *Journal of Marketing Research,* vol. 9 (August 1972), pp. 346–48.

QUESTIONS

1. What is a model? A consumer model? Why is it important to develop and understand models of consumer behavior?
2. Discuss and contrast the several ways that consumer models can be typed.
3. Explain abstraction and realization. What do these terms have in common with consumer behavior?
4. Discuss the difference between models designed to develop consumer theory and models designed to teach consumer concepts. Is the type of model affected by the purpose?
5. Contrast the Freudian psychoanalytic model and the Pavlovian learning model.
6. What models have economics contributed to consumer behavior?
7. Explain the Kotler model of consumer behavior.
8. Contrast the Nicosia, Andreasen, and Engel models of consumer behavior. Demonstrate common variables and differences.
9. Explain the Howard-Sheth model of consumer behavior.
10. Give your personal evaluation of the consumer models presented in the text.

PART TWO

Consumer purchase decisions

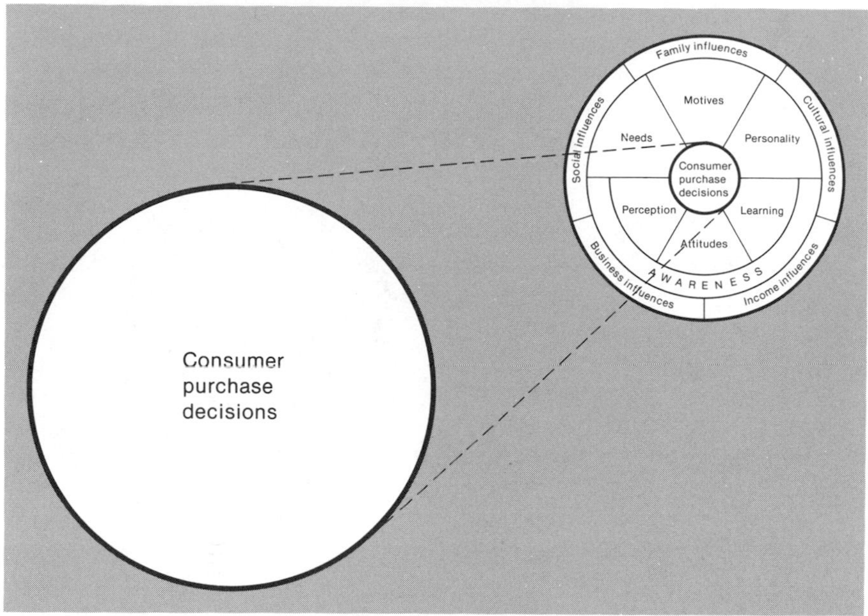

In this Part, we begin a discussion of consumer purchase decisions. With the foundation for consumer behavior in mind, attention can be turned to the model presented in Chapter 1. The remainder of the text is devoted to the explanation of this model. The consumer model is analyzed logically from the inside out. Purchase decisions are the focal point of all consumer behavior, and, as such, represent a beginning for the discussion. There are five chapters in this part built around the consumer purchase process. They are:

4. Introduction to consumer decisions
5. Determine products to purchase
6. Search for market related information
7. Establish consumer preferences
8. Purchase decision and assessment

Chapter 4 introduces and explains consumer decisions and the decision process. The remaining chapters contain a detailed explanation of each step in consumer decision making.

4

Introduction to consumer decisions

Consumer purchase decisions are vital to consumer satisfaction because each decision is a specific committment to a particular brand or store. The making of effective consumer purchase decisions is the central issue of consumer behavior. It is for this reason that consumer decisions are placed at the center of the model. All the individual's basic determinants, needs, motives, personality, and awareness are brought together just so a choice can be made in the marketplace. Any external influences are internalized and utilized by the consumer for that same purpose. With the background information on consumer behavior now complete, we can begin a more detailed discussion of this consumer decision process.

THE CONSUMER'S DILEMMA

Consumers face a serious dilemma in the market. The consumer is caught between the need to make product and store decisions and the inability to make these decisions efficiently. There are a number of reasons why consumers have diffuculty making efficient decisions: too many desires, lack of capital, inadequate information, insufficient time, and poor training.

First, consumers never run out of wants. Consumers want more and better products and services. They want greater variety and a wider range of styles in the products demanded. Fortunately, our society has been able to provide consumers with more and more goods and services, but the sheer weight of the number of product and service decisions reduces efficiency in making them.

Second, it takes money to function effectively in any market, and the consumer market is no exception. Where funds are lacking, this not only limits the total amount of products and services that the consumer can have but it forces the consumer to make compromises on the goods that can be afforded. A mother may be forced to purchase a cheap pair of shoes for her child knowing full well that she will have to enter the market again in a month or six weeks.

Third, consumer information may be inadequate in several ways. The consumer may have too much information, too little information, or incorrect information. Some people argue that mass communication simply confuses people with conflicting information about products. The consumer has so many choices and so much conflicting data on each choice that there may be a tendency to discount all such information.[1] Sellers may withhold pertinent product information that can aid the consumer in deciding on a course of action. The consumer can fail to receive the entire message or may misunderstand the information received. The seller can add to the confusion by deliberately or accidently distorting data.

Fourth, consumer market efficiency is reduced by a lack of time to compare and decide. The average consumer—husband, wife, or child—has more to do in a day than can be done. The consumer must often rely on habit, recommendation, or superficial examination or comparison when selecting merchandise.

Fifth, most consumers are not adequately trained to make sound choices in the market. The American society generally is preoccupied with production rather than consumption. Our entire educational system, and to some extent training in the home, centers around teaching skills in a profession or trade. Practically no effort is given to teaching our youth how to consume—that is how to obtain the most satisfaction out of the fruits of production.

The average consumer cannot tell which size is really the cheapest size of a national brand detergent, and most customers cannot figure the price per can quickly in their heads for a can marked 3/89¢. The situation is actually made worse because the consumer does not appear particularly interested in learning these things.

CONSUMER DECISION PLANNING IS A WAY OUT

The consumer's dilemma in the market is real, and yet one cannot simply throw up one's hands. The difficulties are too serious for the consumer to ignore, and they are too complex to be handled in any casual or ill-considered manner. There are no ideal solutions to consumer problems, but certainly these problems cannot be adequately solved by chance and guess. The consumer must find some sound basis for coping with this dilemma.

It may appear to the reader that the complexity of market problems makes any useful market analysis impossible. Fortunately for the consumer, this is not the case. Consumer decisions can be meaningfully planned. Perhaps we should clarify what is meant by decision planning. When a consumer makes a decision it means that he or she comes to a conclusion. A *decision* can be defined as the selection, from among alternatives, of a specific course of action.[2] *Planning* may be defined as decision making in anticipation of needs or problems.[3] Thus it follows that *consumer decision planning* is the selection from among alternatives of a specific course of action in anticipation of particular needs or problems. We can observe from the definition that consumer decision making does not need to be formal or highly complex. In its essence, it is nothing more than recognizing a problem and choosing how to handle it.

The consumer is generally aware of the products owned, product deficiencies, and the means or preferred ways that existing deficiencies can be corrected. The use of purchase planning improves the consumer's chances of successful buying in three ways. First, purchase planning forces the consumer to establish product goals and to consider specific means for achieving those goals. Thus, planning tends to lead to logical thought processes by the consumer. Second, purchase planning forces the consumer to consider each problem as it arises. In much the same manner as management by exception, the consumer focuses attention on those products, or means of purchase, that are giving trouble at the time. Other decisions can be reduced to routine. The result is that the consumer reduces the number of decisions that must be handled at a given time to manageable proportions while focusing attention for more logical problem solving. Third, overall planning provides a means to give order to the many decisions faced by the consumer. Separate decisions can be assigned priorities by importance or urgency. Some decisions can, perhaps, be deferred, or assigned for future reference when the consumer has been able to obtain more information.

DIFFERENCES IN CONSUMER DECISION PLANNING

The fact that consumers employ decision planning does not mean that all the problems previously mentioned can be overcome. There is no way that the consumer can escape making decisions.[4] Every act of purchase requires one or more decisions: to part with the money or not, to take one product or brand over another, to follow previous purchase patterns or to change, or to approach one salesperson or another. *The difference between consumers is not whether they make decisions, but how well they plan and execute these decisions.*[5] The fact is that consumer planning varies all the way from practically no planning at all to rather formalized, integrated planning. Some consumers are so careful that their plans almost approach the equivalent of a consumer strategy. However, it is safe to say that this degree of decision planning is not characteristic of most consumers. It is a fact of the market that consumers often employ too little planning, improperly placed planning, and incorrect planning. These are the consumers that we refer to as poor marketers. Consumers are perhaps most often guilty of not giving sufficient consideration to the many problems they face. The important point is that consumers do make some effort to plan, and most consumers do employ some type of purchase planning most of the time. This decision planning is at least sufficient to keep them functioning.

The reader must be aware that everything discussed in this book is affected by, and affects, consumer decisions. It must be remembered that individuals either constitute a family or are a part of some family. Thus, the needs, motives, personality, and awareness discussed in Part

Three are at work continually influencing individual family members' purchase decisions. External influences such as cultural, income, family membership, social, and business affect both the individual and the group. These topics are discussed in Parts Four and Five. Our main purpose at this time is to provide an overall view of the decision process to guide the understanding of topics introduced at a later point.

CONSUMER DECISIONS AND RATIONAL BEHAVIOR

The existence of consumer decision making points to the fact that individuals use their mental abilities in the market. That is to say, consumers do not act in a random or undirected manner. There is motivation, no matter how ill-conceived or emotionally based, behind consumer actions. These motives show reasonable patterns that have a degree of predictability. The basis for a specific consumer's actions may not be entirely wise, the actions may not be what we would do under the same circumstances, and these actions are never simple; but reasons of a personal nature do underlie consumer decision behavior. It goes without saying that unless we could ascribe some pattern to consumer actions, the study of consumer behavior would be meaningless. Yet, confusion does exist over whether the consumer is rational or not.

The traditional approach to rationality

The traditional approach to consumer rationality is a direct holdover from economics introduced previously.[6] It is directly related to the concept of economic man. As mentioned earlier, economic man is a person who always attempts to maximize his dollar return or minimize his dollar outlay.[7] In short, economic man attempts to maximize utility, and does not allow emotions to interfere with his decision. Marketers have been generally hard to wean from this concept of economic man. Therefore, when marketers began to specify types of consumer behavior they fell back on economic man. As a result, the traditional concept of consumer behavior is divided into (1) rational, or economic, and (2) emotional, or nonrational behavior.[8] In spite of the historical popularity of these two terms, they do represent a somewhat unhappy choice of words. These two terms give the definite impression that consumer decision behavior is polarized with some actions rational and some actions nonrational. It is conceivable, under the traditional approach, that a consumer is rational at one point in time and nonrational at another point in time.

The argument is that the type of motive the consumer has for purchasing determines the type of behavior that results and whether the consumer is rational or nonrational. In other words, there is a direct correlation between the motive and the type of decision behavior. Thus, if the consumer's motives are based on economic man concepts, then the behavior is rational, and if the motives are based on psychological factors such as feelings, biases, likes, and dislikes, then the behavior is nonrational.[9] Any attempt to increase efficiency, maximize dollar return, or minimize dollar outlay would be considered as rational because of the economic orientation. Nonrational motives are any considerations having to do with the emotions such as love, prestige, pride, power, ego, beauty, and sex. Of course, the reader can readily see that the lists are arbitrary.

The problems with the traditional approach to rationality stem from the rational-emotional dichotomy. It perpetrates the economic man concept, and it represents consumers as rational sometimes and nonrational at other times. Furthermore, the traditional approach implies that consumers are incapable of making effective decisions in the marketplace. Since the term nonrational generally has a bad connotation in our society, it gives the impression that there is something wrong with consumers who purchase on the basis of their psychological wants.

Contemporary view of consumer rationality

The fact is that whether a consumer is considered rational or not depends largely on the definition used. Contemporary marketers reject the economic man concept of rationality in favor of the concept of a problem solver. A problem solver is always considered to be rational, whether maximizing or not.[10] The contemporary view is based on how consumers think and not on how they behave. Thus, rationality is defined as a course of action relative to the solution of a problem arrived at by logically deciding on the basis of known facts about the problem encountered.[11] The key words in this definition are *logically deciding*. A consumer is viewed as rational by contemporary marketers when he or she applies logic to problems, thinks them through carefully, and makes choices.

The contemporary view still requires a coldly calculating individual. It differs from the economic man concept only in the sense that the consumer is no longer required to maximize as a result of decision making. The concept does allow for emotions. The feeling is that the consumer's goals are established on the basis of emotions, but the consumer rationally calculates specific decisions. This position is an improvement over the economic man concept, but it goes almost too far—implying that consumers never do anything rash or stupid. Furthermore, it does not get at the real issue of consumer decision making.

Concept of normal consumer decisions

The whole idea of attempting to justify consumer decisions as rational or nonrational is poorly conceived. Rationality is just not a concept that should be applied to consumer decisions. Generally, in our society, when one speaks of rational or irrational behavior, one has in mind some deviation from reasonable patterns of thought or conduct by an individual.[12] Even the most ardent of the theoretical students of consumer behavior admit that this is not what they have in mind when discussing consumer rationality. Marketers are attempting to develop theories of normal consumer behavior. Normal is used here in the sense of average or acceptable patterns of thought and conduct by individuals in our society. Abnormal persons are sometimes consumers, but their actions do not occupy the center of the marketer's attention. Under the circumstances, one cannot help but wonder why we are so reluctant to part with the idea of rationality.

Man is a thinking animal, and is capable of selecting reasonable courses of action to follow when faced with a problem. This is the point necessary for the marketer to know in order to deal with consumer desires. Consumers are sometimes very careful and sometimes not; they are sometimes logical and sometimes not; they are sometimes efficient and sometimes not; and at some times they attempt to maximize, and at other times they do not. If consumers were not all these things and more, they would not be normal. We might then be able to predict behavior with more precision, but consumers certainly would not be as interesting, nor would they offer the infinite variety of opinions and actions that marketers have come to depend on as the basis for market segments. Therefore, marketers should concern themselves with the normal behavior patterns of consumers.

Normal people have needs. There may be many kinds of needs, but *every* need has a physical and a psychological aspect, and there is no separating the physical from the psychological or emotional. The gnawing sensation in the stomach indicates that there exists a physical need for food and a psychological need for the food to taste good. Nursing a baby is one of the physical aspects of motherhood, but a part of the mother's need is for the psychological sensation from the sucking motion or the feeling of the child's dependency. Fear is psychological, but the physical corollary is apparent when the hair stands on end, the mouth turns to cotton, and the feet begin to move as if of their own free will.

The point is that every decision made by a consumer is based on both physical and emotional needs. A consumer is not reacting to physical needs at one time and emotional needs at another time; therefore the consumer is not rational at one time and irrational at others.

The consumer is motivated when he or she feels a reason to satisfy the simultaneous bundle of needs.[13] When the consumer is motivated, physical and psychological needs have become fused into a requirement sufficiently strong to want to take some action to relieve, modify, or correct the existing situation.

Decision making enters once the person becomes motivated to act. Even though the need is simultaneously physical and emotional, normal decision making is to some degree thought out. The consumer considers, in more or less detail, the possible alternative methods of satisfying the need. The individual acts upon what *appears* to be the most feasible solution at the time. Thus, we don't really question the consumer's rationality. We just don't consider it pertinent to decision making.

Differences in the concepts of consumer rationality

Figure 4–1 demonstrates the differences in the three concepts of consumer rationality presented here. The traditional explanation, based on economic man, is deficient for two reasons. First, it fails to recognize the difference between the reason for a decision or action and the decision or action itself. It is just as normal or reasonable to retreat from the threat of an overpowering emotional fear as it is to attempt to purchase a vacuum cleaner at the lowest price. As a matter of fact, one can argue that it would be abnormal not to run from an overpowering fear.

Second, the economic man concept toward rationality implies that physical and emotional motives are two different things. In fact, we have shown that the two cannot be separated practically in people. Human beings are behaving in a normal manner when, by decision making, they find a preferred solution to a problem. It does not matter

Figure 4–1

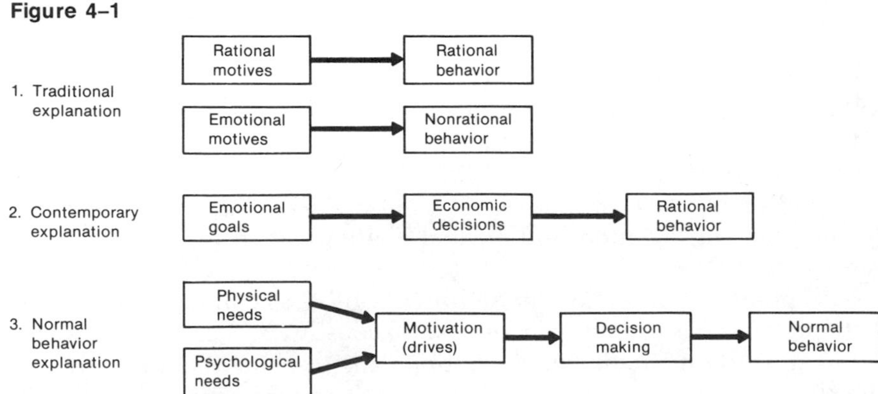

whether the problem is emotionally based, physically based, or, as is more nearly the truth, based on a combination of physical and emotional motives.

The contemporary explanation is equally unsatisfactory. It contains a separation of efficiency factors and emotional factors. The difference is that they supposedly occur in sequence. The actual fact is that emotions and physical considerations operate on the consumer's goals and on his decision processes. Even motivation is not free of emotions. While consumers do decide, in fact *must* decide, all market-oriented questions, they do not necessarily have to decide logically or efficiently. Furthermore, the whole concept of rational and nonrational behavior of consumers borders on the ridiculous. We have defined a decision as the ability to select from among alternatives, and nothing more is required from it.

The normal behavior explanation is a decision making concept, but it emphasizes the meshing of physical and emotional needs. Since the inputs to motivation involve emotions, it follows that motivation, as well as the decision making that follows, has some emotions involved. Just because physical and emotional aspects are involved in every consumer decision does not mean that each is involved proportionally. A given decision may involve more emotional considerations, more physical considerations, or the two may be reasonably proportional. The combination depends on the individual and the circumstance. For example, one consumer may purchase a sport coat primarily for its style (an emotional consideration), while another customer may purchase a coat because of its low price.

Misconceptions about normal consumer decisions

The very fact that the concept of rationality has pervaded the marketer's thinking for so long has led to some common misconceptions about normal consumer decision making. The problem is that instead of simply accepting the decision for what it is, labels of rational or nonrational have to be placed on each decision. It is felt that this tendency is not only incorrect, it is a disservice to the marketing practitioner who must appeal to these consumers. Rational appeals do not necessarily work sometimes and emotional appeals at other times. The soundest course for business leaders is to appeal to the emotions but to provide a rational reason for buying. In other words, a combination of appeals is typically more effective. In order to clarify the point let's look at some common misconceptions about normal, consumer decision making.

Normal decisions and correct decisions. The implication of the traditional explanation of rationality is that if a decision is incorrect it must have been nonrational. The contemporary explanation cannot recognize an incorrect decision. If the consumer was logically deciding on the basis of known facts, it had to be a rational decision *at the time of the purchase*. It is argued that the consumer may change his or her mind later as new facts are introduced, but at the time of the decision, the consumer's action was rational.

The facts are that consumer choices may be either correct or incorrect and still constitute normal decision behavior. A reasonable decision is determined by how it is made, not by whether it is correct or not. The consumer who is deciding is acting normally. In practice, consumers often make incorrect decisions. Four conditions may lead the consumer to make incorrect choices. First, the decision may be based on incorrect assumptions. A person who assumes all hair is green and is told that John has hair will conclude that John has green hair. The decision process is logical. The conclusion is wrong because the assumption was incorrect. A consumer who assumes that a discounted price is a low price can end up paying more for merchandise because the assumption is incorrect. Second, the facts upon which the consumer decides may be insufficient. Consumers often make incorrect decisions on product quality because they depend on price or brand as the determinants of value. Third, the facts may be incorrect. The seller may give the consumer misleading or incorrect information. Fourth, the consumer's judgment may not be sound. The facts may be present but either the consumer perceives these facts incorrectly or uses them ineffectively to make the decision. Nevertheless, the requirements for rationality are met when the consumer decides logically based on *known* facts.

Individual versus social view of normality. Whether decision behavior is socially acceptable or not may depend on the point of view. Certainly, any individual who decides a problem in personal self-interest is acting normally according to our definition. Furthermore the individual believes that the actions taken are reasonable. Society as a whole may view the individual's actions differently. What is normal and reasonable for the individual may be viewed by society as nonrational.[14] For example, the individual consumer may not wear seat belts because they restrict movements. To the consumer, this is a normal and reasonable attitude, although society deems the behavior nonrational because it is life-endangering. A consumer may continue to smoke because the habit is too strong to give up, while society condemns the practice.

The position taken here is that both society and the individual consumer may be correct.[15] The individual may consider his or her behavior perfectly normal, and still not conform to acceptable patterns of behavior prescribed for the group. Social judgment may be that the town drunk, who purchases liquor instead of feeding her family, is nonrational. However, the town drunk may be a weak person and a poor provider, who, in spite of her failure, does not like to see her family suffer. She may think that the liquor she consumes is necessary to preserve her sanity. Thus, how can society say that this person is irrational. Her behavior is normal for her, it is simply not normal for the majority of people. Thus from a social point of view the drunk is nonrational, but from her own point of view she is rational. Society may prefer to see the drunk act differently, but that does not mean that her actions lack reason or thought. It simply makes her behavior different from what the group condones. Notice that society is not necessarily wrong in judging the nonuser of seat belts, the smoker, or the drunk as practicing unacceptable behavior. We may all agree that the total interest would be better served if they acted differently. Society is only wrong in judging their behavior nonrational. There is a real moral and ethical question as to how far society should go in forcing its will on individual consumers.[16]

Habitual and impulse behavior. Habitual and impulse behavior are sometimes presented as examples of nonrational behavior. *Habitual behavior* occurs when, having made a decision once and found it satisfactory, the consumer automatically makes the same decision each time a similar problem arises. Suppose that a person purchases an Arrow shirt after carefully considering the merits of competitive products. This purchase is said to be based on a rational choice. However, when the shirt wears out, if the consumer buys another Arrow shirt without reconsidering the alternatives, he is said to be nonrational because he has allowed habit rather than reason to dictate his action.

The fact is that consumers would be nonrational if they didn't purchase to some extent by habit. Once you have found a satisfactory solution to a problem, it is not reasonable to waste time solving the same problem over and over. Habitual behavior is analogous to the sound management principle of management by exception. You apply your energy to those problems that are giving you trouble. If the consumer did not reduce many decisions to routine, he or she would not have sufficient time for deciding important problems. Besides, a sufficiently strong reason, such as a convincing advertisement of a superior product, can cause the consumer to reconsider habitual behavior. Thus habitual behavior is normal.

Impulse purchases are made on sight with little or no serious comparison of alternatives.[17] Impulse buying is normal because the product receives as much attention as it deserves. Three factors account for impulse purchases: (1) some individuals think faster than others; (2) the decision may not deserve a lot of thought or comparison; and (3) the consequences of being wrong are small. It would seem less than reasonable to devote a lot of time and thought to the purchase of a pack of gum when the consequence of choosing wrong is small. Competing gums are very similar, and if you don't make the best decision you are only out a dime. A normal person allocates more time to the purchase of a house than to the purchase of a car, and the car gets more attention than a new suit.

Rationalization is normal. There is nothing nonrational about rationalizing a purchase. *Rationalization* means the consumer chooses a solution to his or her problem, then justifies the need internally or to others.[18] So long as consumers are using their mind to decide, they are acting normally. There isn't even anything really illogical about this type of decision making. In so far as normal decision behavior is concerned, it does not matter whether the product is selected first and then the reasons, or if the reasons are selected first and then the product. Again, normal behavior results from the way emotional and physical needs and motives are combined into a decision process. Although consumers are sometimes casual in their approach, they are not nonrational. Consumers do plan their moves in the market.[19]

CONSUMER DECISIONS CLASSIFIED

We have pointed out that consumers must make many decisions in the marketplace. Some of these decisions are more complex than others. While we cannot deal with every consumer decision, it is useful to classify the major types of decisions that consumers must frequently make.

Nature of the decision

Decisions classified by their nature tell us something about the decision. There are a number of subtypes of consumer decisions classified according to their nature.

We can classify consumer decisions by the *degree of urgency*. Some consumer decisions are urgent and must be made immediately, as when the sink stops up. Other decisions can be made more leisurely. Usually, the decision to buy a new dress is not urgent, and the decision on a new house can be put off indefinitely.

We can classify consumer decisions by the *frequency of occurrence*. Some consumer decisions are made less frequently than others. Of course, it's a matter of degree between decisions. Toothpaste is purchased more frequently than shoes, but shoes are more frequently bought than sunglasses.

We can classify consumer decisions by *degree of significance*. A decision to buy popcorn at the movie is not as significant as a decision to buy a wiglet. Notice that significance does not just depend on money outlay. Significance refers to the meaning or importance of the decision to the consumer. The purchase of a television set may be significant because of the possible impact on the person or those with whom he or she interacts.

Finally, consumer decisions can be classified by the *amount of routine involved*. Food items are bought on a fairly regular schedule, but perfume, lamps, and watches are bought on a nonroutine basis.

Individual and household decisions

Consumer decisions can be classified by whether the item purchased is for an individual or for the household. Goods typically considered personal items are shirts, dresses, wallets, underwear, jewelry, and key chains. Furniture, automobiles, and food are typically purchased for the household. There is often a difference in the manner of purchase between these two types. Household goods and automobiles are typically decided on by the husband and wife together, but more personal items are decided on by the individual.

Product and store decisions

The consumer must make decisions on the type of product, brand, and so on, to purchase, and on the particular store with which to trade.[20] In a real sense, this entire book is concerned with the reasons why consumers select certain products and stores. However, there are some rather specific factors entering into the decision that can be mentioned at this point. The consumer tends to select the store having the more satisfactory perceived product line, services, prices, and location. Consumers prefer those products that are perceived to offer the greatest satisfaction in terms of the good buy, intended use, prestige, brand preference, and psychic considerations.

It is a mistake to assume that consumers always decide on the product first, then the store. This often happens, but it is often true that the consumer decides on the store first, then the product. The customer, because of location, price, or credit may choose to visit a specific store and take whatever products are offered by that store. The point is that there is no particular sequence to these decisions.

Decision states

One other method of classifying consumer decisions is by the state of decision existing for the consumer at a given time. That is to say, to what degree is the problem fully decided in the consumer's mind. A consumer may be in any of four possible decision states where a particular problem is concerned. They are: (1) rejected, (2) undecided, (3) partially decided, and (4) decided. A solution is rejected when the consumer consciously decides not to pursue that course of action. This state more than any other may cause the individual to seek a different solution. A person is undecided when he or she has no preference for a solution among the alternatives offered. In this state, the consumer cannot make up his or her mind. A person may have decided to buy an iron but be undecided as to which brand to purchase. A consumer in this state will not act. Indecision is a signal to obtain more information about the problem.

A partially decided state covers a wide range of possibilities all the way from practically undecided to practically decided. A person is partially decided when there is a tendency to accept one solution. The consumer may be "sold" on the product but feel that the price is just a little high. Just a little more negotiation can cause the person to act. When the consumer has decided some action, the action may be to buy, not to buy, or to defer the purchase until later. Business attempts to achieve a favorable decided state in consumers.

Interaction of decision types

The types of consumer decisions presented are not alternatives to one another. One of the things that increases the difficulty of consumer decision making is that the person may be, simultaneously, in the process of deciding on more than one of the types presented. The result is often a very complex state of mind for the consumer. Thus, a person may have an urgent household, nonrecurring decision. The decision may simultaneously relate to a product and a store, and the consumer may be partially decided on the course of action to take. As a matter of fact, the average consumer would not consider the above description an unusual situation.

GENERAL CONSUMER DECISION APPROACHES

The question naturally arises, "How does the consumer make decisions?" This is not an easy question to deal with. There is no completely acceptable theory of consumer decision making at this time, but we do know a lot about how consumers make decisions.

Dahl, Haire, and Lazarsfeld describe the three approaches to the study of consumer behavior as distributive, morphological, and analytical.[21] In the *distributive approach,* attention is focused on the outcome of consumer behavior. It is concerned with what people did, where they bought, and what products were involved. The *morphological approach* is descriptive, and it shows how a decision to purchase was made. The *analytical approach,* the one basically used in this book, not only describes how a decision is made but indicates the reasons for or cause of the decision. Thus, the analytical and morphological approaches are very similar.

The analytical method is preferred over the morphological method because it goes one step further to show causal relationships. These two methods are preferred over the descriptive method for the following reasons:

1. Although more complex, these methods provide more in-depth explanation of consumer behavior.
2. Past consumer behavior, as explained by the distributive method, is a less reliable prediction of future consumer behavior.
3. The morphological and analytical methods offer more general explanations of consumer behavior.
4. The distributive method is not as useful for developing marketing strategy.

It is true that the distributive approach is simpler and less costly than the other two approaches. The approach can also be useful for the analysis of specific purchase situations or to explain past consumer behavior. Nevertheless, a general discussion of consumer behavior requires a more analytical decision theory. There are several fundamental assumptions about human behavior that underlie any discussion of consumer decision making. These assumptions are that human behavior is motivated, patterned, learned, and based on assumptions about the behavior of others.[22]

First, human behavior is motivated. People do not act randomly, but with purpose, and a part of their purpose is to buy and consume goods and services. Second, human behavior is patterned in the sense that general behavior is predictable even though specific behavior is not. For example, we can predict that consumers generally take their time in deciding on a new car, but we may not be able to predict the exact factors that enter into the decision. Third, group behavior is learned. People have difficulty tolerating ambiguous situations. Individuals fit their behavior to that observed within the group. This is also true of consumer behavior, and it partially explains our attitudes toward brands, fashion acceptance, and salespeople. Finally, everyone makes assumptions about the behavior of others. These assumptions affect our decisions, including our consumer decisions. A man assumes that his wife wants him to look nice when he buys a new suit, and this influences his choice.

TYPES OF CONSUMER DECISION THEORIES

We are now ready to take a look at the different types of decision theories. For the purpose of discussion, these theories have been divided into partial explanation theories and basic explanation theories. *Partial explanation theories* are so named because they attempt to explain particular types of consumer decisions rather than all consumer decisions. *Basic explanation theories* attempt to develop a broad explanation of all consumer decisions, although exceptions to the rule may be recognized. Each of these groups of theories is discussed in turn.

Partial explanation theories

There are several types of partial explanation theories. Theories that view consumer decisions are based on (1) chance, (2) habit, (3) impulse, (4) social orientation, and (5) heredity are partial explanation theories. Most of these concepts are self-evident. Social orientation is the proverbial "keeping up with the Joneses." It is buying on the basis of what the consumer feels others will think. Purchases based on heredity are made because of the inborn nature of the consumer. None offers a general explanation of how decisions are made by consumers, but at some time or another, consumer decisions may be wholly, or in part, based on these considerations.

The partial explanation theories have two ideas in common. Each theory views consumer deciding as almost entirely based on reaction or emotions, and each emphasizes the lack of factual information upon which consumer decisions are based. It is felt that none of these theories should be discounted. No doubt, at one time or another consumers have made purchase decisions based almost entirely on one or the other of these concepts. Furthermore, almost every consumer purchase decision involves some aspects of the partial explanation theories. For example, who can underestimate the importance of chance or impulse on the individual when shopping or browsing, even when the general product desired is known in advance. Social orientation also is likely to be involved in most decisions to some degree, because all consumers are aware of their relationship with others. Thus, the fact that these concepts are called partial explanation theories indicates nothing of their importance. The name is given because each theory emphasizes a type of decision behavior rather than decision behavior in general.

Basic explanation theories

Basic explanation consumer decision theories consider the consumer as either (1) a risk reducer or (2) a problem solver. These basic explanation theories require some knowledge about the problem on the part of the consumer, but they do not require the perfect knowledge explained earlier for the concept of economic man. Each of the basic explanation theories is discussed below.

Concept of risk reduction. The risk reduction concept is based on the assumption that consumers enter into decision making in the market as a means of reducing risk.[23] The risk reduction theory requires the least amount of information for decision making, and this concept has been popular with many marketers in recent years. The basic idea is quite simple. Every consumer decision involves two elements—risk and consequence. No matter which course of action the consumer takes, there is the risk that the consequence will be unpleasant. The consumer, faced with a market decision, acts to get just enough information to reduce the risk to an acceptable level before acting.[24]

The consumer is faced with the risk of which branded item to buy, especially new product brands, which stores or trade areas to patronize, and which is the best alternative method of allocating his or her funds among all wants.[25] The consumer depends on known risk-reducing strategies such as shopping familiar stores, purchasing only nationally advertised brands, trading with large stores, etc. The risk of information collecting is reduced by accepting more readily favorable information.[26]

Five major types of perceived risk have been identified. They are performance, financial, social, psychological and physical risk.[27] In a recent study of a variety of products it was reported that these five types of risk explained about 74 percent of the variance in the perceived risk of twelve products.[28] Table 4–1 has the rank of these twelve products according to the perceived mean risk of each. The products are ranked according to the degree of perceived risk involved.

The consumer always considers the consequence of any action, and the greater the consequence, the less risk the consumer is willing to assume. Thus expensive products, new products, durables, new stores, etc. call for more information seeking on the part of the consumer. Risk reduction is a normal way for the consumer to handle purchasing because he or she is coping with a difficult situation in a reasonable manner.

Problem solver concept. Another theory of consumer decision making views the consumer as a problem solver.[29] Essentially, the view is that every consumer desire creates a problem situation within

Table 4–1
Ranking of products by mean risk values for each type of perceived risk

Product	Overall risk	Performance risk	Financial risk	Social risk	Psychological risk	Physical risk
1. Sports car	7.18	7.26	7.76	7.42	7.32	5.74
2. Life insurance	6.50	6.58	6.99	4.04	4.73	3.67
3. Color TV	6.17	6.35	6.04	5.82	4.98	3.01
4. Suits	5.91	5.58	6.38	7.13	6.81	1.93
5. Winter coats	5.18	5.00	5.54	6.37	6.16	2.46
6. Dress shoes	4.98	4.59	5.04	5.97	5.47	3.02
7. Deodorants	3.66	4.25	3.80	3.39	3.81	3.14
8. Toothpaste	2.94	2.81	2.61	2.46	2.23	3.57
9. Razor blades	2.92	3.41	3.30	2.04	2.06	4.11
10. Vitamins	2.76	2.66	2.88	1.76	1.77	3.63
11. Aspirin	2.33	2.37	1.94	1.49	1.42	3.54
12. Playing cards	1.60	1.65	1.66	2.20	1.75	1.24

Source: Leon B. Kaplan, "Components of Perceived Risk in Product Purchase: A Cross-Validation," *Journal of Applied Psychology*, vol. 59 (1974), pp. 287–91.

the individual. The consumer acts to solve the problem by deciding on a course of action consistent with his or her subjective desires. When the problem is fully solved, the purchase has taken place. The consumer solves the problem by acquiring information about the situation, determining alternative courses of action, and selecting one course from the alternatives.

John Dewey has been given credit for identifying the steps in problem solving.[30] These steps, in a modified form have become accepted as standard in the study of problems. They are:

1. Problem recognition.
2. Search for information.
3. Evaluation of data.
4. Decision.
5. Post decision evaluation.[31]

As stated, these decision steps apply to any problem—not just consumer problems. What we have is an outline for problem solving. However, it is possible to adapt this outline to the solution of consumer problems. Such an outline is presented at the end of this chapter.

The problem solver theory recognizes that the consumer cannot obtain full information, so risk is involved in any decision. It is also recognized that cost and effort are involved in acquiring information. At some point, the consumer considers the cost of obtaining relevant information too high with respect to the probable need for the information. When this point is reached, the consumer decides on the basis of information already available.

Differences among basic theories. The two primary differences between the risk and problem solver concepts are the definition of rationality and the amount of information needed to make decisions. Each concept requires a reasonable decision process, and each concept allows for emotions. The problem solver concept has a more rigidly defined analysis and it requires more information as a basis for decision making. The risk reduction concept can get by with a great deal of emotion and very few facts. Each theory can serve as an adequate basis for consumer decision making.

STEPS IN CONSUMER DECISION PROCESS

The rationale for consumer decision making is now complete. No single explanation of the decision process is sufficiently complete to stand alone, and a little of each can be identified in most consumer choices. The consumer is a thinker, and decision making is normal activity. The consumer employs a problem solving sequence, but at each step attempts may be made to reduce risk. The consumer may employ the sequence in an effort to maximize return or habit, impulse, social orientation, etc. may modify, or short-circuit, the sequence. In the final analysis, the consumer can probably do no better than to find an acceptabl

Steps in th
a basis for fu
lem solving
with consum
The consume

1. *Determin*
stage, but
deficiency
sumer rec
expand hi
2. *Search fo*
but it is n
it is speci
store type
sumer see
3. *Establish*
evaluation
preference

needed generic products and brands. They also have preferences for store types and the method of shopping.

4. *Purchase decision*. This is the decision stage. It involves the consumer's evaluation of criteria that can be used to make selections from among the various preference alternatives previously established.
5. *Post purchase assessment*. This step corresponds to post purchase evaluation. The word assessment is used to avoid any confusion with the earlier evaluation. At this stage the consumer determines the outcome, or effectiveness of the purchase decision. The results are stored as experience to be used in forthcoming purchase decisions.

Although this sequence of consumer decision steps is not the only manner of viewing consumer decision making, it is a workable method. It is based on accepted analytical stages, and it stands the test of reason. However, the steps should not be looked upon as a rigid sequence nor is every one necessary for each consumer decision. A consumer can proceed from determination of product deficiency to purchase without a search, or a consumer may have sufficient information once the need is recognized to establish preferences. For some types of products, such as convenience goods, there may be very little post purchase assessment. These facts reflect the other decision types previously mentioned. The important point is that the process provides a reasonable approximation of consumer practice, it is sound for discussion, and it does combine aspects of the previously discussed concepts of decision making.

NOTES

... interesting article on the role of ignorance, see Wilbert E. Moore ...lvin M. Tumin, "Some Social Functions of Ignorance," *American ...l Review* (December 1949), pp. 787–95.

...er, *Management* (Homewood, Ill.: Richard D. Irwin, Inc., ...lliam F. O'Dell, Andrew C. Ruppel, and Robert H. Trent, ...*n Making: Analytic Framework and Cases* (Cincin- ...Publishing Co., 1976), p. 5.

...*Demand Analysis for Marketing Decisions* ...D. Irwin, Inc., 1973), p. 16.

...eacock, and Subrata K. Sen, "Purchasing ...ories," *Journal of Consumer Research,* ...4.

..., Sr., "A Comparative Analysis of ...*Journal of Consumer Research,* vol. 2 (June 1975), pp. 29–37; Zarrel V. Lambert, "Product Perception: An Important Variable in Price Strategy," *Journal of Marketing*, vol. 34 (October 1970), pp. 68–76.

6. H. G. Herzberger, "Ordinal Preference and Rational Choice," *Econometrica*, vol. 41, pp. 187–237.
7. George Katona, "Rational Behavior and Economic Behavior," *Psychological Review*, vol. 60 (September 1953), pp. 307–18.
8. E. Jerome McCarthy, *Basic Marketing*, 5th ed. (Homewood, Ill.: Richard D. Irwin, Inc., 1975), p. 155.
9. Jon G. Udell, "A New Approach to Consumer Motivation," *Journal of Retailing*, vol. 40 (Winter 1964–65), p. 6.
10. Rom J. Markin, Jr., *Consumer Behavior: A Cognitive Orientation* (New York: Macmillan Publishing Co., Inc., 1974), pp. 82–84. This book has a good summary of the contemporary view.
11. Kenneth E. Runyon, *Consumer Behavior and the Practice of Marketing* (Columbus: Charles E. Merrill Publishing Co., 1976), pp. 325–26.
12. Elaine Donelson, *Personality: A Scientific Approach* (Pacific Palisades, Ca.: Goodyear Publishing Co., Inc., 1973), pp. 61–62.
13. G. David Hughes, *Attitude Measurement and Marketing Strategies* (Glenview, Ill.: Scott, Foresman & Co., 1971), pp. 11–12.
14. See: A. A. Alchian and W. R. Allen, *University Economics*, 2d ed. (Belmont, Ca.; Wadsworth Publishing Co., Inc., 1964), pp. 19–21; "Business and the Urban Crisis," *Business Week* (February 1968), pp. 57–72; "Perspective on Product Safety," *Final Report of the National Commission on Product Safety* (June 30, 1970), pp. 1–8.
15. Y. Hugh Furuhashi and E. Jerome McCarthy, *Social Issues of Marketing in the American Economy* (Columbus, Ohio: Grid, Inc., 1971), Chap. 2.
16. William Steif, "Why the Birds Cough," *The Progressive*, vol. 34 (April 1970), pp. 47–54; Mort LaBrecque, "Ecology's Dirty Laundry," *The Sciences*, vol. 10 (1970), pp. 5–9; Mort LaBrecque, "Ecology's Dirty Laundry." *The Sciences*, vol. 12 (1971), pp. 10–15.
17. David T. Kollat and Ronald P. Willett, "Customer Impulse Purchasing Behavior," *Journal of Marketing Research*, vol. 4 (February 1967), pp. 21–31; Joe Kent Kerby, *Consumer Behavior: Conceptual Foundations* (New York: Dun-Donnelley Publishing Corp., 1975), pp. 137–38.
18. Robert M. Liebert and Michael D. Spiegler, *Personality: Strategies for the Study of Man*, rev. ed. (Homewood, Ill.: The Dorsey Press, 1974), p. 79.
19. Luis V. Dominguez, "Determining the Nature of the Process of Household Decision Making: An Experimental Gaming Approach," *Marketing Education and the Real World and Dynamic Marketing in a Changing World*, eds. Boris W. Becker and Helmut Becker (Chicago: American Marketing Assn., 1973), pp. 349–53.
20. These decisions are similar to the patronage (choice of store) and selective (choice of product) motives often discussed by marketers. The difference,

of course, is that here we discuss the decisions that result from the motives.

21. Robert A. Dahl, Mason Haire, and Paul F. Lazarsfeld, *Social Science Research on Business: Product and Potential* (New York: Columbia University Press, 1959), pp. 103–104.
22. William J. Gore and J. W. Dyson, eds., *The Making of Decisions* (London: Collier-Macmillan, Ltd., 1964), p. 22.
23. Raymond A. Bauer, "Consumer Behavior as Risk Taking," *Proceedings of the 43rd National Conference of the American Marketing Association,* ed. Robert S. Hancock (Chicago: American Marketing Assn., 1960), pp. 389–98.
24. James W. Taylor, "The Role of Risk in Consumer Behavior," *Journal of Marketing,* vol. 38 (April 1974), pp. 54–60.
25. Joseph F. Dash, Leon G. Schiffman, and Conrad Berenson, "Risk- and Personality-Related Dimensions of Store Choice," *Journal of Marketing,* vol. 40 (January 1976), pp. 32–39; Charles M. Schaninger, "Perceived Risk and Personality," *Journal of Consumer Research,* vol. 3 (September 1976), pp. 95–100.
26. William K. Cunningham, "An Experiment in the Relative Effect of Favorable and Unfavorable Messages on Choice Motivation," *Relevance in Marketing: Problems, Research, Action,* ed. Fred C. Allvine, (Ann Arbor, Mich.: American Marketing Assn., 1971), pp. 450–53.
27. See: J. Jacoby and L. Kaplan, "The Components of Perceived Risk," Proceedings from *Third Annual Conference, Association for Consumer Research,* (University of Chicago, 1972), pp. 382–93; Roselius, "Consumer Ranking of Risk Reduction Methods," pp. 56–61.
28. Leon B. Kaplan, "Components of Perceived Risk in Product Purchase: S Cross-Validation," *Journal of Applied Psychology,* vol. 59 (1974), pp. 288–91.
29. John A. Howard, *Marketing Management: Analysis and Planning,* rev. ed. (Homewood, Ill.: Richard D. Irwin, Inc., 1973), Chap. 3.
30. John Dewey, *How We Think* (Boston: D. C. Heath & Company, 1910). Dewey's original steps were: (1) A difficulty is felt; (2) The difficulty is located and defined; (3) Possible solutions are suggested; (4) Consequences are considered; and (5) A solution is accepted.
31. See: James F. Engel, David T. Kollat, and Roger D. Blackwell, *Consumer Behavior,* 2d ed. (New York: Holt, Rinehard & Winston, Inc., 1973), Chap. 3.

QUESTIONS

1. What is the consumer's dilemma? Explain the reasons why consumers have difficulty making decisions. What is the consumer's way out of this dilemma?
2. Do consumers develop a coherent purchase strategy in the same way as business institutions? Explain.

3. What is meant by rationality? Are consumers rational?
4. Contrast the traditional, contemporary, and normal behavior concepts of consumer decision making. Which of these concepts is the more reasonable position? Explain.
5. Define habitual and impulse behavior. Which, if either, of these types of behavior are normal? Explain.
6. Under nature of the decision, we find degree of urgency and degree of significance as separate types of decisions. Explain the difference between these two.
7. Discuss the consumer's decision states. Give an example of each decision state from your own experience.
8. Contrast partial and basic decision theories.
9. Discuss the interaction of consumer decision theories.
10. Explain the steps in the consumer's decision process.

5

Determine products to purchase

Problems trigger the purchase process
- *Problem recognition*
- *Types of purchase problems*
- *Consequences of problem recognition*

Decide purchase responsibility
- *Function of family purchasing agent*
- *Housewives do the buying*
- *Everybody helps decide need*
- *Responsibility over the decision process*
- *Selection of the purchasing agent*

Product deficiencies begin with the assortment
- *Standard of living depends on the assortment*
- *How assortments satisfy wants*
- *Assortment identification*
- *The assortment and consumer preferences*
- *Problem of assortment upkeep*

Deficiencies discovered by inventory
- *Consumer inventory individualistic*
- *Partial or complete inventory*
- *Casual or formal inventory*

Conditions that signal deficiencies
- *Routine "out" conditions*
- *When expanding the assortment*
- *When deleting products*

Long- and short-run assortments

Degree to which deficiencies specified

In the previous chapter, the reader was introduced to the broad subject of consumer purchase decisions. How consumers make decisions was explained and several decision theories were presented. The previous discussion was general in that it concerned the purchase process as a whole. The steps in the consumer purchase process were introduced, but that was about all. It is now time to begin a detailed discussion of these decision steps with the determination of products to purchase.

PROBLEMS TRIGGER THE PURCHASE PROCESS

The consumer faces many problems when acquiring the goods and services necessary to sustain life and make living really worthwhile. It is the recognition that some problem exists that sets the purchase process into motion. Since personal satisfaction comes from acquiring benefits contained in products, a lack of products is understood to give dissatisfaction or discomfort. Thus the basic problem for consumers is to obtain the products necessary to satisfy needs, wants, and desires. It follows that it is the lack of some specific product or products that acts as the stimulus causing the consumer to become market active. Once the consumer enters the market, other related problems may be encountered. At this time, we seek to understand what it means to recognize a problem, types of consumer problems, and consequence of problem recognition.

Problem recognition

To determine what it means to recognize a problem requires understanding of the definition of a problem and knowledge of what constitutes recognition. A problem has been viewed broadly as either any question to be considered or as any difficulty requiring action. A frequently used definition is that a *consumer problem* exists:

> *any time there is a market related circumstance in which the individual is undecided as to the course of mental or physical action to take.*[1]

Thus the two necessary ingredients for a problem are a goal and indecision.

Problem recognition is primarily a perceptual condition or state. For example, if one's spouse runs off with the mailperson there is a problem, but recognition must wait until the husband or wife perceives that the act has occurred. Thus *problem recognition* is defined as:

> *a state of perception or awareness that there is a significant difference between a desired market circumstance and the actual circumstance.*[2]

Problem recognition brings together experience, memory, forgetting, and sensation in such a way as to activate the conscious mind of the difficulty.

Several conditions must be met before the consumer recognizes that a problem exists. First, the consumer must have some desire that causes dissatisfaction. The dissatisfaction may be based on either physical or mental wants. Second, the consumer must be undecided as to how to proceed toward obtaining a solution to the desire. If the desire is already satisfied, if satisfaction is automatic with knowledge of its existence, or if the solution is known and certain, then there is no recognizable problem. Third, some information is always necessary before a problem is recognized. It is often assumed that all problems arise out of a lack of information, but this assumption is an oversimplification. It is true that the consumer has a problem when there is insufficient information to select a course of action. However, to recognize a dissatisfaction, there must be, at least, sufficient information to indicate the difficulty or some possible solution exists. So long as one knows nothing there is no doubt, and there is no problem. Doubt comes with sufficient information to act, but insufficient information to act in a particular manner.

Types of purchase problems

Consumer problems can be divided into three major types. *Product problems* are those that pertain to the choice of specific items—their features, performance, brand, prices, quality, etc. *Store related problems* involve the choice of retail outlet, store services, location, etc. Problems that involve *method of purchase* include those related to the time to shop, type transportation, number of trips, distance to travel, etc. The consumer is likely to make decisions on most of these problems on any given purchase.

These consumer purchase problems occur and re-occur throughout the purchase process. It is impossible to associate any specific type of decision with a particular step in the decision process. For example, the individual begins to decide issues related to the product at the first stage of the decision process, but some questions of brand, price, etc. may not be fully decided until the moment of purchase. Likewise, during search the consumer considers method of purchase problems but product and store related problems are also important. At the moment of decision, all these problem areas may come together. Although all these consumer problems are important, our attention in this chapter is focused on the determination of products to purchase. The other problems are considered as the discussion of the purchase process continues.

Consequences of problem recognition

Once a problem is recognized, the consumer almost inevitably is faced with certain consequences. The existence of a problem necessitates some action must be taken. The consumer can ignore the problem, defer action until the problem becomes more urgent, or seek some immediate solution. This fact is true no matter which type of problem is being considered. The deferring or ignoring of a problem requires no consumer action, so it is seeking some immediate solution that moves the individual to action.

Problem recognition, by its nature, sets in motion difficult comparisons of complex variables. The individual may compare such factors as stores, brands, prices, time factors, finances, other needs, personal motives, etc. These comparisons may involve the individual in interactions with reference groups, business establishments, or family members. The complexity of the comparisons is one of the major reasons that consumer behavior is so difficult to understand.

Problem recognition leaves the consumer changed. The awareness that a problem exists, coupled with the resulting decisions, cannot help but contribute to the consumer's general education. All types of changes in the consumer are possible. New problems are identified while information acquired and solutions arrived at can make the consumer more conscious of his or her environment. In the process, the consumer becomes a more experienced buyer. Poor problem recognition or inferior solutions make some consumers despondent or callous. Too many problems can cause consumers to give up essentially in their desire for specific products or a better life.

DECIDE PURCHASE RESPONSIBILITY

We have identified the purchase process and discussed the nature of consumer problem recognition, but we have not considered who actually recognizes problems, searches out information, and makes the purchase. We cannot delve further into the purchase process without coming to grips with this question of buying responsibility. In this section we identify and explain the role of the purchasing agent in consumer behavior.

Function of family purchasing agent

In a business, when some department has a need, the product can be acquired in one of two ways. First, the department having a need can go to a supplier directly and negotiate to purchase the product. Second, many firms have a purchasing specialist who assumes the responsibility of buying for the entire business. Each using department makes its product requirements known to the buyer who then engages in search, evaluation, and purchase. It is pretty much the same within the family. Each person with wants must either engage in his or her own buying, or each can indicate their wants to a designated *family purchasing agent* who acts to buy for the group as a whole. Both types of buying are carried out in most families.

Who the family purchasing agent is has a direct bearing on how the buying is accomplished. One family member may not trade with the same store, purchase the same brand, consider price or quality equally important, or select the same time to act as another family member. To some degree, personal biases and preferences are brought to bear by the purchasing agent.

There are two important differences between a family purchasing agent and a business buyer. One major difference is that in the family no single person is permanently designated as the purchasing agent, but this is the case in business. Responsibility varies over time depending on the type product involved, the situation, and the family's life style. Kids ride to the store to purchase candy, dad picks up a six pack on the way home from work, mother purchases dad a new tie while grocery shopping, or dad meets mother downtown after she gets off work to consider dining room furniture. Another major difference is that the family purchasing agent often acts without explict direction from the person with the need. A mother may purchase children's clothing or groceries without specifically asking what is desired. For many types of purchases, the purchasing agent just knows what is required.

Housewives do the buying

In a single member family the individual must act as his or her own purchasing agent in most cases.[3] There is no problem of delegating responsibility. Even in a multi-member family, individuals frequently do their own purchasing. Men, women, and children each tend to purchase most of their personal consumption items such as clothing, toiletries, books, sports equipment, etc. These purchases can constitute a significant market for business firms.

In spite of known purchases by individuals, the fact remains that in most families today, the majority of purchases are concentrated in one person. Typically, this person is the wife, and she easily wins the title of family purchasing agent. This fact is true even if the woman is holding down a full time job besides running the household.[4] Housewives usually purchase groceries which alone account for approximately 20 to 40 percent of total family expenditures; she purchases most convenience clothing such as work clothes, underwear, etc.; and she does most of the gift shopping. It is easy to see why it has been estimated that housewives do the buying of about 70 percent of all family items. A study of 800 grocery store customers yielded the following patterns of search responsibility: the principal shopper was a woman in 75 percent of the cases, 15 percent of the time the principal shopper was a man, and 10 percent of the time the principal shopper was a couple.[5]

Everybody helps decide need

It would be a mistake for business executives to concentrate their sales effort on women based on the false assumption that they are responsible for nearly all purchases. The fact is that the person who actually does the purchasing is not always responsible for determining what is purchased. In a majority of cases, the purchasing agent is acting at the direction of one or more persons who actually possess the wants. The purchasing agent may make final decisions on brand or box size, but the one with the want sets the overall purchase parameters. Evidence indicates that every member of the family can provide input into the purchase of products that are jointly used by the family. The input may be specific to a particular purchase, or it may come in the form of opinions and preferences expressed to the purchasing agent over time.

Even when the purchasing agent is engaged in personal search, other members of the family exert an influence. In the above reported grocery study, it was found that 29 percent of the couples who shopped had children present, 21 percent of the men had children present, and 39 percent of the women shoppers had children present.[6] The principal shopper may perform the physical search for food, but the children provide considerable input, either in the store or before, on the type of cereal to consider, which meat and vegetables to avoid, and the type of snack treats that are desired. The point is that most designated family purchasing agents tend to know member preferences. A study of 100 housewives covering 10 product classes demonstrated that 80 percent of the wives felt they knew the brand preferences of other family members and took these preferences into account when shopping.[7]

The evidence indicates that the husband tends to dominate consumer search and decision for automobiles, tires, beer, liquor, and air conditioners. Wives have greater influence on the search and purchase of cosmetics, clothing, home sewing, silverware, home furnishings,

Table 5–1
Husband-wife decision-making roles in 1955 and 1973

Decision area	*1955 (Percent)*	*1973 (Percent)*
Food and groceries		
Husband usually	13	10
Both husband and wife	33	15
Wife usually	54	75
Number of cases	(727)	(248)
Life insurance		
Husband usually	43	66
Both husband and wife	42	30
Wife usually	15	4
Number of cases	(727)	(247)
Automobile		
Husband usually	70	52
Both husband and wife	25	45
Wife usually	5	3
Number of cases	(727)	(248)
Vacation		
Husband usually	18	7
Both husband and wife	70	84
Wife usually	12	9
Number of cases	(727)	(244)
House or apartment		
Husband usually	18	12
Both husband and wife	58	77
Wife usually	24	11
Number of cases	(727)	(245)
Money and bills		
Husband usually	26	27
Both husband and wife	34	24
Wife usually	40	49
Number of cases	(727)	(248)

Source: Isabella C. M. Cunningham and Robert T. Green, "Purchasing Roles in the U.S. Family, 1955 and 1973," *Journal of Marketing*, vol. 38 (October 1974), pp. 61–81.

and appliances.[8] Table 5–1 demonstrates some of the changes that have taken place in family decision responsibility over the years. These results can be summarized as follows:

1. The husband dominated in 1955 for the purchase of life insurance, and increased this domination by 1973.
2. The wife dominated in handling food and money and bills decisions in 1955, and increased this domination by 1973.
3. Vacations and apartment decisions were jointly determined in 1955 and this tendency increased by 1973.
4. The husband dominated in 1955 for automobile decisions, but his responsibility had greatly declined by 1973.[9]

Responsibility over the decision process

Not only does consumer decision responsibility vary by product and over time, but it varies according to the stage of the decision process. In short, one person in the family may be responsible for problem recognition, another for search and still another for making the decision. There is evidence to support this position.[10] Table 5–2 summarizes the results of one study of 73 households involving the purchase of 25 products.

The study indicates, as we have already shown, that there is consid-

Table 5–2
Husband-wife influence over the decision process

Pattern of influence	*Problem recognition*	*Search for information*	*Final decision*
Husband dominant	Life insurance Other insurance	Life insurance Other insurance Car	Life insurance Other insurance
Autonomic (either party dominant)	Cosmetics Nonprescription drugs Appliances Husband's clothing Housing upkeep Alcoholic beverages Garden tools Saving objectives Forms of saving Car	Nonprescription drugs Appliances Husband's clothing Housing upkeep Alcoholic beverages Garden tools Savings objectives TV/stereo Forms of saving	Nonprescription drugs Alcoholic beverages Garden tools Other furnishings Cosmetics
Syncretic (joint determined)	Children's toys Living room furniture Outside entertainment Vacation Housing School	Children's toys Living room furniture Outside entertainment Vacation Housing School	Children's toys Living room furniture Outside entertainment Vacation Housing School Housing upkeep Appliances Husband's clothing Saving objectives TV/stereo Forms of saving Car
Wife dominant	Cleaning products Kitchenware Child's clothing Wife's clothing Food Other furnishings	Cleaning products Kitchenware Child's clothing Wife's clothing Food Other furnishings Cosmetics	Cleaning products Kitchenware Child's clothing Wife's clothing Food

Source: Harry L. Davis and Benny P. Rigaux, "Perception of Marital Roles in Decision Processes," *Journal of Consumer Research*, vol. 1 (June 1974), pp. 51–61.

erable specialization of responsibility between husbands and wives when purchasing. The search step tends to have more specialization of role than any other step, although problem recognition also displays considerable specialization. There is a clear tendency for the final decision to be made jointly. Notice the tremendous shift of items into the syncretic category at the final decision stage. These results tend to indicate that once information is available within the family about product alternatives, there is considerable communication about these alternatives before buying. This procedure is diplomatically sound, it can lead to better decisions, and improved family harmony from shared satisfaction and blame.

Selection of the purchasing agent

The family purchasing agent is not typically selected formally by appointment or by ballot like government officials. It often happens that the individual gets the job by default because no one else wants it. A housewife may not enjoy buying groceries, but someone has to do it. Certain roles within the family tend to be perceived as carrying specific purchase responsibility. For example, everyone may agree the housewife pays the bills, the husband takes care of automobile repairs, and each spouse purchases their own clothing. These perceptions can vary from family to family. Six factors are especially important in determining who acts as the family's purchasing agent: (1) convenience, (2) type of product, (3) product importance, (4) family organization, (5) purchase competence, and (6) desire to act as a purchasing agent.

Convenience is the most important factor in deciding the purchasing agent where staple purchases are concerned. Groceries and drugs are frequently purchased by the wife while the husband may pick up cigarettes or gasoline. The reason is that each has the necessary information, and it is relatively easy for each to act. The type of product is also important. In many families, search and purchase is divided along product lines. For example, the housewife may handle groceries, children's clothing, appliances, lamps, and car care while the husband may pay the monthly expenses, sports equipment for the children, automobile repairs, and yard equipment. Such items as haircuts, gifts, personal hygiene, and entertainment can only be sought by the user.

The importance of the purchase is a major factor in deciding who becomes the purchasing agent. Importance can be measured by the size of expenditure or the number of family members affected. Nearly everyone in the family may seek information and provide input on the purchase of the automobile because of its psychic importance and the size of the expenditure. Family organization refers to how consumer search and purchase have previously been handled. This factor explains why the housewife acts as the family purchasing agent 90 percent of the time in one family and only 10 percent in another.

Purchase competence is important to the selection of the purchasing agent because it means that the person most capable of handling search and decision is given the task. For example, the person driving the car, eating the meat, cleaning the home, and performing the yard work typically has more pertinent information on these activities. The final factor concerns willingness to act as purchasing agent. A housewife may have to pay the monthly bills because the husband refuses to accept the responsibility. A husband may have to buy gas for the car because the wife does not view this operation with favor. A reluctant purchasing agent may perform poorly until it is better for another family member to undertake search and purchase.

The fact is that no two families act just alike when assigning the purchase task. Who is to act as purchasing agent is either implicitly or explicitly negotiated among the family members. It is possible to have effective buying with either the wife or the husband taking on search and purchase responsibility. Of course, in most families these activities are shared on some reasonable basis. The important point is that every family must have some organization for handling search and purchase decisions.

PRODUCT DEFICIENCIES BEGIN WITH THE ASSORTMENT

Consumer behavior would be much simpler if the individual could deal with one product need at a time. In practice, this situation is never found. Products are not purchased in a vacuum, rather each product must be evaluated in relation to other product needs. To purchase one product means that you either cut down on, or eliminate, the use of some other product. The consumer must plan purchases of individual items so as to meet the more important or more urgent of his or her wants. It follows that, to some degree, the purchase of products must be considered as a group.

Standard of living depends on the assortment

Consumers accumulate over the years large numbers of different types of products which we refer to as assortments. A *consumer assortment* is defined as:

> *that combination of goods and services recognized by the individual, or family, as necessary to maintain or improve the standard of living.*[11]

The assortment is a particular combination of goods and services. This means that every consumer assortment is an individual one. The assortment of no two consumers is likely to be exactly the same. Since each consumer is an individual and each has a different assortment, it follows that each consumer has different needs and wants in the marketplace.

All consumer buying is entered into for the purpose of meeting some assortment goal—to replace goods routinely used up, to modify assortment makeup, or to increase product holdings in the assortment. In fact, one can think of the assortment as the physical manifestations in terms of products and services of a consumer's physiological and physical requirements. The idea of a consumer assortment is too important as the basis for product deficiencies not to require careful understanding.

The consumer assortment is as much a mental condition as it is a physical fact. The consumer acts on the basis of what he or she believes the assortment is, or ought to be, as much as on the basis of what it actually is. Few consumers have an accurate inventory of their total product holdings, but any individual can tell you whether they perceive that their standard of living is being met or not. They can also explain what product priorities are necessary to improve that standard of living. How a consumer perceives his or her assortment relative to those of others affects self-perceptions. If other persons are perceived to have more, we are dissatisfied. If we perceive ourselves to have more, we are happy no matter what the actual standard of living involved.

How assortments satisfy wants

An assortment exists to satisfy consumer desires and to meet contingencies. However, few, if any, consumers obtain any real satisfaction just from the fact that physical goods are in their possession. Some people may have a desire to possess things for their own sake, but even this type of possession is usually related to satisfaction one feels because of the envy of others. That is the point. Physical goods exist for what they can do and not for what they are. Consumers buy and own physical goods because of the real or potential satisfaction seen in those goods. An automobile is not wanted if it does not run, and a cake mix that makes sour cakes is not desired. The goal of consumers in developing target assortments is satisfaction. No matter how noble the idea, how appropriate the materials, or how well designed the product may be, it is not bought unless it satisfies some desire held by a consumer.

Assortment identification

Up until this point, assortments have been discussed as a comprehensive whole. No attempt has been made to delve into the specific makeup, or *composition*, of assortments. The fact is that identification of assortment composition is an integral part of the purchase process. Without a knowledge of what one has, there is no sound basis for determining what one is out of, or which new products can add significantly to the person's want satisfaction. At this time, the attributes of assortment composition are identified, the assortment grid is discussed, and differences between assortments are explained.

Attributes of assortment composition. The composition, or make-up, of an assortment has three attributes: width, variety, and depth. Any understanding of the consumer's assortment is an understanding of these attributes. The existence of these attributes should not surprise us, since all assortments (including business assortments) display these attributes.[12]

The *width* of assortment is defined as the major categories of products that make up the assortment. For example, major categories of consumer needs may be transportation, home furnishings, food, and clothing. *Variety* is the number of different product types that are necessary under each major category. Thus, food has a lot of variety, since it requires canned goods, fruits, vegetables, drinks, and meat. Transportation may require only an automobile and bicycle. *Depth* of assortment refers to the number of individual products of each type carried in the assortment. A consumer may have five steaks, two heads of lettuce, and five cans of corn.

The width, variety, and depth define a particular consumer's assortment, and when we refer to the composition of assortment, we are referring to these three attributes. Any change in the composition of a consumer's assortment must be a change in its width, variety, or depth.

The assortment grid. The essential point of our previous discussion is that consumers possess assortments that can be identified and quantified. A hypothetical assortment inventory can be demonstrated by the use of a grid like the one illustrated in Figure 5–1.

The grid shows a hypothetical assortment composition for a consumer. The assortment composition illustrated on the grid is not necessarily definitive. This particular assortment has a width of four, shown across the top of the table. Variety and depth are listed under each column heading. The amount of detail an individual consumer would ascribe to his grid depends on the thoroughness of the consumer in defining his requirements. A more complete grid may show, besides broad product types and quantities, the specific items desired. These

Figure 5–1
Assortment grid for Consumer *A*

Transportation	*Home and home furnishings*	*Food*	*Clothing, etc.*
2 automobiles	1 house	30 units of canned goods	9 sets of bed linen
	2 davenports	6 items of fresh fruits and vegetables	4 suits
	5 chairs	5 kinds of fresh meat	10 ties
	6 tables	3 loaves of bread	3 pr. shoes
	1 dining room set	40 items of assorted other foods	15 pr. socks
	3 bedroom sets		30 sets of underwear
	30 items of miscellaneous furnishings		12 shirts
			50 pieces of other assorted clothing

items may even be specified by brand name. Notice also that some boxes are vacant. These empty boxes represent the individual's reservations about changing or expanding the assortment at some future time. These empty boxes illustrate the consumer's expectations.

Difference between assortments. Individual consumers have different assortment compositions. These differences may range from minor to greatly different. Perhaps Consumer A lives in the suburbs, has a family, and commutes to work each day. Consumer B, an apartment dweller, single, living downtown, and walking to work may have an assortment similar to the one illustrated in Figure 5–2.

Figure 5–2
Assortment grid for Consumer *B*

Transportation	*Home and home furnishings*	*Food*	*Clothing*
	2 rugs	25 kinds of snack foods	10 suits
	1 liquor bar	8 bottles liquor	30 shirts
	3 etchings	1 qt. milk	8 pr. shoes
		3 bottles aspirin	20 pr. socks
			25 ties
			40 sets of underwear
			60 items of other clothing

Each consumer needs many products in varying quantities to maintain that individual's standard of living. A review of the two hypothetical assortment grids demonstrates that people do have rather definite product requirements at any given point in time and that people do tend to maintain these products at levels sufficient to meet basic needs and provide for contingencies.

Consumer B has fewer product categories in his or her assortment than Consumer A, since B does not use private transportation. The assortment of B is restricted in variety compared to A for all types of products except clothing. Both assortments may be quite satisfactory for the individual involved, but there is an obvious difference in how each consumer views their product needs. The difference lies in the personal characteristics, life styles, responsibilities, and economic conditions of the two consumers. The difference is certainly not due entirely to economic aspects, because Consumer B may have twice the income of A. Consumer B may either spend extra income outside the house or may save a large portion.[13] It goes without saying that the market behavior of A and B will differ due to the differences in their assortment needs.

The assortment and consumer preferences

Based on our observations about the assortment grids of consumers A and B, we can define three important characteristics of assortments:

1. Assortments have a definite structure.
2. Products within assortments have status.
3. Assortments exist to satisfy wants.

A knowledge of these characteristics is important to the consumer for scaling preferences, so let's take a closer look.

All assortments have a structure consisting of the orderly arrangement of interrelated products.[14] The structure of assortments is determined by the width, variety, and depth of products making up the assortment. Structures may differ, and some assortments may be better defined in one consumer's mind than in another, but a structure does exist.

Products within an assortment have status in the sense of importance and/or urgency. A family may give up its living room furniture in order to purchase a second car. Thus, the car has higher status than the furniture. One could conclude that status is directly related to expenditure, but this is not necessarily so. A consumer may part with a second car before greatly reducing the consumption of meat. It is fair to say that, *generally*, a consumer will pay more for goods with higher status in the assortment than for goods with low status.

It was pointed out earlier that there is no reason for assortments except to satisfy wants, and consumers do not enter the market for unwanted products. However, consumers do make mistakes and purchase products that they find out later are unwanted. Such products tend to remain in the assortment indefinitely. Consumption is slow if it occurs at all. It is also true that products no longer needed sometimes remain in the assortment. Many people hang onto possessions long after any possibility of their being used has disappeared.

Problem of assortment upkeep

Consumer assortments can be described as open or closed depending upon whether some products normally on hand are "out" or not.[15] An *open-assortment* is one where some type of deficiency exists. The deficiency may be a routine replacement item or an extension or shift in the holdings of the present assortment. A *closed assortment* exists when all the products required by the consumer are present and the assortment structure is complete. The reader may remember the vacant boxes in the assortment grids presented earlier. These boxes show that these illustrative grids were open assortments.

When the assortment is closed, the consumer has no need for new products and no need to enter the market. On the other hand, when the assortment is open, it does not mean that the household must cease to function. It does not even necessarily mean that the consumer must enter the market to buy. An assortment is a flexible thing. It is very capable of adjustment and reorganization. Most consumers seek closure of their assortments, but until that condition is achieved, they can operate, only at a reduced standard of living. In practice, it seldom, if ever, happens that the household assortment is completely closed.

Not only is the assortment seldom closed, but it is normal that a given consumer's assortment is open with respect to several products at the same time. The children need new shoes, mother wants a dress, it's grocery shopping day again, and the car's radiator needs repair. Over any extended period of time, the entire assortment has to be replaced. Besides the more-or-less frequent and routine purchases of food and clothing, the family will, over time, need a paint job for the house, the addition of a fourth bedroom, the purchase of a second car, two new television sets, bedroom furniture, and a gall bladder operation for father. One basic question individuals in a family face is how to establish some order to the purchase of all these different needs.

DEFICIENCIES DISCOVERED BY INVENTORY

Consumers become aware of deficiencies as a result of comparing their present product holdings to their wants. This comparison requires that consumers have either a formal or an informal inventory of their assortment. Some consumers keep a more inclusive list of their product holdings than others. It is not unheard of for a family to keep a detailed list of its assets. The list may be kept in conjunction with personal property insurance, or it may be kept with the monthly budget for referral purposes. Most consumers probably have no more than a mental impression of their major product holdings. Nevertheless, if you ask a consumer if he or she has a certain item, that person can generally tell you "yes" or "no."

For most consumer product decisions, it is not necessary physically to count the merchandise owned. Most decisions do not involve the entire assortment, so if a physical inventory is necessary, it is usually a partial inventory made where the problem lies. A housewife preparing a grocery list does so based on her holding of groceries. She does not stop to consider her furniture, clothing, appliance, or automobile needs. She may consider one of the other assortment areas if she is doing multiple shopping.

Once the consumer's present holdings are known, a comparison can be made of what the consumer has against what the consumer perceives as his or her wants. The consumer can perceive two types of deficiencies. There may be a deficiency in present holdings. Thus the consumer needs to enter the market to obtain a replacement product. There may also be a deficiency in the sense that the consumer wants some product not contained in his present product holding. In this case, knowledge of what is in the assortment is a stimulus for the consumer to buy what is not in the assortment.

Some consumers plan the products that make up their assortments more than others, and all consumers at some time include one or more products on the spur of the moment. That is to say, the product was not specifically planned into the assortment. The actual evaluation may be as casual as saying, "We need a loaf of bread," or it may involve comparing items in the cupboard to determine what is needed from the grocery store. It can include a periodic check of the condition of lamps, appliances, chairs, and other items to determine if any need replacement or repairs.

Consumer inventory individualistic

It is very difficult to discuss the individual consumer's assortment decisions without it sounding like a completely mechanical process in which the consumer moves logically and relentlessly from one step to another. The fact is that most consumers are not coldly calculating. In spite of this fact, it is difficult to imagine a consumer actually buying a product without first perceiving that he or she has a need for it. The mistake lies in assuming that the consumer's particular awareness of a shortage is based on a thorough product inventory. Often it is, but not necessarily. It would also be incorrect to assume the consumer's perceptions and attitudes concerning his assortment inventory are completely accurate. However, the determinants do affect the care and detail utilized in the inventory.

Many consumers, in certain situations, do not inventory their product holdings at all before purchasing. This situation may exist in the case of impulse, habitual, or insignificant purchases where the need is not great or a particular awareness is at work. The consumer is more likely to make some determination of product holdings when the purchase contemplated is important, when the purchase is expensive, when the purchase is made over time, or when the purchase concerns the entire household. All the basic determinants are important to these latter decisions. For example, the consumer may not inventory holdings before buying candy, cigarettes, jewlery, or some new brand observed in the grocery store. The consumer is likely to inventory holdings when purchasing an automobile, furniture, underwear, appliances, and draperies. One study indicated that consumers maintained stable assortments over time for nine categories of products surveyed.[16] Needless to say, some consumers are more diligent about making a product inventory than others. A lot depends on the consumer's motivation and personality. Some individuals check on everything, while others seldom check on anything. A consumer motivated by thrift is more careful than one without the thrift motive.

Partial or complete inventory

The reader should remember that every individual consumer has an assortment whether that consumer knows what is contained in it or not. The amount of knowledge that the consumer has about his or her assortment depends largely on the extent to which that assortment has been inventoried.[17] One major difference in the efficiency of individual consumers is their knowledge of product holdings. The consumer has a *complete inventory* when everything the household owns is known. A complete inventory of one's assortment is not inconceivable, but it probably occurs only in cases where a relatively few products are involved, or where someone in the family keeps very careful records. The author knows of a student who can name all his possessions. Of course, this student's accumulated goods consist of a well-chosen selection of clothes, expensive stereo equipment, and a Chevrolet van.

Most consumers are not conscious, at a given point in time, of all their possessions. Instead, they have a partial inventory. A *partial inventory* exists when the consumer has knowledge of only a portion of the household's belongings. A partial inventory can exist in several ways. Remember, an assortment displays the characteristics of width, variety, and depth. A consumer may know all the major categories of possessions, such as furniture, automobile, clothing, appliances, etc., but not be aware of the variety or the depth within each category. A consumer may be aware of all the specific items under one category, such as stereo equipment, but not be aware of complete width or depth. The consumer may be aware of how many pairs of pants are owned, but not know either his variety of clothing or the total width of products held. The consumer may know some of the items of width, variety, and depth but not have full knowledge of any category.

Most individual consumers do have at least a partial knowledge of their possessions. For example, the average woman can recall at least a majority of the possessions of her home upon request. This ability to recall indicates a type of prior inventory in the sense that it exists before the actual need. However, the existence of a preinventory is not necessary for the consumer to function. Most people, consciously, or unconsciously, follow the principle of management by exception. That is, they make a partial inventory of products at the time the need arises.

A woman with a flat tire asks herself if she can fit the repair into the monthly budget. A wife checks her canned goods, laundry detergent, and toothpaste before leaving for the grocery store. Other segments of the inventory do not concern the wife.

Casual or formal inventory

When the individual consumer takes an inventory of product holdings, it may vary all the way from very casual to highly formal, just as would be the case for a business. A *casual inventory* is defined as one where the consumer uses mental impressions or observation to determine the products currently owned. Such an inventory can mean that almost no effort is made to survey product holdings. The consumer may assume that daily observation has led to a satisfactory understanding of possessions. The author's wife, a very careful woman, assures him that she can provide an accounting, room by room, of nearly all the family's possessions. The author does not believe everything his wife says. However, it is a fact that consumers continually observe their home and become generally familiar with its contents. A husband may be aware of the missing dining room suite each time he passes that room. The wife is reminded, each time she cuts the back yard, that there is no shed in which to keep tools and lawn equipment.

With a casual inventory, the individual can even mentally count holdings while miles from home or in some store shopping. It should be obvious that consumers who depend on a casual inventory make many mistakes in buying. For example, hardly a week passes that the average shopper doesn't come home either with some grocery item already owned in quantity, or without some needed item. The number of special trips made to obtain items forgotten at the chain grocery store is one factor that has helped make a thriving business of convenience grocery stores. In spite of its faults, a casual inventory can be quite efficient for many consumers. It is the most common type of inventory.

A *formal inventory* is one where the individual actually makes a list, much like a business, based on a first-hand check of household holdings. A complete list of the assortment is seldom undertaken by consumers. When it is, the list is usually associated with some other need such as home protection insurance or the layout of items on a home plan. A partial listing of assortment items is not uncommon. Consumers often make a list of their jewelry in case of theft. Other lists include items placed in a safety deposit box; items placed in storage or in the attic; and landscape plans. The monthly budget kept by many consumers is a partial list of holdings, since the list represents regular payments for goods or services. The reader should not assume that because the consumer has either a casual or formal list of holdings that it is adhered to when purchasing. As we have already observed, and will continue to indicate, a great many factors influence how the consumer purchases. The existence of some assortment inventory probably does add a degree of precision to buying.

CONDITIONS THAT SIGNAL DEFICIENCIES

There are three conditions that signal deficiencies in the individual consumer's assortment, and they are all related to the inventory of holdings. These conditions are:

1. An "out" condition in the present assortment.
2. Making additions to present holdings.
3. Deletions that create new opportunities.

Any of these conditions can signal that the product is a candidate for a high rank in the consumer's preferences.

Routine "out" conditions

The first, and most important, signal of a deficiency is the "out" condition.[18] The assortment is in an "out" condition anytime the consumer is deficient in products normally included in the assortment. When consumers compare, either casually or formally, present assortment holdings to normal holdings, they frequently encounter shortages. Most deficiencies are of this type. An "out" condition can concern routine purchases or special purchases. One study shows that most impulse purchases are out-of-stock same brand or inventory-addition same brand purchases. Routine "out" conditions refer to regular, frequent, and low-cost purchases. Groceries, light bulbs, staple clothing, etc., are routine purchases. Some "out" conditions are not routine, as with the replacement of the wife's wedding ring, the replacement of a couch or bedroom suite, or the replacement of a fishing rod.

When expanding the assortment

Consumer deficiencies can also be indicated when the assortment is expanded. The inventory may indicate that the consumer would like to have products that are not now, and have never been, a part of the assortment. In this case, the present assortment is only "out" in the sense that it does not measure up to expectations. The purchase by a family of its first dining room suite or a storage shed are examples of products that consumers may seek to add to their assortments. Such additions increase the number and variety of product holdings. The consumer is likely to consider product additions when he or she has:

(1) new or different information, (2) expanded desires, (3) expanded means, or (4) changed expectations.

New or different information. New information is introduced to the individual by external sources, and it causes the person to question the performance of some product normally used. For example, aerosol drain openers are causing many consumers to re-assess their use of granulated drain openers. The new pressed potato chips in a can have caused a re-evaluation of traditional potato chips. It often happens that the consumer gets into a habit of purchasing the same product, and it takes some new or different information to shake one out of this pattern. The source of new information may be a friend or acquaintance, business salesman, or some advertisement.

Expanded desires. The assortment may be expanded any time that the consumer experiences increased desires. Expanded desires come from within the individual but may be influenced by the family, reference groups, or business firms. The result is that consumers no longer perceive themselves of their needs the same as previously. The expansion in desires may be for products of a different type or for better products of the same type.

Improved means. Improved means simply refers to the fact that the individuals have an increase in income that can be used to purchase products. The fact that consumers can afford new or different products causes a dissatisfaction with their present situation. Consumers perceive opportunities that were previously closed to the mind, and seeks to improve their standard of living by adding to the assortment.

Changed expectations. Not only do individual's internal desires affect their willingness to expand the assortment, but their expectations have a similar effect. A person's expectations are usually less than one's desires, because expectations bring into play the possibility of achievement. Nevertheless, any change in one's expectations for, say, income, product "out" conditions, needs, etc. may induce the consumer to go ahead and enter the market. Changed expectations can result from business advertising, purchase displays, personal selling, or conversations with friends or acquantances.

The evidence is that consumers with one or more of the following demographic attributes tend to experiment with new or different products: high income, greater formal or informal education, and higher social standing. Personality attributes that lead to product additions include a positive attitude toward innovation, achievement, and group participation, wide interests, high motivation, and a tendency to be opinion leaders. One final factor is communication. People who are quick to purchase new products have wide exposure to communication sources—particularly mass communication.

When deleting products

The deletion of products presently in the assortment can lead to expansion or change in the assortment. When products presently in the assortment are deleted, they make room for new or different types of products. The individual may eliminate the early American furniture in the family room and replace it with contemporary. On the other hand, a family may eliminate one car as the children grow up, and begin to compensate with better food. It is also true that products deleted may not be replaced at all. This condition can occur when the consumer is cutting down on consumption in general, or when the consumer is obtaining an improved or different product. This decision is usually also related to that consumer's expectations.

LONG- AND SHORT-RUN ASSORTMENTS

It is a mistake to consider the individual consumer's assortment in the same short- and long-run terms as a business assortment. A business consciously puts together and maintains, over time, a particular group of goods necessary to manufacture or distribute a finished product to consumers. Most consumers do not say, "I have certain short-run assortment goals and certain long-run assortment goals." Consumers do not think this way, or if they do, it is only in the vaguest of terms. Nevertheless, the idea of short- and long-run assortments does apply to the development of consumer product holdings. There are two ways in which long- and short-run considerations can be applied to consumer assortments.

First, one can compare expectations versus immediate consumption plants.[19] Since expectations concern future consumer desires, it follows that expectations about product desires can be considered a part of long-run assortment determination. Immediate purchase plans are taken to be short-run assortment decisions. By immediate purchase plans is not meant necessarily only today's buying. One may consider normal weekly or monthly purchases as short-run, and future expectations for a new home, automobile, furniture, etc., for which there is no specific time to buy as long-run.

Second, one can consider the total assortment as long-run and any specific purchase requirement as short-run. That is to say, the maintenance of width, depth, and variety of assortment in a proper balance occurs over a long period of time. The purchase of any specific product or products immediately needed to meet balance requirements is a short-run assortment decision.

Furthermore, it should be pointed out that short- and long-run are terms that can be applied to different parts of the same assortment at the same time. A person may plan to replace her air conditioner compressor about every eight years, but this same consumer may replace her groceries approximately four times per month. Thus such items as groceries, gas for the car, and haircuts are short-run needs within the assortment because they require frequent replacement on a relatively short time sequence. Within the same assortment, seed for the lawn, the new carport, and a television replacement are long-run assortment decisions because of their being either infrequent purchases or one-time purchases.

DEGREE TO WHICH DEFICIENCIES SPECIFIED

In even the smallest business enterprise, the management can tell with a high degree of accuracy which products are needed to meet customer wants. The average store can not only tell the specific brand but also the features, price, service, location of the buyer, and how long it will take to receive delivery. Businesses establish elaborate inventory methods to accomplish this degree of precision.

Unfortunately, the same cannot be said for the average American consumer. The evaluation of assortments and the determination of deficiencies is a highly inexact business with consumers. All too often, it is more an emotional experience than a cold-blooded business decision. Many individuals enter the market with no real conception of the products needed. Let us use groceries as an example. One would think that, of all assortment deficiencies, grocery needs would not be left completely to chance. Yet, single men and women often go grocery shopping with nothing more in mind than buying what looks good. The purchase is made for only one or two meals in advance, and there is little planning for the future. Most consumers give their purchases of groceries a little more thought than that. Nevertheless, many housewives go grocery shopping with only the vaguest idea that they need meat, vegetables, and canned goods.

It is possible to specify five degrees to which product deficiencies are recognized in advance of market-related action by the consumer. These possibilities are listed below.

1. Generic product known.
2. Product and brand known.
3. Product, brand, and price known.
4. Product, brand, price, and service known.
5. Product, brand, price, service, and location known.

Of course, the information does not have to be known in the order listed. A person may know the product, brand, and location for example. It is safe to say that in most cases the consumer does not have full knowledge of deficiencies when entering the market. What is perhaps more normal is for the consumer to have a good idea of the generic product desired, a fairly good indication of the brand, or perhaps knowledge of the general price level. Many other decisions related to the purchase are made on the spur of the moment or after the consumer enters the market. It is now time to begin discussion of these market-related actions by delving further into the purchase process.

NOTES

1. Rom J. Markin, Jr., *Consumer Behavior: A Cognitive Orientation* (New York: Macmillan Publishing Co., Inc., 1974), p. 509.
2. James F. Engel, David T. Kollat, and Roger D. Blackwell, *Consumer Behavior,* 2d ed., (New York, Holt, Rinehart and Winston, Inc., 1973), p. 352.
3. "Rise of the 'Singles'—40 Million Free Spenders," *U.S. News & World Report,* (October 7, 1974), pp. 54–56; "Singles, Mingles Boom," *Jackson Daily News,* (Jackson, Ms: June 6, 1974).
4. Harry L. Davis, "Measurement of Husband-Wife Influence in Consumer Purchase Decisions," *Journal of Marketing Research,* vol. 8 (August 1971), pp. 305–12; Robert E. Wilkes, "Husband-Wife Influence in Purchase Decisions—A Confirmation and Extension," *Journal of Marketing Research,* vol. 12 (May 1975), pp. 224–27.
5. "Consumer Behavior in the Super Market," *Progressive Grocer,* vol. 54 (October 1975), pp. 37–59.
6. Ibid.
7. John C. Caulsen, "Buying Decisions within the Family and the Consumer Brand Relationship," *On Knowing the Consumer,* ed. Joseph W. Newman (New York: John Wiley & Sons, Inc., 1966), pp. 59–66.
8. *Sales Management Magazine* (April 7, 1974), p. 14.
9. Isabella C. M. Cunningham and Robert T. Green, "Purchasing Roles in the U.S. Family, 1955 and 1973," *Journal of Marketing,* vol. 38 (October 1974), pp. 61–81.
10. H. L. Davis, "Dimensions of Marital Roles in Consumer Decision-Making," *Journal of Marketing Research,* vol. 7 (May 1970), pp. 168–77; D. H. Granbois and R. P. Willett, "Equivalence of Family Role Measures Based on Husband and Wife Data," *Journal of Marriage and the Family,* vol. 32 (February 1970), pp. 68–72; Davis, "Measurement of Husband-Wife Influence in Consumer Purchase Decisions."
11. Based on Wroe Alderson, *Marketing Behavior and Executive Action* (Homewood, Ill.: Richard D. Irwin, Inc., 1957), p. 199.
12. William R. Davidson, Alton F. Doody, and Daniel J. Sweeney, *Retailing Management,* 4th ed. (New York: The Ronald Press Co., 1975), Chap. 8.
13. We must recognize that outside expenditures are also a part of Consumer B's assortment, although not included in our example.

14. Alderson, *Marketing Behavior and Executive Action,* p. 196.
15. Ibid., p. 197.
16. Eli Seggev, "Brand Assortment and Consumer Brand Choice," *Journal of Marketing,* vol. 34 (October 1970), pp. 18–24.
17. Ibid.
18. Engel, Kollat, and Blackwell, *Consumer Behavior,* p. 356; Kenneth E. Runyon, *Consumer Behavior and the Practice of Marketing* (Columbus: Charles E. Merrill Publishing Co., 1977), p. 328.
19. Philip B. Schary, "Consumption and the Problem of Time," *Journal of Marketing,* vol. 35 (April 1971), pp. 50–55.

QUESTIONS

1. Define problem. What is consumer problem recognition? Give some examples of consumer problems.
2. Discuss the major types of consumer problems. How do these problems relate to the purchase process?
3. Who acts as the family purchasing agent? Why? Is the purchasing agent and the one who decides the need the same? Explain. Discuss the major factors that decide who acts as the family purchasing agent.
4. Define consumer assortment. How is one's standard of living related to the assortment? What is the bearing of assortment knowledge on consumer behavior?
5. Explain the attributes of consumer assortment. Develop a consumer assortment grid for your own major product holdings.
6. What is a consumer inventory? Demonstrate how you have taken a partial or complete inventory of products.
7. Is there a relationship between a casual-partial inventory and a formal-complete inventory? Defend your position.
8. What conditions signal consumer product deficiencies? Which conditions do you consider more important? Explain.
9. Contrast long- and short-run consumer assortments.
10. Do consumers have their assortment deficiencies specified at all times? Discuss.

6

Search for market-related information

Importance of consumer search
The nature of consumer search
Consumer information sources
Personal experience
Reference group sources
Business sources
Use of external sources
Advantages and disadvantages of sources
Determinants of source selection
Overall source effectiveness
How much search?
Value of search
Factors affecting search
Patterns of consumer search
Active or passive search
Continual or intermittent search
Casual or serious search
Geographic search patterns

Once the consumer recognizes that a product deficiency exists, he or she is in a position to deal with the situation. The selection of a sound course of action is improved when it is based on adequate information. That is where consumer search, the second step in the decision process, enters the picture. It may happen that the consumer automatically knows the solution to a perceived product deficiency, but typically this is not the case. It is consumer search that provides the information necessary for decision making, and since search involves overt activity, much of what we refer to as consumer behavior is actually search behavior.

IMPORTANCE OF CONSUMER SEARCH

Consumer search is used to obtain needed goods and services. How nearly persons come to maintaining their standard of living depends significantly on search behavior. When search is effective, it means that the products bought more closely fit consumer wants, and that these products are obtained with less expenditure of time, effort, and money. Poor consumer search can mean that the individual spends more, yet satisfies fewer household requirements. It follows that a knowledge of search behavior is important to both the consumer and the marketer.

Our principal interest is in consumers, and they can benefit from a knowledge of search in several ways. First, a knowledge of the forces helping shape market entry, such as advertising and personal selling, can make consumers more competent in reacting to these forces. Second, a knowledge of the search process can make consumers more astute shoppers. Third, the planning that underlies search and market entry can help make consumers more aware of problems, alternatives, and methods of countering sales attempts made by business executives. When the consumer is a more thoughtful buyer, marketers must become more thoughtful sellers, and everyone benefits.

There are important ways that marketers can benefit from a knowledge of consumer search patterns. First, tactical knowledge is useful for determining target markets. Knowledge of the products sought, stores visited, services requested, method of transportation, distance traveled, etc., can help the marketer account for these patterns when appealing to particular customer groups. Second, a knowledge of the consumer's search pattern provides clues to the type of appeals that the marketer can make. A study of these activities can also point out ways of meeting specific objections to buying. Finally, a knowledge of consumer search is useful for market analysis. Various types of customer analysis comparing before and after search behavior is useful for market planning. The marketer can also compare customer types based on search characteristics. One useful point about search is that much of it is observable which makes the collection of data easier compared to some other steps in the purchase process.

THE NATURE OF CONSUMER SEARCH

In a broad sense, search for information is the activity undertaken to provide data to be used for decision making. All decisions that are not made intuitively involve some search. *Consumer search* is a distinctive type of search, and it can be defined as:

> *the mental and physical activities undertaken by consumers to provide information on products and store alternatives.*

Search behavior is a specific type of activity. It results in the collection of information; it does not relate to the organization or selection from among alternatives. Although some recognized or anticipated product deficiency initiates consumer search, once undertaken, it includes a much wider range of data than that related just to which products are available. Consumer search also includes data on brands, prices, store location, product quality, store services, etc. It stands to reason that consumer search is one of the more important steps in the purchase process.[1] It underlies both the ordering of product preferences and consumer decision to be discussed in coming chapters.

Consumer search may be either internal or external. *Internal search* basically involves recalling information, attitudes, needs, etc. already stored in the mind. This type of search can be accomplished anywhere from the easy chair at home to the place of work. Furthermore, it usually occurs immediately after the problem is recognized. *External search* occurs when the consumer consults friends, relatives, associates, marketers, etc. to obtain information not already accessible.[2] For example, a consumer may have general internal information about how a car works, but may consult several people about features of a particular model before buying. External search can also be done at home, but we think of it as involving some information seeking outside the home. Search can even be unintentional in the sense that much information is obtained by consumers from advertisements, observations in store windows, and casual conversations that do not have to do with immediate consumer product needs. The information is simply stored or forgotten until a situation arises where it is needed.

CONSUMER INFORMATION SOURCES

No matter who is responsible for search within the family, some persons seek one type of information source and others indulge completely different sources.[3] It is important that we investigate these possible sources, because the information obtained by the consumer can be no better than the sources used. Evidence is that all types of consumers use a variety of information sources. One study demonstrated that low-income consumers were quite capable shoppers who use a variety of information sources.[4] Low-income consumers considered newspapers the best source followed by television, advice from friends, and radio. A study of children found that 78 percent reported seeing or hearing of a new toy from television, while the remainder obtained their information from playmates.[5] Another study of over 1,200 consumers led to the conclusion that, while advertising was important to purchasing, other sources were more important.[6] The following broad categories of information sources are available to the consumer.

Personal experience

Personal experience is the consumer's history. It encompasses the individual's previous product problems, success in obtaining information, comparisons made, solutions discovered, and successes or failures encountered. All the market experience of the individual, both conscious and unconscious, is stored in the mind to be called upon as the consumer requires it. Thus personal experience can be called an internal source of information as contrasted with the other two sources that are external. The person does not have to engage in any overt activity in order to obtain the information, but the successful use of personal experience is directly related to the individual's ability to recall.

Reference group sources

Reference group sources of consumer information are based on social contacts the consumer has with others. These contacts may be in family relationships, at work, in community projects, government agencies, and in entertainment groups. The opinion of others plays an important part in consumer search activities.[7]

We can divide reference group influence into family influence and the influence of opinion leaders. Family influences are frequent and significant. Evidence indicates that approximately 50 percent of all durable-goods buyers obtain advice from friends and relatives.[8] The brand bought is often seen first at the home of a relative. Opinion leaders play an important part in the purchase of such products as drugs, appliances, fabrics, dental products, clothing, cleaning agents, hair styles, makeup and movies. Opinion leaders do not have a universal influence. An opinion leader for one type of product is not usually a leader for a completely different type of product. Certain homemakers may lead for detergents while movie stars may lead for fashion clothing.

Business sources

Business information sources utilized by consumers fall into three types: mass media, personal salespeople, and visits to retail stores. Table 6–1 provides some insight into the relative use of these information sources for specified products. It is obvious that consumers use a variety of sources depending on the product. Newspapers and TV commercials are important for most products, but the number one rank for in-store display may surprise many readers.

Table 6–1
Reliance on different sources for product information

	Product category					
	SEA	*SBP &A*	*C &BI*	*OP &A*	*BA*	*KT &G*
In-store displays	30%	46%	41%	41%	49%	49%
Newspaper ads	29	23	24	40	21	20
TV commercials	32	12	16	18	11	21
Ads in women's magazines	15	21	22	7	20	14
Articles in women's magazines	19	21	24	7	19	19
Newspaper articles	9	5	6	12	5	6

Key: SEA—Small Electrical appliances; SBP&A—Serving and buffet products & accessories; C&BI—Cook and bakeware items; OP&A—Outdoor products & accessories; BA—Bathroom accessories; KT&G—Kitchen tools & gadgets

Source: "Housewares Buying Trends," *Stores*, vol. 56 (December 1974), pp. 14–15.

Advertisements provide consumers with a variety of information including brands, price, sales, product features, location, and store name.[9] Consumers use advertisements to gain an overall impression of the store and to make comparisons between brands and prices. Advertisements have different effects on consumers, depending on the product involved. Studies have indicated that when reporting where they received information, 4 percent who purchased sport shirts, approximately 19 to 26 percent who purchased food products, and 25 percent who purchased durable goods said information was obtained from advertisements.[10]

Personal selling is a much less used source of information for consumers. Insurance, cosmetics, brushes, tree surgery, and books are examples of products sold in the home or door to door. Of course, use of this source goes up if one considers retail clerks as a sales source.

A prime source of information for consumers is the retail store. Often it is more difficult to obtain information from a retail store than from mass media. The reason is that there is so much information provided that it often becomes confusing. Consumers tend to simplify by ignoring a large portion of the information. One study shows that, for the purchase of durable goods, 47 percent of the consumers studied visited one store, 15 percent visited two stores, and 26 percent visited three or more stores.[11] In the purchase of sport shirts, 70 percent of the customers visited one store; 7 percent visited two stores, and 18 percent visited three or more stores.

Not only do consumers fail to compare stores but they do not utilize retail stores sufficiently to become knowledgeable about product, service, and price information. Information available at the store that is not available from an ad includes the attitude of store personnel, direct product and brand comparison, service information, product demonstration, and terms and conditions of sale.

USE OF EXTERNAL SOURCES

The previous discussion clearly shows that there are many sources of information available to the consumer. Very seldom does the consumer use all, or even most, of them. Furthermore, the number and types of sources utilized varies with the specific consumer problem. It is time to deal with the factors that affect the use of information sources.

Advantages and disadvantages of sources

It stands to reason that some sources of information are more useful than others. However, we cannot say that one source is more useful than another without specifying how usefulness is measured. Business executives use several methods for determining the usefulness of consumer information sources. Some of these methods include dollar expenditures by consumers, degree of customer exposure, business employment, and the prestige of the source. The consumer is not interested in these business methods of determining source usefulness. Table 6–2 shows some important methods of measuring source usefulness employed by consumers. The consumer is interested in such factors as the amount, cost, quality, availability, and variety of information offered by the source. The problem is that some of the factors overlap, and the consumer may obtain essentially the same quality information from more than one source and must decide between sources.

Table 6–2
Advantages and disadvantages of consumer information sources

Source	Factors favoring use by consumers	Factors hindering use by consumers
I. Business sources. Market Dominated (business institutions; retailers; ad agencies, etc.)	1. Much information available often. 2. Low cost of information. 3. Information available with little effort.	1. Some information biased. 2. Information withheld or wrong. 3. Lack of trust.
II. Reference-group sources. Consumer Dominated (family, friend, associates, etc.)	1. Various information from different sources. 2. Information trusted. 3. Person can select relevant information. 4. Low cost of information.	1. Information may be wrong. 2. Information intermittent. 3. Information often must be sought out.
III. Reference-group sources. Neutral (government, research agencies, magazines, etc.)	1. Information unbiased. 2. Information based on facts. 3. Information trusted.	1. Information costly. 2. Information not regularly available. 3. Information not complete.

Source: Adapted from Donald F. Cox, "The Audience as a Communicator," *Toward Scientific Marketing*, ed. Stephen A. Greyser (Chicago: American Marketing Assn., 1963), p. 72.

Determinants of source selection

There are six principal determinants used by consumers in the selection of information sources. They are: (1) type of product, (2) type of information desired, (3) product life, (4) confidence in the source, (5) usefulness of the information, and (6) previous experience. Each determinant is discussed below.

Type of product. A source may be believed more for one type of product than for another. Consumers trust personal contacts more than mass media for information about durable goods. For some products, such as fashionable clothing, customers tend to depend on the store, but for other items, the manufacturer's brand evokes more trust. When purchasing a convenience product, the consumer may seek little or no information.

Type of information desired. Consumers place different importance on sources, depending on the type of information desired. The tendency is to obtain a variety of information and facts from the mass media while checking its validity from personal sources.[12] Consumers tend also to obtain more general information from the mass media, and specific facts from company salespeople or personal sources. If the information is crucial to the decision, the consumer may seek more trusted personal sources.

Product life. The longer the product has been on the market, the greater the tendency of consumers to utilize reference-group information. Where new products are concerned, the consumer depends more heavily on mass media and on opinion leaders. Opinion leaders can often be a crucial source of information for new fashion products. Personal experience is quite often more important when the consumer is considering a product that has been on the market for some time.

Confidence in the source. A consumer has confidence when he or she believes the information supplied by the source. If the consumer has had good results with products recommended by the source previously, he or she is likely to use it again. If, for example, the consumer has received unreliable information from some reference group source, such as a friend, that source may not be trusted in the future.[13] However, believability does not just apply to reference group sources. Often consumers have lasting relationships with salespersons, and they believe what these persons tell them. Consumers also develop identification with specific firms or their advertising, and they tend to have confidence in those firms with which they have a positive identification.

A problem is that some external sources can be relied on more for one type of decision than for another. It is perhaps not sound to ask a merchant an honest opinion of a competitor's product. This same merchant may be perfectly candid in explaining the performance of his product. A personal friend may give you an honest opinion about some merchant but stretch the truth about some product that he or she owns. After all, the friend does not want it known that he or she purchased a poor product.

It may be that the credibility of the seller of some products can be increased by disclaiming superiority of some product features. This result was discovered in a study using a ballpoint pen, watch, blender, camera, and clock radio. A statement was made that the product had been compared to the industry leader, and several features were listed. Some questionnaires claimed superiority of all features and some did not. The results demonstrated greater confidence in the latter.[14] It would appear that consumers regard consistent claims of superiority for all product features to be just too good to be true.

Usefulness of the information. A consumer is more likely to use a source when the information supplied by that source pertains to the consumer's problem. For example, consumers rely heavily on the local newspaper to keep them up to date on local events including local shopping news. In one study, 64.2 percent of respondents mentioned the local newspaper, and there was an average readership of advertisements of 31.2 percent.[15] It follows that the same source may be used at one time and not at another time. For example, there is a lot of advertising on radio and television, but at any given moment very little of this information may be used, because it does not apply to any specific consumer product need. A consumer is more likely to seek out a friend who likes to fish when seeking information on outboard motors, but a business acquaintance when considering insurance. It is true that consumers often confuse exposure with reliability. They feel a product must be good if it is highly advertised or if many of their friends are talking about it. The fact is that exposure is not always a sound gauge for deciding to place confidence in a product.

Overall source effectiveness

The overall effectiveness of sources of information selected by consumers can be classified into those that have decisive effectiveness, partial effectiveness, and ineffectiveness. A source is decisive in effectiveness when it applies to a particular product and is the most important determinant of the purchase. A source has partial influence so long as it plays some part but is less than decisive. This class can obviously be divided into several subclasses. A source is ineffective when it plays very little or no part in the decision. Information may be obtained, but it is either ignored or disregarded for the purchase decision. In actual practice, the consumer utilizes multiple sources of information. In a given decision, one or two sources may be decisive, several may be partially effective, and some may have very little effect.

HOW MUCH SEARCH?

Consumers in the process of seeking market related information do not all behave alike. We know from experience that some consumers seek more information than others, even when consulting the same type sources. Nearly all consumers engage in more search for some types of products than for others. These points naturally lead to the question, "How much search is necessary?" The answer depends on the value of search and the factors affecting the amount. These points are discussed below.

Value of search

The search for consumer information is costly, but its results are valuable.[16] The values center around the fact that more information can lead to sounder decisions. It can result in lower prices or more suitable products. The costs involved in information seeking are both financial and psychological. It is not possible to make a definitive list of values and costs because they mean different things to different consumers. For example, the time necessary to search and compare products is an advantage to a consumer who wants a more suitable product or lower price. Time is a disadvantage to a consumer who wants the convenience of a quick purchase. To one consumer shopping is fun, but to another it is mental anguish.

Although values and costs cannot be generalized, it does follow that for an individual consumer, search is determined by balancing these factors of information seeking. This balancing is not easy because of the number of variables the consumer must consider. Our next task is to look into these variables, remembering that any one can be a value or a cost to the individual.

Factors affecting search

The factors that make information search valuable and costly can be grouped under five headings.

Experience. Experience is the information already in the consumer's mind. It includes the amount, suitability, and recall of pertinent facts about the purchase. If the amount of information is not sufficient, search is necessary. There is less search for products bought over a long period of time. Not all experience applies to a given problem. Experience is suitable if it contributes to understanding the problem at hand. The problem may be similar to a previous problem, or some anticipated satisfaction may be similar to past satisfactions. A previous solution may be transferable to the present situation. It also follows that if experience cannot be recalled, then search is necessary to fill in the gaps.

Availability of information without search. If the consumer can obtain information without a physical search, so much the better. A great deal of information is available to consumers through the mass media. The consumer often obtains this information whether it is wanted or not. Once obtained it becomes a part of personal experience. Newspapers, television, and radio constantly provide consumers with market information that can help solve current problems without physical search.

Satisfaction derived from search. Among considerations that can lead to search satisfaction are convenience, better information, pleasure from shopping, and social satisfaction.[17] Search can be convenient because more search can lead to better information for deciding or less search can save time. Better information can lead to more suitable products, lower prices, or both. Search may be enjoyable to some consumers, rendering direct satisfaction. A consumer who enjoys shopping is likely to do more of it. A consumer who does not like shopping is likely to make less information suffice. Social values pertain to the psychic satisfactions derived from search—the enjoyment of owning just the correct dress, social acceptance into a particular group, and so on. A consumer placing great value on these psychic considerations may seek more information before deciding on a product.

Perceived consequence of search. The perceived consequence of search refers to the consumer's expected outcome. Important consequences that affect the amount of search are product satisfaction, financial outlay (price and time of payment), social risk, risk of being dissatisfied, and inconvenience. More search is indicated to obtain the correct product, to save money, to avoid social risks, and to reduce inconvenience or the chance of product dissatisfaction.

Value placed on the product. The more valuable the product, the greater the amount of search the consumer is likely to indulge in. A product's worth to a consumer can be measured in several ways: financial worth, worth in terms of the consumer's needs and motivation, and worth as indicated by placement in the target assortment. For example, more costly products get more attention than less costly products, and products that are fundamental to a consumer's needs or motivation get more attention. One study demonstrated that price, convenient location, and services were the most important reasons for a person trading with a particular gasoline service station, and changes in price affected purchase patterns.[18]

PATTERNS OF CONSUMER SEARCH

The specific patterns for seeking market information vary considerably among consumers. Some individuals actively seek facts while others do not, and some persons search continually until the problem is solved, but others do not. Furthermore, some consumer problems are such that the entire family becomes involved in the search for facts, while other problems involve only the individual. Let us consider these different patterns of consumer search.

Active or passive search

All consumers seek product and store information at some time or other, but Figure 6–1 shows that we can distinguish active searchers from passive searchers. *Active searchers* are seekers of market information for its own sake.[19] They enjoy the physical activity involved with external search, and they engage in it even when there is no im-

Figure 6–1
Active and passive searchers

Active searcher

"I liked that dress, but let's stop in *Richard's* before we make up our minds."

Passive searcher

"Hey, *Linskey's* has a sale on pants. They look good, and the price is right."

mediate problem. These consumers often shop for the sole purpose of keeping abreast of what product and store alternatives are available. They ask about the new products that they observe their friends and neighbors using. They read the ads and inquire among reference groups about new ideas observed in the various media. Active searchers tend to be inquisitive persons, they participate in many activities outside the home, they are receptive to new and different products, they are interested in themselves and their community, and they like to be well thought of by others. The market data these consumers obtain is stored for use when a specific problem arises.

The group of *passive searchers* are not willing to expend much effort in seeking product and market facts. It is not that these consumers are not interested in making effective decisions. Mostly, they just perceive themselves as too busy or they feel they have sufficient facts or that the search is not likely to be worth it. Passive searchers seek market information only when it has specific and immediate use. These consumers tend to use external sources, such as television, radio, newspapers, magazines, catalogs, pamplets, etc. that are available without much external search. Passive searchers visit the store primarily to purchase and often their mind is essentially made up when they take action. Passive searchers are frequently preoccupied with work or family, they are introverted, leisure tends to be family oriented, they frequently purchase by habit, and they are not inquisitive about new ideas. Of course, most consumers do not fit either extreme. It is typical to engage in both active and passive search.

Continual or intermittent search

Consumer search can be divided into continual and intermittent. *Continual search* means that the consumer seeks information systematically and regularly until a definitive basis for action is established. A woman who makes several shopping trips in the space of two weeks before buying a dress is engaging in continual search. A husband and wife who visit several automobile dealers, collect and compare dealer literature, and discuss different cars with their friends over a month, are engaging in continual search. The term *intermittent search* refers to information seeking of a sporadic nature that continues until a course of action is chosen. After some period of inconclusive or unsatisfactory search, the individual may cease looking for a period, only to begin again later. A person who does typing at home may periodically check the want ads for a good buy in a used typewriter. A poor child may check the Sears catalog all summer, dreaming about the one or two toys that may be possible at Christmas.

The types of action are the same whether consumer search is continual or intermittent. The three possibilities are: (1) abandonment of the search, (2) storage of the facts discovered, or (3) purchase of a product. Abandonment may occur because the consumer loses interest in the product, because the search is unsuccessful, or because the facts indicate that the consumer should not purchase. Facts may be stored until the consumer has the money to buy or until a more appropriate time for purchase presents itself. Intermittent search is often associated with unsuccessful search, but it can also occur for other reasons. Active seekers, mentioned previously, often engage in intermittent search to check the market. A consumer may engage in intermittent search when the product need is not urgent. Intermittent search may precede the purchase of major durable goods such as a home or furniture.

Either continual or intermittent search may begin with the individual aware or unaware of a specific product need. The consumer may become aware of a product need while shopping around and may engage in continual search until a purchase is made. The consumer may have a generic product in mind, but may engage in intermittent search until the specific item or brand is discovered. It often happens that a consumer cannot afford the time for continual search even though the specific product is known, so the consumer searches sporadically when an opportunity presents itself.

Casual or serious search

Another important pattern of consumer search concerns the seriousness with which the consumer approaches the task. Consumer search is considered *casual* when it is incidental to other activity of the individual. A nonshopper may inquire about a product observed while accompanying a friend downtown. An advertisement may catch the individual's eye while watching television, and it may be noted that the product "looks interesting." Casual search is more likely to be undertaken when the product is of small unit value, unimportant, routinely purchased, or nontechnical. Convenience products and impulse purchases are often based on a casual search.

Consumer search is *serious* when the primary purpose of the activity is to obtain decision information about products, stores, or market conditions. Serious search typically involves more careful consideration, thought, and effort than does casual search. Products that are highly technical, require service, durable, and expensive typically receive serious attention. Shopping products and long-term investment products such as houses, furniture, or insurance are searched more seriously. However, it would be a mistake to assume that serious search is automatically better or more successful than casual search. Either type can result in effective market behavior. The type of search employed depends on the reason for search and the situation.

Geographic search patterns

Consumer search cannot be fully appreciated without taking space considerations into account. Search, more than any other aspect of consumer decision making, requires some overt activity. In fact, consumer search can be meaningfully visualized as the shopper's efforts to overcome problems of space and time. At this point, we consider the geographic search patterns associated with (1) local and extended search and (2) store visitation.

Local and extended search. Shoppers have the choice of purchasing products locally or extending their search to more distant shopping centers, trade areas, or towns.[20] Two generalizations can be made relative to which course of action is followed.

First, all types of consumers tend to resist traveling in their search for products. Most consumers will travel further for shopping products than for convenience products.[21] Even so, approximately five miles is the limit of search for the vast majority of consumers. For example, in a survey of 800 shoppers, *Progressive Grocer* reported that shoppers traveled 1.8 miles one-way to the grocery store on the average.[22] The fact is that the decentralization of retail trade in larger cities has brought a great many product alternatives close to the consumer's residence. There is no need for most shoppers to travel great distances to find desired products.

Second, the size of town has impact on customer willingness to travel. There is a tendency for persons in a relatively smaller town to travel to a larger town to shop. It is the perception of greater product and price selection that attracts. Such extended travel does cost more, but there is the status involved in shopping the larger town. One study of small towns adjacent to Augusta, Georgia found that 84 percent of a sample of 1,543 consumers had shopped in another town recently. Approximately 65 percent of respondents had shopped out of town six or more times over six months.[23] There is a tendency for some people in relatively smaller towns, no matter what the actual size, to shop adjacent larger towns. Thus some persons, even in larger cities, travel to other even larger cities to buy.

There is also a reverse pattern of shoppers traveling from larger cities to smaller one for the purpose of trade. The feeling is that the smaller city, because of less demand, must make a price appeal in order to compete with nearby larger cities. It is entirely possible that this consumer perception is false, but it does persist. A wide range of products are purchased out of town. One study found that some of the more common ones include carpets, men's and women's clothing, curtains, and housewares.[24] Automobiles, furniture, appliances, and jewelry are not purchased as often out of town.

Identification of extended search. Many attempts have been made by business and government agencies to identify and utilize consumer extended search patterns. The two most popular are Reilly's law of retail gravitation and traffic flow maps.[25] Converse used a refined version of Reilly's law with considerable success in Illinois.[26] The basic idea is that persons located in an intermediate town, located between two cities, will divide their shopping in direct proportion to the population of the two cities and in inverse proportion to the distance between them. In other words, population attracts, but the shopper must overcome the disadvantage of traveling longer distances.

Traffic flow maps are similar to road maps, but with one major difference. The width of the lines representing roads vary according to the amount of traffic they carry. One can tell the direction of flow and its source by plotting the points from a city where there is a large drop in line width.

Store visitation. Even when purchasing the same type products, consumers do not display the same patterns of store visitation. Three aspects of visitation are important. They are: (1) the time of day for the visit, (2) the day of the week to shop, and (3) the number of stores to visit.

First, let us look at the time of day. As a general rule, the afternoon hours are more popular for shopping with early evening next most important. The early morning hours are among the less popular for most stores, although grocery stores do a good business at these times. Generally, wives like to do housework in the morning and shop more leisurely in the afternoon. There is a greater likelihood that the husband can shop with the wife in the afternoon or early evening, because both can get off work.

Second, consider patterns of shopping by days. The popularity of shopping days varies by product, type of store, and circumstance. Friday and Saturday are popular for many types of durable goods. A recent grocery study shows that 36 percent of the week's business occurs on Friday, 30 percent on Thursday, and Saturday follows with 17 percent.[27] Shopping on Sunday is increasing in popularity because of the inability to enforce Sunday Closing laws. Monday is the least popular day to visit most stores. Many customers deliberately pick the morning hours and the slow days to do their shopping in order to avoid congestion. Also many customers like to take advantage of specials and sales which firms use to attract customers on the "off days." The importance of Thursday specials in the grocery industry is well known. White sales, and special holiday sales often draw large numbers of customers. Christmas is still the single largest selling season for most stores.

Third, the number of store visits is important to search. Some customers engage in multiple purchases from a single store, while others shop several stores or even different trade areas before purchasing a single product. Even grocery stores, where convenience goods are sold primarily, report customer use of other stores. One study indicated that customers, on the average visited two other supermarkets.[28] Multiple purchases at one store save the consumer time and shopping trips. Shopping several stores or trade areas may insure a more careful purchase with better products at a lower price.

The pattern of store visitation affects the manner of transportation. The automobile is the single most used transportation means, but it is particularly important when shopping several stores because of its speed and flexibility of movement. About 50 percent of consumers use the automobile, 30 percent walk, and 19 percent use public transportation or taxis when shopping.[29] The average grocery shopper makes approximately 2.28 trips to the store.[30] Average shopping trips are less for durable and fashion products.

NOTES

1. Joseph W. Newman and Bradley D. Lockeman, "Measuring Prepurchase Information Seeking," *Journal of Consumer Research,* vol. 2 (December 1975), pp. 216–22.
2. Francis X. Callahan, "Advertising's Influence on Consumers," *Journal of Advertising Research,* vol. 14 (June 1974), pp. 45–48; Patrick Dunne, "Some Demographic Characteristics of Direct Mail Purchasers," *Baylor Business Studies,* (May, June, July 1975), pp. 62–72; "1974 Profile of the Consumer: Housewares Buying Trends," *Stores,* vol. 56 (December 1974), pp. 14–15; Arch G. Woodside and M. Wayne Delozier, "Effects of Word of Mouth Advertising on Consumer Risk Taking," *Journal of Advertising,* vol. 5 (Fall 1976), pp. 12–19; Carl E. Block, "Prepurchase Search Behavior of Low-income Households," *Journal of Retailing,* vol. 48 (Spring 1972), pp. 3–15.
3. An excellent review of information sources types can be found in Peter D. Bennett and Harold H. Kassarjian, *Consumer Behavior* (Englewood Cliffs, N.J.: Prentice-Hall Inc., 1972), pp. 8–9.
4. Block, "Prepurchase Search Behavior of Low-income Households," pp. 3–15.
5. James S. Ferideres, "Advertising, Buying Patterns and Children," *Advertising Research,* vol. 13 (February 1973), pp. 34–36.
6. Callahan, "Advertising's Influence on Consumers," pp. 45–48.
7. Ibid.
8. George Katona and Eva Mueller, "A Study of Purchasing Decisions," *Consumer Behavior: The Dynamics of Consumer Reaction,* ed. Lincoln Clark (New York: New York University Press, 1955), p. 45.
9. Leo Bogart, B. Stuart Tolley, and Frank Orenstein, "What One Little Ad Can Do," *Journal of Advertising Research,* vol. 10 (1970), pp. 3–13.
10. Jon G. Udell, "Purchase Behavior of Buyers of Small Electrical Appliances," *Journal of Marketing,* vol. 30 (October 1966), p. 51; Katona and Mueller, "A Study of Purchasing Decisions," p. 46.
11. Ibid., pp. 45–46.

12. Callahan, "Advertising's Influence on Consumers," pp. 45–48.
13. Woodside and Delozier, "Effects of Word of Mouth Advertising on Consumer Risk Taking," pp. 12–19.
14. Robert B. Settle and Linda L. Golden, "Attribution Theory and Advertiser Credibility," *Journal of Marketing Research,* vol. 11 (May 1974), pp. 181–85.
15. Ernest F. Larkin and Gerald L. Grotta, "Consumer Attitudes Toward and Use of Advertising Content in a Small Daily Newspaper," *Journal of Advertising,* vol. 5 (Winter 1976), pp. 28–31.
16. John D. Claxton, Joseph N. Fry, and Bernard Portis, "A Taxonomy of Prepurchase Information Gathering Patterns," *Journal of Consumer Research,* vol. 1 (December 1974), pp. 35–42.
17. Edward M. Tauber, "Why Do People Shop?" *Journal of Marketing,* vol. 36 (October 1972), pp. 46–49.
18. Gordon L. Wise, "Impact of the Gasoline Price War on Consumer Patronage Motives," *Journal of Retailing,* vol. 48 (Summer 1972), pp. 64–66, 91.
19. Laurence P. Feldman and Alvin D. Star, "Are Active Shoppers Different?" *Business Ideas and Facts,* vol. 7 (Winter 1974), pp. 15–23.
20. Fred D. Reynolds and William R. Darden, "Intermarket Patronage: A Psychographic Study of Consumer Outshoppers," *Journal of Marketing,* vol. 36 (October 1972), pp. 50–54.
21. Arieh Goldman, "Do Lower-Income Consumers Have a More Restricted Shopping Scope? *Journal of Marketing,* vol. 40 (January 1976), pp. 46–54.
22. "Consumer Behavior in the Supermarket," *Progressive Grocer,* vol. 54 (October 1975), pp. 37–59.
23. John R. Thompson, "Characteristics and Behavior of Out-Shopping Consumers," *Journal of Retailing,* vol. 47 (Spring 1971), pp. 70–80; William R. Darden and William D. Perreault, Jr., "Identifying Interurban Shoppers: Multiproduct Purchase Patterns and Segmentation Profiles," *Journal of Marketing Research,* vol. 13 (February 1976), pp. 51–60.
24. Thompson, "Characteristics and Behavior of Out-Shopping Consumers."; Robert O. Herrmann and Leland L. Beik, "Shoppers' Movements Outside Their Local Retail Area," *Journal of Marketing,* vol. 32 (October 1968), pp. 45–51.
25. William J. Reilly, *Methods for the Study of Retail Relationships* (Austin, Texas: Bureau of Business Research, University of Texas Press, 1929).
26. Converse used the formula below to predict the flow of trade to two cities from towns located in between:

$$\left(\frac{B_a}{B_b}\right) = \left(\frac{P_a}{P_b}\right)\left(\frac{D_b}{D_a}\right)$$

where

B_a is the proportion of trade to city A
B_b is the proportion of trade to city B

P_a is the population of city A
P_b is the population of city B
D_a is the distance to city A
D_b is the distance to city B

Paul D. Converse, "New Laws of Retail Gravitation," *Journal of Marketing*, vol. 13 (October 1949), pp. 379–88.

27. Robert F. Dietrich, "They've Changed Their Ways of Shopping," *Progressive Grocer*, vol. 53 (April 1974), pp. 45–47ff.
28. "Consumer Behavior in the Super Market."
29. Daniel J. McLaughlin, "Consumer Reaction to Retail Food Newspaper Advertising in High and Low Income Areas," *Business Ideas & Facts*, vol. 7 (Fall 1974), pp. 21–24.
30. Dietrich, "They've Changed Their Ways of Shopping."

QUESTIONS

1. What is meant by consumer search? Give two examples of how you have recently searched for products. How can it be called search if the consumer does not leave the house?
2. Distinguish between one who has needs and one who acts as a purchasing agent. What is the importance of each to marketers?
3. Who tends to act as the purchasing agent for most American homes? Why?
4. Discuss the factors that are important in selecting a purchasing agent. Does the same person always act as the family purchasing agent? Are you ever a purchasing agent? If so, which of the reasons accounts for your selection?
5. Contrast personal, business and reference group information sources.
6. Why are some information sources more important than others? Can you give examples of important information sources you have used when purchasing?
7. Why would a consumer have more confidence in one source than another? Are business sources ever worthy of the consumer's confidence? Explain.
8. How much search is enough? Discuss.
9. Give examples from your own experience of active and passive search. Continual and intermittent search.
10. What is casual and serious search? Which is the more effective?

7

Establish consumer preferences

Consumer preferences
Individual and family preferences
Individual preference determination
How the individual orders preferences
Factors that influence consumer preferences
Direct and indirect external influence
Preference determination in families
How family preferences are determined
Factors affecting family preferences
The family preference decision
Individual and family preferences differ
Rank of preferences tentative

The third step in the consumer purchase process is the establishment of specific product preferences. This step is extremely important because of its effect on the outcome of the purchase process. The consumer may enter the market with unspecified personal needs, or the consumer may not give adequate attention to the search for information. Nevertheless, the consumer cannot escape the hard conclusion, at some point in time, that certain products are preferred over others. No matter whether the choice is based on insufficient facts and inadequate thought or not, the point remains that there can be no purchase without known preferences for products. In this chapter we deal with how preferences are established by the individual consumer and by the family.

CONSUMER PREFERENCES

Individual consumers have a variety of wants at the same time. Since most persons operate with limited income, all these wants cannot be satisfied. This fact necessitates the ordering of preferences so that those products the individual deems most appropriate or most important as want satisfiers receive proper consideration. Other wants may be put off or not satisfied. This ordering of preferences is nothing more than a priority ranking of product alternatives by importance to the consumer. The establishment of preferences is not the same thing as buying, although buying reflects preferences held. A consumer may have preferences for some time before entering the market. Consumers may even have preferences for products that they never intend to purchase. It is also possible that the order of preferences may change several times before the consumer actually engages in a purchase.[1]

Although consumers can order their preferences, it is not necessary that they know the preferences of every product in their assortment at the same time. The consumer need only be able to determine the order of products under consideration at the moment. A study of consumer preferences for professional sports teams illustrates that the consumer can determine preferences when faced with the necessity to do so. When asked their favorite professional sport, 30.5 percent of respondents ranked football first, 21.9 percent selected basketball, 20.2 percent selected baseball, and the remainer were scattered among other sports.[2]

If this ability to specify what is desired did not exist, then no consumer would ever purchase. It is difficult to imagine a person entering into a purchase agreement when wants are not known, when the mind cannot be made up between desired products, or when there is indifference to the alternative products offered for sale. The very act of sale is prima-facie evidence that the consumer, at that moment, would rather spend money on the designated product than on any other thing, and this is what scaling of preferences means.

INDIVIDUAL AND FAMILY PREFERENCES

The consumer's state of preferences would be much simpler to determine if only the individual's interests were involved. Often this is the case, but there are also situations in which others participate in the ordering process. Actually, the ordering of preferences can be divided into two separate types of situations. One situation involves the individual consumer buying personal requirements. The other situation occurs when the individual participates in establishing priorities for products that affect the family as a whole.[3] Most consumers must contend with both these situations, and in both cases the person is affected by external factors. In the first situation the consumer considers individual wishes in the light of external information. In the latter case, there is the extra consideration of negotiating over differences in each family member's individual priorities. The remainder of this chapter is based on these two types of preference ordering situations.

INDIVIDUAL PREFERENCE DETERMINATION

Now that we understand what is meant by preferences, we are ready for the more detailed discussion of the ordering of product wants. A logical place to begin the discussion is with the individual. If we can understand how the individual orders preferences, then we have a basis for discussing how each person's rank affects family negotiation.

How the individual orders preferences

Traditional economics have made a significant contribution to consumer behavior in the area of preference ranking.[4] The whole concept of marginal utility analysis, since it deals with personal choice, necessarily deals with product preferences. Marginal analysis was introduced and explained in Chapter 3. At this point we want to demonstrate its application to preference scaling and discuss some modifications necessary to apply the concept to the real world.

Preferences ranked by marginal utility. In its essence, marginal analysis specifies that products with more utility to the individual are ranked higher in order of purchase. You may remember from Chapter 3 that utility is the ability to satisfy a human want and marginal utility is the extra satisfaction derived from having one more incremental unit of the product. Table 7–1 shows how marginal analysis can be used to rank consumer preferences for three products.

Table 7–1
Consumer scale of preferences*

Item	Distribution of income per month					
	A		B		C	
A. $\frac{MU}{P}$ of rent	$180	(12:1)	$156	(12:1)	$165	(11:1)
B. $\frac{MU}{P}$ of gasoline	90	(6:1)	78	(6:1)	180	(12:1)
C. $\frac{MU}{P}$ of ham hock	15	(1:1)	13	(1:1)	15	(1:1)
Totals	$285		$245		$360	

( ) means ratio of satisfaction and importance relative to ham hock.
* Two basic assumptions:
a. Total money expenditure is fixed in each case.
b. There is no diminishing marginal utility.

The individual apportions expenditures so that the marginal utility *(MU)* of each product considered is proportional to price *(P)*.[5] In other words, *MU/P* must equal 1/1 for each product. When this condition exists, price measures a products' worth to the consumer and its rank compared to other products. Thus in illustration A, where the consumer has $285 in income, he or she spends $180 on an apartment, uses up $90 in gasoline, and spends $15 on ham hocks. This allocation shows rent is 12 times and gasoline 6 times as important as ham hock on the individual's preference scale.

Suppose our consumer is laid off work (example B) and must resort to welfare. If the consumer's scale of preference is unchanged but income declines to $247, then expenditures must be re-allocated. The person moves to a lower priced apartment and purchases less gasoline and ham hocks. Obviously, total consumer satisfaction has decreased even though shelter is still relatively the most important item.

Another change in circumstance, such as that in illustration C can cause a re-evaluation of the consumer's scale of preferences. Perhaps the person finds a better job than previously held, but it requires considerable driving. Thus gasoline becomes number one on the product preference scale. It is followed by rent and ham hocks.

Modifications in utility preferences. The economic concept of marginal utility is a fair approximation of how consumers order preferences. However, several modifications must be explained in order to relate the concept to the real world.

First, under marginal utility analysis, the individual always attempts to maximize dollar satisfaction between products using cold logic. In practice, consumer emotions get in the way of logic. The consumer may order preferences based on such nonmonetary factors as beauty, comfort, or uniqueness. A lack of sufficient information may often make it impossible to maximize. The consumer may be able to do no better than to optimize preference ranks. Furthermore, the ranking is much less factual than found in economics.[6] The consumer simply says, "We are going to buy a new floor polisher this month, and next month we can see about new clothes for the kids."

Second, most products are not made in infinitely small increments. The consumer must always choose between whole products which are often expensive. That is to say, consumers deal in discrete rather than incremental values. If a car, refrigerator, shoes, or other items could be purchased in one cent increments, these items could rank high on many individual's preferences who cannot even consider the outlay of hundreds of dollars for the items as actually sold. The only choice in reality is to go without.

Third, marginal analysis is based on an explicit comparison of products. Often in the real world, the individual doesn't even think in terms of comparisons. The only consideration absolutely necessary to rank preferences is that the consumer be able to say, "I want that." Such a statement ranks the desired product #1 and all other products collectively #2. For example, as an individual drives home after a difficult day, the thought emerges, "I'm sure tired. I believe I'll stop by the drugstore and pick up a book to relax with this evening." In this case, there is no direct comparison of products, but the consumer is aware that $1.95 spent this way will give more pleasure than to spend the money any other way. If someone pins the consumer down at the time of the purchase, the individual is able to explain the reasons for the action taken.

Fourth, marginal analysis does not consider the reasons that lie behind the scale of preferences. Both individual and environmental factors do influence the decision. These factors are considered more completely in the remainder of the chapter.

Factors that influence consumer preferences

Each individual consumer is responsible for ranking personal preferences, but there are always external influences that affect the decision.[7] Figure 7–1 illustrates the point. The internal factors of preference ranking are the physiological and psychological considerations that, taken together, summarize what the person is.[8] External influences may be derived directly from search as discussed in the previous chapter, or the result of normal human interaction. Even though individuals make up a family, each person's external influences differ in some respects. We discuss in the following paragraphs some of the more important internal and external factors of preference rating.

Figure 7–1
Influences on individual preferences

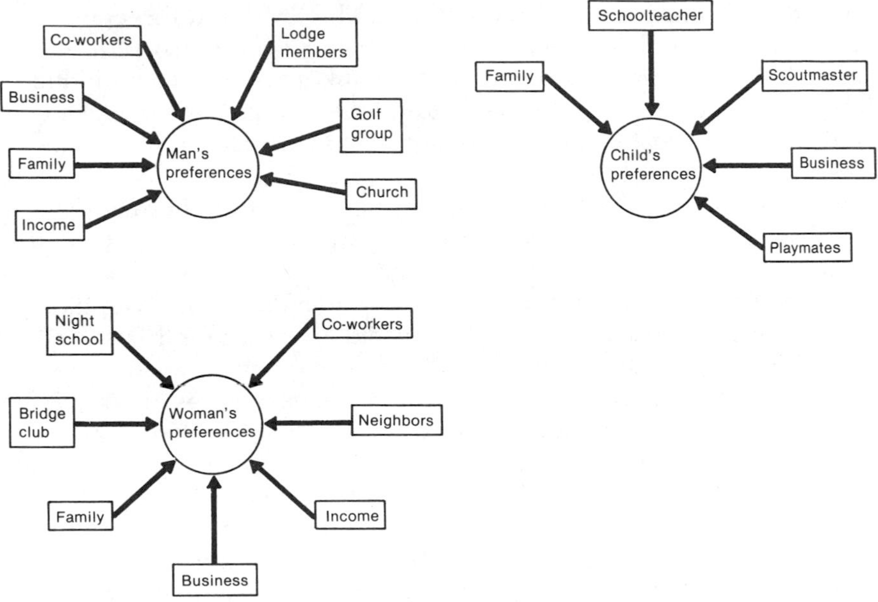

Personal needs. Need is an important consideration to the consumer in scaling preferences.[9] It may be difficult to imagine, but if it's spring and we do not have a lawn mower, we may plan to postpone including golf clubs in our current assortment. The lawn, because it does not stop growing, takes a higher priority. A certain proportion of our income must always go to fulfill our physical needs for such items as nutritious food and basic clothing. However, we must remember that our emotional needs can be just as strong. Therefore, our scale of preferences includes provision for "pretty" clothes and "desirable" food along with the warmth and nutrition provided by these products.

Intended use. Scales of personal preference cannot be separated from the consumer's attitude toward the intended use of the product. As individuals we get more pleasure out of some activities than others, and we favor those products or brands in our assortment for which the use is compatible with our desires. A set of golf clubs ranks higher than a new rototiller on the scale of preferences of a golfer. The rototiller may rank higher for a garden enthusiast. The difference between the two consumers is the attitude toward the activity to which the product is applied. One person's fun is another person's drudgery.

Degree of motivation. The relative intensity of the consumer's motives plays an important part in scaling preferences.[10] No product or brand is included in our assortment scale until the motivation for it reaches a sufficient intensity level. What the individual is motivated toward is also important to the ranking. The level and direction vary among people and between products for the same person. In effect, each product offers interference to the ranking of all other products. The longer a desire is postponed, the higher the product is placed on our preference scale. Also, a product toward which we have a more positive motivation tends to be ranked higher. For example, if the golf clubs have been put off from year to year, the consumer may plan to purchase them instead of the needed lawn mower in spite of the urgency of cutting the grass. The consumer may choose to borrow a lawn mower from a neighbor in order to obtain the clubs, even though this move is personally distasteful. In either case, brand is typically more important in selecting the clubs than the lawn mower.

Experience with product. Past product experience is important for scaling personal preferences. Past experience with products or brands may involve known satisfaction or it may involve known dissatisfaction.[11] Both types of experience affect current ranks. We may have a preference for a particular brand of golf club, such as Wilson, because of our experience using these clubs borrowed from a friend. It should also be noted that our experience with lawn mowers may largely account for our preferring golf clubs to lawn mowers.[12] If we cannot find Wilson golf clubs, we may decide to rank the next best brand in our assortment; but the second choice may rank lower on our preference scale than the original choice. As a result, we may put off the purchase for awhile. An individual's desire for fresh, garden-ripe tomatoes may have to wait for spring. In the meantime, the person may, or may not, decide to take the half-rotten cold-storage tomatoes offered in the grocery store. If the consumer does not like cold-storage tomatoes, then tomatoes are placed further down the list of product preferences.

Price. Price is also a factor that influences consumer preferences. The importance of price rests on its effect on consumer income. Consumers may wish to rank many types of products or brands high on their preference list, but the price of these wants makes it prohibitive. Evidence shows that consumers consider price important in their choice of brands and package size.[13] The evidence is that perceptions have considerable influence on the consumer's conception of price. One study shows that while price is important to the consumer's choice of package size, the consumer lacks perception of relative value between packages.[14] Price is more important in determining rank for immediate wants than for future wants. When individual preferences are related to expectations, the consumer discounts price with the attitude that, "I will worry about that when the time comes." Of course, the consumer cannot put off considering price for purchases that are contemplated in the near future. Thus, a consumer may rank a very much desired, but expensive, product lower on the preference scale because the same money can buy several other needed products. Extra income can push some products, which could not be afforded before, up on the consumer's preferences.

There is evidence to support the fact that consumers can hedge the cost of new products by purchasing smaller quantities. A study of 1,480 individual new brand purchasers discovered this result.[15] The consumer adjusted by purchasing smaller package size rather than purchasing fewer units of the product. As one might expect, the respondents purchased a larger quantity on the second trial. Presumably those who did not like the product did not have a second trial.

Logic of external information. Consumers can be persuaded to rank, or change the rank, of products by the logic of external information. Consumers may not always recognize sound and logical information when it is received, but they do react to perceived logic.[16] If the logic is sound, it can cause a reevaluation of consumer internal needs and motivation. The consumer may seek information from a business, but, if it does not make sense, the consumer will discount or discard it. Even information from a trusted friend is discounted if the consumer does not perceive it as "sound."

Even logical external information may be discarded by a consumer in ranking products if it is not compatible with the consumer's own logic. On a given product ranking, the consumer may receive a great deal of information, some sought and some unsought. The facts are filtered through the individual's thought processes, and that which is incompatible is not used, or it is not given the weight of other data. Of course, sufficient sound external information may cause the consumer to reassess his or her own position.

Purpose for external information. Like businesses, consumers may obtain external information either for objective analysis or for the purpose of rationalization. The consumer is rationalizing when only that information is sought which supports his or her present product ranking. Objective information is sought to test the ranking or as a possible basis for changing it. Either type of information may facilitate preference ranking, and either can lead to effective consumer behavior. When rationalizing, the consumer seeks factual, though biased, support for an emotional preference. It would be difficult to say which type of external information had the greater effect on preferences.

Support for external group ideas. As a general rule, consumer preferences are more influenced by ideas for which there is considerable external group support.[17] If a given product is fashionable with many people, the consumer may give it more attention or feel a stronger desire for it. In other words, the effect is multiplied when there is great support for the consumer's preference. This fact is true, generally, whether the information is favorable or unfavorable to the consumer's product rank. If the consumer wants a certain stove and hears it praised by a friend, a county agent, and a business advertisement, the consumer's preference for the stove is reinforced. If the consumer favors the stove but continues to hear derogatory remarks from several sources, the person may either change his or her mind or become indecisive.

Direct and indirect external influence

External influence on the individual consumer's rank of product preferences occur both directly and indirectly. This is equally true for social groups, business, or cultural influences. Direct influence is defined to exist when an original information source transmits a message that is personally interpreted by the consumer. The interaction does not have to be face to face, but it does have to be an original source. For example, when a consumer observes a television commercial or discusses a product with a salesperson, there is a personal interpretation of an original message from a sender. When a consumer asks a friend about the operating performance of her Buick, there is direct influence.

Indirect influence on consumer preferences occurs when some intermediary receives, interprets, and redistributes a message to the consumer. For example, we have indirect influence when a friend tells the consumer about the product he saw on a commercial last night. We have indirect influence when a consumer's boss tells him or her that all Buicks are excellent automobiles. Indirect influence often operates through family members. That is to say, individual members of the family are influenced by business, social groups, and culture, and these family members repeat and report the effects of such external information to other members who use it when ordering preferences.

PREFERENCE DETERMINATION IN FAMILIES

Over any given period of time the average family buys some products for individual use and some products for use by the group. In fact, there are probably as many, if not more, instances of group need as there are of individual need. A different kind of product ordering is necessary in these instances because the desires of others must be taken into account.[18] In this section, we discuss the manner of establishing product preferences where the entire family is concerned.

How family preferences are determined

The determination of the scale of product preferences for the family is similar to that described for individuals. Figure 7–2 shows the similarity and differences. The external influences are exactly the same as those described for individual preference determination. The difference is that when several products are important to the entire family, individual preferences may be negotiated in order to arrive at a common ranking.[19] The word negotiation sounds very businesslike, but family negotiation does not necessarily resemble that which takes place, say, between management and labor. The lines of battle are not so clearly drawn and the tools used are not so formal in the family. Family negotiations may be more subtle and informal in their application, and while the tools may not be formal they are no less sharply honed or effective. Family members do utilize most of the tools of

Figure 7–2
Influences on family preference decisions

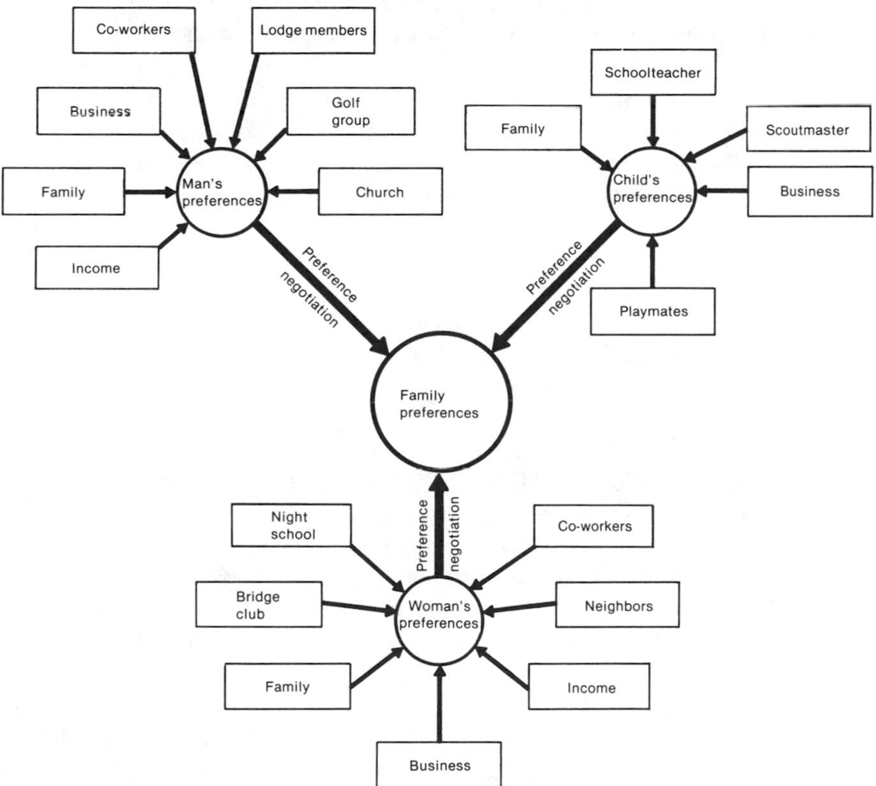

negotiation, including suggestion, persuasion, withholding favors, reprisals, coalitions, and arbitration, that are found in more formal business negotiations. Anyone doubting the effectiveness of family tools of negotiation has only to ask a wife who has ever had a child work on her for a new dress. That wife knows the effects of the relentless pressure to compromise as a result of tears, the social outcast appeal, or the threat of the child's unhappiness. Any husband whose wife wants new drapes is perfectly aware of the pressure to compromise as a result of a few poor dinners or a well-placed headache or two.

Three considerations are important to family negotiation over scales of product preference. They are: (1) personal readiness to negotiate, (2) family member involvement, and (3) type of negotiation. These factors are discussed below.

Personal readiness to negotiate. Family members enter into product negotiations with their scales of preferences set, or they must very quickly place them in order. Three situations may develop at this point. First, if there is general agreement on the order of preferences, the negotiation stops there, and the family's assortment needs are determined. Second, if any family member refuses to compromise on preferences, then the other members must either give in, overrule the holdout, or defer discussion to a later date. If a family member is given his or her way or if a decision is deferred, then the assortment, as of the present at least, is determined, and there is no further need for decision. Third, the family can compromise differences in product ranking through discussion.[20] It is primarily in this third case that there must be a willingness on the part of family members to negotiate their differences. Without a willingness to negotiate, there can be no further progress toward a workable scale of preferences.

Family member involvement. It is not necessary that each member of the family enter into negotiation over every product. Preference negotiation normally takes place between only those family members directly involved in the decision.[21] Parents don't usually consult the children in the negotiation over the inclusion of a new car, furniture, or appliances in the assortment. Mother and daughter may leave father out of the consideration of a new dress. In some cases, when product replacement is routine, no one need be consulted. The mother knows how new shoes for the kids, or a loaf of bread, rank for the family. The reader must be aware at this point that the family assortment is a loose collection of products. At any given time, this assortment exists for the individual family member, for small groups within the family, and for the family as a whole. There is probably never complete understanding as to a final list of preferences except when an actual choice must be made at the moment of purchase.

If the individual is satisfied to remain an observer during the discussion, then no ordering of preferences may be necessary. The consumer may not see the discussion as relating to the problem, or just may not care about the outcome. For example, an individual may remain passive as two friends discuss the merits of going fishing or doing the yard work. In the case of family decisions, the passive individual has no say about the rank of the product under discussion in the family assortment.

If the individual wishes to enter into the discussion, he or she must either have formed prior opinions about the product(s) under consideration, or must be capable of forming on-the-spot opinions about the product or its placement in the assortment. This fact is equally as true between individuals and friends as it is between individuals and the family group. Unless one has opinions about the product's importance, one cannot discuss the problem intelligently. A quick decision is possible because the ordering of an individual's preferences is as much a mental activity as anything else. It does not require significant factual information to back up the opinions expressed. Needed facts can even be obtained during the discussion. When forced to decide, the individual states the feelings of the moment.

Type of negotiation. Once the individual becomes involved in negotiating product preferences, the question becomes, "What type of negotiation is to be undertaken?" Four situations are possible. First, the individual consumer may enter into *direct interaction* with external social group members without any family consultation. This situation is most likely to happen with the single-member family, or when a family member is making a personal product decision that does not involve the family. The consumer may seek advice from these outside parties, or it may be offered without being sought. Second, the individual consumer may enter into a *general discussion* with other family members without any prior consultations among individual family members. The family members, as a group, may discuss such topics as whether to spend money on a vacation which may require curtailing expenditures for the children's clothing and family entertainment. Each member expresses his or her preferences between these expenditures freely, without any prior consultation with other family members or with outsiders.

Third, the individual may enter into *private negotiations* with individual family members prior to the general discussion. No external group advice is sought. It often happens in families that members influence each other before any general discussion takes place. When this prediscussion occurs, there is likely to be joint action in the general discussion. Family members form coalitions or cliques in order to get their way. Children often gang up on parents in order to get a new toy or to gain permission to see a certain movie. Sometimes one parent may side with the children, as when mother announces that everyone prefers a different restaurant to the one selected by father. Fourth, the individual consumer may enter into *prior discussion* with family members, and one or more family members may also be obtaining information and advice from sources outside the family. This latter is the most complicated type of family negotiation. Any type of group agreement prior to general family discussion tends to give strength to one side when scaling preferences. Even when the influence is not intentional, it has the effect of increasing the chance of success of the group.

Factors affecting family preferences

Once there is negotiation over family preferences, no matter which type of negotiation is involved, certain factors come into play. There factors pretty much determine the scale of preference established for the family as a whole. These factors are: (1) ability to persuade, (2) power within the family, (3) family relationships, (4) expected outcome of negotiation, and (5) family income.

Ability to persuade. Often the preferences that result from negotiation depend on the persuasive ability of each individual family member.

Who among us has not observed the ability of children to get their way by a well-timed display of tears. Adults have upon occasion used the same device effectively. Family members use all the art of communications to persuade other family members to place a preferred product higher on the assortment scale.[22] The use of fact, emotion, and outside support are all brought to bear in the negotiation. Also, the ability to use language and present a logical argument affects the outcome.

The status of the individual's own preferences plays an important part in the negotiation. A person resists giving in longer where the product ranks high on his other preferences. It must be noted that a person may have a strong desire for or against a product. In either case, there is a tendency to hold out. The family member is inclined to give in when he or she doesn't care one way or the other about the product. A typical response to a wife's question, "Which hat do you prefer?" is, "Take the one you like." If the husband were given a choice between buying a hat for his wife and not buying one, his reaction might be different.

Power within the family. Each member of a family has some power over the other members.[23] This power may be based on size, strength, recognized position in the group or degree of control over money income. Power can also be founded on apparent weakness. A husband or wife can get their way by appealing to protective instinct of their mate. Where there is power, there is a degree of control over other family members. This control basically centers in the ability to reward or punish. However, the fact that a family member has power may work for or against that member in successfully persuading the group. The person may use his or her power to force personal product desires to a higher position in the assortment, or power can be used to trade off one favor for another. Who can resist the husband who says to his wife, "You let me get the golf clubs and you can have a new camera." A member secure in his or her power may choose not to use it, thus giving in to another member's desires.

The contribution a member makes to the family may be an important source of power. One member's contribution may be in keeping the home and taking care of the children. The other may help with these activities; but their primary contribution may be economic. How the members view their function affects their power in the family. The one may argue a lack of money for the washer, but the other counters by pointing out that the job cannot be done without the washer. The strength of each member's conviction affects the placement of the washer in the target assortment.

Family relationships. Family relationships refer to how the family is organized to handle routine economic problems.[24] Decisions on who handles the money in certain situations, how routine purchases are made, which product brands are routinely preferred, and who makes the purchase come under family relationships.[25] These factors enter into the ordering of product preferences to the extent that one member is attempting to encroach on established routines or change the routines. For example, one of the children may want a brand of bread different from the brand routinely bought. The husband and wife may renegotiate meat purchases for the family. Instead of buying weekly quantities, it may be decided to buy all the meat, a side at a time. This decision may entail further negotiation over the purchase of a freezer that had been low on the family's scale of preferences. In more compatible families, the members have more characteristics in common, and there is a willingness to listen and cooperate. In such families cooperation predominates, and assortment preferences are easier to achieve. In families that are less compatible, the opposite tends to be true. There is argument over products, family members are more likely to act independently of the group, and there is less willingness to compromise. The products held in such families are more likely to reflect individual desires.

The individual's ego needs are a factor of family relationships. An individual may need love, satisfaction, power, recognition, approval, and so on. If a product meets any of these needs, singly or in combination, the individual will hold out longer for its high placement in the assortment.[26] It may be that to give in affects the member's ego even though the product is not personally important. The product becomes secondary, and the important thing becomes the satisfaction of an ego need, such as maintaining one's power. A lot of what one considers obstinate behavior on the part of a mate is probably a desire for power or recognition, as when the husband insists on replacing the station wagon before considering new furniture. An ego-oriented husband is not likely to give in unless some way is found to salvage his ego.

A family member who is secure in his ego needs finds it easier to give in. For example, love or respect for the other family members, can cause one to give in quicker in order to satisfy perceived ego needs of the other family members. A wife may say to herself, "I don't agree, but I love him, and if it makes Harry happy, we can get the new car before replacing the refrigerator." Love can also cause a member to hold out longer if the decision becomes a test of that love.

Expected outcome of negotiation. The expected outcome of negotiation influences a person's willingness to give in on the placement of a product in the target assortment. If a wife feels that her husband does not have his heart in the argument, or if she feels that his knowledge of the product, the situation, or the circumstances is weak, she will hold out longer. Under these circumstances, the wife will also put more effort into her argument, which affects the outcome. If, on the other hand, the wife feels that her husband is unyielding, she may decide that the argument isn't worth the trouble. What wife hasn't run afoul of her husband's unreasoning stubbornness? And what husband hasn't, at one time or another, run up against his wife's unshakable intuition?

Family income. Income is an important factor that can never be ignored when determining product preferences.[27] Income is both an opportunity and a restraint on the group. It is an opportunity because it represents the total amount available to spend. Several factors about income must be considered. First, the number of persons in the group earning income is important. The more earners, the greater the potential of products to include in the assortment. Second, it is important who earns the money. If the wife is working, for example, there may be expenses associated with taking care of children, providing meals, increased clothing for the working wife, etc., that predestine many expenditures. Third, the willingness of family members to share income is important. Generally, the father and mother have no choice in the matter of sharing, although there are families where each member keeps and spends his or her own earnings. Children are another matter. In low-income families, the tendency is for greater contribution by children to the family group. In higher-income families, the children tend to keep their own earnings. Fourth, it is important how many persons the income has to be shared with. A single-member household has fewer required expenditures than a multi-unit household. Fifth, it is important how much money is available, because the more that is available, the more products other than necessaries that can be bought.

The family preference decision

Figure 7–3 demonstrates how the differences of opinion are settled among family members in deciding on family preferences. The decision is essentially one of compromise which involves the individual, reference group, and family factors already discussed.[28] The decision is a narrowing process in which a series of compromises are made con-

Figure 7–3
The family preference decision

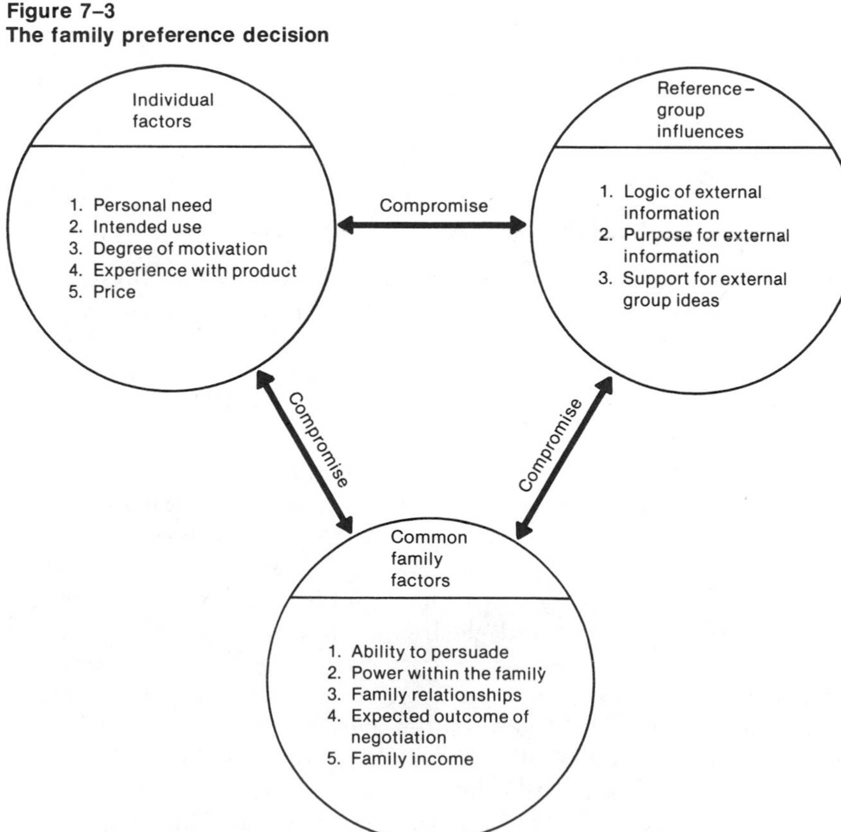

cerning the factors important to the decision.[29] For example, the husband may have a strong personal preference to purchase a boat before the dining room suite—based on his personal needs, intended use, and compatibility of ideas presented by friends and co-workers. However, the husband's ability to push for his desires may be tempered by affection for his wife, knowledge that the boat may not be as important to household operation, and the strong preference of his wife. In the course of discussion, one single factor may become predominant. For example, the husband may give up the boat because of affection for his wife even though his estimate of the situation is that he could have his way. It may even occur that both sides have to give. For example, if the husband wanted a boat and motor they may compromise on a boat and a less expensive dining room suite. Another type of compromise may call for giving up both in favor of a third product or saving the money temporarily.

One fact is sure, every family assortment decision involves some compromise. This fact is as true for the single-member family as for the multi-unit family. Only one compromise may be necessary, or it may take several. The decision may be made quickly or involve considerable time. The decision may be accomplished by formal discussion or by hints and clues dropped here and there by the parties. The decision can be heated or quite calm, but the decision must be made or the family cannot function as an effective unit.

INDIVIDUAL AND FAMILY PREFERENCES DIFFER

How individual consumers or families will decide their preferences is reasonably clear when considering only one factor at a time. The reason is that the complications caused by interaction are eliminated. If the individual or family always considered only its needs, one would only have to know consumer needs to predict behavior. The difficulty is that consumers and families scale their preferences on the basis of all those factors discussed simultaneously. As a result, we cannot predict with exactness the consumer's desire for goods and services. One point is clear: individual and family preferences do differ. No two consumers or families are likely to weigh all the factors mentioned exactly the same way. The result is that each consumer and family is individualistic and desires products to fit its particular requirements.

The effect of influences on preferences also varies between single-member and multiple-member families. In a single-member family that has no contact with any relations, the only factors involved are personal preferences and reference group factors. The family scale of preferences is fully determined any time the individual's ranking is determined. In a multi-member family, all the factors are at work, but even here the effect varies. For example, a consumer living with relatives is not affected as much as one living with a wife or with parents. A child is affected differently than a parent. Even the number of parents or children that make up the family can cause variations in the scales of preference held by the family.

RANK OF PREFERENCES TENTATIVE

The total environment in which the individual functions is dynamic, not static. Thus, the ranking of personal preferences is always tentative until the actual sale takes place. A given circumstance may cause one consumer to act impulsively and immediately to change established preferences. For example, a father may start out to purchase new jeans for his son and end up with a new jacket for himself. The jacket was there, and it was just what the father had wanted, although he had never really considered it as part of his assortment.

New information comes to the consumer right up to the moment of purchase. New information may cause consumers to reevaluate their preference scales. A family may have decided to buy living room furniture before a second car, but a particularly good offer on a new car may cause a quick reshuffling of preferences. The point is that consumers do scale preferences tentatively, and the scales influence their market behavior. Because preferences are tentative, the only positive way to determine a consumer's product preferences is to observe the actual order of purchase.

NOTES

1. Joel Huber, "Predicting Preferences on Experimental Bundles of Attributes: A Comparison of Models," *Journal of Marketing Research*, vol. 12 (August 1975), pp. 290–97.
2. Gordon L. Wise, "Consumer Preference Patterns in Professional Team Sports," *Akron Business and Economic Review*, vol. 5 (Fall 1974), pp. 37–40.
3. Robert F. Kelly and Michael B. Egan, "Husband and Wife Interaction in a Consumer Decision Process," *Marketing Involvement in Society and the Economy*, ed. Philip R. McDonald (Chicago: American Marketing Assn., 1969), pp. 250–58.
4. A. Sen, "Behavior and the Concept of Preference," *Economica*, vol. 40 (August 1973), pp. 241–59.
5. Dennis H. Gensch and Thomas F. Golob, "Testing the Consistency of Attribute Meaning in Empirical Concept Testing," *Journal of Marketing Research*, vol. 12 (August 1975), pp. 348–54.

6. Paul E. Green and Michael T. Devita, "A Complementarity Model of Consumer Utility for Item Collections," *Journal of Consumer Research,* vol. 1 (December 1974), pp. 56–67.
7. Thomas S. Robertson, *Consumer Behavior* (Glenview, Ill.: Scott, Foresman and Company, 1970), pp. 78–79.
8. Richard B. Westin and Peter L. Watson, "Reported and Revealed Preferences as Determinants of Mode Choice Behavior," *Journal of Marketing Research,* vol. 12 (August 1975), pp. 282–89.
9. Paul E. Green and Yoram Wind, "New Way to Measure Consumers' Judgements," *Harvard Business Review,* vol. 53 (July–August 1975), pp. 107–17.
10. Peter Wright, "Consumer Choice Strategies: Simplifying vs. Optimizing," *Journal of Marketing Research,* vol. 12 (February 1975), pp. 60–67; Joel B. Cohen, "An Interpersonal Orientation to the Study of Consumer Behavior," *Journal of Marketing Research,* vol. 4 (August 1967), pp. 270–78.
11. Kent B. Monroe, "The Influence of Price Differences and Brand Familiarity on Brand Preferences," *Journal of Consumer Research,* vol. 3 (June 1976), pp. 42–49.
12. See: John H. Howard, *Marketing Management: Operating, Strategic, and Administrative,* 3d ed. (Homewood, Ill.: Richard D. Irwin, Inc., 1973), pp. 61–77.
13. Kent B. Monroe, "Buyers Subjective Perceptions of Price," *Journal of Marketing Research,* vol. 10 (February 1973), pp. 70–80; Zarrel V. Lambert, "Price and Choice Behavior," *Journal of Marketing Research,* vol. 9 (February 1972), pp. 35–40.
14. Clive J. Granger and A. Billson, "Consumer's Attitude toward Package Size and Price," *Journal of Marketing Research,* vol. 9 (August 1972), pp. 239–48.
15. Robert W. Shoemaker and F. Robert Shoaf, "Behavioral Changes in the Trial of New Products," *Journal of Consumer Research,* vol. 2 (September 1975), pp. 104–09.
16. James E. Stafford, "Effects of Group Influences on Consumer Brand Preferences," *Journal of Marketing Research,* vol. 3 (February 1966), pp. 68–75; M. Venkatesan, "Experimental Study of Consumer Behavior Conformity and Independence," *Journal of Marketing Research,* vol. 3 (November 1966), pp. 384–87.
17. Yoram Wind, "Preference of Relevant Others and Individual Choice Models," *Journal of Consumer Research,* vol. 3 (June 1976), pp. 50–57.
18. Mirra Komarovsky, "Class Differences in Family Decision-Making on Expenditures," *Household Decision Making,* ed. Nelson Foote (New York: New York University Press, 1961), pp. 255–65.
19. Harry L. Davis, "Decision Making Within the Household," *Journal of Consumer Research,* vol. 2 (March 1976), pp. 241–60.
20. Alvin C. Burns and Donald H. Granbois, "Factors Moderating the Reso-

lution of Preference Conflict in Family Automobile Purchasing," *Journal of Marketing Research,* vol. 14 (February 1977), pp. 77–86.

21. Davis, "Decision Making Within the Household."
22. James H. Campbell and Hal W. Hepler, "Persuasion and Interpersonal Relations," *Dimensions in Communications* (Belmont, Ca.: Wadsworth Publishing Co., Inc., 1965), pp. 87–95.
23. Richard Hansen, Gary M. Munsinger, and Jean Draper, "A Dyadic Analysis of Power Roles in the Housing Decision Process," *Relevance in Marketing: Problems, Research, Action,* ed. Fred C. Allvine (Chicago: American Marketing Assn., 1971), pp. 397–401; Kelly and Egan, "Husband and Wife Interaction in a Consumer Decision Process," pp. 250–258.
24. Eli P. Cox, III, "Family Purchase Decision Making and the Process of Adjustment," *Journal of Marketing Research,* vol. 12 (May 1975), pp. 189–95.
25. Robert Ferber and Lucy Chao Lee, "Husband-Wife Influence in Family Purchasing Behavior," *Journal of Consumer Research,* vol. 1 (June 1974), pp. 43–50.
26. Edward L. Grubb and Harrison L. Grathwohl, "Consumer Self-Concept, Symbolism, and Market Behavior: A Theoretical Approach," *Journal of Marketing,* vol. 31 (October 1967), pp. 22–27.
27. John W. Slocum, Jr. and H. Lee Mathews, "Social Class and Income as Indicators of Consumer Credit Behavior," *Journal of Marketing,* vol. 34 (April 1970), pp. 69–74; William Peters, "Relative Occupational Class Income: A Significant Variable in the Marketing of Automobiles," *Journal of Marketing,* vol. 34 (April 1970), pp. 74–77; James H. Myers and John F. Mount, "More on Social Class vs. Income as Correlates of Buying Behavior," *Journal of Marketing,* vol. 37 (April 1973), pp. 71–73.
28. James R. Bettman, "The Structure of Consumer Choice Processes," *Journal of Marketing Research,* vol. 8 (November 1971), pp. 465–71.
29. Harry L. Davis, "Measurement of Husband-Wife Influence in Consumer Purchase Decisions," *Journal of Marketing Research,* vol. 8 (August 1971), pp. 305–12.

QUESTIONS

1. What is meant by consumer preferences? Do you feel that consumers can order preferences? Explain. Give examples from your own experience.
2. What is the basic difference between how individuals order preferences and how families order preferences?
3. How is the ordering of preferences handled in economics? What are the problems with the economic explanation? Explain.
4. Discuss how personal needs affect one's preferences, motivation, experience with the product.
5. Three external factors are important in ordering the individual's preferences. What are they? Discuss the effects of each.

6. How does personal readiness to negotiate enter into family preference negotiation? Discuss.
7. Discuss the types of negotiation that may take place within a family.
8. In family negotiation, discuss the effect of ability to persuade, power within the family, and expected outcome of discussion. Can you give examples from your own experience of the effect of each factor?
9. Explain the effects of family relationships on preference negotiation within the family.
10. Discuss how the scale of family preferences is the result of a compromise.

8

Purchase decision and assessment

Purchase decision
- *Consumption and purchase decision*
- *Consumer decision strategy*
- *The decision process*

Organization of information

Establish decision criteria
- *Sources of criteria*
- *Types of criteria used*

Consumer decision
- *Choice of alternatives*
- *Comparison of alternatives*
- *How the consumer decision is made*

Typical consumer decisions
- *Product decisions*
- *Store decisions*
- *Method of purchase decisions*

Postpurchase assessment
- *Nature of postpurchase assessment*
- *Manner of postpurchase assessment*
- *Purpose and scope of postpurchase assessment*
- *Adjustment in market decisions*

The last two steps of the consumer purchase process are discussed in this chapter. They are purchase decision and post purchase assessment. These steps are the proof of the pudding, so to speak, where consumer behavior is concerned. No matter how carefully the consumer searches for information or orders product preferences, the effort goes for nothing if the consumer cannot make sound decisions. Effective decisions increase the consumer's total assortment and standard of living, and ineffective decisions restrict or compromise the assortment resulting in a reduced standard of living. Thus the discussion of this chapter is extremely important.

PURCHASE DECISION

One may conclude that the purchase decision is the simplest step in the decision process. After all the consumer simply selects the product with the highest rating on the preference list. The truth of the matter is that the purchase decision is never that simple or automatic, and it requires much thought as do the other steps in the purchase process.[1] In fact, consumer decision takes up where the ordering of preferences leaves off. Product preferences establish the *expected* order of purchase for generic products. Consumer decision concerns a whole group of choices related to acquiring these generic products.

To make a decision is to reduce uncertainty to the point where one can specify a course of action. *Consumer decision* is to select, from among alternatives, or preferences, that market related action which is indicated by available information. On a given shopping trip, the consumer, even when knowing the type of product desired, may be simultaneously deciding on the brand, price, store, method of travel, services desired, personal treatment, product line expected, time of purchase, and more. Each of these types of decisions may involve multiple alternatives. Thus the consumer must establish a whole hierarchy of decisions.

The consumer purchase decision is complicated by a general lack of information. Even if search has been extensive, there are typically gaps in what the consumer knows. Judgment is the only ingredient available to fill these gaps. There is also the difficulty of making up one's mind. Problems such as which criteria are more important, how to make judgments between essentially similar alternatives, and how to bring together so many decisions into a single coherent action complicates the problem. The consumer's emotions have to be considered in every decision. All the facts may point toward the conclusion that the purchase of a $40,000 home is illogical, but the consumer may purchase anyway. Logic may indicate to a working couple that too much of the family income goes for clothing, but they still feel the desire to look nice at work. The final decision is sometimes effective and sometimes not, but it is always important.

Another consideration that always affects the consumer's decision is the situation.[2] Such considerations include the purpose of the purchase, who else is involved, alternative products, state of need, etc. Belk, in a study of snack products and meat, found the situational variables to be dominant to the purchase decision.[3] In a test using soft drinks, Bonfield also found support for the importance of situational variables.[4]

Consumption and purchase decision

Consumers make a wide variety of different decisions in a given period of time. When one considers the actual number, it staggers the imagination. Therefore, it is necessary to group these decisions in some meaningful manner if the discussion is to proceed logically. One important method of grouping consumer decisions is based on the reason for the consumer's actions. Based on this criterion, all consumer decisions can be classified as related to the buying of products or the using up of products.

Those consumer decisions involved with using up products are defined as *consumption* decisions. In this category are included such choices as what type of meat to serve for dinner, the type of book to read before bed, which record to place on the stereo, how the children should dress for church or school, when to vacuum the floors, and who was responsible for the lost screwdriver. These are important decisions for any consumer because they relate to their style of living.

The phrase *consumer purchase decision* is defined to mean those choices directly or indirectly associated with buying goods and services. It is logical in a marketing book to be more concerned with the act of purchasing than the act of using up products, although it must be remembered that the one depends to a large extent on the other. Thus, all references to the purchase decision in this book relate to buying. Examples of consumer purchase decisions include the determination of product needs; choices between generic types of goods; selection of brands, prices, and services; which car to take shopping; how many stores to visit; and how to fit shopping into other activities. It is recognized that consumption and purchase decisions are not completely separable. For example, the use of the car to shop or dressing for a shopping trip contain aspects of both using products and buying. However, if the major purpose of the activity is to buy products the decisions are classified as consumer purchase decisions.

Consumer decision strategy

The question arises as to whether consumers utilize a decision strategy as part of their purchase process. The answer hinges on the interpretation one gives to strategy. *Strategy* can be defined to mean the overall plan and adjustment of effort to achieve some specified goal.[5] Based on this definition, one can make a case for or against a consumer decision strategy.[6] Consumers have a goal in the form of desired products. Consumers enter into decision making in order to achieve their goal. Thus, it is possible to consider the consumer's purchase decision the result of strategy. Of course, the effectiveness of the overall group of market-related decisions varies from consumer to consumer. This same statement can be made of any business.

If one compares consumer decisions to those of business, it becomes hard to assign the term strategy to consumer decisions. Consumers lack the factual information, in terms of engineering and price statistics, that most businesses have. Consumers tend to live from week to week to a greater extent than business. Most consumers do not forecast, nor do the majority of their decisions extend over long periods of time. If you doubt this fact, ask any family that has attempted to stick to a budget. Any decision plan of consumers is subject to almost instantaneous change.

One point is clear: consumers are capable of making clear choices in the market. It would be a mistake on the part of business to assume a lack of strategy simply because the choices are sometimes casual and often ineffective. Consumers can show great determination to have their way as business found out during the meat boycott of a few years ago.[7] A recent study was made of similar and dissimilar products to determine if consumers use similar store and brand choice strategies across product categories. The similar products were aluminum foil and waxed paper. The dissimilar products were liquid detergent and facial tissue. The results indicated clearly that: (1) similar strategies were used for similar products, (2) somewhat, although less, similar strategies were used for dissimilar products, and (3) the more similar the products the more similar the strategy.[8]

The decision process

There are specific steps to consumer decision making that can be identified and analyzed. Here we seek to establish what these steps are before beginning a more detailed analysis of each. The definition of decision as specifying a choice from among alternatives suggests three steps. They are: (1) organization of information, (2) establishment of decision criteria, (3) consumer decision.

First, data resulting from search activities and consistent with perceived preferences must be systematized into meaningful groups. This is the organization step so necessary because comparisons are difficult, if not impossible, when based on random facts. Second, the criteria for comparison must be established. Without effective criteria to determine the relative worth of information, no meaningful comparisons of alternatives can be made. Criteria set the standards for measuring worth. Third, the consumer must make a decision. In the making of this decision, reasonable alternatives must be selected from all the facts that have been organized, and these alternatives must be evaluated by making comparisons. The result of comparison is the decision of a specific alternative. Thus the consumer's decision is a natural outcome of the evaluation of data. The next three sections of this chapter contain a detailed discussion of these steps in the decision process.

ORGANIZATION OF INFORMATION

The first step in consumer decision making is to place the data about the problem into a form that can be analyzed. This step can be highly complex when dealing with business problems. It can involve the use of statistics to compile graphs and charts and to provide figures on the relative homogeneity of the data. Consumers typically organize data much more casually, but the reader should not be fooled into thinking that consumers do not organize purchase information. For example, consider consumers who select and compare automobile brochures, tear ads for food specials from the newspaper, and mentally record information given by a neighbor concerning the better of two retail stores.

The consumer, just as a business researcher, may organize data about a market problem formally or informally. An *informal ordering of facts* is mostly mental. It may be nothing more complex than a recognition that certain facts belong to alternative A and certain other facts belong to B. For example, the consumer may say that the Chevrolet has better gas mileage, is cheaper, and has a high trade-in value; while the Pontiac offers prestige, better looks, and a better ride. A *formal organization of facts* requires at least a listing of information. A grocery list provides a basis for comparing prices and brands at the grocery store. The degree of formality a consumer gives to data organization pretty much depends on the importance of the decision to the consumer, the number of alternatives involved, or the amount of information the consumer must bring to bear on the decision.

ESTABLISH DECISION CRITERIA

The second step in the decision process is to establish decision criteria. These criteria become the basis for comparing alternatives later. We will discuss the sources of criteria and the types of criteria that consumers use.

Sources of criteria

Criterion refers to any standard of value or evaluation used as a basis for judgment. Of course, in a given situation, different consumers apply different criteria, so the question naturally arises, Where did they obtain these criteria? Actually, consumer criteria arise from (1) the individual, (2) reference groups, and (3) business.

Personal criteria are among the most important consumer standards, and they involve individual perception, needs, motives, and attitudes. Conservative consumers may have gray or blue as part of their standard in purchasing a new suit, but they may also seek high quality and therefore include high price as a part of the standard. The importance of reference groups cannot be underestimated for establishing consumer criteria. A person may insist that the new car be a Ford product because that is what the family has always purchased. The attitude of friends toward the type of house, car, furniture, and clothing helps determine the criteria for the products. Businesses also furnish consumers with decision criteria because much of what is in consumers' minds about products and services was put there by personal or mass selling. Business has a particular influence on the individual's confidence in product quality, brand, and service.

Types of criteria used

Individual consumers do not always apply the same criteria, and consumers often disagree on the importance of given criteria. Nevertheless, some standard is always necessary for decision.[9] Consumers use many types of criteria, including price, repairs, efficiency, durability, brand, store image, location, and credit. Fortunately, these criteria can be grouped under four major types, as shown in Table 8–1. Cost-related criteria have to do with getting and maintaining the product. Performance and suitability are criteria concerning the use of

Table 8–1
Types of decision criteria*

Cost	*Performance*	*Suitability*	*Convenience*
Price	Durability	Brand	Store location
Repairs	Efficiency	Style	Store layout
Installation	Economy	Store image	Store atmosphere
Operating cost	Materials	Product image	Store services
Cost of extras	Dependability	Time factor	Product extras
Opportunity cost		Appearance	

* Data illustrative rather than inclusive.

the product or desirability of a particular store. Convenience criteria involve time, pleasure, and extras that surround the purchase.

A couple of important points can be made concerning the criteria shown on Table 8–1. First, consumers typically use more than one criterion when evaluating choices.[10] Second, the actual number of criteria used in a given situation is typically small, although it varies by consumer. Third, it is often assumed that product cost is the most important and consistently used consumer criterion. Evidence does not support this position, but it points to a greater importance placed on the less tangible criteria.[11] Finally, it is often true that one particular criterion becomes the focal point of the decision. For example, a consumer may have complete trust in a brand; thus, the consumer selects this brand over similar lower-priced brands.

CONSUMER DECISION

Consumer decision, like consumer search discussed in an earlier chapter, can involve both mental or physical activity. The decision stage may be short or it may take considerable time. One does not take as long deciding the choice between new coats as between new cars. Consumer decision is one of the weakest links in all consumer behavior. First, the success of the evaluation depends, in part, on the type and amount of information received from the search process. All too often the consumer has too much or too little information for effective decision making.[12] Even when information is available, the consumer either does not take the time to consider it or is not capable of analyzing. How many consumers know anything about components of their car, television, furniture, etc.? The author admits that, except in superficial matters, he could not tell the construction of a quality piece of furniture from junk. As a result of a lack of knowledge the consumer too often has to depend on the reputation of the retailer, the brand, or the price of the merchandise as a substitute for effective decisions.

Choice of alternatives

When consumers decide to enter the market for a product, they are immediately faced with many problems, most of which have more than one alternative. It is not possible to specify all the alternatives facing a given consumer because every consumer is different and views the market differently. However, there are three broad types of alternatives faced by all consumers: product, store, and method of purchase alternative. Furthermore, we can specify some of the important market differences upon which these alternatives are based. Table 8–2 illustrates these points.

Table 8–2
Consumer alternatives*

Product alternatives	*Store alternatives*	*Method-of-purchase alternatives*
Brand features	Location differences	Mode of travel
Manufacturer and private brands	Type and quality of service	Store, mail, or telephone differences
Price levels	Width and depth of line	Time of day and will to purchase
Product performance	Layout differences	Single-or-multiple-purchase trip
Product use	Personal treatment	Single or joint decision
	Operational differences	

* Data illustrative rather than inclusive.

At one time or another, nearly every consumer has faced all the alternatives shown in Table 8–2. However, it is not necessary to consider all alternatives in a given purchase. One consumer may not consider private brands an alternative because of a strong preference for national brands. Another consumer may travel to shop only by automobile. In spite of this fact, most shoppers must face most of these alternatives before making a purchase. In one real sense, it is the combination of decisions made concerning each of these market differences that constitutes consumer tactics in the market.

Comparison of alternatives

The heart of consumer decision is the comparison of the available information. At this time, we want to discuss the use of decision criteria, methods of comparison, and consumer use of evaluation.

Use of decision criteria. Any meaningful comparison is always a two-sided affair, as illustrated in Figure 8–1. There must be at least two possible alternatives to compare, and there must be a comparison of each alternative to some decision criteria. In example A, if products

Figure 8–1

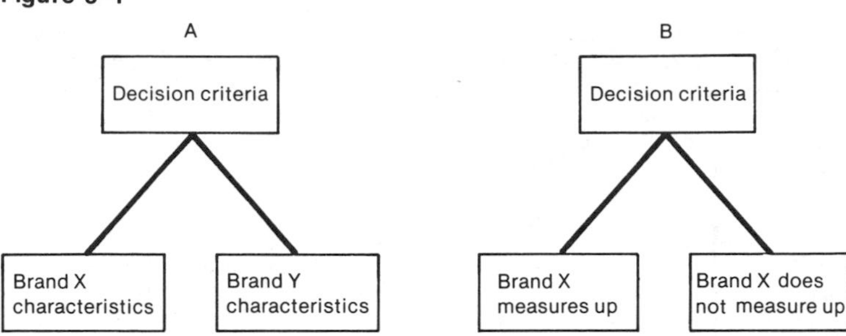

A and B only are compared, we know the differences between the two products, but we have no basis for evaluating our preference based on these differences. In example B, if the product is compared to the criteria, we know of any differences between the product and the criteria. This knowledge has no meaning unless we have an alternative, such as buy if it measures up and don't buy if it doesn't measure up.

It is necessary at this point to clarify how criteria are used in information comparisons. Actually, decision criteria can be used in either of two ways: first, as the basis for selecting various alternatives to evaluate and, second, for evaluating preferences from among the selected alternatives. It can, and often does, happen that these two uses occur almost simultaneously. Thus, a consumer may conclude, "Three television makes are acceptable in terms of price, reputation, service, and convenience of outlet, but I will buy brand A because it is more acceptable."

Method of comparison. In terms of our previous discussion, comparison involves consideration of the type of consumer alternatives compared to the decision criteria. The illustrations in Figures 8–2, 8–3, and 8–4 demonstrate the point. It can be seen from the illustrations that all the criteria do not necessarily apply to every problem facing the consumer. However, a given criterion may be important for the evaluation of product, store, or method alternatives. For example, efficiency and operating cost apply both to product alternatives and to store alternatives.[13]

The comparison process is essentially the same whether it is used to select alternatives or to decide from among alternatives already established. An oversimplified explanation of the difference is as follows. When selecting alternatives, the consumer makes the selection based on whether the alternative possesses the criteria or not. Little attention is given to weighting the criteria. When selecting between already established alternatives, the consumer places greater emphasis on the

Figure 8–2
Product comparison

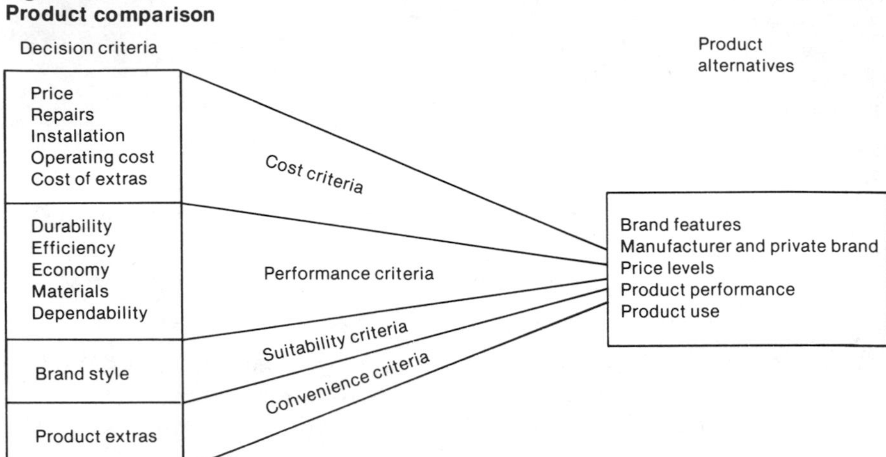

number of criteria possessed by each alternative and the importance, to the consumer, of these criteria. An increasing body of research suggests that the comparison is not a simple adding of product attributes, but rather an averaging of attributes.[14]

How the consumer decision is made

Let us consider some examples of how consumers, as a group, make decisions.[15] The discussion is based on four criteria that are significant

Figure 8–3
Store comparison

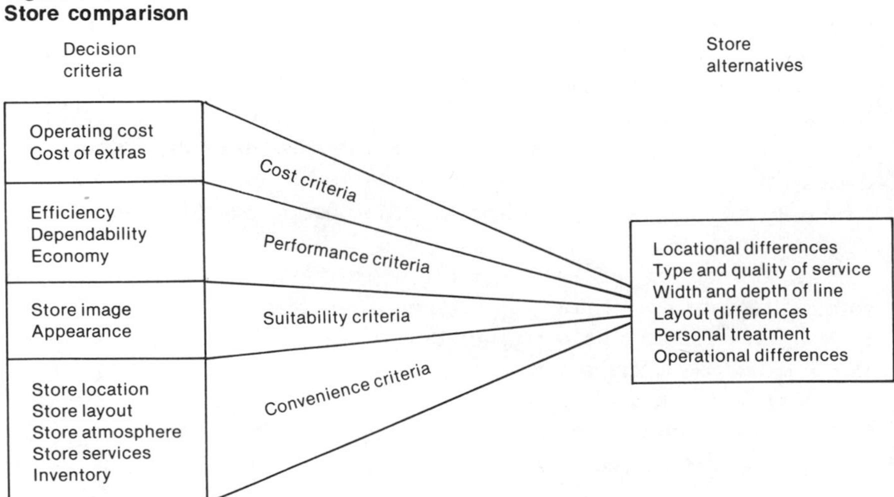

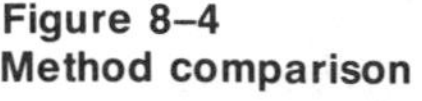

Figure 8–4
Method comparison

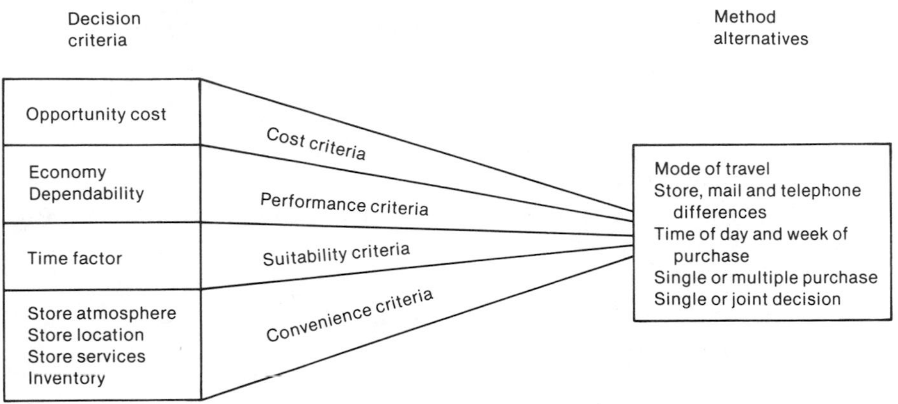

in the evaluation of product, store, and method of purchase: price, location, services, and inventory.

Price differences are important to consumer decision, but their importance varies by product and store.[16] Price is more important for automobile purchases than for groceries, as might be expected, and price varies with the purchase of shirts, appliances, and fashion items.[17] The location of the retail store affects the price of the product and the consumer's attitude toward convenience. Consumers resist traveling downtown because of congestion and parking problems. The suburban stores are also considered more casual by shoppers. For many products, such as convenience goods, location may be the most important consideration in the purchase.

Service and product extras can make a difference in consumer decision, but these criteria are not usually as important as other factors. Inventory reflects the store's assortment. A wide line of merchandise attracts some customers and repels others. The same is true for narrow lines. It is also true that consumers view store inventory differently at different times.

Consumer use of comparison. Logic indicates that consumers must utilize comparison or there could be no decision. However, there is evidence that consumers do not adequately consider alternatives, at least not where products are concerned.[18] For example, it was found that the percentage of consumers considering only one brand of durable goods was approximately 49 percent for television sets, 41 percent for refrigerators, 60 percent for electric irons, and 71 percent for vacuum cleaners. These are not impressive results.

The comparison of consumer alternatives may be made on a direct or indirect basis. A *direct comparison* results when the attributes of two alternatives can be interpreted in terms of themselves without the use of indications. There is a direct comparison when a consumer takes two brands of shirts and observes such product attributes as color, size, and price. An *indirect comparison* occurs when some secondary indicator is substituted as a basis for evaluation because no direct comparison is possible. Consumers often equate advertising, brand, or price with product quality. It is felt that the more highly advertised a brand or the higher its price, the higher its quality. Evidence does not support this belief. Other indicators of product quality are color, texture, and flavor. Prices, advertising, and store design are used as indicators of a quality store.

TYPICAL CONSUMER DECISIONS

A better understanding of how consumers decide can result from illustrating some typical customer decisions. The decisions illustrated are generalizations, and any individual consumer may act differently. The illustrations are grouped around the product, store, and method alternatives presented earlier.

Product decisions

It goes without saying that consumer preferences for different brands vary.[19] Consumers also differ in their attitudes toward manufacturer and private brands, price appeals and deals, and impulse purchases.

Brand decisions. Personal choices of brands are as varied as there are numbers of consumers, but most consumers prefer manufacturer's brands due to a lack of confidence in private brands. Nevertheless, a significant number of consumers apparently prefer private brands.[20] Generally, housewives, consumers with higher education, and members of large families accept private brands more readily. More knowledge or a desire for lower prices and confidence in the retailer probably helps explain why some customers buy private brands.

Price and deal decisions. It has been noted that consumers are affected differently by price. Attitude toward price varies by product and appears to be more important for staple or convenience goods. Some customers display a proneness toward deals such as coupons and price-off products.[21] Deal proneness is more frequent in younger housewives and persons who are less brand loyal. Deal proneness is also less when the consumer buys fewer brands or less units of a product.

Impulse decisions. Consumers often purchase on impulse, and the tendency to do so is greater for convenience goods than for shopping goods. It is no accident that grocery stores place such products as candy, gum, and cigarettes at the check-out counter where consumers must stop. Try getting a child past this point without having to cope with a request for some tidbit. One study shows the following results when grocery shoppers using product lists were compared to those who did not use product lists:[22]

	Users	*Nonusers*
Minutes shopping	30	26
Dollars spent	$30.30	$22.70
Total observed using unit pricing	43%	29%
Total observed using freshness dates	47%	34%
Total redeeming in-ad coupons	17%	9%

Thus list users are more intense shoppers who use unit pricing, freshness dates, and coupons. Users also spend more time shopping, but they do not spend more on the average.

A typical layout of a grocery store is shown in Figure 8–5. This layout is designed to take advantage of the fact that fresh produce makes a good first impression on the consumer. Meat is placed in the rear so that customers must pass through other areas first, increasing the chance of impulse purchases. Evidence exists that only a minority

Figure 8–5
Typical grocery store layout

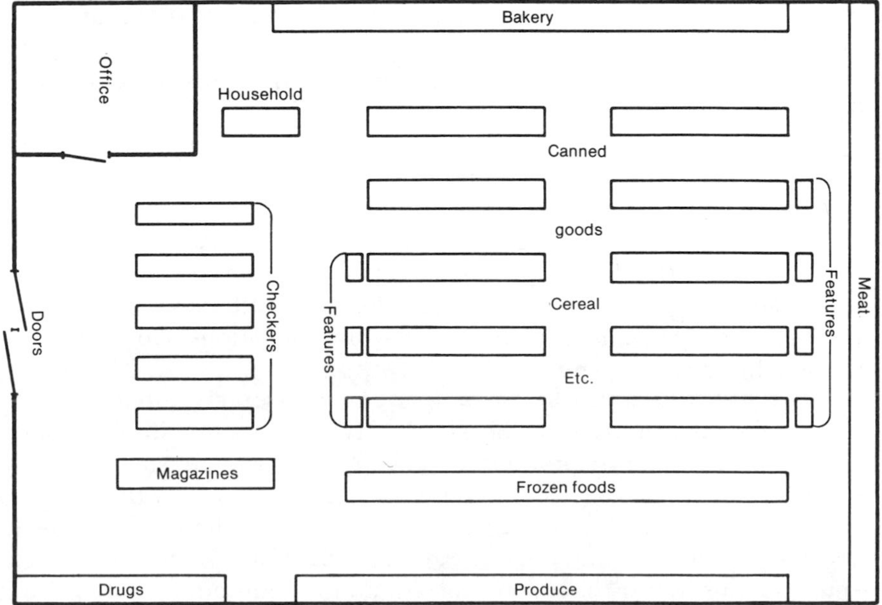

of shoppers have a specified grocery list when buying. At least half of these persons' purchases are impulse purchases.

Department stores, like grocery stores, are designed to obtain impulse sales. Counters, tables, racks, and walls are developed to encourage browsing through the store. Merchandise is placed in the open, and buying is made convenient in order to pick up extra sales. While it is estimated that impulse purchases account for 35 to 50 percent of all retail sales, there is a great variation by individual customers and types of products. Impulse purchases are highest for drugs, frozen foods, toilet items, bathing goods, and convenience household products. Psychology plays a great part in the consumer's decision on purchasing these types of goods.

All types of stores use price incentives in such forms as premiums, deals, and low prices to attract impulse purchases. Furthermore, much of the attention presently devoted to packaging and branding is to develop attractive products that can induce impulse sales.

Store decisions

The attitudes consumers have toward stores, and some typical reactions, can be grouped under choice of store, display and shelf decisions, and store layout.

Choice of store. Consumers look to six main factors in their choice of store: location, price lines, assortment, services, personnel, and atmosphere. The influence of these factors is so varied among consumers that it is impossible to generalize on their effect. Individuals select the store that offers the best combination of advantages to meet their particular desires.

Display and shelf decisions. Consumers do use displays and shelf height and space allocation to make product decisions.[23] Evidence is that the influence of these factors is much less than might be expected. End-aisle displays increase sales some, but the increase varies by products. Sales also vary directly with the amount of shelf space allocated to a product, but again the increase with increased shelf space is not great, and it varies by products. However, there is clear evidence that customers prefer to purchase products located at eye level on the shelf. Their next preference is for waist-high locations. Customers resist reaching or stooping.

Customer reactions to store layout. Customer purchase decisions do vary according to the store's layout. Grocery stores usually follow the rule, fresh produce on the right as the consumer enters, meat in the back, canned and dry groceries on aisles in the middle, and impulse items in display racks and up front. The produce, meat, and check-out areas have the greatest traffic flow. Department stores and discount houses have long recognized the importance of locating products by customer appeals. This fact accounts for impulse fashion merchandise having front locations. Of course, there is considerable variation in store handling of grocery items because of the variations in the merchandise.

Method of purchase decisions

The other broad area of customer decisions concerns the method or manner by which the customer purchases. At this point, we want to consider three decisions in this area: the use of the telephone as an alternative to going to the store, attitudes toward distance traveled, and multiple-shopping decisions.

Use of the telephone. Telephone shopping has been on the increase, although it still accounts for only a small part of total retail purchases. Consumers are particularly likely to use the telephone for purchasing services, such as repair work, and insurance. The telephone is frequently used to fill prescriptions. The principal reason consumers use the telephone is convenience.

Attitudes toward time and distance. Consumers show a clear reluctance to travel much over a half mile to purchase convenience goods or a mile to purchase shopping goods.[24] In most shopping, consumers balance the convenience of closeness against a better choice and/or lower price. A part of the reason for the rapid development of shopping centers is found in the consumer's attitude toward time and distance. Retailers have simply had to go where the consumers are.

Multiple-shopping decisions. Consumers, in recent years, have demonstrated a clear tendency toward multiple-purpose shopping trips. They particularly tend to combine the purchase of: (1) food, hardware, drugs, and houseware items; (2) clothing, services, food, and personal items; (3) drugs, snacks, books, and hardware, and (4) furniture, records, and clothing.

POSTPURCHASE ASSESSMENT

The consumer's purchase tactics are not complete when a decision has been made. It is natural for consumers to evaluate the effect of their decisions. This is the subject of postpurchase assessment. We consider here the nature of postpurchase assessment, the advantages and disadvantages of such an assessment, types of feedback, and the resulting changes in consumer tactics.

Nature of postpurchase assessment

Before proceeding, we need a definition of postpurchase assessment. *Postpurchase assessment* is the consumer's estimate of the result of his or her purchasing activities. It takes place after the product is bought and typically some period of use is involved. Although the consumer may think he or she has made a good buy, the proof is in the using where, sometimes, even the most carefully considered products do not measure up to the consumer's expectations. Table 8–3 shows how a sample of 10,000 consumers viewed the outcome of their buying in 1973 and 1974. A look at the poor ratings for the two years gives some indication of consumer dissatisfaction. In 1973, over half of consumers rated appliance repairs, repairs on home, auto repairs, and movies as poor values. By 1974, a majority of consumers were dissatisfied with children's clothing, but less than half of consumers were dissatisfied with movies. Although some consumers were dissatisfied with every product, most were rated average or better for satisfaction over the two years.

Manner of postpurchase assessment

Postpurchase assessment can be accomplished formally or informally, but it is always a result of new information about the purchase situation.

Formal or informal assessment. Postpurchase assessment may amount to nothing more than a consumer telling a friend that his or her car was a good buy or the lawn mower has worked right since the day it was bought. These are informal evaluations, and the consumer may not make them until some environmental influence forces him or her to consider the purchase. A more formal evaluation occurs when the consumer notes rattles in her new car, keeps figures on gas mileage and repairs, and makes some comparison to other cars or to her own mental criteria of what her car's performance should be.

Based on new information. Postpurchase assessment is always based on new information. The most important type of information is the experience gained as a result of the purchase. Thus, there is an interaction between the individual and the business community that may favorably or unfavorably affect the consumer's attitudes and perceptions. Family members and other reference-group members are likely to express opinions about the purchase or the product that is plugged into the evaluation. These are essentially the same sources used in the original search and evaluation process, but now everyone is expressing opinions and attitudes based on hindsight.

The consumer may begin to have doubts about the purchase even before it is made, and doubts often appear after purchase. The factors listed below are important reasons for doubt concerning a purchase decision.

Table 8–3
Consumer appraisal of value received for money spent, by product category

	1973 Percent distribution			1974 Percent distribution		
	Good	*Average*	*Poor*	*Good*	*Average*	*Poor*
Foods						
Beef	15.8	40.5	43.7	19.7	53.8	26.6
Poultry	29.9	49.2	20.9	44.1	45.1	10.9
Fish	25.9	52.4	21.7	22.2	51.3	26.6
Eggs	41.5	46.1	12.4	39.4	46.4	14.2
Milk	40.3	46.8	12.9	23.0	39.9	37.2
Fresh vegetables	23.8	46.9	29.3	24.1	49.2	26.6
Convenience foods	13.4	48.7	37.9	8.3	42.8	48.8
Restaurant meals	15.2	57.1	27.7	10.9	52.9	36.2
Apparel						
Men's suits	14.2	62.3	23.6	10.0	61.7	28.3
Women's dresses	9.6	50.7	39.6	6.8	48.2	45.1
Children's clothing	8.9	48.1	43.0	6.2	43.6	50.2
Shoes	10.6	50.6	38.7	8.1	45.7	46.1
Homefurnishings						
Upholstered furniture	11.2	58.9	30.0	7.2	56.5	36.3
Wood furniture	13.3	59.5	27.2	10.5	55.7	33.9
Major appliances	24.8	60.1	15.1	19.6	61.1	19.4
Small appliances	27.3	59.7	12.9	21.3	62.1	16.5
Carpets	20.1	66.8	13.1	15.9	67.2	16.9
Home maintenance, utilities						
Appliance repairs	5.3	37.5	57.3	4.1	35.3	60.6
Repairs on home	4.4	38.2	57.4	3.7	37.0	59.3
Telephone	25.0	49.1	25.9	21.4	48.9	29.7
Electricity	28.3	50.7	21.0	19.0	47.3	33.7
Moving expenses	4.0	55.6	40.4	3.2	51.5	45.2
Transportation						
New cars (domestic)	12.5	51.5	36.0	12.0	54.4	33.6
New cars (foreign)	22.0	55.1	22.9	16.0	54.8	29.2
Used cars	10.6	53.5	36.0	12.0	54.1	34.0
Auto repairs	5.8	35.2	59.0	5.3	37.3	57.4
Auto insurance	12.5	47.4	40.1	15.3	53.3	31.4
Local transportation	14.3	46.2	39.5	17.3	48.7	33.9
Air fares (domestic)	16.9	67.1	16.1	11.4	67.5	21.1
Air fares (foreign)	20.8	64.5	14.7	12.8	67.3	19.8
Medical and personal care						
Doctors' fees	13.1	47.4	39.5	12.5	49.9	37.6
Dentists' fees	12.0	44.8	43.2	11.3	47.4	41.3
Prescription drugs	8.7	43.6	47.7	8.5	46.4	45.1
Other drugs	7.5	57.5	34.9	7.1	58.9	34.0
Health insurance	13.7	46.5	39.8	12.8	50.7	36.6
Life insurance	19.4	63.3	17.3	19.0	65.8	15.1
Beauty shop services	14.3	58.0	27.7	13.0	57.5	29.6
Finance						
Credit charges	8.0	42.3	49.7	7.6	43.6	48.7
Bank service charges	18.5	55.8	25.7	17.7	54.0	28.3
Recreation						
TV (black and white)	39.8	51.9	8.4	37.1	55.1	7.8
TV (color)	29.0	53.2	17.8	27.5	56.5	16.1
Movies	5.5	30.1	64.4	16.6	57.2	26.2
Children's toys, games	12.9	51.3	35.8	11.7	52.2	36.1

* See text for definition of this measure.

Source: Fabian Linden, "The Consumer's View of Value Received," *The Conference Board Record* (November 1973), pp. 6–11.

1. The consumer's attitude may change.
2. The consumer may not have understood the product's performance or features.
3. The decision represents a significant mental satisfaction to the consumer.
4. There are other desirable alternatives.
5. The product purchased does not measure up.[25]

Purpose and scope of postpurchase assessment

Postpurchase assessment has three major purposes. First, it adds to the consumer's store of experiences. In a very real sense, it is through postpurchase assessment that experience is taken into the consumer's frame of reference. Thus, it broadens the consumer's personal needs, ambitions, drives, perceptions, and understanding.

Second, postpurchase assessment provides a check on market-related decisions. It gives the consumer an idea of how well he or she is doing in the market. Consumer satisfaction is related to expectations before purchase. One study shows that if product expectations before purchase are too high relative to actual performance, the consumer becomes less satisfied.[26] Consumers rate products higher if performance and expectations fall within a relevant range.

It must be pointed out that postpurchase assessment is not limited to products. Postpurchase assessment includes all the decision alternatives, product, store, and method of purchase, previously mentioned.[27] A consumer may just as logically have doubts about the route taken to shop, or the time spent comparing stores, as about the physical product purchased.

Third, postpurchase assessment provides feedback about the product, store, and method of purchase to serve as the basis for adjusting future purchase behavior.[28] The consumer cannot understand the changes he or she wants to make in his purchase tactics until an evaluation is made.

Adjustment in market decisions

A natural outcome of the consumer's postpurchase assessment is some change in the consumer, because at least experience has been broadened. However, there may, or may not, be a change in purchase tactics. Figure 8–6 shows the kinds of adjustments that may occur in consumer purchase behavior. The illustration is developed around three types of postpurchase feedback. These are consumer satisfied, consumer partially satisfied, and consumer unsatisfied. Of course, the reader must recognize that partial satisfaction can be anything from nearly satisfied to nearly unsatisfied.

Figure 8–6
Adjustment in consumer market decisions

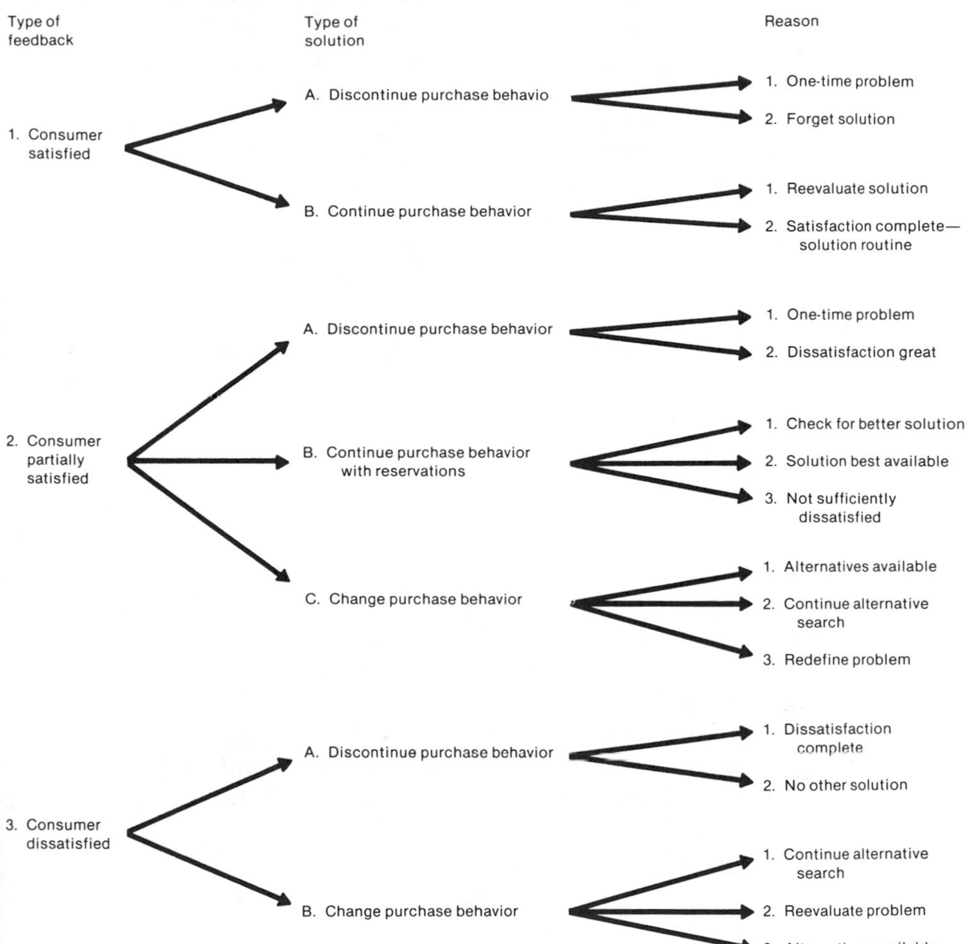

Figure 8–6 shows that there are always alternatives even for the satisfied consumer. It is also apparent that the partially satisfied consumer has more alternatives and, in some respects, the more difficult decisions to make. This is true simply because the partially satisfied consumer may have less strong feelings about the solution than either the satisfied or dissatisfied consumer. The dissatisfied consumer tends to either discontinue purchase behavior or change behavior.

The adjustment in consumer tactics that results from postpurchase assessment most usually depends on (1) the amount of new information; (2) the type of feedback, satisfaction, or dissatisfaction; and (3) the consumer's mental reaction. As we might expect, consumers react differently on all three counts. Consumers seek more information for reevaluation when they are surer of their decision, and consumers sometimes seek information simply to reassure them in their position. Consumers tend to be dissatisfied with a decision when results differ from expectations. This may hold true if the solution exceeds or falls below expectations. It is also true that consumers tend to magnify the differences between expectations and actual results. In any case, the result of postpurchase assessment is that the consumer is satisfied or in a condition of continual search.

NOTES

1. R. A. Mittelstaedt, S. L. Grossbart, W. W. Curtis, and S. P. Devere, "Optimal Stimulation Level and the Adoption Decision Process," *Journal of Consumer Research,* vol. 3 (September 1976), pp. 84–94.
2. Russell W. Belk, "An Exploratory Assessment of Situational Effects in Buyer Behavior," *Journal of Marketing Research,* vol. 11 (May 1974), pp. 156–63.
3. Ibid.
4. E. H. Bonfield, "Attitude, Social Influence, Personal Norm, and Intention Interactions as Related to Brand Purchase Behavior," *Journal of Marketing Research,* vol. 11 (November 1974), pp. 379–89.
5. James F. Engel, Hugh G. Wales, and Martin R. Warshaw, *Promotional Strategy,* 3d ed. (Homewood, Ill.: Richard D. Irwin, Inc., 1975), p. 4.
6. Peter Wright, "Consumer Choice Strategies: Simplifying vs. Optimizing," *Journal of Marketing Research,* vol. 12 (February 1975), pp. 60–67.
7. *Time,* Inc., April 9, 1973, pp. 11–15.
8. Robert C. Blattberg, Peter Peacock, and Subrata K. Sen, "Purchasing Strategies Across Product Categories," *Journal of Consumer Research,* vol. 3 (December 1976), pp. 143–54.
9. James R. Bettman, "A Threshold Model of Attribute Satisfaction Decisions," *Journal of Consumer Research,* vol. 1 (September 1974), pp. 30–35.
10. Lee K. Anderson, James R. Taylow, and Robert J. Holloway, "The Consumer and His Alternatives: An Experimental Approach," *Journal of Marketing Research,* vol. 3 (February 1966), pp. 62–67; Ralph I. Allison and Kenneth Uhl, "Influence of Beer Brand Identification on Taste Perception," *Journal of Marketing Research,* vol. 1 (August 1964), pp. 36–39.
11. A. Gabor and C. W. Granger, "Price Sensitivity of the Consumer," *Journal of Advertising Research,* vol. 4 (December 1964), pp. 40–44; Irving S. White, "The Perception of Value in Products," *On Knowing the Consumer,* ed. Joseph Newman (New York: John Wiley and Sons, Inc., 1966), pp. 101–102.

12. David J. Reibstien, Stuart A. Youngblood, and Howard L. Fromkin, "Number of Choices and Perceived Decision Freedom as a Determinant of Satisfaction and Consumer Behavior," *Journal of Applied Psychology*, vol. 60 (1975), pp. 434–37.
13. Steven Pincus and L. K. Waters, "Product Quality Ratings as a Function of Availability of Intrinsic Product Cues and Price Information," *Journal of Applied Psychology*, vol. 60 (1975), pp. 280–82.
14. C. Michael Troutman and James Shanteau, "Do Consumers Evaluate Products by Adding or Averaging Attribute Information?" *Journal of Consumer Research*, vol. 3 (September 1976), pp. 101–06; James R. Bettman, Noel Capon, and Richard J. Lutz, "Multiattribute Measurement Models and Multiattribute Attitude Theory," *Journal of Consumer Research*, vol. 1 (March 1975), pp. 1–15.
15. T. F. Pickering, "Verbal Explanations of Consumer Durable Purchase Decisions," *Journal of Market Research Society*, vol. 17 (April 1975), pp. 107–13.
16. Stuart U. Rich and Bernard D. Portis, "The Imageries of Department Stores," *Journal of Marketing*, vol. 28 (April 1964), pp. 10–15.
17. "Consumer Behavior in the Super Market," *Progressive Grocer*, vol. 54 (October 1975), pp. 37–59. This is an excellent comprehensive study of consumer grocery purchasers. Price ranked behind cleanliness as a reason for selecting a grocery store.
18. William P. Dommermuth, "The Shopping Matrix and Marketing Strategy," *Journal of Marketing*, vol. 2 (May 1965), pp. 128–32.
19. Kent B. Monroe, "The Influence of Price Differences and Brand Familiarity on Brand Preferences," *Journal of Consumer Research*, vol. 3 (June 1976), pp. 42–48.
20. J. G. Myers, "Determinants of Private Brand Attitude," *Journal of Marketing Research*, vol. 4 (February 1967), pp. 73–81; Ronald E. Frank and Harper W. Boyd, Jr., "Are Private-Brand-Prone Grocery Consumers Really Different?" *Journal of Advertising Research*, vol. 5 (December 1965), pp. 27–35.
21. Frederick E. Webster, Jr., "The Deal-Prone Consumer," *Journal of Marketing Research*, vol. 2 (May 1965), pp. 186–89.
22. "Consumer Behavior in the Super Market," pp. 37–59.
23. Keith Cox, "The Responsiveness of Food Sales to Shelf Space Changes in Supermarkets," *Journal of Marketing Research*, vol. 1 (May 1964), pp. 63–67; "Shelf Merchandising Strategy: A Key to Increased Sales," *Progressive Grocer*, (1964), pp. C-121–C-125.
24. John M. Rathmell, "Discretionary Time and Discretionary Mobility," *Managerial Marketing: Perspective and Viewpoints*, 3d ed. eds. Eugene J. Kelley and William Lazer (Homewood, Ill.: Richard D. Irwin, Inc., 1967), pp. 145–55.
25. G. W. H. Scherf, "Consumer Dissatisfaction as a Function of Dissatisfaction with Interpersonal Relationships," *Journal of Applied Psychology*, vol. 59 (August 1974), pp. 465–71.

26. Rolph E. Anderson, "Consumer Dissatisfaction: The Effect of Disconfirmed Expectancy on Perceived Product Performance," *Journal of Marketing Research,* vol. 10 (February 1973), pp. 38–44.
27. John A. Miller, "Store Satisfaction and Aspiration Theory," *Journal of Retailing,* vol. 52 (Fall 1976), pp. 65–84.
28. Frederick W. Winter, "The Effect of Purchase Characteristics on Postdecision Product Reevaluation," *Journal of Marketing Research,* vol. 11 (May 1974), pp. 164–71.

QUESTIONS

1. What is consumer decision? How does consumer decision differ from the establishment of product preferences?
2. Distinguish between consumption and purchase decisions.
3. What is meant by consumer purchase strategy? Do you feel consumers have a purchase strategy? Defend your position.
4. Explain the overall consumer decision process. Can you give personal examples of how you have employed this decision process.
5. When making decisions, where do consumers find the criteria that are used? Explain the major types of criteria. Which criteria do you consider most important? Explain.
6. What are the three major types of alternatives faced by consumers in the market? Discuss how these alternatives may vary between the purchase of a convenience product and a shopping product.
7. Explain how the decision criteria are used when making comparisons.
8. Select a specific product such as an automobile, furniture, or clothing and demonstrate product, store, and method of purchase comparisons for each.
9. Define postpurchase assessment. Do consumers enter into postpurchase assessment? How important is it to consumer decision making?
10. Why do postpurchase assessments require new information? Discuss the purpose of postpurchase assessment.

PART THREE

The individual: Basic determinants of consumer behavior

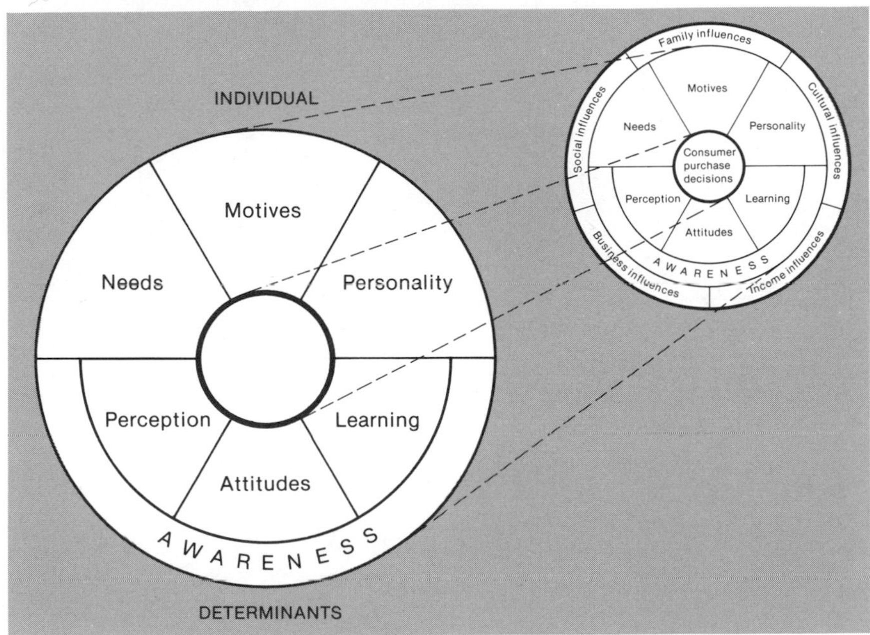

Since we have made the point that it is the individual who is basically responsible for his or her own behavior, it is reasonable to begin our detailed discussion of consumer behavior with this factor. There are seven chapters in this part that relate to the basic determinants of consumer behavior. They are:

9. Introduction to the individual consumer.
10. Consumer behavior founded on needs.
11. Motives stimulate consumer action.
12. Consumers act as they perceive.
13. The effect of consumer attitudes.
14. The effect of learning on consumer behavior.
15. Personality aspects of consumer behavior.

This part develops the middle portion of the model. It develops in detail concepts of needs, motives, personality, and awareness that affect consumer behavior. Since the book emphasizes the individual consumer, Part Three is of particular importance to the reader.

9

Introduction to the individual consumer

Need to understand individual consumers
Self-concept ties basic determinants together
The concept of consumer images
The meaning of image
Types of consumer images
The total person
Preservation of the self-image
Generalizations about the self
The self-concept causes consumers to change
Personal change and consumer behavior
The time element in self
Self-image and mode of living

The discussion of the consumer's decision process in Part Two serves as a good overview of consumer behavior. In it, consumer decision making is detailed, and some of the broad personal and environmental influences on decision making are explained. It is now time to begin dealing with the specifics of consumer behavior in order to provide substance to what was only hinted at previously. The individual consumer acts in a total situation. The actual purchase decision is a result of the individual's makeup, his or her perception, needs, awareness, and the environment that influences this personal makeup. In this part of the book, we explore some of these factors that the individual brings to the purchase situation.

NEED TO UNDERSTAND INDIVIDUAL CONSUMERS

There are several reasons why it is necessary to understand the individual consumer. First, only the individual can interpret market information. In reality, agreement among consumers on a market factor observed can exist, but each individual must separately interpret the factor. Second, only the individual can make decisions. Thus, ultimately all market considerations must be filtered through the individual consumer's mind. Third, it follows that the influence of environmental factors is accomplished through the individual. The individual consumer can be influenced by the environment, but the environment cannot decide for the individual consumer. Fourth, all purchases of goods and services are ultimately enjoyed by individuals. Products may be purchased for group use, but the satisfaction derived is an individual matter. Fifth, and most important, we take the individual consumer point of view because the consumer is the smallest unit of analysis of consumer behavior.

SELF-CONCEPT TIES BASIC DETERMINANTS TOGETHER

It was established in Chapter 1 that the basic determinants of consumer behavior are needs, motives, personality, and awareness. These basic determinants reside in the individual. Therefore, it is around some concept of the individual, or self, that the basic determinants are related to one another.

> *The human being responds not only to objects and persons in the outer environment but to his own body, his own thoughts, his own feelings. In so doing he develops cognitions about the self as a central and valued object.*[1]

What the individual consumer is and how the consumer purchases depend, to a large extent, on his or her view of self. Every individual is simultaneously a physical and a mental entity. That is to say, every individual is a physical fact, an image of self, and an image to others. These images are emotional-mental responses to the fact of the individual that is, in itself, too complex to understand completely. Consumer motives are based on images of one's self and one's environment. Perception is nothing more than the images received by a consumer, and attitudes are the impression held. Even needs are at least partly a result of feelings and impressions. Let us reintroduce the basic determinants at this time and show how the self-concepts are related to each.

In the final analysis, all consumer needs are related to the self, whether derived from the physical self or the mental self.[2] The need for clothing for warmth is physical, but the need for clothing to enhance attractiveness is mental. Consumer needs also arise from how other people view the person. There may be no physical basis for a consumer's need for a new evening gown, but there may be an emotional need based on preserving the image that friends have. The individual's consumer actions depend heavily on awareness and its components. Any awareness of one's self or one's environment depends on existing attitudes, learned experience, and present perceptions. The consumer also depends on awareness to understand the environment. Thus, awareness is at the core of individual identity, and the individual's behavior depends greatly on how one conceives the self in relation to the environment.[3] The important aspect of the individual, so far as consumer behavior is concerned, is not what one is, but what one perceives one's self to be. The consumer acts to bolster his or her self-perception. For instance, in one study of 336 undergraduate students, it was found that beer drinkers saw themselves as more social, confident, extroverted, forward, and sophisticated than nonbeer drinkers.[4]

All consumer behavior is motivated and based on reasonable processes. Motives arise out of the individual consumer's needs as they are perceived by that person. Some of these motives are central to the well-being of the self-image and some are peripheral. Most of our ego-bolstering motives are central to our inner well-being. Here we include love, esteem, affection, status achievement, and recognition motives. The consumer's attitudes revolve around one's self perception.[5] The consumer's self concept is, in fact, an attitude. These attitudes can be looked upon as the culmination of needs, motives, and personality because all these factors aid in forming individual attitudes toward the self and the environment.

THE CONCEPT OF CONSUMER IMAGES

What the individual consumer is, will for the most part, determine what that consumer does. Thus, to understand the individual consumer, it is necessary to gain some insight into the nature of the individual.[6] This is not a simple task. Traditional methods of marketing research do not let us examine the self-concept, since it can only be uncovered by psychoanalysis. The difficulty is that a consumer is simultaneously many things, depending on the perspective taken. Newman points out: "The view of self includes not only one's physical being, but evaluations and definitions of self as strong, honest, good-humored, sophisticated, just, guilty, and a thousand other ideas."[7] These perspectives involve images; so to understand the consumer's nature, we must go into the subject of images and how these images affect consumer behavior.

The meaning of image

Kenneth Boulding says that image is subjective knowledge.[8] That is to say that an image is not the fact of a thing, but it is fact from someone's point of view based on partial and/or inadequate information. The images that consumers have of themselves and others are predicated on the existence of the fact of a person. This existence has five dimensions: space, time, personal relations, organization and emotions.[9] *Space* is a person's physical placement, where the person is. When a person not only knows where he or she is but the sequence of events that led to his or her being there, time is involved. *Relationship* indicates that a person cannot know oneself fully without knowing of those he or she comes into contact with. *Organization* means that a person knows how his or her world operates. One can open the door, turn on the television set, and accomplish other tasks necessary to existence. The person's *emotions* are reactions, feelings, and attitudes concerning the self and the world. When one puts these five dimensions together, the result is a consistent image, or impression, of the person or thing perceived.

Types of consumer images

The consumer image has long been associated with concepts of the self. The difficulty lies in the fact that there exists more than one image of the self. Actually, there are five different concepts of self-image. They are (1) the real self, (2) the ideal self, (3) the self-image, (4) the apparent self, and (5) the reference-group image.[10] Figure 9–1 is designed to aid in understanding these different concepts. The total person is greater than the sum of all the individual images. This fact is indicated on the figure by a dotted line. The person reacts to outside impressions and to his or her own self impression. The manner in which these impressions are internalized with the real self determines

Figure 9–1

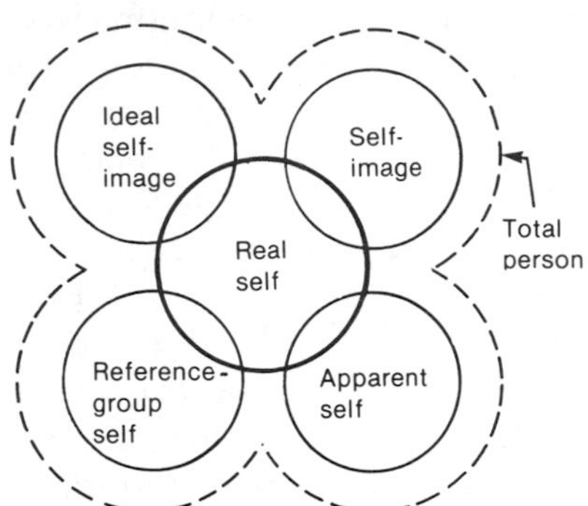

the total person. This point will become more clear as the discussion proceeds.

The real self. The real self is the individual as an objective entity. It is more nearly what a person is fundamentally, and the real self is never completely understood or observed. This fact is as true for an individual who attempts to observe and understand his own nature as it is for an outsider attempting to fathom the nature of that individual. How many of us are aware of the points of pettiness, greed, ambition, loneliness, and affection that reside deep inside our conscious or unconscious minds? It is probably true that most of us could not face the stark reality of perfectly understanding our own nature. We put out of our cognitions (mental processes) those parts of our nature that we cannot, or do not want to, deal with. How many of you know persons who have physical or mental quirks that they are not aware of? It is the same with consumers. We subconsciously prefer a certain color, a particular store clerk, or a particular price.[11] When purchasing products, a consumer follows personal patterns of conservatism or liberalism that may not register on the conscious mind. We get into ruts of travel or trade based on unconscious aspects of our nature.

The real self is extremely important to business. Contained in the real self are a person's basic physical and emotional requirements and characteristics. It is difficult for consumers to stray too far away from their basic nature, even though one may not be completely aware of the motivation. Thus it is the real self that business would most like to research and know. However, it is probably impossible for business to penetrate too far into this realm in any practical sense.[12] What consumers can hide from themselves, they cannot report to business. Sometimes psychological techniques can bring out some parts of a person's nature, but it is difficult and costly.

The ideal self. The ideal self is what the consumer would like to be.[13] This self concerns a person's aspirations, his or her striving and desire to do and be better. The ideal self is never fully achieved, because the consumer cannot let this happen. To do so means the end of hope. A person always finds something new to strive for. Consumer attempts to achieve the ideal self can be seen in the purchasing of prestige products, such as mink coats, diamonds, and yachts. Attempts by consumers to buy products related to social climbing, snobbery, and leisure are also concerned with the ideal self.

The business executive is vitally interested in obtaining information about the consumer's ideal self. Furthermore, the marketer is more apt to have some luck when dealing with this aspect of the consumer, because this part of a person is more apparent. A person tends to be aware of aspirations, and is frequently willing to discuss them. Besides, much can be learned about the consumer's aspirations by observation. Aspirations can be studied by means of observed purchase behavior, style of living, and by surveys. Much of what we refer to as trading up, fashion buying, and keeping up with the Joneses relates to the ideal self. The business manager is also interested because of its effect on discretionary income.

The self-image. The self-image is how consumers see themselves. It is a combination of the real self and the ideal self. It contains consumers' understanding of themselves and their aspirations. The self-image guides much of consumer behavior. In many respects, it is more important in purchase behavior than the real self. A consumer buys products that either support or improve the self-image.[14] A coed who sees herself as sexy may purchase padded bras to augment that image. A boy insists on a mod suit because he sees himself in the swing of things. It is difficult to get the consumer to go against his or her self-image in purchasing.

Knowledge of the self-image is perhaps the most important of all images to business. The self-image controls all normal expenditures that concern the consumer's present life style. In a very real sense, a consumer is what that consumer buys. Information about the self-image can be obtained in the same manner as described above.[15] In some respects, it is even more easily gathered, and business utilizes it constantly. Salespersons deal with the self-image when they feel out a client. Advertisers deal with the self-image when they set the tone and appeals of their advertisements. The clerk in a department store obtains clues to this image by the departments visited by the consumer, the merchandise handled, and questions asked. There is evidence that consumers who have a good image of themselves are more easily dealt with than consumers who have a poor image of themselves.

The apparent self. The apparent self is how outsiders see the consumer. Mainly, what outsiders see is some combination of the ideal self, the real self, and the self-image. The impressions that outsiders hold of the person have a direct bearing on social interaction. If the outsider is impressed, there is a basis for mutual and perhaps favorable interaction; if the outsider is unimpressed, there may be no basis for interaction or it may be unfavorable. Social interactions in turn influence the way the consumer buys. A person tends to copy those he or she admires, and purchases reflect this fact.

Of course, the management of businesses is one group of outsiders who view consumers. One of the problems with business understanding consumers is the failure of the firm to place itself in the consumer's position. The salesclerk, the market researcher, etc. assume that the consumer is what that individual appears to be. Thus a browser is not approached, because it is assumed that he or she isn't going to purchase anyway. A poorly dressed person is assumed to be poor and a well-groomed person is assumed to have money. Business needs to delve deeper into the nature of consumers. The apparent self is the easiest for the business representative to obtain, but it is often misleading.

The reference-group image. The reference-group image is how the consumers think others with whom they associate or identify see them. It is not the image others necessarily have, but the reference-group image is an important motivator, for we tend to behave as we think others want us to. Thus, the way we think others see us is important to our consumption.[16] Consumer purchases related to group identification, group acceptance, pride, and power are associated with the reference-group image. Note that the reference-group image and the image that others have relate the individual directly to his environment. Notice also that all these images are emotional cognitions except for the real self. That is, they are based on emotional-mental responses to facts that cannot be fully understood. Most concepts of self-image develop out of a social situation. Even our aspirations take on meaning in relation to other people.

Obviously, the reference-group self is important to business. However, it is a very complex image. Next to the real-self image, it is perhaps the most difficult for business to pin down. Most of the time the consumer is not completely aware of the reference-group self. Some indications can be obtained by complex psychoanalysis and depth interviewing, but it is a difficult task. Most businesses cannot afford to obtain such information. Yet it is an important motivator, and business needs more knowledge about the reference-group self.

The total person

It would be a mistake to assume that the image types previously discussed constitute the entire person. Actually, none of these concepts is complete. The real self is what the physical and emotional characteristics of a person are, and the other self-concepts are filtered interpretations toward or about that individual.[17] The real self is less than the total person, because the real self is objective. The real self does not account for the mental filtration of its existence through some cognitive process. Thus the total person is the real self plus all the different biased perspectives that exist along with the real self. The total self is the sum of all the images shown on the illustration, and the fact that none of the images match perfectly demonstrates that one's total existence cannot be fully understood. An individual, as we have shown before, is more than either a physical or emotional being; and one is not complete until related to the people around oneself. We are continually learning more about ourselves—our reactions, emotions, attitudes, feelings, capabilities, and so on, and this learning continues throughout life. Only at death does a person experience the final reaction.

Preservation of the self-image

Much of consumer behavior is a result of the individual's attempt to preserve or enhance some concept of the self. There are five main patterns of behavior used by consumers to preserve the self-image.

1. Buy products consistent with the self-image.
2. Avoid products inconsistent with the self-image.
3. Trade up to products that relate to an improved self-image.
4. Purchase products that relate favorably to group norms of behavior.
5. Avoid products that show a radical departure from accepted group norms.

The consumer must act to preserve self-image, real self, and apparent self.[18] The product image which is attractive to the consumer is that which expresses what one thinks he or she is or wants to be. These different images sometimes come into conflict, making it difficult for the consumer to decide. For example, a man may be conservative and introverted by nature, but his wife has him in a group of extroverted people who wear the latest fashions. The man wants to be accepted, but detests the clothing worn by his friends. It is difficult to say what the man's behavior will be. He may compromise by purchasing the more conservative of the latest fashions. The fact is that all the concepts of self can upon occasion come into conflict, causing the consumer some discomfort. Take a woman who has a high opinion of the way she dresses and of how she thinks others view her clothes. Now let a respected friend tell her that her friends like her in spite of her clothes, and the woman has a real conflict. She may solve it by changing her friends or changing her way of dressing.

Consumers also purchase consistent with their ideal-self. One study discovered a positive relationship between a person's self-image and the ideal-self.[19] In spite of this fact, some product intentions correlated better with the self-image and some with the ideal-self. These data support the fact that all the consumer's images play a part in how he or she purchases.

GENERALIZATIONS ABOUT THE SELF

Empirical evidence has led to the development of a number of important generalizations about the self-concept that relate to consumer behavior.[20] First, individuals are more free in disclosing some facts about themselves than other facts. It is for this reason that salespersons and advertisers have difficulty in establishing sales motives and meeting consumer objections to buying. The consumer often cannot or will not disclose certain of his or her reasons.

Second, consumers whose self-concepts agree largely with how others assess them are better adjusted. The purchase behavior of these individuals tends to reflect this stability. It is not that their buying is completely consistent but that their buying behavior is more consistent.

Third, a person's self-concept tends to parallel the attitudes one believes that parents hold toward that person. Thus, a considerable part of consumer behavior is conditioned by the parents. This fact also, in part, provides some continuity to consumer behavior. When the parent-child relationship is healthy and stable, purchase patterns are handed down from parent to child.

Fourth, while in childhood the parents play a dominant role in the child's self-image, later some glamorous figure becomes more important, and finally a composite image begins to develop around some successful adult. The changing nature of a person's self-image accounts, in part, for the changes in a consumer's purchase behavior.

Fifth, individuals with positive self-concepts tend to have more influence on strangers. Thus, salespersons who think of themselves in a positive manner are perhaps more successful. Family and friends with positive self-concepts probably have more influence on the individual's purchase patterns.

Sixth, self-acceptance and the acceptance of others are positively related. Self-acceptance leads to security, and security, in turn, plays an important part in all consumer behavior.[21] A secure person is more willing to change, to adopt new products, to listen to salespeople, and to think positively in a purchase situation. Certainly there can be no question but that the self-attitude one holds is an important factor in consumer purchase behavior.

THE SELF-CONCEPT CAUSES CONSUMERS TO CHANGE

What a consumer thinks he or she is has as much effect on behavior as the factors of behavior that others can observe. The self-concept is particularly important where personal change is concerned. Some personal change is unconscious and takes place over a long period of time, but much of personal behavior change is conscious. A consumer's self-concept is formed out of (1) heredity and environment, (2) reference group associations, (3) membership in social groups, (4) individual roles, and (5) things that just happen.[22] The conscious mind has some degree of control over these factors of change. Of course, the control is absent or limited with heredity and environment, some social group memberships, and chance happenings. The point that is important is that one of the greatest single forces affecting change in the individual is the individual. If a person does not like his or her present image, one can do something about it up to a point.

Personal change and consumer behavior

A person may wish to change the self if: (1) one does not like his or her self-image, (2) one wants to more nearly become the ideal self, (3) one thinks others have a poor or bad image of him or her, or (4) one wants to become associated with some specific reference group. In other words, change comes from within the individual because of one or more of the person's self-concepts. It must be apparent to the reader from our earlier discussions of self-image that no person is ever completely satisfied. It follows, therefore, that personal change is inevitable. The human personality is dynamic in a dynamic environmental setting. Much of consumer behavior is directly related to personal change.

A great deal of personal change is accomplished by the purchase of products. The entire diet industry, manifested in diet foods, diet soft drinks, diet preparations, diet milk, and diet pills, is directly related to individuals' attempts to change. A part of the change desired is phycial, but the motivation may have come from any of the factors we have been discussing.

The desire of a person to change a current image in order to gain entrance into a specific reference group may result in a whole new pattern of purchases. Different furniture, car, clothing, and recreational patterns may be a result of the attempt to impress a group. A desire on the part of individuals to change may lead them to try new products; it may cause changes in the generic type of product bought or the brand purchased; and it may cause persons to purchase more or less than was purchased previously. Marketers, of course, must be constantly aware of these forces at work on the individual. Appeals based on the consumer's desire to be modern, to conform to a particular group's standards, to be popular, to have fun, or to improve health and attractiveness can often exert a strong influence on persons interested in changing their self-concept.

The time element in self

The concept of change within the consumer leads to the conclusion that at any given instant there are time elements that can be applied to the self. There is the present self, the past self, and the future self.

The past self. The past self is the individual consumer as he or she previously existed. The past self exists in the memory. The past concerns a person's characteristics, beliefs, concepts, needs, motives, perceptions, and so on, as they were. Some of these attributes of the self carry over because of the memory and because the individual wants them to last. We remember the enjoyment we received from a particularly exciting football game, or how we stood out because of a flattering dress or a particularly good restaurant. The consumer's past self, because of the memory, contains one's habits and established ways of behaving. The consumer remembers the stores and the products that have given satisfaction in the past. The consumer may frequent these stores and purchase these products, when encountering similar circumstances to those that have previously occurred. Some part of the past always exists in a person. It is this fact that gives behavior continuity.

The present self. The present self develops out of change. It is the consumer's image now. It contains a part of past behavior, but through communication and learning, the present self has become modified and/or expanded. The fact that a consumer forgets partly accounts for the present self. Old habits of consumption are sometimes forgotten. New products, ideas, and associations have taken their places. The consumer has forgotten unpleasant personal and shopping experiences, and the concept of self has moved on to more pleasant associations. Forgetting is one of the better attributes of human nature. People cannot stand up under a lifetime of sadness and disappointment. However, because the consumer forgets, a marketer can never afford to take customers for granted. Customers must be continually resold. The bankruptcy courts are full of cases where this simple fact was ignored.

The future self. The future self is what the consumer can become. Even as the present self exists, it is searching for change—that something new or different that can give life a little more meaning. Thus, the future self is involved with a person's expectations. The future self develops out of the present self and the past self, but it is more than either of these. It is because of the concept one has of a future self that the consumer is not satisfied with today's electric razor, frozen foods, feminine douche, and hair oil. One feels that something different and better will be needed to satisfy the future self, for any or all of the motives we have already discussed. The point is that the present self is never satisfied. Because this is true, marketers can never be satisfied either. They also must change to meet the changing needs of the market.

The business manager can obtain clues to the future from past actions by consumers if he or she is smart enough to pick them up.[23] Observe the recent 1930s trend in women's fashion, the tendency of men to dress in the elaborate, frilly style of the 1600s. However, business executives are most interested in the present and the future self where consumers are concerned. The present self is where sales are today. It is today's fashion, whether in dress, hair, transportation, furniture, or homes. Nearly all business evaluations of sales, profit, inventory, shipments, etc. are based on the immediate past or what passes for the present. Business is concerned with the future self, because it wants to know where opportunities are going to be tomorrow. All business forecasting such as merchandise planning, sales and advertising planning, expense planning, etc. is directed at the future. The predicting of fashion of all types is also business activity directly concerned with the future self. Product innovation is an attempt to determine future needs of consumers before consumers themselves understand their own desires. We label as growth industries those that are better able to predict aspects of the consumer's future self.

SELF-IMAGE AND MODE OF LIVING

No better example of self-image can be found than that depicted in the modes of living in our society. Westfall, using the Thurstone Temperament Schedule, found that differences in personality existed between owners of convertibles and other automobiles. Consumers low in the characteristics "active," "vigorous," "impulsive," and "sociable" were found to be less likely to buy convertibles than the average person. This fact is especially true among persons in the "now generation." Fashions in music, hair styles, dancing, entertainment, and dress are based on this group's self-image. We are all familiar with the images of the "in crowd," the "mods" and the "jet set." Adults also conform to a particular image of their group. In every major city there is a "social elite" and the "middle class." The social elite are always on the lookout for some new fad. These people associate themselves with international groups as much as with local groups. Certainly, self-image is a factor that helps to guide the lives of all consumers.

NOTES

1. David Krech, Richard S. Crutchfield, and Egerton L. Ballachy, *Individual in Society* (New York: McGraw-Hill Book Co., 1962), p. 495.
2. Ira J. Dolich, "Congruence Relationships between Self Images and Product Brands," *Journal of Marketing Research*, vol. 6 (February 1969); Edward L. Grubb and Harrison L. Grathwohl, "Consumer Self-Concept, Symbolism and Market Behavior: A Theoretical Approach," *Journal of Marketing*, vol. 31 (October 1967), pp. 22–27; J. Barry Mason and Morris L. Mayer, "The Problem of the Self-Concept in Store Image Studies," *Journal of Marketing*, vol. 34 (April 1970), pp. 67–69.
3. George A. Field, John Douglas, and Lawrence X. Tarpey, *Marketing Management: A Behavioral Systems Approach* (Columbus, Ohio: Charles E. Merrill Books, Inc., 1966), p. 106; A. Evans Birdwell, "Influence of Image Congruence on Consumer Choice," *Reflection on Progress in Marketing*, ed. L. George Smith (Chicago: American Marketing Assn., 1964), pp. 290–303.
4. Edward L. Grubb, "Consumer Perception of 'Self Concept' and Its Relation to Brand Choice of Selected Product Types," *Marketing and Economic Development*, ed. Peter O. Bennett (Chicago: American Marketing Assn., 1965), pp. 419–22.
5. Thomas R. Wotruba and Joseph S. Breeden, "The Ideal Company Image and Self-Image Congruence," *Journal of Business Research*, vol. 1 (Fall 1973), pp. 166–71.
6. Jack A. Adams, *Learning and Memory: An Introduction* (Homewood, Ill.: The Dorsey Press, 1976), pp. 185–89.
7. Joseph W. Newman, *Motivation Research and Marketing Management* (Boston: Division of Research, Graduate School of Business Administration, Harvard University, 1957), p. 57.
8. Kenneth Boulding, *The Image* (Ann Arbor: University of Michigan Press, 1956), pp. 3–18.
9. Ibid.
10. A different perception of the self-concept is found in John Douglas, George A. Field, and Lawrence X. Tarpey, *Human Behavior in Marketing* (Columbus, Ohio: Charles E. Merrill Books, Inc., 1967), pp. 64–67.
11. Kent B. Monroe, "Buyers' Subjective Perceptions of Price," *Journal of Marketing Research*, vol. 10 (February 1973), pp. 70–80.
12. Ruth Ziff, "Closing the Consumer-Advertising Gap through Psychographics," *Marketing Education and the Real World and Dynamic Mar-*

keting in a Changing World, ed. Boris W. Becker and Helmut Becker (Chicago: American Marketing Assn., 1973), pp. 457–61.

13. Robert M. Liebert and Michael D. Spiegler, *Personality* rev. ed. (Homewood, Ill.: The Dorsey Press, 1974), p. 240.
14. Edward L. Grubb and Bruce L. Stern, "Self-Concept and Significant Others," *Journal of Marketing Research,* vol. 8 (August 1971), pp. 382–85.
15. Mason and Mayer, "The Problem of the Self-Concept."
16. Grubb and Stern, "Self-Concept and Significant Others."
17. E. Laird Landon, Jr., "Self Concept, Ideal Self Concept, and Consumer Purchase Intentions," *Journal of Consumer Research,* vol. 1 (September 1974), pp. 44–51.
18. Christopher Orpen and Adrian Low, "The Influence of Image Congruence on Brand Preference: An Empirical Study," *Psychology,* vol. 10 (1973), pp. 4–6.
19. Landon, Jr., "Self Concept, Ideal Self Concept, and Consumer Purchase Intentions."
20. The discussion of these generalizations is based on E. Earl Baughman and George Schlager, *Personality: A Behavioral Science* (Englewood Cliffs, N.J.: Prentice-Hall, Inc., 1962), pp. 340–41, 375–76.
21. Lyman E. Ostlund, "The Interaction of Self Confidence Variables in the Context of Innovative Behavior," *Relevance in Marketing: Problems, Research, Action,* ed. Fred C. Allvine (Chicago: American Marketing Assn., 1971), pp. 351–57.
22. Paul R. Lawrence and John A. Seiler, "Personality Formulation—The Determinants," *Organizational Behavior and Administration,* rev. ed. (Homewood, Ill.: Richard D. Irwin, Inc., 1965), pp. 273–83.
23. Wayne Delozier and Rollie Tillman, "Self Image Concepts—Can They Be Used To Design Marketing Programs?" *The Southern Journal of Business,* vol. 7 (November 1972), pp. 9–15.

QUESTIONS

1. What is the self-concept? How is it important to consumers? How does the self-concept relate to the basic determinants of consumer behavior?
2. Define image. Discuss the five dimensions of consumer image.
3. What are the types of consumer images? Contrast the real self and the self-image.
4. Discuss how each of the concepts of self is useful to marketers. Which are more important?
5. How does the total person differ from the different concepts of self? Is the concept of a total person useful to marketers? How?
6. Explain how a knowledge of the individual's attempts to preserve the self can be useful to marketers.

7. What factors may cause a consumer to wish to change? Can you demonstrate how these factors have affected your own consumer behavior?
8. What is meant by the time element of self? Explain and contrast the past, present, and future self.
9. Demonstrate the usefulness of the time concept of self to business. Give specific examples.
10. Discuss how self-image affects a person's mode of living.

10

Consumer behavior founded on needs

The previous chapter introduced the idea of the self, because all the basic determinants of consumer behavior reside in the self. Thus the concept of the self underlies this entire section of the book. In this chapter, we are concerned with consumer needs. It is not by accident that the first basic determinant considered is needs. Indeed, needs were chosen deliberately because of their importance to the individual decision process. No basic determinant of consumer behavior, or for that matter no other variable, is more important to our discussion than needs. Without some need to be fulfilled, there is no reason for the individual to become concerned, and therefore no reason to enter the market. In this sense, the entire marketing process begins with a need. We want to discover what needs are, how they relate to motives, and what effect they have on consumer behavior and on business.

NEED DEFINED

Any attempt by business to satisfy a market without some appreciation of personal benefits sought would be chancy at best. Consumers purchase goods and services which they perceive will satisfy needs. For our purpose, a *need* is defined as:

> *any human requirement or ability upon which human performance and efficiency depends.*[1]

Three important points about needs are worth clearing up at this time.

First, needs underlie all human action. As the lowest common denominator of behavior, needs are the building blocks upon which all other factors of consumer behavior rest. Thus it is not possible to explain consumer activity without coming to grips with needs. Needs cause us to replace cells of the body, to blink our eyes, to purchase products, to consume, to seek companionship, work etc. Until there is a need, nothing happens in the mind or body that is related to marketing.

Second, a need is not a deficiency, although the existence of a deficiency can cause one to become aware of a need. A deficiency implies the lack or absence of something, but the body has many of the same needs whether they are currently being satisfied or not. For example, the body needs nourishment, air, water, and comfort, and the fact that the body has a sufficiency of each does not change the fact that they are requirements. The requirement for air is just as real for the body when it is ample as when it is deficient. It is true that a satisfied person may not be aware of the need. We all take satisfied needs for granted, and it is the existence of some deficiency that makes us aware that a need is going unfulfilled.

Third, a need can be physical or psychological. The only consideration is that it be necessary for the body to function. Psychological needs for comfort, safety, affection are as important to most persons as the physical needs.

Fourth, individuals have varying degrees of awareness of needs. It is this awareness that may be associated with a real or perceived deficiency. Need awareness may vary all the way from unaware to an all-consuming attention. The degree of awareness depends directly on the perceived importance of the requirement to the consumer. A consumer may be only vaguely aware of the need for nourishment because it is generally satisfied, but the consumer may be acutely aware of a need for cooling when the air conditioner malfunctions. A young lady may not be deficient in dresses, but she may perceive the need for a new dress based on such psychological considerations as making a good impression at a party or showing others that she can afford a new dress.

A CLARIFICATION IN RELATIONSHIPS

Marketers are guilty of considerable laxity in their handling of the terms need, motive, want, and desire. The result is a considerable amount of ambiguity in meaning. Although we have provided a clear definition of needs, it is necessary to acquaint the reader with the ways these terms are used together.

Need compared to motive

There is a definite tendency in the literature to treat needs and motives as if they were the same thing.[2] Howard and Sheth, two prominent marketing scholars, make the following statement:

> *Motive, goal, need, drive, and want will be used interchangeably here—even though these terms tend to be used in slightly different ways in the psychological literature—because treating them as synonyms facilitates discussion and does not result in serious ambiguity.*[3]

The fact is that there is a distinction between a need and a motive, and that distinction is important both to conceptual accuracy and to practical business activity. A need is a requirement while a motive is a reason to act. It is some deficiency in a need that determines the consumer's unrest, but it is the motive that specifies exactly what the consumer plans to do about the situation. Obviously, marketers are as interested in consumer motives as in consumer needs.

Needs, wants and desires compared

Even in those cases where needs and motives are separated, there is a tendency for marketers to equate needs, wants and desires. Admittedly, there is more justification in this case since each term has to do with a specific type of consumer requirement. Thus a distinction can be made among the terms based on whether the requirement is: (1) necessary or unnecessary or (2) conscious or unconscious. Each is discussed below. The author tends to equate needs, wants, and desires when referring to all types of requirements, but to make a distinction when a specific type is involved.

Necessary and unnecessary requirements. A *need* can be described as a basic (absolutely necessary) body requirement without which life cannot be sustained. Basic needs consist of minimal food, clothing, housing, and medical expenses. A need, used in this sense, cannot be put off long when the body becomes deficient. There may still be further disagreement as to what is basic. Rather than limit needs to physical requirements, as the above definition specifies, the author suggests the term refer to the smallest proportion of any type of requirement necessary to have the individual function efficiently. Thus need would mean basic food, shelter, affection, striving, esteem, etc.

A *want,* on the other hand, refers to any unnecessary requirement—that is it is a requirement only because of anticipated pleasure and not because it is necessary.[4] Thus, a consumer *needs* food but *wants* a candy bar. The consumer *needs* affection but *wants* a steady diet of sex. The consumer *needs* warmth but *wants* a mink coat. A want can frequently be put off because of its nonessential nature. However, notice that wants can be viewed as encompassing needs.

A desire pertains to the consumer's market aspirations. That is to say, a want is a current requirement, whether presently being satisfied or not, while a desire is a forecasted requirement. It is by nature not presently being satisfied. Desires are related to a consumer's dreams and long-range goals. For example, a consumer has a comfortable house, and is presently satisfied with it. However, this consumer realizes someday the house will become old while family income will probably increase. Thus the consumer desires to replace the present home with a bigger and better one when that time arrives.

Unconscious needs—Conscious wants. There is another method of distinguishing needs and wants based on whether the mind is aware of the requirement or not. Under this distinction, a *need* is any unconscious requirement whether necessary to sustain life or not. Thus both red beans and rice that relate to body nourishment and candy that relates primarily to taste can be needs if they are unconscious. The need becomes a *want* when the person senses the existence of a deficiency in the mind.[5] By definition, a need becomes a want automatically after its existence is perceived, and the only distinction between a need and a want is one of awareness. Desires are treated the same way. An unconscious desire is a need and a conscious desire is a want.

It is argued that one of the major functions of marketing is to transform needs into wants by creating awareness on the part of consumers. Needs are said to be insatiable in that they are without limit, and as the consumer acts to satisfy one conscious want, other unconscious needs are brought to mind. Actually, the justification for personal selling and advertising is seen as changing needs into wants rather than creating needs where they did not exist.

Necessities versus luxuries

Needs are often related to products and explained as a simple dichotomy consisting of necessities and luxuries. *Necessities* are defined as products that are necessary to maintain a subsistence level of living. *Luxuries* consist of the purchase of any products above the subsistence level of expenditures. For example, subsistence food is a necessity, but steak is a luxury; basic clothing is a necessity, but a mink coat is a luxury; housing is a necessity, but a summer cottage is a luxury, etc.

The problem with this simple product dichotomy for explaining needs is that what is one person's necessity is another person's luxury. Each person views their present standard of living as necessary to well-being. Most persons do not generally recognize that they own luxuries. Most Americans could not get along without a refrigerator, automobile, vacuum sweeper, freezer, etc. American courts have upheld the view that a necessity is what the person views as necessary. The fact that these items would be gross luxuries to a less fortunate person does not change the dependency. Furthermore, there are differences among nations as to what constitutes a basic standard of living. Our definition identifies a need as a requirement—any requirement.

Positive and negative needs

The polarity of needs has to do with whether they are positive or negative. By our definition, a need can be either positive or negative. A *negative need* is a human requirement based on discomfort, pain, or adverse tension. Such negative needs include a lack of nutrition, physical pain, body odor, or too little life insurance. A *positive need* is one that revolves around satisfaction or feeling good, such as the need for pleasant-tasting food, social interaction, accomplishment, or peace of mind. Many needs can be expressed either positively or negatively. For example, sex can be negatively expressed as the need to avoid mental or physical discomfort, or it can be positively expressed as seeking satisfaction.

THE PURPOSE OF NEEDS IN CONSUMERS

The presence of needs in consumers serves two simple, but vital, purposes. First, the degree to which needs or wants are satisfied is a measure of the consumer's well-being. Consumer need satisfaction can range all the way from low, where few needs are satisfied, to high, where many needs are satisfied. There can even be variation within the range. For example, one consumer may have most basic needs satisfied but few luxuries. Another consumer may have partly satisfied both basic needs and luxuries. Still another consumer may have some needs and luxuries fully satisfied and some partially satisfied or not satisfied at all.

Just because a consumer has satisfied many needs does not necessarily mean that consumer is an unimportant buyer. No one ever satisfies all their needs, so there is always reason to enter the market. Even small purchases can be serious and time consuming to the individual. One also has to be careful in evaluating the effect of money on need satisfaction. Money alone cannot satisfy all needs. Some wealthy persons find certain needs unsatisfied because money cannot purchase the type of human relations that they desire. Wealthy individuals can also be relatively poor consumers because so much of their income goes toward savings or investments. On the other hand, some low-income individuals may have a high degree of need satisfaction because of former accumulation of assets or because their aspirations are more nearly in line with their income. Some low-income consumers don't have much, but they don't expect to have much. Furthermore, low-income consumers can be important buyers for certain types of products. They spend all their disposable personal income, and most of it goes for the basic necessities.

Second, a need deficiency puts into motion cognitive processes that lead to consumer behavior in the form of actions undertaken to correct the tension states. Need deficiencies may be due to many things, such as changed economic status, aspirations, employment, family size, geographic location, age, marriage, etc. A person who has few needs satisfied, may or may not be an important consumer. If the individual has the funds, he or she may enter the market to satisfy some of the existing deficiencies. If the individual does not have the funds with which to act, he or she may have to accept a continued low status of need satisfaction. In this case, the individual may not be an important consumer for some goods. Thus, while slum dwellers may have low satisfaction of their needs, they may not be important consumers of the very products for which satisfaction is low. Not only are the slum dweller's funds insufficient, but there is evidence that the purchase of basic requirements costs more, a fact which further limits buying.[6] One thing is certain, the satisfaction of needs is essential to the physical and mental health of consumers. Any nation that cannot take care of the majority of these needs for its citizens is in for trouble.

STRUCTURE OF CONSUMER NEEDS

It is, of course, understood that every consumer is in some ways different from every other consumer. This statement is certainly true when it comes to their needs. Nevertheless, there are structural patterns to consumer needs when considered in a general context. Now that we have some understanding of what constitutes needs, it is time to delve into need structure. We want to discuss types of needs and their hierarchy.

Classification of needs

There have been many attempts to devise a single, uniform classification of consumer needs.[7] These attempts have met with little success. The problems are twofold. First, there are too many different needs that individuals attempt to satisfy. Second, one classification serves one purpose, and a different classification serves another purpose. The truth is that each of the major ways of classifying needs serves a purpose in that it adds a dimension to our understanding of consumer behavior. A rule of thumb in need classification is that any list should be inclusive enough to illustrate the nature and complexity of consumer requirements, but not so long as to be unnecessarily confusing.

Although there are many variations in the specific lists, nearly everyone agrees that there are two broad types of consumer needs: physiological needs and emotional or psychological needs.[8] *Physiological needs* are those associated with the consumer's basic body functions (hunger, thirst, sex, sleep, warmth, body elimination, replenishment, and activity). These needs are both strong and pervasive. Most physiological needs cannot be put off too long or the individual begins to suffer. *Psychological, or emotional, needs* cover a broad category of requirements associated with positive or negative tensions that result from the consumer's cognitive associations. *Emotion* is a term used here synonymously with *affect* or *feeling*. Characteristics of emotion include (1) outer expression of inner feeling, (2) experience of something felt, and (3) a psychological state.

Maslow's need classification. Maslow was one of the earlier scholars to work with the identification of specific human needs.[9] The original list provided by Maslow has been changed and modified over the years, but it still stands as the classic illustration of need classification. Maslow's original list is presented below.

1. *Physiological needs*—those essential to the biological functions of the body.
2. *Safety needs*—psychological freedom from fear, pain, and discomfort.
3. *Belonging and love needs*—the desire for acceptance, affection, and sexual satisfaction.
4. *Esteem needs*—those associated with prestige, fame, and recognition.
5. *Self-actualization needs*—those related to self expression, energy to act, and personal fulfillment.

Two major modifications to Maslow's list have become generally recognized. They are shown below.

6. *Need to know*—those having to do with curiosity, desire to achieve, and personal fulfillment.
7. *Esthetic needs*—the appreciation of beauty, symmetry, and order.[10]

Note that Maslow's first need is physiological and the remainder are psychological. Thus the list conforms to the basic classification mentioned above.

Other need classification methods. Nearly everyone agrees that humans have physiological needs, but there has been disagreement on the classification of psychological needs. Two lists of psychological needs that differ somewhat from that of Maslow are presented here. One author groups psychological needs into social needs, ego needs, and self-fulfillment needs.[11] *Social needs* are defined by McGregor as those concerning an individual's relationships with others. Social needs include the requirement to be a part of the group, to associate with others, and to be accepted and well thought of by our fellows. Through the products we purchase, we often find it possible to satisfy these needs partially. Examples of products that satisfy social needs include playing cards, fashion clothing, and chip dip which are normally used in association with other persons. Movie patronage is a good example of consumer behavior that satisfies more than one social need. A recent study determined that young and single persons (72 percent are under 30 years) are the typical moviegoers.[12] The research demonstrated that moviegoers attend as couples, and the primary reasons given for patronage were (1) to be with someone and (2) to lose oneself in the picture. *Ego needs* are of two kinds. First, there are those needs that are associated with our self-esteem such as the needs for independence, achievement, knowledge, and self-confidence. Second, there are those needs relating to our reputation such as recognition, appreciation, and respect. All types of products may be bought to meet these needs. Any new item such as the car, the house, furniture may be purchased partly for achievement, independence, recognition, etc. *Self-fulfillment needs* are those related to our desire to actualize our potentials for development. Products associated with our status in life, with providing for our family, or displaying our wealth fit into this category.

Another representative classification of psychological needs that is simple and reasonably comprehensive is that of Bayton. He includes three major types of psychological needs as follow:

1. *Affectional needs*—the needs to form and maintain warm, harmonious, and emotionally satisfying relations with others.
2. *Ego-bolstering needs*—the needs to enhance or promote the personality; to achieve; to gain prestige and recognition; to satisfy the ego through domination of others.
3. *Ego-defensive needs*—the needs to protect the personality; to avoid physical and psychological harm; to avoid ridicule and "loss of face"; to prevent loss of prestige; to seek relief from anxiety.[13]

A careful look at these methods of classification shows that a common thread runs through all of them. The basic differences are in the manner of grouping the needs. Thus, while the combinations differ considerably, there is more compatibility on emotional needs than meets the eye.

Human needs innate

All human needs are innate in the sense that individuals are born fully equipped. Man does not have to learn how to need, and this statement is as true for psychological needs as it is for physiological needs.[14] A child is born with the physical need for body movement, body elimination, food, water, sex, etc. That same child has the innate psychological need for affection, acceptance, satisfaction of the self, etc. Anyone who has ever watched a baby attempt to talk, walk, or to seek comfort in a parent's arms, cannot doubt the soundness of the statement. Thus, while the individual may learn particular motivation or behavior, needs are unlearned. For example, a child's need for food is unlearned, but a child learns to prefer candy or to hate spinach. Furthermore, the child learns specific behavior in the form of crying, playing up to mother, threats, etc., in order to obtain the type of food preferred. If one type of behavior is unsuccessful, the child will attempt another until the correct formula is found. It is the same with adults. One person learned from two bad experiences that a particular tire dealer refused to meet his warranty obligations. A professor also gave up wearing white socks because of criticism of his associates. In this case, the need for acceptance was greater than the need for individualism, and it affected both motivation and purchase behavior.

Hierarchy of needs

Since needs are innate, the question naturally arises as to why consumers attempt to satisfy some needs and not others. The answer, of course, lies in the fact that consumers perceive a definite hierarchy to their needs. The *hierarchy of needs* is defined to mean the consumer's preferences for the order in which needs are satisfied.[15] Most scholars agree that there is a hierarchy of consumer needs, and attempts have been made for years to determine what it is. However, even today, there is no complete agreement on the exact number of needs or the order of human preference.

Figure 10–1 depicts the need hierarchy for Maslow's original list.

Figure 10–1
Maslow's hierarchy of needs

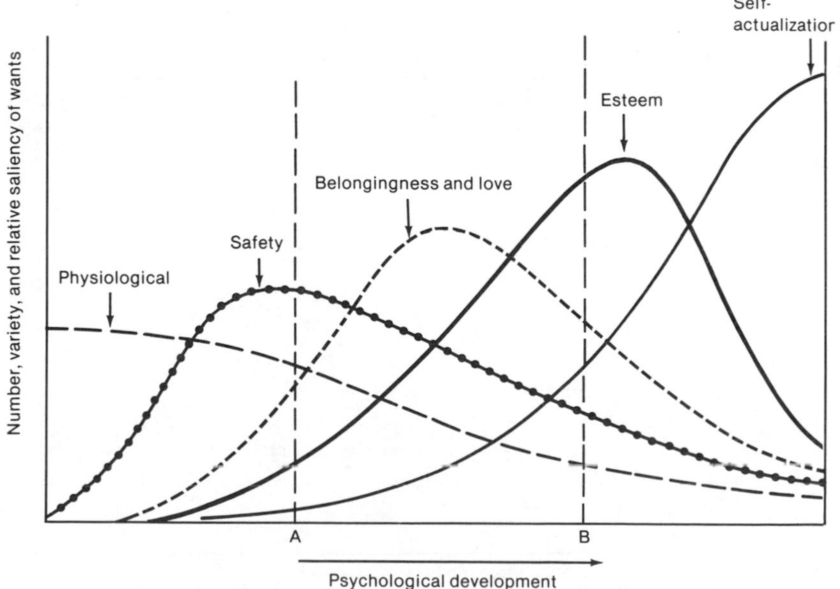

Source David Kreck, Richard S. Crutchfield, and Egerton L. Ballachey, *Individual in Society* (New York: McGraw-Hill Book Company, 1962), p. 77.

Note that the physiological needs are the first to be satisfied, followed by safety, belonging, esteem, and self-actualization. A higher order need must have peaked in satisfaction before the next lower order need can become dominant. The illustration shows that an individual is actually in the process of satisfying most of his or her needs at any given point in time. It is the level of satisfaction that determines the hierarchy.[16]

The sixteen pillars of happiness

Maslow's hierarchy of needs has always been recognized as an ideal. Table 10–1 below adds a realistic dimension to the earlier presentation since it is based on a sample of men and women. Respondents ranked their needs from 1–16 with 1 constituting the highest rank. No individual's hierarchy of needs is necessarily like anyone else's, but the table does indicate averages. Furthermore, a consumer's preferences may change over time and with circumstances. They do not necessarily conform to Maslow's ideal at any given point in time.

Several points can be made concerning the need hierarchy of single men and women compared to married men and women. First, there is more compatibility between singles and between marrieds than among the two groups. Second, single men and women consider the need to belong more important than married persons. Third, married men ranked personal growth needs higher than married women. The

Table 10–1
The 16 pillars of happiness

	Single men	*Single women*	*Married men*	*Married women*
1. Friends and social life	1	1	8	7.5
2. Job or primary activity	2	3	4	7.5
3. Being in love	3	2	2	1
4. Recognition, success	4	4	7	5.5
5. Sex life	5	6	6	4
6. Personal growth	6	5	1	5.5
7. Financial situation	7	9	10	13
8. House or apartment	8	10.5	11	14
9. Body and attractiveness	9.5	8	16	16
10. Health and physical condition	9.5	7	13	9
11. City you live in	11	13	14	11
12. Religion	12	10.5	12	12
13. Exercise, recreation	13	12	15	15
14. Being a parent	—	—	9	10
15. Marriage	—	—	3	2
16. Partner's happiness	—	—	5	3

Source: Phillip Shaver and Johnathan Freedman, "Your Pursuit of Happiness," *Psychology Today* (August 1976), pp. 26–75. Reprinted by permission of *Psychology Today* Magazine. Copyright © 1976 Ziff-Davis Publishing Company.

women ranked being in love higher. Fourth, religion ranked rather low with both groups. Fifth, both marrieds and singles rated the physical needs low. This point is certainly in contrast to Maslow's hierarchy. The finding probably reflects America's higher standard of living where many persons have satisfied their basic physical needs.

Reasons for the need hierarchy

There are two fundamental reasons for the hierarchy of consumer needs. First, some needs are simply more basic than others. The physical need for nourishment or drink take precedence over the need for safety, love, or esteem.[17] There is a feeling that in a modern society, such as the United States, the physiological needs have been sufficiently satisfied for the majority of people, and the psychological needs are becoming correspondingly more important. There is no general agreement as to the specific order of importance of the psychological needs. One should not conclude that a physical need must be completely fulfilled before another need begins to predominate. The law of diminishing returns applies to need as well as other things. As one obtains increased fulfillment of one need, another need lower on the hierarchy begins to become important. It is possible the hierarchy of needs varies among individuals.

Second, there is the consciousness of the need on the part of the individual. To be conscious is to be mentally aware of any life experience. Many needs are hidden in the unconscious mind.[18] These unconscious needs tend to be brought to the consciousness as higher-order needs are fulfilled or as marketing effort makes the consumer aware of the need. Thus a need may have a low, or no, priority for the consumer until he or she is made aware of its existence. Once awareness is achieved, the consumer may place a high priority on its satisfaction. Some aspects of brand switching can be accounted for because of the awareness of a need not previously recognized.

RELATIONSHIP OF NEEDS TO BUSINESS ACTIVITY

The business leader has a vital interest in consumer needs, but it is often less direct than the reader may suspect. In a general sense, the business executive is interested in needs because all motives for buying are founded on needs. There can be no purchase until the consumer has a need. However, the fact is that business does not care particularly what the consumer's needs are. The business leader is more interested in the consumer's reasons, or motives, for purchasing.[19] As we have demonstrated, the consumer has a need for physical activity, but he or she may be motivated to purchase a badminton set, join a health club, purchase golf clubs, or take up bicycle riding. It is the way in which the consumer satisfies the needs that is important to business. Sellers want to understand why certain consumers prefer cycling to golf, and how business can appeal successfully to them. Of course, we must understand needs in order to understand motivation.

There are a couple of ways in which needs directly affect business. First, the hierarchy of motives is directly related to the hierarchy of needs. Business leaders need to develop an understanding of these hierarchies, because appeals to consumers, consumer objections and how to meet them, and basic satisfaction go back to the needs. If a consumer makes a purchase and is dissatisfied afterwards, it may be because his motivation did not get at the solution to his or her need. Second, marketers often segment their markets according to needs. For example, grocery stores, drugstores, dress shops, and shoe stores, are designed around specific needs. Segmentation by benefit is fundamentally a need concept (for example, dividing the market according to economy buyers, status buyers, buyers interested in dependability, low service calls, quality, etc.). Third, most forecasting involves needs. Marketers must produce and sell in anticipation of demand. This statement means that any innovation must be founded on satisfying some consumer need. The basic need must exist before marketers can begin to differentiate by motive. Marketers must forecast need, produce, and distribute products in the correct quantity designed to meet these needs. There can be no escaping this fact.

CONSUMER NEEDS IN CONFLICT

It would be a much simpler world if consumers could deal with their needs one at a time, but this seldom happens in real life. The more usual circumstance is that the consumer must make choices among needs, many of which are in conflict.[20]

How need conflict arises

Conflict among needs arises out of two possible conditions within the person. First, there may be a conflict in the *priority of needs.* In making a purchase, a consumer may be attempting to satisfy, say, three different needs. If the consumer cannot satisfy each of these needs equally, a conflict develops over which one gets priority. The consumer can choose to satisfy one need fully at the expense of the other two, or may find a partial solution to all three. The decision to purchase a new car may result from a person's equal needs for beauty, utility, and economy. The person will be happiest with a car that balances all these needs best. It is not often, however, that the consumer's needs are fully satisfied.

Psychological needs have become increasingly important in advanced Western countries such as the United States. The reason appears clear: the level of living in these nations has been rising. As a result, more and more people have satisfied their basic physical needs within their need hierarchy. Relatively fewer worry about hunger, thirst, or warmth.[21] In accordance with the hierarchy of needs, as these physiological needs are satisfied, the psychological needs take on increased importance. Consumers begin to be more concerned with the type of car or home, and it is no longer sufficient just to be clothed; now the consumer finds a need for better clothes.

Second, conflict can arise because the *needs themselves are opposed.* Lewin points out three types of conflict where needs are in opposition.[22] The first is conflict that occurs between two positive forces (see Figure 10–2). This fact is represented by having to choose

Figure 10–2

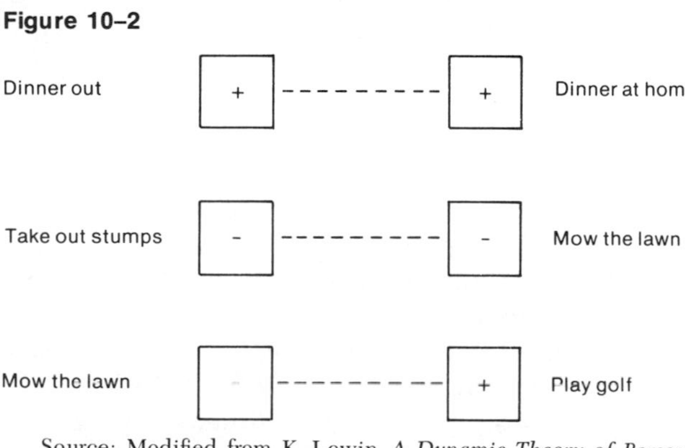

Source: Modified from K. Lewin, *A Dynamic Theory of Personality* (New York: McGraw-Hill Book Co., 1935).

between two desirable alternatives. The decision is relatively painless, and the more positive alternative is decided upon. The second is conflict which occurs between two negative forces. The consumer tries to choose the less objectionable alternative. The third is conflict between one positive and one negative force. The consumer wants to buy a new car, but it means committing more dollars from present savings or future earnings than he or she wants to commit. A decision must be made.

We may find that consumer needs are operating at different levels and strengths at the same time. While some of these needs may be complementary, others may be in conflict. Need conflict occurs when more than one need is operating, and the satisfaction of one need causes another to remain unsatisfied. The opposing tendencies brought about between convenience and cost, dependability and price, prestige and efficiency, and time and money are but a few examples of needs in conflict. Because of the multiplicity of needs, it is essential that the marketing efforts of the firm be directed to appeal to a wide variety of needs. For example, a rather frequent appeal used in advertising perfumes is directed toward the need for affiliation—exhibited with situations showing affection, tenderness, or love—but other appeals may be present in the same advertisement.

Factors affecting the conflict of needs

Factors that have important effects on the conflict of consumer needs are attitudes toward work and leisure, discretionary purchasing power, and balance of leisure and money.

Attitudes toward work and leisure. The amount of leisure available, for most Americans, is on the increase. At the same time, Americans have feelings of uneasiness with respect to leisure. Although individuals have a need for both work and leisure, conflicts develop because of our psychological attitudes toward each. Because we have been reared in a culture which frowns upon idleness, our leisure tends to be of the active variety.[23] We participate in golf, boating, camping, and gardening. As American income increases, this creates pressure for more time in which to spend the additional money. There is always the difficulty of balancing the time to do with the money to do it. Higher productivity leads to more money, and more money creates a need for more leisure. More leisure puts the pressure back on a need for money to utilize the time better.

Discretionary buying power. Discretionary buying power affects the conflict of needs within consumers. *Discretionary buying power* is defined as that part of one's personal income left after paying taxes and providing for basic necessities. Expenditures for taxes and necessities are largely predetermined. One must pay the rent, purchase necessary food, and meet clothing needs, but any income left over can be spent at the discretion of the consumer.[24] Thus the name discretionary buying power. The consumer's purchase of a vacation, or higher-priced food, or a fancy automobile depends on income left after basic needs are provided for. Thus, a natural conflict arises between expenditures for necessities and discretionary expenditures. A consumer who can skimp on food, for example, may be able to afford theatre tickets. It is also true that discretionary purchases come into conflict. The consumer may have to decide between a Caribbean cruise and a better automobile.

Balance of leisure and money. American business executives have considerable amounts of discretionary money but much less discretionary time than other groups. The balance is the opposite for many elderly citizens with more time than money. Some products require a balance of time and money, for example, travel, bowling, spectator sports, camping, and do-it-yourself items. Other products, indirectly affected by this balance, are certain foods, beverages, and home entertainment items. The important point for marketers to consider is the fact that they must literally compete for discretionary time as well as discretionary money.[25] The pressure for more leisure time has made some consumers less patient with shopping around; the trend is toward quick, convenient shopping, which gives the merchant fewer chances at a given consumer.

HOW CONSUMERS RESOLVE CONFLICT BETWEEN NEEDS

We pointed out that consumers are seldom able to satisfy one isolated need at a time. When conflicting needs are present, the individual can act in one of several ways: (1) one can assign a priority to personal needs and attempt to satisfy the most dominant; (2) one can attempt to find one solution for several needs; (3) one can partially satisfy several needs; (4) one can take the all-or-nothing solution; (5) one can take no action; or (6) one can defer the need.

Assign priority to needs

One method for handling conflicting needs is to assign priorities to them. This method is often used by consumers, even though the person may not be aware of it. Because of barriers, such as income limitations, lower-priority needs may have to go unsatisfied at the expense of satisfying needs of a higher priority. A consumer purchasing his or her first new home might prefer a certain neighborhood and style of home that represent spaciousness and refined and dignified surroundings. However, because the dollars to finance the purchase of such a house cannot be obtained, the consumer may compromise and buy a smaller and more functional house in a less desirable neighborhood. In this case, the consumer's purchasing behavior is an attempt to satisfy the high-priority need for shelter at the expense of the low-priority needs for more space and a higher-status neighborhood. One can think of numerous situations where the conflict present between needs is resolved in this manner. Furniture, automobiles, and appliances are but a few of the products where the make and model purchased is determined by the priority given to various needs.

One solution for several needs

Often it is possible for a single product to satisfy more than one consumer need. Finding one solution for several needs is associated with efficiency, because the consumer has made one product do the work of several. This solution may result in some compromise of goals, but often this is not the case. For example, the purchase of items of apparel serves as a means of satisfying more than the basic need for warmth. Clothes can relate to affection by appealing to a mate; to prestige by appearing well groomed at a party; to the ego by providing a good feeling due to confidence. In this case, there is no necessary compromise of goals. On the other hand, if the consumer plans a vacation and knows the money spent on the dress will cut short planned recreation along the way, there is a compromise. Whereas two suits may satisfy a college student's social need, he may still need clothing for the classroom. He might be better served to purchase a sport coat and several pairs of pants so that both needs can be satisfied without great sacrifice of either. It is probably safe to say that most products purchased by consumers serve more than one need. This is normal because the needs themselves are not always mutually exclusive.

Partial satisfaction of needs

In the example above of satisfying several needs, it was assumed that there was no overall reduction in the consumer's satisfaction. In fact, this may not be the case. The consumer may deliberately settle for partial satisfaction of one or more needs. When the consumer has several needs which are in conflict, he or she may attempt to satisfy each partially. This action may be preferred to satisfying one or two completely and having others go unsatisfied. The two-door hardtop automobile of the 1950s, for example, appealed to those who wanted the youthful, sport-car image of the convertible while still needing the practicality of the sedan. The two-door hardtop partially satisfied both needs.[26] A man and woman may purchase less home in order to put more into a car or home furnishings.

The all-or-nothing solution

There are rare cases when a consumer may, in effect, "place all his eggs in one basket" by satisfying one need and letting others go. Of course, every consumer must allow for the basic necessities of life. Thus this solution applies more to things wanted than needed. A man in the military service who has all his basic requirements taken care of may spend almost his entire paycheck on his car and its operation. This person may literally have little money left over to enjoy the use of the automobile. Most of his pleasure comes from riding around in the car. If he dates, it must be car oriented, or the girl must pay her own way.

No action on the need

One choice that business hopes the consumer will not make is to do nothing. A consumer, because of a particular circumstance, may simply allow a need to go unsatisfied. Sometimes a lack of income may cause the consumer to exercise this choice. Sometimes consumers take no action on the need because it has not reached their consciousness that the need exists. This situation is the marketer's fault. Sometimes the consumer just does not consider the need important and does nothing about it. We have all known people who did not care how they look or dress. The author knows more than one couple who have no furniture in one or more rooms of their homes. These individuals just do not consider the furniture necessary, or they have better uses for their money. The reader should not be led incorrectly to believe that just because a consumer has a need, it must be satisfied. We have pointed out that needs are insatiable. At any given time, every consumer has some needs that cannot be satisfied. The consumer simply operates at reduced efficiency.

Defer the need

Many times consumers defer the solution to their needs. That is to say, the consumer does not give up on ever satisfying the need, nor does one, as in the case of the room of furniture cited above, simply have no time limit on meeting the need. In some cases, the consumer, deliberately assigns priorities over time in much the same manner that we have discussed his assigning priorities among needs.[27] The consumer decides a timetable for the handling of specific requirements. The dining room furniture is to be purchased next year, the car is to be replaced the year after, and the carport is to be added the third year. The consumer may consciously plan to stick to these priorities of time. Of course, we must recognize that other things may intervene, and the postponement of a given product may become permanent. It is also possible that the order of purchase, over time, may be changed. As a result, a product thought to be bought in the near future may be put off and another product substituted in its place. In any case, deferment is a conscious choice that the consumer has in handling need conflicts.

Need satisfaction: A compromise

The satisfaction of consumer needs is nearly always a compromise between what the individual would like to have and what the individual can have. A consumer may wish to purchase a new refrigerator to take the place of a troublesome and inefficient one. Although a beautiful coppertone, double-door model is desired, a plain white, less expensive, but more functional model may be purchased. This model may represent the minimum acceptable level of satisfaction for our consumer's need. The consumer is satisfying a higher-order survival need rather than the lower-priority need for beauty. A need of a higher priority may require more complete satisfaction. Of extreme importance are such basic physical needs as food or water. Many persons elect to dine on red beans and rice because this inexpensive food meets a higher-order need for survival. Since we only achieve satisfaction of relatively few of our needs, we must decide which ones we can compromise on and which ones we cannot compromise on.

One difficulty encountered with needs is that people are different. Some people purchase goods to satisfy what to others would appear to be low-priority needs when other items which most would give high priority are not purchased. An individual with a very limited income who purchases an expensive foreign sports car while cutting down on essential food purchases illustrates this point. Because of the high monthly payments, this individual may have an inadequate diet, but she is satisfying certain social or prestige needs. Although such cases appear to be exceptions, they do exist.

CONSUMER ADAPTATION TO UNSATISFIED NEEDS

Even though consumers attempt to gratify needs by goal-directed behavior, often the external barriers, personal defects, or conflicting needs are such that the need remains unsatisfied. When the need that is present is not satisfied, frustration results. Frustration may cause the consumer to try even harder to find a way to satisfy the need. On the other hand, one way out of frustration is to adjust to it. Adaptive processes by which the individual may reduce the intensity of unsatisfied needs are repression, fantasy, and rationalization. Because purchasing decisions are directly influenced by certain of these adjustments, it is necessary that marketers have some understanding of them.

Repression of need by consumer

There are three types of thought repression.[28] The first is *primal repression,* the denial of entry into the conscious mind of any thoughts related to the need or desire. Primal repression occurs when a consumer does not admit that the need exists. The young girl without money for a party dress may just put the prom completely out of her mind.

Second, there is *forgetting*. We have a case of forgetting when thoughts are pushed back into the unconscious recesses of the mind that were once a part of the conscious mind. A boy's need to excel in athletics may be forgotten as he discovers he has no aptitude for sports.

Third, repression of needs occurs in the form of *inhibition*. Inhibition develops as a result of association. Let's say some event occurs simultaneously with feelings of shame or guilt, and the two become connected in the mind of the consumer. Since most people are conditioned to avoid shame or pain, the individual may also avoid the events associated with such feelings. Inhibition is accomplished by inhibiting recall; consciously avoiding stimuli associated with the shame, pain, or guilt feelings; and making substitute responses.

The goal of every sort of repression is entirely to eliminate any necessity for effective action relative to the need. One problem is that learned behavior can be more easily repressed than instinct. The elimination of an instinctive need, such as sex, is seldom attained. The interest in sex still influences consumer purchases, but at a different and less apparent level.

Several conditions are usually present that lead to a repression of needs. Among the needs most likely to be repressed by consumers are (1) needs based on ideas damaging to one's ego, (2) needs that are in disagreement with the individual's moral, cultural, and social code, and (3) needs based on ideas associated with conflicts or guilt feelings. Neither men nor women found midi-length dresses attractive, so this style failed, but both sexes have accepted blow dryers for the hair. In one case, the product did not enhance the ego and in the other case it did. Therein lies the reason for acceptance or rejection of the product.

Motivational research suggests that advertising, to be effective, must appeal to people in such a manner as to give moral permission for them to have fun without guilt. Particular examples of guilt feelings which arise from the purchase and use of certain products are evident. Cigarettes, liquor, and candy are purchased by a major part of the American public, yet people consistently worry and feel self-indulgent and guilty when they use these products.

Consumer needs resolved through fantasy

Most everyone has engaged at one time or another in daydreaming. The flight into fantasy allows a consumer to resolve needs temporarily by imagining something other than actuality. Each of us at times has a "secret life." We may image that we are a millionaire, a great athlete, or an outstanding scholar. Certain products, such as the movies, television, and stage shows, provide the consumer with ready-made fantasy. They allow the purchaser to escape temporarily and to capture a vicarious experience. Advertising for diamonds and perfume often appeals to fantasy in both the layout and the copy. A woman's dreams of male adoration are used to sell certain cosmetics, jewelry, perfumes, furs and automobiles. Men respond to similar appeals from advertisers who show the fellow with the proper cologne or hair cream surrounded by attractive women.

Consumer rationalization of needs

Closely akin to repression is the concept of rationalization. Consumers sometimes find themselves attempting to justify purchasing decisions by searching for reasons for them after the decisions have been made. This is rationalization. Homeowners may purchase expensive furniture for reasons of status, but do not readily confess this. Instead, they prefer to justify the purchase on the basis of the more acceptable reasons that the present furniture is wearing out and that the new furniture has been chosen for its durability.

NOTES

1. James H. Donnelly, Jr., James L. Gibson, and John M. Ivancevich, *Fundamentals of Management*, rev. ed. (Dallas, Texas: Business Publications, Inc., 1975), p. 141.
2. Rom J. Markin, Jr., *Consumer Behavior: A Cognitive Orientation* (New York: Macmillan Publishing Co., Inc., 1974), p. 168.
3. John A. Howard and Jagdish N. Sheth, *The Theory of Buyer Behavior* (New York: John Wiley & Sons, Inc., 1969), p. 99.
4. Keith Davis, *Human Behavior at Work* 4th ed. (New York: McGraw-Hill Book Co., 1972), pp. 52–53.
5. Wroe Alderson, "Needs, Wants, and Creative Marketing," *Cost and Profit Outlook*, vol. 8 (September 1955), pp. 1–3.
6. Walter F. Mondale, "The Challenge of the Ghetto to Marketing," *A New Measure of Responsibility for Marketing*, ed. Keith Cox and Ben M. Enis (Chicago: American Marketing Assn., 1968), pp. 14–17.
7. James L. Gibson, John M. Ivancevich, and James H. Donnelly, Jr., *Organizations* (Dallas, Texas: Business Publications, Inc., 1973), pp. 218–31.
8. Bernard Berelson and Gary A. Steiner, *Human Behavior: An Inventory of Scientific Findings* (New York: Harcourt, Brace & World, Inc., 1964), pp. 240–44; Harold H. Kassarjian and Thomas S. Robertson, *Perspectives in Consumer Behavior*, rev. ed. (Glenview, Ill.: Scott, Foresman and Company, 1973), pp. 113–16.
9. A. H. Maslow, "A Theory of Human Motivation," *Psychological Review*, vol. 50 (1943), pp. 370–96.

10. A. H. Maslow, *Motivation and Personality* (New York: Harper & Bros., 1954), pp. 80–98.

11. Douglas M. McGregor, *The Human Side of Enterprise* (New York: McGraw-Hill Book Co., 1960), pp. 36–39.

12. Lee C. Garrison, "The Needs of Motion Picture Audiences," *California Management Review*, vol. 15 (Winter 1972), pp. 144–52.

13. James A. Bayton, "Motivation, Cognition, Learning—Basic Factors in Consumer Behavior," *Journal of Marketing*, vol. 22 (January 1958), pp. 282–89.

14. James U. McNeal, *An Introduction to Consumer Behavior* (New York: John Wiley & Sons, Inc., 1973), pp. 17–18.

15. Maslow, "A Theory of Human Motivation,"; G. David Hughes, *Attitude Measurement for Marketing Strategies* (Glenview, Ill.: Scott, Foresman & Co., 1971), p. 38.

16. Peter D. Bennett and Harold H. Kassarjian, *Consumer Behavior* (Englewood Cliffs, N.J.: Prentice-Hall, Inc., 1972), pp. 62–65.

17. Freud and some others see sex as the all-encompassing need. See John R. Stuteville, "Sexually Polarized Products and Advertising Strategy," *Journal of Retailing*, vol. 47 (Summer 1971), pp. 3–13.

18. Note our earlier references to Freud, Lewin, and Allport in Chapter 3 for different concepts of the conscious and unconscious mind.

19. Edward H. Asam and Louis P. Bucklin, "Nutrition Labeling for Canned Goods: A Study of Consumer Response," *Journal of Marketing*, vol. 37 (April 1973), pp. 32–37.

20. Joe Kent Kerby, *Consumer Behavior: Conceptual Foundations* (New York: Dun-Donnelley Publishing Corp., 1975), pp. 56–60.

21. As pointed out earlier, the absolute numbers of destitute people are higher than many imagine.

22. K. Lewin, *A Dynamic Theory of Personality* (New York: McGraw-Hill Book Co., 1935).

23. Perry Bliss, *Marketing Management and The Behavioral Environment* (Englewood Cliffs, N.J.: Prentice-Hall, Inc., 1970), pp. 28–29.

24. Lewis Mandell, "The Changing Role of the American Consumer," *Michigan Business Review*, vol. 14 (January 1972), pp. 22–26.

25. Lawrence A. Mayer, "The Diverse $10,000-and-Over Masses," Reported in *Managerial Marketing Policies and Decisions*, eds. Taylor Meloan, Samuel Smith, and John Wheatley (Boston: Houghton-Mifflin Co., 1970), pp. 67–69.

26. William R. Reynolds, "The Wide C-Post and the Fashion Process," *Journal of Marketing*, vol. 29 (January 1965), pp. 49–54.

27. Philip B. Schary, "Consumption and the Problem of Time," *Journal of Marketing*, vol. 35 (April 1971), pp. 50–55.

28. See: Louis Kaplan, *Foundations of Human Behavior* (New York: Harper & Row, Publishers, 1965), pp. 224–45.

QUESTIONS

1. Define need. Is a need and a deficiency the same? Are consumers always aware of their needs?
2. Distinguish between need, want, and desire. What are conscious and unconscious needs? Explain.
3. What purpose do needs serve in consumers? How is the existence of needs related to business activity?
4. Define psychological and physiological needs. Can you give examples of these needs in your own life? Demonstrate how these two type needs affect your buying.
5. What is a hierarchy of needs? Why do these hierarchies develop? What effect do they have on consumer behavior?
6. Discuss the manner in which need conflict develops.
7. Pick any three reasons for need conflict. Demonstrate, using specific examples, how each has affected some purchase. Which factor do you consider most important? Why?
8. Discuss the manner in which consumers resolve need conflict. Rank these different ways of resolving conflict.
9. Explain and illustrate need satisfaction as a compromise.
10. Contrast repression and fantasy as alternative means for adapting to unsatisfied needs.

11

Motives stimulate consumer action

In the previous chapter, we discussed consumer needs. We pointed out that all consumer behavior is founded on needs. However, it is not enough to have a need; the consumer must also want to do something about the need. When a person wants to satisfy a need, we call it motivation. Clearly, there is a very close relationship between needs and motives, although sometimes the difference becomes so small as to be practically nonexistent. This chapter is about consumer motives and motivation.

MOTIVE AND MOTIVATION

The word *motive* derives its meaning from *move,* and a motive is that something within a person that causes him or her to act, move, or behave in a goal-directed manner.[1] A motive is a reason for action. The attempt of consumers to gratify wants through market activities is motivated behavior. Motives act as governors for our system of responses to environmental change. Thus, by definition, consumer behavior based on motives is purposeful; it is directed at achieving goals by engaging in market activities. Motivation is the condition of being motivated. *Motivation* is defined as an active, strong driving force or a "necessity" to reduce an existing state of internal human tension.[2] For a consumer to be motivated, three conditions must exist.[3]

First, there must be need recognition. Motivation indicates to the consumer that some action may be desirable in response to a body requirement. *Need recognition* is an internal mental state associated with motivation. The stimulus for motivation may come from within the individual, as when caused by hunger, or it may be a response to external tension, such as jealousy over a sister's new dress. Second, there must be some *energy mobilization* that causes the consumer to want to do something about his tension. This energy mobilization is strictly internal and comes from the self. Third, there must be some *perceived goal* that the consumer's energies are directed toward. The goal, or at least the means to the goal, usually is in the form of products offered by business establishments. As we shall see, no one or two of these conditions is sufficient for motivation to occur; all three must be present. A consumer may have a need because his only suit is worn out, but it may take a friend's remark about the shabby condition of the suit to mobilize energy toward positive action. Even when a requirement is present and energy is mobilized, the consumer cannot take action until the goal is clear. The consumer must consider all the market related decisions of brand, store, and method of purchase necessary to buy a specific suit. Thus, motivation is a state of mind that directs the consumer's energy mobilization toward a specific market goal.

NEEDS, MOTIVES, AND BEHAVIOR

Consumer needs, motives, and behavior have a definite and definable relationship as illustrated in Figure 11–1 below. Three general principles are demonstrated by the illustration. They are:

1. All human behavior is motivated.
2. All motivated states do not lead to behavior.
3. Motivated behavior is either learned or unlearned.

Figure 11–1
Relationship between needs, motives, and behavior

1. Nonbehavior

Need → Motive → No action

2. Unlearned behavior

Need → Motive → Automatic action

3. Learned behavior

Need → Motive → Thought-out action

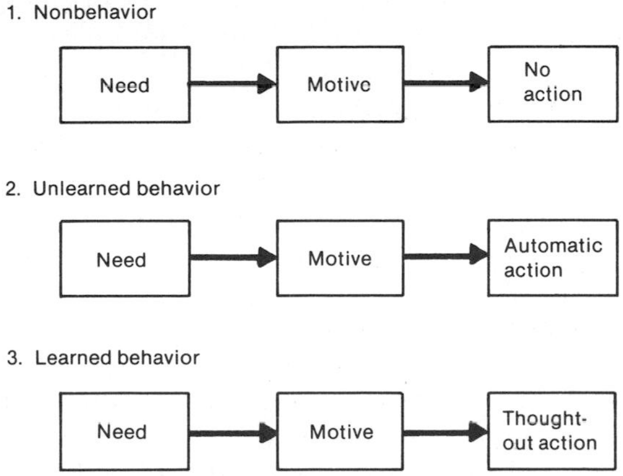

First, whenever any person engages in activity it is motivated. Motives lead to behavior designed to satisfy the need. For example, the body needs nourishment, but it is hunger, that gnawing sensation, that causes one to seek food. Without hunger, there is no reason to believe the person would be aware that body cells were deficient. Thus motives are the link between needs and behavior.

Second, the existence of motivation can lead to *nonbehavior* where no action is taken.[4] The consumer will take no action when there is no opportunity or when the motive can be quieted without taking action. A consumer may be motivated to own a Rolls-Royce or a mink coat but never expect to have the money to act on the wish. A motive long denied can cease to function. It is said that people have been known to starve to death in relative comfort, because, after a period of intense pain, the hunger motive ceases to remind the person that they are starving to death.

Third, motivated behavior is either learned or unlearned. Any inborn action not requiring thought or previous experience is considered *unlearned behavior*. Two types of unlearned behavior have been identified as reflex action and instinct. *Reflex action* is any involuntary, or automatic, response that results from a stimulus. Examples of reflex action include blinking of eyes, heartbeat, sneezing, coughing, and knee jerk. *Instinct* is any inborn tendency to behave in a characteristic manner.[5] At one time Man was thought to have many instincts, but most have been proven false. It may be that such behavior as sucking, activity, crying, and avoidance of pain are instinctive in Man. Breathing is a reflex, but to adapt breathing to an Aqua-Lung is learned. It may be instinctive for a baby to cry, but the use of crying to get a new toy is learned.

Problem solving and experience lead to *learned behavior*.[6] Learned behavior is the most common and the most complex type of human behavior. Because it is so complex it is the least predictable of all types. We have already pointed out the need for nourishment, but a consumer learns to prefer steak over spinach. One may need liquid, but he or she learns to travel to the crossroads for a beer. If the behavior is successful, there is a reduction in tension. If the behavior is unsuccessful, the person remains in a motivated state, and goal directed behavior continues.

A special case of learned behavior is *symptomatic action;* a motive is satisfied rather than the need. Motives are symptoms, but they often receive the attention because they give the trouble. For example, candy, saccharine, or similar substances, which satisfy the hunger motive, can fool the body into thinking it is receiving nourishment. Consumers have to learn to make the proper connection between needs and actions that are in their own best interests, and some learn better than others.

CLASSIFICATION OF MOTIVES

Motives can be classified in various ways, among the more important methods are: (1) generic, (2) physiological or psychological, (3) urgency, (4) primary and secondary, and (5) conscious and unconscious.

Generic motives are distinguished merely according to a simple description of what each is. Typical generic motives are those based on hunger, thirst, sex, striving, pride, sociability, curiosity, fear, and self-preservation.

Any method of grouping motives usually provides more information than a simple generic list, as, for example, does grouping motives by physiological and psychological motives.[7] *Physiological motives* concern basic physical body functions, such as hunger, thirst, sex, elimination, relaxation, exercise, and bodily comfort. *Psychological motives* are those existing in the mind, such as security, love, fulfillment, self-identification, pride, prestige, status seeking, belonging, happiness, sadness, and power. Of course, there is no such thing as a purely physical or purely psychological motive. Love, hunger, striving, and so forth, all have simultaneous physical and psychic sides. Nevertheless, separating the two sides gives us some insight into the nature of consumer motives.

Motives can be classified according to those that must be acted on immediately and those that can be postponed. It is difficult to list these motives because they vary with consumers and over time. Hunger may be more important than pride at one time but not at another. One consumer may find aesthetic reasons more urgent and another may place greater weight on economy.

Motives are often classified as to whether they are primary or secondary.[8] This classification is based on relative importance. *Primary motives* are founded on basic needs necessary to sustain life. *Secondary motives* arise out of social and psychological needs. Secondary motives typically become important only after motives related to primary needs have been satisfied. Secondary motives are derived from the primary motives. It is argued that the basic physical requirements of hunger, thirst, and sex give rise to primary motives. Secondary motives concern how one goes about satisfying hunger, thirst, or need for sex. It is also argued that physical motives are primary, and the psychological motives, such as pride, striving, and so on, are secondary. The American public is pictured as more concerned about secondary motives because our advanced economy has provided for physical needs. There is at present no clear understanding of primary and secondary motives, and any listing would be presumptuous.

Motives can be conscious or unconscious. Few people are ever fully aware of their purchase motives—a fact that makes motivation research difficult. Typically, a given need is associated with several motives, and the consumer may be aware of only one or two of these motives at any one time. Individuals may also not be aware of their true motives. We all rationalize our behavior to conform to what we want to be true. Take a woman considering a new suit for herself. She may be aware that the material is good, the price is right, and the suit will look good on her. She may not recognize her equally real feelings that her husband may not like the suit or that she wants to show up a neighbor.

HOW MOTIVES ARISE

One important consideration relative to motives is to discover how they arise. Up to now, we have just assumed that motives exist. The reader should remember that this question did not arise relative to needs presented in the previous chapter because needs are innate, and, therefore, unlearned. Two concepts new to us at this point are necessary for the discussion of how motives arise. These concepts are *homeostasis* and *dissonance*. Motivation is inevitably tied to these two concepts.

The concepts of homeostasis and dissonance

Scientists use the term *homeostasis* to refer to the tendency in man and the higher animals toward maintaining a relatively stable internal environment within their bodies. The term was originally applied to automatic physical processes such as the maintenance of metabolism, blood sugar content, temperature, and heart beat. Homeostasis was later broadened to include both mental and physical stability. Thus today, homeostasis refers to:

> *any attempt by the body to maintain, or return, to a state of equilibrium where physical or mental body processes are concerned.*[9]

The terms "consonance" and "dissonance" are closely associated with homeostasis. Leon Festinger popularized these terms to explain the relationship between pairs of elements.[10] Two elements are *consonant* with each other when they are in agreement, and two elements are *dissonant* with each other when they are in disagreement, or opposed. Dissonance was originally associated with mental disequilibrium. Over the years, just as homeostasis has come to refer to all attempts by the body to maintain equilibrium, so dissonance has come to mean any nonfitting physical or mental relationship within the individual.[11]

How homeostasis creates motives

Homeostasis in certain aspects of body processes is necessary for human survival. Dissonance occurs anytime an imbalance is present in the body's systems. Since the individual resists change in either its physical or psychological systems, the condition of disequilibrium leads to tension states. This *tension*, in the form of dissatisfaction, discomfort, or anticipated satisfaction, has the power to create motives because the person must act, automatically or through reason, to reduce the dissonance.[12] If tension reduction occurs automatically then there is no motivation, and this situation was explained earlier. The motive is the result of the mental attempts to find a way out of the discomfort or anticipated satisfaction. Thus tension and motivation are closely related, but they are not the same. Tension is a state of being while a motive is a mental process that assumes or prescribes a solution to the tension created.

Homeostasis is not as simple as the previous discussion may lead the reader to believe. First, note that the tension state is not caused just by discomfort but by pleasure as well. One can be motivated to seek a positive, say the pleasure of a family picnic, as much as to avoid a negative, say the "heartbreak of psoriasis." Second, homeostasis is a broader concept than motivation, since it applies to both learned and unlearned behavior. Third, homeostasis can be applied to groups in the sense of society's attempts to maintain relatively stable conditions among masses of people.

Homeostasis of physical body systems

In the definition of homeostasis it was pointed out that the concept applies to physical and psychological stability. Let us consider physical homeostasis which is set into motion by some dissonant factor. *Physical dissonance* refers to any imbalance in a person's physical system. Conditions of disequilibrium that lead to motivated physical actions include the need for food, water, warmth, and sleep. In each of these cases, the body sets into motion a specific motive in response to the physical dissonance. Cells deprived of moisture cause the body to say, in effect: "I'm thirsty, so come on and do something about it." How the body is motivated may vary from individual to individual, but the drive is there. Hunger, a motive designed to aid regeneration of body tissue, can be satisfied by eating at home the food previously purchased or by entering the market for a new food purchase. The consumer may even decide to eat out. In any case, the result should be a reduction in physical tension, and equilibrium of the digestive system.

Homeostasis of mental attitudes

Psychological homeostasis concerns one's attitudes, and it is cognitive dissonance that causes the imbalance. Festinger says, "By the term *cognition* . . . is meant any knowledge, opinion or belief about the environment, about oneself or about one's behavior."[13] Thus *cognitive dissonance* refers to any inconsistent or nonfitting mental attitude or perception. Just as we found for physical functions, individuals value consistency in their attitudes and mental states. Consumers think and act in a manner based on inner conformity. In equilibrium, there is a consistency between what a person knows or believes and what that person actually perceives or does. Inconsistency occurs any time there is a discrepancy between what the consumer knows or anticipates to be true and what one perceives about oneself or the environment. Inconsistency leads to psychological discomfort and results in a motive just as surely as discomfort in body functions leads to motive. The consumer attempts to reestablish equilibrium by removing the source of dissonance.[14] The basic hypotheses about cognitive dissonance are as follows:

1. The existence of dissonance being psychologically uncomfortable will motivate the person to try to reduce the dissonance and achieve consonance.
2. When dissonance is present, in addition to trying to reduce it, the person will actively avoid situations and information which would likely increase the dissonance.[15]

Dissonance often occurs after a purchase has been made. In the purchase of a new automobile, an individual may check prices on several different manufacturer's makes and models. Each of these has certain advantages and disadvantages—power versus economy, styling versus comfort, and combinations of accessories. Once the individual has chosen from among the various alternatives, dissonance may develop.[16] The person realizes that economy might have been sacrificed for additional power. At this point, dissonance may be present because the individual may desire both economy and power. Seeking to reduce dissonance, the consumer will pay particular attention to those advertisements concerned with the automobile purchased.

The cigarette smoker develops dissonance in much the same manner. The pleasure of smoking is inconsistent with the medical reports linking cigarettes with cancer. To reduce the uncomfortable feeling resulting from this psychological inconsistency, the smoker turns off the TV set when medical reports are presented, avidly reads the defenses made by the tobacco industry, or quickly passes over any new government findings. One study of 234 new car purchasers discovered that not all the respondents were dissonant after the purchase.[17] Furthermore, those who had been persuaded to buy had no greater tendency toward dissonance than those who had not been influenced. The results did demonstrate that highly self-confident persons were less likely to show dissonance after the purchase of a car.

Physical and cognitive dissonance have been treated here as if they were entirely different things. In practice, this is not accurate. Most often physical and psychological disequilibrium occur together, as in the case of a young lady who needs body warmth and also food. The lady may be motivated to accept an invitation to a drive-in hamburger stand where both requirements can be satisfied. Hunger, sex, love, physical comfort, etc. all have their physical and their mental side. In most cases they cannot be separated.

CHARACTERISTICS OF MOTIVES

Motives are of fundamental importance in consumer behavior, because they, along with personal needs, give all consumer behavior direction. Therefore, if we can gain some understanding of the nature of motives, we can come to know a lot more about the sources that give rise to actions and make one consumer different from another.

Motives display certain characteristics in common:

1. Motives are founded in needs.
2. Motives give actions direction.
3. Motives reduce consumer tensions.
4. Motives operate in the environment.

Consumer motives founded on needs

The difference between a need and a motive is easy to distinguish in a definitional sense but is difficult to observe in practice. The fact is that motives are founded on needs.[18] Motives cannot stand alone, and every motive has a corresponding need. A need is a physical or mental condition that exists in a person, and a motive is a drive or state of mind taken toward the condition. Table 11–1 shows the relationship between needs and motives. The author has grouped the motives around the consumer needs mentioned in the previous chapter. The

Table 11–1
Needs and motives contrasted

Type of need	*Type of motive*
I. Physical needs	I. Physical motives
A. Food	A. Hunger
B. Water	B. Thirst
C. Sex	C. Tension release
D. Sleep	D. Relaxation
E. Warmth F. Elimination G. Activity	E. Comfort
II. Psychological needs	II. Psychological motives
A. Social needs	A. Social motives
a. Belong	*a.* Security
b. Associate	*b.* Fulfillment, love
c. Acceptance	*c.* Security
B. Ego needs	B. Ego motives
a. Independence	*a.* Identification
b. Achievement	*b.* Fulfillment, identification
c. Knowledge	*c.* Fulfillment
d. Self-confidence	*d.* Security
e. Recognition	*e.* Identification
f. Appreciation	*f.* Love, fulfillment
g. Respect	*g.* Security

physical motives are self-explanatory. There can be as few or as many psychological needs and motives as one desires. We have divided psychological needs and motives into two groups—social and ego—but only four psychological motives were compared to the psychological needs. These four (security, fulfillment, love, identification) are broad enough to contain all the social and ego needs mentioned.[19]

Motives give actions direction

Not only are motives founded on needs, but they direct the type of action the consumer takes in order to satisfy those needs. That is to say, a consumer is always motivated in some specific direction—toward some specific goal. Although motives are directional, they are not always directed in the same way over time. For example, there are many ways that a person can satisfy a need for warmth. The person can purchase a coat, turn up the thermostat, bundle up to a loved one, or perhaps turn up the thermostat and bundle up to a loved one. On one occasion the individual may turn up the heat, but on another may seek warmth with a loved one. The point is that a motive does not allow a person to be neutral about the manner of satisfying a need. The motive directs the person toward a specific type of action that seems appropriate under the circumstances.

Although motives are directional, they do not necessarily lead to correct behavior. Since all motives are filtered through the mind, they have an emotional base. Thus one can be motivated toward what is desirable and socially acceptable, or toward what is undesirable and not socially acceptable. For example, a consumer may spend money on tropical fish when the family is heavily in debt, and the money might be better employed to pay off the loans.

Motives reduce consumer tensions

The basic purpose of consumer motives is to reduce tension. If all tensions were biological, then consumer motivation would be a much simpler matter. Consumer motives are complex because of the problems created by the emotions. If a person needs liquid, we may suppose that he or she drinks water. Unfortunately, motives do not work this way. If a person needs liquid, he or she may consume various kinds of drinks, and some of the least beneficial physically will have the greatest psychological benefit. Any of these drinks may reduce tension and satisfy the purpose of motivation.[20] The physical need of the body may or may not have been satisfied in the process.

Motives operate in the environment

The consumer's environment has a significant influence on motives. The environment can bring out a motive, suppress a motive, or change the direction which a motive may take. A community dance creates a motive to buy a new dress. A girl may reason that a dress acceptable to one group of friends may be criticized by another group. The desire to belong to a particular group may change a person's entire point of view toward the manner of dress. An individual who had never thought much about clothes may suddenly become clothes conscious. Studies show the effect of the situation on consumer motives. In 1950, Mason Haire conducted a classic study of shopper motives based on attitudes toward the use of instant coffee.[21] Respondents were asked to describe the shoppers who prepared two different lists of products—one with a brand of regular coffee and one with instant coffee. Respondents tended to view the shopper for instant coffee as "lazy"; the nonuser of instant coffee had the more favorable image. More recent replications of the Haire study give a different result. "Today, the instant coffee user may actually be more typical than the housewife preparing drip grind coffee."[22] The studies show that the situation has changed since Haire's study, and today's instant coffee users are more likely viewed as modern and involved in the world.[23]

WHY CONSUMERS ARE MOTIVATED DIFFERENTLY

Certain factors associated with motivation make the subject difficult, yet an understanding of them will make clearer why consumers behave differently. To know more about consumer behavior, we must learn more about these aspects of consumer motivation. These important factors of motivation are discussed in the following paragraphs.

Same motive affects consumers differently

Even the same motive does not have an identical effect on different consumers. A desire for security may cause one consumer to spend more on entertainment in order to be with other people. Another consumer may find security by staying at home and saving money. The desire for affection may have many diverse effects on consumers. A person seeking affection may buy flowers, gifts, entertain, buy more clothes, or buy an engagement ring. There is no way to predict the manner of effect that a given motive may have on a consumer.

Just as one motive can lead to many effects, so one effect can come from several very different motives. It is not possible to determine the consumer's motive to any purchase with certainty by observing the effect. One person goes to the movie because he or she wants to see the show, another enjoys the company of a date, a third person is bored and wants to kill some time, a fourth person seeks relaxation after a difficult examination. Each consumer's behavior is essentially the same, but the motives are vastly different.

Some consumer motives are founded on habit, and habit varies among consumers. A shopper may have purchased from a particular grocery store initially because it was located close by, and continues to go to the same store out of habit even when many aspects of its operations are displeasing. This same shopper may get in the habit of buying certain canned goods each week. Daily meals may vary but not the type of food served over a given period of time. Another consumer may have a different pattern of habitual behavior.

Motives can complement or conflict

We have said that most consumer behavior is the result of several motives. Some of these motives complement each other and some conflict. The nature of this interaction between motives is different in different consumers. When conflict in consumer motives is present, there is less chance of a specified market action taking place. A child may desire to buy a candy bar because he is hungry, but conflict arises because of a desire to please one's parents who forbid eating before lunch. When the consumer's motives are in conflict, the direction, strength, and number of supporting motives on each side determine the action that is taken.

Motives vary in intensity

The power of consumer motives is not uniform among individuals. Motives vary in intensity at different times and under different circumstances. The desire for new clothes may be greater at the beginning of each fashion season for one consumer and at the end of the season for another. More consumers tend to eat out on the weekend, but some prefer weekdays. It is interesting to observe a child around Christmas-time. One day he or she wants a new bicycle, the next day a tent, and the day after something different. The desire of a man to visit the barber shop may be stronger on the day before a business meeting than on any other day. Marketers often lose sales because they fail to take into account this variation in the intensity of consumer motives. An enthusiastic customer today may not be as enthusiastic after thinking over the situation.

Motives can be positive or negative

We tend to discuss consumer motives as if their effects were always positive, that is, as if individuals were always motivated to act because they like something. The fact is, a negative motive (dislike for something) can be an equally strong force causing one to take action.[24] Some consumers are motivated positively by a factor, while others are motivated negatively by the same factor. A movie may be exciting to a husband but a bore to his wife. Some consumers have regular car checkups because they fear an accident, but others take no action. Other consumer actions based on negative motives include dental checkups, purchases of deodorant soap, purchases of mouthwash, and termite inspections.

Reaction to risk varies among consumers

Motives direct consumer behavior, and therefore motives involve risk. There is the normal risk of being wrong that is involved in every act or purchase. No one can escape this kind of risk. There is also "perceived risk."[25] Perceived risk is not limited to dollar outlay but includes all disadvantages present in a purchase situation. Perceived risk may involve the consumer's inconvenience, poor product performance, or a threat to social standing that can result from the purchase. The purchase of cologne does not require a large expenditure, but the risks of facial blemish, offending odor, and loss of status are very real.

Even the slightest expenditure may have risk associated with it, but the amount and type of perceived risk present in purchasing decisions does differ among individuals.[26] For example, the period of deliberation over higher-priced durable goods is more extensive for middle-class customers than for lower-class customers. There are two possible reasons for this difference in behavior. First, it may be that the middle-income customer perceives the risk of purchase to be greater than that perceived by the lower-income customer because of a greater investment in career, social standing, and personal property. The middle-income consumer may believe that he or she has more to lose from a faulty decision. Second, the lower-income consumer has less time for deliberation because he or she may be replacing a durable good that is completely worn out.

A relationship exists between the perceived risk of buying certain products and the frequency with which these products are ordered by telephone for delivery. Items perceived as having a high risk associated with them are so purchased much less frequently than were those perceived as having low risk. Among high-risk items are handbags, appliances, and furniture; examples of low-risk items are bed linens, men's and women's stockings, and underwear.

Several strategies may be relied upon by the consumer in an attempt to reduce uncertainty or risk in the purchase. An objective criterion of value may be established by referring to independent source material; purchasing decisions can be made on this basis with reduced risk. Many consumers feel that placing reliance on *Consumer Reports* or some independent seal of approval, will reduce risks. Support acquired from friends to substantiate a purchasing decision is another means of coping with risk.

ASPIRATIONS MOTIVATE CONSUMERS

Aspirations are those goals which consumers set for themselves and subjectively strive to attain. Included in our level of aspirations may be those of owning a $40,000 home, eating steak twice a week, owning two automobiles, or becoming a local fashion leader. Aspirations have a direct relationship to consumer motivation. Once we have acquired the home, the automobile, have become a fashion leader, and can afford all the steak desired, we should experience a reduction in our need for such things. However, consumers often find this not to be the case. Aspirations may be of short or long duration. The acquisition of some products causes the consumer to want more products, different products, better products, or more prestigious products.

Several generalizations can be formulated with respect to consumer aspirations. Included among these generalizations are the following:

1. Consumer aspirations are not static; they are not established once for all time.
2. Consumer aspirations tend to grow with achievement and decline with failure.
3. Consumer aspirations are influenced by the performance of other members of the group to which the person belongs and by that of reference groups.
4. Consumer aspirations are reality oriented; most commonly they are slightly higher or slightly lower than the level of accomplishment rather than greatly different from it.

Consumer aspirations related to motives

Consumer aspirations are directly related to shifts in consumers' motives. For instance, a newly formed household's purchasing behavior may be dominated by the desire for a home, appliances, and furniture. Once these goals have been reached, or other goals take on added importance—the purchase of a color television set, a vacation in Mexico, or a new lawn mower. In addition, aspirations for better appliances, a larger home, or more expensive furniture may arise as the beginning family improves its economic position. Certain of the goals that we establish for ourselves must be viewed as long in duration because of the substantial expenditure that they require. Because of the nature of such goals, the accumulation of assets may be necessary before these aspirations can be attained.

Consumer expectations affect motives

Consumer expectations may be described as the person's subjective notions about the future. Expectations are our estimates of the chances we have to achieve our market aspirations.[27] The expectations consumers hold are influenced by feelings, attitudes, beliefs, personality, reference groups, as well as by the present sense of satisfaction or dissatisfaction. These expectations influence how different stimuli are perceived as well as how we purchase. Individual's expectations about their personal financial situation and the general economic outlook also influence purchasing behavior, purchase motives, and purchase aspirations.[28]

The purchase of products and services today is partly a function of our expectations for tomorrow. Our optimism or pessimism as to what the future holds may be the most important variable in the purchase decision. Even though most consumers are not sophisticated about the workings of our economy, they do have a feeling for what is going on. A college senior, three months before graduation, may purchase a new two-door hardtop priced at $5,500 with a minimum down payment and no present income. Such a decision is not based upon the present situation; it is based on the senior's expectations. It may be that she has accepted her first job, is to be commissioned in the Armed Forces, or will come into her inheritance upon receipt of the degree. The purchase decision is more influenced by expected income than that presently available. What might appear to the outside observer as "overbuying" in respect to income might not be in consideration of the future situation.

Seldom do individuals methodically observe prepared budgets in their purchase patterns. However, even though a written budget may not exist, consumers do allocate their income among various items. The house holder may not have the budget ordered with computerlike efficiency, but is well aware that $250 must be allocated each month for food, rent, and so on. The spend-save patterns of an individual may depend on how price movements, availability of credit, stock upturns or downturns, taxes, and the general economic conditions are interpreted.

BUSINESS INTEREST IN MOTIVES

In some respects, business leaders are more interested in consumer motives than consumer needs. Needs may be important in new-product development and innovation, but motives control the daily decision of the average consumer. It is the motive, not the need, that causes the consumer to act in a specific manner. Study is needed on how consumer motivation affects such marketing factors as (1) store and brand loyalty, (2) impulse purchases, (3) product and store choice, and (4) appeals to specific motives by means of packaging, branding, advertising, pricing, and counter display.

One study found little correlation between retailer and consumer perceptions of what motivates people toward appliances.[29] This study compared price, style, service and warranty, extras, and ease of use. The study found that retailers' misunderstanding of the importance of brand causes misallocation of promotional effort. Repeated exposure to product, packaging, and advertising copy indicates that effects vary according to geographic area. A study of grocery impulse purchases suggests that impulse purchases are due to (1) unclear customer purchase intentions and (2) in-store stimuli.[30] This study further indicated such factors as grocery bill, number of products purchased, type of shopping trip, product-purchase frequency, shopping list, and number of years married affect the amount of impulse purchases.

Promotional effect on customer's motives also requires analysis by businessmen. One study found that in drug and stationery stores the introduction of new carousel displays did not significantly motivate customers to buy more.[31] On the other hand, housewives perceived bread to be fresher when wrapped in cellophane than when wrapped in wax.[32] Obviously, the two wrappers did not motivate housewives the same. Studies of other promotional efforts show differences in motivation. For example, a study of price indicates that customers of low price stores have more valid price perceptions, and price perceptions are no better for those who stress price and those who do not.[33] Only when the factors of motivation are understood can marketers effect significant increases in sales efficiency based on facts rather than guess.

NOTES

1. Joe Kent Kerby, *Consumer Behavior: Conceptual Foundations* (New York: Dun-Donnelley Corp., 1975), p. 68.

2. Thomas S. Robertson, *Consumer Behavior* (Glenview, Ill.: Scott, Foresman and Co., 1970), p. 32.
3. James A. Bayton, "Motivation, Cognition, Learning—Basic Factors in Consumer Behavior," *Journal of Marketing*, vol. 22 (January 1958), pp. 282–89; Elaine Donelson, *Personality: A Scientific Approach* (Pacific Palisades, Ca.: Goodyear Publishing Co., 1973), pp. 222–23.
4. G. David Hughes, *Attitude Measurement for Marketing Strategies* (Glenview, Ill.: Scott, Foresman & Co., 1971), p. 12.
5. Rom J. Markin, Jr., *Consumer Behavior: A Cognitive Orientation* (New York: Macmillan Publishing Co., Inc., 1974), pp. 171–74.
6. Peter D. Bennett and Harold Kassarjian, *Consumer Behavior* (Englewood Cliffs, N.J.: Prentice-Hall, Inc., 1972), pp. 31–33; Robert M. Liebert and Michael D. Spiegler, *Personality: Strategies for the Study of Man* rev. ed. (Homewood, Ill.: The Dorsey Press, 1974), pp. 308–309.
7. Ibid., pp. 183–87; Bennett and Kassarjian, *Consumer Behavior*, pp. 62–65; A. H. Maslow, "A Theory of Human Motivation," *Psychological Review*, vol. 50 (1943), pp. 370–96.
8. Chester R. Wasson, Frederick D. Sturdivant, and David H. McConoughy, *Competition and Human Behavior* (New York: Appleton-Century-Crofts, 1968), pp. 27–28.
9. See: Donelson, *Personality*, p. 223.
10. Leon Festinger, *A Theory of Cognitive Dissonance* (New York: Harper & Row, Publishers, Inc., 1957).
11. William H. Cummings and M. Venkatesan, "Cognitive Dissonance and Consumer Behavior: A Review of the Evidence," *Journal of Marketing Research*, vol. 13 (August 1976), pp. 303–08; Robert Mittelstaedt, "An Experimental Study of the Effects of Experience on Consumer Decision Making," *Science, Technology and Marketing*, ed. Raymond Haas (Chicago: American Marketing Assn., 1966), pp. 617–25.
12. Sadaomi Oshikawa, "The Measurement of Cognitive Dissonance: Some Experimental Findings," *Journal of Marketing*, vol. 36 (January 1972), pp. 64–67.
13. Festinger, *A Theory of Cognitive Dissonance*, p. 3.
14. Del I. Hawkins, "Reported Cognitive Dissonance and Anxiety: Some Additional Findings," *Journal of Marketing*, vol. 36 (July 1972), pp. 63–66; Shelby D. Hunt, "Oosttransaction Communication and Dissonance Reduction," *Journal of Marketing*, vol. 34 (July 1970), pp. 46–51.
15. Festinger, *A Theory of Cognitive Dissonance*, p. 1.
16. Robert J. Holloway, "An Experiment on Consumer Dissonance," *Journal of Marketing*, vol. 31 (January 1967), pp. 39 43.
17. Gerald D. Bell, "The Automobile Buyer After the Purchase," *Journal of Marketing*, vol. 31 (July 1967), pp. 12–16.
18. Kerby, *Consumer Behavior: Conceptual Foundations*, pp. 68–71.
19. The list is only illustrative—it is not suggested that these are the only motives. Furthermore, needs were matched to motives on the basis of

which motive is more important for a given need. Even so, two motives were used in some cases where a clear determination could not be made. Others may find places where more motives can be related to a given need. It is recognized that, typically, a given need does have several motives associated with it.

20. Peter Nulty, "Changing Habits of American Drinkers," *Fortune* (October 1976), pp. 157–66.
21. Mason Haire, "Projective Techniques in Marketing Research," *Journal of Marketing*, vol. 14 (April 1950), pp. 649–56.
22. Johan Arndt, "Haire's Shopping List Revisited," *Journal of Advertising Research*, vol. 13 (October 1973), pp. 5–61; Frederick E. Webster, Jr. and Frederick von Pechmann, "A Replication of the 'Shopping List' Study," *Journal of Marketing*, vol. 34 (April 1970), pp. 61–77.
23. Arndt, "Haire's Shopping List Revisited."
24. Homer E. Spence and Reza Moinpour, "Fear Appeals in Marketing: A Social Perspective," *Perspectives in Consumer Behavior*, rev. ed. eds. Harold H. Kassarjian and Thomas S. Robertson (Glenview, Ill.: Scott, Foresman and Co., 1973), pp. 122–28; John J. Wheatley, "Marketing and the Use of Fear- or Anxiety- Arousing Appeals," *Journal of Marketing*, vol. 35 (April 1971), pp. 62–64.
25. Charles M. Schaninger, "Perceived Risk and Personality," *Journal of Consumer Research*, vol. 3 (September 1976), pp. 95–100.
26. J. Paul Peter and Michael J. Ryan, "An Investigation of Perceived Risk at the Brand Level," *Journal of Marketing Research*, vol. 13 (May 1976), pp. 184–88.
27. Peter D. Bennett and Gilvert D. Harrell, "The Role of Confidence in Understanding and Predicting Buyers' Attitudes and Purchase Intentions," *Journal of Consumer Research*, vol. 2 (September 1975), pp. 110–17.
28. Eugene J. Kelley and L. Rusty Scheewe, "Buyer Behavior in a Stagflation/Shortages Economy," *Journal of Marketing*, vol. 39 (April 1975), pp. 44–50.
29. Peter J. McClure and John K. Ryans, "Differences Between Retailers' and Consumer Perceptions," *Journal of Marketing Research*, vol. 5 (February 1968), pp. 35–40.
30. David T. Kollat, "A Decision-Process Approach to Impulse Purchasing," *Science, Technology, and Marketing*, ed. Raymond Haas (Chicago: American Marketing Assn., 1966), pp. 626–39.
31. Peter J. McClure and E. James West, "Sales Effect on a New Counter Display," *Journal of Advertising Research*, vol. 9 (March 1969), pp. 29–34.
32. Robert L. Brown, "Wrapper Influence on the Perception of Freshness in Bread," *Journal of Applied Psychology*, vol. 42 (August 1958), pp. 257–60.

33. F. E. Brown, "Price Perception and Store Patronage," *Marketing and the New Science of Planning,* ed. Robert L. King (Chicago: American Marketing Assn., 1968), pp. 371–76.

QUESTIONS

1. What is a motive? What is motivation? How are the two related?
2. Explain the conditions that must exist in order for a consumer to be motivated. Is all consumer behavior motivated? Give examples to support your answer.
3. Distinguish between learned and unlearned behavior. How is it possible that each type can result in tension release?
4. Discuss symptomatic action. What is the relationship of symptomatic action to needs? To motives?
5. Explain three methods for classifying motives. In what way are these classifications important to consumer behavior?
6. Define homeostasis. Dissonance. Explain the relationship between homeostasis and dissonance.
7. How do motives arise? Explain how motives arise in physical systems? In psychological systems?
8. Discuss the four characteristics of motives. Show how each is important to understanding consumer behavior.
9. Why are consumers motivated differently? Select a convenience good and a shopping good and contrast your motivation with that of a known friend. Explain how the same motive can affect consumers differently.
10. Explain the importance of risk to motivation. How are aspirations related to risk? How are aspirations related to motives?

12

Consumers act as they perceive

Definition of perception
Perception and sensation are different
Consumer reactions based on perception
Perception relates to consumer needs and motives
Consumer perceptions change
How perception affects marketing
Characteristics of perception that affect consumers
Consumer perception is subjective
Consumer perception is selective
Consumer perception is temporal
Consumer perception is summative
Consumer perceptual process
The consumer as a perceiver
Thresholds of awareness
Importance of cues
Source of the market stimulus
Factors affecting consumer perception
Technical factors
Mental readiness of consumers to perceive
Past experience of the consumer
Mood
Social and cultural factors of consumer perception

Perception, is one of the three variables under awareness that affects the behavior of consumers. It concerns how the individual views him or her self and their world. It is an integral factor in the other basic variables, since an individual's needs and motives are what he or she perceives them to be. Individuals are different, in part, because they perceive differently.

DEFINITION OF PERCEPTION

In the simplest of terms, *perception* can be described as the process of interpreting directly through any of the senses.[1] It also means interpreting in one's mind—to understand and apprehend. Perception can be said to mean the overall process which includes the activity of the person that accompanies or immediately follows the perception acquired through the senses. It is the entire process by which an individual becomes aware of the environment and interprets it so that it will fit into his or her own frame of reference.[2]

Young illustrates perceiving by the use of the following paradigm.[3]

$$\text{To perceive} = \left\{\begin{array}{l}\text{To see}\\ \text{To hear}\\ \text{To touch}\\ \text{To taste}\\ \text{To smell}\\ \text{To sense internally}\end{array}\right\} \text{Some} \left\{\begin{array}{l}\text{Thing}\\ \text{Event}\\ \text{Relation}\end{array}\right.$$

Thus, every perception involves some person who interprets through the senses, some thing, event, or relation which may be designated as the percept. Nearly everything people know of the world around them comes through the senses. When a consumer reports that a particular department store has good bargains, the person is reporting something perceived through sensory experience. The way that consumers think and behave is constantly being affected by their perception of changes in the environment. The way in which consumers handle such new information psychologically, by organizing and interpreting the stimuli impinging on their senses, is what perception is all about.

It should be clear at this point that consumer attitudes, needs, and motives, are conditioned by perception.[4] Perception of needs and motives changes attitudes. Attitudes condition the way consumers perceive. Furthermore, consumer purchase strategy is affected by perception. We perceive products, methods of obtaining products, and consequences of specific actions taken. The consumer's perception of product deficiencies in his assortment may lead to market action.

Perception and sensation are different

If the individual is to relate to the environment, two factors are necessary: sensation and perception. The major distinction made between sensation and perception is one of complexity and elaboration. The term *sensation* is used to designate the effect associated with the stimulation of a sense organ. *Perception* refers to the interpretation of sensation. Perception involves both sensations aroused by external stimuli and past experience.[5]

The senses of vision, touch, hearing, taste, and smell all produce effects that go beyond immediate sensation. The first time a youngster burns a finger on a match, the sensation of pain is related to the match, and the child perceives that the match caused the pain. Thus, sensation coupled with the mental association of two facts produces perception. Because perception involves learning, it carries over time. The youngster will associate the sensation of pain with matches at any future time a burning match is perceived. Thus, sensory experiences are but one component of perception. The child's past experience, his or her background, the result of the encounter, and the activity engaged in at the time all contribute to the way in which matches are perceived. Cantril summed the concept of perception very well with the following story about three umpires who were discussing how they call the game.

> *The first umpire said, "Some's balls and some's strikes and I calls 'em as they is." The second umpire said, "Some's balls and some's strikes and I calls 'em as I sees 'em." While the third umpire said, "Some's balls and some's strikes but they ain't nothin' till I calls 'em."*[6]

Consumer reactions based on perception

If a person sees a red light while out on a boat, he or she does not mistake it for a traffic light, even though the physical object may be quite similar.[7] This same point holds for consumers. A product may be perceived as the answer to a need one time and as an unnecessary expense at another time.

If several customers observe a round, white object several inches in diameter in a retail store, each would most likely react differently to the object based on individual perception. Each person's needs, cultural background, past experiences, and motives will cause perception of the object to differ from that of the other individuals, even though the sensation is the same for all.[8] A round, white object may be perceived as a baseball by the 10-year-old. The boy wants to purchase it. The boy's mother and father may perceive the ball as a hazard or an expense, and the parents may not want to purchase. Since the identical sensation can be interpreted in differing ways, perceptions differ, and the resulting consumer behavior likewise differs. The sign proclaiming a National Football League exhibition game can be perceived as entertainment by the avid football fan, as traffic congestion by the motorcycle policeman, and as a revenue opportunity by the concessionaire. Each person's background and experience have altered individual interpretation of identical sensory data.

Perception relates to consumer needs and motives

Needs, motives, and perception interact in the person.[9] An individual who needs food sees an orange as nourishment. A consumer motivated toward a good time may see an orange in conjunction with a jigger of vodka as a "screwdriver." Another person, with a thirst, sees the orange in terms of a cool drink of orange juice. Someone having none of these needs and motives may not perceive the orange at all—the absence of a strong motivator on the senses may cause this individual to ignore the orange's existence. Thus, it is clear that what we perceive depends on our needs and motives.

It is equally true that consumer needs and motives depend on what we perceive. A person may not be aware of thirst until he or she observes the orange. Upon perceiving it, one suddenly desires a cool, refreshing orange drink. The interaction of perceptions, needs, and motives is extremely important to consumer behavior. Once inside a shoe store, a consumer may suddenly realize the need for a new pair of shoes. The consumer may not have felt this need strongly enough to act until the shoes were perceived. A woman may purchase a small pin because her perception of the item is in line with her needs or motives of the moment. Much of consumers' impulse behavior is explained by this aspect of perception.

Consumer perceptions change

Consumer needs and motives continually change in response to the environment, and this causes perceptions to change both during and between purchase situations.[10] This accounts for the consumer's willingness to try a new product, react to a new advertising campaign, or seek out a different retail store. Individuals trade with a certain retailer, not because of what the store represents, but what that consumer perceives it to represent. Both the consumer and the perceptions the consumer holds about the market change. These changes in turn affect the individual's needs. The advertising campaign may cause a consumer to purchase a previously undesired product. Even though both the market and the consumer are in a state of flux, it must be pointed out that certain aspects of the situation are stable—we do live in a world that is organized and orderly. The things consumers observe and the relations they have with others change, but the changes are usually predictable in the short run. Each individual can rely on the relative accuracy of personal observation. There are always new stores and products, but the bulk of the stores and products available to consumers are reasonably stable.

Numerous studies examining the manner in which perception relates to needs have been conducted. In a study using submarine crews, small groups were asked to look at a screen in a room with low illumination. The crew members were led to believe that a picture had been projected when, in fact, this was not true. They were asked to describe what they saw. The experiment was conducted so that the time since the participants had last eaten varied. When crew members reported what they perceived, there were more responses relating to food by those members having been deprived of food the longest.

Persons participating in experiments in which they are deprived of certain items on a menu later tend to remember best those parts of the menu that were absent (liquids, meats, vegetables). The overestimation in the size of coins by poor children as compared to estimated size by more well-to-do subjects points up the major effects of our needs upon perception.

HOW PERCEPTION AFFECTS MARKETING

Consumers may hold one or more perceptions that directly affect marketing. The more marketers know about these perceptions, the better their chance of appealing effectively to the market. Some of the important perceptions follow.

1. *Store perception* is the impression of the business as a totality. Consumers may view a store as a good or bad place to shop. One study of bank customers found that switching banks was positively related to the perceptions held of the general climate of the two banks.[11] The consumer may also hold an indifferent impression of the store. Business executives are too prone to believe that everyone has a good impression of their store.[12] Furthermore, executives feel that their store holds one consistent impression for all consumers. However, one study shows that consumers may have different perceptions of different departments within a store as well as different impressions between stores.[13] It is even possible that the same store is perceived differently by consumers at various branches or other locations. Each business should learn who it appeals to and why it has a specific appeal as a basis for developing marketing strategy.

2. *Product perception* is the associations of quality, price, service, and warranty made by a consumer toward a particular product or

brand. Manufacturer branded goods generally are perceived as having higher quality than unbranded or private brand products. The products of discount stores are frequently perceived as having lower quality than those of non-discounters. Some customers have a low opinion of product warranties although they may have a good impression of the product.[14] A recent study of consumer product perceptions shows that many consumers have a low opinion of both product quality and warranties. Respondents did not perceive products as built to last and they considered many products too complex. However, nearly 70 percent of the respondents perceived retailers as trying to back up manufacturer guarantees.[15] Small town consumers often trade with major department stores such as Sears or Wards because their perception of service for these stores is higher than for other local stores. Furthermore, products carry varying price images.[16] Here is, obviously, an opportunity for local stores to change customer perceptions of stores and prices. Marketers need to understand how product perceptions are formed, changed, and what affects their duration.

3. *Promotion perception* is the impression of technical and psychological aspects of promotion.[17] Customer perception of promotion is extremely important because promotional effort affects both the store and the product image. Generally, customers are wary of all types of promotion. The advertising industry particularly does not have a good consumer image. Yet, there is no clear understanding of consumer promotional impressions and consumer willingness to purchase based on these impressions. Much promotion, with poor customer perceptions such as the Procter & Gamble ads or the patent medicine ads, sells effectively, while promotion with favorable images sometimes does not sell. The whole area of promotional perception and effectiveness needs more study by marketers.

4. *Perception of honesty and ethics* is the association of the possible outcome of dealing with a business. Perceptions of honesty and ethics are a hot issue in business. Business executives need to ascertain what consumers expect in this area and set about putting their house in order. Generally, business, and specifically marketing, are not perceived as highly ethical or honest, although the consumer may be incorrect in this judgment. Consumers' perceptions of honesty and ethics become all involved in competition, business social attitude, and in store treatment of individuals. It is a difficult area in which to obtain data.

CHARACTERISTICS OF PERCEPTION THAT AFFECT CONSUMERS

Certain characteristics of perception are universal. Perception may differ among consumers, but perception displays four specific characteristics where found: It can be said to be (1) subjective, (2) selective, (3) temporal, or (4) summative. An awareness of these characteristics can greatly aid our understanding of how perception influences consumer behavior.

Consumer perception is subjective

To reiterate, no two consumers perceive the same event or product in the same way. This is true because perception is subjective.[18] It exists in the mind of the individual and only in the mind. As consumers, we often block out those things we don't want to emphasize, such as the price of the item or some possible defect in it. We see what we want to see, and we hear what we want to hear. Thus, the consumer who wants to purchase, perceives the good points of the product as more significant than the bad points. People are predisposed toward accepting certain information and rejecting other information. Consumers accept some data because it is more compatible with their background, feelings, or beliefs than other data. Consumers tend to take in information that is agreeable, so as to protect their self-images and their ego. A person is the embodiment of certain beliefs, attitudes, and prejudices, and consumers buy in such a manner as to leave these factors intact and unchallenged. Figure 12–1 illustrates one form of perceptual bias. Look closely and note what you see. Chances are you first saw the obvious, and the not so obvious only became apparent on further inspection.

Figure 12–1

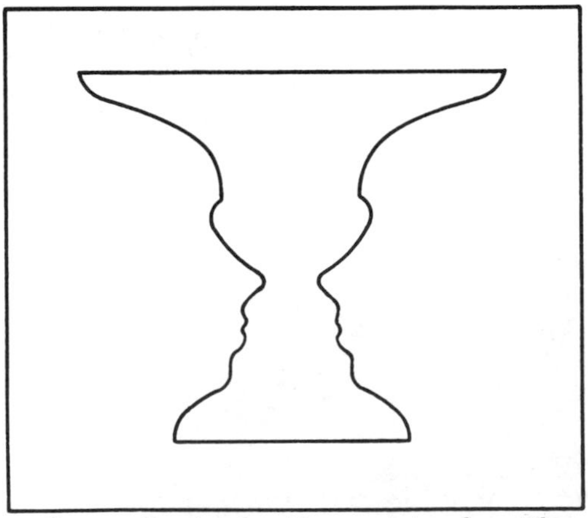

Source: Reprinted with permission from Theodore M. Newcomb, Ralph H. Turner, Philip E. Converse, *Social Psychology: The Study of Human Interaction* (New York: Holt, Rinehart & Winston, Inc., 1965), p. 37.

An awareness of this tendency in each of us to perceive only what we want to perceive may help to make us better consumers by making us more objective.[19] Because of the subjective nature of perception, marketers can take advantage of consumers by playing on their likes, dislikes, prejudices, and attitudes. On the other hand, the marketer who operates under the assumption that his or her perception of the firm, its products, services, and advertising, is the same as that of customers may not do the best job for those customers. The good salesperson learns early that points made in the sales presentation may be perceived differently by a customer than the salesperson anticipated. The salesperson learns that when one stresses high performance and long life, some customers may associate this with high price while others associate it with high quality.

Consumer perception is selective

Perception is selective because individual minds fail to comprehend and interpret all the sensations that bombard the senses at any given time.[20] When a person views a department store window, it is doubtful that one "sees" one third of all the items present. Three mechanisms existing in the perception of everyone determine which stimuli will "get through" to the mind and which will not. These mechanisms are perceptual overloading, selective sensitization, and perceptual defense.[21]

Perceptual overloading occurs because at any given time consumers can only take in and bring up to a conscious level relatively few of the stimuli confronting them. The individual finds it impossible to respond to everything at once. Through perception a consumer is able to select from among the product or store stimuli. In this manner, an individual makes purchases manageable. The selective nature of perception may be regarded as the result of the subjective nature of people and of the limited capacity of a person's sensory equipment. *Selective sensitization* occurs when individuals perceive stimuli more accurately and rapidly because these stimuli are congruous with their value orientation. *Perceptual defense* occurs when a person's value orientation not only contributes to the selection of stimuli but acts to erect a barrier to those stimuli seen as threats. Thus, people are more than normally perceptive to some sensations and less than normally perceptive to other sensations. The result is a type of natural perceptual bias that exists in all purchase situations.[22]

The selectiveness of perception brought about by the physiological inability to take in more than a few stimuli at one time has importance to those in advertising. There are limits to the human capacity to absorb advertising messages accurately. The number of advertisements to which the average American consumer is daily exposed has been estimated to be from 1,500 to 1,800. A marketer's advertisement is thus competing with many others, yet only a small percentage of these are seen and brought to a conscious level by the consumer. Selective perception dictates not only carefully planned media selection but also the number of elements presented in the advertisement and how they are presented. The selective nature of perception also plays a role in merchandising. Merchandising displays and assortments can be an important demand-creating force. However, if displays and merchandising techniques are utilized to the point that too many stimuli are present, they can actually cause business to lose patronage.

Consumer perception is temporal

Most of the things we perceive are temporal in that the perception is of short duration. Thus, products and services have difficulty holding the consumer's attention. This makes selective perception even more important and helps explain how a consumer can filter out an offensive advertising jingle. Temporal perception also partially explains why a well-known product can fail if advertising is cut off. Part of the explanation also lies in the fact that the market is changing.

A stimulus of constant intensity often needs repetition if it is to be brought to the consciousness. A repeated, small ad may be more effective than a single, large ad. The temporal character of perception is the reason that reminder advertising is often successful. Individuals are constantly bombarded by market sensations, and practically none of the initial contacts is lasting. The slogan, "Coke adds life," probably did not register in a lasting form the first time it was heard. It was only after numerous repetitions in a jingle that the idea was brought to a conscious level and remembered.

Consumer perception is summative

Perception tends to be summative. This means that consumers take many sensations that reach awareness almost simultaneously and sum these sensations into a complete and unified whole. Consumers take the separate sensations of observing a building, hearing people move about, and observing various signs and colors, and put these facts together as a retail store. Consumers do the same thing when they observe an advertisement, a store sign, or a product design. Most sales messages are more effective when both audio and visual techniques are utilized rather than when either one or the other is used singly. The reason is that each sense message reinforces the others and aids in forming a consistent, unified impression. Consumers will add up a brand name, color, package features, approximate price, quality, past experience in using the product, and so on, to arrive at a purchasing decision. It is difficult to conceive how consumers could ever make up their minds to buy, if it were not for the fact that perception is summative.

CONSUMER PERCEPTUAL PROCESS

It should be clear to the reader that perception involves a mental process. There are three elements to this process: conveyance, elaboration, and comprehension.[23] First, *conveyance* is the act of getting sensations to the brain. Consumers possess a number of sensory organs, as already mentioned, that convey to the mind stimuli from the external world. The more important are those of vision, hearing, touch, temperature, pain, taste, smell, and common chemical sense. For example, in Figure 12–2 the boy observes the girl by means of his

Figure 12–2

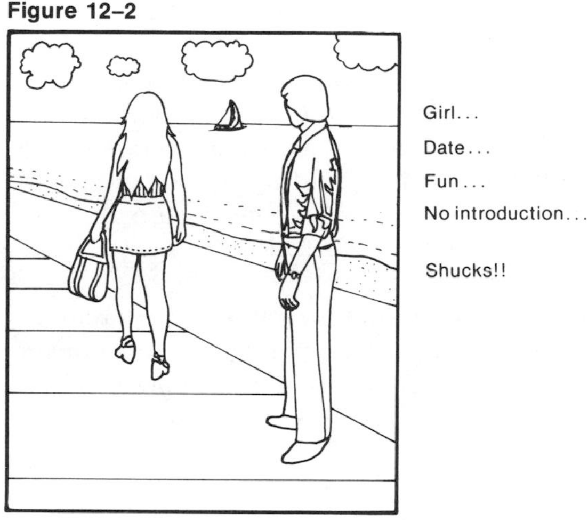
Girl...
Date...
Fun...
No introduction...
Shucks!!

sight and probably hearing. After the external environment has excited one or more of the sensory organs, the stimuli are conveyed to the brain via the central nervous system. The stimuli may affect any one of the different sensory organs or may affect several simultaneously. Second, the stimuli are *elaborated*. This is a step that is primarily mental. It involves the mind classifying the sensations according to knowledge and experience. In this way, the person finds out what the sensations are, whether there has been some past experience with them, and so on. It is also at this point that the sensations are related to the person's motives, predispositions, feelings, attitudes, and previous sensations. The third element, *comprehension,* is not actually a separate stage in the process. Rather, it is the natural result of the elaboration stage. Comprehension occurs when understanding of the sensation has been gained by the mind.[24] In other words, the sensation has become a perception. In the figure, the boy comprehends the girl but is also aware of the fact that they have not been introduced. Thus, the boy's mental image of fun is not likely to actually occur.

THE CONSUMER AS A PERCEIVER

The process of perceiving relates to every aspect of a consumer's mental activity. It is related to action, as when a woman, upon seeing a piece of furniture marked down, quickly "stakes a claim." Perception is related to memory when the same woman recognizes a product she has not seen for some time and thought was no longer available. The relationship of perception to emotion can be seen when a man becomes angry and berates the store manager for not having in stock the item featured as a special in yesterday's newspaper. When this same customer read the newspaper and began to make the decision to buy that item, his thinking was initiated by his perception of the printed word. Another consumer may see a dress in a store window on her way to the supermarket and enter the store to look at it more closely. Perception is related to motivation in that the need was there, and her perception of the dress in the window brought about her action of entering the store.

Several characteristics of the consumer as a perceiver are important for understanding the effect of perception on consumer behavior. Among these factors are (1) thresholds of awareness, (2) importance of cues, and (3) source of the market stimulus.

Thresholds of awareness

Each bit of perceptual information must be assigned some priority if our actions are to achieve continuity and direction. The factors that assign these priorities to the incoming data are not primarily the stimulus factors but factors such as interests, needs, and attitudes that can be measured by observing how a person reacts to various standard stimuli. Of particular importance to advertising, merchandising, and marketing research is the fact that the attention-getting value of the market stimulus depends not so much on the stimulus itself as on the individual the stimulus affects. We have pointed out that consumer behavior is very rarely controlled by a single stimulus affecting a single sense. Rather, consumer behavior is affected by a pattern of stimulation. The value and meaning of the market stimulus depend upon the context in which it is perceived. All of our senses have some limit to responsiveness to stimulation. In the literature these limits are referred to as thresholds.

There are three thresholds that correspond to each sense. They are as follows:

1. *Lower threshold:* Point beyond which the market stimulus is not sufficiently strong to be noticed by the consumer.
2. *Upper threshold:* Point beyond which increased stimulation produces no increased response.
3. *Difference threshold:* The smallest increment of stimulation that can be noticed by a consumer.[25]

These upper and lower thresholds do not correspond to the physical limits of market stimuli. Physical stimuli can be lower or higher than the threshold limits. Furthermore, these threshold limits apply to individual consumers and not to groups. Each consumer has a personally unique upper and lower threshold.

The consumer may be influenced by considerations he or she may not be able to identify, by responding to cues that are below the threshold of recognition. The product package is often spoken of as the "silent salesman." A good package design has the ability to attract the customer's attention. The size of the package, its color, and its design may be influential, even though consumers may think they are interested only in price, brand name, or contents. The package may be so well designed that it breaks through the consumer's lower threshold. In advertising, marketers often observe that it is some simple, inexpensive bit of data that determines the way the entire advertisement is perceived. It is extremely important for marketers to gauge those factors people respond to, while at the same time acknowledging that this is not always possible.

Importance of cues

All consumers utilize cues taken from the environment to aid their perception. Cues are perceived signals that can stand for something else.[26] Typical cues used by consumers to identify and evaluate merchandise include product brand, product package, store signs, advertisements, the smile of a sales person, personal treatment in a store, and so forth. The consumer may allow a brand name to stand for the product, or a store sign may cause the customer to form an impression of the entire retail organization.

One study of brand choice, where the number of information cues and number of brands were varied, provides interesting results.[27] The study was made using 153 college students. The results indicated that:

1. The greatest accuracy for selecting the best brand occurred when fewer brands had the greatest amount of information.
2. The poorest accuracy for selecting the best brand occurred when the subjects had the least amount of information per brand.
3. Accuracy in selecting the best brand declined as more information was provided with more brands.

The first two conclusions can be expected, but the third conclusion is surprising. It suggests that the consumer can have too much information when making decisions.

When consumers are required to form difficult perception judgments, they may respond to irrelevant cues.[28] A merchant's smile, for example, may serve as the cue for some consumers to judge honesty, although such a cue is relatively worthless in such a complex assessment. Yet, cues can be called irrelevant, incomplete, or redundant only in respect to the consumer perceiving them. What is irrelevant to one consumer may be relevant to another. The brand "Jax" may mean nothing to a consumer outside the South, but in that area consumers recognize it as a popular beer. The greatest variation in perception occurs where the incoming information is incomplete or ambiguous to the consumer. The correct context to irrelevant or incomplete cues may be either guessed at or assumed to be complete until additional information is presented.

Source of the market stimulus

Consumers weigh perceptual evidence coming from respected or favored sources more heavily than that coming from other sources. This accounts for the fact that a friend may influence a consumer's choice of a product to a greater extent, even in a casual conversation, than thousands of dollars worth of advertising. It also explains why some advertising is believed more readily than others. Often the success of a firm's marketing effort may depend on how a small group of fashion leaders perceive these marketing efforts. This is particularly true of stores that place heavy reliance on the opinions of persons who are looked up to. Firms take advantage of personal influence on consumers in many ways, including the testimonial advertisement. If a consumer already has a favorable impression of the product or store, it is much easier to influence that consumer through sales effort.

FACTORS AFFECTING CONSUMER PERCEPTION

The nature of the percept and the act of perceiving are affected by physical factors and subjective factors. It is impossible to discuss every factor that affects consumer perception, but the major considerations can be grouped under five headings: (1) technical factors, (2) mental readiness, (3) past experience, (4) mood, and (5) social and cultural factors.

Technical factors

When we refer to technical factors, we mean the actual things that are perceived by consumers. We do not mean the person's interpretation of the thing but rather the thing as it actually exists. There is evidence that technical (physical) cues affect price-quality judgments of products more than non-physical cues such as price or store image.[29] In one study of hosiery the physical cues far outweighed price and store image on the respondents perception of quality.[30] Whatever the consumer perceives is based on the actual thing, no matter how much the perception may become distorted in the beholder's mind. A pencil is a technical fact, but the reason that one person sees a pencil as an instrument with which to write a letter home, another sees it as a means to curl hair, and another person sees it as a ruler is due to perception in response to a need. Technical factors refer to the things perceived, but these objects may be nonphysical. Consumers focus their perception on such abstractions as success, profit maximization, competition, efficiency, sales, and cost. The existence of these concepts are technical, but the differences consumers observe in them are perceptual.

Briefly outlined in the following paragraphs are some important technical attributes of objects that affect consumer perception. Some of these attributes apply primarily to physical objects, and some can apply to both material and abstract objects.

Size. Larger objects generally attract more attention than small objects, although there is no direct incremental relationship. Larger cans, larger ads, and larger stores attract more consumers. To some, size may also connote quality. Many people consider a large store to be automatically better than a small store.

Color. Color attracts more attention and makes a greater impression than black and white. An object in color is perceived quicker and is more likely to be remembered. Color can also emphasize various parts of an object, thus aiding learning. Used on labels, signs, and store fronts, color influences consumer perception. Color ads are 50 percent more effective than black and white, and newspapers using color have higher readership.

Intensity. *Loud, bright, important,* and *significant* are words that convey intensity of an object. Greater intensity attracts and focuses attention. Intensity also affects memory and learning. Bright colors, important consumer decisions, and significant past experiences affect present consumer behavior.

Movement. Movement is a particularly good attention getter. Movement is an important element in TV commercials, point-of-sale aids, and in demonstrating products. Store signs that employ movement attract more customers.

Position. Where a thing is located affects perception. Consumers buy more products located shoulder-high on store shelves. The left-hand side of a page and the upper half of a page get more of a person's attention. The placement of components in an advertisement help create interest and affect memory. Placement of products in a store can achieve the same effect.

Contrast. Contrast gains attention and creates interest much as color does. Contrast is used effectively in ads, for interior and exterior store designs, for product placement, and on product labels. Contrast is achieved by varying the thought, color, size, pattern, or intensity.

Isolation. Isolation can also be used effectively to gain attention and to influence people's perception. Even a small object, such as a knife, uniquely displayed attracts more attention than a window full of products.

It must be remembered that these attributes interact. High contrast may offset greater size. An object has its greatest impact on perception when several of the attributes function together.

Mental readiness of consumers to perceive

Mental readiness refers to a consumer's mental attitude toward and state of readiness to perceive. The following factors influence mental readiness: (1) perceptual fixation, (2) perceptual habit, (3) confidence and caution, (4) attention, (5) mental set, (6) familiarity, and (7) expectations.

Perceptual fixation. The tendency of consumers to stabilize their perceptions of the environment is known as "perceptual fixation." Consumers tend to anticipate certain market stimuli in the environment and thus to stabilize their effects over time. You can say that individuals generalize some of their perceptions, and retain them even after the basis for them has changed. Perceptual fixation is illustrated by the consumer who perceives a quality image for a retail store even after evidence accumulates that the store has gone downhill. In the same way, consumers tend to resist changing their image of a particular brand. They will continue to use inferior products long after better ones are available.

Perceptual habit. There is a certain habitual pattern present in the perceptions of consumers. We are all creatures of habit, and we perceive accordingly.[31] Individuals only break down old perceptions when forced to reorganize them. A customer's performance in any situation may be partially determined by habitual reaction toward the situation. Those in the habit, for example, of shopping in small specialty stores giving a great deal of service may be slow to accept the discount house.

Confidence and caution. The extent to which the consumer is confident or cautious affects perception.[32] The confident perceiver tends to size up a complex situation more quickly, to see more favorable elements in it, and to take in more detail. One may even see details in the situation that are not actually present. Cautious observers take more time in viewing a situation, but their perceptions are likely to be more accurate. The confident consumer is quick to make up his or her mind; the cautious one takes more time to make a purchase.

Attention. Before perception can take place, the consumer's attention must be secured. If consumers are not attentive to a stimulus, there is no awareness. Attention consists essentially of focusing an awareness upon certain sensory processes aroused by the percept.[33] Consumer awareness is usually characterized by the persistence and duration of the actual sensory processes or of the imagery set up by them.

Two factors affecting the attention process are the span of attention and fluctuation in attention. A consumer's *span of attention* is simply the number of discrete objects related to products or other market factors that a person is able to apprehend simultaneously. This can be tested experimentally by asking subjects to report the objects they can remember from a large number shown them for a brief period. It has been found that the average number reported correctly under such conditions is around eight. For maximum attention, therefore, consumer messages must be kept simple and to the point so as not to exceed the individual's span of attention. Familiar phrases, simple layouts, and fewer propositions all contribute to the success of staying within the limits of the consumer's span of attention.

Fluctuations in attention occur because consumers are unable to concentrate on one object for too long a period. Every four or five seconds, attention shifts. Radio advertisers using announcements repeated at intervals do so in recognition of fluctuations in attention. Although the listener's attention shifts, in this way it is shifted to the same message. Attention-getting visuals are often relied upon in television commercials, but these also may incur the danger of shifting the viewer's attention to the visual rather than the message intended.

Package designs, merchandising displays, point-of-purchase materials, radio and television commercials, and printed advertisements must all take into account both the span of attention and fluctuations in attention as factors in the perceptual process.

Mental set. Closely related to the attention factor is the concept of mental set. Psychologists refer to mental set as a person's tendency, or readiness, to react to a given stimulus. This condition may be illustrated by the preparatory commands given by a drill sergeant or a pro football quarterback. When the quarterback gives such signals at the line as "down–hup–32–64–28," he knows that his team has been "preset" to react to the number 28 by charging forward.

In the same manner, consumers are also "set" to perceive objects and events. Consumers perceive the way they are set to perceive by their cultural, social, and personal makeup. Mental set involves the direction that our attention takes; it is not just a readiness to react but a tendency to react in a certain way. Sales trainers constantly put to use the concept of mental set in their everyday training of junior salespersons. Sales personnel, for example, are told to be constantly alert to overt responses of prospective customers. Thus, the sales person is "set" to observe and adjust the sales presentation according to reactions that previously might have been ignored. The training is aimed at placing in the trainee's "mental set" as many such helpful elements as possible.

Familiarity. Familiarity, as used here, connotes more than the mere acquaintance with a situation or object perceived. It implies some prior pattern of experienced phenomena into which the present percept fits. Familiarity results from the relationship of the percept to a recognized scheme that supplies meaning to the percept. Consequently, the ability to understand the meaning of the percept is closely related to its familiarity.

In a study of 326 beer drinkers in which each was given six-packs of unlabeled beer followed with six-packs of labeled beer, it was found that:

1. Participants could not discern taste differences among different brands, but labels did influence evaluations, that is, product differences resulting from marketing rather than physical product differences are what mattered.
2. Loyalty toward their brand increased when positive brand identification was possible.
3. Participants could not identify "their" brand of beer in a blind comparison test.[34]

In designing promotional campaigns, a firm must consider the ease with which a customer can become familiar with the company's product. If the product is complicated, then the problem of securing familiarity with it becomes even more important. Designers of promotional campaigns try to develop familiarity toward the brand, store layout, service, price range, sales people, and so on. The concept actually touches on everything a consumer does.

Expectations. Expectations are a type of mental set, but they are so important to perception that we discuss them separately. Expectations affect perception because people tend to perceive what they expect to perceive.[35] If aspects of the object are missing, the mind tends to fill in the gaps and complete the picture, a tendency known as closure. For example, given a price, the consumer fills in expectations concerning product quality.[36]

Past experience of the consumer

What a consumer perceives today is influenced by experience. Individual expectations, too, will be based on past experience. A consumer recognizes a life preserver or an oar because he or she has previously identified these objects. The individual expects a life preserver to remain essentially the same over time. Thus, one may not correctly identify a boat seat life preserver the first time it is seen on display in a store. One perceives the object as a cushion and not as a life preserver because that conforms to experience. A brand of canned beans is perceived as being of high quality because of past experience with that brand. A large part of the total perception we have of a business is based on our past experience in dealing with it.

Mood

Mood refers to our feelings, present attitude, or state of mind. It is a factor of great importance to consumer perception. A person in the mood induced by illness does not perceive the world in the same way as does the person who feels well. An optimist will view a situation favorably that a pessimist sees as bad. Although a good mood does not assure that a consumer will buy, a consumer in a good mood is more inclined to buy more and better things. Of course, some products may be more quickly bought when the consumer is in a bad mood. A person depressed by the future may more readily purchase insurance.

Because one derives enjoyment out of the buying situation, a person in a buoyant mood may take longer to purchase. Mood can be reflected in how the product, brand, store, and advertisement are presented. A product depicted as exciting has a greater appeal than one that appears dull. We have all had the experience of looking at a label and getting the impression that the product represents something old, traditional, and out of date. Another product label using a different combination of language, design, color, and typography may give us a feeling that the product is fashionable and will give prestige.

Social and cultural factors of consumer perception

How consumers perceive will be affected by factors related to the society and culture in which they live. The role one plays, or conceives oneself to play in society; social class or status; and certain aspects of the culture in which one is immersed will all influence how the person perceives products and the marketer's attempts to sell them.[37] It therefore is of greatest importance that the marketer should understand these social and cultural differences and be able to adapt strategies to them.

Everyone has a role to play in society. This role will be determined by such factors as age, sex, occupation, ethnic or national group, and social class. Perceptions of products will differ according to role, and advertising to the old cannot be based on the same appeals as advertising to the teen-age group. Recently a new advertising agency has been founded on the principle that those who think "white" cannot effectively reach black consumers; the perceptions are not the same.

The Starch Readership Reports illustrate the differences required in making appeals to male and female readers of advertisements. The same copy and layout for a Volkswagen ad varied greatly in readership scores by sex. Media selection, copy, and layout all must be directly related to perceptual differences resulting from sex distinctions. Such differences are a result of cultural training of the sexes in their different roles. The recent development of "unisex" products has resulted from present-day tendencies toward confusion of sexual roles and tendencies of male and female to want the same types of clothing, personal adornment, and so on.

While many Americans do not like to think so, it is a fact of life that social classes do exist in our country, and they greatly affect consumer perceptions. Sociologists and other social scientists have, as we have discussed elsewhere in this book, classified the social classes from "lower-lower" through the middle levels to "upper-upper." They have pointed out that consumers tend to perceive products in ways conditioned by their level in the social structure. Consumers differ, too, in the importance they place on "upward mobility." A consumer oriented toward social climbing may perceive certain products as being inferior because it is known that upper-class families do not buy them. Yet a consumer who has it made socially and financially may show contempt for prestige products and brands and practice a kind of inverse snobbery.

A status-conscious consumer perceives the automobile as a status symbol, a means of keeping up with the Joneses. A less status-conscious individual will perceive the car as a means of transportation. The sales appeals directed to each must be varied accordingly.

Factors present in the culture may affect the consumer's perceptions favorably or may set up barriers to them. Among such factors are traditions, customs, norms of modesty and of social behavior, relative value systems, fatalism, and attitudes toward innovation. In addition to the general culture, many subcultures influence perception—for example, the hippies.

The American culture is more receptive to technological change than most others. In underdeveloped countries, change is often resisted.

If people perceive, in terms of their cultural norms, a product to be improper, illogical, inappropriate, inefficient, or undignified, their purchasing behavior toward it will be influenced.

NOTES

1. Good discussions of perception can be found in Perry Bliss, *Marketing Management and The Behavioral Environment* (Englewood Cliffs, N.J.: Prentice-Hall, Inc., 1970), Chap. 6; Thomas S. Robertson, *Consumer Behavior* (Glenview, Ill.: Scott, Foresman & Co., 1970), Chap. 2.
2. Adapted from Paul Thomas Young, *Motivation and Emotion: A Survey of the Determinants of Human and Animal Activity* (New York: John Wiley & Sons, Inc., 1961), pp. 289–99.
3. Ibid., p. 298.
4. See: John A. Howard and Jagdish N. Sheth, *The Theory of Buyer Behavior* (New York: John Wiley & Sons, Inc., 1969), Chap. 5.
5. James H. Meyers and William H. Reynolds, *Consumer Behavior and Marketing Management* (Boston: Houghton Mifflin Co., 1967), p. 3.
6. Hadley Cantril, "Perception and Interpersonal Relations," *American Journal of Psychiatry,* vol. 114 (1957), pp. 119–26.
7. Meyers and Reynolds, *Consumer Behavior and Marketing Management;* Harold H. Kassarjian and Thomas S. Robertson, *Perspectives in Consumer Behavior* (Glenview, Ill.: Scott, Foresman and Co., 1973), pp. 1–9.
8. J. R. Brent Ritchie, "An Exploratory Analysis of the Nature and Extent of Individual Differences in Perception," *Journal of Marketing Research,* vol. 11 (February 1974), pp. 41–49.
9. Albert H. Hastorf and Hadley Cantril, "A Case Study of Differential Perception," *Journal of Abnormal and Social Psychology,* vol. 49 (1954), pp. 73–79.
10. Ronald J. Dornoff, Clint B. Tankersley, and Gregory P. White, "Consumers' Perceptions of Imports," *Akron Business and Economic Review,* vol. 5 (Summer 1974), pp. 26–29; William O. Adcock, Jr., Ugur Yavas, and Anthony J. Alessandra, "Consumer Reactions to a New Money Machine," *Atlanta Economic Review,* vol. 26 (September-October 1976), pp. 52–54.
11. Benjamin Schneider, "The Perception of Organizational Climate: The

Customer's View," *Journal of Applied Psychology*, vol. 57 (1973), pp. 248–56.

12. Peter J. McClure and John K. Ryans, "Differences Between Retailers' and Consumers' Perceptions," *Journal of Marketing Research*, vol. 5 (February 1968), pp. 35–40.
13. C. Glenn Walters, "Retail Store Image: Fact or Fantasy," *Business Ideas and Facts*, vol. 6 (Summer 1973), pp. 15–25.
14. George Fisk, "Guidelines for Warranty Service After Sale," *Journal of Marketing*, vol. 34 (January 1970), pp. 62–67.
15. Robert E. Wilkes and James B. Wilcox, "Consumer Perceptions of Product Warranties and Their Implications for Retail Strategy," *Journal of Business Research*, vol. 4 (February 1976), pp. 35–43.
16. F. E. Brown, "Price Perception and Store Patronage," *Marketing and the New Science of Planning*, ed. Robert L. King (Chicago: American Marketing Assn., 1968), pp. 371–76; Arch Woodside, "Relation of Price to Perception of Quality of New Products," *Journal of Applied Psychology*, vol. 59 (Fall 1974), pp. 116–18.
17. Irwin A. Horowitz and Russell S. Daye, "Perception and Advertising," *Journal of Advertising Research*, vol. 15 (June 1975), pp. 15–21.
18. Kent B. Monroe, "Buyers' Subjective Perceptions of Price," *Journal of Marketing Research*, vol. 10 (February 1973), pp. 70–80.
19. John A. Howard, "New Directions in Buyer Behavior Research," *Relevance in Marketing: Problems, Research, Action*, ed. Fred C. Allvine (Chicago: American Marketing Assn., 1971), pp. 375–80.
20. James F. Engel, "The Influence of Needs and Attitudes on the Perception of Persuasion," *Toward Scientific Marketing* (Chicago: American Marketing Assn., 1964), pp. 18–29.
21. Leo Postman, J. S. Bruner, and Elliott McGinnies, "Personal Values as Selective Factors in Perception," *Journal of Abnormal and Social Psychology*, vol. 42 (1948), pp. 142–52.
22. Homer E. Spence and James F. Engel, "The Impact of Brand Preference on the Perception of Brand Names: A Laboratory Analysis," *Marketing Involvement in Society and the Economy* ed. P. R. McDonald (Chicago: American Marketing Assn., 1970), pp. 267–71; D. P. Spence, "Subliminal Perception and Perceptual Defense: Two Sides of a Single Problem," *Behavioral Science*, vol. 12 (1967), pp. 183–93.
23. Adapted from M. A. Vernon, *The Psychology of Perception* (Baltimore: Penguin Books, Inc., 1912), pp. 12–15. Vernon suggests five factors of perception as (1) stimulus, (2) conveyance, (3) elaboration, (4) comprehension, and (5) response. This list almost duplicates the steps in the broader concept of communications discussed later. The essential factors of perception appear to be the three mentioned.
24. Jerome S. Bruner, "On Perceptual Readiness," *The Psychological Review*, vol. 64 (1957), pp. 123–52.
25. Meyers and Reynolds, *Consumer Behavior and Marketing Management*, p. 11.
26. Beverlee B. Anderson and J. D. Culea, "The Influence of Information

Cues on Expectations and Taste Perceptions," *Proceedings: Southern Marketing Assn., 1973*, ed. Robert L. King, pp. 98–103; Rom J. Markin, Jr., *Consumer Behavior: A Cognitive Orientation* (New York: Macmillan Publishing Co., Inc., 1974), p. 242.

27. Jacob Jacoby, Donald E. Speller, and Carol A. Kohn, "Brand Choice Behavior as a Function of Information Load," *Journal of Marketing Research*, vol. 11 (February 1974), pp. 63–69.
28. Gail Tom and Margaret Rucker, "Fat, Full, and Happy: Effects of Food Deprivation, External Cues, and Obesity on Preference Ratings, Consumption, and Buying Intentions," *Journal of Personality and Social Psychology*, vol. 32 (1974), pp. 761–66.
29. See: I. R. Andrews and E. R. Valenzi, "Combining Price, Brand Name, and Store Cues to Form an Impression of Product Quality," *Proceedings of the 79th Annual Convention of the American Psychological Association, 1971*, vol. 6, pp. 649–50; J. Jacoby, J. C. Olson, and R. Haddock, "Price, Brand Name, and Product Composition Characteristics as Determinants of Perceived Quality," *Journal of Applied Psychology*, vol. 55 (1971), pp. 570–79; J. C. Olson and J. Jacoby, "Cue Utilization in the Quality Perception Process," *Proceedings of the 2nd Annual Convention of the Association for Consumer Research*, vol. 2 (1972), pp. 167–79.
30. George J. Szybillo and Jacob Jacoby, "Intrinsic Versus Extrinsic Cues as Determinants of Perceived Product Quality," *Journal of Applied Psychology*, vol. 59 (1974), pp. 74–78.
31. Howard and Sheth, *The Theory of Buyer Behavior*, pp. 168–69.
32. Alan G. Sawyer, "The Effects of Repetition of Refutational and Supportive Advertising Appeals," *Journal of Marketing Research*, vol. 10 (February 1973), pp. 23–33.
33. James U. McNeal, *An Introduction to Consumer Behavior* (New York: John Wiley & Sons, Inc., 1973), pp. 83–85.
34. Ralph I. Allison and Kenneth P. Uhl, "Influence of Beer Brand Identification on Taste Perception," *Journal of Marketing Research*, vol. 1 (August 1964), pp. 36–39.
35. David A. Zellinger, Howard L. Fromkin, Donald E. Speller, and Carol A. Kohn, "A Commodity Theory Analysis of the Effects of Age Restrictions Upon Pornographic Materials," *Journal of Applied Psychology*, vol. 60 (1975), pp. 94–99.
36. A. Oxenfeldt, D. Miller, A. Shuettman, and C. Winick, *Insights Into Pricing* (Belmont, Ca.: Wadsworth Publishing Co., Inc., 1961), pp. 79–83.
37. Frederick E. Webster, Jr., "Determining the Characteristics of the Socially Conscious Consumer," *Journal of Consumer Research*, vol. 2 (December 1975), pp. 188–96.

QUESTIONS

1. What is perception? How are perception and sensation related? Give examples of your perception using each of the six senses.
2. Discuss the manner in which consumer reactions are related to percep-

tion. Demonstrate the relationship between perception and needs. And motives.

3. Explain, using examples from your experience, how perception affects marketing.
4. What is subjective perception? Demonstrate how subjective perception affects purchasing. Do the same for the other three characteristics of perception.
5. Explain and demonstrate the perceptual process. What are thresholds of awareness? The lower threshold? The upper threshold? The difference threshold?
6. Explain the importance of cues to the perceptual process. Give examples of cues that have affected your purchasing.
7. What are the technical factors of consumer perception? Give examples of the effect of each.
8. Explain mental readiness. Contrast perceptual fixation and perceptual habit. Discuss and illustrate mental set.
9. What is mood? How does it affect consumers?
10. Discuss the social and cultural factors of consumer perception.

13

The effect of consumer attitudes

Attitude defined

Types of attitudes

Attitudes and values systems

The function of consumer attitudes

Properties of consumer attitudes

Readiness to act

Consumer attitudes have polarity

Consumer attitudes vary in intensity

Attitudes display structure

Completeness of attitudes varies

Formation of consumer attitudes

Personal experience

External authorities affect attitude formation

Cultural effects on attitude formation

Consumer attitude stability

Consumer behavior conforms to attitudes

Factors affecting attitude stability

Factors of instability

How consumer attitudes change

Change in the product

Perceptual change

Change in strength of the attitude

Change in store of information

Change in product importance

Change in communications

Consumer attitudes and business policy

The second component of awareness is the consumer's attitudes. Generally speaking, a person's behavior is greatly affected by the disposition or attitude toward that subject. It is not an easy matter to get to the individual's underlying attitudes—they are not directly observable. We observe the behavior that results from attitudes, but not the attitudes themselves. Since a given behavior can result from several different attitudes, this behavior may not be a good guide to attitudes. Yet, we must make the attempt to understand attitudes because they guide everyday consumer actions.[1] People seldom act in opposition to their attitudes, just as they seldom go against their motives.

ATTITUDE DEFINED

The term *attitude* can be used to denote how an individual thinks or feels about something: "From a cognitive point of view, an attitude represents an organization of valenced cognitions."[2] From a motivational point of view, an attitude represents a state of readiness for motive arousal.[3] For our purposes, an attitude is the relatively lasting manner whereby the perceptions and motives of consumers are organized toward certain market objects, events, or situations. Thus, said simply, consumer preference or predispositions to act toward some specific market-oriented goal is that individual's consumer attitude.

TYPES OF ATTITUDES

Such words as *beliefs, feelings, opinions, inclinations,* and *biases* are often used to depict attitudes.[4] While an attitude is any predisposition, each of the above terms denotes a particular type of attitude. Of course, any type of attitude may be conscious or unconscious. We tend to detect shades of difference in personal predispositions according to what specific individuals do or say. However, the attitude itself is a combination of cognitive processes (such as thought and memory) and motivational processes (involving emotion and striving).[5]

Opinions, beliefs, and feelings are usually thought of in relation to a person's preference for one viewpoint in matters which are controversial or on which there is more than one side. Store loyalty, brand preference, store atmosphere, product quality, and prices are consumer subjects on which individuals often have beliefs and opinions. However, the types of predispositions differ among consumers and situations in several important respects.[6] The most important differences relate to their duration and intensity.

Beliefs are predispositions accepted as truth and supported by strong facts or other information. Most beliefs are reasonably permanent, but they may, or may not, be important. For example, a consumer may have a strong belief about a Kenmore washer and Borden's milk, but they are not equally important. *Opinions* are predispositions not based on certainty. There may be some facts, but they are only suggestive of the conclusion drawn by the consumer. Opinions tend to relate to current questions, and they are relatively easily changed. Nearly everyone has an opinion on the reason for the current energy crisis, but a few facts could change a lot of minds. *Feelings* are predispositions of a basically emotional nature. They can be quite durable and deep-seated, but they are not usually supported by relevant facts. The feelings that a woman's place is in the home, or that men who shop with their wives are sissies are deeply entrenched in many minds. We can think of feelings as sentiment, opinions as impressions, and beliefs as values. Attitudes, then, can be any type of conviction—weak or strong, permanent or temporary—based on fact or emotion.

Inclinations and bias can refer to any type of attitude. An *inclination* is a partially formed attitude when the consumer is in an essentially undecided state. For example, between Phillips 66 and Exxon a buyer may be inclined toward Phillips 66 because of the reputation of the dealer, but still undecided because of a preference for Exxon's brand. *Bias* is a mental prejudice believed in spite of the fact that there is evidence to the contrary. A consumer may have biased feelings, opinions, or beliefs. Bias can work for or against a retailer. For example, product preference is a type of bias.

ATTITUDES AND VALUE SYSTEMS

Attitudes comprise a person's total value system, and because these are subjects on which there is no consensus, they take on more importance for some groups than for others.[7] Southerners have a positive attitude toward grits, but northerners have a negative attitude. Thus grits sell in the one region but not in the other. One fact is becoming increasingly clear. The value system upon which attitudes depend, begins to develop in early childhood. There is clear evidence that some of the more effective advertising reaches children before the age of five. Our values are modified as a result of the learning process and experience, but many early predispositions remain essentially unchanged throughout our lives. Marketers can take advantage of this fact. The author knows a man who has purchased the same make car throughout his adult life. Certainly, we can determine a consumer's values to some extent by observing the choices made and the attitudes taken both before and after the purchase. The attitudes taken determine the consumer's interest patterns and are reflected in the consumer's actions.

THE FUNCTION OF CONSUMER ATTITUDES

There are several functions which attitudes perform that affect consumer purchase behavior.[8] Among these are (1) the adjustment function, (2) the ego-defensive function, (3) the value expressive function, and (4) the knowledge function. All of these functions are aspects of the way we adapt to our environment, but one must keep in mind that the need on which the attitude is formed may be different for different persons.

The *adjustment function* concerns how a consumer relates to the environment. The adjustment function recognizes that individuals usually attempt to maximize or at least optimize pleasure, or the rewards of the environment, and minimize pain, or the penalties inherent in the environment. In order to accomplish these desired ends, generally favorable attitudes are formed toward products, brands, or stores giving pleasure, and unfavorable attitudes are formed toward those that displease.

Ego-defensive mechanisms are those which we use to reduce anxieties and protect the ego from our own unacceptable impulses or from forces in the environment which we view as threatening.[9] This tendency of individuals has been documented for political campaigns. An example of how the ego-defensive function affects consumers is found in attitudes toward cigarette information: a large percent of nonsmokers read articles about the effect of cigarettes on health, but only a few smokers read these articles. All types of fear appeals used by marketers such as those used for insurance, beauty aids, patent medicines, and diet food concern the ego-defensive function.[10] One author suggests that such appeals can be used effectively when "(1) The feared condition is avoided through use of the sponsor's product. (2) There is no psychological investment in not using the product. (3) What is feared is damage to the *social image* of the self rather than to the *physical self*."[11]

Many attitudes have the function of hiding the true nature of ourselves or of expressing central values that reflect the type of person we envision ourselves to be. These attitudes serve a *value-expressive* function.[12] It is not the nature of these attitudes to serve a negative function of reducing tension, but to allow the individual to take a positive stance toward obtaining self-identity. The person's reward comes from expressing any attribute associated with the ego. The value-expressive function also serves to adjust the person more nearly in conformity with personal ambitions. Consumers express their values in the products they purchase, the prices they pay, and the businesses that they patronize.

The *knowledge function* consists of the means whereby individuals give meaning to the unorganized world around them.[13] This meaning comes from the standards and frames of reference that attitudes supply. In performing their knowledge function, attitudes lead consumers to seek information and guide them in accumulation of a standard of living. By helping to establish standards of understanding, the attitudes of consumers become a personal means of growth and development that is reflected in the products and services purchased.

PROPERTIES OF CONSUMER ATTITUDES

The properties displayed provide the basis by which attitudes serve their functions. Important properties of attitudes are readiness to act, direction, intensity, structure, and completeness. A discussion of each of these properties can be of benefit to our understanding of consumer attitudes.

Readiness to act

In some ways, consumer attitudes are like the trigger of a pistol. Just as the trigger sets the reaction of the pistol into motion, so attitudes initiate the reaction of consumers.[14] In another sense, attitudes are a device for simplifying consumer behavior. The mind cannot process, catagorize, and evaluate all the necessary market information that leads to logical purchases in every situation faced. Attitudes provide the consumer with an immediate and appropriate response that bypasses much of the learning and thinking process. Consumer attitudes function somewhat like a program functions for a computer. A computer acts as it is programmed to act. Consumers, through their attitudes, also act according to how they are "programmed." Attitudes are learned over a long period of time, and not only do attitudes make the consumer's market reactions simpler and less time-consuming, but they also reduce the amount of information that has to be learned. Because consumers have formed attitudes, they do not need to relearn how to react to each market situation.

Consumer attitudes have polarity

The position taken toward a market problem can be based on positive or negative attitudes. *Positive attitudes* predispose people to act or react favorably to product or stores. *Negative attitudes* predispose people to avoid some situation by market action, but it does not preclude purchasing.[15] A consumer with a negative attitude toward burnt orange is not likely to purchase a sweater of that color. A consumer may have a positive attitude toward a pair of shoes and a negative attitude toward insurance because it is unpleasant to think about death. The consumer may purchase in both cases. Thus, a negative attitude can act as a stimulus to buy in the same way as a positive attitude. It is difficult to determine the difference between a surface annoyance and deeper, more meaningful attitudes. A consumer may be annoyed by a particular door-to-door salesperson, but the annoyance is not deep. However, if the person is predisposed to hate all salespeople, then an attitude is involved. A mèrchant can overcome a negative annoyance fairly easily, but to change the attitudes held by customers is difficult.

Consumer attitudes vary in intensity

The recognition that consumer attitudes have a positive or negative direction is not enough. There are degrees of feeling involved with consumer attitudes, no matter which *direction* the attitude takes.[16] Consumers can evaluate their attitudes toward a product as very positive, slightly positive, or positive, and the same type of evaluation can be made for negative attitudes. Actually, consumer attitudes can be visualized to lie somewhere along a continuum such as the one shown below. The number of predispositions a consumer can hold along the continuum is infinite.

Very positive Neutral Very negative
I______________I______________I

Notice that some predispositions may tend toward neutral. That is to say, the consumer has no strong predisposition. Although it is virtually impossible to measure precisely the degree to which an attitude is favorable or unfavorable, it is possible to determine its relative position in the scale.

Attitudes display structure

Consumer attitudes display a type of structure, and this is important in simplifying consumer behavior.[17] *Structure* refers to the fact that there is a pattern or element of consistency to the beliefs and feelings a person has. Although a consumer may have thousands of attitudes, the attitude that one feels toward one purchase situation is often quite similar to that felt toward another purchase situation. Attitude structure is particularly important as an indicator of consumer behavior, because a person's purchase behavior can sometimes be determined by observing general behavior. For example, a person who is a conservative in politics is likely to be conservative in dress, eating habits, and spending. Behavior shows a pattern based on one attitude that is held in several situations. It is also possible to obtain clues about how a consumer may purchase one product, say, a suit, by observing that person's purchase of another product, say, shoes.

Completeness of attitudes varies

Consumer attitudes tend to show a property that may be called *completeness.* It sometimes happens that consumers base their attitudes on insufficient information. In spite of this fact, the consumer assumes that the attitude is accurate and acts on it. For example, a consumer may, because of one poor performance, consider a television repair man to be incompetent or dishonest. Because of the tendency toward completeness, this attitude may well carry over to the store and management that hired the repair man. A consumer develops an attitude toward a particular brand of television as well made and dependable. This consumer may transfer this attitude to all products made by the manufacturer of the television set. People do not like things incomplete. They tend to fill in the missing details, and this is true of attitudes.

FORMATION OF CONSUMER ATTITUDES

Attitudes come about as a result of personal experience, external authorities, and culture. There is increasing evidence that consumer attitudes result from specific cognitive processes.[18] The consumer internalizes information, both supportive and contrary to presently held beliefs, evaluates it and either maintains or adjusts attitudes as a result. The evidence is that the consumer relies primarily on internal mental responses to the message rather than the content itself when forming or adjusting attitudes.[19] It is still not clear whether supportive or contrary information has the greatest effect in attitude formation. Let us consider how experience, external sources, and culture operate in the formation of attitudes.

Personal experience

Consumer attitudes are formed as a result of personal learning based on experience. As we shall see later, this personal experience is affected by other people and culture. Several elements in personal experience affect the formation of consumer attitudes.

First, the needs and motives the person has developed play a part.

As consumers we do not like high prices, but we like high-quality products. A learned attitude can strongly favor either physical or emotional needs and motives. A consumer may have acquired a favorable attitude toward diamonds when other products are more useful.

Second, the amount, type, and soundness of information accumulated influences attitude formation. To some extent all consumer attitudes are based on information. The more the consumer knows about a product or store the easier it is to have an opinion. Consumers often hold unsound attitudes because of incorrect or insufficient information. The author knows of a retailer merchandising primarily groceries and drugs who has built a reputation as a discounter. Actually, this store has low prices only in the drug department. A recent study of product warranties concludes that consumers have become oriented, through experience to expect product failure.[20] Furthermore, the study shows that when faced with a problem, consumers would much rather deal with the retailer for an adjustment than with the manufacturer.

Third, as the above example shows, the selective nature of consumer perception, based on personal experience, also influences attitude formation. Consumers have tended to ignore high grocery prices in evaluating the retailer mentioned.

Fourth, the consumer's personality affects attitudes. Some consumers have a strong immunity to some attitudes but are susceptible to others. Personality characteristics in one consumer may accompany certain attitudes; in another consumer these characteristics may be correlated with other attitudes.

Fifth, consumers tend to hold attitudes consistent with the aspirations they have developed. A consumer who wants to move into the middle-income class tends to emulate this group's attitudes toward cars, homes, and styles of dress. This fact is reflected in the consumer's purchases.

External authorities affect attitude formation

The formation of individual consumer attitudes is affected by external authorities, including friends, authors, teachers, parents, ministers, co-workers, and many others. The evidence of this influence is supported by research. A study was made of coffee, where a control group was compared to an experimental group with prior information of varying types.[21] The experimental group was significantly influenced by the prior information about the product. However, the uniformity of consistency of external opinions did not materially affect the respondent's opinions.

Although external authorities may provide consumers with what appear to be facts, the attitudes formed may depend on which set of "facts" the consumer believes.[22] The extent to which one authority is believed over another depends on the feeling of trust and respect the consumer has for the authority. Recent advertising has taken advantage of the fact that consumers tend to identify with people like themselves rather than with movie stars or public figures. This identification is based on the fact that consumers trust the opinions of people like themselves. The consumer may feel that someone similar can better appreciate the consumer's problems. A problem arises when facts are available from two authorities such as competing salespersons or ads. If the facts support each other, the individual's attitudes are more likely to be influenced and strengthened. If the authorities disagree, the consumer may select the more respected authority, compromise his attitude to conform to some aspects of all authorities, or distort the facts to fit into a private reality.

Cultural effects on attitude formation

A consumer's present and past cultural environment affects the formation of attitudes. The influence derived from customs and mores, traditions, and social exposure condition attitudes toward new situations. A consumer raised in a conservative atmosphere is likely to reject, at first, new clothing fashions that incorporate extreme styles or colors. Of course, given time to adjust, this consumer may be induced to accept the new fashion. The present attitudes of consumers develop out of past attitudes, and it is easier to accept attitudes compatible with previous values. For example, a consumer who has always believed in saving is more likely to take the attitude that a low-priced product of lower quality is a good buy. Most consumer tastes for food, clothing, and entertainment are shaped by the surrounding culture.

The reader should be aware by this time of the interrelationships between all the individual factors of consumer behavior. It is simply impossible to keep these variables completely separate. Furthermore, the environment cannot be separated from the individual. The reader is simply reminded that any division of needs, motives, perception, and attitudes is arbitrary.

CONSUMER ATTITUDE STABILITY

As just demonstrated, the attitudes consumers have do not just happen. Consumers are not born with their attitudes established; yet, once formed, attitudes have a tendency to persist.

Consumer behavior conforms to attitudes

There can be no doubt that most consumer behavior conforms to individual attitudes.[23] Consumers generally act according to their predispositions. This fact was reinforced by a recent study of soft drinks where test results reinforced the conclusion that stated preference is a significant predictor of choice behavior.[24] A consumer with an attitude of thrift is likely to spend less and save more than a good-time Charlie. Consumers favor those merchants whose appeals to buy are compatible with their individual basic attitudes. Even so, attitudes are not infallible guides to behavior, and consumers do occasionally go against their customary attitudes in buying.[25] This is borne out in a study of the brand preferences, purchase intentions, and actual purchases of 465 Chicago housewives:[26]

1. Brand preference and purchase intention were very close with 52.4 percent of respondents buying the specified brand, and another 14.9 percent fulfilled their goal by purchasing the specified brand plus another brand also. Only 15.3 percent completely changed brands.
2. Brand preference was a good indicator of purchase, but 15 percent did purchase differently from their stated intentions.
3. Brand preference did not predict the amount of purchase. Overall, 61.4 percent of respondents purchased more units than they had expected to.

An appeal of the moment, such as price, salesmanship, merchandise availability or a desire to try something new, may account for the differences.

Factors affecting attitude stability

Attitudes, as guides to consumer activity, must show a degree of stability, at least in the short run.[27] Actually, attitudes tend to stabilize and become stronger with the length of time held. Three factors are particularly important for exploring the stability of consumer attitudes: attitude structure, causality of attitudes, and attitude congruence.

Structure of attitudes provides stability. It was pointed out earlier that consumers hold similar attitudes toward products or market situations that they consider to be in the same class. Consumers, in their acceptance of new products, are often reflecting the structure of their attitudes toward the product class rather than the new product. A housewife may reject a new cold-water detergent because of her attitude toward all cold-water detergents, even though the new product may be superior to any she has used. Consumers tend to find a balance in their beliefs about various products. When consumer attitudes are in balance, they tend to be stable. We can say that where balance exists, attitudes tend to reinforce one another. Thus, there is a tendency to resist change. Furthermore, the consumer has more at stake when several beliefs are at stake rather than one. The consumer tends toward self-protection by holding on to personal attitudes. A consumer's attitude toward products or stores of the same class affect each other if they are strengthened or weakened. If the housewife's attitude toward the new cold-water detergent product is weakened by new information, the attitude toward all other detergents in the same class may be changed in either of two ways. The attitude toward all cold-water detergents may be weakened or she may disassociate this product from all others in the class. In the latter case, she has reorganized the perceived class of objects.

Causality of attitudes affects stability. If consumers view something as having been the cause of something else, they associate the cause and effect through attitudes. A husband who feels very strongly that grocery prices are unjustifiably high, may carry his negative attitude over to trading stamps or other merchandising techniques. In addition, consumer attitudes toward certain means resemble consumer attitudes toward the ends to which they apply. Cause-effect relationships tend to strengthen and stabilize our attitudes because we can observe direct relationships. A consumer's attitude toward a business is likely to be the same as that toward the salesperson who represents the business.

Congruence conditions attitude stability. Congruence means agreement or harmony of the attitudes of the individual consumer with those of others.[28] Consumers compare attitudes toward the same products or market situations in the same way that they compare other things. Since all consumers justify their own attitudes, it reinforces this opinion to find other consumers in basic agreement. Thus, the attitude tends to be stabilized. Individuals perceive the person who is in agreement with their attitudes as being compatible. This is of particular importance in personal selling, where the situation dictates agreement between the customer and salesperson if the sale is to take place. It also holds for customers' choice of store or trade area.

Factors of instability

Even though consumer attitudes are stable in the short-run, changes do occur.[29] Actually, some consumer attitudes are always changing. When we refer to stability, we mean only a tendency for most consumers' attitudes to remain stable in the short-run. Thus, we actually find a kind of stability in the midst of constant change. The principal reasons for attitude instability are (1) conflict of attitudes, (2) the effect of the situation, (3) the multiplicity of attitudes, and (4) traumatic experience.

Conflict of attitudes affects stability. Consumers have many attitudes, and every individual is a bundle of contradictions. That is to say that, in the thousands of attitudes held by a person, there is never complete consistency. A consumer may have a very favorable attitude toward the color blue, but this person may not like blue on his wife. When attitudes are in conflict, the consumer may have to make compromises. It is a question of which attitude is more important. A man may buy a convertible in spite of an attitude against this style. We would be hasty to conclude that the person was going against his attitudes. We seldom really go against our attitudes. What probably happened to this consumer is that the person, a father, also had a favorable attitude toward his family, and it was the family members who wanted the convertible. In this case, the father compromised the two attitudes in favor of pleasing his family. He still gets a car, but his attitude toward the family determines the type of car. A consumer may favor expensive clothes; but this consumer may purchase more modest clothes because of an attitude toward thrift.

Situation affects attitudes. Because of variations in the situation, one finds a considerable amount of variation in consumer behavior. Some of this variation appears opposed to the consumer's known attitudes. However, this is usually not the case. In spite of the fact that we expect behavior to reflect attitudes, we must remember that consumer behavior results from many stimuli. In addition to the direct stimuli found in the situation, there are many indirect stimuli that are at work on the individual.[30] As the total situation becomes more complex, it becomes more difficult for the person to respond in any simple way. Consumer behavior is strongly influenced by the individual's background and experience, as well as what the person perceives in the present situation.

A consumer may purchase a given bedroom suite because the salesperson was very persuasive, or because a friend prompted the action, or because the consumer's guard was not up sufficiently at the time of the purchase. In short, the situation may have a great bearing on its outcome in spite of the consumer's specific attitude.[31] The consumer's attitudes are not necessarily changed, but, at the time of the purchase, these attitudes were not as strong as some others. It must be remembered that an individual who has thousands of attitudes on a great many subjects cannot wear them all on his or her sleeve. It is actually possible that an attitude may momentarily become lost in the complexity of the mind. Of course, this is not likely with an attitude the consumer considers important. We must also make room for simple impulse when considering the influence of the total situation on attitudes. Political pollsters must face the fact that a nominal Republican promises to vote Republican, but casts a straight Democratic ticket on election day. The same thing happens to consumers. The trade-in allowance, doubts about safety, or impulse may cause a person to override established attitudes.

Multiple attitudes and instability. The more complex a purchase situation is, the more of the thousands of attitudes held by a person that are likely to apply to the situation. These multiple attitudes often come into conflict, but rather than compromising, as we previously explained, the individual may choose one attitude, or one group of attitudes, over others. Thus, the conservative consumer who buys a gaudy suit may be expressing the totality of his or her complex attitudes. The consumer is not going against these attitudes, but is simply allowing one attitude to be dominant over the others. The strength of the attitudes held plays an obvious part in the decision. Attitude strength may also combine with the situation to lead to a specific action. Take the case of a woman considering a new dress. This woman may simultaneously have attitudes toward the color, style, price, the impression she will make, and comfort. Who is to say that she is being inconsistent to buy the dress in which she will make the greatest impression rather than the one with the color she likes best?

Traumatic experience. Attitudes may develop quickly as a result of some traumatic experience involving a great deal of emotion. The attitude one has toward seat belts can be changed very quickly from neutral to positive as a result of an accident. Unexpected good treatment by a salesclerk can create a positive attitude toward a store. Normally, the formation of attitudes is not so quick but depends on repeated exposure. Attitudes that result from traumatic experience often are not as lasting as those that develop more slowly.

HOW CONSUMER ATTITUDES CHANGE

Although there is a necessary degree of stability in the attitudes held by consumers, these attitudes are not static. As a matter of fact, it is just as important to the consumer that attitudes change over time as it is to have short-run stability of attitudes. Attitude stability gives our actions continuity, but attitude change allows one to develop as a person and as a consumer.[32]

It would be a dull world indeed if no one ever changed their mind, if no enemy could be won over, if no woman who said no could be convinced to marry. A person's attitudes are the best guide to what a person feels and believes. These attitudes really constitute what a person is. If it were not for a willingness of people to change, there could be no improved technology, because people would not accept the improvement. It is interesting to note that American consumers not only are willing to change but they seek change. Ours is a nation built on technology. Our people are not satisfied with the status quo. All these changes are brought about through changing attitudes. There are a number of specific factors which cause a consumer's attitudes to change.

Change in the product

If the product itself is changed and information is received by consumers about the change, their attitudes may be affected. Often this is the simplest and easiest way to get people to change their attitudes. A slight change in the packaging of a consumer product may quite literally be 10 times more effective than all other advertising or personal selling efforts. A change in the properties of the product are readily observable to people, and sellers do not have to rely as much on persuasion and argument to convince the customer that something is different from before. There are many things a seller can change besides the product. The seller can change service, the attitude of salespeople, or prices. It is often very effective to change the physical appearance of the store. Modernizing can lead to a completely new attitude toward it on the part of the customers. A new location can have the same effect.

Perceptual change

There are many instances where attitude change can be brought about by new perceptions even though the product or store remains the same. The receipt of new information may modify consumer attitudes because it changes perception of the properties of the product or the situation. A change in product price or product content can cause the consumer to reevaluate his or her conception of the product. A change in promotion can also be effective. For example, many marketers have been concerned about the effect of putting blacks in advertisements. The worry was that the whites, who comprise the bulk of the market, would reject products that use blacks in their appeal. A recent study, although not conclusive, sheds some light on the current white attitude.[33] This study reported the attitudes toward the purchase of soap of over 13,000 white respondents. Three end-isle, point-of-sale purchase displays with life-sized female models were used. Some displays used black models and some white. The results show no significant difference in the purchase of soap by whites as a result of the use of black models or white models.

The subjective characteristic of perception may lead to a change in attitude even though there is actually nothing new in the situation. The important thing is that the consumer believes that the situation has changed. New information that does not fit well with our preexisting attitudes may be ignored or misinterpreted. Thus, there may be no change in attitude where a change is actually called for. An effective sales or advertising campaign can lead to a perceived change in a company's operations whether such a change has actually occurred or not.

Change in strength of the attitude

It appears that weak attitudes are more susceptible to change than those attitudes which are stronger or more extreme. A weak consumer attitude may be either positive or negative. The weakest attitude is a neutral feeling. In a study of 405 college students' attitude change toward legalized gambling, abstract art, and accelerated programs, it was found that students with either strong favorable or unfavorable attitudes underwent the least change in their original position upon the addition of new information. Those students without strong favorable or unfavorable attitudes and relatively weak attitudes toward the topics underwent the greatest change. Even a strong attitude can be changed if it is systematically attacked. It may be necessary to give a strong, but sound, reason for the change. Repetition is also effective for changing strong attitudes. The attitude is chipped away a little at a time.

Change in store of information

Consumers having a limited amount of information about the product or firm are more susceptible to a change in attitude than are those with greater storage of information.[34] With limited information, contradictory information is more likely to bring about an attitude change than when a large amount of information is present. Marketers are well aware of the difficulties involved in breaking into a market where large doses of effective informational advertising has caused brand preference. The attitudes of children and poorly educated persons are more easily influenced with respect to certain attitudes than are those of adults or people with higher education. Children are exposed to different types of information, to some degree, than adults. One rather comprehensive study of children's responses to advertising provides the following results:

1. Children 5–9 watched more children's programs, movies, and family programs. The 9–12 age group watched more adventure, education, and sports programs.
2. The younger children were exposed to more food, gum, and toy commercials, while older children viewed more drug, patent medicine, and "all other" type commercials.
3. Both groups gave full attention to the television before the commercial, but only about 39 percent of the older children continued to give full attention during the commercial. Younger children tended to continue giving full attention during the commercial.
4. About 20 percent of older children, compared to many fewer younger children, expressed a negative reaction to commercial onset.[35]

Children are usually brought up to respect their elders' judgment, because these children have little information with which they can evaluate many objects. Thus, the effects of advertising vary due to the educational level of the appeals used in the ads. The amount of information present is not only limited by age and education. Even highly educated persons may revise their attitudes when given new information. Certainly, this fact accounts for much of the brand switching that goes on in the market.

Change in product importance

Attitudes toward products that are psychologically important to consumers and central to everyday actions are not likely to change. These are the objects about which consumers have amassed the most information, and attitudes toward them tend to be stable. Those attitudes held toward products that are less important are more susceptible to change with the presence of additional information. A housewife responsible for the weekly grocery shopping and subsequent feedings of her family, finds products related to these activities more central than the remote problem of the United States' balance of payments. Although she may have some meaningful attitudes toward the balance-of-payments problem, these are based on little information and may be readily changed by rather small amounts of new information. Accomplishing a change in attitude toward her family's food requirement is not easy.

Change in communications

Attitudes are not easily changed from unfavorable to favorable or vice versa. This is because consumers tend to avoid information that is inconsistent with their present attitude structure. Crane suggests that to bring about a change in attitudes by marketing communications, three alternatives are possible.

1. Existing products may be given new labels which affect both their content and evaluation of them.
2. The product itself may be changed by changing the attributes that are used in constructing it or by urging audiences to move toward larger or smaller classifications.
3. Changes may be made in the way the product is evaluated. This can either be done directly or by influencing the values of related categories.[36]

In effect, communications can be used to change the product, change the consumer's perception of the product, or change the way a consumer evaluates an object. A change in one attitude affects others, due to consumer attempts to make information and attitudes hold consistent. Consumers tend to rely on nationally advertised brands because they trust the communications to be truthful, and because consumers feel no one can afford to spend a lot of money on communications without a good product. We must also remember that the effectiveness of the presentation also influences consumers.

CONSUMER ATTITUDES AND BUSINESS POLICY

It is impossible to cite all the ways that consumer attitudes affect business policy. At every point where there is either direct or indirect contact between customers and business, there are attitudes formed on both sides. In designing promotional strategy, marketers use a knowledge of attitudes to appeal to favorable opinions and beliefs. A knowledge of attitudes can be helpful in getting consumer attention and in meeting objections to the product. Of course, the promoter hopes to be able to appeal in a positive way to positive, deep-seated beliefs held by a large number of consumers.[37] Marketers also use a knowledge of feelings and opinions as a basis for inducing brand patronage switching. It is easier to get consumers to switch where their feelings or opinions are concerned.

The store strategy of marketers also reflects consumer attitudes. Store locations take into account customer attitudes toward travel, specific sites, congestion, traffic flow, etc. The exterior and interior design and layout are used to attract attention to make shopping easier and generally build favorable attitudes toward shopping in the store. Most marketers work hard to get employees to build customer goodwill by knowing their products and by treating customers honestly, promptly, and with respect. Many stores emphasize services as a means of creating favorable attitudes on the part of customers.

Product strategy also builds on creating positive attitudes. Marketers focus on specific product features that create a good impression, and they tend to avoid negative features. Stores cater to the positive attitudes customers have toward shopping for several products at a time and their belief in comparing, where large-ticket products are concerned. Product price is featured when the executive feels it can create a favorable attitude; and other product features are stressed when price is felt not to be favorable or competitive.

There is a great need for more attitude research. Advertisers probably do the most in this direction. Advertisers investigate consumer attitudes toward entire-advertisement and specific-ad features. This information is used in designing ads. Advertisers are also noted for their work in motivation research. More work is needed on customer attitudes toward new products and brands; sensitive messages; identification of features affecting shopping behavior; store and product images; attitude formation and change; and attitudes affecting product choice.

NOTES

1. Michael B. Mazis, Olli T. Ahtola, and R. Eugene Klippel, "A Comparison of Four Multi-Attribute Models in the Prediction of Consumer Attitudes," *Journal of Consumer Research,* vol. 2 (June 1975), pp. 38–52.
2. Thomas S. Robertson, *Consumer Behavior* (Glenview, Ill.: Scott, Foresman & Co., 1970), pp. 53–55.
3. Robert A. Baron, Donn Byrne, and William Griffitt, *Social Psychology* (Boston: Allyn and Bacon, Inc., 1974), pp. 164–65.
4. G. David Hughes, *Attitude Measurement for Marketing Strategies* (Glenview, Ill.: Scott, Foresman & Co., 1971), pp. 9–10.
5. Ibid.
6. Milton Rokeach, *Beliefs, Attitudes, and Values* (San Francisco: Jossey-Bass, Inc., 1968).
7. John Petrof, "Attitudes of the Urban Poor Toward Their Neighborhood Supermarkets," *Phylon,* vol. 31 (Fall 1970), pp. 190–301.
8. D. Katz, "The Functional Approach to the Study of Attitudes," *Public Opinion Quarterly,* vol. 24 (Summer 1960), pp. 163–204.
9. Robertson, *Consumer Behavior,* p. 61.
10. Homer E. Spence and Reza Moinpour, "Fear Appeals in Marketing—A Social Perspective," *Journal of Marketing,* vol. 36 (July 1972), pp. 39–43.
11. John R. Stuteville, "Psychic Defenses against High Fear Appeals: A Key Marketing Variable," *Journal of Marketing,* vol. 34 (April 1970), pp. 39–45.
12. Robertson, *Consumer Behavior,* p. 62.
13. Ibid.
14. D. A. Oaker and G. S. Day, "Dynamic Model of Relationships Among Advertising, Consumer Awareness, Attitudes and Behavior," *Journal of Applied Psychology,* vol. 59 (June 1974), pp. 281–86.
15. Michael B. Maxis, Robert B. Settle, and Dennis C. Leslie, "Elimination of Phosphate Detergents and Psychological Reactance," *Journal of Marketing Research,* vol. 10 (November 1973), pp. 390–95.
16. Hughes, *Attitude Measurement for Marketing Strategies,* pp. 10–11.
17. Albert V. Bruno and Albert R. Wildt, "Toward Understanding Attitude Structure: A Study of the Complimentarity of Multi-Attribute Attitude Models," *Journal of Consumer Research,* vol. 2 (September 1975), pp. 137–45; J. R. Bettman, "Relationship of Information Processing Attitude Structures to Private Brand Purchasing Behavior," *Journal of Applied Psychology,* vol. 59 (Fall 1974), pp. 79–83.

18. Peter L. Wright, "The Cognitive Processes Mediating Acceptance of Advertising," *Journal of Marketing Research,* vol. 10 (February 1973), pp. 53–62.
19. Ibid.
20. Robert E. Wilkes and James B. Wilcox, "Consumer Perceptions of Product Warranties and Their Implications for Retail Strategy," *Journal of Business Research,* vol. 4 (February 1976), pp. 35–43.
21. Robert E. Burnkrant and Alain Cousineau, "Informational and Normative Social Influence in Buyer Behavior," *Journal of Consumer Research,* vol. 2 (December 1975), pp. 206–15.
22. Terrence V. O'Brien, "Tracking Consumer Decision Making," *Journal of Marketing,* vol. 35 (January 1971), pp. 34–40.
23. Jon G. Udell, "Can Attitude Measurement Predict Consumer Behavior?" Journal of Marketing, vol. 29 (1965), pp. 46–50; Hughes, *Attitude Measurement for Marketing Strategies;* George S. Day, *Buyer Attitudes and Brand Choice Behavior* (New York: The Free Press, 1970).
24. Frank M. Bass, Edgar A. Pessemier, and Donald R. Lehmann, "An Experimental Study of Relationships Between Attitude, Brand, Preference, and Choice," *Behavioral Science,* vol. 17 (November 1972), pp. 532–41.
25. Martin Fishbein, "The Search for Attitudinal-Behavioral Consistency," *Perspectives in Consumer Behavior,* rev. ed., eds. Harold H. Kassarjian and Thomas S. Robertson (Glenview, Ill.: Scott, Foresman & Co., 1973), pp. 210–20.
26. Seymour Banks, "The Relationships between Preference and Purchase of Brands," *Journal of Marketing,* vol. 15 (1950), pp. 145–57.
27. John U. Farley, John A. Howard, and L. Winston Ring, *Consumer Behavior: Theory and Application* (Boston: Allyn & Bacon, Inc., 1974), Chap. 7.
28. Paul E. Green, Yoram Wind, and Arun K. Jain, "A Note on Measurement of Social-Psychological Belief Systems," *Journal of Marketing Research,* vol. 9 (May 1972), pp. 204–08.
29. Farley, Howard, and Ring, *Consumer Behavior: Theory and Application,* Chap. 7.
30. R. Ted Will and Ronald W. Hasty, "Attitude Measurement Under Conditions of Multiple Stimuli," *Journal of Marketing,* vol. 35 (January 1971), pp. 66–70.
31. Russell W. Belk, "Occurrence of Word of Mouth Buyer Behavior as a Function of Situation and Advertising Stimuli," *Relevance in Marketing: Problems, Research, Action,* ed. Fred C. Allvine (Chicago: American Marketing Assn., 1971), pp. 419–22.
32. James L. Ginter, "An Experimental Investigation of Attitude Change and Choice of a New Brand," *Journal of Marketing Research,* vol. 11 (February 1974), pp. 30–40; C. A. Kiesler, B. E. Collins, and N. Miller, *Attitude Change: A Critical Analysis of Theoretical Approaches* (New York: John Wiley & Sons, Inc., 1969).
33. Ronald F. Bush, Robert F. Gwinner, and Paul J. Solomon, "White Con-

sumer Sales Response to Black Models," *Journal of Marketing*, vol. 38 (April 1974), pp. 25–29.

34. Vithala R. Rao, "Changes in Explicit Information and Brand Perceptions," *Journal of Marketing Research*, vol. 9 (May 1972), pp. 209–13.
35. Scott Ward, "Advertising and Youth: Research Problems," *Sloan Management Review*, vol. 14 (Fall 1972), pp. 63–82.
36. E. Crane, *Marketing Communications* (New York: John Wiley & Sons, Inc., 1965), pp. 65–66.
37. Harper W. Boyd, Jr., Michael L. Ray, and Edward C. Strong, "An Attitudinal Framework for Advertising Strategy," *Journal of Marketing*, vol. 36 (April 1972), pp. 27–33.

QUESTIONS

1. What is an attitude? How does it differ from perception? Discuss the different types of attitudes.
2. Contrast the adjustment function, ego-defensive function, and the value expressive function. What is their importance to consumer behavior?
3. What is meant by attitude properties? Explain readiness to act. Relate attitude polarity to intensity.
4. What is attitude structure? How does this structure affect consumer behavior? Give examples from your own experience.
5. Discuss personal experience, external authorities, and culture as possible sources of attitudes. Which is most important?
6. Does consumer behavior conform to attitudes? Why or why not? Defend your position.
7. Explain the effect of structure, causality and congruence on attitude stability. Contrast causality and congruence.
8. What is meant by attitude instability? Can you give examples from your own experience? Explain the factors of attitude instability.
9. Explain how consumer attitudes change. Of what importance is this fact of change to business executives? Explain.
10. Discuss the importance of attitudes to business.

14

The effect of learning on consumer behavior

Consumer attitudes, perceptions, and motives are not automatically acquired, nor do these determinants always occur fully developed. Consumer positions are developed over a period of time as a result of learning. While the behavior of an infant is sometimes random and often diffused, the adult's energy is mobilized toward specific goals in a more selective manner. The difference between the behavior of the adult and that of the child is based on learning. In this chapter, we consider the important questions associated with learned behavior.

LEARNING DEFINED

Like most ideas, learning can be viewed in more than one way.[1] Psychologists generally consider *learning* to be:

> *any change in an individual's response or behavior resulting from practice, experience or mental association.*[2]

To some, learning is the change that results, and to others, it is the process of arriving at the change through practice, experience, or mental association. Actually, learning implies both as the definition points out. The difficulty is that the learning process cannot be observed—only the results of learning or of what has been learned is observable.[3] We see that a consumer is continually drawn to a single brand of watch (brand loyalty) or that after watching several TV commercials, a consumer changes his or her habit of purchasing a certain brand of dog food. We cannot observe the actual learning that led to these behavior patterns or to changes in them, only the behavior itself. It is known that learning (1) is goal oriented, (2) involves associations that may lead to habitual responses, and (3) requires reinforcement of responses taken. More is said about these factors later.

LEARNING AND FORGETTING

Consumer learning and consumer forgetting go hand in hand.[4] *Forgetting* is the loss, or extinction, of a thought process once held in the mind. A particular purchase pattern, once learned by the consumer, can never be unlearned, but the pattern can be repressed into the unconscious mind.[5] This repression of thought is essentially what we mean by forgetting. The fact that thoughts are never completely lost to the mind is indicated by ability of persons to remember with vivid clarity, under hypnosis, things forgotten.

Forgetting serves a useful purpose in consumer behavior. It is difficult to imagine the effect on a person of total recall. The mind would be continually cluttered with useless or unnecessary information about products, stores, buying experiences, etc. Furthermore, it would be almost impossible for a person to face up to the constant reminder of all pleasant, embarrassing, desirable, or painful market experiences. Forgetting allows the mind to file away unneeded or unwanted information, thus making room for new experiences, current experiences, or relevant experiences. It focuses the person's mind on the anticipation of the future rather than a re-living of the past. This is an altogether healthy situation. Of course, forgetting works both ways. If one can forget that which is unpleasant, it is necessary to forget that which is pleasant. The knife cuts both ways.

Frequently, information that has been forgotten can be brought back by careful, intense concentration. Thus ideas about products, stores, advertisements, etc. that have been forgotten can be recalled when the need arises again. Sometimes forgotten information is brought back to the conscious mind without further experience or effort. This unaided recall is referred to as *spontaneous recovery.*[6] Spontaneous recovery can occur at any time when the consumer is least expecting it, or even when the information is not particularly needed.

The effects of forgetting

The fact that individuals forget affects consumer behavior in three important ways. First, forgetting makes purchase reinforcement necessary. Because consumers do not automatically remember products, brands, stores, services, and prices, information or rewards must be repeated over and over to effect desired responses. This is why repetitive advertising can sometimes be more effective than one-time advertising. Second, forgetting fosters consumer change.[7] Consumers forget old brand loyalties, purchase strategies, and assortment preferences. This opens the door for new brands and preferences. Third, the fact that consumers forget makes continuous repetition necessary, at least on a periodic basis. This is true even where the consumer is sold on the store, brand, price, or service. The use of reminder advertising is based on this principle.

Patterns of consumer forgetting

Four points are important concerning forgetting.[8]

1. Consumers forget information at about the same rate no matter how important or meaningful it may be.
2. Consumers forget very rapidly just after learning.
3. Understanding the information retards the consumer's forgetting.
4. Consumers recognize brands, slogans, sales appeals, and so forth, easier than they can recall this information.

These facts help explain why consumers sometimes cannot recall advertisements or other information just perceived. These points also add weight to the use of reminder advertising; presentation of nonsense slogans, brands, and jingles, courtesy calls by salesmen; use of increased shelf space; and catchy brand names.

WHAT CONSUMERS LEARN

Consumer behavior involves learning at two different levels, one essentially mental and the other essentially physical.[9] On the first, and more basic, level, the consumer must learn thought processes. These thought processes involve the consumer's beliefs, preferences, feelings, opinions, and mental associations:

1. A consumer learns to associate a green giant with canned vegetables.
2. A consumer learns that one department gives efficient service and another doesn't.
3. A consumer learns to prefer Manhattan shirts.

On the other level, the consumer learns specific physical behavior. This behavior may be in the form of a direct action to satisfy an inner desire or a specific reaction to an unforeseen market stimuli. Thus, learned physical behavior always involves previously learned attitudes:

1. A consumer learns that one route to the shopping center is faster than another.
2. A consumer learns that one haggles over the price of furniture in one store but not in another.
3. A consumer learns a specific reaction to an advertisement for a detergent.

Nearly all consumer behavior involves learning at both levels, but the learning does not necessarily occur at the same time. Actions may be learned long after the attitudes have been formed. New attitudes may be formed as a result of specific behavior. For example, a young lady requires both types of learning for the purchase and use of makeup. She learns attitudes toward the use of makeup, attitudes toward particular brands, specific actions in applying makeup, and specific actions in obtaining the makeup.

Whether dealing with thought processes or behavior, the consumer learns both what is right or acceptable and what is wrong or unacceptable. We have a habit of thinking of learning in terms of its positive aspects, perhaps as a result of its association with school. Certainly, everything learned is both new and useful. However, new and useful information can just as easily pertain to *avoidance* thoughts or behavior as to *seeking-out* thoughts or behavior. Consumers learn, often by trial, to avoid certain clerks in a store. They learn that specific brands are not suited for their purposes, and they learn to avoid certain stores.[10] Consumers also learn to avoid shopping during the rush hour, to avoid putting off the payment of bills, and to avoid unlawful market activity.

ELEMENTS OF CONSUMER LEARNING

There are various methods by which one can learn, but three factors are basic to all these learning processes: the existence of some stimulus, a response to the situation, and reinforcement of the response.[11] We say that learning has occurred when the person can make the correct response each time the stimulus occurs. The three factors are common to all learning, but, of course, we are interested in how consumers learn.

Need for an object stimulus

The first requirement necessary for learning is an object stimulus.[12] The *object stimulus* is any environmental object, perceived by the individual, that can trigger market action. Actually, for a stimulus to exist, there must be a perceived object and motivation.

Perceived object. The *object* referred to in the definition of an object stimulus is a type of learning goal. It is the focus of attention that makes learning necessary to acquire the object. This object has three characteristics worthy of mention: It can be a direct or indirect goal, physical or mental, or market related or not.

As used here, the word object does not refer necessarily to a physical thing. The consumer can be stimulated by such physical things as products, brands, size, location, or number, but intangibles such as service, quality, and satisfaction can also be the object stimulus to consumer learning. Although the object is a consumer-learning goal, the object can be either a direct or an indirect goal. With a *direct object* the consumer learns because of direct satisfaction anticipated from the object. A consumer may learn the brand, price, and location of a new type of watch because of the direct satisfaction of ownership. An *indirect object* causes learning about an intermediate product necessary to satisfy the object. Thus a young man may learn how to obtain a particular cologne because of the indirect goal of a date with a specific young woman. In any case, it is the object that stimulates the consumer to learn and not necessarily the physical thing. Notice in the above example that the cologne desired for its own sake is a market-related object. A date is not a market-related object, but it leads to market-related learning.

Stimulus motivation. It is not enough that the consumer perceive the object. There can be no learning unless the consumer is motivated to seek the object. We have already discussed motives, and there is no need to repeat the discussion at this point. Suffice it to say that the consumer must perceive the object, and he must have a desire to obtain the object, before learning can occur. The longer the consumer is deprived of the goal, the greater the attempt to learn. Also, the stronger the motivation, the quicker the consumer learns. For example, a male consumer learns the brand, slogan, and so on, quicker from a commercial featuring a fishing reel he has wanted for some time than he learns the same facts about hair spray.

Consumer response to the situation

The response a consumer gives regarding a situation, like the object stimulus, can be physical or mental. A *response* is any action, reaction, or state of mind taken because of a particular object stimulus. The same response to a stimulus may occur several times before one can say that the response is learned. When a person jerks the hand from a fire, he or she has made a simple response to the heat of the fire. A more complex response is illustrated by a person moving from the sun into the shade. A man rushing downtown to buy three suits for $100 is making a physical response, but a woman taking a favorable attitude toward a beer commercial is making a mental response. In order to understand learned responses, we must delve into response characteristics and stimulus-response associations. We must also consider correct and incorrect responses.

Response characteristics. Consumer responses display the characteristics of speed, frequency, and amplitude. *Speed* is the quickness with which the response occurs. Speed can vary from almost immediate to considerably delayed. Some situations require more immediate responses than others. For example, a person can react immediately to a salesperson, but the response to a television commercial must necessarily take some time. On the other hand, the consumer may take more or less time before buying after either the sales pitch or the commerical. *Frequency* is the number of responses or the number of correct responses in a given time period. The more frequently the consumer responds in a manner consistent with the marketer's desires, the more nearly habitual is that consumer's behavior.[13] Some products require more frequent responses than others. *Amplitude* is the positiveness of the response. Even if a consumer buys a given product, the purchase may be made with high or low conviction and enthusiasm. For example, a consumer who is simply trying out a product does not have the same positive attitude as a long standing purchaser. It is a general rule that learning increases as the speed of the response, the frequency of correct responses, and the positiveness of the response increases.

Stimulus-response association. The idea of association is basic to learning. It is by association that the stimulus and responses are brought together.[14] The accomplishment of association is not always easy. For example, one of the more difficult tasks any marketer faces is to get consumers to associate some specific satisfaction with a product. In spite of repeated advertising and personal selling, many consumers never get the message.

Three factors that make association difficult for consumers are discrimination, generalization, and sampling.[15] *Discrimination* is a tendency of some consumers not to associate a response with a similar stimulus. A consumer likes Schlitz beer but does not associate this like with another brand. *Generalization* is the tendency of some consumers to have the same response when faced with a similar stimulus. A marketer's use of a family of products takes advantage of this tendency. General Motors associates the goodwill of its name with several brands of automobiles. *Sampling* refers to a consumer tendency to consider only a few stimuli out of a whole hierarchy that affect a given stimulus. Only the response associated with the sampled stimuli are learned. Thus, a similar situation, where different stimuli are sampled, may lead to a different response by the consumer.

Correct and incorrect responses. The question of whether the learned response of a consumer is correct or not may depend on the point of view. In a market situation, the executive may want one type of response from the consumer, and the consumer may want to give an entirely different response.[16] For example, a proper response from the business point of view may be to purchase brand X.[17] Thus, the consumer responded incorrectly if he or she purchases brand Y. The consumer may find the response incorrect should brand Y prove to be unsatisfactory. Because consumers fail so frequently to respond in a manner desired by marketers, a great deal of money is spent by business on personal selling and advertising. This is also why marketers must attempt to sell to some target market where there is an improved chance of obtaining a desired response.

Consumers often make incorrect responses from their own point of view. Perhaps the consumer makes an incorrect association, or perhaps the association doesn't register, or it could be that the association is not strong enough to evoke a correct response. For example, soft-drink commercials may repel some older customers because of the emphasis on youth and "way-out" music. A housewife may pass up a better detergent because she dislikes the company's advertising. When the consumer becomes aware that incorrect responses have been made, he or she should forget these responses and attempt to develop the correct responses.[18] If an incorrect response has become firmly entrenched, it can be difficult to change.

Reinforcement of the response

The third factor that directly affects consumer learning is reinforcement.[19] There is some confusion in the literature over the meaning of reinforcement. The tendency among psychologists, even though the language does differ among sources, is to equate reinforcement and reward when referring to learning. This is the manner in which the terms are used in this discussion.

Reinforcement, or reward, can be defined in either of two ways depending on the intended use. Viewed as a result, *reinforcement*, or *reward*, is the satisfaction resulting from successful behavior which triggers human memory of how the satisfaction was obtained.[20] Viewed as an inducement, reinforcement is the probability that a given response to a specific stimuli will re-occur given the same stimuli and situation. That is to say, reinforcement is the thing that causes the individual to relate the response to the stimulus correctly. In this latter sense, reinforcement is more or less repetitive behavior that establishes future behavior. In the following paragraphs, we discuss the function of reinforcement, types of reinforcement, and the three laws of reinforcement.

Function of reinforcement. Some reward is necessary for learning to take place. It is the fact that rewards occur in conjunction with stimuli that cause responses to be learned. The learning occurs because the reward is desired. Thus, because a housewife has neighbors call twice a week for coffee made with a certain brand (stimulus) and comment on the flavor of the coffee served (reward), the housewife may learn to prefer that brand of coffee (response). There is evidence that the timing of the reward, or reinforcement, affects learning. Learning tends to increase:

1. As the number of reinforcements increase.
2. When there are rest periods between responses.
3. As the size of the reward increases.
4. When rewards are intermittent or varied.
5. When there is little time lapse between the response and the reward.[21]

Types of reinforcement. Reinforcement can be classified as: (1) tangible or intangible, (2) positive or negative, and (3) primary or secondary. A *tangible reward* is derived from making a correct response to the stimulus. For example, the good health one obtains from proper eating habits is a tangible reinforcement causing one to continue eating properly. A successful purchase is also a tangible reinforcement. *Intangible rewards* are mental, and they are derived from participating in the response. The good feeling one gets while swimming or the pleasure of viewing a well stocked retail store are mental reinforcements. There is no definitive evidence to suggest that one of these types of reinforcement is more effective than the other. Each can lead to effective learning.

Positive and negative reinforcement have to do with compensation and penalty.[22] *Positive reinforcement* is compensation oriented. The idea is that one is more likely to make the correct response to a stimulus if some pleasure, favorable treatment, payment, etc. is expected.[23] We return to stores where clerks are pleasant and attentive; we make repeat purchases of products that satisfy, and frequent trade areas that are accessible. *Negative reinforcement* is penalty oriented. It is based on the concept that a person will repeat certain behavior in order to avoid the penalty of not performing. For example, a child may be good to avoid getting spanked. Consumers purchase hairpieces to avoid the penalty of showing their baldness, individuals do not shoplift for fear of legal action, and some persons avoid shopping downtown to avoid the penalty of heavy traffic and parking problems.

Scholars debate whether positive or negative reinforcement is more effective. The answer is not easily determined. In a broad sense, every consumer decision involves both compensation and penalty. They travel in pairs. If one avoids pain, one obtains the compensation of feeling good. However, for a particular consumer, making a specific purchase, one or the other factor typically dominates learning. Importance varies with the person and the situation. A woman buying perfume is hardly conscious of the penalty of doing without. On the other hand, she may be acutely aware of the penalty of not putting anti-freeze in the car.

Primary reinforcement occurs when there is a direct bond between a stimulus and a response as a result of a reward. When a customer drinks a coke, primary reinforcement takes place. *Secondary reinforcement* occurs because some stimulus occurs in conjunction with the primary stimulus. The secondary stimulus becomes associated with the primary satisfaction. Thus, if the consumer meets a good friend while drinking the coke, the two satisfactions tend to become fused, increasing the pleasure of the coke and aiding the response to buy a coke next time the person is thirsty.

Three laws of reinforcement. The laws of effect, exercise, and readiness greatly influence consumer learning. First, the *law of effect* concerns the repetition of a satisfactory response. Once an association, or bond, is established between a stimulus (food), a response (eat out), and satisfaction (hunger relief) the connection is strengthened by repetition. A very strong consumer association may become habit. If an association is followed by dissatisfaction, the connection is weakened. However, there is evidence that disuse does not lessen the bond.

Once a connection has been made, a type of conditioning may take place. If the subject is placed in the same situation again, it takes him or her less time to discover the solution to the problem. This process is called the *law of exercise*. Just as an athlete gets better with exercise, so a consumer gets better at finding the way to a shopping center, deciding where to go for certain types of purchases and discovering reasonable interest charges to pay on credit, as he or she exercises his responses.

The *law of readiness* refers to the fact that no learning can take place unless the subject has the ability and willingness to solve the problem. Some consumers qualify on this point more than others.

CONSUMERS LEARN IN DIFFERENT WAYS

All consumers learn, but not all consumers learn the same things, nor do they learn at the same speed or in the same manner.[24] The basic elements, stimulus-response-reinforcement are found in all learning, but there are differences in their use and application. There are two broad categories of learning theory—connectionist and cognitive—and each has its own variations.

Connectionist theories

The connectionists explain learning almost entirely by the association of stimulus and response. The proper response is learned by rote memory, and there is little room for perception and insight. There is little question but that much learning is of this type. Although there are differences among the connectionists, these differences can be demonstrated by the classical conditioning and pleasure-pain theories.

Classical conditioning. Classical conditioning holds that learning is a matter of conditioning.[25] The basic idea is that two ideas presented together are considered together providing there is something to connect them in the individual's mind. It is the possibility of a reward that connects the objects or ideas. Pavlov's experiments with dogs are now famous.[26] By associating the ringing of a bell with food, Pavlov was able to get dogs to secrete saliva by ringing the bell alone. Thus, two completely unrelated ideas can be related by having each idea associated with a reward. The method can be reversed, causing extinction or forgetting. If the stimulus is given without the reward, the response will gradually cease. Furthermore, the method is not perfect. An incorrect response can occur even after many correct responses.

Marketers often rely on conditioned responses to reach consumers. Most reminder advertising falls in this category. In all kinds of selling, some reward is associated with the seller's product in an attempt to get the consumer to buy. Habitual purchasing is another example of conditioned response. Individuals can be conditioned to favor products, brands, stores, prices, and services.

Pleasure-pain theory. The pleasure-pain theory is similar to the classical conditioned response theory. The idea is that people seek pleasure and avoid pain. Individuals must learn by association which things give pleasure and which give pain. Certainly, the pleasure-pain concept helps to explain consumer behavior. A consumer may give in to a salesperson because it is painful to argue further. Products are bought to avoid the pain of embarrassment or rejection by the group. Because shopping involves the pain of inconvenience, a consumer may purchase at the nearest location in spite of higher prices.

Cognitive theories

The cognitive theories are founded on Man's ability to think and associate facts to solve problems. These theorists discount reinforcement and conditioning for learning and emphasize Man's insight. The attitude of the cognitive theorist is that individuals learn from past history *plus insight.*[27] A person observing a stimulus and a response can think through the connection between the two. The reward may be nothing more than solving the problem. The two important cognitive theories are problem solving and experience.

Problem-solving theory. Problem solving does not depend on conditioning the central nervous system; rather, it depends on thinking through to solutions. When a subject is presented with a problem, logic is used to arrive at a solution. Sometimes the solution results from inspiration when the connection suddenly happens. More likely, answers result from logically connecting elements, systematically considering alternatives, and so on. Thus, thinking individuals employ organized behavior to seek the solution to a problem. The original solution is not left to chance.

Consumers use problem-solving techniques every day. A consumer, new to a city, uses problem solving to decide on preferred stores. Problem solving may be involved when a person tries a new product. A consumer observing a new product for the first time may, by its very features, determine both its use and its benefit.

Experience theory. The concept of learning through experience is similar to problem solving, and in some elementary forms it is similar to the conditioned response. The basic idea is that when faced with a problem, the consumer will apply previous methods or solutions to the problem. If the theory involves only trial and error to discover a solution coupled with reinforcement, then it is a connectionist theory.[28] The theory becomes cognitive in nature when insight is applied to experience. For example, insight may be used to apply previous solutions to similar problems or the person may perceive that if certain individual elements used in the past were applied together, they will work for the present problem.

Consumers use experience to build upon. For example, experience with a long established detergent may be used to evaluate a new detergent by the same company. A new brand is perceived for its function and benefit because of previous knowledge about competing brands. Of course, experience is also used to establish purchase routines in terms of stores to visit, time of the day to shop, and brand to buy.

THE LEARNING CURVE

What we refer to as learning does not usually take place all at once. Learning is an incremental process. That which we learn increases with the number of experiences or trials. Figure 14–1 shows this process. This graph is known as the learning curve.

Figure 14–1

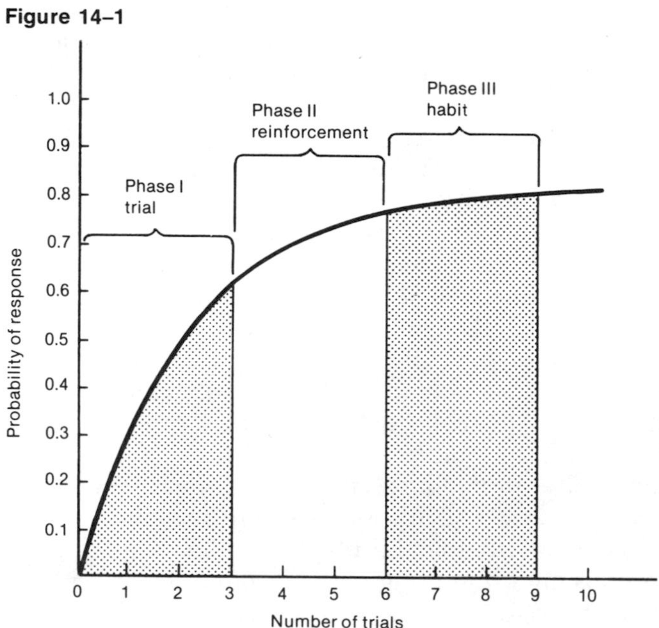

Reprinted, with modification, by permission from John A. Howard, *Marketing Management: Analysis and Planning*, rev. ed. (Homewood, Ill.: Richard D. Irwin, Inc., 1963), p. 36.

On the graph, the number of trials is plotted on the horizontal axis and the probability of a given response is plotted on the vertical axis. The learning curve may apply to a product, a service, a store, or anything that is capable of being learned.[29]

If we assume that the curve refers to the purchase of a particular brand of merchandise, then we find that, after three trials, there is about an 0.62 probability that the person will buy the same brand on the next purchase. The probability of a repeat purchase of the brand is about 0.76 on the sixth trial. By the time we reach the upper limit of the curve, behavior is instantaneous. The rate of learning is small.[30]

The curve is divided into three phases. Phase I is the trial phase. The consumer is problem solving. More time is taken with the decision, and the outcome is less sure. In phase II, decision time has been reduced, and the probability of repeat purchase is greatly increased. At phase III, learning is almost complete, and repeat purchases are automatic and based on habit.

IMPLICATIONS OF LEARNING FOR MARKETERS

There can be no question, from the previous discussion, of the importance of learning to consumers. However, there is ample evidence that learning is equally important to marketers. Several important implications for marketers can be drawn from concepts of learning.

1. Consumers learn in different ways, and what works on one consumer may not work on another. Thus, marketers must study their customers, and marketers must continually relate methods of learning to specific customer types.
2. Marketers, in utilizing promotion, should always associate their product with one or more specific rewards. The importance of rewards to learning has been demonstrated. Consumers respond to benefits, and it is this that marketers must sell rather than physical goods. Consumers tend to be more loyal to brands that satisfy their needs.
3. Time and frequency of product exposure are crucial to purchase. One study shows: *a*. Consumers who frequently purchase orange juice are more likely to purchase it again; *b*. the probability of brand purchase decreases as time between stimuli increases; *c*. buying a particular brand depends on when the brand was last purchased; and *d*. brand loyalty is never absolute. A consumer can be induced to switch by proper methods.
4. Habit introduces efficiency into the purchase process.[31] Habit is learned from repetitive promotion or purchase. Habit aids the business by making the customer more loyal, and habit aids the consumer by reducing purchase decisions where problems have been satisfactorily solved.

5. To induce consumers to purchase new products or to change from previously used products may require large amounts of money and energy on the part of marketers. This fact is true because learning new ideas is more difficult than augmenting those already known. However, the cost can be reduced by associating new products with established products.

6. Credibility of the source is important to how the consumer purchases. Thus, marketers should work to build good reputations for themselves and their products. Exorbitant claims, untruthful promotion, or other devious methods of sale should be avoided. The marketer should work to build repeat sales based on customer satisfaction. Other implications of learning on marketing strategy can be determined. However, these are some of the more important ones.

NOTES

1. For a good review of learning see: Scott Ward and Thomas S. Robertson, *Consumer Behavior: Theoretical Sources* (Englewood Cliffs, N.J.: Prentice-Hall, Inc., 1973), Chap. 2.
2. Jack A. Adams, *Learning and Memory: An Introduction* (Homewood, Ill.: The Dorsey Press, 1976), p. 6.
3. Gregory V. Jones, "A Fragmentation Hypothesis of Memory: Cued Recall of Pictures and of Sequentional Position," *Journal of Experimental Psychology*, vol. 105 (1976), pp. 277–93.
4. Harold H. Kassarjian, "Applications of Consumer Behavior to the Field of Advertising," *Journal of Advertising*, vol. 3 (Summer 1974), pp. 10–15.
5. Chester R. Wasson, *Consumer Behavior: A Managerial Viewpoint* (Austin, Texas: Austin Press, 1975), pp. 96–97.
6. Ward and Robertson, *Consumer Behavior: Theoretical Sources*, pp. 87–88.
7. Edward E. Smith, Susan E. Hariland, Lynne M. Reder, Hiram Brownell, and Nancy Adams, "When Preparation Fails: Disruptive Effects of Prior Information on Perceptual Recognition," *Journal of Experimental Psychology*, vol. 2 (May 1976), pp. 151–61.
8. Benton J. Underwood, "Forgetting," *Scientific American*, vol. 210 (March 1964), pp. 91–92.
9. Rom J. Markin, Jr., *Consumer Behavior: A Cognitive Orientation* (New York: Macmillan Publishing Co., Inc., 1974), pp. 152–53.
10. Joseph W. Newman and Richard Staelin, "Purchase Information Seeking for New Cars and Major Household Appliances," *Journal of Marketing Research*, vol. 9 (August 1972), pp. 249–57; Leo Bogart and Charles Lehman, "What Makes a Brand Name Familiar?" *Journal of Marketing Research*, vol. 10 (February 1973), pp. 17–22.
11. Joe Kent Kerby, *Consumer Behavior* (New York: Dun-Donnelley Publishing Corp., 1975), pp. 308–12.

12. The object stimulus is sometimes referred to as a cue in the literature.
13. Alan G. Sawyer, "Repetition and Affect: Recent Empirical and Theoretical Development," Paper Presented at the *Symposium on Industrial and Consumer Behavior*, (University of South Carolina, March 25, 1976).
14. John A. Howard, *Marketing Theory* (Boston: Allyn Bacon, Inc., 1965), pp. 100–12.
15. Jack A. Adams, *Learning and Memory: An Introduction* (Homewood, Ill.: The Dorsey Press, 1976), pp. 20–23.
16. Arno K. Kleimenhagen, Donald C. Leeseberg, and Bernard A. Eilers, "Consumer Response to Special Promotions of Regional Shopping Centers," *Journal of Retailing*, vol. 48 (Spring 1972), pp. 22–29.
17. Peter O. Peretti and Chris Lucas, "Newspaper Advertising Influences on Consumers' Behavior by Socioeconomic Status of Customers," *Psychological Reports*, vol. 37 (1975), pp. 693–94.
18. Alfred A. Kuehn, "Consumer Brand Choice as a Learning Process," *Journal of Advertising Research*, vol. 2 (December 1962), pp. 10–17.
19. J. Ronald Carey, Steven H. Clicque, Barbara A. Leighton, and Frank Milton, "A Test of Positive Reinforcement of Customers," *Journal of Marketing*, vol. 40 (October 1976), pp. 98–100.
20. Adams, *Learning and Memory*, pp. 9–10.
21. Sidney Stegel and J. M. Andrews, "Magnitude of Reinforcement and Choice Behavior in Children," *Journal of Experimental Psychology*, vol. 63 (1962), pp. 337–41; John F. Hall, *The Psychology of Learning* (Philadelphia: J. B. Lippincott Co., 1966), pp. 208–80.
22. Martin Fishbein and Icek Ajzen, *Belief, Attitude, Intention and Behavior: An Introduction to Theory and Research* (Reading, Pa.: Addison-Wesley Publishing Co., 1975), pp. 430–31.
23. Arch G. Woodside, "Over-Rewarding the Consumer," *Marketing Education and the Real World*, eds. Boris W. Becker and Helmut Becker (Chicago: American Marketing Assn., 1972), pp. 396–99.
24. Frederick W. Winter, Jr. and James L. Ginter, "An Experiment in Inducing and Measuring Changes in Brand Attitudes," *Relevance in Marketing: Problems, Research, Actions*, ed. Fred C. Allvine (Chicago: American Marketing Assn., 1971), pp. 411–15; Fishbein and Ajzen, *Belief, Attitude, Intention and Behavior;* John J. Wheatley and Sadaomi Oshikawa, "Learning Theories, Attitudes and Advertising," *University of Washington Business Review*, (Summer 1968), pp. 24–33.
25. Ivan P. Pavlov, *Conditioned Reflexes* (London: Oxford University Press, 1927).
26. James A. Schellenberg, *Social Psychology* (New York: Random House, 1970), pp. 108–09; Adams, *Learning and Memory*, Chap. 4.
27. Markin, *Consumer Behavior: A Cognitive Orientation*, pp. 238–39.
28. Hull has been given credit for much work along these lines, particularly in the area of primary and secondary reinforcement. See: Clark C. Hull, *A Behavior System* (New Haven, Conn.: Yale University Press, 1952).

29. Howard, *Marketing Theory*, pp. 100–12.
30. Ibid.
31. Thomas S. Robertson, *Consumer Behavior* (Glenview, Ill.: Scott, Foresman & Co., 1970), p. 32.

QUESTIONS

1. What is learning? Forgetting? How are the two related? Explain.
2. Relate learning to motivation and perception. What is the importance of learning to consumer behavior?
3. Discuss the effects of forgetting on consumer behavior. What do consumers learn? Explain.
4. What are the elements of consumer learning? Discuss the part played by reward in learning. Explain and relate the response characteristics.
5. What is reinforcement? How does it relate to learning? Use examples of reinforcement from your own purchase experience and demonstrate how it works.
6. What is meant by connectionist theories of learning? Explain and contrast classical conditioning with the pleasure-pain theory.
7. What are the cognitive theories of learning? How do the cognitive theories differ from the connectionist theories? Give examples you know of in which the two broad type theories apply in consumer purchasing.
8. Discuss the problem solving theory of learning. Use specific examples to demonstrate how the theory works.
9. Discuss how the experience theory of learning differs from classical conditioning.
10. What is the learning curve? Does it have any application to consumer behavior or is it just theory? Explain.

15

Personality aspects of consumer behavior

Does a consumer's personality determine that person's awareness, needs, and motives, or is it the other way around? It is difficult to determine. Does one conclude that an individual has a favorable attitude toward a conservative retailer because the individual has a conservative personality? Or is it more likely that a consumer has a conservative personality because that person consistently purchases from conservative retailers and otherwise displays conservative attitudes. To what extent do learning and perception play a part in determining personality? Scholars can be found that take either side of these issues. The disagreement tends to point up a deeper truth—that personality and consumer behavior are inevitably entwined. The fact is that the relationship is not one of dependence but one of interdependence. In this chapter, we shall deal with consumer personality.

WHAT PERSONALITY IS AND IS NOT

Human personality is a complex subject. Although all persons differ in personality structure, it is still possible to examine basic dimensions of human personality in order to develop a better understanding of how consumers think and behave.

The term personality is encountered in popular usage in phrases such as "personality kid" and "she has personality." There was even a song entitled "Personality." The term has come to mean whatever one person sees in another. In this casual usage, "personality" has a good connotation—to "have personality" is not a bad thing.

The truth, however, is that personality has broader and deeper connotations than its popular usage would indicate. One view is that personality means the total inner organization of the person. This type of definition says that personality is the summation of the person. It focuses on the internal self. Another definition of personality focuses on differences. "Personality refers to all the characteristics which make one individual different from another."[1]

Each of these definitions has something to offer. In the most basic sense, *personality* is the summation of the characteristics that make the person what he or she is and distinguish each individual from every other individual.[2] By this definition, personality can be used in two quite different ways: Personality thought of as the sum total of a person provides a basis for studying and attempting to understand the individual; personality viewed in terms of individual differences provides a means of comparing one individual to another in order to understand their essential differences.

Just so there can be no misunderstanding about the term, we want to make clear what personality is not. Personality does not refer to an ability to get along with others, nor is it the same thing as being popular within the group. Personality is not the ability to get votes. Personality is sometimes used to refer to an oddball or loner, but this is not personality. In fact, personality can *never* be any of these things, and yet personality may include all of them. What we wish to emphasize is that personality constitutes a much broader concept that indicated by any of the above statements. Yet, because a person is uniquely what he or she is, that person may be popular, respected, or considered different. Thus, the term is used to describe such superficial things as popularity and friendliness, but personality itself goes to the very core of the individual's being.

CONSUMER PERSONALITY AS A SOCIAL PRODUCT

It is increasingly recognized that personality is a social product. The way a person feels and thinks, acts and talks, or even what the person dreams or wishes, results from that person's experiences with other persons, events, and objects throughout a lifetime. Everytime a consumer meets another person he or she reacts, in part, in terms of the interpretation of the other person's behavior—an interpretation which comes from past experience. If the consumer's actions, judged by responses received, proves inappropriate, the individual takes this fact into account before taking further action. A consumer may attempt to haggle over the price of a product only to meet criticism from the clerk and stares from other customers. A consumer whose personality tends toward independence may pay no attention and continue to haggle, but a consumer whose personality tends toward meekness will probably back down from the situation and seek to find a way out of the dilemma.

An example can serve to demonstrate the effect of personality on consumer actions. In a study of persons who buy audio visual equipment, where one group purchased from a specialty store and another purchased from a department store, different personality attributes were discovered. The specialty store customers were found to be more self-confident, perceived less risk related to their purchase, and considered the product area less important than was found for department store customers.[3]

CONCEPTS OF PERSONALITY

In one discussion of personality it is said that "the student is immediately impressed with the number of personality theories available today."[4] Anyone attempting to classify these concepts is also impressed by the large number of variations in each theory.[5] It is never easy to classify concepts. Many seemingly different ideas are found to be similar when one gets past the terminology used. Also, it must be remembered that any classification scheme is an oversimplification. Finally, all classification schemes involve judgment. The statements of others must be interpreted by the one doing the classifying. Unfortunately, all this does not relieve one of the problems of bringing order to a complex subject. Some type of classification method is usually necessary.[6] For our purposes, the major concepts of personality can be grouped under four classes: (1) psychoanalytic theory, (2) trait theory, (3) type theory, and (4) Gestalt theory. The remainder of the chapter is devoted to these personality concepts.

THE INFLUENCE OF PSYCHOANALYTIC THEORY

The psychoanalytic theory of personality is derived from the work of Sigmund Freud.[7] Freud based much of his life's work on the study of dreams in which he found clues to the unconscious. He laid the foundations for psychoanalysis in the methods he developed for the treatment of hysteria. Freud saw sex or sexually related biological feeling as the basic determinant of personality. Freud believed that as a child develops he passes through several stages—the oral, anal, phallic, and genital periods—and these sensuous periods determine the dynamic nature of personality.

Freud pointed out that the personality is controlled by the *psyche* (mind), which exists on three levels, called the id, ego, and superego. The *id* is the unconscious part of the psyche from which instinctual impulses and demands for the satisfaction of primitive needs arise. The demands of the id are unlimited. A newborn child is practically all id, since it has not yet learned conscious behavior. The *ego* derives from the id through contact with reality. It is the largely conscious part of the mind, ruled by reason and mediating the unlimited demands of the id and bringing them in accord with everyday reality, in the interests of self-preservation. The *superego* is mostly unconscious, though partly conscious. It develops out of the ego through processes of internalization and introjection of influences and disciplinary actions of parents especially, but also other authority figures. Thus, the superego is a person's "moral law" that directly guides behavior and keeps the person in line with the rules of society. It is "built up" more or less at random out of childhood experience with parental and others' warnings, threats, punishments, advice, and example. The child looks upon these parental and authority figures as being omnipotent and omniscient.

Freud saw wishes as originating in the id to be met by the reason of the ego and the morality of the superego. If the wish is contrary to the standards set by the ego and superego, it is suppressed into the unconscious mind. If the wish is deemed acceptable, it is permitted to affect behavior.

The great influence of Freud on scholars and practitioners cannot be underestimated. The great names in psychiatry and psychology tend to be either disciples or critics of Freud.[8] As a result of criticism and modification much of Freudian theory has been discarded by scholars, but it constitutes the original breakthrough in understanding personality. Alfred Adler believed that striving for superiority rather than sex was the basic factor of personality. Karen Horney saw personality as the result of anxieties a child learns to cope with that stem from the parent-child relationship. Eric Fromm considered man alone in society, and personality to him was the result of striving for love, brotherhood, and security. In short, the biological basis for personality advocated by Freud has been greatly broadened by the recognition that individuals have many characteristics that influence human personality development.

The practitioners are even more inclined to stay with Freudian personality concepts. Freudian influence is observed throughout branding, advertising, and personal selling. The practice of making products sex symbols, as with "Mr. Clean" and the "Man from Glad" is strictly Freudian. The use of sex such as Branniff's "mid-air strip" and the Hathaway shirt ads using the man with the eye patch also indicate the continuing power of Freud. Every salesperson who gains attention with a sensuous story is utilizing Freud. It is safe to say that Freudian appeals to sensuality, sex, and related subjects are the personality concepts most used by advertisers.

CONSUMER PERSONALITY TRAITS

It has been pointed out that personality is a complex subject, but one way to deal with its complexity is to break the totality of personality down into simpler constructs. The personality trait is one of the simpler constructs of personality, but when one breaks personality down this way, the hope is that the totality is not lost in the process. Our task now is to give meaning to trait theory, and to relate human traits to consumer behavior.

Traits and trait theory defined

Trait theory goes back to before the 19th century. In its simplest form, trait theory is based on the idea that people have powers or qualities that are located in the mind, and these powers determine behavior.[9] A more complex development of trait theory was offered by Allport.[10] Allport reasoned that traits were attributes that identify a person and make the person both whole and functional. Traits acted as regulators, and people with similar traits were believed to behave in a similar fashion. These persons were thought to have similar goals, and therefore it was concluded that the striving to achieve the goals would be similar also.

Each of us has a unique way of responding to environmental stimuli, and our responses are described by others as personality traits. A *personality trait* is any human characteristic, distinctive from other characteristics and consistent in effect, that distinguishes the behavior of one individual from another.[11] If we know that a person laughs, walks, or dresses, we know nothing to distinguish that person from others. However, if we know a person has a cackling laugh, walks with a limp, or dresses in the latest fashion then we have an identifiable personality. This is the reason that characteristics of personality must be distinctive. Personality traits must also be consistent—we cannot identify and classify people unless their distinguishing characteristics are reasonably stable.[12] Abilities are special types of traits that determine what people can do with body and mind.

Differences between consumer attitudes and traits

Consumer attitudes, as we have seen, are formulated in reference to some particular object, such as a product or store. This is not the case with traits. Traits are not directed at anything in particular. An attitude is a predisposition to act *toward* something; a trait is a characteristic manner of acting toward everything.[13] Thus, a consumer may hold certain attitudes toward retailers, downtown congestion, and high prices; yet, when speaking of any of these topics, the individual may speak slowly and use certain mannerisms that distinguish personality.

Consumer attitudes result in our taking preferential action with respect to the market situation, whereas, traits are more generalized tendencies to act in a certain manner given the situation. Traits, because of their nature, may be appropriate or inappropriate to a specific situation. Attitudes are favorable, unfavorable or neutral toward the situation, but traits do not refer to acceptance or rejection. Thus, the consumer's favorable attitude toward buying an electric can opener when combined with the trait to be cautious leads the consumer to deliberate before buying. The general trait of a consumer to be selfish or extravagant differs from the attitudes he or she may hold toward a retail store. A person may like the store but because of a frugal trait not want to purchase clothes there. A consumer may count pennies just as carefully when buying a suit he or she likes as when buying fly spray that he or she does not particularly care for.

Inventory of consumer personality traits

One may well imagine that as the study of personality proceeds, the number of recognized traits tends to increase. One source lists 17,953 different words distinguishing one's human behavior.[14] Furthermore, the complexity of the human personality has not lent itself to any easy agreement on a single, unified list of personality traits. Several lists have been advanced, and there is some overlapping among them.

Common traits in consumers. When we consider consumer personality traits, we are likely to consider only common traits. Common traits are those held in some degree by nearly everyone. One list of common traits includes (1) activeness, (2) vigor, (3) impulsiveness, (4) dominance, (5) stability, (6) sociability, and (7) reflectiveness.[15] Another list includes (1) general activity, (2) calmness, composure versus nervousness, (3) objectivity, (4) confidence versus inferiority feelings, (5) agreeableness, (6) cooperativeness, (7) sociability, (8) ascendance versus submission, (9) masculinity versus femininity, (10) restraint versus rhathymia, (11) reflectiveness, (12) depression and (13) emotionality.[16]

Listed below are 11 traits that appear common to most people. Each trait has its distinguishing characteristic, and each definitely affects consumer behavior.

1. *Activity.* Even babies have different activity levels. Activity shows up in consumers in their willingness to shop and spend time searching in the market.
2. *Masculinity.* Gestures, speech, habits, and attitudes found in one sex but not in the other. This trait is manifested in the type of products and stores favored by consumers. It is the basis for manufacturers giving their products sex attributes. All consumer behavior reflects this trait.
3. *Independence.* All people differ in their reliance on other people. A consumer's independence is reflected in dress, eating habits, preference for entertainment, and manner of shopping, just to name a few.
4. *Achievement.* Some people are characterized as achievers and others are not. Achievement is not dependent entirely on intelligence. Consumers with high achievement motivation are conscious of what others think of their behavior, manners, dress, and so on. These consumers may or may not conform to group norms.
5. *Anxiety.* Individuals display different degrees of sureness of themselves. Consumer anxiety shows up in the manner in which an individual handles the purchase situation. Salespeople do not usually intimidate a consumer who has self-assurance.

6. *Sociability.* The desire for interaction with others varies among people. Sociability affects shopping because shopping is social behavior, and some consumers are more willing to participate than others.
7. *Dominance.* Dominance is the desire to cause others to submit, and this important trait varies among people. Shopping for products gives individuals an outlet to display their need to dominate others. This trait makes a consumer aggressive and difficult to deal with in the buying process.
8. *Adaptability.* Some people can adapt to conditions of reality to a greater degree than others. If a desired product is not available, such consumers take a substitute.
9. *Aggressiveness.* Consumer aggressiveness shows up in many ways, including willingness to try new products, attitude toward price and service ngotiation, and the seeking out of products and stores.
10. *Seriousness.* Some people take life seriously and others are carefree. A serious consumer gives more attention and consideration to a purchase.
11. *Emotional control.* People vary considerably in their ability to control their emotions. A certain amount of emotional control is necessary by consumers in all purchasing, but it is perhaps more important in situations where service is slow or inadequate, when prices are exorbitant, when dishonesty is present, and when promises are not kept.

Of course, all these traits interact, the points made above apply only when considering each trait separately in connection with an individual consumer. For example, a consumer who is active, sociable, adaptable, and emotionally stable will consume differently from one who is active, sociable, aggressive, and serious.[17] What a consumer actually does may be based on an internal compromise of traits, such as sociability and independence.

Individual consumer traits. In addition to the common traits found in most people, there are traits, called individual traits, that are found in only one or a few persons. There are so many of these traits, and they vary so greatly, that it is impossible to provide a list. However, as an example, individual traits include: a person's particular guilt feelings, ego-defensive mechanism, and concept of self, taste, concept of beauty, and so on. These traits are crucial to consumer behavior because they play an important part in making each consumer's market reaction unique. Furthermore, there is interaction within the consumer between common and individual traits that affects market behavior.

Personality traits are extremely important for understanding consumer behavior, but traits are also important for identifying consumer groups. One point of particular interest to marketers is the continuing attempt to identify systems of traits in consumers. That is to say, a market segment is really a group of consumers displaying some common personality traits. The marketer wants to put together a system of common traits from those in the list provided previously. Given these common traits, the marketer can discover the basic appeals to make to this group of consumers. This approach recognizes that groups of traits can in fact be a motivating force influencing consumer behavior.[18] For example, a marketer can motivate through appeals, groups of consumers who display anxiety or independence or aggressiveness. Groups of consumers can also be appealed to who display several of the traits.

CONSUMER PERSONALITY TYPES

If we are asked to describe a friend to someone, there is a natural tendency for us to type that person. In our description, we would assign the person to one or more categories such as introverted-extroverted. In describing a person by type, we tend to focus on one or more outstanding characteristics of that person and not on less obvious aspects of behavior. In this section, we discuss the definition of personality types, consumer types and stereotypes, and the empirical evidence on personality types.

Type theory and types defined

Theories of personality based on human types are similar to trait theories. *Type theory* categorizes people into groups (types) based on either physical or psychological attributes. Personality types can be based on such physical attributes as color of hair and skin, sex, and so on. Psychological attributes include intelligence, emotions and emotional stability, and mental traits. The physical theory sees all human behavior as dependent on the physical structure of the person. This concept of personality goes all the way back to the Hippocratic school of medicine and the bodily humors of medieval physiology. The psychological concept of personality type considers behavior to be controlled by the mind and not the body. The perceptual process and attitude formation play an important part in these theories.[19] Jung built his concept of personality around the manner in which a person perceived and developed attitudes toward his environment. Both the physical and psychological concepts of personality are self-restrictive. These concepts do not deal with the whole person, although they do provide for human change. The concepts are at best oversimplifications of human personality.

There are similarities and differences between type theory and trait theory. A human trait is the smallest single component of personality. A trait concerns specific individual mental or physical characteristics. A *personality type* is defined to mean a compatible group of human characteristics that, taken together, control behavior and distinguish between individuals. The characteristics upon which types are classified can be either physical or mental. A personality type is a larger unit than a trait because several traits or other characteristics are necessary to constitute a personality type. The essential point of personality types is that people are classified according to a few key traits or characteristics.

Consumer types and stereotypes

Stereotypes are sometimes used synonymously with personality types, but there is a difference. *Stereotype* refers to a fixed notion held about a group of people and based on one, or a few, human characteristics. We are using stereotypes when we ascribe fiery tempers to redheads and scheming minds to people with narrow eyes. When we discuss Frenchmen as wine-drinking, fun-loving lovers, we are stereotyping Frenchmen. When we say that middle-income American consumers are conservative, home-oriented, wife-dominated consumers, we are speaking in stereotypes. Both Frenchmen and middle-income Americans are more complex than the stereotypes indicate. Furthermore, no individual in a group will conform to the stereotype because stereotypes indicate average behavior.

There exists no more agreement on personality types than was found earlier for personality traits.[20] Furthermore, personality types are found not to be an infallible guide to consumer behavior.[21] Two individuals may be classified as the same type but purchase differently. The reason is, of course, that the stereotyping of people is an oversimplification of the true complexity of these people. Still, personality types do give us insights into the nature of people that are important for understanding their behavior.

Types based on characteristics. One important classification of personality types is based on physical and psychological characteristics of people.[22] This classification divides people into five types as follows:

1. *Systematic classification*—a system of mutually exclusive types. For example, some people believe there is a black consumer type and a white consumer type.

2. *Ideal types*—social stereotypes of personality. These are idealized images rather than real people. Examples are the tightwad and the clotheshorse types.
3. *Discontinuous types*—here people are classed by color, sex, disease, hair color, size, and shape. For example, men are not supposed to enjoy shopping with their wives, and blondes are supposed to have more fun.
4. *Types based on test scores*—here people with similar scores are grouped together.
5. *A group of traits*—these are the same traits mentioned under our discussion of personality traits in the previous section.

This classification of personality types is very broad; it covers most of the possibilities. One problem with any such classification is that a consumer may fit in more than one category. Thus, what the typing gains in breadth of understanding of consumers, it tends to lose in preciseness. The classification can be useful to marketers for understanding the basic characteristics of personality types and in segmenting markets and differentiating products.

Types based on basic values. Another method of typing consumers places the emphasis on values that people hold.[23] This method identifies six classes of people, and it refers to both males and females:

1. *Theoretical Man.* The theoretical person is a seeker after truth and fundamental values. The scientist fits this group. A consumer fitting this group would be fact oriented, interested in change, and broad-minded.
2. *Economic Man.* This person is concerned with utility and maximizing. Many consumers fit this category to a degree. Such consumers are price conscious or interested in the good buy.
3. *Aesthetic Man.* This is the artistic person concerned with beauty in the world. All consumers fit this group to some degree.
4. *Social Man.* Here we have the consumer motivated by love of others. He or she is motivated by group norms, and their purchases reflect this.
5. *Political Man.* This consumer is concerned with power. They surround themselves with products that feed this power requirement.
6. *Religious Man.* This type is a mystic and is not completely bound to this earth. This consumer is more detached. He or she is not market or product oriented, and they purchase out of necessity almost as an afterthought.

This classification is more nearly in line with personality as understood by marketers. It deals with values that can be appealed to as motivating forces within the individual.

Types based on social values. An even more useful list for marketers focuses on the social values of consumers.[24] It divides people into the:

1. *Tradition directed.* These persons are oriented toward the past and resist change. Tradition-oriented consumers are not fashion leaders except where traditional fashions are concerned, and they tend to purchase by habit more often.
2. *Inner directed.* These persons have their own internal value systems and keep command of their own activities, including their consumer behavior. They are independent nonconformists who are not easily influenced by others.
3. *Other directed.* The characters of these people are formed mainly by external influences. These people respond to and need others. Such consumers buy group-oriented products, and they tend to be fashion followers.

Personality types can be used in much the same manner as personality traits. They provide a simplified picture of consumer personality that can be used as a basis for discovering consumer appeals, meeting objectives, and increasing or creating motivation by means of either personal selling or advertising. Since type theory focuses on one or a few prominent traits or values, it is simpler to work with, and data can more easily be gathered. However, personality types are not as fundamental as traits, and many factors of human behavior can be hidden by a blind reliance on type.

GESTALT PERSONALITY THEORY

The term "Gestalt" was coined by the German psychologist von Ehrenfels. Gestalt is derived from configuration, and it generally refers to the totality of a situation. "Thus the term *Gestalt,* pattern, or configuration came to describe a unity of perception in which the parts derived their meaning from the whole and could not be separated from the total pattern or organization without losing their identity.[25] Some outstanding contributors to the development of Gestalt psychology were Kurt Lewin, Kurt Koffka, Wolfgang Köhler, and Max Wertheimer.

Gestalt is intimately tied up with personality. The basic idea is that the whole of a person is greater than the summation of his or her parts, and personality cannot be determined by a consideration of separate characteristics. Personality is as much a product of the environment as it is of the individual's mind. Experiments prove that individuals respond to stimuli in relation to their experiences.[26] In Gestalt theory, personality is viewed as the result of the interaction between the person and the total environment—the two must be considered together as a patterned event. It is consistent with Gestalt theory that attitudes, perception, aspirations, self-concepts, satisfaction, frustration, motivation, etc., are all necessary to explain and understand human personality.

Consumers attempt to stabilize their psychological field by providing meaning to the surrounding world. Consumers strive to reduce tension and conflict between themselves and their environmental perceptions by the type of market decisions made. For example, the use of average looking people in television commercials is consistent with Gestalt theory. Such commercials assume that consumers can better identify with people like themselves. There are other examples. Business executives take advantage of the concept when they provide tension-reducing products such as deodorants, cosmetics, and life insurance. Personal selling and advertising that stress social acceptance or show people having fun, such as the beer commercials, are following Gestalt principles.

THE PROMISE OF CONSUMER PERSONALITY CONCEPTS

So far our time has been spent discussing the major concepts of personality and relating these concepts to specific types of consumer behavior. It is now time to turn our attention to the evaluation of personality as a factor of consumer behavior. What is its importance? Is it important, and what is its present state of effectiveness? What are the problems associated with the use of personality concepts to explain consumer behavior?

Personality is basic to consumer behavior

There is little question among scholars that personality is a major factor of consumer behavior.[27] After all, we have shown that personality is related to the basic attributes of a person's nature, and a person seldom acts in opposition to his nature. We have also demonstrated that personality is affected by the environment. It is this sure knowledge that accounts for so much experimental work on personality. After all the promise is so great. To be able to generalize, from the basic attributes of individuals, to specific consumer behavior means that the prediction of consumer action reaches the realm of possibility.

The fact that there is a clear relationship between personality and general behavior has been recognized in the literature for some time.[28] Furthermore, it requires no more than personal intuition to recognize the logic of the relationship. Most of us can recognize specific personality traits or types of acquaintances. We are aware of how specific people tend to relate to their environment. The introvert or aggressive types tend to behave in expected ways. Persons who have the trait of hypertension show it in their actions. The problems are (1) making the connection between theory and practice and (2) relating general human behavior based on personality to specific consumer behavior. At the present time, we do not fully understand these relationships.

What the research shows

Most personality research undertaken by marketers centers on comparing personality traits or types to a wide range of products. Little work has been done to test the psychoanalytic or Gestalt theories. This fact is a real weakness in personality research. A summary of major personality studies can pinpoint the present status of the marketer's understanding of the effect of personality on consumer behavior. The studies have been grouped, for comparison purposes, into those that (1) show a strong relationship, (2) those that show a mixed relationship, and (3) those that show little or no relationship.

Strong personality and purchase relationship. Mason Haire set the pattern for personality studies. In his now famous study, Haire found that (1) many products have meaning far beyond their physical attributes, (2) these personality attributes are a major factor in purchases, and (3) the identification of these personality factors requires indirect approaches.[29] Haire compares the personality traits of lazy, poor planner, thrift, spendthrift, poor wife, and good wife for two national brands of coffee. This study was recently duplicated with the same results.[30] Another study compared the owners of Chevrolet and Ford automobiles for such personality traits as active, vigorous, impulsive, dominant, stable, sociable, and reflective. In this study, it was found that the personality factors do have a significance for predicting the owners of the two types of cars.[31] It has been shown that there is a positive correlation between personality factors and promotion.[32] Kassarjian used inner-directed and other-directed people for commercials promoting such products as telephone service, high-fidelity turntable, Ralph's market, Sea & Ski, IBM typewriter, Bayer aspirin, Kodak, and Fairchild's restaurant. It was found that (1) inner-directed people preferred inner-directed commercials, while other-directed persons preferred that type commercial, and (2) both groups felt that other-directed commercials would appeal to the largest number of persons.

Mixed personality and purchase relationships. Some personality studies show mixed results. One important study can be summarized as follows:

a. There were significant differences between aggressive, complaint, and detached personality types for shirts, men's deodorant, after-shave lotion, razors, and aspirin.

b. There were no significant differences among the types of cigarettes, toilet or bath soap, men's hair dressing, and toothpaste.
c. The different personality types did tend to view different television programs differently, and the difference corresponded to the type of personality.[33]

Some specific findings included the following. High-aggressive men preferred van Heusen shirts. High-complaint-oriented people preferred a mouthwash. High-complaint people tended to have brand preferences for toilet or bath soap. High-aggressive personality types preferred a manual razor as compared to low-aggressive or complaint-oriented people. High-detached people were greater consumers of tea. High-complaint people preferred Bayer aspirin.

A recent study compared personality types to extreme body types. It was hypothesized that heavy-set persons are extroverts, and thin persons are introverts. It was also hypothesized that the heavy-set types prefer mod or currently stylish clothing, while the thin types prefer conservative clothing.[34] In this study, a relationship was found between personality and body type, but the relationship between body type and clothing preference was not validated. In fact, just the opposite of the hypothesis was discovered. Heavy-set types preferred conservative clothing perhaps because it helped to disguise their figures.

Poor personality and purchase relationships. The majority of the studies surveyed show little direct relationship between personality and product choice or use. One study compared headache remedies, new fashions, vitamins, cigarettes, mouthwash, alcoholic drinks, deodorant, automobiles, and chewing gum to the personality traits of ascendency, responsibility, emotional stability, and sociability.[35] The result was a very weak, but positive, correlation. Another study by Koponen found little or no meaningful relationship when such personality factors as dominance, achievement, dependence, assistance, aggression, and change were compared to cigarettes and magazines.[36] The study, like some others, did show a relationship between personality and advertising response. Sparks and Tucker used the traits of ascendancy, responsibility, emotional stability, sociability, cautiousness, original thinking, personal relations, and vigor in a comparison of such products as headache remedy, mouthwash, men's cologne, hair spray, shampoo, antacid, *Playboy,* alcoholic beverages, fashion adoption, complexion aids, vitamins, haircut, cigarettes, coffee, chewing gum, and after-shave lotion.[37] Little or no meaningful relationship was found in the study. Brody and Cunningham compared personality variables to family brand loyalty and found practically no relationship.[38] Evans found personality factors to be of no value in determining whether a consumer owns a Ford or Chevrolet automobile.[39] Similar studies have found the same general results.

Several important conclusions can be drawn from a review of all the relevant studies of personality and purchase behavior. First, the data supports the connection between personality and consumer behavior. There is too much positive data to think otherwise, in spite of the obvious weak correlation in many cases. Second, the data indicates clearly that personality traits are not the only variables at work where consumer behavior is concerned. The weak correlation and the mixed results of one study clearly point to other considerations being at work. Third, the data indicates that the relationship between personality and purchase is much more complex than may have originally been suspected. Fourth, the data indicates hope that continued research and study can bear meaningful results where personality is concerned.[40]

Problems in using personality theory

There is a clear discrepancy between the promise of personality theory and the findings of researchers. The question arises as to why the difference exists. Actually, the answer is not too difficult to come by. The basic problem lies in assuming a simple relationship between personality traits and purchase patterns. This assumption leads to several fallacies.

First, there is the fallacy of the dominant attribute. It is assumed that one, or a few, attributes control consumer behavior. Actually, the total number of personality characteristics has never been determined. There is no question but that on any problem faced by the consumer, more than one of these attributes is at work. Furthermore, the attributes vary in intensity. Thus, a person may be shy but have a strong urge to excel; or the person may be aggressive and dislike conflict, but be highly sociable. The question is which trait, or traits, is going to control the purchase situation. The answer, of course, for any consumer depends on the number and strength of traits brought into play on a given purchase.

Second, there is the fallacy of attribute consistency. The notion is that if a person is dominant oriented in one situation he or she is dominant in all situations, or if that person is emotionally stable at one time, he or she is emotionally stable at all times. The fact is, that the effect of a personality trait depends a lot on the situation and the object being considered. A man may be a tiger at the office, but meek as a lamb when with the "little woman." A woman may be personable and easy going in social situations, but conflict oriented at the office. Thus, what is true about personality in one purchase situation may not be true in the next.

Third, there is the fallacy of time consistency. This is the notion that a person's personality does not undergo change over time. The fact is that a person can modify his personality as he or she develops as a person. Introverts can learn to be more outgoing, and aggressive persons can develop restraint. The changes show up in purchases. The author's experience is that a person who is shy and intimidated by clerks tends to become more aggressive as income increases over time.

Fourth, there is the fallacy that personality is the total person. This notion runs through all the research that has been cited. The fact is that personality attributes, whether traits or types, are just one of the variables of human nature. The environment, needs, motives, perceptions, and attitudes also enter into any purchase decision, as has been shown. A shy person may turn aggressive when his or her kids are hungry and he or she is out of work. A sociable person may become belligerent if a salesclerk ignores her or is discourteous.

Fifth, there is the fallacy that people with similar attributes purchase alike. The fact is that most personality traits have more than one possible product outlet. A social person can as easily display this fact by purchasing a dress as by purchasing a meal with a friend. A man's masculinity can be demonstrated in the shaving lotion purchased, style of clothes, or manner of wearing his hair. Thus, consumers with similar personalities may purchase in entirely different ways.

Future of personality variables to consumer behavior

The reader should not be discouraged about the future of personality as a factor of consumer behavior. A clear relationship has been demonstrated. The studies that have been made are beginning to develop understanding of both how personality affects the purchase process and how complex the subject actually is. That constitutes more than a beginning. From this point on, both the research methods and the results are very likely to get better.

NOTES

1. James H. Meyers and William H. Reynolds, *Consumer Behavior and Marketing Management* (Boston: Houghton Mifflin Co., 1967), p. 122.
2. Elaine Donelson, *Personality: A Scientific Approach* (Pacific Palisades, Ca.: Goodyear Publishing Co., Inc., 1973), p. 3.
3. Joseph F. Dash, Leon G. Schiffman, and Conrad Berenson, "Risk- and Personality-Related Dimensions of Store Choice," *Journal of Marketing*, vol. 40 (January 1976), pp. 32–39.
4. Robert M. Allen, *Variables In Personality Theory and Personality Testing* (Springfield, Ill.: Charles C. Thomas, Publisher, 1965), p. 31.
5. The French sociologist, Fourier, classified human personality into 3 classes, 12 orders, 32 genera, 134 species, and 404 varieties, all equaling 810 types of personalities.

6. Harold H. Kassarjian, "Personality and Consumer Behavior: A Review," *Journal of Marketing Research,* vol. 8 (November 1971), pp. 409–18.
7. See: Sigmund Freud, *Collected Papers* (London: International Psychoanalytic Press, 1922).
8. Kassarjian, "Personality and Consumer Behavior," p. 410.
9. See: J. McCosh, *Psychology: The Cognitive Powers* (New York: Charles Scribner's Sons, 1888).
10. G. W. Allport, *Personality: A Psychological Interpretation* (New York: Henry Holt & Co., 1937).
11. Robert M. Liebert and Michael D. Spiegler, *Personality,* rev. ed. (Homewood, Ill.: The Dorsey Press, 1974), pp. 148–54; Kassarjian, "Personality and Consumer Behavior."
12. Kathryn E. A. Villani and Yoram Wind, "On the Usage of 'Modified' Personality Trait Measures in Consumer Research," *Journal of Consumer Research,* vol. 2 (December 1975), pp. 223–28.
13. Arnon Perry, "Heredity, Personality Traits, Product Attitude, and Product Consumption—An Exploratory Study," *Journal of Marketing Research,* vol. 10 (November 1973), pp. 376–79.
14. G. W. Allport and H. S. Odbert, "Trait Names: A Psycholexial Study," *Psychological Monograph,* vol. 47, no. 211 (1936).
15. *Thurstone Temperament Schedule,* 2d ed. (Chicago: Science Research Associates, Inc., 1953).
16. J. P. Guilford and W. S. Zimmerman, "Fourteen Dimensions of Temperament," *Psychological Monograph,* vol. 70, no. 417 (1956).
17. Daniel W. Greeno, Montrose S. Sommers, and Jerome B. Kernan, "Personality and Implicit Behavior Patterns," *Journal of Marketing Research,* vol. 10 (February 1973), pp. 63–69; Mark I. Alpert, "Personality and the Determinants of Product Choice," *Journal of Marketing Research,* vol. 9 (February 1972), pp. 89–92.
18. W. Gruen, "Preference for New Products and Its Relationship to Different Measures of Conformity," *Journal of Applied Psychology,* vol. 44 (December 1968), pp. 361–66.
19. C. G. Jung, *Psychological Types* (New York: Harcourt, Brace, & Co., Inc., 1946).
20. *Are There Consumer Types?* (New York: Advertising Research Foundation, Inc., 1964), p. 25.
21. It has been pointed out on several occasions that many factors affect consumer behavior and that personality is only one of these factors.
22. B. Notcutt, *The Psychology of Personality* (New York: Philosophical Library, Inc., 1953).
23. G. W. Allport, P. E. Vernon, and G. Lindzey, *A Study of Values,* rev. ed. (New York: Houghton Mifflin Co., 1959).
24. David Riesman, *The Lonely Crowd* (New Haven, Conn.: Yale University Press, 1950).
25. Allen, *Variables in Personality Theory,* p. 55.

26. Kurt Lewin, *Principles of Topological Psychology* (New York: McGraw-Hill Book Co., 1936).
27. T. K. Chakrapani, "Personality Correlates of Brand Loyalty," *Psychological Studies,* vol. 19 (1974), pp. 27–33; L. E. Boone, "Personality and Innovative Buying Behavior," *Journal of Psychology,* vol. 86 (March 1974).
28. See: G. W. Allport, *Becoming: Basic Considerations for a Psychology of Personality* (New Haven, Conn.: Yale University Press, 1954); R. Stagner, "Homeostasis as a Unifying Concept in Personality Theory," *Psychological Review,* vol. 58 (1951), pp. 5–17; W. B. Cannon, *The Wisdom of the Body* (New York: Norton, 1932).
29. Mason Haire, "Projective Techniques in Marketing Research," *Journal of Marketing,* vol. 14 (April 1950), pp. 649–56.
30. Frederick E. Webster, Jr., and Frederick von Pechman, "A Replication of the 'Shopping List' Study," *Journal of Marketing,* vol. 34 (April 1970), pp. 61–77.
31. Ralph Westfall, "Psychological Factors in Predicting Product Choice," *Journal of Marketing,* vol. 26 (April 1962), pp. 34–40.
32. Harold H. Kassarjian, "Social Character and Differentual Preference for Mass Communications," *Journal of Marketing Research,* vol. 2 (May 1965), pp. 146–53.
33. Joel B. Cohen, "An Interpersonal Orientation to the Study of Consumer Behavior," *Journal of Marketing Research,* vol. 4 (August 1967), pp. 270–78.
34. Lee A. Graf, "Personality Derived from Body Type as a Predictor of Consumer Preferences in the Male Clothing Market," *Applications, Issues, Developments and Strategies in the Decision Sciences,* ed. Thad Green and S. Roland Jones (Mississippi State: American Institute of Decision Sciences, 1973), pp. 256–57.
35. W. T. Tucker and John J. Painter, "Personality and Product Use," *Journal of Applied Psychology,* vol. 45 (October 1961), pp. 325–29.
36. Arthur Kopenen, "Personality Characteristics of Purchasers," *Journal of Advertising Research,* vol. 1 (September 1960), pp. 6–12.
37. David I. Sparks and W. T. Tucker, "A Multivariate Analysis of Personality and Product Use," *Journal of Marketing Research,* vol. 8 (February 1971), pp. 67–70.
38. Robert P. Brody and Scott M. Cunningham, "Personality Variables and the Consumer Decision Process," *Journal of Marketing Research,* vol. 5 (February 1968), pp. 50–57.
39. Franklin B. Evans, "Psychological and Objective Factors in the Prediction of Brand Choice," *Journal of Business,* vol. 32 (October 1959), pp. 340–69.
40. Parker M. Worthing, M. Venkatesan, and Steve Smith, "A Modified Approach to the Exploration of Personality and Product Use," *Relevance in Marketing: Problems, Research, Action,* ed. Fred C. Allvine (Chicago: American Marketing Assn., 1971), pp. 363–67.

QUESTIONS

1. Define personality. Contrast what personality is with what it is not. Why do you think personality is important to consumer behavior?
2. What is psychoanalytic theory of personality? Where does this concept originate from? Who is Freud? What were Freud's contribution to personality theory?
3. Explain and relate the Psyche, Id, ego, superego. How do these concepts relate to consumer purchasing? Give examples.
4. What is a trait? Trait theory? Explain. Can trait and the psychoanalytic theory of personality be compared?
5. List and explain the eleven traits considered common to personality. Give examples of how each can affect consumers in a purchase situation.
6. Define types and stereotypes. What is the heart of type theory? Classify and explain personality types based on basic values. Can you give examples of how these types appear in people?
7. Discuss types based on social values. Is it possible to combine types based on social values with types based on basic values? Explain.
8. What is the Gestalt concept of personality theory?
9. Discuss what the research on personality shows. Is it favorable or not? What do you think is the future of personality in explaining consumer behavior? Explain.
10. What are the problems encountered in using personality research? In conducting research? Can they be overcome?

PART FOUR

Environmental influences on consumers

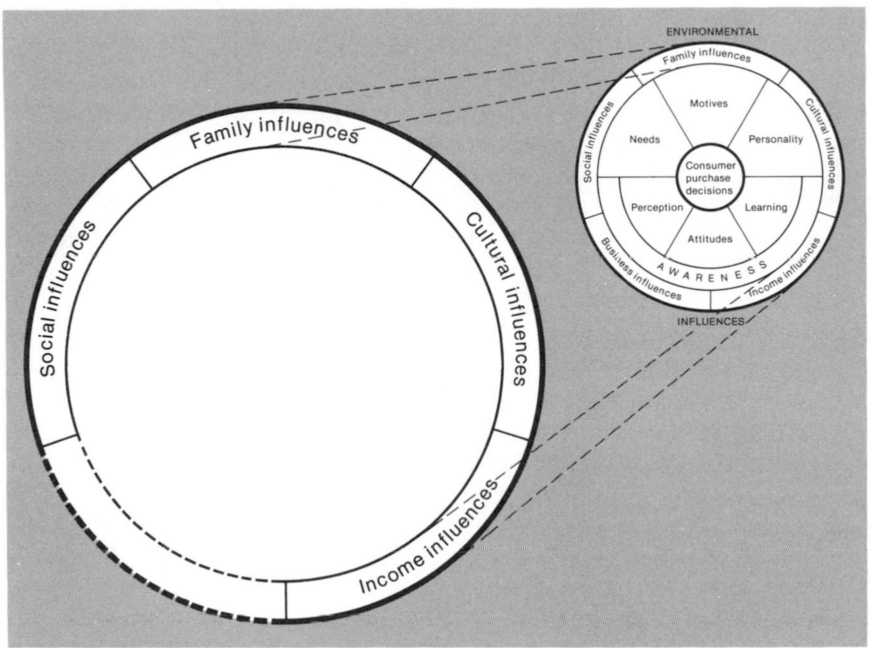

This part is the first of two which investigate the consumer's environment. It has seven chapters, as follows:

16. Introduction to environmental influence
17. Family influences: Internal behavior
18. American household structure
19. Income influences on consumer behavior
20. Consumers and social groups
21. The consumerism movement
22. Cultural aspects of consumer behavior

The intent of this part of the book is to show how nonbusiness environmental factors affect consumer purchase strategy by acting through the basic determinants. Business firms have not been overlooked in the discussion, but the permeating influence of business upon consumers makes it necessary to give this variable special attention. The business environment is the subject of the next part.

Part Four proceeds, generally, from the most compact external group (the family) that affects the individual to the broadest group (the culture). The purpose of the first chapter in this part is to bridge the gap between the individual and the environment. Of course, this bridge consists of communications.

16

Introduction to environmental influence

Influence between consumers

Communication defined

One-way or two-way communications

Types of communication

The communications process and consumer behavior

The communications process

Elements of communication

Noise in the communication process

Consumer acceptance of communications

Two-step flow of communications

Significance of the two-step flow

Importance of opinion leaders

Who are the opinion leaders?

Factors affecting how consumers are influenced

Beliefs held by the consumer

Consumer attitude toward the communications

Consumer use of symbols affects influence

Acceptance of change

Consumer influence on others

Type of consumer affects influence

The subject of this part of the book is the relationship between the individual consumer and the external environment. The consumer influences the environment and, in turn, is influenced by the environment. These interactions are numerous and complex, but the unifying factor is communications. Thus, basically, the section involves how consumers communicate and the effects of these communications on individual consumer behavior.

INFLUENCE BETWEEN CONSUMERS

Influence refers to the fact that the attitudes, feelings, actions, and so on, of individuals are affected by communications from others with diverse social and cultural backgrounds.[1] In simple terms, influence is the effect people have on each other as a result of social contact.[2] This definition points to the fact that there are three broad elements of influence: people (individually or in groups), the external environment, and a means of communications between the two. People are necessary to influence and be influenced. Social, cultural, and income factors provide the source of similar and different behavior patterns that lead to interaction. It is communications that then relates the individual to the environment. We have indicated previously that there is very little that a consumer accomplishes that is not affected to some degree by others.[3] However, we have only scratched the surface of group communications and influence. Now we shall delve into the subject in some detail.

Interpersonal communication has four main functions in any society. First, communication is a *social connector*. It is the only method of relating people of diverse feelings, attitudes, economic placement, and backgrounds to one another. Second, communication does more than relate individuals, it serves as a *common denominator*. The sharing of experiences often reduces the differences among individuals and groups, leading to understanding, joint effort, and similar behavior patterns. Third, through the pressures of persuasion and new insight, communication can give the communicator a measure of *control* over the thoughts and actions of others. Fourth, although communication can be a common denominator, it can also be an *instigator of social change*. When situations are made clear through communications, the individual may decide they need to be changed. Furthermore, perceived differences in wealth, social placement, ownership of things, and attitudes lead to dissatisfactions. The individual may be stimulated to want similar or different things.

COMMUNICATION DEFINED

There are several facets of the meaning of communication that require our attention. First, communication is not easy to define. Communication is "really a synonym for social interaction," since all social interaction *takes the form* of some communication.[4] "The word *communicate* is sometimes used to mean the sending or transmitting of information but it actually means to make common or to share. . . .[5] Following these leads, we define *consumer communication* as an interchange of market-related information.[6] In other words, consumer communication is the result of any action, physical, written, or verbal, that conveys meaning about consumption problems between an individual and others in the environment.

The word *communication* is used interchangeably to refer to the message transferred, the media through which the message is relayed, and the entire process, including message and media. Marketers consider an advertisement (message) as a communication, the television station (media) is considered a means of communication, and the Columbia Broadcasting system (sender) is considered as a communications system. We use *communication* to refer to the process by which social interaction occurs. The message refers to that which is communicated, and the media refers to the agency through which the communication takes place.

One-way or two-way communications

Communication is often viewed by marketers as either one-way or two-way.[7] *Two-way communications* occur in a person-to-person relationship such as in the case of a personal selling situation. There is typically one sender and one receiver with immediate feedback between the two. The feedback can occur in several forms, such as sight, sound, smell, and so on. Since feedback is immediate, it is also continuous. This type of communication offers opportunities for improved understanding between the sender and receiver. It accounts, in part, for the effectiveness of personal selling.

One-way communication occurs between a sender and a mass audience. There is either no feedback or the feedback is delayed, and the sender has difficulty determining how much of the message was actually received. One-way communication can typically reach many more people at reduced cost per person reached, but the ability to cause action, as in the case of advertising, is low. The sender must anticipate needs, appeals, messages, and objections. The chances for misunderstanding are great where one-way communication is used.

A question arises as to when actual communication has taken place. Is there communication when a message is received or is understanding or agreement necessary for communications? The attitude taken here is that communication requires more than simply receiving the message. Some degree of understanding is necessary, but it is not necessary that there be agreement on the ideas communicated. If there is no agreement, the communication may be considered ineffective by the sender, but it is still communication if it was understood. Thus, the effectiveness of communications depends on the goal sought. If an advertiser attempts to create a quality brand image, but the consumer associates the brand with lower quality but still buys, has there been communication? The answer is that there has been communication, and if the goal is sales, then the communication was effective. If the goal was a favorable consumer frame of mind toward the quality of the product, then the communication was ineffective.

Types of communication

There are several ways that communications can be classified, and all are meaningful depending on the intended use of the information. First, communications can be classed by *type of coverage* into personal or mass communications. Personal communications take place between two individuals, or between a business and an individual, and mass communications are designed to reach the general public.

Second, classed by *method of communicating*, there are written, verbal, and physical communications. Included in physical communications are all body movements, odor, and such other factors as clothing. In short, all things communicate, but they do not communicate the same things to different people.

Third, communications can be classed by *purpose* into casual, informative, persuasive, or reminder. Casual communication is the backyard variety, usually indulged in to pass the time. Yet, some of the most important communications affecting consumer behavior result from this backyard variety. The other types of communication mentioned are designed specifically to change the consumer's thinking or behavior. Each differs primarily in the intensity of the effort. Persuasive communication has the greatest commitment to changing the opinions, feelings, attitudes, or behavior of the consumers. It is the most influential of all communications.

Fourth, communications can be classed by the *groups that a consumer relates to*. The major types of groups that consumers relate to are the family, various social groups, cultural groups, ethnic groups, religious groups, and business groups.

THE COMMUNICATIONS PROCESS AND CONSUMER BEHAVIOR

Communication does not just happen. It requires some order, some planning. Even the function of speaking is not a reflex, but must be controlled by the speaker. Furthermore, from the moment one contemplates a communication until it is finished, there is a regular process involved that is based on specific elements.

The communications process

The very idea of communication is the establishment of some common ground of understanding—to share feelings or attitudes. The process by which this sharing takes place is illustrated in Figure 16–1.[8] The communications process consists of two basic components, three activities, and one output. These elements are defined below:

Figure 16–1

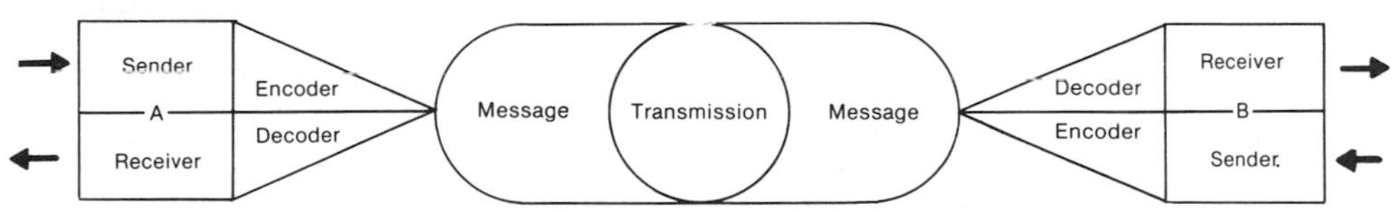

Source: Adapted from Wilbur Schramm, "How Communication Works," *Advertising Management: Selected Readings,* ed. Harper W. Boyd, Jr. and Joseph W. Newman (Homewood, Ill.: Richard D. Irwin, Inc., 1965), p. 79.

These elements are defined below:

I. *Components*
   A. *Sender*—the person or group of persons who have some thought, idea, or concept to be transmitted to others.
   B. *Receiver*—the person or persons who are the target of the thought that is transmitted.

II. *Activities*
   A. *Encode*—to translate what the source wishes to communicate into effective symbolism for transmission.
   B. *Decode*—to interpret the symbolism transmitted for the receiver.
   C. *Transmission*—conveyance of the thought or idea through some effective channel between the sender and the receiver.

III. *Output*
   A. *Message*—the thought, idea, or concept which is transmitted between components.

Communication is typically a push-pull process, as illustrated, in which a message is sent and some response, called feedback is evoked. This *feedback* is just reverse communication, and no special device is needed to demonstrate it on the figure.[9] Feedback contains all the elements of the original communication. In the figure, individual A has some thought to transmit to individual B. Individual A translates the thought (encodes) into a message that is transmitted through some channel. Individual B interprets (decodes) the message and internalizes it. One complete communication has occurred at this point. However, should B wish to respond to A's message, which is fairly typical in cases of social interaction, then the roles of the parties are reversed. Here we have feedback where individual B becomes the sender and A the receiver. This reverse communication is exactly like the original in execution. However, it is generally referred to as feedback because the message is made in response to a previous communication. In practice, the two parties may communicate for some time with each alternately reversing their role in the communication process.

Elements of communication

We are now in a position to discuss the elements of the communication process in more detail. The sender-encoder and the receiver-decoder are considered together for this purpose.

Sender-encoder. The sender of market-related communications can be a family member, people with whom the consumer associates, or business establishments. No factor of communication is more important than the sender. Some people, Hitler and Churchill, for example, had a knack for language and a way of presenting information that made believers out of large numbers of people. Such businesses as General Electric, Procter and Gamble, Macy's, Goodyear, General Motors, and Korvettes have been unusually successful in communicating through personal selling and advertising.

The encoder may be the same person as the sender, or the sender and encoder may be different. For example, the managers of Sears may be considered the senders of communications about a new line of furniture handled by the organization. However, the advertising department is the encoder because the employees of this department must translate the information about the furniture into terms the customers will understand. People differ in their encoding of essentially similar information. Thus, the communications used by Sears to sell the furniture differ from those used by a furniture store.

The message. The sender communicates by use of messages, and any writing, speaking, wave of the hand, lifting of the eyebrow, or other signal that can be interpreted is a message.[10] Messages always involve symbols. Symbols stand for the thought, and thought must be translated into symbols to be transmitted. Symbols are considered in detail later in the chapter. These symbols are the basis of all communications.

Some consumers respond more to emotional appeals and some respond more to appeals to reason. All consumers respond to both types of appeal. Studies indicate that four considerations are important to message effectiveness:[11]

1. The message must gain attention.
2. The message must be built around symbols that relate to a consumer's experience.
3. The message must arouse personality needs.
4. The message must suggest solutions to the needs aroused.

The type of message is also important. A favorable response can be gained using either positive or negative appeals, but not everyone responds favorably to the same type of appeal.

Transmission. Message transmission takes place through a channel. A channel may be ink, paper, electric current, pictures, or visual light. In other words, anything that is capable of transmitting a message is a channel. Certain consumers respond to one type of channel and others to a different type. One consumer deliberately reads the newspaper ads while another ignores them. Radio is not listened to and television is not watched equally by everyone, and even when listening and watching consumers do not all turn to the same program.

The decoder-receiver. The receiver and decoder are typically the same person, but for a particular message, there may be an intermediary decoder, as in the case of the priest who interprets the Lord's message or a teacher who explains a math problem to a pupil. In marketing, a fashion leader is one who interprets current style messages and relates this information to large numbers of consumers. Of course, the interaction between the intermediary and the individual may also be considered a separate communication which the receiver must decode. Much of what we refer to as miscommunication or ineffective communication is a result of faulty decoding. The full message isn't received, or it is interpreted in a way other than that intended by the sender.[12]

Individual consumers differ in their reactions to messages. Some personality types are more easily persuaded to accept ideas and messages than others. Some important general conclusions relating to this point are the following:

1. Consumers who relate to others (other-directed) are more persuasible than those who are self-centered (inner-directed).
2. Consumers with low intellectual ability are more influenced by one-sided communications than consumers with higher intellectual ability.
3. Consumers of high intellectual ability are more influenced by presentations showing more points of view.
4. Consumers who are socially withdrawn remain relatively uninfluenced by persuasive communications.

5. Consumers of high intelligence are less easily persuaded by false or irrelevant arguments than those of low intelligence.[13]

Feedback. Feedback is essential to effective communication. In one study, various types of feedback were tested for their effectiveness in aiding learning and reducing frustrations within a group. The results demonstrated that feedback increases the accuracy of results and aids confidence.[14] Feedback is most effective when it provides for questions and answers. Market feedback can be in the form of an answer, a purchase, or a change of attitude that may affect future purchases. Many types of feedback are received by businesses concerning consumers. Some of these are sales results, complaints, compliments, returned merchandise, failure to respond (lack of sales), and so on. Feedback provides a basis for adjustment and change in the communication so that it may be made more effective.

Noise in the communication process

Noise is used to mean any type of interference with the communication process.[15] Noise was not included in the elements of communication because it is usually a disruptive and not a constructive force. Interference can occur anywhere in the process where there is interaction. The major points are shown in Figure 16–2. Several types of noise are possible in the communication.

Figure 16–2
Noise in the communication process

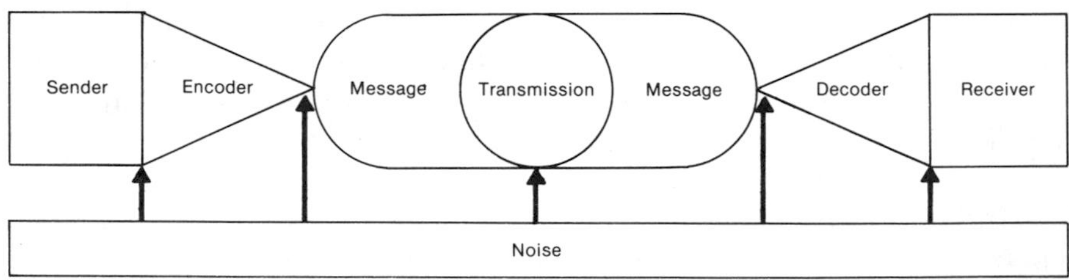

One kind of noise occurs when the environment of the sender and receiver have nothing in common. Of course, feedback can sometimes alleviate this situation. Noise can occur because the idea presented by the sender may not be clear, the thought may not be properly encoded, or the decoding may be at fault. Noise may result from channel selection, since a consumer may miss the message or it may not get sufficient attention to register. The net effect of noise is to reduce the effectiveness of communications.

CONSUMER ACCEPTANCE OF COMMUNICATIONS

Of course, a major reason for any communications is to influence the thoughts or actions of consumers. Thus, the adoption by the receiver of the ideas communicated is a natural objective of communications. Five stages may be identified in the *adoption process.*[16] These stages indicate how consumers evaluate new ideas and make decisions on whether to accept or reject them.

1. *Awareness.* At this initial stage, the consumer has been exposed to the idea but does not have sufficient knowledge about it. An example can be found in a new product that the consumer has just heard about. The consumer has no strong opinion.
2. *Interest.* At this stage, the consumer becomes interested in the new product and seeks additional information about it.
3. *Evaluation.* Here, the consumer mentally relates the product to his or her present need situation and decides whether or not to try it.
4. *Trial.* At this stage, the consumer pretests the product on a small scale to determine its particular utility. The product may be rejected here or at any previous stage. The consumer becomes motivated somewhere between stage 3 and stage 4.
5. *Adoption.* Finally, at the adoption stage, the consumer decides to accept the product. It becomes a part of the consumer's normal purchase behavior.

Research shows that consumers use different sources of communicated information over the adoption process. Table 16–1 has data on communication sources for a wide range of farm products. Notice that the mass media are more used at the awareness and interest stage of adoption. Reference group sources and specialists become more important as the consumer approaches evaluation, trial, and adoption. Dealers and salespeople did not rank high as a communication source at any stage of adoption.

It is not necessary for a consumer to go through each stage before adoption. For example, a person observing a package of chewing gum for the first time may move directly from awareness to trial. Generally, the higher the price of the product or idea or the more complex it may be, the greater the likelihood that the consumer will go through all the stages. It should also be noted that a consumer need not begin the adoption process at the awareness stage. It is possible that a person has already gone through the process to evaluation and rejected the product or idea. Some new situation or information may cause the person to reconsider at a later date and pick up either at the evaluation stage or at the trial stage.

Table 16–1
Rank order of information sources by stage in the adoption process

Awareness:	*Interest:*	*Evaluation:*	*Trial:*	*Adoption:*
Learns about a new idea or practice	Gets more information about it	Tries it out mentally	Uses or tries a little	Accepts it for full-scale and continued use
1. Mass media—radio, TV, newspapers, magazines	1. Mass media	1. Friends and neighbors	1. Friends and neighbors	1. Friends and neighbors
2. Friends and neighbors—mostly other farmers	2. Friends and neighbors	2. Agricultural agencies	2. Agricultural agencies	2. Agricultural agencies
3. Agricultural agencies, Extension, Vo-Ag.	3. Agricultural agencies	3. Dealers and salesmen	3. Dealers and salesmen	3. Mass media
4. Dealers and salespeople	4. Dealers and salespeople	4. Mass media	4. Mass media	4. Dealers and salespeople

Personal experience is the most important factor in continued use of an idea.

Source: William Lazer and William E. Bell, "The Communications Process and Innovation," *Journal of Advertising Research* (Sept 1966) pp. 2–7.

The acceptance of ideas found in communications can be either immediate or delayed. *Immediate reaction* to communications occurs when the message is received and the consumer response follows directly or nearly so. An immediate purchase based on the recommendations of a friend or neighbor is an immediate reaction. A *delayed reaction* means that the consumer is influenced by the communications, but the decision is put off until some later date. This type of reaction is most likely to occur with mass communications. An advertisement may convince the consumer to buy, but the actual purchase is put off until the next trip to the store. Another example is where it takes several ads to convince the consumer to take action. A residual of goodwill is built up until it becomes sufficiently strong to cause the consumer to act. Sometimes the reaction desired on the part of the consumer is some change in attitude, but even this change can be immediate or delayed.

TWO-STEP FLOW OF COMMUNICATIONS

Up until now we have discussed influence as if it always resulted from direct communications between a sender and a consumer. The fact is that influence is seldom that simple. Indeed communication is often direct, but it also occurs in two steps, with an intermediary between the original source and the final destination.

Significance of the two-step flow

Evidence exists to indicate that the flow of mass communications is much less direct than often supposed.[17] Figure 16–3 illustrates the basic nature of the two-step-flow concept. The tendency is for influence to flow from the mass media to opinion leaders who are receptive to the idea presented, and from these opinion leaders to the general public. The original contention was that opinion leaders influenced others as a result of their interest and placement in the communications network.[18] It was also felt that opinion leaders exerted pressure on the masses for social conformity. While evidence exists to support the first position there is considerable doubt about the ability of opinion leaders to exert pressure on the group.

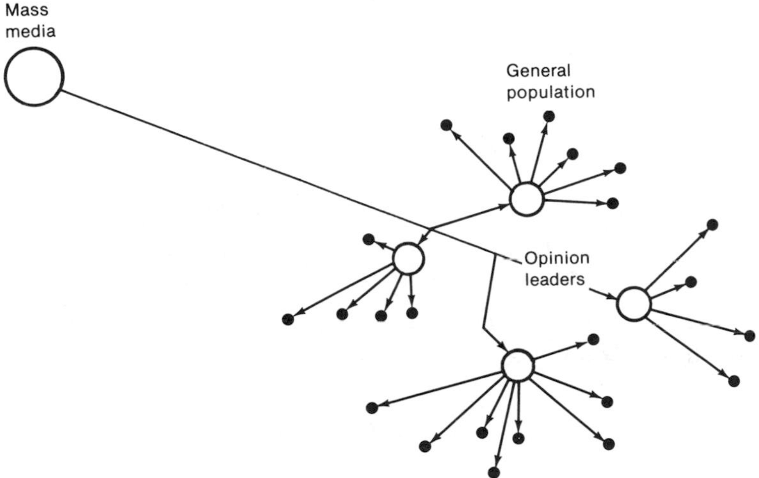

The market is composed of a relatively few active information seekers and a large number of passive information receivers.[19] These information seekers may be different from innovators because they may seek information only about the product or service that interests them. The opinion leader may be conservative in all respects except this one interest. Innovators, on the other hand, seek change for its own sake. One fact has become clear about opinion leaders, their influence can be horizontal as well as vertical.[20] A *vertical flow* is from high status, socially elite individuals to the average consumer. A *horizontal flow* occurs when people are affected by others in their own peer group. There is a growing feeling that a horizontal two-step flow is more important than the vertical type. Consumers tend to be influenced by people of their own type with whom they regularly come in contact.

Importance of opinion leaders

The significance of group influence on consumer behavior cannot be overestimated. The opinion leader is a trend setter who accepts the risk and uncertainty of new products, services, and market innovations. This is true whether the instigator is a political figure, a movie star, or the next door neighbor. The opinion leader interprets, evaluates, and guides the general acceptance by other consumers of new ideas. Personal influence has been shown to be more important for the purchase of new products and in switching stores.[21] Even so, one cannot discount the influence of the mass media. Remember, the media influence consumers directly and also influence the opinion leaders. A classic study of the effects of informal influence was made by *Fortune* magazine in Philadelphia neighborhoods. The number and brand of air conditioners were plotted in house windows and compared to the patterns of social contact and influence in the neighborhood. The purchase patterns were found to follow the patterns of personal influence even to the brand purchased.[22]

The automobile industry provides a good example of the failure to recognize the importance of opinion leaders. In the 1950s, the industry considered the owners of small foreign cars as a little strange and unworthy of notice. Unfortunately for the auto makers, these consumers turned out to be real opinion leaders, and the small car caught on. Detroit had difficulty cracking the small-car market as a result.

Who are the opinion leaders?

The use of the term "opinion leader" is perhaps a mistake, because it assumes someone who has control over others who must follow.[23] As a result, there is a tendency to associate opinion leaders with prominent people or people in the public eye. As a matter of fact, for certain products such as fashion clothing, jewelry, shoes, etc., politicians, movie stars, presidents and their wives, athletes, and nouveau riche make excellent opinion leaders. These persons have a lot at stake in keeping up with fashion and being in the public eye. However, the facts are that in specific situations, anyone can dictate fashion and other product trends.[24] Some of the more lasting consumer trends have been established by quite ordinary persons. For example, high school students tend to set the fashion for music; college students are important in men's clothing fashion; housewives (who worked in the war plants of World War II) started the fashion for slacks; and young adults greatly influence the fashion in small sports cars.

There is a growing body of evidence, although not conclusive, that opinion leaders fall into some general patterns. One study found that,

"(1) socially integrated individuals are highest in fashion interest, fashion magazine readership, and interpersonal exposure, and (2) socially independent individuals are highest in self-confidence."[25] Robertson and Kennedy found that the most important characteristics of consumer innovation are venturesomeness and social mobility, although participation, financial standing, and interest outside the community were also important.[26] In any case, it is clear that a variety of persons can be product innovators, depending on the product and the situation.

FACTORS AFFECTING HOW CONSUMERS ARE INFLUENCED

Among the more important of the factors that affect the influence of communications on consumers are (1) the beliefs held by the consumer, (2) the consumer's attitude toward the communications, (3) the use of symbols, (4) the willingness of the consumer to accept change, (5) the consumer's influence over others, and (6) the type of consumers involved.

Beliefs held by the consumer

The ability of a persuasive argument to affect change in a consumer depends, in part, on the type of belief brought into question.[27] Consumers are willing to change some beliefs much more quickly than others. Professor Milton Rokeach has outlined five important types of beliefs, and the following discussion is adapted from his classification.[28]

1. *Primitive beliefs.* These are deep-seated beliefs in the physical and social world and of the self. We believe to save is good, that right will prevail, that competition is fair, that one's car is as good as any made, and that one's home is comfortable. These beliefs are uncontestable facts to the individual. Everyone else is aware of these types of beliefs.

2. *Beliefs of deep personal experience.* These are beliefs that one holds no matter whether others hold them or not. These beliefs are facts to the individual, and they are usually about ourselves. We believe ourselves to be intelligent, easygoing, yet ambitious. Some of these beliefs relate to what we like, and some relate to our fears. For example, a consumer feels he or she is a capable buyer, but does not trust a certain retailer.

3. *Authority beliefs.* These are beliefs which relate to physical and social alternatives which are too complex to verify within ourselves. Therefore, we tend to accept the word of some authority. These beliefs are broad in scope. Students tend to take the word of their

teachers. Up to a point, children believe their parents. The point is that these are important beliefs *we* hold—and we look for others who support our belief in them. Testimonials in advertising are effective partly because they support the consumers' authority beliefs.

4. *Peripheral beliefs.* These are beliefs that are derived from outside sources. A Ford owner derives the belief that his or her car is more soundly constructed than other cars from company sales material. Some consumers buy a particular shaver because a prominent athlete recommends it. Consumers believe these ideas because of faith in the source and not because of personal experience.

5. *Inconsequential beliefs.* These are beliefs of no great importance to the consumer. There is no great harm if the belief is proved wrong. Some beliefs that fall in this group are: an electric razor is better than a blade, suburban shopping beats city shopping, and similar convenience goods are priced about the same.

Beliefs that are taken for granted are basic to a person's existence, and these beliefs are the most resistant to change. Consumers even become upset when these beliefs are challenged. Beliefs of personal experience are almost as difficult to change. Consumers cling to these beliefs no matter whether others agree with us or not. Authority beliefs can be changed, but the easiest way to make the change is to bring the authority into question. The same reasoning holds for derived beliefs. The individual is willing to revise his or her position on these beliefs if the authorities or sources are shown to be in error. Inconsequential beliefs can be changed with no difficulty, because they do not affect the core of one's system of values.

Consumer attitude toward the communications

The ability to influence is not only affected by the type of belief held but influence is also affected by the receiver's attitude toward the ideas communicated.[29] One's response may be described as (1) no attitude, (2) idea understood and rejected, (3) idea understood and ignored, or (4) idea understood and believed. Only the fourth attitude is favorable to a change in the consumer's behavior. The communicator's task is more difficult if the receiver is not aware of the idea, or if one understands but has rejected the idea. If the consumer already believes, then the sender's task is easy. It is only necessary to move the receiver to action. The results of three years of research surveying hundreds of books and magazines has convinced the Leo Burnett Company, first, that no ad is likely to be completely believable if its purpose is to change the consumer's mind and, second, that ads do not need to be completely believed to be effective.[30] No single ad can change a consumer's mind, but several ads may accomplish that end over time.

A consumer may have no attitude because the communication has not been received or because the communication was not understood. It is difficult for a person to remain neutral toward an idea once that idea is understood. The consumer will ignore the idea only if it has no bearing on his or her life—that is, if it is a completely irrelevant idea to the person. It is more likely that communication will be understood and either accepted or rejected. The problem of ignored communication is persuading the consumer that the idea does relate to his or her life. A rejected communication is most difficult to handle because the persuader must first convince the consumer that the rejection was wrong and then convince the person that the idea should be believed.

Consumer use of symbols affects influence

It is through the use of symbols that the consumer interprets and gives meaning to the market environment. All communications are founded on the use of symbols, and one difficulty with communications is that the symbols used do not always convey exactly the intended thought.[31]

How symbols are used. Symbols, by their nature stand for something else, as Figure 16–4 demonstrates. There is no direct relation-

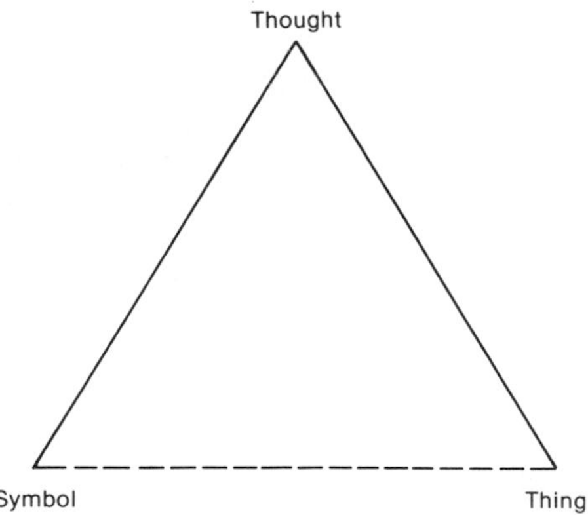

ship between the symbol and the thing. There is a relationship between the symbol and the thought it produces. There is also a relationship between the thought and the thing. The accuracy of these relationships is subject to attitudes, experience, expectations, perception, and present needs. There can always be misunderstanding when communication is based on "thing" substitutes. Almost anything can be a symbol. Symbols are:

> . . . *such familiar things as written and spoken words, religious beliefs and practices, including creeds and ceremonies, (the several arts,) such familiar signs as the cross and the flag, and countless other objects and acts which stand for something more than they are.*[32]

It follows that although symbols affect both the conscious and unconscious mind, the symbol should not be confused with the actual thing it refers to. The symbol is no more than a communications shortcut.

Importance of symbols to consumers. The symbol that produces thought may be more important to the buyer than the thing itself. In one sense, all things that people buy are merely symbols that stand for satisfaction. The things people buy have personal and social meanings that are completely outside the products' material functions. Since products are recognized by their symbolic meaning, shopping is made easier with less conflict or indecision than would otherwise be the case. Consumer choices are made more routine, and more goods are bought on impulse, because one object is symbolically more harmonious to that individual's goals. We select our furniture not only for utility but also to serve as visible symbols of our taste, wealth, and social position. We often choose our residence because it offers us a "good address." We trade a perfectly good automobile in for a later model, not always to get better transportation, but to give evidence to the community that we can afford the new car.

Persuaders may use "poison" words, or bad symbols, to arouse fear.[33] For instance "B.O." and "bad breath" are used to arouse fears of ruined careers and wrecked love affairs. The testimonial employs the voice of experience to cause consumers to accept or reject persons, products, or ideas. The association of prestige and the product can make advertising highly successful. Consider the testimonial, "Aren't you glad you use Dial soap—Don't you wish everybody did?" However, unless the person and the message are associated or credible, there can be a negative reaction. It is hard for the average consumer to imagine a glamorous movie star washing dishes and reciting the merits of brand X.

Characteristics of symbols. Symbols display certain characteristics that are important for the understanding of consumer behavior. These characteristics are gender, social participation, conventionality, and self-expression. A basic characteristic of symbols is *gender*. In any society, roles are assigned by sex, and we refer to physical acts as well as innate objects as if they were male or female. A large part of marketing communications is designed to create or change the sex of products. Mr. Clean and Ajax have male images, and who doesn't know of the attempt to change the sex of Marlboro cigarettes by the use of cowboys with tattoos on their hands.

Symbols of *social participation* are based on the fact that one can make inferences about the nature of an individual by the products one owns. Automobiles, homes, and clothes are associated with a person's social position or aspirations. One can gain insight into people's attitudes, manner of speaking, and so on, by the products they own. *Conventionality* symbols make use of the fact that some products are staple and bought for their function rather than for status: milk and bread fall in this group. Other products are associated with *self-expression symbols,* even though the product may be generally staple in nature. Dishes, silverware, and tablecloths fall in this category. These products have a measure of personal identification.

Individual and group symbolism. Two systems of symbols, sometimes in conflict, are important to consumer behavior: the symbols associated with the desire for individuality and those associated with a desire for group recognition and participation. Examples of the first are the symbols associated with secret societies, fraternities, and so on. Patriotic groups, each having its own symbols but all associating themselves with the American flag, are examples of the second. Consumer individuality can be observed in attempts to purchase unique products or prestigious brands that cannot be purchased by everyone. Group participation can be observed in the individual consumer's loyalty to accepted suburban stores and by loyalty to accepted brands, such as Kodak and Ann Page. The point is that it is desirable for the consumer to be associated with some brands or methods of purchase, but the consumer seeks individuality in certan other brands and methods of purchase. Marketers need to know the symbolism associated with consumer behavior in order to reach those consumers more effectively.

Acceptance of change

The decision to accept change is made on the basis of the consumer's views about the purchase situation. The consumer's understanding of the relationship among all the business and human components that make up his or her environment is referred to as his cognitive structure. Any decision to accept change in purchasing behavior is a decision, by that consumer, to modify his or her cognitive structure. Both face-to-face and mass communications make attempts to modify the consumer's cognitive structure.[34] The adoption of an idea requires that the message must not only be received but must be accepted. The consumer may be willing to receive information but not to accept it. The consumer may also be unwilling even to receive the message. The latter case may occur when an ad in a magazine is deliberately passed over by the consumer or when the ratio is turned off.

The prune industry offers a good recent example of using effective symbolism to cause change. The sale of prunes had been declining. Advertising of prunes had been focused on their value as a laxative, and many people considered prunes a symbol of age and linked the product with medicines, constipation, and childhood reprimands. A new image was created to persuade people to eat prunes—California's new "wonder fruit." Bright colors replaced black-and-white in advertisements; "wrinkles" were described as resulting because prunes "pack-in so much sunlight energy, ready to pop." Advertisements used such lines as, "Eat them like candy right out of the box."

Consumer influence on others

Some consumers change and affect others, and some do not, but it is true that aggressiveness of a person has a lot to do with the extent of his or her influence on others. In this respect, consumers can be typed as follows:

1. *Active adopters* adopt the idea, product, or service and attempt to influence others to do so.
2. *Active rejecters* reject the idea, product, or service and attempt to influence others to do so.
3. *Passive adopters* adopt the idea, product, or service but do not attempt to influence others to do so.
4. *Passive rejecters* reject the idea, product, or service but do not attempt to influence others to do so.

Opinion leaders may be active adopters or active rejectors. They influence other individuals to accept or reject technological changes.[35] Passive consumers in our society rarely, if ever, actively stimulate demand for change. Yet these consumers are often found to influence change by the example they set for the group. The passive group can also affect change by slowing down the acceptance of new ideas.

Type of consumer affects influence

The type of consumer to whom the message is directed affects the extent of that message's influence. Consumers have been classified according to their willingness to accept change and innovations that they have been made aware of into the following categories:[36]

1. *Innovators.* This niche in the innovativeness continuum is generally occupied by venturesome consumers who are eager to try new ideas, who rise at once to meet the challenge of risk and uncertainty which surrounds change.[37] They are usually more worldly and associate with other tastemakers and trend setters. And considerable wealth and intellect are usually a part of their composition, for innovating is expensive and often requires complex technical skills.

2. *Early adopters.* These consumers are a more integral part of the community's social fabric than their rash and radical cousins, the innovators. And as such, they are the most effective opinion leaders in society. As catalysts of change who are closer to the "average" consumer, these early adopters are respected by their peers and considered highly effective tastemakers.

3. *Early majority.* Consumers in this group adopt new ideas just before the "average" member in the community. These consumers are usually recognized for their role in making innovations legitimate, for they are the vital link between the very early and the relatively late adopters.

4. *Late majority.* These consumers adopt innovations just after the "average" member of the community. A conservative approach is usually taken, but the adoption of these innovations may eventually become an economic or social necessity. Public opinion and the pressure of peers are often necessary to reinforce their decision to adopt.

5. *Laggards.* Included within this category are the near-isolates—the last members of a community to adopt ideas. These consumers are almost exclusively tradition oriented; their frame of reference is always the past. Adoption of ideas always lags far behind the original awareness of the idea, for laggards are often suspicious of change and innovation. Consumers in this group defy any attempt to alter their traditional values.

The adoption process by consumers is not as discrete as these classes indicate, but the types can be observed.[38] A consumer may be an innovator for one product and a laggard for another. Laggards may lead change when style is moving in the direction of conservatism. Individuals may also move between classes over time.

NOTES

1. For an excellent treatment of how people deliberately try to influence the values, beliefs, and behavior of others, see Erwin P. Bettinghaus, *Persuasive Communications* (New York: Holt, Rinehart & Winston, Inc., 1968).
2. James Hulbert and Noel Capon, "Interpersonal Communication in Marketing: An Overview," *Journal of Marketing Research,* vol. 9 (February 1972), pp. 27–34.
3. Ibid.
4. Chester A. Wasson, Frederick D. Sturdivant, and David H. McConaughy, *Competition and Human Behavior* (New York: Appleton-Century-Crofts, 1968), p. 145.
5. George A. Field, John Douglas, and Lawrence X. Tarpey, *Marketing Management: A Behavioral Approach* (Columbus, Ohio: Charles E. Merrill Publishing Co., 1966), p. 348.

6. See: Keith Davis, *Human Behavior at Work* (New York: McGraw-Hill Book Co., 1972), p. 379.
7. Elihu Katz, "The Two-Step Flow of Communication: An Up-to-date Report on an Hypothesis," Reported in *Dimensions of Communications,* Ed. Lee Richardson (New York: Appleton-Century-Crofts, 1969), pp. 246–62.
8. For other concepts of the process see: L. Thayer, *Communication and Communication Systems* (Homewood, Ill.: Richard D. Irwin, Inc., 1968); William V. Haney, *Communication and Organizational Behavior* (Homewood, Ill.: Richard D. Irwin, Inc., 1973), pp. 179–95; M. L. DeFleur, *Theories of Mass Communication* (New York: McKay Publishers, Inc., 1966).
9. Jon Eisenson, J. Jeffery Auer, and John V. Irwin, *The Psychology of Communication* (New York: Appleton-Century-Crofts, 1963).
10. Thomas S. Robertson, *Consumer Behavior* (Glenview, Ill.: Scott, Foresman & Co., 1970), pp. 49–50.
11. Wilbur Schramm, "How Communication Works," *The Process and Effects of Mass Communications,* ed. Wilbur Schramm (Urbana: University of Illinois Press, 1954), pp. 3–26.
12. Max Wales, Galen Rarick, and Hal Davis, "Mesasge Exaggeration by the Receiver," *Journalism Quarterly* (Summer 1963), pp. 339–42.
13. Irvin L. Janis and Peter B. Field, "A Behavioral Assessment of Persuasibility: Consistency of Individual Differences," *Personality and Persuasibility,* eds. Irving L. Janis and Carl I. Hovland (New Haven, Conn.: Yale University Press, 1959), pp. 29–61.
14. H. J. Leavitt and R. A. H. Miller, "Some Effects of Feedback on Communications," *Human Relations,* vol. 4 (1951), pp. 401–10.
15. Wilbur Schramm, "Information Theory and Mass Communication," *Journalism Quarterly* (Spring 1955), pp. 131–46.
16. William J. McGuire, "Some Internal Psychological Factors Influencing Consumer Choice," *Journal of Consumer Research,* vol. 2 (March 1976), pp. 302–19.
17. William R. Darden and Fred D. Reynolds, "Backward Profiling of Male Innovators," *Journal of Marketing Research,* vol. 11 (February 1974), pp. 79–85.
18. Lawrence G. Corey, "People Who Claim to be Opinion Leaders: Identifying Their Characteristics by Self-Report," *Journal of Marketing,* vol. 35 (October 1971), pp. 48–53.
19. James H. Myers and Thomas S. Robertson, "Dimensions of Opinion Leadership," *Journal of Marketing Research,* vol. 9 (February 1972), pp. 41–46.
20. Francesco Nicosia, "Opinion Leadership and the Flow of Communications: Some Problems and Prospects," *Reflections on Progress in Marketing,* ed. L. George Smith (Chicago: American Marketing Assn., 1964), pp. 340–58.

21. James W. Taylor, "A Striking Characteristic of Innovators," *Journal of Marketing Research,* vol. 14 (February 1977), pp. 104–07.
22. William H. Whyte, Jr., "The Webb of Word of Mouth," *Fortune,* vol. 50 (November 1954), pp. 140–43, 204–12; Shlomo I. Lampert, "Word of Mouth Activity during the Introduction of a New Food Product," *Consumer Behavior: Theory and Applications,* eds. John U. Farley, John A. Howard, and L. Winston Ring (Boston: Allyn & Bacon, Inc., 1974), Chap. 4.
23. Robertson, *Consumer Behavior,* pp. 83–84.
24. See: Edward M. Tauber, "Why People Shop," *Journal of Marketing,* vol. 36 (October 1972), pp. 46–59; Corey, "People Who Claim to Be Opinion Leaders," pp. 48–53; John O. Summers, "Media Exposure Patterns of Consumer Innovators," *Journal of Marketing Research,* vol. 36 (January 1972), pp. 43–49.
25. Fred D. Reynolds and William R. Darden, "Mutually Adaptive Effects of Interpersonal Communication," *Journal of Marketing Research,* vol. 7 (November 1971), pp. 449–54.
26. Thomas S. Robertson and James N. Kennedy, "Prediction of Consumer Innovators: Application of Multiple Discriminant Analysis," *Journal of Marketing Research,* vol. 5 (February 1969), pp. 64–69.
27. Martin Fishbein and Icek Ajzen, *Belief, Attitude, Intention and Behavior* (Reading, Pa.: Addison-Wesley Publishing Co., 1975), pp. 467–70.
28. Milton Rokeach, "Images of the Consumer's Changing Mind On and Off Madison Avenue," (paper delivered at the 1963 regional convention, American Association of Advertising Agencies), pp. 4–7.
29. John O. Summers and Charles W. King, "Interpersonal Communications and New Product Attitudes," *Marketing Involvement in Society and the Economy,* ed. Philip R. McDonald (Chicago: American Marketing Assn., 1969), pp. 292–99.
30. J. A. Maloney, "Is Advertising Believability Really Important?" *Journal of Marketing,* vol. 27 (October 1963), pp. 1–8.
31. An excellent general discussion of symbols can be found in: Glenn M. Vernon, *Human Interaction,* 2d ed. (New York: The Ronald Press Co., 1972), Chap. 3.
32. W. Lloyd Warner, *American Life, Dreams, and Reality* (Chicago: University of Chicago Press, 1953), p. 2.
33. Michael L. Ray and William L. Wilkie, "Fear: The Potential of an Appeal Neglected by Marketing," *Journal of Marketing,* vol. 34 (January 1970), pp. 54–62; Brian Sternthal and C. Samuel Craig, "Fear Appeals: Revisited and Revised," *Journal of Consumer Research,* vol. 1 (December 1974), pp. 22–34; Homer E. Spence and Reza Moinpour, "Fear Appeals in Marketing—A Social Perspective," *Journal of Marketing,* vol. 36 (July 1972), pp. 39–43.
34. John A. Czepiel, "Word-of-Mouth Processes in the Diffusion of a Major Technological Innovation," *Journal of Marketing Research,* vol. 11 (May 1974), pp. 172–80.

35. David F. Midgley, "A Simple Mathematical Theory of Innovative Behavior," *Journal of Consumer Research,* vol. 3 (June 1976), pp. 31–41.
36. "The Process of Mass Acceptance," *Modern Packaging Magazine,* (1959), pp. 75ff.
37. Summers, "Media Exposure Patterns of Consumer Innovators," pp. 43–49; James H. Donnelly, Jr. and John M. Ivancevich, "A Methodology for Identifying Innovator Characteristics of New Brand Purchasers," *Journal of Marketing Research,* Vol. 11 (August 1974), pp. 331–34.
38. Ronald B. Marks and R. Eugene Hughes, "The Consumer Innovator: Identifying the Profile Of the Earliest Adopters of Community Antenna Television," *Marketing: 1776–1976 and Beyond,* ed. Kenneth L. Bernhardt, (Chicago: American Marketing Assn., 1976), pp. 568–71.

QUESTIONS

1. Define influence. What are the four main functions of interpersonal communication? Explain.
2. What is communication? How does it differ from influence? How is the message, the media, and the process related to communications?
3. Explain and contrast one-way and two-way communications. What is their importance of consumer behavior?
4. Explain the major ways in which communications can be classified. Demonstrate how each is important to consumer behavior.
5. What is the communications process? Explain. Why is it referred to as a push-pull process? Define the major elements of the communication process.
6. Discuss the manner in which noise affects consumer behavior. What do you think that business can do about noise?
7. Explain the steps in the acceptance process. Is acceptance immediate or delayed? Discuss.
8. What is the two-step flow of communication? Is it a valid concept? Are opinion leaders important to this process? Explain.
9. How do consumer beliefs affect the influence of communications? Explain the major types of beliefs. How do attitudes affect communications effectiveness?
10. Explain the effect that symbolism has on influencing consumers. What are the characteristics of symbols? How do consumers influence each other? Explain.

17

Family influences: Internal behavior

The basic behavioral unit in almost all societies is the family. The development of socialized patterns, including consumer patterns, in children is heavily dependent on the family unit. The effect, during the formative years, of the various family members on the behavior of children exerts a continual influence on the individual throughout life. When the child "leaves the nest," he or she begins to form new relationships. Most people eventually marry and form a new family unit. As a child, the individual's role was subordinate; as a parent, the individual's role takes on increased importance. Family relationships discussed here underlie not only the family target assortment, but many of the other influences on individual consumer behavior.

FAMILY AND HOUSEHOLD DEFINED

In a general way, the human institution referred to as a family or household can be viewed from the perspective of a behavioral unit or a statistical unit. Although the terms family and household are often used interchangeably, differences in their meaning can be pinpointed. The behavioral view focuses on the internal relationships of the group, including structure, relationships, problems, and thought processes. Thus a *family* can be defined as a social group related by birth, marriage, or adoption, sanctioned by the system, with individuals acting according to well defined social roles.[1] Although families normally consist of two parents and one or more children, either natural or adopted, it is not necessary that both parents or children be present to constitute a family. In most societies, families are formalized through the institution of marriage, and they display well-developed systems of symbols, language, and rituals.

The *household* refers to a statistical unit, and its primary use is to analyze economic activity. The household is the unit used in the collection of almost all census data. It deals mostly with location and characteristics of the group. The term household is defined as *all individuals living alone or people living together under one roof.*[2] It does not require either a blood or legal relationship. Thus a household is a broader unit than the family.

Marketers are vitally interested in both the family as a behavioral unit and in the household as a statistical unit. Most of the time there is no need to distinguish between the two, but where such distinction is necessary, it is pointed out. The reader should note that the family unit or the household unit can and often does consist of individuals. For example, the basic determinants of consumer behavior discussed in Part Three involved families or households in the sense that every individual either is one or is a member of one. Since our attention in this chapter is behavioral, the term *family* is used as the basis for our discussion. In the next chapter, where the emphasis is on statistical considerations, the term *household* is used.

FUNCTION OF FAMILIES

The family could not exist if it did not perform four basic functions: (1) the function of procreation, (2) the economic function, (3) the social functions, and (4) the child-rearing function.[3] These four functions are basic because the human race, as we know it, could not exist without the performance of each. Children must be born, educated, and provided for. The human child cannot provide for itself. The child does not inherit a knowledge of social values and behavior. These things must be taught. These ends cannot be achieved without the economic activity necessary to provide income. The family unit is the best means that society has discovered for handling these functions.

Each of the basic functions of the family can be associated with consumer purchase behavior.[4] Sex and procreation affect nearly all consumer behavior. There are, of course, products to aid procreation and products to interfere with the process. Of more importance, are the indirect effects of sex on consumer behavior. The desire to attract and hold a mate directly affects the consumers' choice of clothes, jewelry, perfume, hair preparations, food, and recreation. Much consumer advertising has some sex connotation because of the importance of this factor in our everyday lives. Child rearing and social activities are almost as important as sex to consumer behavior. The consumer's home, mode of dress, recreation, and eating habits are influenced by social contacts. Furthermore, the children in the family have their own individual needs.

Economic activity is entered into in order to obtain consumer desires. The things consumers want greatly affect their ambitions, work habits, the kind of work they do, and their attitudes toward work. Income also places limitations on what consumers can have and forces choices among products.

FAMILY ORGANIZATION

Products are bought for the individual members of the family or for the group as a whole. Furthermore, each member of the family exerts some influence on the other members for most products purchased. To improve our understanding of the needs of the family as a unit, we want to take a look at the family as an organization.

Characteristics of family organization

As a group, the family exhibits all the aspects of any organization.[5] The differences among families that affect their consumer behavior lie not in whether they are organized but rather in how they are organized. The family has all the following characteristics: (1) common purpose, (2) specialization among members, (3) leadership and status relationships, (4) cooperation among members, and (5) communication. Let us consider these organizational factors.

1. *Common purpose.* Purpose is found in the function of the family. It is common purpose that holds families together. This purpose may be centered on the children, work, or social activities, and the purchase patterns of the family and its members usually reflect individual and group purpose. A career-oriented family will purchase differently from a child-oriented family, and so on.

2. *Specialization of members.* There is a division of labor in all families. Husbands traditionally work at outside jobs, wives keep house, while children play and learn. These traditional roles are breaking down today, and over 30 percent of women are also working outside the home. This fact does not change the fact of family specialization; it only makes for a different type of specialization. Families do differ in how responsibilities are divided among members. Specialization affects consumers in several ways. Perhaps the most important effect is on the purchasing agent. Each family member tends to purchase for the activity over which he or she specializes.

3. *Leadership and status.* The husband leads in some families; the wife in others.[6] Leadership denotes status. The family leader exerts a large influence on the products, stores, and methods of purchase of the family. Of course, it should be remembered that leadership varies at different times.

4. *Cooperation.* There is overall cooperation within families, although at a given time, various members may be competing. Families at least cooperate with respect to the broader economic, educational, and organizational goals. This fact leads to agreement on product groups to purchase as well as the type and order of purchase.

5. *Communication.* All family members communicate with one another, but some communicate better than others. It is through communications that family members influence the product and store choices of other family members.

Organizational interaction and influence

When the basic determinants of every family member (needs, motives, personality, and awareness) differ, there must be some compromises based on organizational factors. Take a family that is career oriented, has a working mother, and communicates effectively. It should be easy to get across the notion that the mother must spend relatively more on clothing than if she stayed at home. In a home where the mother is the leader in most family decisions, it may be that relatively more is spent on unnecessary household items and items for the kids. The mother may be softhearted where the kids are concerned, so the parents go without. In highly specialized but cooperative families, the rule may be that each family member can spend personal funds as he or she chooses. Little monetary support may come from the parents. It is not even unheard of that each parent keeps and spends their own income. On the other hand, some families with multiple members pool their resources in order to take care of common expenditures. Even the children may contribute to the pool.

Smaller families have organizational patterns that differ from those of large families.[7] Cooperation, on such things as sharing clothing, rooms, toys, and so on, is much more important in the large family. Smaller families may leave parents more time to indulge in social or community work, requiring expenditures for clothing, entertainment items, and eating out, not as common in larger families. No specific guidelines can be stated because the number of combinations of organizational factors is large.

TWO-FAMILY MEMBERSHIP

The average American is a member of two families. Individuals are members of the family they are born into, and they are also members of the family they help to establish. Arising out of this fact, we observe six general patterns of family influence on the individuals composing the family.

First, as children grow up and form their own families, parents are left alone with the empty nest. The older family members constitute separate markets, and they show characteristic independence in their purchases. Second, marriage in our society leads to the establishment of a new family—characteristically, Americans do not continue to live with parents after marriage. Whereas the impact on consumption is not great when a husband and wife move in with parents, this is not true when a new household is formed. The new family must begin its consumption almost from scratch. Third, because families continually break up, the size of the American family is limited. The average family has a husband, wife, and two to four children. Actual size varies over time. The result is that products are made for this average size of family. The sizes of houses, kitchen furniture, automobiles, refrigerators, washers, dryers, milk cartons, and so forth, reflect the average size of American families. As a result some mis-matching of products occurs where the family is more or less than average.

Fourth, new families lead to new patterns of authority. The authority of the parents is rejected, and new family heads tend to become independent. The younger family members eventually begin to show their independence of thought in their purchase patterns. Fifth, status is lacking in the newly formed families. Thus new families must establish their own status, internal relationships, and social contacts. They are therefore more inclined to emphasize status symbols and status products. Sixth, the change from child to head of household is drastic in American life. The individual is placed quickly and uniquely on his or her own. There is no gradual transition as where families remain together, and there is less reliance on the experience of elders. The new family brings product and store biases, tastes, authority, concepts, and so on, from the previous family, but these patterns begin to break down rather quickly. In the final analysis, the new family increasingly becomes a separate unit to be reckoned with in the market with its own tastes, preferences, and desires.

FAMILY DYNAMICS AND CONSUMER BEHAVIOR

Because of their effect on consumption, it is useful to have an awareness of the changes taking place in American families. Some of the more important of these changes are summarized below:

1. The role of the husband as family leader is decreasing in importance over time.
2. There is less emphasis on providing for the necessities of life.
3. There is a lessening of family unity.
4. Women and children are becoming increasingly independent.
5. Family members have greater mobility outside the home.
6. There is an increase in leisure activities.
7. More leisure is family oriented.
8. Husbands are participating more in family recreation.

There are many factors that contribute to the changes occurring in American families.[8] The more important factors of family change include (1) the growth of cities, (2) improved communications, (3) improved economic conditions, (4) advances in technology, (5) emancipation of women, (6) influences outside the home, (7) women working, (8) the automobile, and (9) the shorter workweek.[9] For example, the growth of cities and the automobile have thrown large numbers of people together and increased associations outside the family. These associations, coupled with increased freeom of women, the increased economic contributions of working wives to the family, and better communications, have significantly reduced the husband's authority and have tended to lessen family unity and stability. On the other hand, the improved financial status of most families and a shorter workweek have combined to increase leisure time and to allow all members of the family to participate together in recreation. It is easy to see that all the factors mentioned interact.

The changes taking place in the family are basic to changes in consumer purchase behavior. The family has been shown to be the basic spending unit. It is not possible to list all the effects, but some illustrations can serve to underscore the importance of family changes on consumer behavior. Women are making more decisions in the family, and they are making more consumer decisions. Perhaps some of the male's recent emphasis on high fashion, particularly the more colorful fashions, is a subconscious attempt to gain back some of his lost power in the family. As a result of outside associations more consumer purchase decisions are being influenced by people other than family members. Keeping up with the Jonses is becoming even more important in our society. More leisure has increased the sales of recreation equipment, and do-it-yourself tools and supplies, casual dress, and trips to Europe.

TYPES OF FAMILIES

Families can be typed in several ways, but perhaps the most useful methods of classifying families are by structure, orientation, and composition. These classifications are important to the discussion because each has its effect on the way the family purchases. Insight into these influences can be gained by discussing each family type separately.

Type based on structure

Family structure refers to the relationship between the family head and the other family members. The structural parts are husband, wife, children, and relatives. The following three family breakdowns are based on structure:[10]

1. *Nuclear.* This is the basic and most elemental family type in our society. It consists of husband, wife, and children who are living together.
2. *Extended.* This family is much larger and is made up of the nuclear family of two or more generations related by blood. This family includes other relatives such as grandparents, uncles, cousins, and so on.
3. *Compound.* The compound family is that in which the husband has more than one wife or the wife has more than one husband.

This type of family is not important in our society because our laws, religion, and customs forbid it. However, in some cultures it is essential for economic reasons.

Since the nuclear family is the most prominent in our industrial society, it will be considered in greater detail in this chapter than the other types. However, we should be aware that in other cultures the extended or compound family may take on greater importance. The maintenance of the kinship system and the continued emphasis on the family as a producer of goods account for the importance of the compound type of family in many societies, but in America present-day physical and socioeconomic mobility make such families difficult to maintain.

The isolation of the American family from relatives is the basis for referring to the family as the basic spending unit. This separation also tends to break down potential influences after the children are married. Thus, family members in their spending tend to rely more on their own judgment and that of opinion leaders than on that of parents or grandparents. For example, a Gallup survey has shown that 61 percent of young women polled selected a different style or period of furniture for the living room than that chosen by their mothers.[11]

Type by orientation

Family orientation refers to the particular preference patterns the family is oriented toward. In a given family, there may be a whole hierarchy of these preferences. On the basis of preference patterns, we have divided families into four major classes or types: family-centered families, career-centered families, consumption-centered families, and combination families.[12]

Family-centered families. A family-centered group exists where a high valuation on "family togetherness" is present.[13] Families exhibiting this type of life style are those we sometimes refer to as being "closely knit." The typical patterns for such families might be the following: Marriage occurs at a young age for both the male and female, and a short span in which the wife as well as the husband works follows marriage. During this time, the family tries to accumulate some savings. Within a relatively short time, children are born, the wife quits her job, and the life of the family begins to center around the children. A strong child-centeredness continues for many years. Such a family tends to remain close over the years. The so-called generation gap is less pronounced in such families. An extreme example is found in Chinese families. Chinese families are very cohesive. Even several generations in the United States have failed to break down the close identification. In these families juvenile delinquency is very rare and because "face" is important, children do not do those things that reflect poorly on their parents.

An orientation symbolic of the family-centered preference patterns is easily illustrated. The family curtails social activities rather than entrust the children to a baby-sitter. It decides to move to the suburbs because it would be better for the children; allocates a large part of the family budget for educational insurance policies for the children, and selects a vacation spot acceptable to the children.

Career-centered families. Success at a career is the dominant theme displayed by families with this orientation.[14] Such family units are often described as those which have a high degree of "upward mobility." The amount of time, money, and energy spent is primarily directed toward career enhancement. The family itself may even be neglected, for there appears to be an inverse relationship between the family-centered and career-centered orientation. Extreme examples of this preference pattern would result in marriage being delayed and children postponed. Placing emphasis on a big new home appropriately located in the proper section of the community, the "right" kind of car, and membership in certain clubs, along with products that symbolize status, is characteristic of families of this type.

Consumption-centered families. A third family pattern is that in which the desire is neither for a career nor for family life.[15] This type of family prefers to have as high a present standard of living as possible.[16] The family is usually very easy going. Family units with this preference pattern spend a large proportion of both their time and money on products and services associated with "enjoying life and having a good time." Sports cars, extensive and expensive leisure-time activities, along with frequent travel are typical of the activities and expenditures of these families.

Combination families. The previous patterns are not mutually exclusive. Most families combine in their orientation a certain amount of family-, career-, and consumption-centered patterns. Some persons by birth and favorable economic placement have certain orientation patterns prescribed for them. On the other hand, some families, because of low income, social placement, age, and so on, may not be able to choose the particular family orientation they would prefer. The following combination family types are all possible.[17]

1. *Family-career centered.* Both family and career receive equal emphasis in this mode of living. However, little emphasis is given toward consumership.
2. *Family-consumption centered.* This manner of living is depicted by a balance between family and consumption. This is the family

that enjoys life and doing things together. Little emphasis on a career is present.

3. *Career-consumption centered.* Little emphasis on familism is present, as most activities and expenditures are directed toward career success and consumption for enjoyment.

In urban societies, a wide variety of orientations may be found present in varying degrees. Even in the combinations described above, it is possible for one to dominate more than another. It is also possible that a family can have a sufficiently broad orientation to include family, career, and consumption aspects. As one can see, the structure of families and their influence on purchases is a very complex subject.

Type by family composition

Family composition also affects purchase patterns. Family composition is the makeup of the family, that is to say, the number of types of members. A family without one of the parents does not function like a family where both parents are present. If the father is missing, the mother may have to work. As a result, the mother needs more and better clothes. The family may eat out more or buy cheaper foods or consume more TV dinners. When the mother is missing, there will be greater costs for housekeepers and child care and other expenditure patterns will change.

Family consumption patterns will differ according to the number, sex, and influence of children.[18] There are the obvious differences in needs for girls and boys, but other differences can also be noted. Where girls are concerned, there will be greater costs for dresses and formals for parties, cosmetics, and perhaps music and dancing lessons. Boys cost more for transportation; recreation, including camping; Boy Scouts; and sums spent on dates with girls. Both boys and girls make large demands on the family for goods and services.

FACTORS OF FAMILY PURCHASE INFLUENCE

Factors that have a significant influence on how the family purchases are family goals, family organization, family compatibility, family role structures, family life cycle, and family life styles. Family organization has already been discussed, and at this point, we give consideration to what each of the remaining factors is, and how it influences the family.

Family goals

The types of goals aspired to by the family affect family relationships and purchases. In any family, three types of goals can be identified; goals influenced by society, goals influenced by individuals, and family group goals.

The family has certain *social goals* that are directed or greatly influenced by outsiders. These social goals are often protected by law. Among these goals are education of children, provision for adequate food and clothing, and the absence of cruelty. A less definite goal is the adherence of family members to the cultural, moral, and ethical standards of the society. These goals affect family purchases in many ways. The family must pay for the education of children, and basic clothing expenditures have high priority. The moral and ethical codes affect how consumers deal with businesses.

Personal goals, such as the desire for status, a better home, and a more comfortable living, are brought into the family by individuals before marriage or emerge during the life experience of the family.[19] These goals directly affect consumer behavior because they relate to the individual's aspirations. He or she may be willing to work harder to obtain such goals, and often the goal cannot be separated from specific products.

Some *family goals* are shared jointly by the individual and the family as a whole. The purchase of a home, certain types of furniture, and vacations fall into this category. Frictions are likely to occur in the family when personal, social, and family goals do not coincide. Of course, friction is likely to be less where family goals are concerned. Frictions can still arise over details of style, brand, design, and so on.

Family compatibility

A compatible family means one characterized by a high degree of harmony. Love and affection are demonstrated, and arguments are not serious. An integrated family is one that is organized and functions as a unit. The members know their places, there is a large measure of agreement on actions and decisions, and family members seldom step out of place. Based on these concepts, we can describe four conditions of family compatibility:

1. Compatible-integrated.
2. Compatible-nonintegrated.
3. Noncompatible-integrated.
4. Noncompatible-nonintegrated.

The *compatible-integrated* family approaches an ideal, the members get along, and the family functions as a unit. In such a family, there is a lot of democracy. Members talk over purchase decisions, and goods are bought with considerable agreement.[20] Members are willing to compromise on purchases, and often bow to the judgment of other members who feel strong product needs.

The *compatible-nonintegrated* family is the sloppy family. There is a great deal of love, but the family isn't organized. The house may be unkempt, and family members exert considerable individuality in their friendships, behavior, and purchase habits. Purchases are not discussed as often, and there is less agreement on the course of action to take.

Noncompatible-integrated families show less affection. The husband and wife have little in common. It may be that the family is held together by the parents' feelings for the children. There is, however, outward unity. This is what may be called the "modern" family. The husband and wife do not allow private feelings to interfere with normal household duties. This family functions as a unit but has no common bond of feeling. In private matters, the parents may seek separate identifies. There is a great deal of agreement on all purchases related to household operations, but practically no agreement on products of a personal or recreational nature.

Noncompatible-nonintegrated families cannot long exist. This family has no common bond to hold it together. The purchase behavior of such a family, while it exists, is erratic. Of course, it goes without saying that there are degrees of family compatibility that lie between the ones described.

Family role structure

The individual plays not one but several roles in associations with others.[21] A role refers to the individual's interpretation of his or her part or activity within the group. For example, in a family the wife not only is a housewife but she plays the role of a housewife with the other family members. Thus, the wife interprets how she feels a housewife should act, and she attempts to act in that manner. The husband plays the role of a father. Each family member also plays the role of a consumer, and the individual interprets how a consumer should act, what a consumer should buy, and how a consumer should buy.[22]

Two types of role combinations are particularly important in the family: instrumental versus expressive roles and external versus internal roles.

Instrumental versus expressive roles. *Instrumental values* relate to functions and are primarily economic.[23] *Expressive values* relate to things valued for themselves and not because of functions. An instrumental leader is called a functional leader, and an expressive leader is called a social leader. Husbands and wives may engage in either type of role.

The difference in family roles is reflected in the family's purchasing behavior. In buying decisions involving products which may be thought of as primarily being instrumental or functional, the male member may exert more influence than when the product is viewed as having primarily expressive value. This distinction may hold even when the user of the product is not the purchaser.[24] An example of this is found in the case of women who buy a high proportion of male sports shirts, ties, and shorts. It is important to remember that these items are expressive, even though they are intended for and used by men.

If one were to observe the purchase of household furniture by a husband and wife, one could witness an example of this functional and expressive distinction. While the wife looks at the upholstery and finish (expressive values), her husband could be observed to more closely examine the joints, springs, and structure (the functional aspect).

A recent study of instrumental and expressive requirements in product satisfaction sheds some light on their importance. It was found that respondents tend to satisfy instrumental requirements in their products first, then their expressive requirements.[25] The evidence was that customers do not pay much attention to instrumental satisfaction so long as the product performs satisfactorily, but they get concerned if the product fails to perform as expected.

External and internal roles. Husbands in our society are normally more concerned with matters external to the family. Among these would be included those activities that involve or relate the family with major external institutions, such as legal questions and appearances, government activities or requirements—the license plates or income tax—and the arrangement for a mortgage, insurance, and the like. The wife's role, however, may be primarily concerned with matters internal to the family, such as the interior decoration and maintenance of the home, the children's health and appearance, and those other tasks traditionally thought to belong in the realm of the female.

Family role differentiation by the internal or external division becomes less and less important as wives become more active outside the home. Working wives and social class differences will directly affect the degree of importance this distinction has in any particular family. An example of such overlapping of roles might be a situation in which both husband and wife share an interest in home repairs (instrumental-internal), and the decision is one involving both members. Entertainment outside the home (expressive-external) is also decided jointly. However, each spouse makes his or her own special contribution to most purchase decisions, and it cannot be simply stated that one or another makes an independent decision because a passive influence is present by the very nature of the family structure.[26]

Family life cycle

The stage at which a family finds itself in its life cycle affects purchase behavior. Family life cycle is extremely important for determining consumer behavior, so we must devote some time to discussing the concept. We must define family life cycle and demonstrate its effect on consumer behavior.

Life cycle defined. The idea of a family cycle has come into wide use because of the importance of age on consumer purchase patterns. The family life cycle is defined as the identifiable stages in a family life that are determined by a combination of the age of the family head and the number of children in the family.[27] The stages in the life cycle can be identified in several ways. One method includes baby, youth, teens, young adult, adult, and senior citizen. Another method goes by age of the family head and includes the following groups: under 25, 25–34, 35–44, 45–54, 55–64, and 65 and over.

The most widely used method of classification is based on age of the family head, marital status, and ages of children living at home. This method has five life-cycle classes as follows:

Table 17–1
Family life cycle

Life cycle stage	*Title*	*Characteristics*
First stage	Bachelor	Single persons, below age 34
Second stage	New married	Young couples, no children, below age 34
Third stage	Full nest I	Young couples, young children, below age 34
Fourth stage	Full nest II	Older couples, older children, age 34–54
Fifth stage	Empty nest	Older couples, no children, over 54
Sixth stage	Solitary survivor	Single persons, age over 54

Source: William D. Wells and George Guber, "Life Cycle Concepts in Marketing Research," *Journal of Marketing Research*, vol. 3 (November 1966), pp. 355–63.

Of course, all families do not conform to such a life cycle classification. For example, a solitary survivor may be below 54 years of age, and a single person who has never married may be over 34 years of age.

However, these six stages do conform to the majority of American families; they are a useful device for viewing consumer market behavior.

Life cycle affects consumer behavior. It is possible to make some generalizations concerning the effects of the life cycle on family earnings and patterns of buying.[28] It is true that no single family will conform to these generalizations.

In stage one, individual earnings are typically low, but except for older male and female bachelors, needs are also lower than in later stages. The individual may be living at home or attending college. If he or she is working it is often part time. However, many of the persons needs are still being handled by parents. The person's needs are mostly personal at this stage.

In stage two, family needs suddenly increase at a time when family earnings are at their lowest. The family, by its formation, needs almost everything, including a house, furniture, food, soft goods, appliances, and perhaps transportation. These needs occur when the family head has just entered the work force full time and has not fully developed employment skills. This fact is reflected in pay. One result, is that the new family must purchase carefully. Parents shop and compare products, they frequent sales, and they hold off purchases until they find the "good buy." The spouse may also enter the work force at this stage to help the family get started. It is a busy, but often happy time for the family.

In stage three, earnings of the family head have begun to increase, but, with the birth of children expenses continue to mount from the first stage. The *basic* products for household operations have, for the most part, been acquired, but the advent of children greatly increases expenditures for clothing, hospital and medical care, and recreation. The cost of education begins to be felt. Parents find themselves putting off the satisfaction of personal wants in order to provide for children. Increased travel associated with children may make a second automobile necessary. This period is often associated with anxiety and frustration for parents.

In stage four, the family begins to stabilize expenditures, while earnings are beginning to peak. Parents finish furnishing the home or replace poorer temporary furniture with more durable types, purchase or upgrade their home, begin to take vacations, buy a higher priced automobile, and perhaps take part in community activities such as the PTA and church. The one exception to more stable expenditures concerns children. As children mature, their requirements increase rather than decrease. Children's clothing and recreational requirements become more complex and there is a great increase in educational expenditures. One major offsetting expense is that medical costs tend to decrease drastically at this stage. If one parent is ever to quit work, this is the time.

In stages five and six, family expenditures take a drastic drop. The income of the head drops with retirement or death, but needs are also greatly reduced. The family has accumulated its major possessions, and most purchases are of the replacement type. There are no great expenditures for children. The parent(s) may move to a smaller home, eliminate one car, and adopt more restricted eating and recreational activities. The one major exception is that medical expenses, that decreased earlier in life, now mount again with increased age. Happiness at this life cycle stage greatly depends on the individual.

Family life-style

Consumption is partially explained by the concept of life-styles. It was William Lazer who is given credit for introducing the life style concept.[29] *Life-style* is defined as a person or a family's distinctive or characteristic mode or manner of living. Marketers tend to determine life-style by AIO (Activities, Interests, and Opinions).[30] Some life-style determinants are shown in Table 17–2.

Table 17–2
Life-style determinants

Activities	*Interests*	*Opinions*	*Demographics*
Work	Family	Themselves	Age
Hobbies	Home	Social issues	Education
Social events	Job	Politics	Income
Vacation	Community	Business	Occupation
Entertainment	Recreation	Economics	Family size
Club membership	Fashion	Education	Dwelling
Community	Food	Products	Geography
Shopping	Media	Future	City size
Sports	Achievements	Culture	Stage in life cycle

Source: Joseph T. Plummer, "The Concept and Application of Life Style Segmentation." *Journal of Marketing*, vol. 38 (January 1974), pp. 33–37.

It is the family life-style that aids in explaining why families, even those with approximately the same income, do not live and consume alike.[31] Some families continually live beyond their means. Other families skimp on purchases in order to save for a rainy day. One family puts its income into conspicuous consumption items, such as a bigger home, and car and expensive clothing. Another family spends for the children's education and an insurance plan for retirement.

Table 17–3 indicates some of the important regional differences in life-style for Americans. The great difference in life-styles is apparent

Table 17–3
Regional life-style profile

Item	Percentage agreeing Total	East	South	Mid-west	West	South-west
Prefer a traditional marriage with the husband assuming the responsibility for providing for the family and the wife running the house and taking care of the children	52	39	52	59	45	61
When making important family decisions, consideration of the children should come first	52	49	62	51	48	50
Every vacation should be educational	48	49	54	52	38	47
I am considering buying life insurance	19	14	30	17	17	21
I nearly always have meat at breakfast	29	14	52	22	26	34
Went out to breakfast instead of having it at home at least once last year	57	57	42	61	71	61
Worked on a community project at least once during the past year	35	39	50	34	31	34
Attended church 52 or more times last year	28	23	37	31	20	30
I like to visit places that are totally different from my home	72	79	63	72	75	65
I would like to spend a year in London or Paris	33	40	36	27	38	24
Went on a trip outside the U.S. last year	14	24	8	12	19	15
Rode a bus at least once last year	32	49	26	28	40	24
It is hard to get a good job these days	77	82	83	77	65	80
Used a bank charge card at least once last year	43	52	43	41	52	50
Returned an unsatisfactory product at least once during the past year	65	67	52	70	65	64
Used a "price off" coupon at a grocery store	63	67	50	72	60	53
My days seem to follow a definite routine—eating meals at the same time each day, etc	62	68	66	58	53	64
Cooked outdoors at least once last year	81	86	82	84	80	84
Went on a picnic at least once last year	75	78	65	79	79	73
Had wine with dinner at least once during the past year	60	70	38	62	72	49
Had a cocktail or drink before dinner at least once last year	70	78	59	75	77	53
I am interested in spice and seasoning	43	46	44	41	54	35
Visited an art gallery or museum from 1 to 4 times in the past year	30	29	27	32	40	34
Went bowling at least once last year	36	42	20	44	34	24
Went hiking at least once during the past year	46	49	47	43	59	45
Went backpacking at least once last year	6	8	7	4	16	5
Went hunting at least once last year	32	18	43	29	32	40

Source: Needham, Harper & Steers Advertising Inc., *Life Style Survey*, 1975.

from the table. We can only summarize these differences here. First, Easterners think of themselves as cosmopolitan. They are more likely to travel, have a cocktail before dinner, cook outdoors, prefer traditional marriages, use bank charge cards, and read the evening newspaper. Second, Southerners tend toward a conservative life-style. They are most likely to attend church, cater to children, and be community active. Southerners are political conservatives. Third, Midwesterners think of themselves as average. They are above average in returning unsatisfactory products, preferences for popular music, and bowling. They prefer traditional marriage, are above average in reading the evening newspaper, and having a cocktail before dinner.

Fourth, Southwesterners are traditional in that they prefer traditional marriage, are less likely to drink before dinner, and desire less travel. They are above average in reading the morning newspaper, and in their preference for time saving appliances. Fifth, Westerners tend toward liberalism. They are above average in riding the bus, visits to art gallerys, hiking, and backpacking. They are also above average in use of appliances, color TV, and charge cards. Westerners tend to feel secure.

Before leaving the factors that influence family spending, a word of warning is in order. The factors mentioned affect each other. There is considerable interaction among the factors. For example, a family may be in stage two of the life cycle but have a high life style. It is the fact of these interactions that makes a specific prediction of how an individual family will consume difficult to ascertain.

NOTES

1. See: Glenn M. Vernon, *Human Interaction,* 2nd. ed. (New York: The Ronald Press, Inc., 1972), Chapter 26.
2. U.S. Department of Commerce, Bureau of the Census, *Statistical Abstract of the United States,* 1972, p. 3.
3. Adapted from Bernard Berelson and Gary A. Steiner, *Human Behavior: An Inventory of Scientific Findings* (New York: Harcourt, Brace & World, Inc., 1964), p. 314.
4. Harry L. Davis, "Decision Making Within the Household," *Journal of Consumer Research,* vol. 2 (March 1976), pp. 241–57.
5. See: Scott Brier, "The Family as an Organization," *Social Service Review,* vol. 38 (Summer 1964), p. 250.
6. Berelson and Steiner, *Human Behavior,* p. 314.
7. W. Thomas Anderson, Jr., "Identifying the Convenience-Oriented Consumer," *Journal of Marketing Research,* vol. 8 (May 1971), pp. 179–83.
8. W. F. Ogburn, "Why the Family is Changing," *Perspectives in the Social Order,* (New York: McGraw-Hill Book Co., 1963), p. 299.

9. Eva Mueller, "A Look at the American Consumer," *On Knowing the Consumer*, ed. Joseph W. Newman (New York: John Wiley & Sons, Inc., 1966), pp. 25–28.
10. Elane Donelson, *Personality: A Scientific Approach*, (Pacific Palisades, Ca.: Goodyear Publishing Co., Inc., 1973), p. 400.
11. *Los Angeles Times*, February 16, 1964.
12. Wendell Bell, "Social Choice, Life Styles, and Suburban Residence," *Suburban Community*, ed. William Dobriner (New York: P. Putnam's Sons, 1958), pp. 225–42.
13. Ibid., p. 240.
14. Ibid.
15. Anderson, Jr., "Identifying the Convenience-Oriented Consumer," pp. 179–83.
16. Bell, "Social Choice, Life Styles, and Suburban Residence."
17. Ibid.
18. Scott Ward and Daniel B. Wackman, "Children's Purchase Influence Attempts and Parental Yielding," *Journal of Marketing Research*, vol. 9 (August 1972), pp. 316–19.
19. Brier, "The Family as an Organization," p. 250.
20. Barbara E. Harrell-Bond, "Conjugal Role Behavior," *Human Relations*, vol. 22 (1969), pp. 77–91.
21. Harry L. Davis, "Dimensions of Marital Roles in Consumer Decision-Making," *Journal of Marketing Research*, vol. 7 (May 1970), pp. 168–77; Richard A. Scott, "Husband-Wife Interaction in a Household Purchase Decision," *Southern Journal of Business*, vol. 5 (July 1970), pp. 218–25.
22. Davis, "Decision Making Within the Household," pp. 241–60.
23. Isabella C. M. Cunningham and Robert T. Green, "Purchasing Roles in the U.S. Family, 1955 and 1973," *Journal of Marketing*, vol. 38 (October 1974), pp. 61–65.
24. G. H. Brown, "The Automobile Buying Decision within the Family," *Household Decision Making, Consumer Behavior*, vol. 4, ed. N. W. Foote (New York: New York University Press, 1961).
25. John E. Swan and Linda Jones Combs, "Product Performance and Consumer Satisfaction: A New Concept," *Journal of Marketing*, vol. 40 (April 1976), pp. 25–33.
26. David M. Heer, "The Measurement and Basis of Family Power: An Overview," *Marriage and Family Living*, vol. 25 (1963), pp. 133–39; "A Pilot Study of the Roles of Husbands and Wives in Purchasing Decisions," *Life*, Parts 1–10 (1965).
27. William D. Wells and George Guber, "The Life Cycle Concept in Marketing Research," *Journal of Marketing Research*, vol. 3 (November 1966), pp. 355–63.
28. Rose Laub Coser, ed. *Life Cycle and Achievement in America* (New York: Harper and Row, Publishers, 1969); Douglas J. Tigert, Richard

Lathrope, and Michael Bleeg, "The Fast Food Franchise: Psychographic and Demographic Segmentation Analysis," *Journal of Retailing*, vol. 47 (Spring 1971), pp. 86–87.

29. William Lazer, "Life Style Concepts and Marketing," *Toward Scientific Marketing*, ed. Stephen A. Greyser (Chicago: American Marketing Assn., 1963), pp. 130–31.
30. Joseph T. Plummer, "The Concept and Application of Life Style Segmentation," *Journal of Marketing*, vol. 38 (January 1974), pp. 33–37.
31. George P. Moschis, "Shopping Orientations and Consumer Uses of Information," *Journal of Retailing*, vol. 52 (Summer 1976), pp. 61–70.

QUESTIONS

1. Define family. Define household. Distinguish between the two terms. Why is family or household referred to as the basic spending unit?
2. Explain the four functions of a family. In what way are these functions related to consumer purchasing? Explain.
3. What is family organization? Explain the characteristics of family organization. Demonstrate how each characteristic affects consumer behavior.
4. Define two-family membership. Discuss six ways in which two-family membership affects the way we purchase.
5. What trends can you cite that have been important in families in recent years? What factors have contributed to these trends? Do these trends have any bearing on consumer behavior?
6. Discuss family types based on structure.
7. Discuss family types based on orientation.
8. How do family goals affect consumer purchases? Family compatibility?
9. What are family roles? Define instrumental and expressive roles. Internal and external roles. Show how these roles affect your own purchase behavior. Use specific examples.
10. Define family life cycle. Define family life style. Relate the two concepts. Show how each affects consumer purchases.

18

American household structure

Market structure defined

Total U.S. population

The base of population

The birthrate

Significance of total population

Geographic distribution of population

Regional population distribution

Regional migration

Urban and rural trends

The growth of metropolitan areas

Concept of metropolitan area

Expansion of metropolitan areas

Interurbia

Effects of geographic shifts on consumers

Population segments based on demographic characteristics

General trends in age and sex

Segments based on education and occupation

Other factors of population segments

The previous chapter dealt with the American family as a social unit. Its internal relationships were emphasized, and they were found to be meaningful to consumer behavior. However, the American family is far too important to consider only from an internal, individualistic point of view. Its economic aspects must be considered along with its social aspects.

While we cannot always predict the consumer behavior of individuals, we do often get patterns when we aggregate. Thus in this chapter, the family is discussed from the point of view of its market structure. This view necessitates moving away from the relationships of the individual family and considering the family as composites, or what we commonly call markets. It is also convenient to shift from the use of family to the use of household because most market statistics are kept in the latter terms. As we shall see, the American household displays many different market structures which constitute a wide variety of consumption possibilities. Furthermore, we can obtain much more specific data on size and expenditures when discussing markets than when we dealt with individual families.

MARKET STRUCTURE DEFINED

Since people in households spend money, they naturally constitute markets available to be tapped by business. Our first task in discussing the nature of these markets is to identify what constitutes a market. We have skirted this issue previously, but it can no longer be put off.

Like so many terms used in marketing, a market can be defined in many ways. Most of these definitions are perfectly reasonable and valid depending on the use to be made of them. Thus, a market can be defined as (1) a type of business, such as a supermarket; (2) a geographic area, as when the sales manager refers to his "southern" market; (3) a place, such as the Chicago market or the suburban market; (4) a group of people such as the teen-age or senior citizen market; or (5) a place where buyer and seller come together, as used in economics. One of the more popular definitions used by marketers is based on the ability to buy. Thus a *market* can be defined as individuals or organizations who are actual or possible buyers of specific groups of generic type products.[1] In truth, this latter definition is emphasized in this text, but nearly all the above concepts are used at one time or another in this chapter.

The problem with markets is that there are many different ways to view them. Most consumers are heterogeneous (different) in some respects, and this fact means that they do not want exactly the same products. It follows that there is no one mass market in the United States, but many market segments.[2] A market segment is defined as *any part of a total market that displays similar human characteristics that result in similar purchase patterns.* The characteristics used in this chapter to differentiate household markets are primarily demographic. They include the following:

1. Age.
2. Sex.
3. Race.
4. Occupation.
5. Education.
6. Location.
7. Family size.
8. Family life cycle.
9. Marital status.

Most of these demographic factors are discussed in this chapter.

TOTAL U.S. POPULATION

Figures on total U.S. population show the size and direction of change in the American market. Total population underscores all other changes in the economy. The population of the United States has been increasing since the beginning of our nation, and, as Table 18–1 shows,

Table 18–1
Total U.S. population, 1910–80

Year	*Total population*	*Population change*
1900	75,994,575	
1910	91,972,266	15,978,000
1920	105,710,620	13,738,000
1930	122,775,046	17,065,000
1940	131,669,275	8,894,000
1950	150,697,361	19,028,000
1960	179,323,175	28,626,000
1970	203,211,926	7,516,926
1975	212,965,000	9,753,074
1980*	249,420,000	36,455,000

* U.S. Census estimates.
Source: U.S. Department of Commerce, Bureau of Census, *Statistical Abstract of the United States* (Washington, D.C.: U.S. Government Printing Office, 1975), p. 5.

this increase has been consistent, although there are variations in the numbers. The slower increase in population caused by the depression between 1930 and 1940 is demonstrated by the figures. The significant increase in population after each world war is also evident, but the big upturn in population occurred after 1940. The decade of the 1950s witnessed a larger increase than ever before, but in the 1960s the steep climb dropped drastically. The Bureau of the Census estimates that the nation's population will continue to increase through 1980. The underlying explanations for these figures are a progressively larger base of population and a high birth rate relative to a lower death rate.

The base of population

The *base of our population* means the total number of people in the United States at any point in time. So long as the birth rate remains at some constant value above that necessary to reproduce ourselves, the base of population will be larger each succeeding year. Even assuming that the number of children born to each family remains constant, population increases, because each year there are more families to have children. If the birth and death rates were constant, population would expand at a constantly increasing rate. It is the fact that the birth and death rates do not remain constant that causes the base of population to increase more in some years than in others.

The birthrate

The national birthrate, or number of live births per 1,000 population, was high between 1945 and 1958, although not as high as in some former years. These and other figures can be checked in Figure 18–1.

Figure 18–1
Birth rate per 1,000 population, 1910––67 (plotted at five year intervals until 1940, then for individual years)

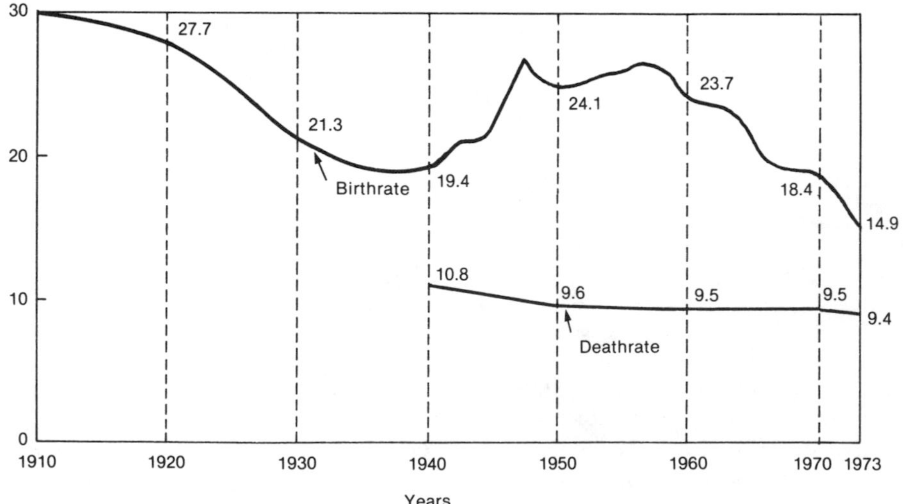

Source: U.S. Department of Commerce, Bureau of the Census, *Statistical Abstract of the United States* (Washington, D.C.: U.S. Government Printing Office, 1975), p. 53.

The birthrate increased substantially from the low of 18.7 in the depression year of 1935 to the 25.0 of the cold-war year of 1955. After 1957, the birthrate declined continuously each year to the 14.9 figure shown for 1973. This latter figure is an all-time low for the United States. It is even lower than the birthrate of the depression years of the 1930s.[3] At this figure, the population of the nation is just about at the point of reproducing itself. Thus the goal of a zero, or declining population, sought by some is a distinct possibility. Of course, it will take into the next century for the effect to take place because of the effect of the base of population. People are having fewer children, but there are more people of childbearing age because of more recent high birthrates.

One also has to consider the possibility that the birthrate can change again, perhaps increasing. The fact is that the birthrate cannot be taken for granted. There are many influences which have an effect on the birthrate. Among the more important influences are economic and psychological considerations. These two are certainly sufficiently important for us to give them more attention below.

Economic influences on births. Until 1957, the birthrate had a tendency to follow fluctuations in economic conditions. When income increases, people at all income levels tend to have more children. When income declines, people at all income levels tend to have fewer children.[4] However, when income rises, the birthrate tends to increase faster for low-income families, and when income falls, the birthrate declines fastest for high-income families. Thus, low-income families tend to have more children at all levels. The assumption is that they have little else to do. Although income and the birthrate do not follow exactly the ideal relationship described, income change is a basic influence on the number of children born each year.

Psychological influences on births. Income alone cannot account for changes in the birthrate. There must be other factors involved, and we refer to those as psychological factors or those dealing with mental attitudes. The psychological attitudes of people toward family size, income, and future prospects affect the number of children born, but there is no single psychological factor at work. It is important to note that people's changed attitudes toward family size tend to follow some traumatic experience in the society. The depression of the 1930s is an example of such an experience. The depression caused unemployment and a decline in income. It led to delayed marriages and young couples doubling up in homes with parents. The resulting attitude of pessimism toward the future was not compatible with large families.

World War II created conditions that caused people to change their attitudes toward family size. The war increased income and reduced most of the psychological tensions created by the depression, and the economic climate of the country was one of optimism. Most goods were available, although some were scarce, and everyone who wanted employment was working. People began to marry earlier and to have more children. Then, in the late 1950s, fear of a population explosion led to a slowing of the birthrate. Communications had advanced to the point where the suffering of people around the world became immediately known. The problems associated with overpopulation received such a big play in the mass media that one could not avoid feeling that family planning was a duty to society. The first birth control pill, introduced in February of 1963, made family planning easier.[5]

The life expectancy, at birth, of a person at the time of the Civil War was approximately 35 years. A child born in 1920 could reasonably expect to live to 54, but by 1973, an infant had a life expectancy of 71 years. The natural tendency is to assume that adults are living longer, but this does not appear entirely accurate. An adult in 1967 could expect to live only two or three years longer, on the average, than his or her Civil War counterpart. Improved medical techniques, shorter working hours, and a more healthful diet largely account for this increase. However, the big difference in life expectancy lies in the fact that fewer are dying in infancy, and this pushes the average up.

Table 18–2 shows that Americans are having smaller families. Family size increased through 1965 in the nation primarily because more families are having three or more children. But a declining birthrate began to lower family size after 1965, the largest decline was in families with three or more children.

Table 18–2
Family size, 1950–71

Number of children under 18	*Percent of total families*		
	1974	*1965*	*1950*
Without children	46.2	43.4	48.3
One child	19.2	17.7	21.1
Two children	17.9	16.8	16.5
Three or more children	16.9	22.1	14.1
Total	100.0	100.0	100.0

Source: U.S. Department of Commerce, Bureau of Census, *Statistical Abstract of the United States* (Washington, D.C.: U.S. Government Printing Office, 1975), p. 42.

Significance of total population

All of the people of the United States are consumers, but two facts should be made clear at this point concerning these consumers. First, people alone do not constitute markets. People in mass may be potentials, but these potentials do not become realized markets unless the consumers have income and an inclination to buy. Second, each and every consumer is an individual, and purchase behavior is dependent on many factors. In the coming sections, we show how factors of geography and personal characteristics such as age, sex, education, and occupation tend to lead to different purchase patterns among consumers. Each more or less similar group of consumers can be a completely different market segment. In short, our task now is to break down the total population figures into meaningful subgroups.

GEOGRAPHIC DISTRIBUTION OF POPULATION

Total population of the United States is increasing, but there are important regional differences in consumption patterns associated with these increases. A look at the geographic patterns of population affords further insight into the nature of market segments. Besides the distribution of population, there are two other important geographic considerations that need attention: regional migration and urbanization.

Regional population distribution

The distribution of population in the United States is shown in Figure 18–2. The northern and eastern sections of the nation have the largest population, but the South and West are increasing in population at the fastest rate. The differences between regions are reflected in consumer purchase patterns. Families in the South spend more than the national average for such products as cereals, sugar, sweets, beverages, fats, and oils.[6] Northeastern families spend more for meat and fish. Dairy products and potatoes take a larger share of the budget for consumers in the North Central region. Families in the West spend more on fruits and vegetables. A study by A. C. Nielson shows that soft-drink consumption by people in Chicago was 22 percent above the nation's average, cigarette consumption in New England was 29 percent above average, consumers in the Pacific were purchasing 60 percent more frozen foods, and Middle Atlantic consumers bought 28 percent more prepackaged meats than the average.[7]

Regional migration

That the people of the nation have been on the move since 1955 is amply demonstrated by Figure 18–3. Americans are a restless people, and approximately 9.2 percent of the total population moves each year. There are 22.3 percent of the total that move within the same county,

Figure 18–2
Regions and geographic divisions of the United States*

	Population 1975	Population 1970	Population 1960	Percent change 1960-1970
United States	216.6	203.2	179.3	+13.3
Northeast	51.6	49.1	44.7	+ 9.8
North Central	59.7	56.6	51.6	+ 9.6
South	66.8	62.8	55.0	+14.2
West	38.4	34.8	28.1	+24.1

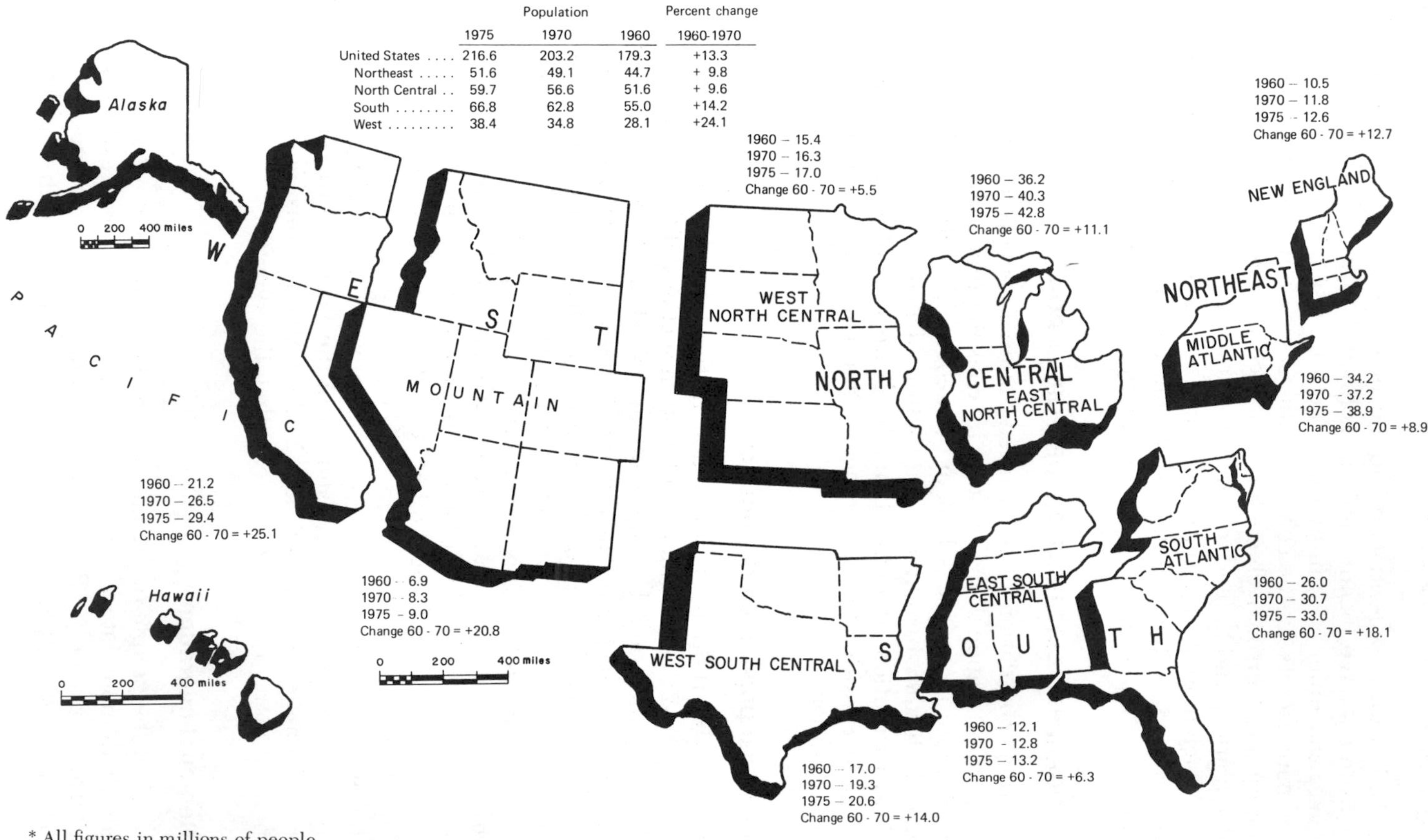

* All figures in millions of people.
Source: U.S. Department of Commerce, Bureau of the Census.

Figure 18–3
Population mobility (proportion of each group moving, excluding persons in group quarters, March 1970 to March 1974)

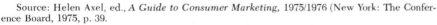

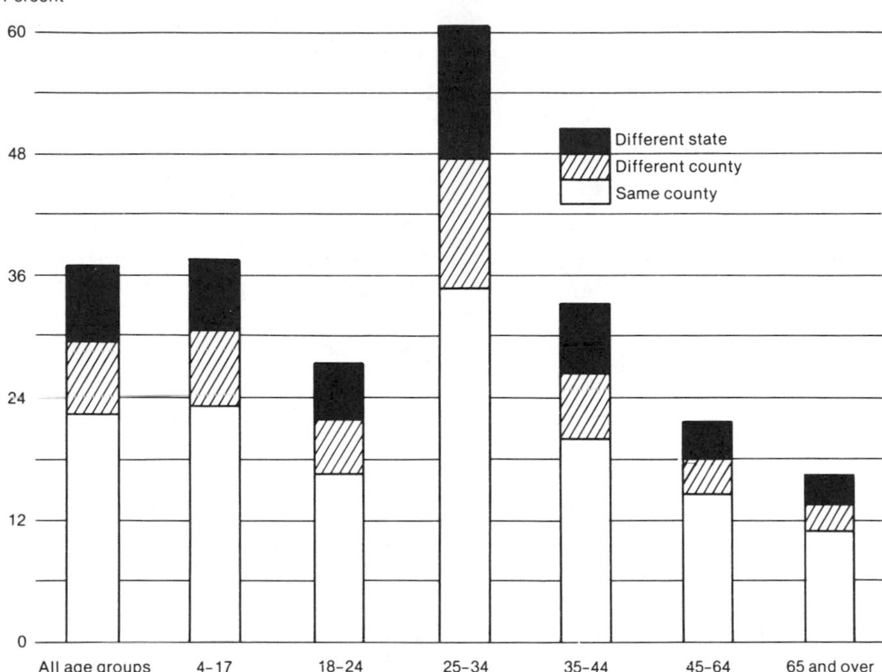

Source: Helen Axel, ed., *A Guide to Consumer Marketing*, 1975/1976 (New York: The Conference Board, 1975, p. 39.

7.3 percent who move out of the county but within the state, and 7.6 percent who move to another state.

One study found that geographic mobiles could be characterized by a tendency to be concentrated in managerial or professional-technical occupations and by both a higher average level of education and a higher than average income.[8] Mobile persons tend to have a previous record of moving, and they are generally motivated to move by the chance for a better job or by the chance to improve their social status. Adults between the ages of 25 to 34 tend to be the most mobile groups within our society. As a general rule, nonwhites, nonfarm, and southern and western regions have the highest percentage of mobiles.[9]

Geographic mobiles tend to represent an exceptional market segment in comparison to the remainder of the population in terms of their above-average occupations, educations, and incomes. These households, when compared to local movers and nonmovers, are likely to be important customers for particular products and services. They tend to be more flexible in terms of the extent to which they are willing to switch brand, store, and product during the period of adjustment following the move. New consumers in a neighborhood have problems associated with finding satisfactory products, stores, and shopping areas. There is likely to be considerable shopping around by these people initially.

Urban and rural trends

The American people are not only moving between states and regions, but they are deserting the farms in favor of the industrialized cities. The United States changed from a rural society to an urban society between 1850 and 1900. As Table 18–3 shows, by 1920 the

Table 18–3
Farm and nonfarm population (millions of persons)

Year	*Total*	*Farm*	*Nonfarm*	*Farm as percent of total*
1920	106.5	31.9	74.5	30.0
1930	123.2	30.5	92.7	24.8
1940	132.1	30.5	101.6	23.1
1950	151.7	23.0	128.6	15.2
1960	180.7	15.6	165.0	8.7
1970	204.8	9.7	195.1	4.7
1971	207.0	9.4	197.6	4.6
1972	208.8	9.6	199.2	4.6
1973	210.4	9.5	200.9	4.5
1974_p	211.9	9.3	202.6	4.4

$_p$ = Preliminary.

Note: Farm population figures are as of April 1; total population (including armed forces overseas) as of July 1.

Source: Helen Axel, ed., *A Guide to Consumer Marketing,* 1975/1976 (New York: The Conference Board, 1975), p. 41.

country was 70 percent urban, and by 1960 the urban percentage had jumped to 91.3. By 1974, only 4.4 percent of the population was rural. The reader should bear in mind that this small percentage of rural population has provided the essential food and clothing needs for the greatest industrial nation in the world. Even these figures are not reflective of the facts. Of the 9.4 million people in rural areas, only 2.3 million, or 24.4 percent were actually employed in agriculture. Thus, either the majority of the rural population were retired, rural landowners, or they depended on the city for their source of income. By 1974, approximately 70 percent of the American population was living on 1 percent of the land area. The American economy had certainly become characterized as highly industrialized.

This industrialization has been both a blessing and a curse. First, it has provided the United States with the highest standard of living that the world has ever known. It has concentrated people, making large retail stores, mass merchandising, direct selling, effective promotion, and low-cost goods possible. Second, it has caused a rapid deterioration of the environment in which we must all live. The ghettos of our cities, smog, water pollution, crime, drugs, and poverty can, at least partly, be laid at the door of industrialization and the concentration of population.

In spite of the now small size of the rural market, it is a mistake for marketers to ignore this group. Rural consumers are major purchasers of many products. Like their city cousins, the rural family has become sophisticated and discriminating in its tastes. For example, rural consumers have become more aware of the role that household appliances play in making life easy. The rural market today is not only composed of farm families but also of commuting business employees, retired people, and others interested in personal convenience. More than 60 percent of the rural population have a food freezer as compared to only slightly above 24 percent for cities. The expansion of power to rural households has created a new source of market potential for many appliance manufacturers, even though this market constitutes only 26.5 percent of the total population.

THE GROWTH OF METROPOLITAN AREAS

The urbanization of the American people has become manifest in the development of large metropolitan areas. The influx of people into cities and their subsequent exodus to the suburbs has completely restyled the American manner of living. The influx of people has necessitated recognition that the economic existence of a city may differ from its political existence. In this section, we examine the impact of metropolitan growth on market segmentation.

Concept of metropolitan area

We have become a nation of city dwellers. The decline of rural population has been more than compensated for by the emergence of large cities as shown by Figure 18–4. These cities began to spill over their political boundaries as early as the 1920s in some places, and what has become known popularly as "the flight to the suburbs" was in full swing by the 1950s. Thus a new concept of city had to be devised that kept the political entity of the city but recognized the reality of the suburbs. The consideration of markets in particular do not recognize political boundaries.

Figure 18–4
Standard metropolitan statistical areas (areas defined by office of management and budget, February 1971)

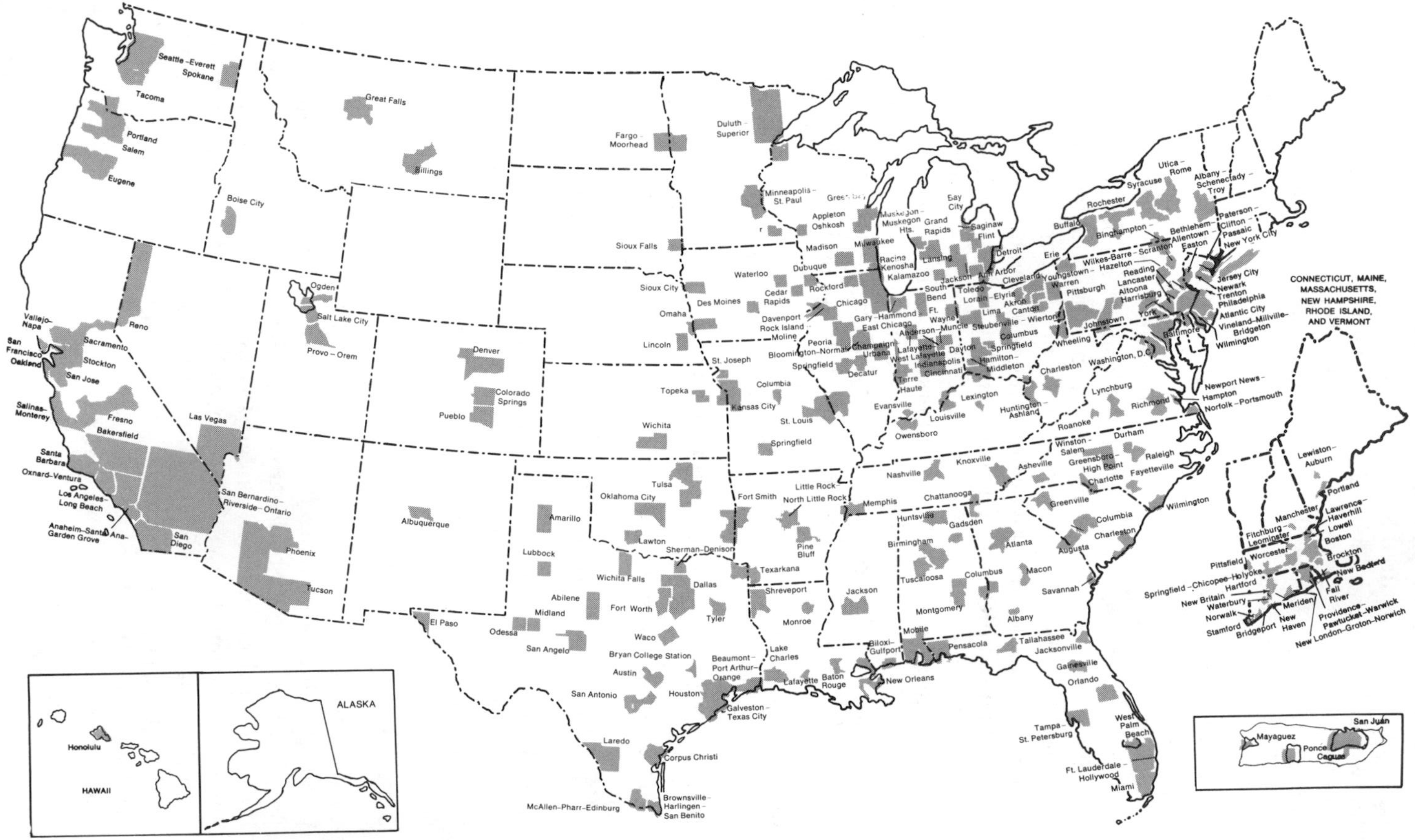

Source: U.S. Department of Commerce, Bureau of the Census, 1971.

The new concept of a city is the Standard Metropolitan Statistical Area, sometimes referred to as a Standard Metropolitan Area or SMA.[10] *A Standard Metropolitan Area* consists of a central city (political boundary) of 50,000 persons or more and all contiguous counties. Contiguous means citylike in the sense of population density, lights, paved streets, sewage, water, etc. Sometimes dual cities are used to obtain the 50,000 population if they are located close together. As a general rule, except in New England, only total counties are used, based on whether the county is over half contiguous. In New England the population of small towns in the county is included but not the entire county. This fact makes comparisons difficult between New England and the remainder of the country. The present usage of SMA has come to include (1) CBD, central business district; (2) central city, political boundry including CBD; and (3) suburbs, areas outside the central city but inside the SMA.

Expansion of metropolitan areas

By 1973, the American population was distributed among 266 metropolitan areas in the following manner: 7 areas of over 3 million; 28 areas between 1 and 3 million; 37 areas between 500,000 and 1 million; 66 areas between 250,000 and 499,999; 103 areas between 100,000 and 249,999; and 25 areas under 100,000.[11] People have been attracted to the cities by better employment opportunities, higher pay, and greater cultural and entertainment opportunities.

As Table 18–4 demonstrates, the expansion of the Standard Metropolitan Statistical Areas since 1950 has been great, but the rate of change has slowed considerably. Even so, approximately 68 percent of the American people live in these metropolitan areas. This fact adds to the concentration of the American market with its advantages and disadvantages as already mentioned. There is even a certain type of geographic concentration, since the bulk of the metropolitan areas is located in the northeastern part of the United States and California.

The suburbs of the metropolitan areas have increased in population much faster than the central cities. As a matter of fact, the central cities have decreased proportionately in population, as Figure 18–5 shows. Over 37 percent of the population of the United States in 1970 lived in metropolitan suburbs. These suburbs offer more room, a slower pace of living, and freedom from the noise, smog, crowds, and fear of the central city. Land values are often cheaper in the suburbs, although this is changing as the suburbs develop. Besides these obvious suburban advantages, there is a certain feeling of prestige to be gained from living in the suburbs.

The central cities of the metropolitan areas tend to attract the low-

Table 18–4
Population of metropolitan areas (millions of persons, except percent)

Residence and race	1950	1960	1970	1973	Percent change 1950–1960	Percent change 1960–1970	Percent change 1970–1973
Total	151.3	179.3	203.2	209.8	18.5	13.3	3.2
Metropolitan areas*	94.6	119.6	139.4	142.9	26.4	16.6	2.5
In central cities	53.8	60.0	63.8	63.6	11.4	6.4	−3.1
Outside Central Cities	40.8	59.6	75.6	79.3	46.3	26.8	4.9
Nonmetropolitan areas	56.7	59.7	63.8	66.9	5.3	6.8	4.9
				1974			*1970–1974*
White	135.2	158.8	177.7	181.5	17.5	11.9	2.1
Metropolitan areas*	85.1	105.2	120.6	121.9	23.6	14.6	1.1
In central cities	46.8	49.4	49.4	46.8	5.7	†	−5.6
Outside central cities	38.3	55.7	71.1	75.1	45.5	27.6	5.6
Nonmetropolitan areas	50.1	53.7	57.2	59.6	7.2	6.6	4.2
Nonwhite	15.0	18.8	22.6	26.6	25.5	20.2	1.8
Metropolitan areas*	8.8	12.7	16.8	20.3	43.6	32.0	2.1
In central cities	6.6	10.0	13.1	15.1	50.6	32.1	1.5
Outside central cities	2.2	2.8	3.6	5.3	23.1	31.5	4.7
Nonmetropolitan areas	6.1	6.1	5.8	6.3	−.6	−4.5	8.6

* Data refer to 243 areas as defined in 1970 and are based on census enumerations.
† Less than 0.5 percent.
Source: Helen Axel, ed., *A Guide to Consumer Markets, 1975/1976* (New York, The Conference Board, 1975), p. 35.

income, unskilled workers from the rural areas and small towns. As Table 18–4 shows, Blacks move to the central city in much greater proportions than do whites. Blacks are economically depressed in the United States today, with 1974 incomes relatively 60 percent those of Whites, down from 65% in 1970.[12] Both Blacks and Whites that move to the central city are looking to better their lot by working in the factories and improving their skills over time. The suburbs directly attract the higher-income people from outside metropolitan areas and second-generation core city dwellers whose incomes have increased as they gain technical competence.[13] The suburbs also draw the children of central city dwellers whose incomes have increased with more education and greater adaptation to city employment opportunities. Most suburban dwellers continue to depend on the city core for their employment, but this is changing.

The consumer's location within the metropolitan area affects purchase patterns. Consumers in central cities spend less on transportation than suburban consumers, but purchases associated with outdoor or casual living are greater for residents of the suburbs. The person who has left the city is forced into home ownership, since apartments

Figure 18–5
Population by residence (total population each year = 100 percent)

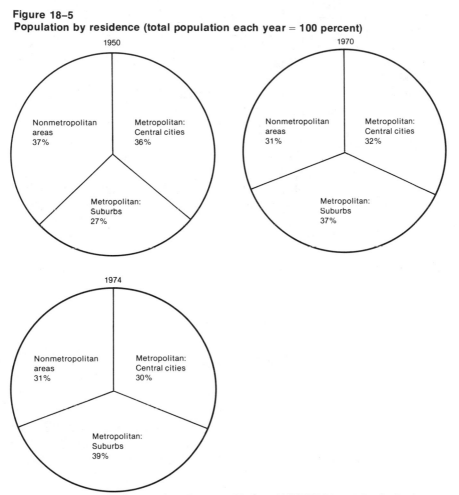

Source: Helen Axel, ed., *A Guide to Consumer Markets, 1975/1976* (New York: The Conference Board, 1975), p. 34.

are not easily available. One builder discovered that the purchase of a new home led directly to 17 other purchases, including furniture, appliances, drapes, garden tools, new car, and, in many cases, a second car.[14]

Interurbia

Although the rate of growth is likely to slow in the future, the general tendency of people to move to the suburbs will continue. Already, in some sections, metropolitan areas are beginning to fuse, giving rise to a new type of supercity even larger than the standard metropolitan area. The name *interurbia,* or *megalopolis,* has been given to these supercities. Today a person can travel from Boston, Massachusetts, to Norfolk, Virginia, a distance of over 600 miles, without effectively going outside the "city." This area is known as the Atlantic Seaboard megalopolis and contains over 20 percent of the U.S. population on 6 percent of the land area. A look at Figure 18–6 will show other examples of emerging interurbia.[15] The Lower Great Lakes megalopolis spreads from Pittsburgh, Pennsylvania, to Buffalo, New York, on the east, and to Chicago, Illinois, and Milwaukee, Wisconsin, on the west. The Great Lakes and Atlantic Seaboard megalopolises are beginning to merge through Ohio and Pennsylvania. Two other developing interurban areas are the California megalopolis, running from San Francisco–Oakland through Los Angeles to the Mexican border, and the Florida megalopolis that curves from Orlando through Tampa–St. Petersburg to Miami. This latter region is the fastest growing of all the supercities. Not only will the consumer of the future be a city dweller but the consumption of products associated with clean water, recreation, waste disposal, and environmental pollution will increase.[16]

Effects of geographic shifts on consumers

Two major consumer market changes have resulted from the rapid growth of American cities. First, metropolitan markets have become so large and scattered that consumers do not identify with the downtown trade area. Consumers increasingly identify with the suburban shopping areas, and all types of retail stores have had to move to the suburbs. Shopping centers, both planned and unplanned, have sprung up all around the outskirts of cities, and in many larger cities, there are more stores in these shopping centers than there are downtown.

Second, the expansion of our city population has modified the living habits of the nation. Briefly stated, some of the important changes include:

1. More informal social patterns.
2. More home-centered recreation.
3. Greater dependence on the automobile.
4. More problems associated with congestion.

City families are dependent on the automobile for social and marketing activities, and suburban consumers tend toward multipurpose shopping trips. The automobile saves time when the consumer is comparison shopping between stores located in different shopping areas.

Figure 18–6
Changing patterns of interurbia, 1985

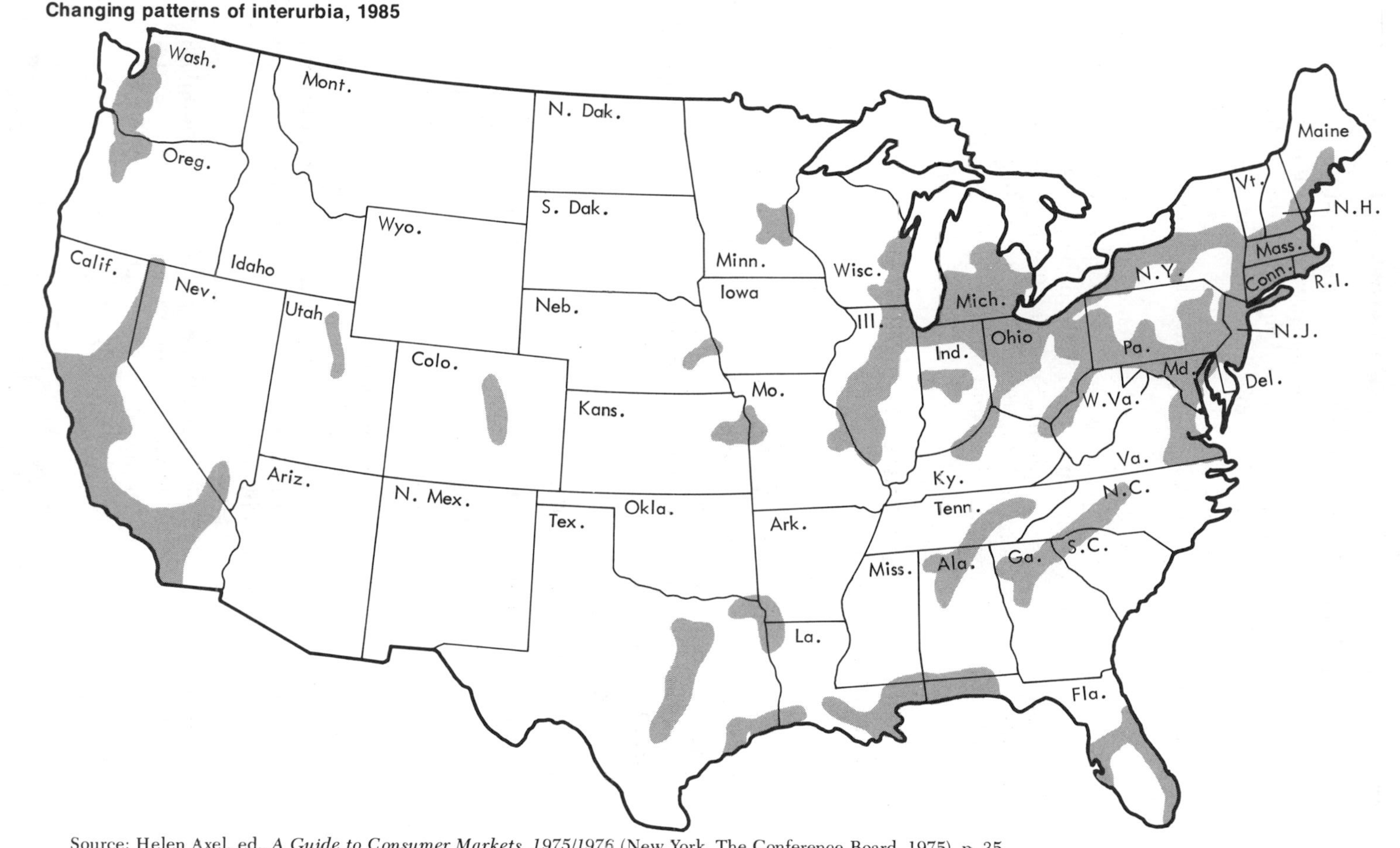

Source: Helen Axel, ed., *A Guide to Consumer Markets, 1975/1976* (New York, The Conference Board, 1975), p. 35.

Consumers prefer the shopping centers because of their informality, and parents feel more free to shop there with children. The shopping centers are also easier to get to, and they provide ample parking space. The tendency toward informal living and home-centered activities has greatly increased the sale of such products as stereos, TV sets, barbecues, lawn mowers, tools and hardware, and outdoor furniture.

Congestion problems of all types have taken away some of the convenience and ease of city living but have created new markets in the process. Traffic congestion, smog, parking problems, and close living are common sources of complaint. Some of the resulting consumer products that have increased in importance are antismog devices, fences for the yard, compact cars, and planned recreational areas.

POPULATION SEGMENTS BASED ON DEMOGRAPHIC CHARACTERISTICS

Important changes have occurred in the composition of the U.S. population. Along with the total and regional changes already discussed, market segments are often distinguished on the basis of sex, age, education, occupation, and similar demographic factors. Certainly, no in-depth knowledge of consumer behavior is possible without some feeling for the differences in the behavior of various segments of the population.

General trends in age and sex

Figure 18–7 shows trends in the American population by age and sex between 1974 and 1985. A number of facts of importance to market segments can be obtained from this chart. It shows the preponderance of young people in our population in 1974. The figures clearly demonstrate the changes in the birthrate previously discussed. The figures show the drop in the number of children in the 0 to 10 age group, and the large number of children and young adults in the 10 to 29 age groups in 1974. The bumper crop of "war babies" during the period 1940–1950 shows up today in the 25 to 35 age group, and the depression babies of the 1930s show up as the smaller group between 35 and 45 years old. Of course, after 35, all age groups begin to decrease in numbers because of the effect of the death rate on the population. Notice the direct benefit of advancements in food, medicine, and recreation in the larger proportion of the population in the 50–60 age group. Of course, this group also is partly accounted for by the higher birthrate before the 1930s.

Figure 18–7
Population by age and sex

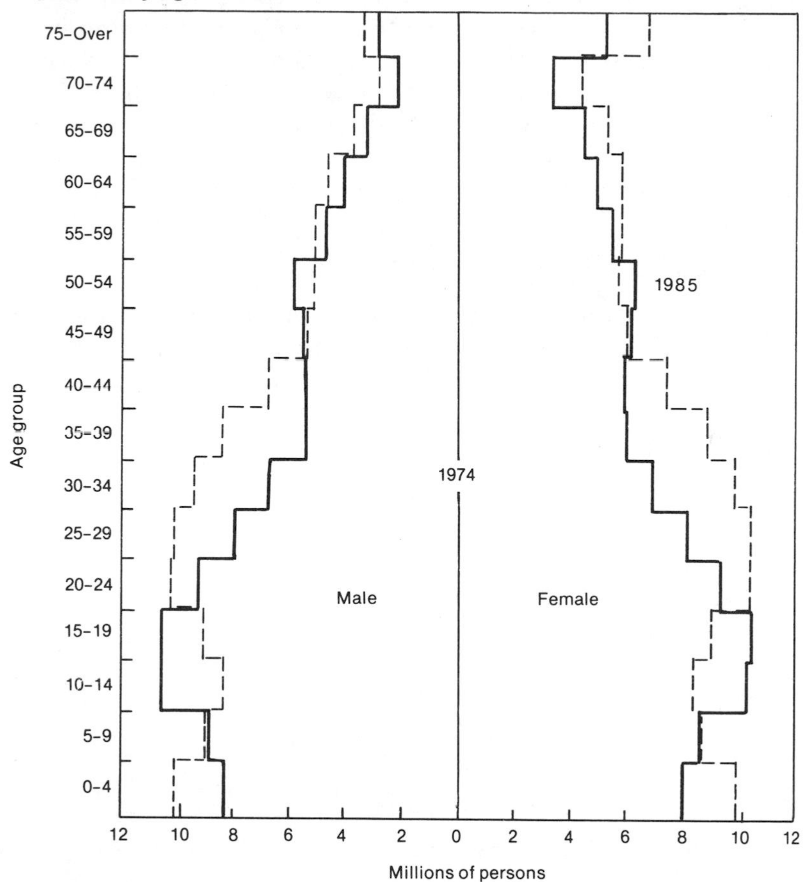

Source: Helen Axel, ed., *A Guide to Consumer Markets, 1975/1976* (New York: The Conference Board, 1975, p. 19.

Since age is a moving average, we can tell a good deal about the future composition of the population by making projections. The number of children between 5 and 19 will decrease by 1980. Teens will increase in the 1970s. The evidence is clear that women outlive men, and this fact shows up in both the 1974 and 1985 projections. Men tend to hold their own with women up until about age 30, but after that the faster death rate of American men begins to take its toll. The difference is significant in the upper age groups. Not directly shown in the table is the fact that between 1950 and 1960, the over-65 population increased about twice as fast as the total population.

The figures give clear evidence of the past importance of the youth market, but they indicate that a change is on the way. By 1984, the young adults, who by a natural process will become more conservative, will become the large market. One can predict a trend back to slightly more conservative buying habits. This fact is particularly true when considered in conjunction with the increased number of senior citizens. Even today, baby foods, childrens' clothing, etc. are finding it necessary to diversify because of declining markets. These were the rapidly increasing products of the 1950s and 1960s.

Segments based on education and occupation

Our nation is rapidly becoming one of skilled workers. Table 18–5 shows the more significant occupational trends. The increase in the

Table 18–5
Employed persons by occupation: 1960–1975

					Percent change		
Major occupation	*1960 (000)*	*1965 (000)*	*1972 (000)*	*1975 (000)*	*1960–1965*	*1965–1972*	*1972–1975*
White-collar workers (professional, technical, managers, officials, proprietors, clerical, and sales workers)	28,725	32,104	38,892	42,092	11.8	21.1	8.2
Blue-collar workers (craftsmen, foremen, operators, and laborers)	24,210	26,466	27,744	27,216	9.3	4.8	−1.9
Service workers (private household and others)	8,349	9,342	11,066	11,493	11.9	18.5	3.9
Farm workers	5,395	4,265	2,926	2,747	−26.5	−45.8	−6.5
Totals	66,681	72,179	80,627	83,549	8.2	11.7	3.6

Source: U.S. Department of Commerce, Bureau of the Census: *Statistical Abstract of the United States* (Washington, D.C.: U.S. Government Printing Office, 1975), p. 359.

white-collar group reflects a continuing influence of women in the labor force. Women accounted for 20.4 percent of the work force in 1920, 32.1 percent in 1960, 35.1 percent in 1965, and 39.7 percent in 1975.[17] It also reflects a continuing trend toward upgrading all types of labor in our society. Blue-collar and farm workers declined as a proportion of the labor force. The increase in service workers was almost as significant as that of white-collar workers. Overall, the labor force of the United States showed a significant increase over the period shown.

Table 18–6 shows a summary of important educational characteristics of the population. Several educational trends are evident. First, over 53 percent of school-age people in the country in 1973 were

Table 18–6
School enrollment by selected characteristics, 1973 (thousands of persons, except percent, as of fall opening)

Characteristic	Population 3–34 years	Number enrolled	Percent of population: Enrolled in school*	Enrolled in college	Not enrolled; H.S. grad.
Total	111,109	59,392	53.5	7.4	31.5
Age					
3–4	7,000	1,692	24.2	—	—
5–6	6,731	6,228	92.5	—	—
7–9	11,131	11,036	99.1	—	—
10–13	16,376	16,253	99.2	—	—
14–15	8,326	8,118	97.5	.1	.1
16–17	8,196	7,236	88.3	3.5	2.6
18–19	7,649	3,284	42.9	32.9	41.0
20–21	7,114	2,144	30.1	29.1	54.1
22–24	10,474	1,515	14.5	14.0	70.0
25–29	15,369	1,309	8.5	8.3	73.5
30–34	12,744	580	4.5	4.3	71.8
Sex					
Male	55,088	30,889	56.1	8.5	29.3
Female	56,021	28,504	50.9	6.3	33.6
Race					
White	95,393	50,617	53.1	7.7	32.6
Black, other races	15,716	8,775	55.8	5.4	24.7
Black	14,032	7,834	55.8	4.9	24.1
Residence					
Metropolitan	76,853	41,269	53.7	8.2	32.4
Central cities	33,311	17,798	53.4	8.5	30.7
Outside central cities	43,542	23,471	53.9	7.9	33.7
Nonmetropolitan	34,248	18,123	52.9	5.5	29.4

* All levels, including college.
Source: Helen Axel, ed., *A Guide to Consumer Markets, 1975/1976*, (New York: The Conference Board, 1975), p. 70.

enrolled in school. This is a favorable figure. Second, there were slightly more males than females enrolled. Third, the total enrollment figures did not differ much by race, but significantly more whites attended college than did blacks. This figure, no doubt, reflected differences in economic conditions of the two races. Fourth, place of residence was not important to the proportion of persons attending school. By comparison, in 1973, 59.4 million of 111.1 million Americans 25 years or older, had finished high school as compared to 40.8 million in 1960. Persons 25 years or older completing college jumped from 16.4 million in 1960 to 20.7 million in 1974.[18]

Education and occupation have similar, but not identical, effects on consumer needs, and the extent and level of education have been increasing in the United States. People who have not finished high school typically read movie magazines and scandal magazines. There is good evidence that people of different occupations do not view their needs alike. One study shows that upper working-class members (primarily skilled laborers) place great importance on owning a middle-class home; a late model, medium-priced car; a houseful of modern furniture; many appliances in the kitchen; and up-to-date clothing. Better-educated consumers, on the other hand, go in for higher-priced homes and automobiles, tend toward traditional and antique furnishings, and high-fashion clothing. The better-educated person's reading is more likely to center around such magazines as *Harper's, Fortune, Atlantic Monthly,* and *Business Week,* or scientific and professional journals. College graduates usually spend less on food and clothing than noncollege graduates of the same income level, and this is true regardless of the actual level of income earned by the graduate. College graduates also tend to spend more on their cars than noncollege graduates of the same income level.

Other factors of population segments

It can be very useful to classify markets by race, which is discussed fully later, religion, and national origin. For example, much of the objection to birth control pills has been based on religious beliefs, and, at one time, meat sales declined in many cities during Lent and on Friday. The sale of religious artifacts is big business in the United States, the two periods of greatest yearly expenditure centering around Christmas and Easter. People of different national origin have tastes that develop out of the culture and environment of their mother countries. When these people enter the American social system, they bring their national tastes with them, introducing new products into our culture—for example, Polish sausage, pizza, kimonos, mumus, spaghetti, and Danish Modern furniture.

NOTES

1. Henry Assael and A. Marvin Roscoe, Jr., "Approaches to Market Segmentation Analysis," *Journal of Marketing,* vol. 40 (October 1976), pp. 67–76.
2. Philip Kotler, *Marketing Management: Analysis, Planning, and Control* (Englewood Cliffs, N.J.: Prentice-Hall, Inc., 1972), p. 89.
3. Lawrence A. Mayer, "It's A Bear Market for Babies, Too," *Fortune,* vol. 90 (December 1974), pp. 134–37.
4. Genevieve Millet Landau, "Why Small Families are Back in Style," *Parents and Better Family Living,* vol. 48 (July 1973), pp. 40–42.

5. In recent years, live births in the United States have exceeded deaths by a ratio of about two to one. Calculated from statistics on births and deaths in U.S. Department of Commerce, Bureau of the Census, *Statistical Abstract of the United States* (Washington, D.C.: U.S. Government Printing Office, 1972), p. 50.
6. U.S. Department of Agriculture, *National Food Situation* (Washington, D.C.: U.S. Government Printing Office, 1967).
7. Finding Food Patterns," *Marketing Insight,* February 12, 1968, p. 3.
8. Alan R. Andreasen, "Geographic Mobility and Market Segmentation," *Journal of Marketing Research,* vol. 3, no. 4 (November 1966), pp. 341–48.
9. Helen Axel, ed., *A Guide to Consumer Markets, 1975/1976* (New York: The Conference Board, 1975), p. 39.
10. Bureau of the Census, 1970.
11. U.S. Department of Commerce, Bureau of the Census, *Statistical Abstract of the United States* (Washington, D.C.: U.S. Government Printing Office, 1975), p. 20.
12. Axel, *A Guide to Consumer Markets, 1975/1976,* p. 126.
13. Fabian Linden, "The Changing Cities and Suburbs," *The Conference Board Record,* vol. 13 (February 1976), pp. 14–17.
14. "Interurbia: The Changing Face of America," Memo of J. Walter Thompson Co., May 10, 1960.
15. Compare this map to the one showing metropolitan areas (Figure 18–6).
16. Jerome P. Pickard, *Dimensions of Metropolitanism* (Urban Land Institute, 1968).
17. *Statistical Abstract of the United States,* 1975.
18. Ibid., p. 118.

QUESTIONS

1. What is a market? Why are there so many different concepts of a market? What is the importance of the different ways to view a market?
2. Discuss the significance of total population on consumer behavior.
3. Why has population been going up? Explain the effect of the base of population on this increase. How has the birthrate affected the growth in population? What is the significance of these changes on consumer purchasing?
4. Explain the major points concerning the location and change in the population of the United States. How do these factors influence consumer behavior?
5. What is regional migration? What has been the trend in regional migration in the last six years? How do you account for the shifts?
6. Define a SMSA. Central City. Suburb. How are they related? Summarize the population changes in these SMSA's.

7. Discuss the recent trends in population by age and sex.
8. What trends do you see in the future for marketing based on age and sex trends in the United States? Why?
9. Discuss important trends in education in the nation. Do the same for occupation. What is the effect on consumer behavior? Of what significance is the rapid increase of women in the labor force?
10. Give your general impressions of the effect of population on consumer behavior.

19

Income influences on consumer behavior

Total U.S. income
Income trends in the united states
Importance of income changes

Belief in a middle-income america
Rationale of a middle-income nation
Reasons advanced for income leveling
Assumption of a leveling of tastes
Income rising but not leveling

Regional purchasing power
Income distribution by regions and states
Income shifts to metropolitan markets

Income by family characteristic
Income by age of head
Income and family size
Income by sex
Income by education
Income by occupation
Other aspects of income

Patterns of income deployment
The american market basket
The effect of inflation on expenditures
Family spending power

Income is as important in influencing consumer behavior as any other factor that we have discussed. As a matter of fact, its importance has made it impossible to ignore completely even when discussing other variables. Income represents what the consumer has to operate with in the marketplace. The consumer's standard of living and life style reflect the particular manner in which income is spent. This chapter is primarily a discussion of income, with some resulting expenditures shown. The same general demographic factors employed for household structure are used as the basis for the chapter. This organization is used because income affects all aspects of household structure. It also provides a logical basis for the discussion.

TOTAL U.S. INCOME

The household is the basic spending unit of our society. Income is the lifeblood of the household. Without income the household, as we know it, cannot survive. It is predicted that by 1980 there will be approximately 77 million households.[1] We are interested in how well these households are doing in an economic sense, and what their expectations are for the future. Trends in income provide clues to the magnitude, change, and direction of change in the American standard of living.

It is useful at this point to provide a brief description of what is meant by income. There are several measures of income, and all are important, but some are more important to consumer behavior than others. *Gross national product* (GNP) is the total of all goods and services produced by a nation, measured at market prices. All other measures of income are computed from GNP. *Personal income* includes all money received by individuals, unincorporated businesses, and nonprofit organizations. This measure is important because it encompasses everything that consumers earn; but consumers cannot spend all their personal income because it includex taxes. *Disposable personal income* is the amount retained by the individual after taxes. It is the amount that the consumer has available to spend. Whatever income remains after all personal outlays is personal savings. *Discretionary income* is disposable personal income after all outlays for necessities required to maintain the individual's level of living. Expenditures for basic food, clothing, and shelter have first priority on the consumer's income. After these payments have been met, the consumer has more latitude, or discretion, in how to spend the remaining income. Discretionary income, or discretionary buying power, is important to the consumer, because they are influenceable where this money is concerned.

Income trends in the United States

The productivity of the American economy has been increasing about 2 to 4 percent each year since the mid-1930s.[2] This increased productivity is reflected in income as shown in Figure 19–1. The GNP in 1940 was only slightly higher than it had been in 1930. The slow rate of increase over the period was due to the depression of the 1930s when GNP declined. Between 1940 and 1950, GNP almost tripled due primarily to the effect of World War II. The decade of the 1950s, with its hot and cold wars, led to another doubling of GNP. Gross national

Figure 19–1
Gross national product, disposable income, personal income, 1930–1970 (current dollars)

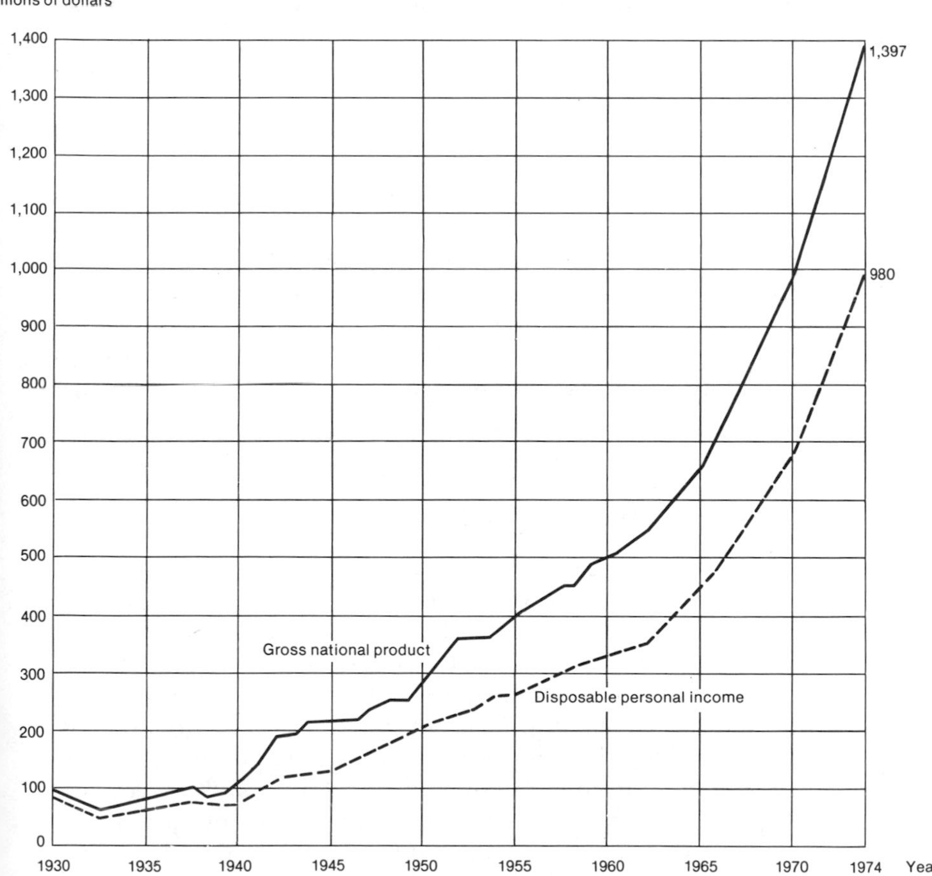

Source: U.S. Department of Commerce, Bureau of the Census, *Statistical Abstract of the United States* (Washington, D.C.: U.S. Government Printing Office, 1972 and 1975), p. 311 and p. 385.

product increased approximately 2.8 times between 1960 and 1974 and about 4.9 times between 1950 and 1974. Disposable personal income increased approximately 4.7 times between 1950 and 1974. The difference between the two values is due to expanding government services and a resulting increase in taxes.

Median family income was $6,691 in 1947; $6,800 in 1950; $9,358 in 1960; $12,531 in 1970; and $12,836 in 1974—measured in 1974 dollars. This increase was about 5 percent per year in current dollars. In 1974, about 64 percent of all families are earning as much as $10,000, or more.

Importance of income changes

Income data show that American consumers are better able to buy the products desired and that their level of living is rising. However, the increase is not as great as might be desired, because American families continually need more income. The average urban family of four needs $12,000 for a modest standard of living. Approximately 50 percent of this needed income is a reflection of a higher level of living. That is to say, families need more income because more products are considered basic.

Some recent changes in living standards are indicated by greater expenditures for health, auto ownership, and clothing. Increased informality in life styles of consumers is reflected in a tripling of sales of women's casual shoes. More sports outfits and short-sleeve shirts and fewer suits and dress shirts for men also show this tendency toward informality.

BELIEF IN A MIDDLE-INCOME AMERICA

One of the great popular beliefs of Americans is that theirs is an essentially classless society in which the great and the small visit the same stores, purchase the same merchandise, and share in the good life together. The assumption is that the great bulk of the market falls within the same general income bracket, and that because incomes are leveling, the tastes of American consumers are also leveling. If consumers earn alike, they must consume alike. Much has been written and said about the leveling of consumption between the rich and the poor and the emergence of a middle-income market in the United States. However, there are those who believe in the concept and those who do not. The investigation of the facts can shed light on which point-of-view is correct while also providing insight into consumer behavior.

Rationale of a middle-income nation

The proponents of the concept of a leveling of income and buying patterns among Americans were very vocal during the 1960s. A typical statement was, "What we have in the U.S. today, by income standards at least, more nearly resembles a diamond than a pyramid—i.e., there are more people in the middle than there are at the top or bottom."[3] Seligman's reasoning was generally held to be true in the early 1960s, and it could be supported by the data in Figure 19–2. The table in

Figure 19–2
The changing income pyramid (total families each year = 100 percent; based on 1974 dollars)

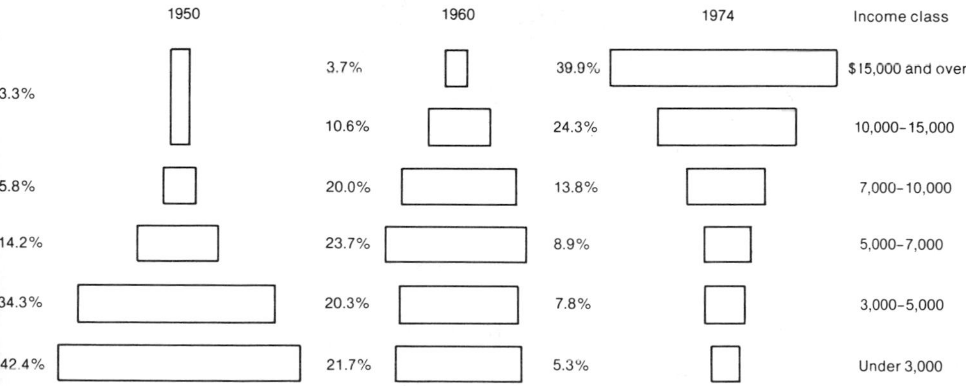

Source: U.S. Department of Commerce, Bureau of the Census, *Statistical Abstract of the United States* (Washington, D.C.: U.S. Government Printing Office, 1975), p. 390.

1960 does slightly resemble a diamond with the mass of the market falling between $3,000 and $10,000. In 1950, the data looked like a pyramid, with most families below $5,000. A review of the 1970 figures is even more optimistic, since it appears that the pyramid has turned upside down with most Americans falling in the high-income categories over $10,000. Based on a cursory investigation of these data, one might conclude that we have truly become an affluent society. Perhaps the figures deserve a little more careful study.

Reasons advanced for income leveling

Several reasons have been advanced for the leveling of American income. First, there is the high progressive income tax. It is argued that the income tax reduces disposable income of high-income families and redistributes it to low-income groups through government services and unemployment compensation. Second, there is the incidence of households having more than one person employed. The argument is that multiple employment raises the income of the poor because they are the group most likely to indulge in double employment. Table 19–1 summarizes important facts about multiple household employment. Nearly 42 percent of all husband-wife families had a working wife. This percentage has been increasing steadily since the turn of the century, and it has certainly become a significant factor in the American labor market.

Table 19–1
Working wives by family income class, 1973

	Husband-wife families			*Percent with working wife*
Income class	*Total*	*Wife working*	*Wife not working*	
Total (millions)	46.8	19.5	27.3	41.6
(Percent)	100.0	100.0	100.0	—
Under $3,000	3.7	1.2	5.4	13.5
$3,000–5,000	6.8	3.0	9.5	18.3
5,000–7,000	8.4	4.9	10.8	24.3
7,000–10,000	14.5	12.6	16.1	36.1
10,000–15,000	27.2	27.5	27.0	42.0
15,000–25,000	29.0	38.4	22.3	55.1
25,000 and over	10.5	12.6	9.1	49.9
Median income (dollars)	13,028	15,237	11,418	—
Mean income (dollars)	14,594	16,439	13,281	—

Note: Data refer to wife in paid labor force.
Source: Helen Axel, ed., *A Guide to Consumer Markets, 1972/1973* (New York: The Conference Board, 1972), p. 137.

There is a direct correlation between the percent of wives working and household income. There can be no doubt but that wives are important to the family standard of living.[4] The difference is clearly shown when median income of families with working wives is compared to those where the wife does not work. Third, there is the incidence of moonlighting. More and more men are holding down two or more jobs, and these figures are not shown in Table 19–1. Although the second job may be part-time or low paying, it does add something to the family's income. Thus the argument goes that these three factors are at work leveling incomes and buying.

Even if we grant that incomes are leveling, *which we do not,* there is no evidence to support the leveling of tastes. Evidence indicates that the very means of acquiring the extra income causes variations in expenditures. The spending patterns differ in families in which the wife works and/or the husband moonlights compared to families with the same income where one spouse stays home. This difference is found not only in the quantity of expenditures but in the quality of goods purchased. Families with multiple workers spend more on childcare, apparel, restaurants, and transportation. For example, a government study shows that husbands of working wives spend about 5 percent more on their own apparel than do husbands of nonwage earning wives. The cost of the wife's wardrobe is about 25 percent more than that of the nonworking wife.

Income rising but not leveling

Some marketers find little comfort in the concept of a leveling of American family income. These marketers question the validity of the concept. There is no question but that the incomes of Americans have increased. We have cited this fact in Figure 19–2. However, the incomes of all Americans have been rising, and that includes the rich as well as the poor. The question is whether there are fewer poor if the purchasing power of the rich has been increasing as fast as that of the poor. In short, have we mistaken an increase in income generally for a leveling, or did it simply cost more to be poor in 1974? Figure 19–2 does not take into account the fact that the poverty level has also been increasing between 1950 and 1974 along with income.

Table 19–2 shows how American families were distributed income-wise between 1950 and 1974. There is little in the figures to

Table 19–2
Percent of aggregate, income of families by fifths (1947 to 1974)

Item and income rank	*1950*	*1960*	*1970*	*1974*
Families	100.0	100.0	100.0	100.0
Lowest fifth	4.5	4.8	5.4	5.4
Second fifth	11.9	12.2	12.2	12.0
Middle fifth	17.4	17.8	17.6	17.6
Fourth fifth	23.6	24.0	23.8	24.1
Highest fifth	42.7	41.3	40.9	41.0
Highest 5 percent	17.3	15.9	15.6	15.3

Source: U.S. Department of Commerce, Bureau of the Census, *Statistical Abstract of the United States* (Washington, D.C.: U.S. Government Printing Office, 1975), p. 392.

encourage the leveling theory. Families with the lowest fifth and second lowest fifth of income actually increased slightly between 1950 and 1974. Thus the number of poor families showed no improvement over the period. There was only a slight drop in families in the highest fifth for income. This latter fact would give some credence to the progressive income tax argument, but it had little total effect. These data show that the United States has not found the solution to poverty.[5]

It may actually be a disservice to our society to preach a leveling of income when so many people are left out of the good society.

There is no question but that the standard of living of the nation has improved. Any real increase must be based on productivity, and these figures were cited previously. However, it appears that most productivity increases are going to families that are already reasonably well off in the society rather than to the very poor. This fact is logical since poor people are in that category either because of some personal or technical problem or because of discrimination. Nevertheless, there has been a change in the nature of families on poverty. The percent of blacks and others living below poverty was 55.9 percent in 1960, measured in current dollars, and the figure decreased to 29.6 percent in 1973. Over the same period, whites below poverty decreased from 17.8 to 8.4 percent.[6] While minorities constitute the bulk of the low-income families in America, there has been some decrease in the incidence of poverty among these groups. Much more work has to be done before the situation changes greatly. Total persons living below poverty decreased from 22.2 percent in 1960 to 11.1 percent in 1973.

REGIONAL PURCHASING POWER

Important differences in the purchasing power of consumers can be found among regions. People's wants and needs differ in various parts of our nation, and the difference that exists in incomes affects the behavior of consumers. Within regions, differences can be found within cities. We now turn our attention to these regional differences.

Income distribution by regions and states

The regional distribution of income, as well as regional changes in income, follows closely the distribution of population. Table 19–3 has state and regional income figures. The more important trends in regional income are summarized as follows:

1. Income increased in all states between 1960 and 1974.
2. The largest total purchasing power is located in the New England section of the nation.
3. The far Western and Southeastern areas are increasing in purchasing power the fastest.
4. The net shift of purchasing power is toward the West.
5. Incomes are leveling between the "have" regions and the "have-not" regions.

A closer look at the figures. A closer look at the geographic income figures can give meaning to the changes. Every region and every

Table 19–3
Personal income, 1960 to 1974, by states and regions (represents a measure of current income received from all sources during the calendar year by the residents of each state)

	Amount (bil. dol.)				*Per capita*								
									Percent state per capita of U.S. per capita				
State	*1960*	*1970*	*1973*	*1974 (prel.)*	*1960*	*1970*	*1973*	*1974 (prel.)*	*1960*	*1970*	*1973*	*1974 (prel.)*	*Rank, 1974 (prel.)*
U.S.	399.9	808.2	1,057.8	1,148.7	$2,222	$3,966	$5,041	$5,434	(X)	(X)	(X)	(X)	(X)
N.E.	25.6	51.1	63.3	60.2	2,430	4,304	5,216	5,697	109.4	108.4	103.5	104.8	(X)
Maine	1.8	3.3	4.2	4.6	1,881	3,309	4,040	4,439	84.7	83.4	80.1	81.7	43
N.H.	1.3	2.9	3.7	4.2	2,126	3,850	4,615	5,143	95.7	97.1	91.5	94.6	29
Vt.	.7	1.5	1.9	2.2	1,868	3,328	4,185	4,588	84.1	83.9	83.0	84.4	38
Mass.	12.7	24.8	30.6	33.2	2,463	4,347	5,268	5,731	110.8	109.6	104.5	105.5	13
R.I.	1.9	3.8	4.7	5.0	2,210	3,960	4,869	5,376	99.5	99.8	96.6	98.9	20
Conn.	7.2	15.0	18.3	20.0	2,828	4,923	5,931	6,471	127.3	124.1	117.7	119.1	3
M.A.	88.5	166.8	206.6	224.9	2,582	4,475	5,525	6,033	116.2	112.8	109.6	111.0	(X)
N.Y.	46.2	86.0	104.2	113.1	2,742	4,712	5,720	6,244	123.4	118.8	113.5	114.9	6
N.J.	16.7	33.9	43.0	46.8	2,728	4,705	5,874	6,384	122.8	118.6	116.5	117.5	4
Pa.	25.7	46.9	59.4	65.0	2,267	3,970	5,010	5,490	102.0	100.1	99.4	101.0	17
E.N.C.	86.8	166.7	217.7	235.9	2,391	4,130	5,333	5,773	107.6	104.1	105.8	106.2	(X)
Ohio	22.8	42.9	54.5	59.6	2,345	4,011	5,070	5,549	105.5	101.1	100.6	102.1	15
Ind.	10.2	19.6	26.5	28.1	2,174	3,768	4,998	5,263	97.8	95.0	99.1	96.9	25
Ill.	26.7	50.2	64.8	70.5	2,649	4,504	5,801	6,337	119.2	113.6	115.1	116.6	5
Mich.	18.4	37.2	50.2	53.9	2,351	4,175	5,540	5,928	105.8	105.3	109.9	109.1	10
Wis.	8.7	16.9	21.7	23.8	2,187	3,809	4,781	5,210	98.4	96.0	94.8	95.9	27
W.N.C.	31.8	61.4	85.5	86.8	2,061	3,749	5,137	5,206	92.8	94.5	101.9	95.8	(X)
Minn.	7.1	14.7	20.0	21.3	2,074	3,839	5,144	5,450	93.3	96.8	102.0	100.3	18
Iowa	5.5	10.6	15.3	15.1	1,986	3,755	5,347	5,302	89.4	94.7	106.1	97.6	22
Mo.	9.2	17.7	23.0	24.2	2,116	3,775	4,831	5,056	95.2	95.2	95.8	93.0	30
N. Dak. ...	1.1	2.0	3.6	3.5	1,751	3,191	5,730	5,547	78.8	80.5	113.7	102.1	16
S. Dak. ...	1.2	2.1	3.3	2.9	1,792	3,101	4,771	4,218	80.6	78.2	94.6	77.6	48
Nebr.	3.0	5.6	8.1	7.5	2,113	3,786	5,299	4,877	95.1	95.5	105.1	89.7	33
Kans.	4.7	8.7	12.1	12.3	2,165	3,857	5,338	5,406	97.4	97.3	105.9	99.5	19
S.A.	48.1	111.3	152.9	168.5	1,843	3,618	4,690	5,073	82.9	91.2	93.0	93.4	(X)
Del.	1.3	2.5	3.3	3.6	2,788	4,527	5,813	6,227	125.5	114.1	115.3	114.6	7
Md.	7.3	17.0	22.2	24.1	2,342	4,318	5,446	5,881	105.4	108.9	108.0	108.2	12
D.C.	2.3	3.8	4.8	5.4	2,963	5,036	6,566	7,479	133.3	127.0	130.3	137.6	1
Va.	7.4	17.3	23.6	25.8	1,863	3,720	4,868	5,265	83.8	93.8	96.6	96.9	24
W. Va.	3.0	5.4	7.1	7.9	1,621	3,070	3,974	4,390	73.0	77.4	78.8	80.8	44
N.C.	7.2	16.6	22.6	24.7	1,585	3,256	4,258	4,612	71.3	82.1	84.5	84.9	37
S.C.	3.3	7.8	10.6	11.9	1,390	2,992	3,885	4,258	62.6	75.4	77.1	78.4	47
Ga.	6.5	15.5	20.9	22.8	1,649	3,357	4,343	4,662	74.2	84.6	86.2	85.8	40
Fla.	9.7	25.6	37.8	42.4	1,948	3,741	4,820	5,235	87.7	94.3	95.6	96.3	26
E.S.C.	18.1	38.3	52.3	57.3	1,497	2,990	3,935	4,279	67.4	75.4	78.1	78.7	(X)
Ky.	4.8	10.1	13.5	15.0	1,578	3,118	4,050	4,470	71.0	78.6	80.3	82.3	41
Tenn.	5.6	12.3	16.9	18.5	1,571	3,124	4,124	4,484	70.7	78.8	81.8	82.5	40
Ala.	5.0	10.2	13.7	15.0	1,522	2,947	3,864	4,198	68.5	74.3	76.7	77.3	49
Miss.	2.7	5.8	8.2	8.7	1,222	2,630	3,546	3,764	55.0	66.3	70.3	69.3	51
V.S.C.	30.9	66.1	88.3	95.1	1,819	3,406	4,355	4,622	81.9	85.9	86.4	85.1	(X)
Ark.	2.5	5.6	8.1	8.8	1,389	2,886	3,956	4,280	62.5	72.8	78.5	78.8	46
La.	5.4	11.3	14.8	16.2	1,668	3,097	3,950	4,310	75.1	78.1	78.4	79.3	45
Okla.	4.4	8.7	11.6	12.4	1,879	3,381	4,331	4,566	84.6	85.2	85.9	84.0	39
Tex.	18.6	40.5	53.9	57.7	1,935	3,600	4,558	4,790	87.1	90.8	90.4	88.1	34
Mt.	14.4	30.1	42.5	46.7	2,087	3,601	4,615	4,965	93.9	90.8	91.5	91.4	(X)
Mont.	1.4	2.4	3.4	3.5	2,035	3,504	4,626	4,776	91.6	88.4	91.8	87.9	35
Idaho	1.2	2.4	3.4	3.9	1,857	3,294	4,381	4,934	83.6	83.1	86.9	90.8	32
Wyo.	.8	1.3	1.7	1.9	2,274	3,816	4,696	5,156	102.3	96.2	93.2	94.9	28
Colo.	4.0	8.6	12.3	13.3	2,266	3,851	4,966	5,343	102.0	97.1	98.5	98.3	21
N. Mex. ..	1.8	3.1	4.3	4.6	1,860	3,092	3,877	4,137	83.7	78.0	76.9	76.1	50
Ariz.	2.7	6.6	9.7	10.7	2,021	3,665	4,687	4,989	91.0	92.4	93.0	91.8	31
Utah	1.8	3.4	4.7	5.2	1,982	3,218	4,096	4,452	89.2	81.1	81.3	81.9	42
Nev.	.8	2.3	3.1	3.5	2,803	4,563	5,712	6,073	126.1	115.1	113.3	111.8	8
ac.	55.8	116.5	148.7	164.3	2,612	4,383	5,413	5,903	117.6	110.5	107.4	108.6	(X)
Wash.	6.7	13.8	17.7	19.6	2,358	4,053	5,151	5,651	106.1	102.2	102.2	104.0	14
Oreg.	3.9	7.8	10.8	11.9	2,216	3,717	4,845	5,270	99.7	93.7	96.1	97.0	23
Calif.	43.0	89.9	113.7	125.4	2,709	4,496	5,508	5,997	121.9	113.4	109.3	110.4	9
Alaska	.6	1.4	2.0	2.4	2,806	4,632	5,926	7,023	126.3	116.8	117.6	129.2	2
Hawaii ...	1.5	3.5	4.6	5.0	2,365	4,263	5,525	5,882	106.4	116.6	109.6	108.2	11

X Not applicable.
Source: U.S. Bureau of Economic Analysis, *Survey of Current Business,* August 1974 and April 1975.

state had an increase in income between 1960 and 1974. In 1974, the East North Central and Middle Atlantic regions ranked first and second for total dollar income, and both of these were in New England. The South Atlantic region was third in total income.

The advance of the South and West in income and the leveling between regions is also shown by the figures. The fastest rates of growth in total income between 1960 and 1974 by region were (1) South Atlantic (3.5 times); (2) East South Central (3.2 times); (2) Mountain (3.2 times); and (3) West South Central (3.1 times). Thus, the South was increasing in income faster than other areas.

Families distributed by income. Table 19–4 shows how families were distributed on a regional basis for income. These data can aid in explaining the trends just noted. In 1953, when the other three regions each had less than 30 percent of their families earning less than $5,000, the South had 45.5 percent of its families earning less than this amount. After starting from this low base, Southern families moved rapidly into the higher-income brackets. By 1973, the South had as many families above $10,000 as the North Central region, and it was closing in on the others. The Northeast region that began on about a par with the Pacific and North Central regions in 1953 increased in income faster than the other regions. By 1973, the Northeast region had more families in the higher-income brackets than any other region.

Income shifts to metropolitan markets

Income, like population, has been shifting rapidly to the metropolitan areas, as Table 19–5 shows. The median income of metropolitan areas in 1974 was $12,961, or $910 above the national average of $12,051. Both the central cities and the suburbs had higher median income than nonmetropolitan areas. The figures also show that there were fewer families in the below-$3,000 category in metropolitan areas. Even so, all was not rosy in the metropolitan areas. Blacks fared much less well in these areas than did whites. The median income for blacks was a whopping $4,999 below that of their white counterparts. Even so, blacks made out better, incomewise than families outside the metropolitan areas. There can be no doubt but that the bulk of the American purchasing power resides in the metropolitan areas.

INCOME BY FAMILY CHARACTERISTIC

No matter whether income is rising or leveling, there are important distinguishable family differences that can be identified by income. Income is not evenly distributed among the population. Some people have and some have not. These differences are significant enough for us to devote some attention to them.

Table 19–4
Families by income class and region (1973 dollars)

Region and income class	Families (percent)				
	1953	1960	1965	1970	1973
U.S. Total	100.0	100.0	100.0	100.0	100.0
Under $3,000	16.5	13.0	9.8	7.2	6.0
$3,000– 5,000	13.6	11.9	10.6	8.8	8.6
5,000– 7,000	19.2	13.6	11.0	9.8	9.4
7,000–10,000	25.6	23.6	20.1	16.8	14.9
10,000–15,000	17.4	23.7	27.3	27.6	25.5
15,000 and over	7.6	14.4	21.4	30.0	35.5
Median income (dollars)	7,054	8,436	9,792	11,277	12,051
Northeast Total	100.0	100.0	100.0	100.0	100.0
Under $3,000	9.2	7.6	6.2	5.2	4.6
$3,000– 5,000	11.9	9.8	8.4	7.3	8.3
5,000– 7,000	22.1	13.7	9.9	8.5	8.5
7,000–10,000	28.4	26.0	20.3	15.9	13.9
10,000–15,000	20.1	25.9	30.5	29.3	26.1
15,000 and over	8.3	17.2	24.8	33.9	38.8
Median income (dollars)	7,642	9,093	10,675	12,164	12,850
North Central Total	100.0	100.0	100.0	100.0	100.0
Under $3,000	13.6	11.8	7.4	5.6	4.7
$3,000– 5,000	11.2	11.8	9.4	8.3	7.2
5,000– 7,000	18.7	12.6	10.3	9.1	7.8
7,000–10,000	27.9	24.2	20.8	16.0	14.6
10,000–15,000	19.6	26.0	29.4	29.1	27.2
15,000 and over	9.0	13.5	22.7	31.8	38.6
Median income (dollars)	7,641	8,686	10,282	11,767	12,831
South Total	100.0	100.0	100.0	100.0	100.0
Under $3,000	27.4	21.7	16.5	10.8	8.8
$3,000– 5,000	18.1	15.9	14.2	10.3	10.1
5,000– 7,000	17.9	15.4	13.0	11.9	11.6
7,000–10,000	20.4	20.8	20.1	18.4	16.2
10,000–15,000	11.4	17.1	21.8	24.7	24.2
15,000 and over	4.6	8.9	14.2	24.0	29.2
Median income (dollars)	5,503	6,583	7,897	9,780	10,627
West Total	100.0	100.0	100.0	100.0	100.0
Under $3,000	13.1	7.7	6.1	6.0	5.3
$3,000– 5,000	13.0	8.6	8.9	8.6	8.5
5,000– 7,000	17.9	11.4	10.6	8.8	9.1
7,000–10,000	26.1	23.5	18.3	16.3	14.7
10,000–15,000	20.1	27.7	28.5	28.2	24.7
15,000 and over	9.8	20.9	27.2	22.2	37.7
Median income (dollars)	7,638	9,825	10,845	11,712	12,470

Note: 1953 distributions for total United States estimated.
Source: Axel, ed., *A Guide to Consumer Markets, 1975/1976,* p. 130.

Table 19–5
Money income of families—race and residence by income level: 1974*

	White						Black					
		In metropolitan areas			*Outside metropolitan areas*			*In metropolitan areas*			*Outside metropolitan areas*	
Item and income level	*United States*	*Total*	*In central cities*	*Outside Central cities*	*Nonfarm*	*Farm*	*United States*	*Total*	*In central cities*	*Outside Central cities*	*Nonfarm*	*Farm*
Number (1,000)	49,451	32,850	12,388	20,462	14,768	1,833	5,492	4,240	3,271	970	1,159	99
Percent	100	100	100	100	100	100	100	100	100	100	100	100
Below $3,000	3.3	3.4	4.1	3.1	5.4	10.9	14.4	12.3	13.1	9.9	21.7	28.9
$ 3,000–$ 3,999	3.1	2.5	3.3	2.0	4.2	4.5	8.9	8.6	9.0	7.1	9.7	12.0
$ 4,000–$ 4,999	3.7	3.1	3.9	2.6	4.9	4.7	8.2	7.6	8.1	6.1	10.2	7.4
$ 5,000–$ 6,999	8.4	7.4	9.1	6.4	10.1	11.5	13.5	12.8	12.8	12.9	15.8	15.7
$ 7,000–$ 8,999	8.8	7.8	9.4	6.8	10.9	11.3	11.5	11.3	11.7	10.4	11.8	12.2
$ 9,000–$11,999	15.2	14.2	15.3	13.5	17.4	15.4	13.4	13.9	13.5	14.8	11.8	10.5
$12,000–$14,999	14.6	14.7	14.0	15.1	14.9	10.4	10.7	11.4	12.1	9.1	8.7	5.1
$15,000 and over	42.1	47.0	40.7	50.7	32.3	31.2	19.4	22.2	19.7	29.9	10.5	8.1
Median income (dollars)	12,595						7,596					

* As of March 1971. Includes members of the Armed Forces living off post or with their families on post but excludes all other members of the Armed Forces. Eludes inmates of institutions. Based on Current Population Survey.

Source: U.S. Bureau of the Census, *Current Population Reports*, Series P-60, No. 80.

Income by age of head

Income by age of family head tells us much about the ability of families to consume. On the basis of income related to age, families may be subdivided into those in the formative years, the good years, and the retirement years.

The formative years. Median income is below the national average for people in the ages up to age 25 (Table 19–6). Many marriages

Table 19–6
Projections of households by age and income level (percent distributions, based on 1972 dollars)

		Age of Household Head					
Income class	*Total*	*Under 25*	*25–34*	*34–44*	*45–54*	*55–64*	*65 and over*
1972—Total:							
Millions	68.3	5.5	13.6	11.7	12.8	11.2	13.5
Percent	100.0	100.0	100.0	100.0	100.0	100.0	100.0
Under $3,000	14.0	15.5	6.0	5.0	6.5	13.5	35.5
$3,000– 5,000	11.0	16.5	7.5	6.0	6.5	10.0	23.0
5,000– 7,000	10.5	17.5	10.0	8.0	7.5	10.5	13.5
7,000–10,000	16.0	24.0	20.0	15.5	14.0	16.0	12.0
10,000–15,000	23.0	19.5	32.5	28.0	25.0	23.0	8.5
15,000–25,000	19.5	6.5	20.5	29.0	29.0	19.0	5.5
25,000 and over	6.0	.5	3.5	8.5	11.5	8.0	2.0
Median income	12,595	9,151	13,294	15,850	17,059	14,137	7,518
1980—Total:							
Millions	77.3	6.0	18.3	13.1	11.8	12.4	15.6
Percent	100.0	100.0	100.0	100.0	100.0	100.0	100.0
Under $3,000	11.0	12.0	4.5	4.0	5.5	11.5	28.5
$3,000– 5,000	9.5	12.5	6.0	5.0	5.0	7.5	22.0
5,000– 7,000	9.5	15.5	7.5	5.5	6.0	9.5	15.0
7,000–10,000	13.5	22.0	14.5	11.5	10.5	13.5	12.5
10,000–15,000	21.5	23.5	29.0	23.0	20.0	21.0	11.5
15,000–25,000	25.5	13.0	32.0	35.5	34.0	25.5	7.5
25,000 and over	9.5	1.5	6.5	15.5	19.0	11.5	3.0

Note: Projections are high series and are consistent with a 4 percent average annual real growth in GNP.

Source: Helen Axel, ed., *A Guide to Consumer Markets, 1975/1976* New York: The Conference Board, 1975, p. 135.

take place before the groom is 25. Thus, at a time when the family is being formed and many types of products are needed, it is least able to purchase. New families need more of everything, but 49.5 percent of these families have income below $7000. Thus, goods must be accumulated slowly on a strict priority basis. Credit is important to this group, particularly installment credit.

The good years. Median income increases with age of family head up to the age of 55. The years between 25 and 55 are the good years for most families. Family potential to consume is great, and although most families continue to spend most of their disposable personal income, living is better. The average family can afford the better things of life, such as a second car, a dishwasher, garbage disposal, and stereo, as well as many recreational and service products. The necessities of life take a smaller proportion of total family income, so discretionary purchases and savings tend to increase. The family can also afford products of higher quality. In short, this is the period in which the family lives at its highest level.

The retirement years. Median income declines after age 54, but most families in the 55-to-64 age group still earn between $7,000 and $25,999. Generally, the good life continues but at a reduced scale for most. Some families actually improve their ability to consume, as children begin to reach adulthood and leave the home, reducing the total number of claims on the family's income. Most durable goods have already been accumulated by the household, and the styles of living are pretty well established by age 54.

After 65, the median family income takes a sharp drop to $7,518. The family head has reached retirement, and the family typically must greatly reduce expenditures. During the current period of inflation, the plight of the aged living on fixed incomes is far from enviable. Since the women statistically outlive the men, the number of widows is large and these widows generally live on still further reduced incomes. However, with the number of people over 65 increasing rapidly, due to improved medical, nutritional, and sanitation techniques, the over-65 market is still an important one.

Income and family size

Children have a significant impact on the way family income is spent. The demands on family income increase with the number of members in the family. Given two families, one with three members and one with six members, each having the same income, we can reason that each member of the smaller family has more actual material wealth than each member of the larger family.

Table 19–7 shows the distribution of children by families in the United States from 1950–74. Median family size is approximately 3.1. The figures show that there are a large number of families with no children in all years. By 1960, there is a significant drop in the number of families with four or more children.

We can make several points concerning consumer behavior based on income and family size. First, high-income families can better meet

Table 19–7
Households by size (thousands)

Household size	*1950*	*1960*	*1970*	*1974* *Total*	*1974* *Male head*	*1974* *Female head*
Number (000)						
Total	43,468	52,610	62,874	69,859	53,862	15,997
One person	4,737	6,871	10,692	13,368	4,742	8,626
Two	12,529	14,616	18,129	21,495	18,043	3,451
Three	9,808	9,941	10,903	11,913	10,172	1,741
Four	7,729	9,277	9,935	10,900	9,902	998
Five	4,357	6,064	6,532	6,469	5,885	584
Six	2,196	2,976	3,505	3,063	2,772	292
Seven or more	2,113	2,865	3,178	2,651	2,347	304
Percent distribution						
Total	100.0	100.0	100.0	100.0	100.0	100.0
One person	10.9	13.1	17.0	19.1	8.8	53.9
Two	28.8	27.8	28.8	30.8	33.5	21.6
Three	22.6	18.9	17.3	17.1	18.9	10.9
Four	17.8	17.6	15.8	15.6	18.4	6.2
Five	10.0	11.5	10.4	9.3	10.9	3.7
Six	5.1	5.7	5.6	4.4	5.1	1.8
Seven or more	4.9	5.4	5.1	3.8	4.4	1.9

Source: Helen Axel, ed., *A Guide to Consumer Markets, 1975/1976* (New York: The Conference Board, 1975), p. 62.

the basic needs of their families with a smaller proportion of disposable income. This leaves more discretionary buying power for the better things of life. Second, large, low-income families tend to spend a larger percentage of their income for the basic necessities of life. Third, families with no children represent a large potential market. Fourth, purchases for children's products take a substantial part of the family budget anytime they are present in the home.

Income by sex

Nearly all males in the United States of employment age have jobs, and it is no secret to most Americans that women have entered the labor force in large numbers since 1940 as shown on Table 19–8. About 71 percent of the nation's women were receiving incomes in some form—job-associated, pensions, retirement, and so on—by 1974. This figure compares with only about 43 percent in 1950. However, approximately 59 percent of these women in 1974 received less than $4,000 per year, and of these, 49 percent received less than $3,000.

Discrimination against women is apparent, because only 27 percent of American males earned less than $4,000 in 1974 and only 21 percent

Table 19–8

Money income–percent distribution of recipients, by income level, by sex: 1950 to 1974 (covers persons 14 years old and over as of March of following year)

	Total persons		*Income level of persons with income (percent distribution)*							
Sex and year	*With income (percent)*	*Without income (percent)*	*Below $3,000*	*$3,000–$3,999*	*$4,000–$4,999*	*$5,000–$5,999*	*$6,000–$6,999*	*$7,000–$9,999*	*$10,000 and over*	*Median income*
Male										
1950	90.1	9.9	58.7	20.9	9.6	4.6	2.0	2.0	2.0	$2,570
1955	92.1	7.9	44.2	16.5	15.8	10.3	5.4	5.1	2.9	3,354
1960	91.4	8.6	37.8	11.1	12.0	12.7	8.9	11.3	6.1	4,081
1965	91.5	8.5	22.4	8.6	8.9	10.6	9.8	18.1	11.8	5,023
1970	92.1	7.9	25.6	6.8	6.2	6.7	7.0	21.0	26.7	6,670
1974 total	92.5	7.5	20.5	6.0	5.5	5.4	5.4	15.7	41.6	8,379
Female										
1950	43.2	56.8	93.5	4.5	1.2	0.3	0.1	0.2	0.2	953
1955	49.3	50.7	83.7	10.7	3.4	1.2	0.4	0.4	0.3	1,116
1960	56.0	44.0	76.8	11.1	6.7	3.1	1.2	0.9	0.2	1,262
1965	59.4	40.6	70.0	11.1	7.8	5.1	2.6	2.4	0.8	3,093
1970	66.5	33.5	58.6	10.3	8.8	6.9	4.9	7.5	3.0	2,237
1974 total	70.8	29.2	49.1	10.0	8.3	7.2	6.0	11.5	7.9	3,093

Source: U.S. Bureau of the Census. *Current Population Reports,* Series P-60, No. 80, and unpublished data.

of males earned less than $3,000. The apparent small earnings for women would at first appear to be in error. Much of this discrepancy in earnings is the result of the large percentage of women in the labor force who are only employed on a part-time basis. Nevertheless when only full-time equivalents are considered, this difference still exists and, in fact, has widened in the past few years. In 1950, median wages and salaries of fully employed women was $953 as compared with $2570 for their male counterparts. However, by 1974, the median income for women had increased to $3,093, or by 3.2 times; but men's incomes had risen to $8,379, or by 3.3 times.

There are several reasons, some economic and some emotional, that help explain the pattern of wage discrimination between men and women. First, women have historically had a higher employment turnover rate than men. This difference in turnover has narrowed considerably as more and more women seek full time employment as a career alternative. The latest government figures available (1968) show a 2.6 percent turnover for women and a 2.2 percent turnover for men.[7] The figures may have declined further. The important point is that many executives are still conditioned to the higher figure, and they pay accordingly. The prevailing attitude is that women are higher employment risks. Second, more women have part time jobs than men, and these jobs typically pay less. In 1974, only 5 percent of men compared to 27.6 percent of women held part time jobs.[8] Some women work primarily to help the family over periods of financial strain or to provide personal or family extras. Third, women tend to find employment in lower paying jobs due partly to historical hiring practices of industry. The 1974 figures show 67.2 percent of women were employed in clerical, service, and operative jobs.[9] Fourth, many executives pay women less simply because they feel that women are less productive. This attitude is beginning to change as there is little concrete evidence to support the position for most jobs. Fifth, some managers pay women less because they have been able to get away with paying women less.

Income by education

The American consumer is becoming better educated, and the education is paying off. This trend will continue through the early 1980s. Two facts are clear from Table 19 9. First, income increases with age, and presumably with experience, through age 54. Second, income of all age groups increases with additional formal education. The age group with the highest income level is the 45 to 54 group, and this group combines formal education and experience to achieve peak earnings. The main lesson to be learned from these data is that median

Table 19–9
Family income by age and educational level, 1973 (income in dollars for family heads 25 years and over)

		Years of school completed				
Age group	*Total families*	*Elementary or less*	*Some high school*	*High school graduate*	*Some college*	*College graduate*
Median income, total	$12,513	$ 7,649	$10,742	$13,188	$14,753	$19,367
Age of head						
25–34	12,206	7,491	9,428	11,759	13,221	16,337
35–44	14,307	9,444	11,269	13,988	16,320	20,862
45–54	15,223	10,261	13,036	15,828	18,564	23,247
55–64	12,781	9,155	11,992	14,039	17,248	21,701
65 and over	6,426	5,465	6,525	7,710	9,392	13,655

Source: Helen Axel, ed., *A Guide to Consumer Markets, 1975/1976* (New York: The Conference Board 1975), p. 138.

income, and therefore purchasing power, increases with additional education. No doubt, education also changes a person's tastes and affects patterns of consumption. There are 33.5 million households in the United States with incomes over $10,000. This number is 60.7 percent of total households. The importance of the over-$10,000 group cannot be underestimated. For example, these consumers purchase 35 percent of all built-in dishwashers, 42 percent of all clothes dryers, 35 percent of all washers, and 41 percent of all air conditioners.

Income by occupation

The overall market segments based on occupation can be determined from Table 19–10. Managers, professionals, and sales had the highest median income in 1973 for males. The rank was essentially the same in 1963. Among women, professionals, managers, and clerical occupations had the highest median income in 1973, but in 1962, the place of clerical and managers was reversed. Females earned less for every occupation, each year, than their male counterparts. Females often earn less than half of what men earn for the same occupation. One might expect this situation to change in the future as a result of Title VII of the 1964 Civil Rights Act which prohibits discrimination on the basis of sex. The figures do not support much change through 1973. Only among service trades did the income of women increase more rapidly than that of men. The increase was the same for professionals and craftsmen.

Table 19–10
Median money income of persons with income, by sex and occupation group, 1962 and 1973

Sex and occupation group (in survey group)	*1962*	*1966*	*1970*	*1973*	*Times increased 1962–1973*
Male employed civilians	5,754	6,856	8,966	11,186	
Professional, technical, and kindred workers	7,621	9,205	12,255	14,306	1.9
Farmers and farm managers	2,490	3,547	3,881	6,697	2.7
Managers, officials, and proprietors, except farm	6,907	8,826	11,665	14,519	2.1
Clerical and kindred workers	5,613	6,542	8,652	10,627	1.9
Sales workers	6,225	7,553	9,765	12,296	2.0
Craftsmen, foremen, and kindred workers	6,247	7,161	9,253	11,245	1.8
Operatives and kindred workers	5,335	6,135	7,644	9,503	1.8
Service workers, except private household	4,386	5,117	6,964	7,937	1.8
Farm laborers and foremen	1,881	2,576	3,355	4.427	2.5
Laborers, except farm and mine	4,377	5,133	6,462	8,158	1.8
Female employed civilians	3,412	3,946	5,323	6,335	1.9
Professional, technical, and kindred workers	4,840	5,779	7,850	9,093	1.9
Managers, officials, and proprietors, except farm	3,744	4,472	6,369	7,667	2.0
Clerical and kindred workers	3,826	4,315	5,539	6,469	1.7
Sales workers	2,607	3,066	4,174	4,650	1.8
Craftsmen, foremen, and kindred workers	(B)	4,213	4,955	6,144	–
Operatives and kindred workers	3,156	3,387	4,465	5,358	1.7
Private household workers	1,138	1,334	1,990	2,069	1.8
Service workers, except private household	2,223	2,695	3,875	4,588	2.1

Source: U.S. Department of Commerce, Bureau of the Census, *Statistical Abstract of the United States* (U.S. Government Printing Office, 1975) p. 370.

Although the prestige occupations have higher median income, it would be a mistake to overlook other occupations as unimportant purchasers. Any income group can be individually important, and it is significant that income between the different occupations began to level out between 1962 and 1973. Even with this rise and leveling of incomes, there is still considerable variation in consumer purchasing by occupation. Among these differences are the following:

1. Prestige occupations have higher absolute but lower percentage expenditures for necessities.
2. Less prestigious occupations spend more absolutely and percentagewise on house furnishings and automobile-associated purchases.

3. By age groups, expenditures vary more in prestige occupations than for less prestigious occupations.
4. Each occupation peaked family income after age 45.

Other aspects of income

Income can be considered by means other than those discussed here. Some of these other methods include segmentation by religion, ethnic background, personality, and family history. Any of these factors can, and often do, affect consumer behavior. When a person tithes to a church he or she reduces personal ability to consume. Family history can affect the amount of income a person has to spend. The person may inherit millions or only be left debts. Not everyone is able to rise above poor surroundings. The point is that there are many ways to classify market segments based on income. We have attempted to discuss some that we consider of general importance. Other specific needs may lead one to a different breakdown.

PATTERNS OF INCOME DEPLOYMENT

We have said that income creates both an opportunity and a restraint on the consumer—an opportunity to purchase, and a restraint on what and how much can be bought. It is interesting to observe the types of choices that the consumer has made and the differences that exist between various groups of consumers. These subjects are taken up in this section.

The American market basket

Table 19–11 points out graphically how the consumer's dollar was spread among major types of products required for the household. Of course, these are aggregate figures, and there would be important differences for specific households. The demand for goods and services produced by the American economy increased over three times in a 20-year span. In dollar amounts, we find that consumers are buying at a rate never before equaled in our history; but there are changes in how these consumers allocated expenditures among product classes. Personal consumption tends to change slowly for broad product groups, as Table 19–11 shows, although change may be sudden for individual items within a category. The figures show that food is the number one market basket item for Americans. Although the proportion spent on food decreased, it retained its position over the period. Housing, that was in fifth place in 1950, jumped to third place in 1973, while household operations retained its second place position. Transportation and

Table 19–11
Personal consumption expenditures by type of product, 1950 to 1970

Item	1950 (percent)	1955 (percent)	1960 (percent)	1965 (percent)	1970 (percent)	1973 (percent)
Food, beverages, and tobacco	30.4	28.4	26.9	24.8	22.9	22.2
Clothing, accessories, and jewelry	12.4	11.0	10.2	10.0	10.2	10.1
Personal care	1.3	1.4	1.6	1.8	1.7	1.5
Housing	11.1	13.3	14.2	14.7	14.7	14.5
Household operations	15.4	14.7	14.4	14.3	14.2	14.6
Medical care expenses	4.6	5.0	5.9	6.5	7.7	7.8
Personal business	3.6	3.9	4.6	5.1	5.7	5.6
Transportation	12.9	14.0	13.3	13.5	12.6	13.6
Recreation	5.8	5.5	5.6	6.1	6.6	6.5
Other	2.4	2.8	3.3	3.5	3.9	3.6
Totals	100	100	100	100	100	100
dollars (in billions)	191.0	254.4	325.2	432.8	617.6	805.2

Source: Percentages calculated from statistics in U.S. Department of Commerce, Bureau of the Census, *Statistical Abstract of the United States* (Washington, D.C., U.S. Government Printing Office 1975), p. 383.

clothing and accessories also dropped one position between 1950 and 1973. There were other minor shifts in position. Thus, the figures show that there were important shifts in the manner in which consumers distributed their income.

THE EFFECT OF INFLATION ON EXPENDITURES

No doubt the changes over time in consumer expenditures reported above were the result of varied and complex motives of individuals.[10] However, inflation was an overriding factor that had its effect on expenditures for everyone. Table 19–12 below has inflation figures. The

Table 19–12
Consumer price index, selected groups, 1960–1974

Item	1967	1970	1974
Food	100	114.9	161.7
Apparel	100	116.1	136.2
Personal care	100	113.2	137.3
Housing	100	118.9	150.6
Household operations	100	107.6	150.2
Medical care	100	120.6	150.5
Transportation	100	112.7	137.7
Recreation	100	113.4	133.8
All items	100	116.3	147.7

Source: *Statistical Abstract of the United States*, 1975, p. 422–23.

figures show that inflation was accelerating for all categories of products over the period. Medical care, housing, and apparel had the highest rates of inflation between 1967–1970, but food, household operations, and housing led, in that order, for inflation over the entire period. There is no question but the higher prices of these items between 1967–1974 account partly for the shifts in expenditures observed earlier.[11] Income was being shifted out of the less inflationary items to compensate for the higher prices of housing items and medical expenditures. It is also obvious that rising American incomes were not sufficient to offset inflation completely. There is no doubt that American purchasing power was erroded over the period, and the erosion was greatest between 1970–1974.

The figures support the fact that consumers handle rising food cost better than some other costs. Even though food led all items for price increase over the period, consumers still managed to spend less, proportionally, on food in 1973 than in 1950. As food prices increase, the consumer shifts to lower priced foods and shops more carefully. For example, cheese and eggs can be substitued for meat. Lesser known canned goods, such as off brands or private brands, take the place of the more expensive national brands. Consumers can also purchase smaller quantities of foods and reduce cost. The recent rage for home gardens is another method of cutting corners on food to reduce total cost. There is much less chance to reduce household and medical expenditures.

Family spending power

The changes in consumption already cited are significant, but they do not indicate the variation in the ability of different groups of consumers to purchase. Table 19–13 can shed some light on this subject. This table compares the number of families, by characteristic, to their spending power or total money income. First, we observe that the greatest purchasing power is concentrated in the 35–54 age group. This figure is consistent with peak family earnings cited earlier. Second, whites have a disproportionate percent of spending power compared to blacks. Third, spending power tends to be concentrated in higher-education groups, and in the prestigious occupations. Fourth, the metropolitan area families have greater spending power than they have families. However, the two figures are abut proportional for the central cities. The difference lies in the fact that suburban families have a disproportionate percentage of income compared to their numbers. The difference is greater for the larger metropolitan areas than for the smaller ones, but the general trend is the same. Fifth, the South is the only region that has less proportion of spending power than it has

Table 19–13
Distribution of family spending power, 1973

Family characteristic	Per Cent distribution: Families	Spending power*
Total	100.0	100.0
Age of head		
Under 25	7.7	4.9
25–34	22.4	21.0
35–44	19.5	22.2
45–54	20.4	25.5
55–64	15.7	17.0
65 and over	14.3	9.5
Race of head		
White	88.9	92.4
Negro, other races	11.1	7.6
negro	9.9	6.4
Education of head†		
Elementary or less	23.1	15.4
Some high school	15.8	13.2
High school graduate	33.1	33.6
Some college	12.2	14.0
College graduate	8.5	12.1
Postgraduate	7.2	11.8
Occupation of head‡		
Professional, tech	14.8	19.3
Mgrs, administrators	15.4	20.4
Clerical workers	8.1	6.9
Sales workers	6.0	6.8
Craft workers	21.5	20.2
Operatives	17.1	14.1
Service wrokers§	7.6	5.5
Other employed	9.4	6.9
Residence		
Metropolitan areas	67.8	72.3
1,000,000 or more	38.5	43.1
Central cities	15.4	14.9
Outside c.c.	23.1	28.1
Under 1,000,000	29.3	29.2
Central cities	13.7	12.9
Outside c.c.	15.6	16.3
Nonmetropolitan areas	32.2	27.7
Nonfarm	28.5	24.5
Farm	3.7	3.3
Region		
Northease	23.2	24.4
North central	27.0	28.1
South	32.0	29.0
West	17.7	18.5

* Total money income accruing to families
† Distribution based on family heads 25 years and over
‡ Distribution based on employed civilians only
§ Except private household
Source: Helen Axel, ed., *A Guide to Consumer Markets, 1975/1976* (New York: The Conference Board, 1975), p. 137.

proportion of families, although the North Central region is about proportional. Thus these data demonstrate the wide differences in the ability of Americans to consume.

NOTES

1. U.S. Department of Commerce, Bureau of the Census, *Statistical Abstract of the United States* (Washington, D.C.: U.S. Government Printing Office, 1975), p. 39.
2. Ibid., p. 382.
3. David Seligman, "The New Masses," *Fortune*, May 1959, p. 107.
4. "A Powerful New Role in the Work Force, But . . . . . ," *U.S. News &*

World Report (December 8, 1975), pp. 58–62; Rena Bartos, "Insight on Selling the Working Woman," *Marketing Times* (May-June 1976), pp. 3–6

5. A recent study by Congress based on a sample of states shows that malnutrition is widespread all across the United States.
6. Helen Axel, ed., *A Guide to Consumer Markets, 1975/1976* (New York: The Conference Board, 1975), p. 140.
7. *1975 Handbook on Women Workers,* (Washington, D.C.: U.S. Department of Labor, Employment Standards Administration, Women's Bureau), p. 6.
8. *Statistical Abstract of the United States,* 1975, p. 348.
9. Axel, *A Guide to Consumer Markets, 1975/1976,* p. 101.
10. Hans B. Thorelli, "A Consumer View of Inflation and the Economy," *Business Horizons,* vol. 17 (December 1974), pp. 25–31.
11. George Katona, "Psychology and Consumer Economics," *Journal of Consumer Research,* vol. 1 (June 1974), pp. 1–8.

QUESTIONS

1. If the household is the basic spending unit, what is the relationship between households and income? What are the different types of income? Explain. Which is more important for consumer behavior?
2. What has been the trend in overall income in the United States? What is the significance of these trends?
3. Are individual incomes leveling in America? Why or why not? Support your answer with sound logic and experience. Would a leveling of income mean a leveling of consumer tastes? Explain.
4. Distinguish between the have and have not regions where income is concerned. What do you feel accounts for the differences? Is the situation changing? Explain.
5. What has been happening to incomes in metropolitan areas? What does this change mean to consumption patterns in the United States? Explain.
6. Discuss the pattern of income distribution among families, and show how this distribution affects buying.
7. What part does family size play in affecting purchasing? What part do sex and education play?
8. Explain the patterns of difference in the distribution of income between blacks and whites. Between males and females. How do these patterns affect buying?
9. How are consumer expenditure distributed? What is the pattern of change in this distribution?
10. Why do we know more about how consumers purchase in the aggregate than we do for individuals? Do you feel that this situation will change? Why or why not?

20

Consumers and social groups

We have made the point that no one makes purchasing decisions in isolation. Consumer behavior is affected by the social implications of the actions taken, and it is necessary to appreciate how the consumer's market outlook, values, and attitudes are conditioned by the social structure. The nature of social interaction and the effect of social pressures on purchasing behavior are discussed in this chapter.

SOCIAL INTERACTION

The fabric of a given society is woven from many threads of interpersonal relationships. The behavior of every individual is influenced in some way by other individuals.[1] *Social interaction* is the exchange that goes on between people—the reciprocal action of the person and the social environment.[2] Anything having to do with human beings living together in groups may be termed social. Interaction refers to mutual action or effect—thus, social interaction is the intereffect of people within groups. These interactions among individuals provide satisfaction for the participants, and individuals condition their actions in such ways as to continue these satisfying relationships. Consumer social interaction is how the individual consumer interacts with social groups with respect to purchasing behavior.

Our definition of social interaction places great importance on groups. The group is the foundation for social interaction. Although the meaning of group seems obvious, the definition is complicated by the fact that there are many different kinds of groups, for example, crowds, mobs, and social or organized groups. A *crowd* is a group by virtue of its consisting of a large number of people in close proximity. A large number of people waiting at an airport, fans at a football game, and the people at a rock festival are examples of crowds. These people are identified only by their proximity and their common purpose, whether it is waiting for a plane or watching a football game. A *mob* is a large and disorderly collection of people, frequently tending to violence. It is a group only by virtue of proximity, and it has no organization.[3] A *social group* is more than a conglomeration of individuals; to be a social group there must be a purposeful interaction among members. Specifically, we define a *group* as an organization of two or more interrelated individuals having a common purpose or function with identifiable role and status relationships among members.[4]

CHARACTERISTICS OF GROUPS

The following characteristics, common to all groups, can be derived from the previous definition: (1) Groups have a common function or purpose, (2) group members play distinct roles, (3) group members vary in status, (4) groups have a class structure, and (5) group members influence one another. These characteristics establish a common ground for the remainder of the chapter. They are defined as follows:

1. *Common function or purpose.* A function or purpose is that factor that ties social groups together and provides for identification. Thus, senators constitute a group because of a common function, and a church congregation qualifies as a group because of a common purpose. Groups can be classified by function or by aspects related to function.
2. *Member roles.* Roles identify the prescribed behavior of members composing the group, depending upon their placement and status in the group. The leader plays one role, the followers play another.
3. *Status of members.* Status identifies the position or function of the individual members of the group.
4. *Class structure.* Social class identifies people of equal position or prestige within the group. The social position of a person can be determined by that person's status, role, and function in the group. For example, a team leader has a different status from that of an ordinary member of the team because he or she performs a different function.
5. *Influence.* All members of a group interact. This interaction leads to influence. The influence may be purposeful or accidental, but it occurs.

REFERENCE GROUP

The term *reference group,* as the name implies, is used to designate a group to which individual consumers relate. The consumer does not necessarily have to be a member of the reference group, but it is necessary that the reference group exert some influence, either direct or indirect, on the consumer.[5] This influence is present because the group perspective is used by the individual as a frame of reference for decisions. The reference group, in fact, may be one in which it is impossible to become a member. A young crippled boy, identifying with the Green Bay Packers, may be influenced by this identification to purchase and collect athletic equipment as a hobby. The often discussed but never identified "Joneses" with whom we are forever trying to keep up represent an intangible reference group. Other reference groups are found in our fellow workers, movie stars, and "women."[6] The use of testimonial advertising is often quite effective because an individual can identify with the reference group represented by the person in the ad. Witness the success of Arnold Palmer brand of golf equipment with the weekend golfer.

The consumer can identify with the group because of general knowledge of the group's existence or because of some personal knowledge or acquaintance with an individual in the group. The influence the reference group has on the consumer operates through purpose, roles, and status.[7] The consumer may purchase in a certain way to accomplish the same purpose as the group, to become a member of the group and to play a similar role, or to obtain status like that held in the group. In the following sections, groups are classified by function and related aspects; status and roles in groups are discussed; group influences are explained; and social class is discussed as it affects groups. These characteristics are related to consumer behavior.

HOW GROUPS ARE CLASSIFIED

While there are several ways that groups can be classified, most of the classifications relate to function or purpose, degree of participation, or nature of membership. At this time, we want to clarify the major types of groups to which consumers may belong or draw opinions from. We discuss functional groups, then turn our attention to groups classified by degree of participation and by type of membership.

Groups classified by function or purpose

Man is a social animal who seeks out other human beings for social, protective, and economic purposes. These and similar purposes form a basis for classifying groups. Thus, we find work groups, football teams, church groups, the Army, and a supper club. The development of these functional groups is inevitable, some on a voluntary basis and some forced. All groups tend to be selective. Individuals tend to leave groups whose purpose, function, or group opinion differs from their own. This selectivity of association results in common views within groups where people freely associate. There is less similarity of view where the associations are forced. We expect more agreement within the church group than within the army. The fact that consumers belong to these groups brings them into contact with group opinions. These opinions are bound to influence the desires, attitudes, perceptions, and so on, of the consumer. In turn, the consumer's purchase behavior is directly influenced. Thus the number and type of groups to which the consumer belongs, as well as the reference groups with which he or she identifies, affect that consumer's behavior.

Groups classified by degree of participation

Consumers do not participate to the same degree in all groups. Thus, based on participation, we can divide groups into primary and secondary groups. Although the degree of participation differs in these two types of groups, each may have significant influence on consumers.

Primary groups. Primary groups are characterized by the face-to-face association and high degree of cooperation among members. Primary groups are basic in forming the social nature of a consumer, since it is within these groups that a person's most direct and most frequent interaction with others takes place. Primary groups to which consumers are exposed are: the family, neighbors, bridge clubs, car pools, and a regular golf foursome. Notice the overlapping with functional groups. This overlapping is natural, since all groups are based on some common function. From childhood to old age, consumers find many of the everyday purchasing decisions affected by the opinions, experiences, and biases expressed by members of their primary groups. Sue files for future reference Mary's statement that a certain deodorant caused her to break out in a rash. A fellow worker complains continually of mechanical trouble with a car, and this affects the consumer's attitude when the time comes to buy a new car. A neighbor puts down new carpeting in her house, and her associates suddenly realize that the old place could use a little repairing.

Secondary groups. Secondary groups, unlike primary groups, are characterized by a more conscious and deliberate choice by those making up the group's membership. You may have heard such groups referred to as "special-interest" groups. This characterization may well be appropriate because secondary groups often do represent specialized interests, fundamental beliefs, or needs. Although direct contact of the members occurs, it is not depended upon. The Democratic or Republican party, the AFL–CIO, the church, and Sigma Chi fraternity are all examples of secondary groups. In each of these secondary groups, one usually finds many primary-group situations. Communication within primary groups usually reflects immediate feedback, but secondary groups experience a greater delay in feedback. Secondary groups affect consumer behavior through individual beliefs. For example, union members are careful to buy union-made goods. Individuals with strong religious beliefs do not attend movies banned by their church. Consumers are also influenced directly by the primary interactions within the secondary group.

Groups classified by type of membership

There are four types of groups classified by type of membership: (1) participation, (2) automatic, (3) anticipatory, and (4) negative.[8]

Participation groups. The participation group is one in which the consumer actually takes part. These may be either large or small. Small face-to-face communication groups, such as the family or social organization, are examples of such groups. Direct associations between the members are the rule in small groups. On the other hand, there can be larger groups in which larger membership is held, but there is an absence of personal association, active participation, or face-to-face association. Such is the case of political party membership. Participation groups tend to affect consumer attitudes directly, and they usually affect attitudes having to do with the group. For example, standards of dress may be established in the group.

Automatic groups. Automatic reference groups are those in which a person automatically belongs because of age, sex, marital status, race, education, and so on. Thus, mothers, teen-agers, college students, Americans, and millionaires constitute automatic reference groups. Membership in such groups may be loose and identification among members may be low, but one is aware of belonging to the group. The individual in an automatic reference group assumes the role that is expected of all those who belong to the group, and these roles affect consumer behavior. A newlywed, in her role as a housewife, may wonder what other wives would do in a similar situation. The dominating influence of automatic reference groups results from the consumer's perception of what society expects him or her to do in certain circumstances. These people's purchase behavior can be influenced by augmenting their role or increasing their feeling of belonging. A salesperson, for example, may point out to the young wife that the brand of cookware he or she is selling is preferred by most housewives.

Anticipatory groups. The anticipatory group is one to which the consumer aspires but in which he or she does not presently hold membership. We can observe anticipatory group behavior in persons who wish to join the country club, move into a better neighborhood, or climb into the better social circles of the city. These people make comparisons with the anticipatory group when making purchase decisions. They are apt to adopt the standards of dress, talk, ethics, and entertainment followed by the anticipatory group.

Negative groups. Negative groups are the opposite of anticipatory groups. A person avoids association with negative groups. A person may not wish to be identified with bums, hippies, the nouveau riche, Ku Klux Klansmen, the NAACP, politicians, communists, or criminals. Notice that very often, but not necessarily, the attitude held toward a negative group is based on group biases of those outside the negative group. The negative reference group influences consumer decisions in that people do not take certain actions or purchase certain products that may identify them with these groups. The person may or may not actually belong to the group, but one's actions are an attempt to disassociate one's self, nevertheless. The beer industry has had difficulty disassociating beer from the lower classes.

A person can be a member of a functional, primary, and secondary reference group at the same time. Furthermore, a person can belong to all the types of membership groups. For example, a person can be simultaneously a member of a family, the Democratic party, the Elks, the National Guard, a young men's Christian group, and the church.

BUSINESS INTEREST IN SOCIAL GROUPS

It was established earlier that social groups, through communications, have a decided influence on consumer behavior. This influence can be greater than the direct effect of business promotion.[9] It follows that businessmen have a high vested interest in knowing about group influence.

Business executives have several types of specific interest in knowing about groups. *First, business managers need to identify important groups in our society and communities.* It is important to know why people join certain groups. What patterns of socio-demographic factors can be identified in these individuals that can give clues to selecting promotional appeals and methods of presentation to these consumers? Are there social conscious and independent types of consumers? How do they differ? How can they be reached in the market?

Second, business needs to understand the inner organization and operation of groups in general. Such consideration as how is status determined, what are the rewards and sanctions of belonging to specific groups, and how are these rewards and sanctions administered? Of particular importance to business management is how influence flows through the various types of social groups. We actually know little about the process of word-of-mouth communications as it applies between coworkers, neighbors, church and social groups, consumer groups, etc.[10] How strong and in what directions are specific effects on individual consumers?

Third, business executives need to know who the opinion leaders are in various groups. Do these leaders vary from group to group? Do different opinion leaders influence in different ways?[11] If business knew this it could direct specific types of promotion to the masses and other types to the opinion leaders. The total effect of promotion would be much greater. Clues to opinion leaders might be found if business could determine how leaders obtain and maintain their position of influence.

Fourth, business managers need to know the effect of consumers belonging to several groups at the same time. What type of purchase conflicts arise and how the consumer resolves them?[12] Which groups have the most influence on consumption patterns? How does the type source affect consumer believability on matters pertaining to consumer behavior?

Fifth, business needs to know the effect of consumer status or position in the group. Does the individual have status because he or she conforms to group standards or do the standards determine the status? How does role playing in the group affect consumption?

Sixth, business executives need to know how consumers that are new to a community utilize groups. How do new members of the community establish group membership? Are these memberships lasting? What effect does the new membership have on the consumer's initial choice of specific stores, banks, and service institutions? This type of knowledge about social groups can have a tremendous effect on developing consumer market strategy by businessmen.

EFFECTS OF STATUS AND ROLE ON CONSUMERS

One important attribute of all groups is that group members have positions of status within them, and certain roles are associated with the status position held. *Status* is defined as the place occupied in a social group relative to other members of the group; status relates to a person's prestige position in the group. The term *role* is used to designate the sum total of the cultural patterns associated with a certain status. Role is the way people behave in social positions with reference to how others expect them to behave. Everyone has an idea of how a millionaire and a garbage person should behave. The fact is that the millionaire and the garbage person also have an idea about how they are expected to behave in certain situations, and each usually acts accordingly.

Function of status and role affects consumption

Status and role serve several important functions in our society. First, status and role determine an individual's placement in various groups and, as a result, the individual's placement in the society. Second, status and role form the basis for many social interactions. Social placement, in part, determines who people associate with and the manner of the association. Third, status and role determine many of the life styles maintained by individuals. The individual's social placement, interactions, and life-styles directly affect consumer behavior.[13] Social placement directly affects consumer attitudes toward the house one lives in, the car one drives, the clothes one wears, and the food one eats, because we tend to imitate what we see our peers doing. Thus, consumer behavior results, in part, from social interaction. Patterns of consumption developed early in a person's life tend to follow him or her, with modification, of course.

Multiplicity of roles affects consumers

Since status and role are affected by the social organizations in which a person participates, it follows that a person can simultaneously have more than one type of status. The person can also play a variety of roles based on the status held. However, no one can exercise all these roles simultaneously. A person operates on the basis of one, or a relatively few, roles at one time. In effect, consumers are continually jumping back and forth between the many roles demanded of them. A woman is a mother and housekeeper during the day and a wife and companion at night. This mother's purchasing action differs at various times dependent on the role she is playing at the time. As a practical housewife, she may watch every penny, only to splurge on a new nightgown because she knows her husband will like it.

There are many factors that affect the status and roles of individuals within groups, but the most important are age, sex, family structure, occupation, social class, and ethnic origin.[14] It is obvious that a person's role and status changes over time. A part of the explanation for changes in consumer purchase patterns can be traced to this fact. A man gets a promotion and a raise, creating a new status. As a result he may move into a better neighborhood, buy a bigger car, and take up golf. Some aspects of status cannot be changed, such as ethnic group or age. Consumers may attempt to compensate for this in the manner of their purchases.

Role conflict and consumer behavior

In spite of the fact that individuals occupy multiple roles, most people are able to meet their role obligations, most of the time, with a fair degree of success. However, there are times when roles come into conflict, and consumer behavior is affected by this conflict. There are several ways in which this occurs. First, conflict may arise when the expected behavior of a person does not conform to what is socially acceptable. A woman in a traditionally male occupation, such as that of a jockey, is going to be subjected to this type of role conflict. Such a person may go out of her way to purchase and use feminine products after working hours. Second, conflict occurs when a person steps out of traditional behavior patterns. In the process of growing up, one develops rather clear ideas of how fathers and mothers act, including their consumer actions. When one reaches adulthood, he or she is likely to pattern his or her consumer behavior after that of their parents. However, standards of conduct and consumption change over time, and conflicts can result. Third, conflict can result from a plurality of roles which may make legitimate, but conflicting, demands on the person. The father of young children who works must constantly face this situation. He has difficulty finding time for the two roles, and it is difficult for him to decide which to place first. The kids should come first, but the job is necessary to provide properly for the children.

A recent study confirms that in families where the woman's role is changing, new patterns of decision making may develop.[15] It was found where the wife holds contemporary attitudes of her role, the husband's decision making decreases and the wife's increases. Advertisers are recognizing this change in the woman's role. A survey of advertisements shows that the portrayal of working women in promotion has more than doubled in recent years.[16]

GROUP INFLUENCE ON CONSUMER BEHAVIOR

The ways in which groups influence behavior are many and varied. Groups influence immediate behavior, and they influence plans for the future through aspirations. Groups provide the goals for the individual's purchase behavior by acquainting individuals with the life styles of others.[17] Groups also provide the standard for measuring social successes and failures. Individuals compare their social and economic achievements to those of other members of the group.

Acceptance of group influence

Group influence is not the same to all people at all times. Compliance, identification, and internalization describe degrees of acceptance of social influence. Compliance occurs when an individual's actions are influenced by the social structure but the group influence is superficial. The individual adopts the behavior of the group, not because he or she believes as the group believes but because one feels that agreeing can produce a satisfying social effect. The individual's fundamental values remain unchanged.

The effect of social pressures has been laboratory tested. In a classic study, subjects were asked to state which of three lines were equal. Subjects were exposed to the obviously incorrect opinion of a majority. Over one-third of the subjects gave the same opinions as the majority. Some thought they had perceived the lines incorrectly, others doubted their own judgment, but a third group did not want to appear different from the majority.[18]

Purchases made to gain the influence of others fit this category perfectly. In the case of identification, an individual adopts group behavior in order to identify with some person or persons in the group. An example ot this is the young man who identifies with the movie star and copies his style of dress, hair style, and walk. The man believes in his actions, but not because they are personally satisfying. The influence is not continual but occurs only when the appropriate role definition is activated by some stimulus.

Internalization represents the highest order of social influence. It is distinguished by the fact that the individual accepts actions because they have been internalized as part of his value system. As such, they have been incorporated into the individual's makeup in such a way that they need not be monitored to assure that they enter into the decision process—they do so automatically.

The significance of various degrees of acceptance of social influence rests on the extent to which consumers act but have reservations about the wisdom of their actions. This point is illustrated by people who adopt particular fashions that they find neither appealing nor flattering. When in doubt, consumers tend to conform. In a study of conformity to group pressure and its result in restricting product choice, it was found that information from peer groups regarding style and quality were accepted on the basis of group conformity because it could not be evaluated objectively.[19] Products that are visible, in the sense that attributes can be verified, or have small social meaning are more often purchased on the basis of personal taste.

Strength of group influence on consumers

Group influence varies between consumers and over time. Group influence also varies by the type of decision the consumer is making. For example, influence may not be the same for product, brand, store, services, or method-of-purchase decisions. Furthermore, the influence felt by the consumer relative to any decision may be either strong or weak. Figure 20–1 illustrates the different strengths of group influence on a consumer where product and brand are concerned.[20]

Four conditions can be described, based on the table. The group may exert (1) strong product–strong brand influence; (2) strong product–weak brand influence; (3) weak product–strong brand influence; or (4) weak product–weak brand influence. There are some types of products, such as cars, cigarettes, beer, and drugs, where the groups exert a strong influence on both the choice of product and choice of brand. Other products have only a small group influence on the brand choice but greatly affect the product choice. Such products as instant coffee, air conditioners, and television sets, fit this group. A weak product–strong brand influence by the group is found for such products as furniture, clothing, magazines, refrigerators, and toilet soaps. Many convenience goods such as soap, canned goods, underwear, and

Figure 20–1

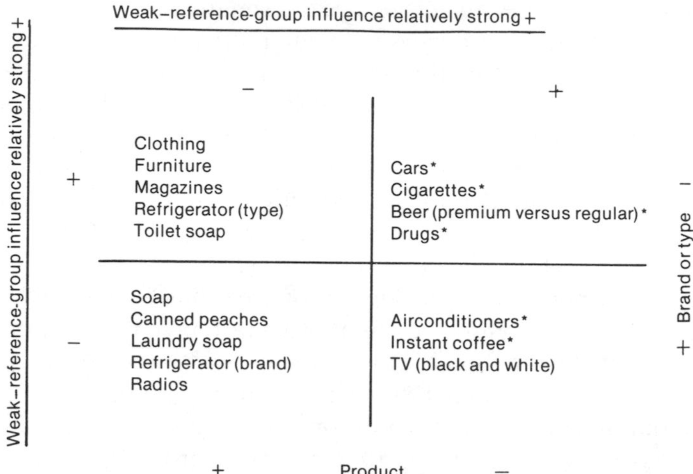

Note: Products and brands of consumer goods may be classified by the extent to which reference groups influence their purchase. (The classification of all products marked with an asterisk(*) is based on actual experimental evidence. Other products in this table are classified speculatively on the basis of generalizations derived from the sum of research in this area and confirmed by the judgment of seminar participants.)

Source: Bureau of Applied Social Research, Columbia University.

so on, have both a weak product and weak brand influence by the group or consumer.

EFFECTS OF SOCIAL CLASS ON CONSUMERS

Americans have traditionally steered away from the concept of social class. As a nation founded on democratic principles, we like to think of all people as equal. The American dream of a land where everyone has an opportunity to rise to the top prevails. Rather than face up to a contradiction between the ideal of equality and the concrete fact of social difference, we look the other way. When we do this, however, we fail to recognize an important part of our society's way of life. Social class enters into every aspect of our lives—marriage, family, business, government, work, and consumption. It is an important factor in determining personality development as well as the kinds of skills and abilities an individual may possess. Even though the principle of social class is often oversimplified and misunderstood, when applied in a realistic manner it can be proved invaluable to an understanding of consumer behavior.[21]

Social classes are groups of people who are, more or less, equal to one another in prestige and community status. Social class is the culmination of the group interactions discussed. Persons belong to a particular social class by virtue of (1) the willingness and regularity of formal and informal interaction, (2) the extent to which they share the same goals, and (3) the common views held toward their environment. This total life-style of the various social classes makes them significant to marketers.

One study of the effect of social class on purchasing found that two important dimensions of social class (occupational prestige and education) were directly related to the purchasing and switching of automobiles.[22] Social class was also found to be related to brand loyalty among these automobile buyers. A recent study of the urban poor, who occupy the lowest class of the social strata, have special purchase problems. The urban poor are penalized by shopping local stores where prices are abnormally high.[23] These shoppers gave as reasons for their purchase patterns: store convenience, friendship, and availability of credit. Transportation was also a factor. Over one fourth of the respondents reported that they wanted to purchase from their own kind of people. Another study led to the conclusion that advertising has a greater impact on the lower socioeconomic class than on middle class.[24]

Methods of social classification

There are several ways in which social classes can be determined. First, one or more of the factors of status can be used. Thus, individuals may be classified by occupation or income into high, middle, or low social classes. Such a classification does not always reflect the facts of a person's class role.[25] A $20,000-a-year truck driver is accorded a lower social position than an $18,000-a-year college professor. Nevertheless, in many instances this can be a satisfactory method of classification.

There are three other methods for determining social class. The subjective approach is one whereby each of us classifies ourselves and others based primarily on emotions. Classed this way, nearly everyone falls in the middle-class group. A second approach is to classify people by reputation. This method is seldom accurate, but can be useful for casual observations. The third, and most accepted, approach is objective evaluation. Since this approach is so important, we want to cover it in detail.

Four items appear to be most important indicators of social class. These are occupation, source of income, type of housing, and location of residence. Table 20–1 describes six social classes based on these items. It provides us with meaningful types of social class.[26]

It is clear from these data that most consumer markets fall into the

Table 20–1
The Warner social class structure*

	Social class	*Membership*	*Population percentage*
1.	Upper-upper	Locally prominent families, third- or fourth-generation wealth. Merchants, financiers, or higher professionals. Wealth is inherited. Do a great amount of traveling.	1.5
2.	Lower-upper	Newly arrived in upper class. "Nouveau riche." Not accepted by upper class. Executive elite, founders of large businesses, doctors and lawyers.	1.5
3.	Upper-middle	Moderately successful professionals, owners of medium-sized businesses and middle management. Status conscious. Child and home centered.	10.0
4.	Lower-middle	Top of the average-man world. Nonmanagerial office workers, small-business owners, and blue-collar families. Described as "striving and respectable." Conservative.	33.0
5.	Upper-lower	Ordinary working class. Semiskilled workers. Income often as high as two next classes above. Enjoy life. Live from day to day.	38.0
6.	Lower-lower	Unskilled, unemployed, and unassimilated ethnic groups. Fatalistic. Apathetic.	16.0
	Totals		100.0

* These estimates are based on Warner and Hollings' distributions in rather small communities. However, an estimate of social class structure for America approximates these percentages.

Source: Adapted from Charles B. McCann, *Women and Department Store Newspaper Advertising* (Chicago: Social Research, Inc., 1957).

lower-middle class and upper-lower classes. Anthropologists describe the upper-upper class as "international in their residence, friendships, and relationships." In America, clothing, sports, and education favored by this class bear the mark of British influence. The lower-upper class has the goals of the class above and the class below themselves, and their purchase patterns also follow those of these classes. The upper-middle class housewife shops in her neighborhood, visits over the back fence, and engages in local activities. Members of this group read *Time, Fortune,* and the *New York Times,* play bridge, attend plays and symphonies, and many belong to the golf or yacht club.

The lower-middle class is oriented toward television, movies, and bowling. They read *Reader's Digest Condensed Books, Sports Illustrated, Good Housekeeping, American Home,* and *Ladies Home Journal.* They purchase at the neighborhood shopping centers and Sears. A high degree of price sensitivity is reflected in this group. The man is often a union member and belongs to some lodge.

The upper-lower class is oriented toward enjoying life, and their purchases do not reflect the desire for middle-class respectability. However, they do try to keep up with the times and live comfortably. Entertainment centers on television and the movies. The group does not read very much.

The lower-lower class tends to be fatalistic. The group has only 8 percent of the purchasing power of the economy. Marketers generally tend to overlook this group. However, there is evidence that not only do low-income groups constitute good markets for particular types of products, but that they are individualistic.[27] One fact is clear: Most consumers use a variety of information sources. Blacks or poor are not different in this respect, and everyone includes some social group information in his market activity.

Attitude differences by social class

There are differences in preferences and attitudes among the various social classes. Figure 20–2 summarizes the attitudes one study indicated that each social class took toward all other social classes. Notice that each class has a good image of itself.

In another study, some of these same points showed up in conversations. When women were asked to pick words which they thought best described themselves, working-class women picked such words as "fun-loving," "curious," and "easygoing." The middle-class woman didn't see herself as fun-loving but instead her self-conceptions revolved strongly around "moral," "responsible," and "serious."[28]

In still another study, sophisticated women, who were listeners of radio, "scornfully ridiculed daytime serials" which they referred to as soap operas. These serials had tremendous appeal for the mass-audience woman. The radio daytime serial seemed to embody many of the working-class woman's basic beliefs about the "scheme of things."[29]

When asked to state the first thing that came to mind when they heard the word "baby," middle-class women responded with "darling," "sweet," and "mother." However, the bottom half of the market turned up with such reactions as "pain in the neck," "more work," and "a darling, but a bother." Such a reaction may have resulted from larger families in this group combined with fewer baby aids.[30]

On a broad exploration of lamp styles, furniture styles, and home styles, the lower half of the market selected completely different styles from the top half. The lower classes did not want the modern ranch homes or the two-story colonial so popular with the upper classes. Nor did they choose the severely plain, functional styling of furniture preferred by the top segment of the market.

Figure 20–2
The social perspectives of the social classes

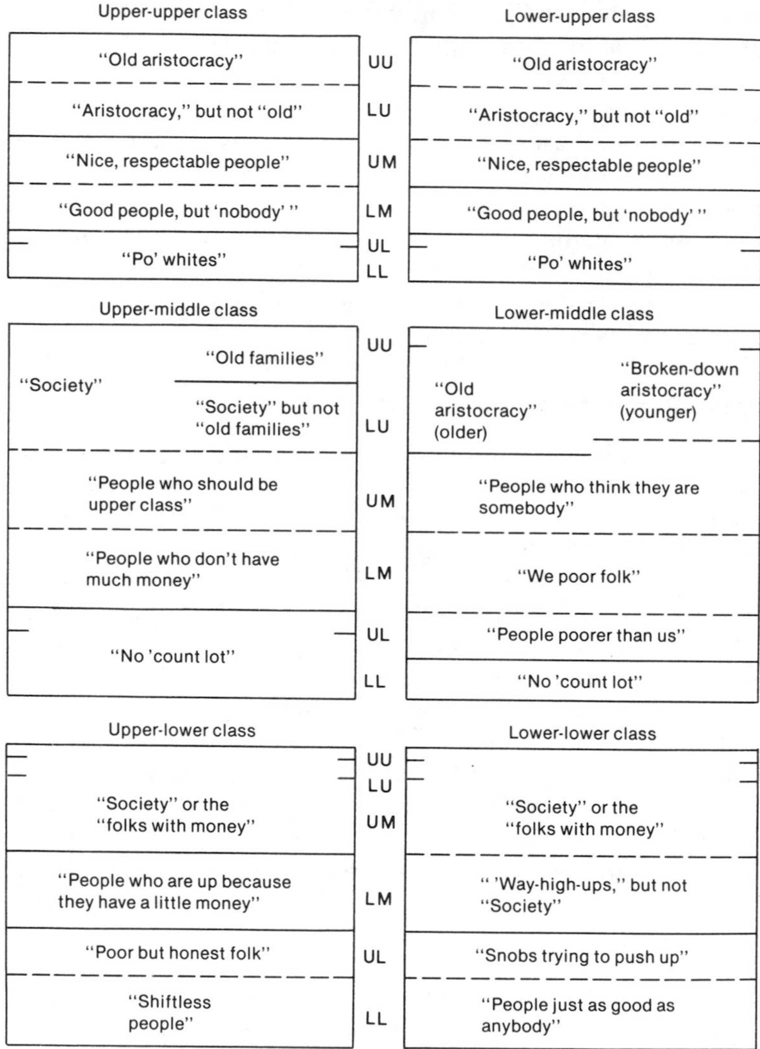

Source: A. Davis, B. B. Gardner, and M. K. Gardner, *Deep South* (Chicago: University of Chicago Press, 1941).

Social class and consumer choice

A vast amount of difference can be observed in the shopping and spending habits of the various social classes. Upper-class people consume more services than do members of other classes. This group is an important reference group for others. The upper-middle class family spends a relatively large share of its income on housing, expensive furnishings, clothing from quality stores, and on cultural amusements or club memberships.

The lower-middle class family may have a better house than an upper-middle class family in the same income bracket, but the neighborhood is probably not as fancy. The lower-middle class family is likely to have a full wardrobe, though not as expensive, and probably more furniture but none by name designers.

The middle-class wife normally finds it necessary to stretch her budget to include those extras she desires for herself and her family. For this reason, she is careful in her spending and compares prices. The working-class family, though they may have the same income as the upper- and lower-middle class families, is apt to have a less pretentious house in a neighborhood of lower status. The lower-class family is likely to have a bigger and later model car and more expensive appliances than a middle-class family in the same income bracket. The lower-class family spends more on clothing and furniture.

NOTES

1. Frederick E. Webster, Jr. and Yoram Wind, "A General Model for Understanding Organizational Buying Behavior," *Journal of Marketing*, vol. 36 (April 1972), pp. 12–19.
2. Scott Ward, "Consumer Socialization," *Journal of Consumer Research*, vol. 1 (September 1974), pp. 1–14.
3. George C. Homans, *Social Behavior: Its Elementary Forms* (New York: Harcourt, Brace & World, Inc., 1967).
4. Adapted from John W. McDavid and Herbert Harari, *Social Psychology: Individuals, Groups, and Society* (New York: Harper & Row, Publishers, 1968), p. 237.
5. Jean E. Weber and Richard W. Hansen, "The Majority Effect and Brand Choice," *Journal of Marketing Research*, vol. 9 (August 1972), pp. 320–23.
6. A. Benton Cocanougher and Grady D. Bruce, "Socially Distant Reference Groups and Consumer Aspirations," *Journal of Marketing Research*, vol. 8 (August 1971), pp. 379–81.
7. Robert E. Witt and Grady D. Bruce, "Group Influence and Brand Choice Congruence," *Journal of Marketing Research*, vol. 9 (November 1972), pp. 440–43.
8. Francis S. Bourne, "Group Influence in Marketing and Public Relations," *Some Applications of Behavioral Science Research*, ed. Rensis Likert and Samuel P. Hayes, Jr. (Paris: UNESCO, 1957), pp. 217–24.
9. Edward M. Tauber, "Why Do People Shop?" *Journal of Marketing*, vol. 36 (October 1972), pp. 46–59.

10. Russell W. Belk, "Occurrence of Word-of-Mouth Buyer Behavior as a Function of Situation and Advertising Stimuli," *Relevance in Marketing: Problems, Research, Action,* ed. Fred C. Allvine (Chicago: American Marketing Assn., 1971), pp. 419–22.
11. John O. Summers, "Generalized Change Agents and Innovativeness," *Journal of Marketing Research,* vol. 8 (August 1971), pp. 313–16.
12. Joseph T. Plummer, "Life Style Patterns and Commercial Bank Credit Card Usage," *Journal of Marketing,* vol. 35 (April 1971), pp. 35–41.
13. James H. Myers, Roger R. Stanton, and Arne F. Haug, "Correlates of Buying Behavior: Social Class versus Income," *Journal of Marketing,* vol. 35 (October 1971), pp. 8–15; William W. Curtis, "Social Class or Income?" *Journal of Marketing,* vol. 36 (January 1972), pp. 67–68; H. Lee Mathews and John W. Slocum, Jr., "Social Class and Commercial Bank Credit Card Usage," *Journal of Marketing,* vol. 33 (January 1969), pp. 71–78.
14. Donald J. Hempel, "Family Buying Decisions: A Cross-Cultural Perspective," *Journal of Marketing Research,* vol. 11 (August 1974), pp. 295–302.
15. Robert T. Green and Isabella C. M. Cunningham, "Feminine Role Perception and Family Purchasing Decisions," *Journal of Marketing Research,* vol. 12 (August 1975), pp. 325–32.
16. Louis C. Wagner and Janis B. Banos, "A Woman's Place: A Follow-up Analysis of the Roles Portrayed by Women in Magazine Advertisements," *Journal of Marketing Research,* vol. 10 (May 1973), pp. 213–14.
17. George P. Moschis, "Social Comparison and Informal Group Influence," *Journal of Marketing Research,* vol. 13 (August 1976), pp. 237–44.
18. Solomon E. Asch, "Effects of Group Pressure upon the Modifications and Distortion of Judgment," *Group Dynamics,* ed. Dorwin Cartwright and A. Zander (New York: Harper & Row, Publishers, 1953).
19. M. Van Katesan, "Experimental Study of Consumer Behavior Conformity and Independence," *Journal of Marketing Research,* vol. 3 (November 1966), pp. 384–87.
20. The table is only illustrative for products and brands. There is little empirical evidence concerning group influence on stores, services, and method of purchase.
21. Arun K. Jain, "A Method for Investigating and Representing Implicit Social Class Theory," *Journal of Consumer Research,* vol. 2 (June 1975), pp. 53–59; Gordon R. Foxall, "Social Factors in Consumer Choice: Replication and Extension," *Journal of Consumer Research,* vol. 2 (June 1975), pp. 60–64.
22. Frederick E. May, "The Effect of Social Class on Brand Loyalty," *California Management Review,* vol. 14 (Fall 1971), pp. 81–87.
23. Louis E. Boone and John A. Bonno, "Food Buying Habits of the Urban Poor," *Journal of Retailing,* vol. 47 (Fall 1971), pp. 79–84.
24. Peter O. Peretti and Chris Lucas, "Newspaper Advertising Influences on

Consumers' Behavior by Socioeconomic Status of Consumers," *Psychological Reports*, vol. 37 (1975), pp. 493–94.

25. James H. Myers and John F. Mount, "More on Social Class versus Income as Correlates of Buying Behavior," *Journal of Marketing*, vol. 37 (April 1973), pp. 71–75; Myers, Stanton, and Haug, "Correlates of Buying Behavior: Social Class versus Income," pp. 8–15.
26. William Lloyd Warner, Marcia Meeker, and Kenneth Eells, *Social Class in America* (New York: Harper & Bros., 1960), p. 5.
27. Carl E. Block, "Prepurchase Search Behavior of Low-Income Households," *Journal of Retailing*, vol. 48 (Spring 1972), pp. 3–15.
28. Pierre Martineau, *Motivation in Advertising: Motives That Make People Buy* (New York: McGraw-Hill Book Co., 1957), p. 38.
29. W. Lloyd Warner, *The Radio Daytime Serial* (Chicago: University of Chicago, 1937).
30. Ibid.

QUESTIONS

1. What is social interaction? How is it important to consumer behavior? Distinguish between group, crowd, and mob interaction.
2. Discuss the five characteristics of groups. Provide examples of how each characteristic may affect a particular purchase.
3. Define reference group. To what reference groups do you belong? In what ways do each affect your purchase behavior?
4. Discuss groups classified by participation. To what primary groups do you belong? To what secondary groups? How does each influence you?
5. What are membership groups? Define automatic, participation, anticipatory, and negative groups. Give examples of each that affects your behavior.
6. Explain why business is interested in social groups. Can business, in your opinion, do much to affect these groups?
7. What is status? What is role? How are the two related? Illustrate some roles that you play. Do these roles involve any consumer behavior? Explain.
8. What is the multiplicity of roles? Does multiplicity affect roles conflict? Explain.
9. Discuss the effect of group influence on consumer behavior.
10. What is social class? Explain how social classes are grouped. How does social class affect consumer attitudes? Consumer choices? Discuss.

21

The consumerism movement

Consumerism defined

Historical development of consumerism

- *The period of innocence*
- *The period of public awareness*
- *The period of consumer achievement*

Consumerism today

- *Current issues of consumerism*
- *Types of consumer organizations*
- *Objectives of consumerism*
- *Tools of the consumer movement*

What consumerism has accomplished

- *Possible courses of action*
- *Consumer bill of rights*
- *Legal protection for consumers*
- *Increased social awareness by business*

Future of consumerism

For the most part when one thinks of consumer behavior, a picture comes to mind of the solitary shopper making the rounds of the grocery, drug, discount, and department stores. It's an image of one person against the business system attempting to overcome high prices, confusing product claims, sales inefficiency, and sometimes dishonesty in an attempt to provide the necessary goods for a family's operation. Although it may not be entirely correct, one tends to think of consumer behavior as an unequal confrontation, with the individual pitted against the power and organization of the business enterprise. Well, that picture is beginning to change.

Consumers are learning that they, too, can display the power of organization and numbers. Whereas even 15 years ago, the notion of concerted action by consumers was considered impossible by most marketers, today it has become a reality. At the moment when the first spontaneous action of a group of consumers caused some business to change its attitude or policy, consumerism, a weak and sporadic ideal, became a market force to be reckoned with. This chapter concerns the development, present status, and future of this consumerism movement. If business decisions are to be adequate to meet consumerism's pervasive impact on the marketplace, the movement must be systematically appraised and understood.

CONSUMERISM DEFINED

As we shall see in a later section, the consumer movement is quite old, but consumerism is a term of recent origin. Its very inclusion in the language attests to the growing impetus our society is placing on the consumer. Consumerism is a rejection of the doctrine of *caveat emptor* in which the buyers were viewed as having both the will and the means to protect themselves in the market.[1] Like most new doctrines, consumerism has been advanced from more than one perspective. Consumerism has variously been shown to be organized consumers, a social force, and the activities of various agencies. Buskirk and Rothe indicate: Accordingly, consumerism, is defined as the organized efforts of consumers seeking redress, restitution, and remedy for dissatisfaction they have accumulated in the acquisition of their standard of living.[2] Aaker and Day define consumerism as: The widening range of activities of government, business and independent organizations that are designed to protect individuals from practices that infringe upon their rights as consumers.[3]

Both definitions are somewhat restricted—the first, because it ignores agencies other than consumers; and the latter, because it deemphasizes individuals. Furthermore, consumerism, as it has evolved, includes much more than consumer protection or redress of wrongs. A broader definition is needed, and for the purpose of this book, consumerism is defined as:

> *an organized effort by consumers within the environment designed to aid and protect consumer rights by efforts directed at, and through, government, business and private organizations.*[4]

HISTORICAL DEVELOPMENT OF CONSUMERISM

The beginning of the consumer movement is, of course, lost in time.[5] However, it is safe to say that the first disgruntled consumer probably occurred simultaneously with the first marketing institution. After all, there is some basis for natural antagonism between buyers who seek the lowest price for goods and sellers who seek the highest price. Most consumers feel that everything they purchase costs too much, since, if each item cost less, the consumer could spread his or her income further.

There is no general agreement on the specific causes for the rise of modern consumerism as an organized protest. When business, consumer, and government representatives were given 28 reasons popular in the literature, to explain the rise of consumerism, there was little agreement. A consensus existed on only the seven items listed below:

1. The political appeal of consumer protection legislation.
2. The mechanical and impersonal nature of the marketplace.
3. The language of advertising.
4. A bandwagon effect.
5. Greater public concern for social problems.
6. A feeling that business should assume greater "social responsibilities."
7. A change in national attitude.[6]

A complete history of consumerism is not necessary or desirable at this time, but a summary of the high points of progress can place consumerism in proper perspective.[7] The consumer movement can be divided into three periods: (1) the period of innocence, (2) the period of public awareness, and (3) the period of consumer achievement. This definition is sufficiently flexible to encompass most institutions involved in consumerism, and it points to the need for consumer aid as well as protection.

The period of innocence

The period of innocence is so named because the mass of people naïvely believed that they had no right to more, or because they had faith in the system to provide for their requirements. This period lasted from the dawn of history until approximately 1900. The early part of the period was characterized by suppression of the masses. The barons of England had achieved a measure of freedom from King John with the signing of the Magna Charta in 1215, but the benefits had not been passed on to the average person. A very strict class system existed in all nations. The gentry ruled and enjoyed the good life, which was supported on the backs of the commoners who had little or nothing. Even so, there were isolated, and usually spontaneous, instances of resistance to the low standard of living. Occasionally, the serfs would rise up against the baron, or commoners would wreck the local trade center. The legendary tales of Robin Hood, although fictional, depict true situations in which the poor attempted to gain better economic conditions.

The roots of the American revolution in 1775 were founded in the consumer-related problems of tariffs, sales tax, and product shortages. Only later did it become a fight for freedom. The Boston Tea Party is a notable example of an early consumer uprising and product boycott. The French Revolution in 1789 was largely due to a desire of the common people to share more in the good life. These two struggles changed the course of history and gave the ordinary person a large measure of freedom.

The 19th century continued the advance in human freedom in America, but saw no real upswing in consumer action from the sporadic types that had previously occurred. The writings of Alfred Marshall and Adam Smith had popularized a concept of economic balance that precluded any opportunity to change the inevitable. Most people believed, in spite of the evidence of their eyes, in pure competition in which resources were perfectly allocated automatically. The "unseen hand" controlled the system, and the individual consumer was caught in its power. Furthermore, the average person's recently won freedom worked against any concerted consumer movement in an organized sense. Individualism, pride in self-achievement, and self-sufficiency were the order of the day. Americans did not want to depend on group action, the government, or private agencies to achieve their goals. This dependence was viewed as a restriction of freedom. People wanted the American dream of advancement based on personal merit and hard work. There was not much chance for organized consumer action under this type of atmosphere.

The period of public awareness

What has become popularly termed the consumer movement, or consumerism, had its beginning around 1900, although the first consumer protection law was passed in 1872.[8] The period of awakening occurred between 1900 and 1960, and it is so named because a real change in the American attitude toward consumer problems occurred during this period.[9]

The late 1800s and early 1900s contained factors that caused people to become increasingly aware of the existence of market inequities. The builders of the transcontinental railroad, completed in 1869, had, with government cooperation, made tremendous profits from land grabs, exploitation of labor, and the abuse of Indians and settlers alike. The Grangers were instrumental in bringing these abuses to light, and this knowledge began to open some eyes. The growth of large business after 1880 with some instances of conspiracy, interlocking directors, price fixing, dividing up territories between companies, etc. added impetus to the awakening.

Like most causes, the consumer movement needed leadership and a catalyst to get it moving. The leadership was beginning to appear by 1891 when the first Consumer League was formed, and by 1898 this organization had become a national federation.[10] The catalyst came in the form of two books published between 1900 and 1930. *The Jungle* was a graphic expose of working conditions in Chicago's meat packing industry.[11] This book told of rats, dirt, and even humans finding their way into the packaged meat. The book became popular and was instrumental in the passage of the landmark Food and Drug Act of 1906. *Your Money's Worth* was one of the first attacks on advertising and high-pressure selling.[12] Thus by 1930, the consumer movement was an established fact, but it still had not gained cohesion as a movement.

Consumerism grew slowly but steadily during the 1930s. Writers continued to focus attention on consumer problems. *100,000,000 Guinea Pigs* dealt with the manner in which business experimented on the American public with new products, and *American Chamber of Horrors* focused on unsafe cosmetics and quack medical cures.[13] When the Federal Drug Administration pushed for new protective legislation in the early 1930s, only the American Economic Association and the National Congress of Parents and Teachers were interested. Due largely to these two books, the scope of the problem was brought home to the public, and 16 national women's organizations joined the fight.[14] As a result, new legislation was passed in the food and drug area.

The period of consumer achievement

The period of consumer achievement began in the 1960s and continues to the present. In this period, consumerism began to reach its potential. The period is characterized by consumer action on several fronts.[15] In the 1960s, much legislation dealing with labeling of products, food and drug standards, lending, product safety, and promotion truth and honesty was passed. Furthermore, the general public was finally made aware to the point of identification with the consumer movement. It is for these reasons that the period is identified with achievement.

Consumerism has become a popular cause with government officials, better-business bureaus, academicians, movie stars, and even business leaders.[16] The movement began to show some efforts toward organization, and by 1969 there were over 29 states with consumer leagues or similar organizations. The most active consumer groups were in Louisiana and Arizona.[17] Even so, the movement was still characteristically identified with specific personalities. Ralph Nader is probably the name most identified with the modern consumer movement. However, Betty Furness, Vance Packard, David Caplovitz, and Jessica Mitford are also important symbols of consumerism.[18] In the next sections of this chapter, we can more clearly identify the present status and accomplishments of consumerism today.

CONSUMERISM TODAY

It is apparent from the previous discussion that consumerism has come a long way since 1900. Even so, the movement remains largely fragmented and lacking in overall direction. Just getting the attention of a group as large and diverse as American consumers is a monumental task, and obtaining cooperative action from them staggers the imagination. The immensity of the group is, perhaps, consumerism's chief enemy. Group size probably accounts for the fact that the peaks and valleys of interest in consumerism follow closely publicity of emotion-charged national issues associated with purchasing power or health problems. Only such issues are capable of obtaining broad consumer support over periods of time. A discussion of the issues, objectives, organizations, and tools of consumerism can greatly aid in clarifying these points.

Current issues of consumerism

Consumerism finds its reason for being in a great many current problems and issues. These issues range from inflation and business ethics to pollution and protection of minorities.[19] Fortunately, these issues can be meaningfully grouped around three broad topics: (1) economic issues, (2) social issues, and (3) issues of business ethics.

Economic issues. The general operation of our business system gives rise to economic issues. Of these issues, inflation causes the greatest concern among consumers, although the abuse of technology, depletion of resources, and productivity are important. Inflation, which reflects the general price level of goods, affects every consumer's pocketbook. Americans have learned to live with a little inflation, since it is preferred to any deflation. However, any sharp rise in prices, such as has occurred in the late 1960s and 1970s, erodes real income and leads to discontent.

The abuse of technology is a broad area of consumer concern that involves business stewardship over tools, methods, and techniques of production. Americans believe in technology, because it leads to productivity and a higher standard of living. We have even come to recognize that some unemployment is tolerable because it occurs while unskilled workers are being moved to more skilled and higher paying jobs. However, there is a growing feeling, whether right or wrong, that excesses in technology are not sound because of their effect on people and the environment. Business is criticized for moving too fast technologically, as seen by criticism of the expenditures on space, opposition to atomic energy plants, and the scrapping of the SST. Business is also criticized for too slow a rate of technology, as seen by the current attacks on the internal combustion engine; failure to install pollution abatement devices in industry; and the federal interstate highway system, railroads, and rapid transit.

Consumers are becoming increasingly concerned about the failure of productivity to keep in step with rising prices. The American public has become astute enough to recognize the tie-in of productivity with the balance of U.S. payments abroad and foreign imports.

The depletion of resources has suddenly been introduced to consumer issues in recent months. The most striking example is the continuing gasoline shortage, but many of our natural mineral, wildlife, and scenic resources are rapidly being depleted. Of course, it can easily be seen that these economic problems are often directly related to social and ethical goals.

Social issues. The major social issues directly related to consumerism are environmental protection, protection of minorities, and protection of health and safety.[20] There is no question but that the environment is a real social problem. However, consumers appear about as confused over how to handle it as does business. Consumers insist on a lessening of pollution, but refuse to give up their oversized, dirty automobiles or the products of polluting factories. Consumers actively seek improvement in the safety of products, such as flammable materials, dangerous toys, poisons, etc, but refuse to use their seat belts, object to the cost of safety devices, and do not remove medicine from children's reach or safely dispose of old refrigerators. The attitude often appears to be that it is up to business to find a way to protect the environment and the consumer without the individual giving up anything. The interesting fact is, that given sufficient time, business will probably do just that.

Protection of minorities has been a social issue in America for over 15 years. Several factors are tied together that affect consumerism. They include: equal rights for minority groups, better housing, more livable cities, and more job and income opportunities. The minorities in question include blacks, Indians, Asians, women, children, poor, etc. Most Americans have come to recognize the importance, too, of solving the problems of minorities, although there are admittedly still holdouts for the old order. Progress has been good—even spectacular—by previous standards, but still most would consider results unsatisfactory. There are many reasons for the lack of results which include: human biases, lack of clear objectives by concerned parties, inefficiency and corruption in some government agencies, failure of minorities to respond to aid, lack of funds, and distractions by radical groups. One overriding problem is the sheer immensity of the undertaking. No nation in history has ever undertaken so vast a program of social reform, or achieved such good results—no matter how unsatisfactory.

Some responsible persons have concluded that we have moved too far too fast with social programs. Total public expenditures on welfare rose from $77 billion in 1965 to a colossal $287 billion in 1975.[21] Social security payments, unemployment insurance, pensions, Medicare, etc. have followed the rising trend in expenditures. One author concluded that welfare is no longer for poor people since welfare is the essence of the state itself.[22] There is a growing feeling that these social programs must be brought under control with more benefits to the real needy but less overall expenditure.

Issues of business ethics. Business has always been under attack by some group. The criticism is sometimes justified and sometimes not. It is the author's experience that businesspeople are about as honest and ethical as the average of the population. It should be understood that the above statement leaves plenty of room for improvement. The fact is that business is an easy target for disgruntled members of society. Some businesspeople are often stupid, inefficient, and dishonest, and the first two may be more serious than the latter. Thus, any attack is likely to contain some elements of truth. Consumers feel that business is so impersonal that no one is really hurt by such attacks. Besides, the industry is really too vast to fight back on a personal basis.

The overriding issue of business ethics is fair, honest, and equitable treatment for consumers.[23] Of course, this issue can be broken down into several problem areas, including truth in promotion, unit pricing, high-pressure selling, restraint of trade, service standards, etc. The problem is that the great variety of stores, the number of generic products, and the specific brands available make it impossible for the consumer to be fully informed when buying. Therefore, the consumer is an easy target for various types of deceptions by dishonest, misinformed, or just poor business firms. Some of the more common types of deceptions include: promoting a No. 303 can as larger than a No. 2 can; selling factory seconds or damaged merchandise without identification; using large packages not completely full to give the appearance of more; use of bait pricing; making false and misleading statements about the store or its merchandise; selling essentially the same merchandise for different prices; charging exorbitant interest on credit purchases; overcharging merchandise; and misidentifying merchandise for pricing purposes.

It does not matter that the majority of businesspeople are honest. The consumer measures the worth of the entire group by the bad encounters. Besides, where abuses take place, the consumer has a right to have these abuses corrected. The problem is that no amount of consumer vigilance or government action can completely eliminate dishonest or unethical business practices. However, there is no question but that such action can act as a deterrent and improve the overall performance of business.

Types of consumer organizations

The consumer movement has attracted a wide variety of groups with diverse interests, and it is difficult to keep these groups working together. The current situation is that temporary coalitions are formed as the interests of specific groups coincide, but they seldom include a majority of available organizations, nor are they of long duration when organized. Herrmann says:

> *the constituent groups in these coalitions include labor organizations, consumer cooperatives, credit unions, consumer educators, the product-testing and consumer education organization (Consumer Union), state and local consumer organizations, plus other organizations with related interests such as senior citizens groups and professional organizations.*[24]

To this list should be added such federal agencies as the Federal Trade Commission, The Food and Drug Administration, the Federal Communications Commission, and the Department of Agriculture. Furthermore, there is clear evidence that the consumer movement depends heavily on the favor of the White House for any legislative improvement.[25] Presidential support has been particularly important in the Kennedy and Nixon terms. Perhaps the most consistent consumer participants are Consumer Union and the state and local consumer organizations.

Objectives of consumerism

There are, of course, as many different consumer objectives as there are consumer organizations. Labor unions may be primarily concerned with wages, cooperatives may want favorable legislation to extend their sphere of influence, credit unions may want to become involved in legislation relating to lending and interest rates, and educators may be primarily concerned with student understanding of the consumer movement. However, there are three logical objectives of consumerism that underlie all the above organizations, whether recognized or not. They are:

1. Consumer education.
2. Consumer self-protection.
3. Business acceptance of responsibility.

First, consumers must be informed. Information provided may include tips on when and where to shop, how to determine merchandise quality, when to compare and when not to, tips on good buys, how to compare prices, and how to take advantage of sales. Other types of information include lists of ethical and cooperative dealers and lists of businesses caught, or suspected, of actions detrimental to consumers. There is evidence that a lack of information concerning rights is one of the more serious problems of consumerism.[26] Second, consumer self-protection takes two forms. Consumers, under the guidance of some agency, may attempt redress by refusing to buy from certain stores or by refusing to purchase certain types of merchandise. The meat boycott of 1973 is an example of this type of action.[27] Consumer organizations also seek self-protection of consumers through the support of, or opposition to, specific legislation that affects consumers. Third, consumer organizations, by direct action and education, seek to get business voluntarily to accept its responsibility to consumers and society.

Tools of the consumer movement

Publicity, is, and has been thoughout the history of consumerism, the single most important tool of the movement. We have already cited the effect of books used to expose specific conditions in business. Other publicity tools include news releases, published lists of offending firms, and newsletters. Consumer organizations work hard at uncovering genuine news items that the news media can pick up. Newsletters are sent primarily to the membership of the various consumer organizations and are one of the prime methods of consumer education.

Political action is the second most important tool of consumerism. It ranks behind publicity because political action is so dependent on publicity. Consumerism uses three types of political action. First, organization members study the platforms of political candidates, give support to those in line with consumer goals, and educate consumers on candidates to support. Second, there exists both an organized and unorganized lobby in favor of consumerism in Washington. The lobbyists are mostly unpaid, but often quite effective, especially when supported by spontaneous write-ins from constituents. Third, write-in campaigns are sometimes organized at the local level to support candidates or legislation favorable to the consumer movement. These campaigns can be quite effective.

Direct action is the least important of the consumerism tools. The prime means of direct action is the consumer boycott or threat of boycott. The effectiveness of a boycott is limited because it is difficult to organize group action and sustain it over any length of time. Thus the boycott is used only as a last resort, or when it is the result of spontaneous action. The meat boycott of 1973 was organizationally successful, but it had mixed effect on meat prices.[28] The prime reason being that there were sound economic reasons for meat prices to be high.

WHAT CONSUMERISM HAS ACCOMPLISHED

We now have some feel for the history and current status of American consumerism. It is, therefore, time to deal with the accomplishment of the movement. There is no question but that these accomplishments have been significant.

Possible courses of action

Everyone has an opinion about consumerism, and consumers, business, and the government has objectives relative to the movement.[29] Of course, little can be accomplished in meeting the needs of the various groups without objectives. The problem is that objectives of the principal parties do not coincide. Table 21-1 demonstrates how consumers, government, and business view the broad courses of action necessary to the consumerism movement. There was general agreement among the three groups except on the need for more legislation. Business representatives did not agree with this need to the extent of the other two groups. Business representatives did express a greater desire for more voluntary business efforts than consumers did. We can now turn our attention to how well these somewhat conflicting objectives have been achieved.

Consumer bill of rights

Perhaps the most important single accomplishment of modern consumerism is the recognition that consumers have certain rights. In

Table 21–1
Business, government, and consumer views of the needs of consumerism (by group)

	Percent who agreed			*Percent who disagreed*			*Percent who were uncertain*		
	*I**	*II**	*III**	*I*	*II*	*III*	*I*	*II*	*III*
1. More cooperation among government, business and consumers	74%	64%	75%	13%	22%	8%	13%	14%	17%
2. New "consumer relations" thinking	74	81	92	13	13	8	13	6	0
3. More voluntary business efforts	88	56	67	8	19	9	4	25	24
4. Additional legislation at the federal level	17	94	92	58	0	0	25	6	8
5. Additional legislation at state level	21	88	92	62	0	0	17	12	8
6. Stricter enforcement of present laws	60	94	92	16	0	8	24	6	0
7. Broad consumer education program	87	100	100	9	0	0	4	0	0

* Group I —Business Spokesmen
Group II —Consumer Spokesmen
Group III—Government Spokesmen
Source: Ralph M. Gaedeke, "What Business, Government and Consumer Spokesmen Think about Consumerism," *The Journal of Consumer Affairs,* vol. 4 (Summer 1970), pp. 7–18.

1962, the late President John F. Kennedy in a *Special Message on Protecting the Consumer Interest* outlined consumer rights as: (1) the right to safety, (2) the right to be informed, (3) the right to choose, and (4) the right to be heard.[30] No doubt, other factors such as specific acts of legislation have had a more immediate impact on consumers. However, the clear statement of consumer rights means more in the long run. First, their publication by the president puts everyone on notice that consumer interests are to be served. Second, the list of consumer rights provides a standard for evaluating business service to the community. Third, the bill of rights will provide a basis for future legislation of far-reaching impact. Thus, the existence of a consumer bill of rights overshadows all other accomplishments of consumerism. Let us take a closer look at these rights.

The right to safety. This is the right of the consumer to be protected against the sale of products hazardous to health or life.[31] The right is not absolute and must be applied with reason, since any product can be potentially dangerous. Gasoline used in automobiles can explode, screwdrivers can put out eyes, some people are allergic to specific chemicals, and appliances can short-circuit. However, no one seriously wants these products removed from the market. The right to safety is directed at unusually hazardous products such as narcotics, unclean food, fire hazards, defective products, or products where the consumer cannot be aware of the hazard. No amount of government action can eliminate all health and safety hazards, and the consumer is expected to use intelligence and reasonable caution when using any product.

The federal government has been active in the area of consumer safety by (1) limiting the sale of diseased meat, narcotics, and dangerous patent medicines; (2) regulating the use of drugs and chemicals by consumers themselves; (3) initiating programs of highway, waterway, and air safety; and (4) establishing standards that eliminate or control conditions of manufacture and sale of goods. The Consumers Product Safety Commission puts out an index of hazardous products. The most hazardous products according to the index are:

1. Bicycles and bicycle equipment.
2. Stairs, ramps, landings.
3. Doors, other than glass doors.
4. Cleaning agents.
5. Tables, non-glass.
6. Beds.
7. Football, activity-related equipment.
8. Swings, slides, seesaws, playground equipment.
9. Liquid fuels, kindling.
10. Architectural glass.[32]

Of course, all these products bring consumer benefits, and the difficulty is to balance safety against consumer wants. It is not an easy decision to make.

The right to be informed. This consumer right concerns protection against fraud, deception, and grossly misleading information, promotion, labeling, and other practices. It also establishes the consumer's right to have the facts needed for intelligent product choice. The right to information does not relieve the consumer of responsibility of market awareness. Each seller has the right to present his or her product most favorably, and there is nothing that requires such full disclosure as: do better or cheaper competitive products exist, exact performance, or features that are unsuited or unnecessary to the specific consumer. It is still the consumer's responsibility to shop, compare, and use relevant market information efficiently.

The right to be informed deals with some sticky moral and ethical questions to which no absolute answers are yet available. The most difficult question is where to draw the line between truth and untruth or fact and deception. For example, is the use of cartoons untruthful because cartoons are not real? How about the use of actors to depict average persons in commercials? Is it deceitful of an aspirin manufacturer to advertise that its product is the best, when, in fact, there are none better—although several are just as good? Is it ethical to promote toys on the morning TV cartoon shows for viewing by the susceptible young? Are appeals to sex, beauty, and happiness factual in promoting drugs and cosmetics? Ask your acquaintances about these and similar questions of information presentation, and you may be surprised at the variety of answers you receive. Marketers are equally in doubt. They must wait for clarification by the legislatures and courts. The federal government has already passed significant legislation in this area. Furthermore, the government supports efforts of the Bureau of Home Economics, the Department of Agriculture, and the Food and Drug Administration to provide consumers with product standards and market information.

The right to choose. The right to choose is to be assured, when possible, a variety of products and services at competitive prices. It is understood that in such industries as public utilities, government regulation substitutes for the competitive mechanism to provide these goods and services. Government action in the arena of consumer choice has focused primarily on the passage of legislation affecting competition. The most active watchdogs of American competition within the government are the Department of Justice, the Federal Communications Commission, the Federal Trade Commission, and the U.S. Patent Office.

There are important issues of consumer choice that have not been effectively clarified at this time—questions like: How much choice is enough? Consumer sovereignty? Which products do consumers want? and Product warranty?[33] These are not easy questions for either business or the consumer to answer. It may take years, and many court decisions, to settle these questions.

The right to be heard. This is the right of consumers to be assured that their interests will receive full consideration in the establishment of government policy, and quick and fair treatment in administrative agencies. Agencies are urged to begin to develop a dialogue with consumer groups and individual consumers.

In July 1962, the Consumer Advisory Council was established to study this particular right of consumers. After lengthy investigation, the council reported ten critical areas needing attention. They are:

1. Consumer standards, grades, and labels. To study governmental consumer standards of identity, quality, quantity, safety, and product performance, including assessment from the consumer point of view of systems of grades, labels, and quality designation.
2. Two-way flow of information and opinion between government

and the consumer: To prepare recommendations for improving the two-way flow of information and opinion between government and the consumer public.

3. Effective consumer representation in government: To examine and advise on different structures and procedures for achieving effective representation of, and participation by, the consumer in government.
4. Consumer credit: To examine consumer credit (including mortgage credit) in order to assess its effect on the family and the nation, to evaluate contract terms as they facilitate or inhibit efficient and intelligent use of credit by consumers, and to appraise procedures used in cases where consumers have made excessive use of credit.
5. Interrelation among Federal agencies and between Federal and State agencies in areas of consumer protection: To examine and advise on such relationships with a view to improving the effective administration, enforcement, and scope of their programs.
6. Acceleration of economic growth: To examine and advise on the process of economic growth with the objective of submitting the consumer's point of view on basic economic policies designed to promote a higher level of national product, income, and employment—with special attention to the factors determining consumer decisions to save or consume and the improvement of economic opportunities.
7. Improvement of levels of consumption of low-income groups.
8. Antitrust action and prevention of price fixing.
9. Provision of adequate housing for the Nation's families.
10. Medical care.[34]

As a result of the council's report, the government has begun to move on a broad front of consumer rights. It will probably be some time before the action of the council and the government agencies can be evaluated.

Legal protection for consumers

The immediate accomplishments of consumerism are most apparent in the legal sphere.[35] We have deliberately skirted the question of legal action so that the pertinent laws can be presented together and in sequence. This has been done in Table 21–2.

It is difficult to evaluate the impact of these consumer protection laws individually. They cover such a wide range of violations. Generally speaking, consumers are not as aware of their rights as they might be. One study of 234 consumer found mixed results concerning awareness of the Truth in Lending Law.[36] While over 58 percent of the

Table 21–2
Significant consumer legislation: 1906–1976

1906	*Food and Drugs Act of 1906.* It regulates misbranded and adulterated foods, drinks, and drugs in interstate commerce.
1914	*Federal Trade Commission Act.* It established the Federal Trade Commission has among its responsibilities "unfair methods of competition" including deceptive advertising.
1938	*Federal Food, Drug, and Cosmetic Act of 1938.* It added cosmetics and devices to the Food and Drug Act of 1906; required clearance prior to distribution of new drugs; and established standards of identity, quality, and fill for food in containers.
1938	*Wheeler-Lea Amendment.* It gave the Federal Trade Commission power to prosecute for deceptive advertising or sales practices.
1939	*Wool Products Labeling Act.* It requires labeling wool products for the kind and amount of wool contained.
1951	*Fur Products Labeling Act.* It prohibits misbranding, false advertising, and false invoicing of fur products.
1953	*Flammable Fabrics Act.* It prohibits transporting easily ignited wearing apparel or material in interstate commerce.
1958	*Automobile Information Disclosure Act.* It requires posting of the suggested retail price on all new automobiles.
1959	*Textile Fiber Products Identification Act.* Added most textile products not covered by the Wool or Fur Products labeling Acts.
1960	*Federal Hazardous Substances Labeling Act.* It required the labeling of hazardous household chemicals.
1960	*Color Additives Amendment.* It gave the FDA, under the Food and Drug Act, the right to regulate conditions of safe use for color additives to foods, drugs, and cosmetics.
1962	*Kefauver-Harris Drug Ammendments.* It amended to Food and Drug Act requiring manufacturers to list new drugs with the FDA; to provide generic labeling; and to provide pretesting.
1965	*Drug Abuse Control Amendments.* It gave several powers to the Food and Drug Administration including: requiring drug handlers to keep records of suppliers and sales; power to seize illegal supplies; power to serve warrants and to arrest violators.
1965	*Fair Packaging and Labeling Act* (Truth-in-Packaging). It regulates the packaging and labeling of consumer goods.
1966	*National Traffic and Motor Vehicle Safety Act.* It provides the Department of Transportation power to set safety standards for new and used tires and automobiles.
1966	*Child Safety Act.* It amended the Hazardous Substances Labeling Act of 1960 to prevent marketing potentially harmful toys, and it allowed the Food and Drug Administration to remove harmful products from the market.
1966	*Cigarette Labeling Act.* It required manufacturers to place, "Caution:

Table 21–2 *(Continued)*

	cigarette smoking may be hazardous to your health," on all cigarette packages.
1967	*Wholesome Meat Act.* It required high standards for meat inspection and to cleanup of unsanitary meat plants.
1967	*National Commission on Product Safety Act.* It set up a commission to review hazardous household products and to file recommendations for legislation.
1968	*Consumer Credit Protecting Act* (Truth-in-lending). It established full disclosure of annual interest rates and financial charges on consumer loans and credit.
1968	*Wholesome Poultry Products Act.* It required states to have inspection systems for poultry and poultry products.
1968	*Hazardous Radiation Act.* It established performance standards to limit or prevent radiation emissions from electronic products.
1969	*Child Protection and Toy Safety Act of 1969.* It amended the Federal Hazardous Substances Act to include electrical, mechanical, or thermal hazards.
1970	*Fair Credit Reporting Act.* It regulated the reporting and use of credit information by business.
1972	*Consumer Product Safety Act.* It protected against the unreasonable risk of injury from unsafe products.
1974	*Fair Credit Billing Act.* It required that a creditor must take steps if a debtor complains of an error within 60 days of the receipt of a bill.
1974	*Real Estate Settlement Law.* It required the disclosure of all real estate costs to buyers prior to the transaction.
1975	*Magnuson-Moss Warranty, Federal Trade Commission Improvement Act.* It required that warranties disclose the terms of the warranty in simple readable language.
1976	*Preservation of Consumers' Claims and Defenses, Unfair or Deceptive Acts or Practices.* It required credit contracts to contain provisions warning the consumer as to what would happen if there is non-payment.

respondents stated that they were aware of the law, only about 27 percent could answer questions about it. Of course, knowledge is necessary if the application of the law is to be effective. It was also found that knowledge varied by demographic factors.

The reader will observe a clear trend of wider and more comprehensive coverage over time. Basic drug protection in 1906 had been extended to include such areas as child protection, credit, environmental quality, smoking, product safety, and packaging. There can be no doubt of the progress made over the period. On an individual basis certainly, the Food and Drug Act of 1906 was a milestone that opened the door for consumer protection. The "Truth-in-Packaging" Act of 1965, the "Truth-in-Lending" Act of 1968, and the Consumer Product Safety Act of 1972 were also extremely important in establishing legal trends. The impact of consumerism can almost be measured by the snowballing of legislation between 1900 and 1972. The total impact of the legislation has been to change the thinking of the nation on the subject of consumer protection. The American economic system has gone from "let the buyer beware" to one approaching "let the seller beware."[37]

Increased social awareness by business

Another area of accomplishment for consumerism lies in business awareness.[38] There are two sides to business awareness. One side is the recognition of public responsibility, and the other side is to see opportunity in public service.

Business acceptance of responsibility. Business leaders are generally aware of the consumer movement—its social goals, organization, and leadership. Of course, awareness is not acceptance, but it is a necessary first step in that direction.[39] Table 21–3 provides an indica-

Table 21–3
How chief executives and controllers rank responsibility to selected groups

Group	*Percent of chief executives giving rank of 1*	*Percent of controllers giving rank of 1*	*Average rank*
Stockholders	81.9	86.2	1
Employees	12.1	10.5	2
Customers	26.1	0.0	3
Creditors	11.8	11.0	4
Society	5.5	0.0	5

Source: Arthur W. Lorig, "Where Do Corporate Responsibilities Really Lie?" *Business Horizons*, Spring 1967, pp. 51–54.

tion of how chief executives and controllers in some 300 major firms view their business responsibility. These results indicate that the business managers polled are basically inward looking where responsibility is concerned. However, the results are encouraging. Chief executives, who have the greatest long-run influence on business policy, rank customers third in importance even though chief executives were not included on the questionnaire.[40] No significant percentage of either chief executives or controllers recognized responsibility to satisfy society as a whole. Thus the problem now is to turn business awareness into acceptance of responsibility.

One of the principal problems for business in meeting social responsibility is the failure to communicate between business and environmental leaders. Table 21–4 indicates the extent of this failure to communicate. Common terms used by the two just do not mean the same things. This gap in communications has to be bridged before business can take the initiative for providing social needs.

Table 21–4
Models of the consumer's world

	Businessman's view	*Key words*	*Critic's view*
1.	Product differentiation	Competition	Price competition
2.	Differentiation through secondary function	Product	Primary function only
3.	Any customer desires on which the product can be differentiated	Consumer needs	Correspond point-for-point to primary function
4.	Any customer decision that serves the customer's perceived self-interest	Rationality	Efficient matching of product to customer needs
5.	Any data that will (truthfully) put forth the attractiveness of the product in the eyes of the consumer	Information	Any data that facilitates the fit of a product's proper function with customer's needs.

Source: Raymond A. Bauer and Stephen A. Greyser, "The Dialogue that Never Happens," *Harvard Business Review*, vol. 45 (November–December 1967), p. 2 ff.

Any improvement requires a continuing change in the attitude on the part of business toward consumers and the environment—a new code of conduct to replace self interest. Fortunately, such a code is available. It establishes business priorities for policy making as follows.

1. The professional manager affirms that the interest of the company will be placed before self-interest.
2. Duty to society will be placed above duty to the company and above self-interest.
3. The manager has a duty to reveal facts in any situation where self-interest is involved with that of the company, or where the interests of the company are involved with those of society.
4. The manager must subscribe wholeheartedly to the belief that when business managers follow this code of conduct, the profit motive is the best incentive of all for the development of a dynamic economy.[41]

This code of conduct is basically an extension of the marketing philosophy already known to business. Its acceptance can lead to effective self-regulation of business, thus reducing the influence of government in business affairs.

Marketing opportunities of consumerism. A positive attitude toward consumerism by business can lead to new opportunities. After all the route of least resistance in acquiring profits is to produce and market what society wants.[42] The trick is now, as it has always been, finding out what consumers want. When Ford attempted to promote a safe car in the 1950s, consumers rejected the move.[43] This situation has changed today as a result of the consumer movement, and the car would be accepted today. As a result, the marketer can find significant opportunities for successful marketing in social needs.

Kotler defines four major categories of product opportunities.[44] *Desirable products* have high immediate satisfaction and long-run benefit to consumers (new "miracle drugs," automobile engines, and fabrics). These products should receive the marketer's greatest effort. Their very nature make them easy to sell and highly profitable. *Pleasing products* have high immediate satisfaction, but are harmful to consumers over time (cigarettes, narcotics, and alcohol). There are great marketing opportunities here, but they lie in developing alternatives to the harmful products. The development of alternative products include: low-lead gasoline, products that aid in stopping smoking, antipollution devices for cars and factories, rapid transit systems, and safe sugar substitutes. Of course, there is a risk associated with such products because consumers are not always willing to change. Some are successful and some are not. *Salutory products* have low appeal to consumers but are highly beneficial over time (nonflammable cloth, safety belts, and foods made from algae, soybeans, or seaweed). Since the lack of basic consumer appeal is inherent in such products, the challenge for marketers is to make the product pleasing or to promote an effective change in attitude toward it. These actions are more difficult than the opportunities previously cited, but the rewards can be great when successful. *Deficient products* have no immediate appeal and no lasting benefit. The marketer should simply avoid these products since there is no basis for successful marketing. However, it is clear that the marketing opportunities of consumerism are there, and the payoffs are great for far-sighted business leaders.

FUTURE OF CONSUMERISM

The future of consumerism is bright. In fact, the movement is likely to pick up momentum in the next few years. Kotler says,

Consumerism was inevitable.
Consumerism will be enduring.
Consumerism will be beneficial.
Consumerism is promarketing.
Consumerism can be profitable.[45]

These points have been the focus of attention of this entire chapter. The movement needs to move away from dependence on personalities and toward a closer, cleaner organization. Effort must also be directed toward clarifying objectives and getting these objectives across to the several agencies participating in the movement and to the average person. These are difficult chores, but they are inevitable.

NOTES

1. Warren C. Magnuson, "Consumerism and the Emerging Goals of a New Society," *Consumerism*, ed. Ralph M. Goedeke and Warren W. Etchenson (San Francisco: Canfield Press, 1972), pp. 3–7.
2. Richard H. Buskirk and James T. Rothe, "Consumerism—An Interpretation," *Journal of Marketing*, vol. 34 (October 1970), pp. 61–65.
3. David A. Aaker and George S. Day, "A Guide to Consumerism," *Journal of Marketing*, vol. 17 (July 1970), pp. 12–19.
4. Adapted from David W. Cravens and Gerald E. Hills, "Consumerism: A Perspective for Business," *Business Horizons*, vol. 13 (August 1970), pp. 21–28.
5. The modern consumer movement is of much more recent origin. Most scholars date it from about 1900. See Robert O. Herrmann, "Consumerism: Its Goals, Organization, and Future," *Journal of Marketing*, vol. 34 (October 1970), pp. 55–60; Ralph M. Gaedeke, "The Movement for Consumer Protection: A Century of Mixed Accomplishments," *University of Washington Business Review*, vol. 29 (Spring 1970), pp. 31–40.
6. Ralph M. Gaedeke, "What Business, Government and Consumer Spokesmen Think about Consumerism," *The Journal of Consumer Affairs*, vol. 4 (Summer 1970), pp. 7–18.
7. William J. Wilson, "Consumer Reality and Corporate Image," *California Management Review*, vol. 16 (Winter 1973), pp. 85–90.
8. Gaedeke, "The Movement for Consumer Protection."
9. Herrmann divides the modern consumer movement into three eras: (1) early 1900, (2) 1930s, and (3) 1960s. See Robert O. Herrmann, *The Consumer Movement in Historical Perspective* (University Park, Pa.: Department of Agricultural Economics and Rural Sociology, 1970), pp. 2–31. The first two eras coincide with our period of public awareness, and the third period coincides with the period of consumer achievement.
10. Ibid.
11. Upton Sinclair, *The Jungle* (New York: Doubleday, Page and Co., 1906).

12. Stuart Chase and F. J. Schlink, *Your Money's Worth* (New York: The Macmillan Co., 1927).

13. Arthur Kallet and F. J. Schlink, *100,000,000 Guinea Pigs* (New York: Grosset and Dunlap, 1933); Ruth de Forest Lamb, *American Chamber of Horrors—The Truth About Food and Drugs* (New York: Farrar and Rinehart, 1936).

14. Herrmann, *The Consumer Movement*, pp. 2–31.

15. W. Thomas Anderson, Jr. and William H. Cunningham, "The Socially Conscious Consumer," *Journal of Marketing*, vol. 36 (July 1972), pp. 23–31.

16. Paul N. Bloom, "How Marketers Can Help Consumer Educators," *The Journal of Consumer Affairs*, vol. 10 (Summer 1976), pp. 91–95.

17. Herrmann, "Consumerism: Its Goals, Organization, and Future."

18. See Ralph Nader, *Unsafe at Any Speed* (New York: Grossman, 1965); Jessica Mitford, *The American Way of Death* (New York: Simon and Schuster, 1963); David Caplovitz, *The Poor Pay More* (New York: Free Press of Glencoe, 1963); and Vance Packard, *The Hidden Persuaders* (New York: D. McKay Co., 1957).

19. See Lee E. Preston, ed., *Social Issues in Marketing* (Glenview, Ill.: Scott, Foresman & Co., 1968) and William T. Greenwood, ed., *Issues in Business and Society*, 2d ed. (Boston: Houghton Mifflin Co., 1971).

20. Preston, "The High Price of Being Poor," *Changing Times*, vol. 22 (August 1968); William Stief, "Why the Birds Cough," *The Progressive*, vol. 34 (April 1970), pp. 47–54; "Black America 1970," *Time*, April 6, 1970, pp. 13ff.; Ian Shaw, "Consumer Opinion and Social Policy: A Research Review," *Journal of Social Policy*, vol. 5 (January 1976), pp. 19–32.

21. John A. Davenport, "The Welfare State vs. The Public Welfare," *Fortune*, (June 1976), pp. 132–36ff.

22. Ibid.

23. Larry J. Rosenberg, "Retailers' Responses to Consumerism," *Business Horizons*, (October 1975), pp. 37–44; Stephen A. Greyser and Steven L. Diamond, "Business is Adapting to Consumerism," *Harvard Business Review*, (September-October 1974), pp. 38–58.

24. Herrmann, "Consumerism: Its Goals, Organizations and Future," pp. 55–60.

25. Ibid.

26. William H. Cunningham and Isabella C. M. Cunningham, "Consumer Protection: More Information or More Regulation?" *Journal of Marketing*, vol. 40 (April 1976), pp. 63–68.

27. *Time*, vol. 101 (April 9, 1973), pp. 11–15.

28. Ibid; *U.S. News & World Report* (April 8, 1974), p. 20.

29. Thomas P. Hustad and Edgar A. Pessemier, "Will the Real Consumer Activist Please Stand Up: An Examination of Consumers' Opinions About Marketing Practices," *Journal of Marketing Research*, vol. 10 (August 1973), pp. 319–24; Hiram C. Barksdale and William R. Darden,

"Consumer Attitudes Toward Marketing and Consumerism," *Journal of Marketing,* vol. 36 (October 1972), pp. 29–35.

30. *Consumer Advisory Council, First Report,* Executive Office of the President (Washington, D.C.: U.S. Government Printing Office, 1963), pp. 5–8, 18–31.
31. Paul Busch, "A Review and Critical Evaluation of the Consumer Product Safety Commission: Marketing Management Implications," *Journal of Marketing,* vol. 40 (October 1976), pp. 41–49.
32. *Consumers Product Safety Commission Annual Report,* (Washington, D.C.: July 1, 1973–June 30, 1974), p. 50.
33. Etienne Cracco and Jacques Rostenne, "The Sociological Product," *Business Topics* (Summer 1971), pp. 27–34; George Fisk, "Guidelines for Warranty Service After Sale," *Journal of Marketing,* vol. 34 (January 1970), pp. 62–67; William Trivoli, "Has the Consumer Lost His Sovereignty?" *Akron Business and Economic Review,* vol. 1 (Winter 1970), pp. 33–39.
34. *Consumer Advisory Council, First Report,* pp. 5–8, 18–31.
35. Lee Richardson, "Consumers in the Federal Decision-Making Process," *California Management Review,* vol. 16 (Winter 1973), pp. 79–84; Mary Gardiner Jones, "The Consumer Interest: The Role of Public Policy," *California Management Review,* vol. 16 (Fall 1973) pp. 17–24.
36. William H. Bolen, "Consumer Awareness of Truth in Lending," *College of Business Ideas and Facts,* vol. 7 (Fall 1976), pp. 37–41.
37. John A. Prestbo, "Seller Beware—Consumer Proposals Bring About Changes in American Business," *Wall Street Journal,* June 21, 1971.
38. Louis L. Stern, "Consumer Protection Via Self-regulation," *Journal of Marketing,* vol. 35 (July 1971), pp. 47–53.
39. See: "How Business Responds to Consumerism," *Business Week,* September 1969, pp. 94–108; Stern, "Consumer Protection Via Self-regulation,"; and Chamber of Commerce of the United States, "Business-Consumer Relations," *Policy Declaration, 1970–71* (Washington, D.C., 1970), pp. 9–12.
40. Out of 152 executives, 34 (representing over 22 percent) wrote in customers.
41. *Business Week,* June 19, 1961, p. 166.
42. E. Patrick McGuire, "New Opportunities in Consumerism," *Conference Board Record,* December 1970, pp. 41–43; David R. Leighton, "Responding to Consumerism," *Social Marketing,* ed. William Lazer and Eugene J. Kelley (Homewood, Ill.: Richard D. Irwin, Inc., 1973), pp. 124–33.
43. Philip Kotler, "What Consumerism Means for Marketers," *Harvard Business Review,* vol. 50 (May–June 1972), pp. 48–57.
44. Ibid.
45. Ibid.

QUESTIONS

1. Define consumerism. What is the relationship between consumerism and other social groups?
2. Why do you feel consumerism has been so slow to catch on among people? Explain.
3. Contrast the period of innocence, period of awareness, and period of achievement. Do you feel the consumer movement has peaked or not? Explain.
4. What are the more important current issues of consumerism? Which do you feel are more important? How do these issues affect your attitude toward business and buying?
5. Do you feel consumers are correct in their criticism of business practice? Explain. Give personal examples to support your position.
6. What are the objectives of consumerism? What organizations are involved? Which types of tools are involved?
7. Explain the consumer bill of rights. What is its importance? Is it adequate? Why or why not? What modifications would you add to this bill?
8. What legal protection do consumers have? Is it adequate?
9. Is business aware of consumer attitudes? Do they care? What can be done?
10. Discuss the marketing opportunities offered by the consumerism movement. Do businesses take advantage of these opportunities? Why or why not?

22

Cultural aspects of consumer behavior

When we observe individuals going about their everyday activities, it is difficult at first to see any order or pattern in their behavior. It is even more difficult to understand the relationships between the activities of many different people. On closer inspection, however, we can observe a fairly high degree of consistency and regularity in the interaction between people. In this chapter, we consider a number of aspects of culture in which these regularities can be seen.

THE MEANING OF CULTURE

Every individual is a product of culture; everyday actions and decisions of all people are affected by their cultural backgrounds.[1] Man has always congregated into groups. At first, the primary reason for banding together was probably for protection, but additional reasons for joining forces were later found. As people began to develop a common body of thoughts, feelings, techniques, and beliefs, they realized that the benefits of the culture were greater than could be attained by any individual alone. Culture is this thinking, feeling, and believing that binds individuals together. It is not limited to the "fine" arts, but embraces all the by-products of man's activities. Because of the comprehensiveness of such a concept, it is difficult, if not impossible, to agree on what is or is not included in culture.

The concept of culture is sufficiently broad to encompass all aspects of the man-made environment. For our purposes, *culture* is defined to be:

> *a set of learned beliefs, values, attitudes, habits, and forms of behavior that are shared by a society and are transmitted from generation to generation.*[2]

Instinctive behavior and the primitive needs or tensions that provide the ultimate motivation for behavior, although influencing culture, are not a part of it. The function of any culture is twofold. First, culture exists to establish norms of behavior. Culture is the standard that people use for guidance when they are not sure which type of action or behavior is proper. How does a young girl behave on her first date? What is the proper role of a millionaire toward charity? What will be the neighbor's reaction to my purchasing a high-priced automobile? These and other questions can be partly answered on the basis of cultural standards. Second, culture functions as a type of enforcer of group standards. By using cultural characteristics, it tends to force prescribed types of behavior. The often used phrase, "society's point of view," refers to this type of pressure. Society as a whole can both reward and punish, and this fosters individual conformity.[3] Obviously, some conformity is good and is needed in any group activity, but society can become oppressive. When culture becomes too formalized, it can stifle change and innovation. Some changes, as some standards, are needed for any social order to survive.

HOW CULTURE AFFECTS CONSUMERS

All consumer behavior is conducted within the framework of the society in which we live.[4] Individuals begin to learn at a very early age the benefits of culture as well as the restrictions that culture places on all behavior, including consumer behavior. The significance of this influence can be determined from Figure 22–1. As we have pointed

Figure 22–1
How culture operates to affect consumers

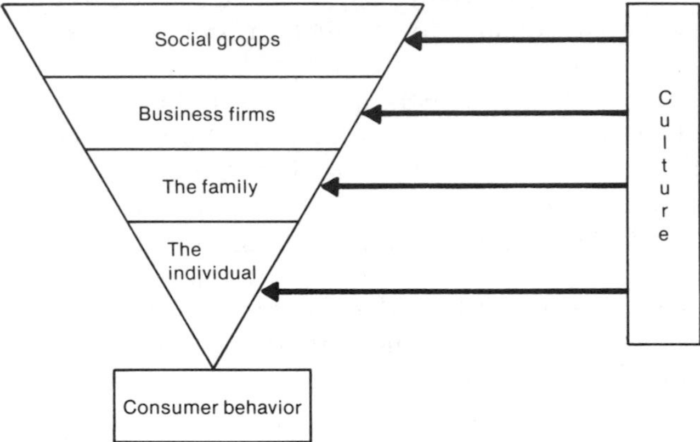

out before, the individual is the smallest unit of consumer behavior, and the pyramid rises from there according to the increasing size of the unit with which the individual identifies. Culture affects all levels of the society, as shown. Culture operates on the individual consumer directly in many ways. For example, the individual knows that he or she must buy needed goods rather than steal them. The individual also knows that one is expected to deal honestly, honor all contracts made, make payment, pay on time, register complaints in legitimate ways, observe store rules, and so on.

Culture also affects consumer behavior indirectly by operating through the family, business firms, and social groups. This effect occurs in two ways. First, culture directly affects each of these groups helping to shape the attitudes, feelings, biases, and opinions that the individual consumer may draw upon. Second, the various groups render rewards to the consumer for correct behavior and punish incorrect behavior. For example, jail may await the consumer who steals or does not honor contracts. Thus, we see that culture is an important determinant of consumer behavior.

BASIC FACTORS OF CULTURE

The depth of the influence exerted by culture can be understood by examining the basic factors of all cultures. All human beings, regardless of their differences, have much in common, and these common aspects are susceptible to scientific analysis. Let us consider seven basic factors which are thought to underlie all cultures.[5] We can say that culture is: (1) learned, (2) handed down, (3) social, (4) ideational, (5) gratifying, (6) adaptive, and (7) integrative.[6]

First, culture is learned; it is not present at birth but must be acquired.[7] Second, culture is passed from one generation to another. Inculcation involves not only the passing on of techniques and knowledge but also the disciplining of the child's animal instincts and impulses in order to adjust him to social life. Third, culture is social by nature and consists of groups of habits formed in relationship with others. In effect, culture prescribes the manner of social interaction. Fourth, group habits, to an extent, are conceptionalized as ideal norms of behavior. Most people show an acute awareness of their own cultural norms. Fifth, culture always satisfies some basic or secondary need. Its elements are tested habitual techniques for gratifying human impulses in man's interaction with the external world. Any product of culture that is not gratifying tends to be changed over time.[8] Sixth, culture tends to adjust to the geographic environment by borrowing from the social environment of neighboring peoples. It also tends to adjust to the biological and psychological demands of the people composing the culture. Seventh, elements of a culture tend to form a consistent and integrated whole. Thus, there is consistency in culture.

CULTURAL UNIVERSALS

There are many characteristics that are universal to all cultures. Among these common characteristics are athletics, cooking, art, education, food taboos, language, law, status, marriage, and government.[9] Some cultural universals are compelled and some are prohibited, as Table 22–1 shows. Although some of the universals may vary, modern societies follow the same practices as did the 25 primitive societies upon which these findings are based.

The principal variation between cultures lies not in the existence of these characteristics, but in the manner in which they are employed in the culture.[10] Marriage exists in all cultures, but the ceremony itself may differ. Football is popular in the United States, but the American form of the sport is practically unheard of elsewhere. All cultures provide housing, but houses range from the igloo of the Eskimo, to the paper and wood structure of the Japanese, to the highly complex American home of brick and wood.

Table 22–1
Cultural universals prohibited and compelled in 25 primitive societies

Compelled universals	*Prohibited universals*
Protection, sleeping, mourning, giving, generosity, hospitality, weeping, cleansing, friendliness, seeking good luck, avoiding bad luck, obeying, learning, concealing body parts, grief, pacifying others, fighting.	Adultery, murder, stealing, hating, deceiving, cannibalism, harming food, incest, biting, crying, playing, jealousy, treason, suicide, destroying goods, anger, interfering with war, laziness.

Source: C. S. Ford, "Society, Culture, and the Human Organism," *Journal of General Psychology*, vol. 20 (1939), pp. 135–79.

Within any culture there are characteristics that must be learned by everyone. For example, everyone must learn the language and manner of dress. Some characteristics do not have to be learned by everyone, and the members of the culture may select from among alternatives. In most countries there are several language dialects. The methods of cooking and favorite dishes vary between regions of the United States, and there are also differences in dress between sections of the nation. Some cultural characteristics apply only to specific groups, for example the work group, private societies, and so on.

THE ATTRIBUTES OF CULTURE

The understanding of culture revolves around knowledge of certain attributes that make up the core of any culture. Although these attributes persist in all nations, there may be differences in the specifics of their employment in different nations. These attributes are socialization, group norms, and rewards and sanctions. The three attributes go hand in hand. Each is dependent on the other three and the end result of their interaction is culture. It is necessary to delve deeper into each of these subjects. We begin our discussion with socialization and end with rewards and sanctions.

Socialization

It is fortunate that each generation does not have to reinvent everything that the previous generations created. If this were necessary, it is likely that not much progress would be made and that the pace of any progress would be slow. Man would be too busy catching up to ever advance much beyond an elemental level of knowledge. It is socialization that makes progress possible.[11] Let us define socialization and discuss how communication and the use of symbols contribute to the process of socialization. We must also relate socialization to consumer behavior.

Except for differences of perspective, socialization is like interaction. Interaction concerns the present and deals with people communicating about current problems and interests. *Socialization,* on the other hand, refers to the communication between generations and is the process whereby the norms, folkways, morals, ethics, technology, organizations, and so on, of one generation are passed on to the next.[12] We can say that socialization is the basic human urge that causes people, both at present and over periods of time, to seek out each other for the purposes of communicating and preserving ideas. Because of socialization, each generation begins with a head start of knowledge over that of the previous generation.

Basic to any system of culture is communication—all socialization depends on it. Man is unique in the world because, by using communication, one can describe where he or she has been, what was seen and done, and how goals were accomplished. Man can remember and reproduce from memory things learned in the past. Since we have already described the communication process, there is no need to spend more time on the subject at this point.

As previously pointed out, symbols are vital to communication. Although we do not intend to repeat previous discussions, a point or two about symbolism relative to culture may be stated here. The ability to use symbols allows man to reproduce thoughts and concepts. Whereas concepts are fragile, many types of symbols used are relatively permanent. Thus, the ability to symbolize ideas makes it possible over time to accumulate the components of culture.

The importance of socialization to the knowledge of consumer behavior can be stated rather succinctly. First, consumer behavior, because it involves an interaction between an individual and a business, is a part of the socialization process. Second, consumer behavior, like all behavior, depends on the ability to express ideas as symbols and to communicate. Third, the very products that consumers buy are but symbols of consumer satisfaction and are based on technology that has been passed on from generation to generation. Finally, much of the act of shopping, negotiating, and buying is symbolic. That is to say, it is done to impress, to please, or to signify some aspect of our culture.

Norms of culture

The second attribute of culture that requires our attention is referred to as group norms. A *culture norm* is defined as a standard way of acting or behaving prescribed by the society as a whole. Norms sometimes change and are often unclear and ambiguous, but norms do exert a powerful influence on our daily lives.

A norm can be any kind of social standard. In the American social system, it is understood that one does not take the head of one's neighbor. Yet, in the primitive social system of head hunters of certain areas, a youth was not considered a man until he had taken a head or two. The point is that nothing is socially just or correct, ethical or moral, except what the norms of a society declare to be just or correct, ethical or moral. In some societies, a consumer is expected to haggle with the merchant over every purchase, but in the American society most purchases are made without haggling. Although many prices are negotiated, our economy is characterized as a one-price economy in the sense that the retailer sets the price, and the consumer has the choice of accepting or rejecting it.

Society makes norms to suit its own purposes, and it is the nature of norms to serve the society in which they exist. The following four aspects of norms are important to the understanding of this service.[13]

1. Guide to action. Norms guide action in several ways. First, norms keep us informed as to what we can do. Sex is permissible after marriage, and there is nothing wrong with owning two cars. Second, norms prescribe what we must do. We must feed, clothe, and care for our children; we must respect our neighbor's property; and we must drive on the right-hand side of the road. Third, norms prescribe how we must behave. We must whisper in the library and observe the social proprieties everywhere. Fourth, norms establish when we can act. One waits until the age of 16 in many states before he is allowed to drive, and marriage before the age of 18 is frowned upon. Fifth, norms proscribe what we cannot do. We cannot appear on the street in the nude, we cannot commit crimes against our neighbor; and we cannot swindle others out of their money.

2. Standards to judge behavior. Norms serve as standards by which we judge our own behavior as well as the behavior of others. The prime question here is whether individuals are conforming to the social standards, which serve as a measure of our actions and form the basis for rewards and sanctions. Thus, this subject is vitally interwoven with the next.

3. Paired norms. The norms established by a society are frequently paired. That is to say, the norms prescribe what can be done and proscribe what cannot be done. We are required to do something on the one hand, and forbidden to do it on the other. Examples are found in our marriage and driving laws and in prescribed social graces. We are required to wear clothing (prescribed), but, at the same time, we are prohibited (proscribed) from going naked. We are required to honor our contracts and we can be prosecuted if we do not honor our contracts.

4. Pervasiveness of norms. Some norms, such as laws against stealing and murder, are pervasive. The customs of shaking hands, kissing, and savings are also universal customs in our society; these norms apply with equal force to everyone. Other norms are group oriented. Examples of group-oriented norms can be found in hair cuts, styles of dress, attitudes toward bathing, and bias toward people and things. Our purchases tend to conform to these cultural norms.

Types of norms. There are many types of cultural norms that can be identified, but the most important are laws, mores, and folkways or customs.[14]

Customs, or folkways, are devised by people and refer to traditional ways that people interact with each other. Observance of these folkways is not required by law; their only enforcement is by the people themselves. People conform to them because they want to—because they believe in them. We eat three meals a day, observe retail store hours, and purchase the latest fashions because we feel it is the right thing to do.

Mores are those customs or usages of a society that are regarded as being essential to its welfare and even survival. They include moral attitudes and are the more formal rules and customs prescribed by the society. Although there are no agencies to enforce mores, the penalties for breaking the rules can be severe. Whereas deviations from customs are not serious, deviations in moral conduct are considered a threat to the entire society. Thus, family responsibility, sexual behavior, and business ethics are considered very serious matters by the society.

Laws are the most formal of all social norms and pertain to deviations from accepted conduct so serious that they cannot be tolerated by the society. Laws are formally enacted by the courts or some duly authorized governmental body and may be enforced by various agencies such as the police, national guard, or army. The legal structure has a direct bearing on the operation of business. Laws prescribe many of the relationships between business and the consumer.

The effect of cultural norms. The effectiveness of cultural norms should not be judged by the amount of formality associated with them.[15] Mores are more formal than folkways, and laws are more formal than mores, but the degree of formality associated with each does not insure the degree of conformity associated with each. Laws act as deterrents on certain actions, but individuals break laws regularly. The real effectiveness of norms, therefore, lies in the willingness of people to conform to the standard. Prohibition did not keep consumers from drinking, just as chain grocery stores and discount houses grew in spite of formal opposition by traditional retailers.

People conform to norms for a number of reasons. First, norms bring a high measure of order into daily interactions among people.[16] We know what to expect from the behavior of others because we conform to the same norms. Second, norms are a partial substitute for judgment. Because of established norms, we know what is right or wrong and what is acceptable behavior without worrying about it. Third, people like the approval of their peers that results from conformity to norms. Fourth, most people do not care for the disapproval that results when norms are broken. Finally, it is often easier to conform than not.

Norms affect market behavior because they apply to both the buyer and the seller. Such everyday business ethics as honoring contracts, offering honest service, and competing fairly are based on norms. Laws such as the Robinson-Patman Act, Federal Trade Commission Act, Pure Food and Drug Act, Fair Trade laws, and the Truth in Lending law place direct limits on the actions of business.

Other facets of marketing are affected by mores and customs, such as the hours for opening and closing stores. The practice of closing on Sunday is partly custom and partly legal. In short, there is very little of business life that is not affected by norms.

Rewards and sanctions

Norms of culture are enforced by the use of rewards and sanctions.[17] *Rewards* are the favors that society can bestow in appreciation for conformity; *sanctions* are the penalties society can bring to bear on the nonconformist. Either rewards or sanctions can be effective in assuring a large measure of social conformity. Both rewards and sanctions can be formally or informally structured into the system.

Formal rewards are such things as diplomas, awards, plaques, medals, and testimonals. Informal rewards usually take the form of approval by our friends—a handshake, a pat on the back, an acceptance of a dinner invitation, or flattery.

Formal sanctions result from the laws previously mentioned. These sanctions vary in form from money payments for minor deviations, such as parking violations, to long prison terms for more serious crimes, such as stealing. Informal sanctions are in the form of disapproval by our peers. The ostracized person, or the social outcast, knows informal sanctions. These sanctions may take the form of a look, a gesture, silence, or avoidance, and any one of these can be effective.

THE ACQUISITION OF CULTURE

Just as a child has no conception of the world at birth, an infant does not possess culture at birth. Language, morality, and other norms of behavior, alien at birth, are all aspects of culture that must be acquired. Each infant enters a society with certain possibilities for acquiring the necessary information that will be made available to him, and the consequence of all the influences brought to bear result in one's competencies, standards, judgment, and attitudes.

However, impulses are not controlled, values acquired, or norms conformed to automatically. Adult standards are not assumed by the child without some transformation. The child interacts with mature persons who behave in accordance with some system of rules which we call culture. These value systems have not been explicitly formulated by the adult whose behavior is governed by them and will not be explicitly formulated by the child who acquires them. The child possesses what he or she perceives of adult behavior and in this way extracts the rules system implicit to it.

The first task of Man is to live. Recognized needs to support life are soon followed by efforts to satisfy these needs, and in the process of trial and error, other needs are also recognized and satisfied. As a result of these efforts to satisfy needs, consumers develop habits, routines, and skills. Each person benefits from the experience of neighbors, which leads to some group agreement that proves to be expedient. Eventually, all persons adopt the same rules for the same purposes, and in this way customs and mores are developed to replace instincts as guides to behavior. The process occurs from a combination of conformity and consensus.

The behavioral norms of each culture present the guidelines by which the participants of the culture judge each of their activities. Whether this process is conscious or subconscious, the important thing to remember is that it does take place. Marketing can determine the structure or order of the culture which is delineated by behavioral norms and ascertain to a considerable degree those predictable patterns of behavior for most events and activities. However, each culture is slightly different even within the same society.

Sources of cultural values

Culture is learned from almost any source of social contact. It is not necessarily passed down from senior to junior citizens. However, in every society there are certain institutions that become the focal points of cultural accumulation. In primitive tribes, this function was often handled by the village elders; but as societies advanced, more complex institutions had to be developed to deal with cultural knowledge. Today, the primary sources of cultural knowledge are (1) family, (2) school, (3) church, (4) political institutions, and (5) other institutions.

It is difficult to pinpoint which institutions are responsible for which cultural values, because they all interact. However, some institutions do tend to take the lead where certain values are concerned. It can be helpful to identify some of these tendencies.

The basic institution of cultural accumulation in the American society is the family, followed by the school.[18] The other institutions influence in varying degrees that are impossible to serialize. The family is pervasive because not only do family members begin their influence at birth when the individual is most susceptible, but most other cultural knowledge is filtered through the family. Thus it is safe to say that every type of cultural value is influenced, to a substantial degree, by the family. Even so, the family is particularly important in establishing values of personal identity, pride, sharing, affection, honesty, social status, and biases.

The school also reaches the child at a very early and impressionable age. Thus it greatly influences cultural values. The school is particularly important in shaping social values, sex values, work values, competition, achievement, and social reward and sanctions. The church tends to affect a person's moral, ethical, and religious values, and this fact is true whether the person is an agnostic or avidly religious.[19] After all, a rejection of church is as much an effect as is acceptance. Political institutions augment social values, but play a great part in creating the values of national culture such as perception of one's heritage, pride in country, flag, and national achievement.

Cultural institutions vary in influence

In a given society, and at a given time, the institutions of cultural knowledge vary in their importance. For example, the family was at one time the major source of sex values in America; but more and more this influence is being taken over by the schools. The family's effect on political attitudes has been greatly shifted to political parties, largely as a result of the mass media. The social graces, once taught in the home, are increasingly being shifted to social groups and schools. The result is a decline in family influence on cultural knowledge and an increase in the influence of schools and political groups. There is some evidence that the church, which has been out of favor for some time, is back on the rise as a cultural influence.

It is important to consumer behavior where cultural values are derived. For example, the decline of church and family influences has profoundly affected people's attitudes toward marriage, family planning, and abortion. Products related to these issues have also undergone changes. The bias of schoolteachers at lower grades toward girls has been frequently cited. This bias not only affects the attitude of boys toward school, but could be a factor in the unisex trend and the tendency of males to accept more readily female-oriented products such as long hair and ornate clothing.

CULTURAL CONTRIBUTIONS TO BUSINESS STRATEGY

Culture is important to business in many ways, but its effect is often felt through the operation of social groups. One important way that business can take advantage of culture is on a regional basis. In many ways Southern culture differs from Western culture, and Western culture differs from Eastern culture. For example, the evidence is that Westerners are more liberal and tolerant of others. While Southerners are conservative in most attitudes. Easterners, especially those in large cities, are self-reliant and not disposed to becoming involved in the problems of others. Of course, these are simply examples and not meant to characterize either individuals or regions.

These regional differences can become the basis for successful market differentiation. Southerners purchase more Early American furniture than any other section of the nation, while Westerners tend toward contemporary and new styles of furniture. Southerners dress more conservatively and wear lighter clothing than Easterners. Magazines recognize cultural differences by regions. Many magazines now run regional issues. The general content of the magazine is the same nationally, but regionally sensitive editorial comments and advertisements are varied. For example, for a long time, editorials and ads dealing with racial issues were promoted in the North but shunned in Southern editions. Television has long been noted for making special promotional appeals to local cultural attributes of people.[20]

Specific cultural appeals are becoming popular for marketers.[21] Business emphasizes positive cultural values and attempts to avoid values that can offend. For example, nearly all successful beers have been associated with the German culture. Contraception and abortion products are avoided in promotional material in strong Catholic communities because of long-standing values. Even the symbols used by marketers often must take into account cultural factors. Certain cleaning liquids and even one automobile used sex symbols to promote their products. In some countries fashion clothing in white cannot be sold because this color is associated with mourning. Products that fall outside cultural norms are not likely to be successful, and when they are it usually takes massive selling efforts to overcome the ingrained beliefs. Crawfish, prized in Louisiana, have not been successfully promoted in other parts of the nation. Consumers in America reject seaweed and grasshoppers that are important foods elsewhere.

Sometimes marketers can, even must, change cultural values in order to market their products successfully. Such changes typically require long periods of time. Some successful products based on cultural change include:

1. Men wearing high-heeled shoes.
2. American purchasing of oriental cars, electronic products, and textiles.
3. Women using short-cut food products.
4. Dishwashers.

Products where culture change is being undertaken include garbage compactors, fish meal and algae food products, and lettuce cigarettes.

Marketers can also use a knowledge of cultural rewards and sanctions to advantage in product design and promotion. Feminine hygiene products, foot powder, and deodorants are examples of specific products that make such appeals. There are cultural aspects involved with the acceptance of fashion and with brand acceptance and loyalty. It is easy to see that knowledge of culture is an integral part of the marketer's strategy. All too often this aspect is left to chance.

THE AMERICAN CULTURE

Although we do not directly observe culture, we do abstract it from patterned actions, reactions, dress, and appearance. The clothes worn, food eaten, and gifts given express a society's norms and modes. In turn, these are the foundations of markets. American culture has been described as resting on the foundations that the universe is mechanistically conceived, that Man is its master, and that people are equal and perfectible. These foundations in turn result in specific values, such as our work emphasis, material well-being, and conformity patterns.[22] Others postulate that one of the basic characteristics of American culture is its high level of achievement motivation.

Seven characteristics of American culture

The above, and similar views, lead to the conclusion that the American culture is characterized by the following basic values:[23] (1) religious belief, (2) material comfort, (3) equality, (4) conformity, (5) technology and innovation, (6) youthfulness, and (7) humanitarianism.

First, we are a religious people, and religion conditions our attitudes toward work, morality, other people, and consumption. We generally subscribe to the Protestant ethic. All religious groups in the United States generally believe that: *(a)* work is good, *(b)* belief in God is fundamental, *(c)* God rewards industry and hates idleness, *(d)* one should strive for practicality and efficiency, and *(e)* a moralistic attitude is the only sound approach to life.

Second, material comfort is an American way of life. A rising level of living is considered the reward for hard work. Thus, a consumer is justified in owning whatever he or she has earned, but should purchase prudently and deal fairly.

Third, there is the idea of equality. The American culture values achievement rather than birth. We all admire personal success. We honor individualism and the individual's right to rise above his or her background.

Fourth, Americans value conformity. Conformity is awareness of the group. How we live, what we buy, our attitudes toward leisure, and so on, are conditioned by group awareness. To some degree all Americans conform, yet we all try to be a little different. The little difference explains why consumers don't like buying the same dress or furnishing their houses the same.

Fifth, there is no question but that Americans prize technological advances and innovation. Ours is a society built on change. Everyone wants more and better and different products and services. We damn obsolescence but could not do without it.

Sixth, youthfulness is increasingly a prized cultural characteristic.[24] It shows up in the music we listen to, the cars we drive, the clothes we wear, and our presence at sports events.

Seventh, Americans recognize the individual's responsibility to others. This is humanitarianism. This is demonstrated by our tax system, which provides for the transfer of government funds for welfare programs, and by the many charities which flourish in America.

American cultural attitudes

Attempts have been made to define the basic cultural factors of all Americans. These attempts center on delineating the cultural attitudes of an average American. Of course, such attempts are doomed to failure because there is no average American, nor is there any average American culture. What we are likely to get is a composite view of what Americans *perceive* their culture to be, and the facts may be quite different from the perceptions. Even so, the knowledge is useful, since we have established that individual consumers vary much in accordance with their perceptions.

A. *Personal data*

Native born and educated; protestant; first, middle and last name after Anglo-Saxon use; speaks English; no accent; causal sense of humor; warm; conformist; playful; fair; vivacious; healthy; good sport; happy-go-lucky; self-sufficient; tough.

B. *Personal likes*

American papers and books only; protein eater; coffee, milk, fruit juice, cola, milk shakes; whiskey, gin, rum and beer with food; women drink with men; non-organized relaxation; spectator sports and gambling; popular American music; American holidays.

C. *Appearance*

Dress based on local American fashion; relaxed; casual and informal; gestures; slender, youthful appearance.

D. *Personal attitudes*

Food is nourishment; emphasize hygiene, vitamins and calories; quickly prepared dishes; no sauces or spices; large amounts served; leftovers thrown away; American culture only one known and unaware of differences; parents viewed as friends and guides—not punitive; authority evenly divided between parents; women emancipated and status not related to marriage; women seen as equal to men; success measured by money and popularity.

E. *Residence*

Resides in areas decided by class membership; mixes with neighbors.

Although this list was compiled in the 1940s and perceptions are changing, it still depicts the impression that many Americans hold of themselves. Five general modifications are required in the list to suit the culture of the 1970s. First, there is a continued emergence of women as a social and economic factor. Second, Americans are more tolerant toward minorities and all types of new ideas. Third, there is degeneration of health standards, particularly with respect to cancer, nutrition, and diet. Fourth, Americans are becoming much less self-sufficient, and there is a greater tendency to seek aid from others, particularly government. Fifth, there is a lessening of parental ties, and a general breaking-up of the traditional concept of the family. This slow change in cultural attitudes is not surprising since culture moves like molasses, usually taking long periods to show significant shifts.

SUBCULTURES

There is no such thing as a completely homogeneous society. Every society is made up of large groups of people who demonstrate basic differences, which can be based on physical factors, religion, race, or nationality.[25] Each major culture is in many ways the result of a fusion between all the subcultures that constitute the major culture.

Customs, attitudes, and mores are taken from each group and molded into the whole.

Subculture refers to the manner of behaving peculiar to a group that is a part of some larger group. A subgroup shares many customs with the major group, but the subgroup also has distinctive roles, status, and values of its own. Thus, longshoremen, university professors, gangsters, pilots, football players, hippies, blacks, Mormons, and middle-aged people are all examples of subcultures.

The question naturally arises, "What is the difference between a reference group and a subculture?" The answer is that in one sense there is no difference, and in another sense a difference exists. First, every reference group is a subculture, but every subculture is not necessarily a reference group. The subculture is a group, homogeneous in some important way, while the reference group is any subgroup to which a person relates. A person may be a member of the middle-income subculture but pattern his behavior after that of a higher-income group. The black subculture is said to relate to both its own group and the white middleclass group. Subcultures in our society are usually referred to as minority groups. There are four major types of subcultures recognized in the United States—those based on age, race, religion, and nationality.

The Spanish subculture

Subcultures based on national origin stem from distinct customs, mores, and folkways brought from the homeland. Among the national minority groups in the United States are the Irish, Italians, Polish, Mexicans, Puerto Ricans, Chinese, Germans, and English. We use the Spanish subculture to illustrate differences among consumers brought about by national origin.

Some 10.6 million people of Spanish heritage live in the United States today.[26] Members of this group comprise the second largest ethnic market (after the black) and the largest ethnic group based on nationality. The Spanish market is subdivided into three different groups—the Mexicans of the Southwest, the Cubans of Florida, and the Puerto Ricans of New York City. About 6.2 million Spaniards live in California, Texas, and New York, accounting for about three fourths of the Spanish market.[27] This market, because of its geographic concentration, is rather easy to reach by the use of communications through specialized media.

A majority of the family heads of Spanish families emigrated from a comparatively simple economy and culture in which custom and tradition dominate behavior, and family life is influenced to a large extent by community opinion. The husband, who is the principal wage earner, dominates the family and has strong authority over buying decisions. Family ties are strong, and in spite of immigration, urban living, and minority group status, marriage and family life have been slow to change. Domination of the father, however, has declined with Americanization. The youthful members of the family are not as subordinate to parents as they once were.

The degree to which a minority takes on the customs and mores of the majority is an important measure of its adjustment to a new social system. The assimilation of the Spanish group into U.S. culture has been slowed because of its folk background. Most first-generation Spanish people, as well as second- and third-generation families, maintain their own language and customs. Although most Spanish immigrants quickly take on the more obvious external aspects of culture, the essential values of the American culture are assimilated more slowly. A part of the lack of adaptability is explained by their poverty and a slowness of Americans to adjust to the Spanish people. Assimilation is always a two-way street. The Spanish-American upper class is the most nearly assimilated into American culture. The members of this group are important opinion leaders among their people. The upper-class Spaniards are watched closely, and when they succeed, others in the group follow suit. Because this upper-class group is respected for its assimilation into American culture, it is often the key group to reach when introducing new products or attempting to influence the Spanish-speaking American market.

Spanish traditions and customs have resulted in some significant differences in buying. The Spanish market is highly individual in its choice not only of products but of brands as well. Spanish Americans tend to rent rather than own their homes. They resist the substitution of new types of food products for their traditional low-income tropical diet. Spanish Americans tend toward traditional home furnishings, and their low incomes allow for few luxuries. The Puerto Ricans tend to accept new products to a greater degree than other Spanish-speaking people, probably because more of them are younger.

The Jewish subculture

Subcultures can be based on a group's system of worship. Some important religious subcultures in the United States are the Jews, Catholics, Mormons, and Protestants. As of 1975, there were approximately 250 religious bodies in this country with 330,460 churches and 131,245,000 members.[28] Protestants have 221 different bodies and each one can be considered a subculture. Jewish people were chosen for our discussion of subcultures based on religion.

The average Jewish family has only lived in the United States for about two generations. According to estimates by the American Jewish Committee, there were approximately 5.6 million Jews in 1960 and 6.0 million in 1976, comprising slightly less than 3 percent of the American population.[29] This figure seems surprisingly low when we consider the extent to which this group contributes to American commerce and intellect. However, a look at the socioeconomic factors that differentiate this ethnic group from others explains why this minority stands out.

Characteristics of the Jewish subculture. In the Western world, the Jews have a longer history as a people than the rest of the population in the countries they inhabit. Their culture is growing at a rate much slower than that of other cultures. The Jewish family structure may be best described as family-centered, and joint decision making is often more of a practice with this group than with other groups where one family member dominates.

Two types of concentration are found in the Jewish population in America: economic and geographical. There is a tendency toward occupational concentration in relatively few areas of economic enterprise. A high proportion of Jews are employed as professionals—doctors, lawyers, professors—or as entrepreneurs in retailing or light industry.[30] A high proportion of the Jewish population in this country resides in metropolitan areas. It is said that as much as 40 percent of the Jewish population resides in New York City. This high degree of concentration makes it an easy group to reach through specialized media.

In the United States, Jews, comprising 3 percent of the population, make up 8 percent of the college educated. Education, according to some, is the major instrument of Jewish unity. With above-average educations, we find Jewish people in occupations with above-average status and above-average incomes. The extremely high education level found among members of this group not only results in their being an affluent market but also a discriminating one.

Jewish purchasing behavior. There are several products that appeal only to the Jewish population because of their separate identity. Many of these products are seasonal, while some are used every day. Items such as kosher foods, Hanukah candles, matsos, and dradels are but a few of the many types of items for which the primary market is the Jewish population. However, in addition to these favored specialized products, there are also numerous product categories that find little favor among Jews. Second-generation Jewish housewives exhibit a marked antagonism toward preprocessed packaged foods, and most Jewish families state a clear preference for fresh or canned foods. Jews rank low among ethnic groups in the acceptance of frozen red meat, cake mixes, and dehydrated soups. Jewish dietary laws and "ethnic tastes" explain some of these differences in grocery consumption, and distinctive baked goods and kosher meats explain this group's reluctance to purchase many packaged convenience food items.

Although the Jewish population may not receive certain consumer convenience items well, the high educational level of this group causes it to be an important consumer group for cultural items. As this group has become more affluent, they have become patrons of the arts and collectors. In addition, it has been pointed out that "their independence of the American tradition makes Jews a market for the new."[31]

The American Jew is modern minded, as is often reflected in the architecture of the Jewish synagogues. The willingness of Jewish consumers to purchase new items often leads to their being innovators or early adopters. Persons of Jewish or French descent are more likely to purchase new products than are people of British, German, or Italian descent. However, this is not always the case. Jewish families, in spite of their income and social standing, often find barriers to residing in certain communities, belonging to certain clubs, enrolling in certain schools, and following certain occupations. This fact alone would have developed a uniqueness of the group. Cultural identification, although continuing strong, has declined in recent years. Today, American Jews are becoming less bound to religious mores and traditions. As a result, the American Jew is becoming more identifiable with the rest of American society. The growing conformity has altered even those forms of living which have throughout the ages been directly tied with Jewish religious and social views. As the attachment to Jewish values becomes slightly weaker with each generation, distinctive purchasing behavior becomes less discernible.

The black subculture

People with a common biological heritage, consisting of certain permanent physical distinctions, may be classified as a subculture based on race. Different races are distinguished by color of skin and eyes, color and texture of hair, stature, and bodily proportions. Among the more important racial groups in the United States are the black, the American Indian, and the Oriental subcultures. Blacks have been selected to illustrate racial subcultures.

Characteristics of black consumers. The black market in the United States is important and large.[32] In 1974 there was a total of 24.2 million blacks in the country.[33] This number is roughly the equivalent of the white population of Washington, Oregon, and California. Blacks represent approximately 11.4 percent of total American population. Black population has been increasing faster than white population for some time. In spite of the overall rate of growth in the number of blacks, some states actually show declines in black population. The South was the only region to have a smaller percentage of blacks in 1970 than in 1960, although more than 50 percent of all blacks still live in the South.[34]

There has been a noticeable improvement in black purchasing power. Although 15.4 percent of nonwhite families had incomes of less than $3,000 in 1973, this was an improvement over the 31.7 percent 13 years earlier.[35] Still, median income of nonwhites in 1973 was $7,596 compared to $12,597 for whites.[36] Black unemployment was about two times that of whites.[37] Blacks, even more than other minorities, do not assimilate into the white community. The bulk of the black market in most cities is concentrated in an area seldom encompassing more than a total of two square miles. The white population takes up the remainder of the city's area. Blacks display high self-identification and compactness as a group brought about by geographic concentration, common economic conditions, and white rejection. Most blacks are in the lowest economic strata, and the family tends to be dominated by women. Whereas approximately 14.5 percent of previously married whites live alone, approximately 26.6 percent of blacks are in this situation.[38] Thus women have a great influence on the attitudes and behavior of black children and on purchase behavior generally.

Purchase patterns of black consumers. A great many of the wants held by blacks are just like those of their white counterparts. Blacks want to provide for the necessities and still have some money left for luxuries. A middle-income black is not so different from a middle-income white in this respect. However, there is enough evidence available to show that black buying is not identical to that of the white consumer.[39] Table 22–2 summarizes the result of one study, and shows differences in black and white purchasing patterns.

The activities of blacks are often stunted by legal, quasi-legal, or psychological means. Blacks cannot live, work, or play with the same freedom as whites.[40] Often the black is prohibited from belonging to good clubs, restricted in the purchase or rental of housing equal to income, and restricted in enjoying the privileges of entertainment and vacation resorts. Even when not prohibited, the black often prefers to stay home to avoid snubs. The net result of certain restrictions and the drive to belong has given the black consumer a special kind of market orientation. Blacks hesitate to put money in a home or a new automobile. The home often must be built in a slum where it can depreciate by one half when the last brick is placed. An automobile is a high-risk item to purchase in ghetto areas because of theft and depreciation. Instead, blacks tend to spend their income on personal consumption items for

Table 22-2
Negro versus white distribution of family expenditures for current consumption (controlled for income: $1,000–$14,999 income inclusive)

	Average percent of current consumption	
Expenditure category	*White*	*Negro*
Total food expenditures	25.7%	24.4%
Food prepared at home	20.7	20.0
Food away from home	5.1	4.4
Tobacco	1.8	2.0
Alcoholic beverages	1.7	2.3
Shelter	16.1	16.1
Rented dwelling	8.5	11.3
Owned dwelling	7.1	4.7
Other shelter	0.5	0.1
Fuel, light, refrigeration and water	4.8	4.6
Household operations	5.8	6.3
House furnishings and equipment	4.6	5.3
Clothing, material and services	8.9	12.5
Personal care	2.8	3.8
Medical care	7.1	4.5
Recreation	3.5	3.7
Reading	1.0	0.9
Education	0.9	0.5
Transportation	13.1	11.9
Automobiles	11.4	9.5
Other travel and transportation	1.8	2.4
Other expenditure	2.2	1.4
Expenditure for current consumption	100.1%	100.3%

Source: Raymond A. Bauer and Scott M. Cunningham, "The Negro Market," *Journal of Advertising Research*, vol. 10 (April 1970), pp. 3–13.

which they can obtain full value. They spend more for clothing, home furnishings, nonautomobile travel, and savings. Even so, it would be a mistake to lump all blacks together when it comes to purchase patterns.

There is evidence that some blacks tend to emulate their white counterpart, while others attempt to be distinctly different. For example, the black consumption of Scotch whiskey, clothing, and luncheon meats may be patterned after mental perceptions of middle-class Americans.[41] Other blacks attempt to reject the white ideal by consuming in just the opposite patterns. This can be observed in some of the dress of the black cults, patterns of entertainment, and preference for stores operated by blacks. However, it is probably true that the great bulk of black consumers simply base their purchase of products on the same personal taste preferences that guide most whites.

Subcultures based on age

Important subcultures can be identified based on the age of individuals.[42] For our purpose, four broad age groups can be discussed: adolescents, teen-agers, young adults, and senior citizens.

Adolescents. The average family contains about 3.2 members, and adolescents are the recipients of a great deal of attention from grown-ups.[43] The smaller family size combined with a relatively high family income has meant more for everyone. Children are rewarded for passing from one grade to another in school, cleaning up their rooms, or going on errands. When accompanying parents on shopping excursions, the child receives consumer training by observing the parents. Children between seven and nine years old are asked questions by their parents with regard to household purchases.

Consumption patterns are beginning to be established by the age of five. Five-year-olds make purchase suggestions, mainly for personal items, but a small percentage actually make suggestions about such family items as meat, canned goods, cake mixes, and other food products. Many of these suggestions are identified by brand name with the child's principal source of information being television.

By the age of seven, a child has taken on more attributes of older consumers. Income comes from the performance of small tasks and from a regular allowance. The seven-year-old makes independent selections of personal items and independent choices of such group products as cereal, frozen juices, cookies, and luncheon meat. The adolescent also makes a number of purchase suggestions to parents.

Many nine-year-olds are dissatisfied with parents' purchases made for them and prefer to buy their own personal items. It is common for the nine-year-old to make frequent trips to retail outlets, and the child is actively engaged in, and aware of, the marketing process. The child in this age group is aware of the differences in cost among products and has an acute awareness of TV commercials. When asked, the nine-year-old shows a preference for products that have prestige value.

The teenage group. The main source of income for teenagers is in the form of an allowance. The allowance represents a bare minimum, as parents are almost always willing to supplement it with emergency loans or gifts. Money received from part-time or full-time jobs also represents a substantial source of income for teenagers. Teen buyers represent a highly profitable market segment for certain producers, since most of their money is available for recreational, luxury, and impulse spending. With no food, clothing, or shelter to draw heavily upon incomes, members of this group spend money on goods they want.

One must remember when considering the teenage, or youth, market that there are several peculiarities common to this group. It is extremely fluid, and things change so rapidly that obsolete products and fads can occur almost overnight. The real problem when marketing to this group, however, is the danger of alienating its members. Not only are the young people changing because of the constant flow into and out of the teenage group, but the youths themselves do not like to be figured out. The young often take pride in being different from their parents. Thus, it does not follow that if you sell mama, you sell daughter. It may well be that daughter will reject the product just because her parent uses it.

Young adults. The young-adult market is made up of people between the ages of 18–25. This is really two market segments comprising the college group and the young married group. It is estimated that nearly 65 percent of young people between the ages of 16–21 are in college.[44] College students are big spenders on wearing apparel, furnishings, books, and recreational equipment. They are also among the heavier users of beer.

"More girls marry at 18, as a part of this youth market, than at any other age."[45] These young marrieds are better informed than their parents were. New families need more of all types of products, so the evidence points to more spending by this group in the future. However, the need to increase spending comes at a time when earnings are low. The young family has not reached its peak earning capacity. Thus the young marrieds tend to be discriminating buyers. One way out for the newly married is for the wife to work. Where the wife works, the family sometimes splurges on recreation, entertainment, travel, and eating out. Of course, the young married market can be further subdivided along product lines, such as for homes, clothing, food, and home furnishings.

Senior citizens. In 1974, the United States had 19.9 percent of families with the head of household 65 years of age or over. This group is growing at a substantially faster rate than the population as a whole. While the total population is expected to increase by 40 percent between 1950 and 1975, the population of the 65 and over age group will increase by 75 percent.

Senior citizens constitute a different but significant market for products. Children have left the nest, income has declined to that of retirement level, and the senior citizen is often left alone. People in this group spend much of their time at home, frequently with a health problem. The senior citizen has already accumulated most of the products needed for home operation. These consumers require smaller homes, less transportation, and fewer clothes and accessories;

but they need more insurance, recreation, medical care, and services. The tastes of senior citizens tend toward the conservative. This group is not so venturesome as teens or young adults.

The mere fact that a person reaches retirement age does not obviate their need for products and services. In fact, in many cases, the senior citizen offers a better market for those products and services that satisfy more complex psychological needs, such as social and self-fulfillment needs. This, however, is a difficult group to reach because of attitude and outlook. Products and appeals which single them out as a unique and special group may have negative results. Although they feel that more attention should be given to members of this age group, they tend to resent special marketing treatment, especially that which makes them feel inferior because of age considerations.

NOTES

1. Harold H. Kassarjian and Thomas S. Robertson, *Perspectives in Consumer Behavior* (Glenview, Ill.: Scott, Foresman & Co., 1973), pp. 450–464.
2. Peter D. Bennett and Harold H. Kassarjian, *Consumer Behavior* (Englewood Cliffs, N.J.: Prentice-Hall, Inc., 1972), p. 123.
3. Harold G. Grasmick, "Social Change and Modernism in the American South," *American Behavioral Scientist*, vol. 16 (July–August 1973), pp. 913–33.
4. Douglas J. Dalrymple, M. Y. Yoshino, and Thomas S. Robertson, "Consumption Behavior Across Ethnic Categories," *California Management Review*, vol. 14 (Fall 1971), pp. 65–70; Ronald D. Michman, "Culture as a Marketing Tool," *Marquette Business Review* (Winter 1975), pp. 177–83; Walter A. Henry, "Cultural Values Do Correlate with Consumer Behavior," *Journal of Marketing Research*, vol. 13 (May 1976), pp. 121–27; Joseph Franklin Hair, Jr. and Ralph E. Anderson, "Culture, Acculturation and Consumer Behavior: An Empirical Study," *Marketing Education and the Real World*, eds. Boris W. Becker and Helmut Becker (Chicago: American Marketing Assn., 1973), pp. 423–28.
5. Omar K. Moore and Donald J. Lewis, "Learning Theory and Culture," *Phychological Review*, vol. 59 (September 1952), pp. 380–88.
6. Frederick D. Sturdivant, "Subculture Theory: Poverty, Minorities, and Marketing," *Consumer Behavior: Theoretical Sources*, eds. Scott Ward and Thomas S. Robertson, (Englewood Cliffs, N.J.: Prentice-Hall, Inc., 1973), pp. 473–75.
7. Jules Henry, *Pathways to Madness* (New York: Random House, 1971).
8. David T. Kollat, Roger D. Blackwell, and James F. Robeson, *Strategic Marketing* (New York: Holt, Rinehart & Winston, Inc., 1972).

9. Bernard Berelson and Gary A. Steiner, *Human Behavior: An Inventory of Scientific Findings* (New York: Harcourt, Brace & World, Inc., 1964), pp. 646–47.
10. Charles E. Osgood, "It's the Same the World Over," *Parade* (February 1972), p. 22.
11. Scott Ward, "Consumer Socialization," *Journal of Consumer Research*, vol. 1 (September 1974), pp. 1–14.
12. Glenn M. Vernon, *Human Interaction: An Introduction to Sociology*, 2d ed. (New York: The Ronald Press Co., 1972), p. 385.
13. Rom J. Markin, Jr., *Consumer Behavior: A Cognitive Orientation* (New York: Macmillan Publishing Co., Inc., 1974), pp. 457–58.
14. Vernon, *Human Interaction*, pp. 229–32.
15. Ibid., pp. 235–36.
16. Ibid., pp. 238–42.
17. Ibid., pp. 242–47.
18. Joe Kent Kerby, *Consumer Behavior: Conceptual Foundations* (New York: Dun-Donnelley Publishing Corp., 1975), pp. 573–76.
19. *Time*, vol. 97 (June 21, 1971), pp. 56–63; William S. Cannon, *The Jesus Revolution* (Nashville, Tenn.: Broadman, Inc., 1971).
20. Jean Cazeneuve, "Television and the Human Condition," *Communication*, vol. 1 (1974), pp. 197–211.
21. Philip Kotler and Gerald Zaltman, "Social Marketing: An Approach to Planned Social Change," *Journal of Marketing*, vol. 35 (July 1971), pp. 3–12.
22. Seymour M. Lipset, "A Changing American Character," *Culture and Social Character*, eds. Seymour M. Lipset and Leo Lowenthal (New York: Doubleday & Co., Inc., 1971), pp. 136–71; Geoffrey Gorer, *The American People* (New York: W. W. Norton & Co., Inc., 1964).
23. Conrad M. Arensberg and Arthur H. Nichoff, *Introduction to Social Change: A Manual for Americans Overseas* (Chicago: Aldine Publishing Co., 1964), pp. 153–83; R. M. Williams, *American Society, A Sociological Interpretation* (New York: Alfred A. Knopf, Inc., 1951), pp. 388–442.
24. Charles A. Reich, *The Greening of America* (New York: Random House, 1970).
25. D. O. Arnold, *The Sociology of Subcultures* (Berkeley, Ca.: Glendasary Press, 1970).
26. Helen Axel, ed., *A Guide to Consumer Markets*, 1975/1976 (New York: The Conference Board, Inc., 1975), p. 23.
27. Richard P. Jones, "Spanish Ethnic Market Second Largest in U.S.," *Marketing Insights* (November 27, 1967), p. 10.
28. *Statistical Abstract of the United States*, 1975, p. 47.
29. Axel, *A Guide to Consumer Markets*, 1975/1976, p. 42.
30. N. Glazer and P. Moynihan, *Beyond the Melting Pot* (The MIT Press and Harvard University Press, 1963).

31. Ibid., pp. 173–74.
32. George Joyce and Norman A. P. Govoni, eds., *The Black Consumer: Dimensions of Behavior and Strategy* (New York: Random House, 1971); Raymond A. Bauer and Scott M. Cunningham, "The Negro Market," *Journal of Advertising Research,* vol. 10 (1970), pp. 3–13.
33. Axel, *A Guide to Consumer Markets,* 1975/1976, p. 11.
34. Ibid., p. 30.
35. Ibid., p. 128.
36. Ibid., p. 127.
37. Ibid., p. 99.
38. Ibid., p. 44.
39. Thomas E. Barry and Michael G. Harvey, "Marketing to Heterogeneous Black Consumers," *California Management Review,* vol. 17 (Winter 1974), pp. 50–57; John P. Maggard, "Negro Market–Fact or Fiction?" *California Management Review,* vol. 14 (Fall 1971), pp. 71–78.
40. Waylon D. Griffin and Frederick D. Sturdivant, "Discrimination and Middle Class Minority Consumers," *Journal of Marketing,* vol. 37 (July 1973), pp. 65–68.
41. "Negro Food Buying Differs," *Marketing Insights,* vol. 2 (January 29, 1968); D. Parke Gibson, "Why There is a Negro Market," *The Black Consumer* (New York: Random House, 1971), pp. 39–48.
42. Stephen J. F. Unwin, "How Culture, Age, and Sex Affect Advertising Response," *Journalism Quarterly,* vol. 50 (1973), pp. 735–43.
43. Axel, *A Guide to Consumer Markets,* 1975/1976, p. 66.
44. Ibid., p. 70.
45. Ibid., p. 67.

QUESTIONS

1. Define culture. What is the purpose of culture in our society? Explain.
2. Discuss the basic factors of culture. How does culture affect consumer behavior?
3. What are cultural universals? Give some examples.
4. Explain the meaning of cultural attribute. How does the attribute of socialization affect consumers? What is the effect of norms on consumer behavior? Explain the types of norms.
5. What role do rewards and sanctions play in culture? How does each affect consumer behavior?
6. Discuss the manner in which culture is acquired. What are the sources of cultural values?
7. Discuss the seven characteristics of American culture. How valid are these characteristics? Do they effect the way consumers behave? Explain.

8. What is a subculture? How does a subculture differ from a reference group?
9. Contrast the Spanish subculture and the Jewish subculture. Give examples of how these subcultures are important to consumer behavior.
10. Discuss the black subculture. Discuss the differences in purchase patterns based on age. Explain.

PART FIVE

Business effects on consumer behavior

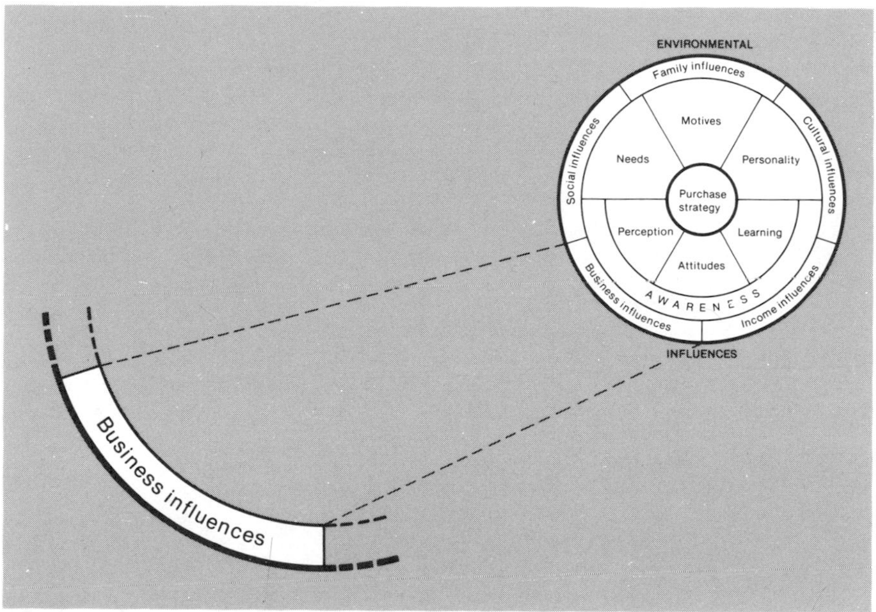

Business is a part of the consumer's total environment, but requires special treatment, because all consumer behavior deals with the interaction between the individual consumer and some business. The business affects consumer behavior through the basic determinants that cause consumers to adjust and modify purchase strategy.

Part Five encompasses five chapters:

23. Introduction to Business Influence.
24. Consumer Research.
25. The Consumer's Product Image.
26. The Consumer's Store Image.
27. Effect of Promotion on Consumers.

The purpose of this part of the book is to more clearly illustrate how consumers react to policies and decisions made by business. The chapters do not investigate how a business establishes policies, but rather explore the effect of business policies and decisions on consumer decision processes.

23

Introduction to business influence

Perspectives of marketing strategy
Business influence on consumers
Influence and persuasion
Influence and manipulation
Restraints on business influence
Business influence benefits consumers
Purpose of business influence
Business and personal influence on consumers
Similarities in business and personal influence
Differences between business and personal influence
Business influences consumers through image formation
Image-building process
Characteristics of business images
Business images classified
Differences in consumer images
Image stability and change

Business is another environmental factor which greatly affects consumer behavior. Often the influence that family, friend, and neighbor have on consumer behavior is an incidental result of other human interaction. A chance comment about some product by a friend may cause a person to try the product. A neighbor may make a casual comment about a store in the course of describing a trip downtown. This information may eventually be the reason that the consumer visits that store.

Although many customers may purchase from a given business because of chance information, the enterprise cannot depend on chance to attract customers. The business must take direct and positive action designed to attract and hold customers. For this reason, the most important external influence on consumer behavior is that exerted by business. Not only do businesses influence the consumer directly, but businesses also affect the consumer through others. In this chapter, we lay the foundation for Part Five by discussing business influence.

PERSPECTIVES OF MARKETING STRATEGY

The concept of marketing strategy is very familiar to every marketing student. It is perhaps the principal subject related to the study of marketing. However, the consumer's view of this strategy is seldom emphasized and that is the subject of this presentation. *Marketing strategy* is typically defined as the overall plan put together to guide business activity.[1] Marketing strategy consists of two major components.

1. *The target market.* A specific group of consumers to be satisfied.
2. *The marketing mix.* The coordinated product, place (marketing channel), promotion, and price policies of the firm.

There are in fact two, rather than one, perspectives of marketing strategy—its development and its implementation. The consumer plays a different role with each of these perspectives.

It is usual to discuss marketing strategy in terms of how it is developed by the firm. This position is illustrated in Figure 23–1. Here the perspective is that of the firm's management. That is to say, the view is from inside the firm looking out at the market.[2] When developing strategy, the consumer is the objective of the marketing mix. Management takes data on consumers (location, numbers, wants, income, etc.) and coordinates product, place, promotion, and price policies to appeal to this market. Most discussions of marketing strategy are concerned with this development of the marketing mix.

Consideration of the implementation of marketing strategy requires

Figure 23–1
Marketing strategy: Consumer effects on the mix

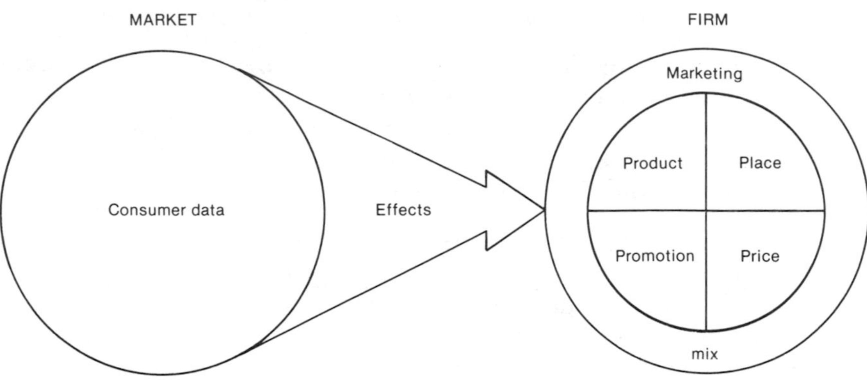

a different perspective as illustrated in Figure 23–2. The view is that of the consumer who is faced with several different marketing strategies by varying types of business. The consumer must satisfy his or her wants based on available products, prices, promotion, and place of purchase. The assumption is that firms already have more or less effective marketing mixes, and the question becomes, "What effect does this mix have on consumer behavior?"[3] *This latter perspective is the one taken in this book.* The discussion is in no way a duplication or summary of the elements of marketing management. The discussion is exactly one hundred and eighty degrees out of phase with the typical discussion of marketing strategy. The view taken here is that the firm is the external factor, and decision making is the prerogative of the consumer. Our concern is how consumers view marketing strategy, and not how business executives construct such a strategy.

Figure 23–2
Marketing strategy: Mix effects on the consumer

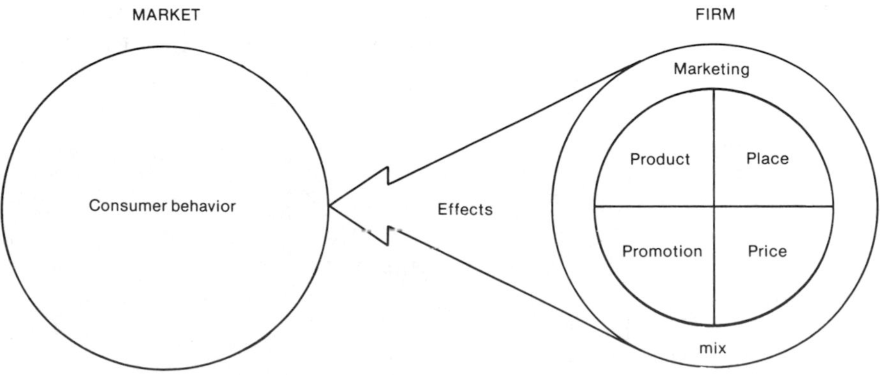

Because the perspective is that of the consumer, the treatment of the marketing mix must be adjusted. Three modifications in the concept of product, place, promotion, and price are worth noting.

1. Product and price decisions are combined because the consumer typically considers price as another product attribute.
2. Place considerations for consumers concern the type, location, and layout of retail stores rather than channel decisions.
3. Promotion to the consumer is viewed as information or influence.

Furthermore, the consumer typically has fewer facts than does a businessperson, so the overall emphasis is more on product, promotion, and store images or impressions when dealing with consumers. Consumer decisions are greatly influenced by these impressions. However, it should be clear that these modifications do not change the basic nature of the subject. We are still discussing the marketing mix.

BUSINESS INFLUENCE ON CONSUMERS

Business organizations are by nature designed to influence consumers. Exerting this influence is one of the principal activities of business, for it is through influence on consumers that the objectives of the firm are achieved.[4] We shall begin our discussion of business influence by defining influence and persuasion, explaining the difference between influence and manipulation, and describing the restraints placed on the use of business influence.

Influence and persuasion

The term *influence* is not used here in any derogatory manner—we are not referring to any immoral, illegal, or unethical activity undertaken by business. We are referring to one of the basic functions of business, that of motivating people to do something—take an action, form an opinion, or accept an idea. Thus, business influence is defined as *the effect a business has on consumers as a result of appeals made by advertising, personal selling, and other means of persuasion directed at the consumer's reason or emotions in order to accomplish the firm's objectives.*

Business influence implies that reasoning, urging, emotional appeals, and various other kinds of inducements are used to evoke some response from the consumer favorable to the firm. However, influence is the result of inducement and not the inducement itself. Influence is the ability to evoke a specified response from consumers and can only be measured by the results obtained. The means or inducements offered to achieve a state of consumer influence is referred to as *persua-*

sion. The business uses the persuasive forces of advertising, personal selling, brand, publicity, price, product quality, and so on, in order to gain a condition of influence over consumer attitudes or behavior.[5]

Influence and manipulation

Influence is sometimes equated with manipulation as in the statement "Dirty Dog influenced dear old dad to change his will, leaving us poor kids without a dime." *Manipulation* connotes an unreasonable or unfair use of power by one person over another. Manipulation also implies that the manipulator is gaining something at the expense of the one manipulated.[6] Thus, manipulation is defined as getting someone to do something against their will. If a seller makes a consumer buy when the consumer does not want to, there is manipulation.

Influence, as used in this book, has nothing in common with manipulation.[7] *Influence* simply indicates that business is an external environmental factor to the consumer which plays an important part in shaping the consumer's thinking and behavior. To some extent, business influences consumers by its very presence, whether it attempts to do so or not; but our attention is focused on influence resulting from information supplied by business to the consumer. This information usually takes the form of personal or mass communications concerning the company or its products that can benefit the consumer. Thus, business influence, as used here, is a positive force which functions for the benefit of consumers.

We do recognize that not all businessleaders are honest and that business information is designed to persuade. The vast majority of businessleaders are honest within the acceptable meaning of the term, and dishonest business is not a subject specifically handled in this book. Business information must be persuasive or it has no purpose, but by persuasion we mean presenting facts in the most favorable light. We mean appeals to a person's reason or emotions. These types of appeals are sometimes referred to as propaganda. *Propaganda* is the making of deliberately one-sided statements to a mass audience.[8] The information is slanted, emotion charged, sometimes deceptive, but usually has some basis in fact. Even propaganda cannot force the consumer to act against his or her will. Propaganda begins to border on manipulation when excessively false or misleading information is employed.

Restraints on business influence

Many believe that American business is characterized by manipulation or excessive influence. Our attitude is that this point of view is essentially unfair to business. Besides the honesty of businessleaders, there are restraints that affect the willingness and ability of business to influence consumers. First, business' code of self-protection places restraints on its influence.[9] Most firms are built on repeat sales, and it is not good business to do anything that will reduce such sales. Thus, most executives and owners try to build goodwill for their firms instead of destroying it.

Second, competition restrains business influence. If one firm does not serve the customer honestly, another will step in to do the job. People favor those firms that sell them benefits. Thus, firms that attempt to influence people unduly are not likely to remain in business long, even though in any given short-run period, there will always be some organizations which are not acting in the public's interest. Third, consumers themselves are more knowledgeable than ever before. These consumers may not have sufficient knowledge in all respects, but they are better informed, and it is more difficult today to persuade people. The increased knowledge is a result of better general education and more particularly, of better communications.

Fourth, the influence on public opinion of such critics of business as Vance Packard and Ralph Nader tends to place restrictions on business influence. Fifth, consumers have more legal protection than ever before. The legal structure is not perfect, but it does provide some basic protection. The existing laws also act as a warning to businessmen that flagrant violations of consumer rights can lead to further restraints.[10]

BUSINESS INFLUENCE BENEFITS CONSUMERS

If we simply state that business influence is not manipulative, we have not said much to recommend it. The fact is that in its attempt to influence, business works a positive good for consumers. Business influence benefits consumers by providing information, and the fact that businesses compete provides a variety of different information. The consumer can evaluate the different data and reach an independent decision as to which business offers him the best advantage.[11] Business advertising and personal selling tell the consumers such things as (1) types of products made available, (2) product features, (3) where products can be bought, (4) business attitudes, (5) product quality, (6) prices, (7) services offered, and (8) store hours. Consumers would be hard pressed to find as much up-to-date, descriptive, and pertinent information by any other means. We can say that business images serve as a basis for individual consumer action, to reduce consumer decisions, and to reassure the individual concerning choices made.

PURPOSE OF BUSINESS INFLUENCE

Generally speaking, business influence aims to motivate the consumer to purchase the company's products and services. More specifically, business influence has four purposes. First, it is used to implant and win acceptance for a new idea, as with a new product or a new method of sale. In order to create a market for margarine, the industry had to get across the idea that margarine, even though less expensive, was as nutritious and tasty as butter.

Second, business influence is designed to change human behavior. People tend to resist change, and it can take generations to build substantial markets. Preprepared food had to wait for wide public acceptance until women found greater incentives for spending less time in the kitchen. Thus, the development of a greater interest in leisure activities aided the wider use of prepared foods.

Third, business influence is often designed to move consumers to specific action. Most personal selling and advertising are designed to accomplish this end.

Finally, business influence is used to change consumer attitudes. Housewives resisted accepting TV dinners and other frozen precooked products because they felt guilty about taking the easy way. The manufacturers attempted to change this attitude by picturing housewives who served frozen dinners as efficient family members who thereby reduced their time in the kitchen in order to spend more time with their families.

BUSINESS AND PERSONAL INFLUENCE ON CONSUMERS

There are many similarities between the personal factors of consumer behavior discussed in Part Three and business influence discussed in Part Five. There are also many differences between the two. Let us look into these aspects of business influence.

Similarities in business and personal influence

The most important similarities between business and personal influence are discussed in the following paragraphs.

1. All influence is based on the power to affect consumers by other than physical means. The power may be derived from trust, respect, knowledge, proficiency, communications, or strength of character.[12]

2. Influence is conditioned by perception. It is not truth or facts which affect behavior so much as it is the consumer's perception of truth. Consumers base their actions on the facts as they see them.

3. All influence affects the consumer's attitudes. One cannot be influenced and remain the same. The change may not be the one desired, but some change in attitude is necessary for influence to take place. A business may advertise the power of a deodorant to reassure the consumer about the effectiveness of the product. Some consumers may get the intended message and purchase, but others may not purchase because they feel that a strong deodorant is harmful to the skin.

4. All favorable responses to influence are based on some perceived physiological or psychological need that the consumer has. It is difficult to influence a consumer who has no need for the product.

Differences between business and personal influence

Now attention can be turned to the differences between personal and business influence on consumers. Most of these differences stem from the fact that business attempts to influence consumers in some specific way.

1. Business influence is directly or indirectly associated with some product. In its dealings with consumers, the firm attempts to generate short- or long-run sales, whereas personal influence may be for many purposes, including such things as the loan of money, a divorce, marriage, or recognition.

2. The intent of business influence is known to the consumer, and the consumer is placed on guard. This may not be true where personal influence is concerned.

3. Since consumers are aware of the purpose of business influence, a natural distrust of business results. This makes it more difficult for the businessman to influence consumers.

4. In an effort to overcome the natural distrust of consumers, business influence is well organized. Very little is left to chance in business communications.

5. Not only are business communications well organized, but business makes a more intense use of a wide variety of media to get its message across.

BUSINESS INFLUENCES CONSUMERS THROUGH IMAGE FORMATION

It is not easy to specify why a consumer prefers one brand of goods over another or why people will go far out of their way to trade with a preferred retailer. No factor is more important than the attitude, or feeling, or overall image that the consumer assumes toward the product or firm. We find that there are several perspectives that one may take toward business images. However, nearly everyone agrees that these images do concern attitudes. A business image is *the subjective attitude, feeling, or impression that the consumer takes toward a business or some activity of a business institution.*[13]

The term *business image* is always used to denote any type of image that can be associated with the organization, whether it relates to the product or the store. In other words, *business image* is a catchall term used when it is not convenient to specify a particular type of organizational image or when referring to several images together. One could say that any business image is the consumer's concept of the store's personality. This feeling is subjective and exists in the mind of the consumer, although it can be assumed that the consumer's attitude is based on something the company does or does not do. On the whole, this point is well taken. Consumers react to business policies, but consumers may also form a mental picture of a business from no more than hearing the company name. Product, store, service, and price images are specific examples of impressions that come under business images. These images concern only some part of the firm's operations.

Image-building process

Business images are formed in the minds of consumers, but these images result from interpretation of business activities. Our point of view emphasizes the consumer. We are not so much interested in what business must do to influence consumers as we are in the effect of business activities on the consumer.

Figure 23–3 illustrates, in simplified form, the image-building process that consumers go through. Of the total number of market-related messages, or impressions, received by the consumer, some penetrate the conscious mind and form a picture, and some do not.[14] The thing perceived can be a product, store, or some other business factor. It may be that the consumer cannot perceive the entire thing at one time. At any rate, the individual constructs a total consistent image on the basis of available information. If necessary, the consumer fills in missing facts in order to complete the picture. This point is illustrated by elaboration on Figure 23–3 where the consumer takes a point of information and expands it into a consistent whole. Show a person a "Pepsi" and he or she may form a complete picture of fun and fellowship. Mention "Macy's" and the average New York consumer has a complete idea of the store, even though it is not possible to see and know everything and everyone connected with Macy's. Some consumers may have a mental picture of Macy's, even though they have never seen it outside of their advertisements.

Figure 23–3
Selected mental impressions

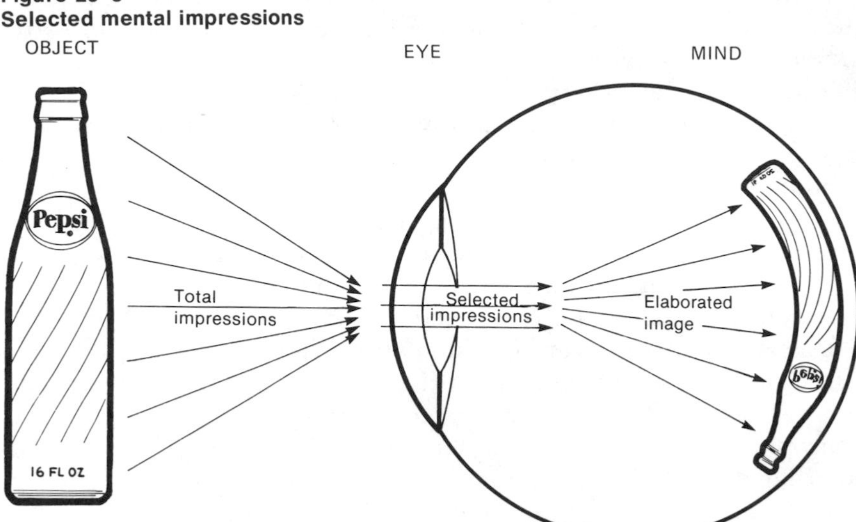

Characteristics of business images

Our discussion of the image formation process points to a number of important characteristics of business images that need further clarification. First, the images held by the consumer are emotional responses to the fact of the business. The image constitutes what people believe about a product or company as opposed to what actually constitutes the product or company. This attitude is based partially on feelings rather than completely on knowledge. For this reason, there may be considerable difference between how the consumer sees the business and what the business is.

Second, business images are always oversimplifications in the mind of the consumer. The image depends on filtered messages and filtered perception.[15] The human mind has difficulty coping with all the impressions received about a given situation. The problem becomes even more complex when we consider the number of situations encountered in a given time period. A person takes her car to the local dealer for repairs, and the repairs are excellent. Although the customer receives messages about the building, people, location, and prices, her image of the dealer is that of a good repair department.

Third, the consumer can expand and elaborate the image of a product or business almost at will.[16] One does this by transferring known facts about the product or business to the unknown aspects. The consumer assumes that, given no information to the contrary, whatever is true about one part of business is true about other parts. The customer mentioned may assume that the new-car department of the automobile dealer is good because the repair department is good.

Fourth, business images are subject to almost instantaneous change. Since images are based on emotions and perceptions, they are easily modified. One bad experience with a business can undo years of good service by that business.

Business images classified

There are several meaningful ways of classifying business images, but particularly important to consumers is the classification of images as institutional, functional, or commodity.

Institutional images. Classification of business images as institutional is based on the consumer's attitude toward the enterprise as a whole. The two types of institutional images are corporate image and store, or company, image. The *corporate image* is the consumer's impression of the business as a member of the community. Corporate image has more to do with how the firm operates as a citizen than with what it sells or to whom it sells. Most organizations have a fuzzy corporate image, but some businesses have been very successful in building their images. Procter and Gamble, General Motors, Mattel, Sears, International Business Machines, and General Foods have excellent corporate images. *Store image*, or *company image*, is similar to corporate image, but store image is more narrowly conceived. The store image is the consumer's attitude toward a particular store's ability to satisfy that consumer's needs. Thus, store image is built on customer experience and relates to the products, policies, personnel, and prices offered by the store.[17] Store image and corporate image may be essentially identical for small, single-store organizations, but they are seldom the same for large multiunit or chain operations.

Functional images. Business images typed according to activity are called functional images. The three major types of functional images held by consumers are (1) the service image, (2) the price image, and (3) the promotional image. All functional images have to do with some particular aspect of the firm's operations. *Service image* is the consumer's attitude toward specific services offered—their amount, adequacy, and efficiency. *Price image* is the consumer's impression of the price level, price lines, discounts, and other aspects of price that are important to consumers. The *promotional image* concerns consumers' attitudes toward the manner in which the company advertises.

Commodity images. Brand images can be classified along commodity lines into product image, brand image, and brand-line image. Commodity images involve attitudes toward the company's merchandise offering. The *product image* is the broadest of the three. This image is the consumer's feeling concerning all aspects of the product offering. Product image concerns product quality, suitability, and assortment. *Brand-line image* is the consumer's attitude toward the product of specified manufacturers. It includes design, packaging, and product attributes, but it consists mainly in the identification of these product attributes with a specific maker or seller.

The importance of the commodity image is illustrated by research findings which indicate most consumers can't tell the difference between one gasoline and another and yet they show strong preferences for particular brands. A majority of the subjects analyzed cannot distinguish among unlabeled brands of cola drinks, cigarettes, and beer.

Differences in consumer images

The consumer's image of an enterprise may differ because of three circumstances. First, an individual may have more than one image of a given company. The customer may consider the service to be good, but prices out of line. Second, the consumer's attitude toward the enterprise may vary over time. A person's image of a brand prestige store may change considerably as that person's income increases. The business may also institute changes that affect the consumer's attitude. Third, attitude varies among consumers. No two people are likely to perceive a business in exactly the same manner. These differences make it possible for a business to adjust its image to particular market segments.

Consumer attitudes toward businesses are seldom indifferent. The very idea of an image assumes some predisposition toward the firm. Thus, it is difficult to separate the consumer's image of a business from the consumer's mental disposition toward it. Different consumers may have any of four mental dispositions toward a business or some part of the business: (1) a favorable image, (2) a confused image, (3) an inadequate image, and (4) an unfavorable image. The reader may note that three out of the four dispositions are likely to operate against the business' achieving its objectives.

A *favorable image* means that the consumer is pleased with his or her concept of the organization. A *confused image* occurs when the consumer obtains conflicting impressions of the firm and cannot decide what the organization stands for. An *inadequate image* occurs when the consumer lacks information upon which to reach a decision about the enterprise. An *unfavorable image* occurs when the consumer is displeased with his or her concept of the business. The images received of some businesses by consumers are clear and distinct, while other businesses fail to get across to customers any consistent personality. Consumers are more likely to base their actions on clear images, because the consumer has more faith in the information obtained. A business image is more likely to be favorable when the image is (1) definite, (2) consistent in point of view, (3) to the point, (4) believable in its symbolism, and (5) related to the values of the consumer and his or her reference groups. A clear image is not the same as a favorable image—an image can be clear in the consumer's mind but unfavorably received. Not everyone will like the personality portrayed by a business. However, if the image is clear in the consumer's mind, the person has a basis for accepting or rejecting the personality presented. A confused image appeals only rarely to any large segment of the market. A clear image becomes a favorable image when large numbers of consumers see values that agree with theirs contained in the image.

Image stability and change

It is characteristic of business images that they change, but it is more difficult to change some images than others. There are six principles that relate to business stability and change.[18]

1. *Stable business images depend on internal consistency and external support.* A consumer's attitude toward business remains constant as long as that individual's perception continues to support the image held and as long as peer groups agree that the consumer's image is the correct one.

2. *Both internal and external opposition to stable images are resisted.* Consumers resist, up to a point, any challenge to business images held because (1) it is easier to continue to believe as before than to develop a whole new image, (2) any threat to the image held brings the person's judgment into question, and (3) the threat tends to force the person to question peer opinion.

3. *Unstable business images are best attacked by creating further doubt.* The task is easier with unstable images because the consumer is already unsure of his or her attitude.

4. *New business images should be presented in the most favorable light.* One important method of presenting new images favorably is to manifest already accepted consumer values.

5. *The clarity and frequency of the business image affects consumer acceptance.* Consumers are more likely to accept ideas or attitudes that are clear and presented often.

6. *New business images must attract the attention of large numbers of people to stimulate development.* Not everyone can be expected to accept the new image, but giving wide exposure to it and causing large numbers of people to take positions toward it will speed its acceptance.

NOTES

1. E. Jerome McCarthy, *Basic Marketing: A Managerial Approach,* 5th ed. (Homewood, Ill.: Richard D. Irwin, Inc., 1975), Chap. 4; Philip Kotler, *Marketing Management: Analysis, Planning, and Control,* 2d ed. (Englewood Cliffs, N.J.: Prentice-Hall, Inc., 1972); Ben M. Enis, *Marketing Principles* (Pacific Palisades, Ca.: Goodyear Publishing Co., Inc., 1974), Chap. 3.
2. An overview of the business perspective of consumers can be found in the following: J. Howard Westing and Gerald Albaum, *Modern Marketing Thought* (New York: Macmillan Publishing Co., Inc., 1975); James F. Engel, Henry F. Fiorillo, and Murray A. Cayley, *Market Segmentation: Concepts and Applications* (New York: Holt, Rinehart & Winston, Inc., 1972); George P. Morris and Robert W. Frye, *Current Marketing Views* (San Francisco: Canfield Press, 1973).
3. Kenneth J. Roering, Robert D. Schooler, and Fred W. Morgan, "An Evaluation of Marketing Practices: Businessmen, Housewives, and Students," *Journal of Business Research,* vol. 4 (May 1976), pp. 131–44; Hal Pickle, Royce Abrahamson, and Alan Porter, "Customer Satisfaction and Profit in Small Business," *Journal of Retailing,* vol. 46 (Winter 1970–1971), pp. 38–49; Stephen K. Keiser and James R. Krum, "Consumer Perceptions of Retail Advertising with Overstated Price Savings," *Journal of Retailing,* vol. 52 (Fall 1976), pp. 27–36.
4. Charles J. Dirksen and Arthur Kroeger, *Advertising Principles and Problems,* 4th ed. (Homewood, Ill.: Richard D. Irwin, Inc., 1973), p. 4.
5. George J. Szybillo and Richard Heslin, "Resistance to Persuasion: Inoculation Theory in a Marketing Context," *Journal of Marketing Research,* vol. 10 (November 1973), pp. 396–403.
6. Alvin A. Achenbaum, "Advertising Doesn't Manipulate Consumers," *Journal of Advertising Research,* vol. 2 (April 1972), pp. 3–13.
7. Harry A. Lipson, Eugene J. Kelley, and Seymour Marshak, "Integrating Social Feedback and Social Audits into Corporate Planning," *Social Marketing,* eds. William Lazer and Eugene J. Kelley (Homewood, Ill.: Richard D. Irwin, Inc., 1973), pp. 174–91.
8. Edmund D. McGarry, "The Propaganda Function in Marketing," *Journal of Marketing,* vol. 23 (October 1959), pp. 131–39.
9. Louis L. Stern, "Consumer Protection via Self-Regulation," *Journal of Marketing,* vol. 35 (July 1971), pp. 46–58.
10. The recent legislation dealing with lending and packaging are examples.
11. "What Does Advertising Do for the Consumer?" *Journal of Advertising,* vol. 2 (1973), pp. 22–27.
12. Barry E. Collins and Harold Guetzkow, "Direct Sources of Power and Interpersonal Influence," *A Social Psychology of Group Processes for Decision Making* (New York: John Wiley & Sons, Inc., 1964), pp. 121–25.
13. This definition has been adapted from Pierre Martineau, "The Corporate Personality," *Developing the Corporate Image,* ed. Lee Bristol, Jr. (New York: Charles Scribner's Sons, 1960), pp. 3–13.

14. William H. Reynolds, "The Role of the Consumer in Image Building," *California Management Review*, vol. 7 (Spring 1965).
15. Walter Lippman, *Public Opinion* (New York: MacMillan Co., 1922), pp. 79–81.
16. S. I. Hayakawa, *Language in Thought and Action*, 2d ed. (New York: Harcourt, Brace & World, Inc., 1964). A good discussion of the inference process.
17. Thomas J. Stanley and Murphy A. Sewall, "Image Inputs to a Probabilistic Model: Predicting Retail Potential," *Journal of Marketing*, vol. 40 (July 1976), pp. 48–53; V. Parker Lessig, "Consumer Store Images and Store Loyalties," *Journal of Marketing*, vol. 38 (October 1973), pp. 72–74.
18. Bordin H. Nelson, "Seven Principles of Image Formation," *Journal of Marketing*, vol. 26 (January 1962), pp. 67–71. The principles presented here are liberal modifications of those presented by Nelson.

QUESTIONS

1. What is marketing strategy? How does the perspective of strategy differ in consumer behavior from others?
2. Define influence. Contrast influence and persuasion. Contrast influence and manipulation. What does each have to do with consumer behavior?
3. Discuss the restraints that affect business' ability to influence consumers. Which is more effective? Why?
4. In what way does business influence benefit consumers.
5. Discuss the purpose of business influence on consumers.
6. Explain the ways that business and personal influence are alike. Are these similarities good or bad?
7. Explain the ways that business and personal influence are dissimilar. Are these differences good or bad?
8. What is an image? How are images formed? What part do images play in consumer decision making? Explain.
9. Explain the characteristics of consumer images. Define the important types of business images, and show the importance of each.
10. Discuss the factors of business stability and change.

24

Consumer research

Marketing research and consumer research
Uses for consumer research
Sources of data
Government sources
Private sources
Company sources
Consumer sources
Research ethics
Consumer research methods
Demographic research
Customer profile based on demographic factors
What the profile shows
Cognitive research
Association tests
Recall tests
Projective tests
Scaling tests
The use of statistics

No discussion of consumer behavior can be considered adequate that does not devote some attention to consumer research. We are interested in consumer research because it is a basic tool of the business environment, and it can make marketers better servants of consumers. Thus, consideration must be given to how consumer information can be obtained and to how consumer data can be applied.

MARKETING RESEARCH AND CONSUMER RESEARCH

In its broadest sense, research is the search for truth. Marketing research is the search for truth about marketing. Marketing research is defined as:

> *the gathering, recording, and analyzing of facts about problems relating to the transfer and sale of goods and services.*[1]

Consumer research seeks truth about consumers. Thus consumer research is a subclass of marketing research.[2] Consumer research is defined as:

> *the gathering, recording and analyzing of facts about problems relating to final household consumers.*

Consumer research attempts to discover the essential nature of individuals and groups in the market—their numbers, location, characteristics, needs, motives, decision processes, and actions. Nearly every section of our society can benefit from a greater knowledge of consumers. Government can use consumer research as a basis for devising better laws to protect consumers in the market. Consumer groups need a better understanding of purchase behavior in order to help people buy more efficiently. Business needs consumer information as a basis for its marketing strategy.

There are various ways that consumer research can benefit business.[3] The scientific method, upon which all consumer research is based, provides system to the analysis of consumer problems. Then, too, consumer facts provide a sounder basis for action than hunches or guesses. Even good executives cannot always make sense out of facts. Thus, wrong decisions can result even when facts are available, but the chances of wrong decisions are reduced. Martilla and Carvey identify four common problems that result in poor research. They are:

1. Using interval scale statistics for ordinal scale data.
2. Equating statistical significance and practical importance.
3. Interpreting confidence intervals as measures of total research error.
4. Employing false criteria for causality.[4]

Even with these problems, research does tend to assure that consumers receive adequate attention from executives. It is difficult to ignore research when it is available, and most executives are aware of a shortage of information upon which to decide. These executives are not likely to pass up available data. Finally, the availability of data suggests to managers solutions to consumer problems that they would otherwise defer or fail to recognize. Even so, there is the question of how much research is enough.[5]

USES FOR CONSUMER RESEARCH

Consumer research has many uses. The most important one is determination of the drives that cause people to buy. However, this is not the only application. Some of the more important uses are classified below.

A. Nature of markets
   1. Customer location
   2. Customer characteristics
   3. Customer change
   4. Market comparisons
   5. Determine market potentials
   6. Estimate sales
B. Motivation
   1. Analyze motives for purchase
   2. Evaluate factors influencing motives
   3. Establish motives behind product and store preferences
   4. Analyze motives for shopping and comparing products
C. Attitudes
   1. Establish attitude toward store
   2. Establish attitude toward product brand
   3. Determine problems of consumer dissatisfaction
   4. Analyze relative strength of attitudes
   5. Determine store image
   6. Determine product image
   7. Analyze attitude toward distance traveled to shop
   8. Evaluate attitude toward purchase planning
D. Preference
   1. Determine store preferences
   2. Determine product preferences
   3. Estimate store loyalty
   4. Estimate product loyalty
   5. Establish trade area preferences
   6. Determine purchase frequency

E. Intentions
   1. Estimate purchase intentions
   2. Analyze relationships between aspirations and purchase intent
   3. Determine degree of intent realization

SOURCES OF DATA

There are a great many sources of data available for consumer research. These sources can be grouped under the following headings: (1) government sources, (2) private sources, (3) company sources, and (4) consumer sources. Some of the most important sources in each category are summarized in the following paragraphs.

Government sources

The federal government is a most fertile ground for consumer information. Of particular interest to managers is the *Census of Population,* which contains data on population, population characteristics, and income. These data are subdivided by U.S. totals, states, standard metropolitan areas, counties, and cities. Other vital sources are the *Census of Business: Retail Trade* and the *Census of Business: Service Industries.* These two publications have data on number of stores, employment, and sales for a large number of product categories. The data are subdivided in the same manner as in the *Census of Population.* Three other general information sources are: the *Statistical Abstract of the United States,* the *City County Data Book,* and the *Survey of Current Business.* Each issue of the *Abstract* contains a "Bibliography of Sources of Statistics."

Private sources

One of the most important private sources of consumer statistics is *Sales Management: The Magazine of Marketing,* a semimonthly publication aimed at business. Each year a special spring issue of *Sales Management* presents selected data comparable to that in the *Census of Business* (made available every five years in years ending with 2 and 7), and *Census of Population* (available every ten years). Another source is the *Life Study of Consumer Expenditures,* which has a large number of consumer statistics based on the years 1960–61. *Chain Store Age, Advertising Age,* and *Marketing Communications* (formerly *Printers' Ink*) are examples of periodicals that carry articles for businessmen. These publications often have articles dealing with consumers. The major marketing journals include the *Journal of Mar-*

keting, the *Journal of Retailing,* and the *Journal of Marketing Research.*

Company sources

Most business firms have a wealth of information about consumers available in their own records. Very often this information is overlooked, or it is not put to full use by the company. The first place to begin searching for answers to any problem is in company records. Company sources include (1) credit records, (2) inventory records, (3) sales slips and tapes, (4) credit application records, and (5) accounting records.

We wish to say a word about the use of credit and sales records as sources of customer information. For firms selling on credit, this source should not be overlooked.[6] Typically, the credit application records of a company contain information on the customer—name, residence, occupation, income, marital status, sex, age, and payment record. The sales slips usually have information on type of merchandise sold, price, quantity sold, date sold, selling department, and/or name of salesperson. This information is exactly the type included later in this chapter on the customer profile. It is, therefore, possible for the store to construct profile data using these two prime information sources.

Consumer sources

No source of consumer information is more important than consumers themselves. This source requires original research directed at some sample of consumers.[7] Most consumer analysis that deals with motivation and attitudes must be obtained directly from these consumers. A considerable proportion of this chapter is devoted to explaining methods of obtaining data directly from consumers.

RESEARCH ETHICS

There has been increased concern in recent years about government, business, and private agencies prying into the private lives of citizens. The concern is greatest when some agency elicits information without the individual's knowledge. It is possible for researchers to use hidden tape recorders, microphones, one-way mirrors, disguised questionnaires, etc. to obtain consumer information.[8] There is evidence that such techniques are currently being used by marketing executives, and the question of ethics is being asked.

It is felt that any attempt to gain information directly from an individual without the individual's knowledge is unethical. An exception may be made for purely observational type activity. However, there does not appear to be anything ethically wrong with using raw data collected with consent for a variety of purposes not specifically stated to the respondent. For example, asking questions about purchase behavior when the researcher is actually interested in the return rate of questionnaires. A recent survey of executives found they were generally opposed to the use of ultraviolet ink, hidden tape recorders, and one-way mirrors for research purposes.[9] It was discovered that line managers were more tolerant of these methods than were the researchers. This probably reflects the line managers need for information which is often scarce.

CONSUMER RESEARCH METHODS

Consumer research is a much broader area of study than is often realized. There is a tendency to equate consumer research with motivation research, but, whereas motivation research concerns why consumers do certain things or act in some specified manner, consumer research concerns all the vital aspects of understanding consumers. Consumer research can be classified into broad methods according to the nature of the research: (1) demographic research and (2) cognitive or motivation research.

Demographic research deals with vital statistics about consumers—their numbers, location, sex, occupation, income, age, ethnic group, and marital status.[10] It attempts to chronicle what consumers are in terms of observable attributes. Primarily concerned with nose counting, this type of research is easily quantifiable. The importance of demographic studies cannot be overestimated. Some of our most important work on consumer behavior has developed from such studies.

Cognitive, or what was historically termed motivation research, deals with a consumer's mental process and his or her relationship to his environment.[11] Cognitive research deals with the consumer's mental processes—attitudes, perception, motivation, personality, learning, communications, beliefs, and convictions. It also relates the consumer's mental processes to the environment by means of investigation of social class, group influence, culture, and family operation. Cognitive research also deals with the consumer decision processes. Boyd and Westfall said, "Research on motivation is not limited to any specific type of behavior, but includes the entire area of human behavior that may be related to marketing."[12]

Cognitive studies attempt to get below the surface of observable attributes and discover why consumers behave in specific ways. Cognitive research concerns the recognition, classification, and evaluation of the fundamental motivating forces manifest in consumer behavior. Consumer motives, perceptions, beliefs, etc. are difficult to quantify, and research in this area depends heavily on judgment.

DEMOGRAPHIC RESEARCH

Demographic research is usually based on secondary data, most of which are furnished by government sources. Demographic data are often used as a basis for classifying motivational information. For example, consumer product preferences may be classified by age, sex, or income. It may be useful to classify consumer attitudes toward advertisements by region or occupation. Brand loyalty of customers can be meaningfully analyzed by age groups. Since the next section of the book deals with demographic data, there is no need to spend more time on the subject at this point. We will limit our discussion here to an example showing how a retail store manager may effectively use demographic data.

Customer profile based on demographic factors

A customer profile is a composite picture of the firm's market based on some customer characteristic. Table 24–1 offers a customer profile

Table 24–1
Profile of customers for a hypothetical retail store

	Marital status (percent)			*Occupation (percent)*		
Age, income, and sex	*Living with spouse*	*Not living with spouse*	*Totals*	*Blue collar*	*White collar*	*Totals*
Age						
Under 30	13	17	30	18	12	30
30–45	45	5	50	17	33	50
46–60	9	2	11	8	3	11
Over 60	3	6	9	4	5	9
Total	70	30	100	47	53	100
Income						
Less than $5,000	4	9.0	13.0	10.0	3.0	13.0
$5,000–$9,999	57	17.0	74.0	36.5	37.5	74.0
$10,000–$15,000	8	3.5	11.5	0.5	11.0	11.5
Above $15,000	1	0.5	1.5	0	1.5	1.5
Total	70	30.0	100.0	47.0	53.0	100.0
Sex						
Male	25	15	40	23	17	40
Female	45	15	60	24	36	60
Total	70	30	100	47	53	100

Source: Thomas Greer and Glenn Walters, "The Effective Use of Credit Records," *Northwest Business Management*, vol. 4, no. 1 (Fall 1966), p. 3.

based on selected demographic factors for a retail firm. The profile is nothing more than a convenient way of summarizing demographic data. The data are usually expressed in percentage form so that comparisons can be easily made. In our illustration, age, income, and sex are compared to marital status and occupation. By using such information, we can tell, for example, the proportion of our customers of different marital status and occupation that are in each age group.

What the profile shows

Once the customer profile is summarized, the retail manager can tell at a glance the types of customers that potentially compose his or her market segment.[13] An evaluation of Table 24–1 shows that most customers are married females between 30 and 45 years of age. They are white-collar workers and earn between $5,000 and $9,999 per year. Given this picture of what most of his customers are like, the retail store management can plan a basic product, price, and service assortment. Decisions can be made on the width and depth of merchandise lines, the amount of current fashion in the merchandise, the advertising appeals, brands, and prices that would be most consistent with the characteristics of the majority of the store's customers.

The profile also provides the retailer with clues on how to vary the basic assortment in order to account for individual preferences.[14] For example, in the hypothetical retail store, some provision should be made to give special attention to single and male customers, since 40 percent of the store's potential customers are male and 30 percent are single. Furthermore, since 13 percent of this market earns $10,000 or more, policies should be developed to appeal to the needs of the higher-income customers. A detailed analysis using more characteristics can point up other opportunities.

COGNITIVE RESEARCH

Because demographic data are more readily available and easier to quantify, we seem to know more about *how* consumers behave than we do about *why* they behave as they do.[15] Yet we can never hope to understand consumers until we get at the reasons which underly their actions. This fact, no doubt, accounts for the upsurgence of motivation research in recent years.

Cognitive research can be divided into four types according to the nature of the response required from the consumer: (1) association tests, (2) recall tests, (3) projective tests, and (4) scaling tests.

Association tests

Association tests are among the oldest tests of motivation, and they are simple to administer. All association tests are based on the idea that a proper stimulus leads to an immediate response. The respondent is asked to respond to a series of key words or ideas with the first thought that comes to mind. These words are those associated with the product or service about which information is desired. In addition, a number of unrelated words are included which provide concealment and make responses easier. By carefully structuring the sequence of words or phrases, a rhythm is established so that the responses become automatic. In this way, it is felt that the inner motives of the respondent can be brought out. The most important types of association tests are the free word association, successive word association, and sentence completion tests.

Association tests can be very useful for a variety of marketing problems. They can be used to determine consumer attitudes toward products, stores, advertising appeals, product features, store services, and store personnel. In short, the technique can be used in any instance where attempts are made to determine consumer attitudes.

Free word association. Free word association involves presenting the respondent with a series of words one at a time.[16] The subject responds freely to each word presented with the first word that comes to mind. The group of words presented to the respondent usually contains some *neutral* and some *stimulus* words. The stimulus words pertain to the study, the neutral words do not. For example, in a study of margarine or cooking-oil purchasing, key words included might be *health, cholesterol, convenient, butter, cost,* and so on. As each word is read, the time it takes the respondent to answer is recorded. Thus, the researcher can determine which responses are automatic and which are reasoned. Of course, the researcher is looking for automatic or free responses. The respondent is not allowed to write replies, because this gives time to think. The researcher may write the answers or check them off from a prepared list of typical replies.

Although the collection of data is simple using the free word association technique, the interpretation of results is not.[17] The typical method of tabulating results is to divide responses by frequency of occurrence into typical responses, thought-out responses, and nonresponses. Thought-out responses and nonresponses are useful only to the extent that they denote resistance to answer or indecision or weak attitudes toward the subject. Typical responses are usually further categorized by type to indicate respondent attitudes.

Successive word association. Successive word association is the same as free word association except that instead of asking for a single-word response, a series of single-word responses are sought for each word asked. The respondent may be asked to give the first three or four words that come to mind. These words are ranked in order by the researcher. It is felt that this technique can obtain information on several layers of responses. The data are analyzed in the same manner as for free word association.

Controlled word association is a variation used to measure the impact of advertising. Vicary asked a cross section of adults to name the first business that came to their minds when such words as *hotel, bread, bank, house paint,* and *dairy,* were presented. The words were then rearranged, and the same question was asked, followed by a list of the agency's clients. The association of products and services with certain advertisers was obtained as well as the linking of advertisers with products and services.

Sentence completion test. The sentence completion test is also similar to the free word association test. The main difference is that the respondent is given a series of incomplete statements designed to evoke responses about a particular subject rather than single words. Also, since the answers can be written, the respondent has some time to think about the reply.

The respondent is asked to complete the sentences with the first "idea" that comes to mind. In comparing margarine and butter, one might state, "A housewife using margarine instead of butter is . . . . ," or "The healthfulness of margarine is . . . ." The sentence completion test may give more information about the respondent's inner feelings, since he or she has a chance to qualify statements, but it does give the respondent an opportunity to consider the answer. In order to adjust to this factor, the subject is timed. Responses that take too long are classified as "thought out."

Recall tests

Recall tests are based on the assumption that people can accurately remember the past. The test is designed to induce the respondent to remember and report on some past emotion, attitude, response, or behavior, or some past event in which the respondent played a part. Recall tests may be either verbal or written, and are of four principal types: (1) written questionnaire, (2) depth interview, (3) focused group interview, and (4) behavior sampling.

Written questionnaire. The written questionnaire is based on a standard list of questions about some subject.[18] Little attempt is made to disguise the purpose of the questions. The respondent is usually asked to select the best answer to each question from a group of alternatives, and each question seeks one complete attitude or belief.

The questionnaire can be made more selective by designing sequence questions which give different perspectives on the same attitude or belief. In this way some idea of the degree, intensity, or consistency of beliefs can be obtained. Sequence questions are scored as a group, and the important consideration is the pattern of response rather than the answer to a single question. A large number of different types of questions can be employed in a questionnaire to determine respondent attitude. Questions may range from simple "yes-no" types up to very complex rankings of preferences. In any case, the questionnaire is a very flexible means of investigating consumer attitudes and beliefs.[19]

Depth interview. The depth interview as used in consumer research is an adaptation of the method employed by clinical psychologists. It is simple to describe, difficult to practice. Depth interviewing is not usually undertaken without the services of highly trained interviewers.

The interviewer makes the respondent as comfortable and relaxed as possible. He or she then asks many questions about the subject, product, or problem under investigation. The order of questioning is determined as the interview progresses and fruitful avenues for investigation arise. The questions are usually indirect, but designed to evoke responses, and the respondent is prompted to give as much detail as possible. The interviewer either types the interview or makes notes. These records become the basis for the analysis of findings. The researcher may spend hours or days analyzing the results before reaching final conclusions.

Depth interviewing is designed to obtain a large amount of information about a limited subject.[20] Its greatest market use is for determining underlying reasons or motives that help explain buyer behavior. The major problems with depth interviewing are: Few quantifiable results are obtained; it lacks structure; and it is difficult to obtain qualified researchers.

Focused group interview. The focused group interview is similar to the depth interview, but it differs on two counts.[21] First, several people are involved. Second, the focused group interview depends largely on the interaction of ideas between members of the group. The basic concept of depth interviewing is followed in the group interview. A group of typical consumers is brought together and prompted, by questioning, to provide detailed information on their feelings or attitudes or beliefs about some product or problem. Group depth interviews have been used to explore corporate image, political issues, container design, advertising themes, and new-product research. The results are recorded and analyzed in much the same manner as with depth interviewing.

Behavior sampling. In behavior sampling, the respondent is asked to relive certain specified buyer situations. The respondent is placed in a relaxed atmosphere and asked to recall every detail involved with the buyer situation under study. Even seemingly irrelevant information, such as the time of day or the color of the sky, are sought. It may be that some seemingly unimportant factors were actually crucial in the purchase decision.

Behavior sampling is useful for analyzing the buyer's decision processes and for determining the factor of buyer influence and the sequence of activities involved in purchasing.

Projective tests

Projective tests operate on the simple principle that a person will answer more freely and truthfully if relieved of direct responsibility for personal expressions.[22] Motives exist which are below the respondent's level of verbalization, and these motives are related to the decision to purchase or not to purchase. However, they can only be identified by approaching them indirectly. Thus, the problem is to have respondents project themselves into someone else's place or into some ambiguous situation. The respondent is then asked to give meaning to the other person's actions or to the situation. The response is unstructured, and the respondent is asked only to answer in any way that seems appropriate.

Projective techniques are designed to break through the bias and natural desire for secrecy felt by most people and to get down to the bedrock of human emotions. The purpose is to uncover the unconscious motivation of human behavior. Like most techniques that delve below the level of human consciousness, projective techniques require highly trained personnel. Problems arise in administering the test and in interpreting the results of unstructured answers. Particular problems are the overemphasis of projective techniques to the exclusion of other methods.

Pictorial projectives. Several pictorial methods are used in the projective method. The three most popular are the Rorschach inkblot test, the thematic apperception test, and cartoons.

The *Rorschach test* is a device used primarily in clinical psychology. A series of non-structured "pictures" composed of inkblots are shown to the respondent. The subject is asked to explain what he or she sees in the picture. Evidence demonstrates that persons will project their own personality into explaining the blots. The organization that the subject imposes upon an unstructured form is revealing of underlying personality structure.

The *thematic apperception test* (TAT) provides the subject with a series of ambiguous pictures, which the subject is asked to explain. The respondent may be asked such things as what conditions gave rise to the situation, what is happening, and what the outcome will be. The assumption is that in explaining the picture, subjects will tell something about themselves. This occurs because subjects are asked to tell a story about a picture where few clues are available. This means that they must resort to their own experience and imagination. The theory behind such a technique rests on the assumption that when persons are called upon to structure an unstructured or ambiguous situation, it is necessary for them to rely on their own personality attributes. The TAT test is useful for obtaining customer reaction to products or product features and for gaining insight into the personality or personality traits of individuals in social situations.

A variation of the TAT method is found in the use of cartoons (Fig. 24–1). The principle is the same, but cartoons are simpler and easier to administer and interpret. The respondent is shown an ambiguous cartoon—for example, the one shown in Figure 24–1. One housewife

Figure 24–1

WHAT DO YOU THINK
OF SAMUEL'S DEPARTMENT
STORE?

asks, "What do you think of Samuel's Department Store?" The respondent is asked to give the reply of the other housewife. Like the TAT, the cartoon projective uses an indirect approach to get at basic human traits, feelings, and attitudes.

Other similar projective techniques include attitude batteries, psychodrama, puppetry, and finger painting. Most of these methods vary only in the manner in which the information is gathered.

Verbal projectives. The difference between verbal and pictorial projectives is in the use of words instead of pictures to describe a social situation. The basic technique is to describe a product, situation, or problem and ask the respondent what others would do under the described circumstances. For example, in a now famous and classic case, an auto manufacturer asked people what *they* wanted in a car. The answer came back that these people wanted a safe, functional, conservative car. When this same manufacturer asked respondents what *their neighbors* wanted in a car, they obtained a different answer. People said their neighbors wanted a flashy car with lots of chrome, horsepower, and style. Very few respondents, in this case, mentioned safety.

Scaling tests

A more recent innovation in cognitive research is the use of scales to rate or rank consumer attitudes.[23] As we have indicated, it is practically useless to ask people direct questions about their attitudes because none of us fully understands these attitudes. Since attitudes are not directly observable, some indirect method is needed to get at an understanding of feelings, beliefs, and attitudes. Rating scales have proved to be a useful device for researching consumer attitudes, cognitions, and dissonance.[24]

The basic idea behind all rating scales is that respondents can rate themselves along some attitude continuum. Scales can be conveniently divided into four major types: bipolar or unstructured scales, Likert or summated scales, Thurstone or equal-appearing interval scales, and semantic differentials or paired-word comparisons.[25]

Bipolar scales. The simplest of all scales is an unstructured bipolar scale. In this type of scale, the respondents are asked to rate themselves with respect to two bipolar factors.[26] For example, a respondent may be asked, "Do you feel the majority of TV advertising is honest or dishonest?" The respondents, in answering the question, are classified into two categories—those who believe TV advertising is honest and those who believe TV advertising is dishonest.

The unstructured scale is very flexible. Almost any type of question can be asked, and, should the researcher desire more detail about a given attitude, a sequence of questions bearing on the point can be asked. Another variation is to ask open-end questions. For example, we could ask, "What do you feel about the honesty of TV advertising?" In this manner we would receive a variety of answers that could be ranked into several categories by the intensity of the attitude expressed.

Likert (summated) scales. Likert scales involve three considerations.[27] First, a group of statements about some subject is constructed, such as the following statements about candy:

1. Candy provides energy.
2. Candy is fattening.
3. Candy causes tooth decay.
4. Candy tastes good.
5. Candy is messy.

Each of these statements has about equal attitude value. Second, a group of agreement-disagreement responses is provided:

1. Strong agreement.
2. Agreement.
3. Undecided.
4. Disagreement.
5. Strong disagreement.

The responses are given numerical values as indicated. Third, a respondent is asked to match the statement to the number of the response that most nearly expresses his or her attitude.

The responses are summed based on the numbers 1 to 5. The sum total of all responses is the score for each respondent. In the example described, low scores indicate agreement with the statements, and high scores indicate disagreement. Cohen offers an example of the use of a Likert scale in his study of the relationship between consumer market behavior and complaint, aggression, and detached interpersonal orientations.

Thurstone (equal-appearing interval) scales. The Thurstone method recognizes the difficulty in assigning quantitative values to highly qualitative attitudes.[28] The method assumes that a person can tell the difference between attitudes represented by widely varying statements.

In practice, the Thurstone method is similar to the Likert method.[29] A large number of statements about a subject is collected, judged, and sorted into 11 piles.[30] The piles are arranged in descending order beginning with favorable statements, to a neutral statement at position 6, and continuing with increasingly unfavorable statements to position 11. A three-position list of statements about student attitude toward teachers is:

1. Teachers are the most important ingredient in the educational process.
2. Teachers don't add to education but they don't interfere with education.
3. Teachers are the greatest barrier to education.

Respondents are asked to agree or disagree with each statement. Logically, if the scale is a good one, the respondent's choices should cluster around those positions that more nearly reflect his or her attitude toward the subject. The individual's score is usually computed as the median of the positions with which he or she agrees. In the Thurston scale, the lower the score the more positive the attitude toward the subject.

Semantic differentials. The use of semantic differentials is increasing in importance in marketing.[31] This method has a variety of uses, but it is presently more important in the study of store and brand images, store loyalty, and in attitude research.[32] The semantic differential is based on a series of bipolar scales like the ones depicting the product and company image for beer shown in Figures 24–2 and 24–3.

There are seven positions designated on the scale between such bipolar words as good—bad or like—dislike.[33] The fourth position can be considered a neutral position on any positive-negative scale since it divides the scale equally and there are three positions for bad and three positions for good. Respondents are asked to place a check by the

Figure 24–2
Specific product image

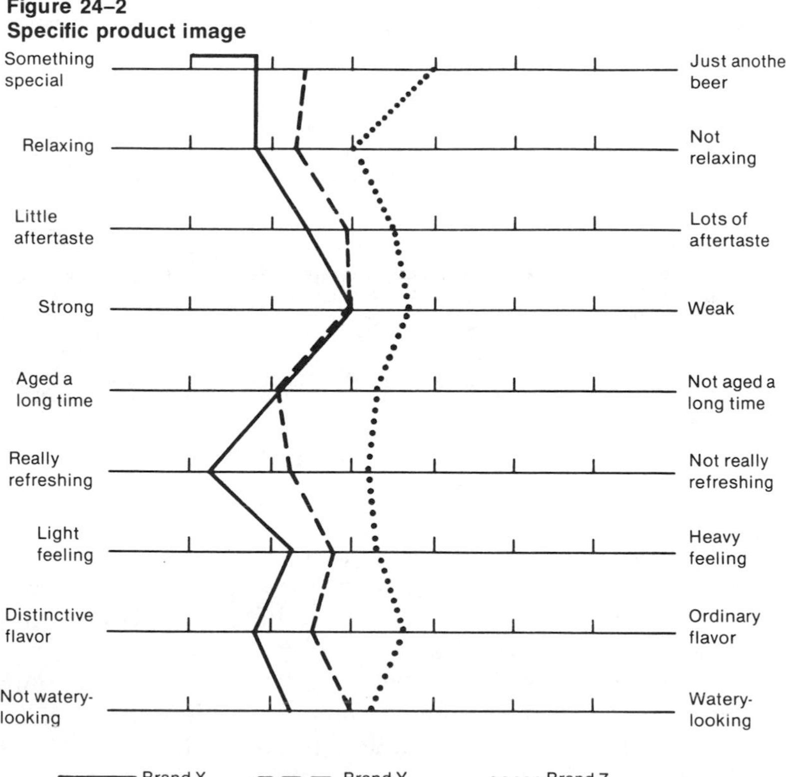

Source: William A. Mindak, "Fitting the Semantic Differential to the Marketing Problem," *Journal of Marketing*, vol. 25 (April 1961). Reprinted by permission of the American Marketing Association.

Figure 24–3
Company image

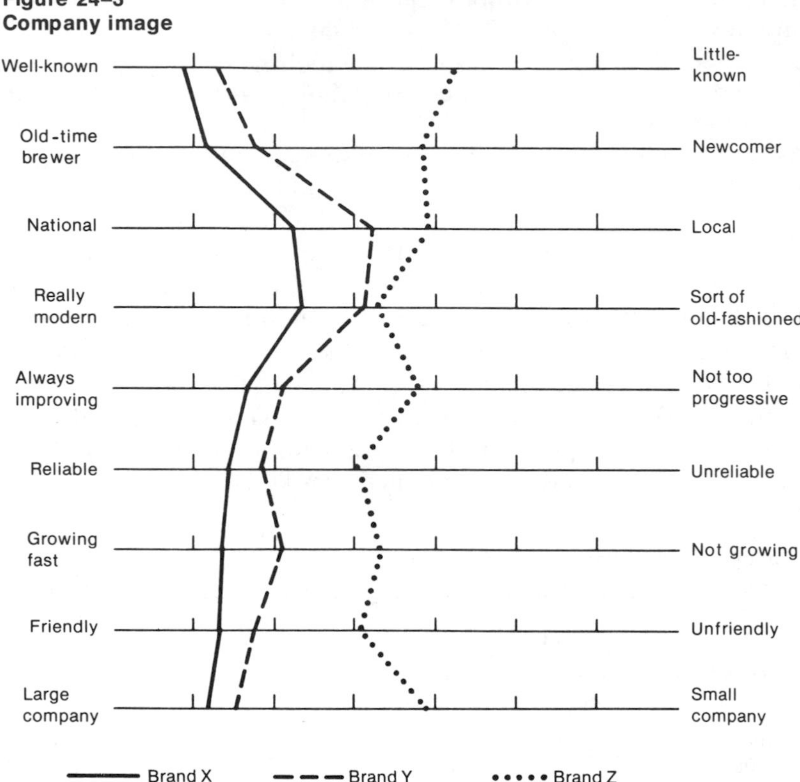

Source: William A. Mindak, "Fitting the Semantic Differential to the Marketing Problem," *Journal of Marketing*, vol. 25 (April 1961). Reprinted by permission of the American Marketing Association.

position that most nearly describes their attitude toward the product, store, or subject under investigation. A line connecting each of the points provides the researcher with a composite picture of the respondent's attitudes toward the subject. Figures 24–2 and 24–3 show composites.

A seven-position scale has been historically used in defining semantic differential scales, but actually there is nothing magic about the number.[34] Five- or three-position scales could just as easily be used, since any odd number provides a neutral point of reference. Some researchers have even used even-numbered scales. An even number of positions has the advantage of forcing the respondent to take a stand because there is no neutral position. It is often found with the seven-position scale that answers tend to congregate at the neutral position. Of course, forcing respondents to take a positive or a negative position may distort the results if the respondents are really neutral in their attitude. There is no reason why any scale is necessary. The respondent can simply be given the two bipolar words and asked to indicate which word more nearly described his or her attitude.

THE USE OF STATISTICS

The discussion of consumer research presented here has been limited to some of the more important methods of obtaining the information. It is beyond the scope of a book such as this to develop either the methodology or the specific statistical techniques necessary to conduct consumer research. It is felt there is a great need for a book on this particular subject. However, for those who are interested in further investigation of consumer research, we take this opportunity to mention some of the more important statistical techniques currently in use.

One important technique is multidimensional scaling which depicts respondent's similarities and preference judgments as points in geometric space.[35] Another, and even more popular, tool is multivariate analysis which involves the use of factor analysis and discriminant analysis. This type of analysis makes it possible to handle the multitude of intervening factors that affect any analysis.[36] Cluster analysis concerns ways of grouping multivariate profiles. Canonical analysis is also becoming popular. Canonical analysis has three objectives. They are: (1) to determine vectors of weights for each set of variables, (2) to determine independence between two sets of variables, and (3) to explain the nature of relationships.[37] It must be made clear to the reader that these are all highly complex statistical techniques involving the classification and evaluation of masses of data. None of these techniques could be employed without the computer, and it is an integral part of any modern consumer research.[38]

Of course, the problem with any technique is that it is no better than the person behind it. Sometimes it is possible to become so involved with the technique that the goal of understanding consumer behavior is forgotten.[39] It is encouraging that the tools of the consumer behavior researcher continue to improve, and the results of analysis show the improvement.

NOTES

1. R. S. Alexander, Chairman, "Report of the Definitions Committee," *Journal of Marketing*, vol. 7 (October 1948), p. 210.
2. Gerald Zaltman and Philip C. Burger, *Marketing Research: Fundamentals and Dynamics* (Hinsdale, Ill.: The Dryden Press, 1975), Chap. 5.
3. John A. Howard, "Buyer Behavior and Related Technological Advances," *Journal of Marketing*, vol. 34 (January 1970), pp. 18–21.
4. John A. Martilla and Davis W. Carvey, "Four Subtle Sins in Marketing Research," *Journal of Marketing*, vol. 39 (January 1975), pp. 8–15.

5. John J. Wheatley, "Research Methodology—How Much Emphasis?" *Journal of Marketing,* vol. 37 (April 1973), pp. 58–59.

6. Thomas V. Greer and Charles G. Walters, "Credit Records: Information Tool for Planning," *Journal of Retailing,* vol. 42 (Spring 1966), pp. 11–18.

7. Peter Hodgson, "Sampling Racial Minority Groups," *Journal of the Market Research Society,* vol. 17 (April 1975), pp. 104–06.

8. C. Merle Crawford, "Attitudes of Marketing Executives Toward Ethics in Marketing Research," *Journal of Marketing,* vol. 34 (April 1970), pp. 46–52; Robert L. Day, "A Comment on 'Ethics in Marketing Research'," *Journal of Marketing Research,* vol. 12 (May 1975), pp. 232–33; Alice M. Tybout and Gerald Zaltman, "A Reply to Comments on 'Ethics in Marketing Research: Their Practical Relevance'," *Journal of Marketing Research,* vol. 12 (May 1975), pp. 234–37.

9. Ibid.

10. Donald S. Tull and Del I. Hawkins, *Marketing Research: Meaning, Measurement, and Method* (New York: Macmillan Publishing Co., Inc., 1976), Chap. 15.

11. See: Robert J. Holloway, Robert A. Mittelstaedt, and M. Venkatesan, eds., *Consumer Behavior: Contemporary Research in Action* (Boston: Houghton Mifflin Co., 1971); Stuart Henderson Britt, ed. *Psychological Experiments in Consumer Behavior* (New York: John Wiley & Sons, Inc., 1970); David T. Kollat, Roger D. Blackwell, and James F. Engel, eds. *Research in Consumer Behavior* (New York: Holt, Rinehart & Winston, Inc., 1970).

12. Harper W. Boyd, Jr., and Ralph Westfall, *Marketing Research: Text and Cases,* 3d ed. (Homewood, Ill.: Richard D. Irwin, Inc., 1972), p. 617.

13. M. S. Moyer, "Market Intelligence for Modern Merchants," *California Management Review,* vol. 14 (Summer 1972), pp. 63–69.

14. Kit G. Narodick, "What Motivates the Consumer's Choice of an Airline?" *Journal of Retailing,* vol. 48 (Spring 1972), pp. 30–38.

15. Nariman K. Dhalla and Winston H. Mahotoo, "Expanding the Scope of Segmentation Research," *Journal of Marketing,* vol. 40 (April 1976), pp. 34–41.

16. Paul E. Green, Yoram Wind, and Arun K. Jain, "Analyzing Free-Response Data in Marketing Research," *Journal of Marketing Research,* vol. 10 (February 1973), pp. 45–52.

17. Ibid.

18. John J. Wheatley, "Self-Administered Written Questionnaires or Telephone Interviews?" *Journal of Marketing Research,* vol. 10 (February 1973), pp. 94–96.

19. A. Marvin Roscoe, Dorothy Lang, and Jagdish N. Sheth, "Follow-up Methods, Questionnaire Length, and Market Differences in Mail Surveys," *Journal of Marketing,* vol. 39 (April 1975), pp. 20–27.

20. Laurence Siegel and Irving M. Lane, *Psychology in Industrial Organizations* (Homewood, Ill.: Richard D. Irwin, Inc., 1974), pp. 442–45.

21. Keith K. Cox, James B. Higginbotham, and John Burton, "Applications of Focus Group Interviews in Marketing," *Journal of Marketing,* vol. 40 (January 1976), pp. 77–80.

22. William A. Yoell, "The Fallacy of Projective Techniques," *Journal of Advertising,* vol. 3 (1974), pp. 33–35.

23. Paul E. Green and Vithala R. Rao, "Configuration Synthesis in Multidimensional Scaling," *Journal of Marketing Research,* vol. 9 (February 1972), pp. 65–68.

24. William J. Lundstrom and Lawrence M. Lamont, "The Development of a Scale to Measure Consumer Discontent," *Journal of Marketing Research,* vol. 13 (November 1976), pp. 373–81; Tull and Hawkins, *Marketing Research: Meaning, Measurement, and Method,* Chap. 10.

25. Green and Rao, "Multidimensional Scaling and Individual Differences," pp. 71–77.

26. Edward J. Lusk, "A Bipolar Adjective Screening Methodology," *Journal of Marketing Research,* vol. 10 (May 1973), pp. 202–03.

27. For the basic work in the field, see Rensis Likert, "A Technique for the Measurement of Attitudes," *Archives of Psychology,* vol. 22 (June 1932), p. 55. Further material is presented in G. Murphy and Rensis Likert, *Public Opinion and the Individual* (New York: Harper & Bros., 1938), p. 316.

28. L. Thurstone and E. Chase, *The Measurement of Attitudes* (Chicago: University of Chicago Press, 1929).

29. However, differences do exist. For a comparison between the two, see L. W. Ferguson, "A Study of the Likert Technique of Attitude Scale Construction," *Journal of Social Psychology,* vol. 13 (February 1941), pp. 51–57.

30. Thurstone originally used 11 positions, and this number is still common. Actually, any odd number of positions is sufficient for analysis.

31. Del I. Hawkins, Gerald Albaum, and Roger Best, "Stapel Scale or Semantic Differential in Marketing Research?" *Journal of Marketing Research,* vol. 11 (August 1974), pp. 318–22; Ronald F. Bush and Joseph F. Hair, Jr., "Consumer Patronage Determinants of Discount Versus Conventional Motels," *Journal of Retailing,* vol. 52 (Summer 1976), pp. 41–50.

32. William A. Mindak, "Fitting the Semantic Differential to the Marketing Problem," *Journal of Marketing,* vol. 25 (April 1961), pp. 28–33.

33. John Dickson and Gerald Albaum, "A Method for Developing Tailormade Semantic Differentials for Specific Marketing Content Areas," *Journal of Marketing Research,* vol. 14 (February 1977), pp. 87–91.

34. James Hulbert, "Information Processing Capacity and Attitude Measurement," *Journal of Marketing Research,* vol. 12 (February 1975), pp. 104–06; Warren S. Martin, "The Effects of Scaling on the Correlation Coefficient: A Test of Validity," *Journal of Marketing Research,* vol. 10 (August 1973), pp. 316–18.

35. Paul E. Green, "Measurement and Data Analysis," *Journal of Marketing*, vol. 34 (January 1970), pp. 15–17; Howard, "Buyer Behavior and Related Technological Advances," pp. 18–21.

36. Jagdish N. Sheth, "The Multivariate Revolution in Marketing Research," *Journal of Marketing*, vol. 35 (January 1971), pp. 13–19; David L. Sparks and W. T. Tucker, "A Multivariate Analysis of Personality and Product Use," *Journal of Marketing Research*, vol. 8 (February 1971), pp. 67–70.

37. Mark I. Alpert and Robert A. Peterson, "On the Interpretation of Canonical Analysis," *Journal of Marketing Research*, vol. 9 (May 1972), pp. 187–92.

38. Lloyd M. DeBoer and William H. Ward, "Integration of the Computer into Salesman Reporting," *Journal of Marketing*, vol. 35 (January 1971), pp. 41–47; George Fisk, "Computer-Aided Marketing Instruction," *Journal of Marketing*, vol. 35 (January 1971), pp. 20–27.

39. Purnall H. Benson, "How Many Scales and How Many Categories Shall We Use in Consumer Research?—A Comment," *Journal of Marketing*, vol. 35 (October 1971), pp. 59–61; Paul E. Green and Vithala R. Rao, "A Rejoinder to 'How Many Scales and How Many Categories Shall We Use in Consumer Research?—A Comment'," *Journal of Marketing*, vol. 35 (October 1971), pp. 61–72.

QUESTIONS

1. Define marketing research. Define consumer research. Contrast the two types of research. What is the importance of consumer research?
2. Discuss and illustrate some of the more important uses for consumer research.
3. What are the two major methods of conducting consumer research? Define and contrast demographic and cognitive research. Which is more important? Explain.
4. Explain and illustrate a consumer profile. Discuss the possible uses for such a profile.
5. Define association tests. What is a free word and successive word association? Explain, illustrate, and contrast.
6. How does a recall test differ from an association test? Define a recall test. Discuss the use of written questionnaire and depth interview. Illustrate the use of each.
7. Define projective tests. Contrast projectives, recall tests, and association tests. How are Rorschach tests used? How are Thematic apperception tests used?
8. Discuss the use and meaning of verbal projectives.
9. What is meant by scaling tests? How are bipolar scales used? In what way does the nature and use of Likert scales differ from bipolar scales?
10. Define semantic differential. How is the semantic differential used? Explain and illustrate the use of the semantic differential.

25

The consumer's product image

We discussed in Chapter 23 the fact that business firms influence consumers to purchase the products they sell. Consumers spend their income for these products, and it is from the use of them that the consumer derives satisfaction. Business influence may be said to begin with the product. In this chapter, we want to take a close look at products and the role played by the products themselves in shaping consumer behavior.

THE NATURE OF PRODUCT INFLUENCE

Product can refer to different things according to the perspective taken. The engineer sees a product as a set of engineering specifications, and the accountant sees a product as a group of related costs. Too often the marketer views the product as a physical thing that must be sold at all cost. From the consumer's perspective, the product may be defined as follows:

> *A product is a complex of tangible and intangible attributes, including packaging, color, price, manufacturer's prestige, retailer's prestige, and manufacturer's and retailer's services, which the buyer may accept as offering satisfaction of wants and needs.*[1]

As viewed by the consumer, a product is more than a physical thing. The attitudes taken toward products depend not only on their physical composition but also on the consumer's concept of the product. A product may be a haircut, legal advice, architectural service, lawn mower repair, or public transportation. Services are just as much products as candles, hair spray, soap, floor polish, airplanes, and electric blankets. People sacrifice income for services, and the satisfaction realized from a service may be every bit as beneficial as the satisfaction derived from a physical good. The fact is that the total product is always greater than the physical product. Every physical good has some service associated with it. The product that the consumer purchases is this physical good and the bundle of services that surround it. The nature of the total product can be changed by changing the services.

What consumers buy, and what businesses have to sell, is satisfaction. People are not interested in metal, fabric, plastic, wood, mineral, and plants per se. People are interested in what these things can do for them. It is not the thing, but the idea of the thing, that attracts consumers. A diamond is not polished carbon to the young man in love. Rather, a diamond is the gleam in his fiancee's eye. The automobile is not a combination of metal, plastic, and fabric. The automobile represents freedom, mobility, esteem, success, pride, and more. Products are simply the means necessary to achieve some desired satisfaction.

This is true whether the product is a service or a combination of physical good and service.

How the product motivates

Most promotion is meaningless unless it is based on product attributes. There are four product benefits that play a part in motivating consumers.

First, the product serves the consumer as a means of *identification*.[2] Features and design, as well as brand and package, draw attention to the product, and distinguish one product from another. Identification is necessary before purchase, and often people recognize the product when they do not know the producer. How many of us can associate more than two or three of the many consumer products made by Procter and Gamble with that company?

Second, we tend to *associate satisfaction* with the physical thing used. Thus, seldom do we think of services that surround the physical good or the seller when we consider satisfaction. We consider the producer only to the extent that the brand name and producer are the same. We think, "That was a good Bulova watch," instead of "That Bulova Company sure makes, and Sears sure distributes, a good watch." Our satisfaction is associated with the product, because most directly we receive satisfaction from the product.

Third, the product *reassures consumers* as to their judgment. Each time a person reuses a familiar product to find the same quality, it proves the soundness of the initial decision.

Fourth, products give consumers *psychic satisfaction*. A person may obtain status or prestige in the eyes of associates by owning products.

Elements of product image

Business managers build into products features designed to influence customers. Taken together these features constitute the product image. There are five elements that make up the product image: (1) product design, (2) product development, (3) brand, (4) package, and (5) price. We define these terms as follows:

1. *Product design* is a combination of the attributes, characteristics, or performance factors that constitute a product's existence. Product design is the embodiment of what a physical product is. What a product is, of course, largely determines what the product can do for the consumer.

2. *Product development* consists of the ideas, research, and engineering necessary to discover, test, and certify new products. Prod-

uct development makes it possible for the consumer to have new and different products.

3. *Brand* is any name, term, symbol, or design, or combination thereof, which identifies the good or service of one seller or a group of sellers and distinguishes them from those of competition.[3] The brand identifies the product for the consumer and relates it to the maker and to quality.

4. The *package* is the container and/or wrapper within which the product is contained. The package protects the product for the consumer and aids in identification. Packaging is closely related to brand and product design.

5. *Price* is the dollar amount the consumer must spend for the product. The price places limits on what the consumer can have and acts as a guide to product quality and desirability.

These five elements of product image are discussed in detail over the remainder of this chapter. For the sake of convenience and organization, design and development, and packaging and branding, are discussed together. We now turn to design and development.

ATTITUDES TOWARD DESIGN AND DEVELOPMENT

Product design and development affect the consumer's image because these two determine what the product can do for people, and what new and/or different products are available through innovation. The producer designs into the product specific features, or attributes, that management thinks likely to appeal to the largest number of consumers. The consumer's image of the product depends, in part, on how the product design is interpreted. Four factors have a direct bearing on the individual's interpretation of the suitability of products.

First, consumer attitudes toward products differ because of innate differences in people.[4] There is the obvious difference between men and women which leads to giving products "sex" when products have no "sex" of their own. Cigarette brands can be placed on a continuum by gender. In a study of cheese ads, it was found that respondents gave gender to the setting of the advertisements. An ad showing a wedge of cheese sitting on a brown wooden cuttingboard with black bread was thought masculine, but the same cheese shown in a setting using lighter colors and flowers led respondents to report the scene as feminine.[5] The differences between married and single people, adults and children, tall and short people, and so on, lead to different impressions of suitability.

Second, consumer tastes differ for specific product features. Even when two people agree on the suitability of a generic type of product, variations in taste cause different attitudes toward the suitability of specific product features. One consumer views a six cylinder engine in an automobile as a desirable feature because it makes the car economical to drive. Another person sees the same car as underpowered, and he or she may be concerned about passing safety in a car with a six cylinder engine.

Third, purely emotional responses of people are seldom the same. Two products are perceived differently because of emotional responses to purely superficial or nonexistent factors. A consumer may not purchase one national brand of wax beans because the color combination on the label is not pleasing to that person. Another consumer may find pleasing the equal parts of red and white used on the product of a national manufacturer of soup.

Fourth, perceptions of suitability differ among people. Product desirability is a highly abstract concept. A product deemed best from an engineering standpoint may not be considered suitable in the minds of consumers because of its high price. Another problem is that a product seen as being of high desirability in one situation may be viewed differently in another situation. A Volkswagen is a more desirable product than a Cadillac if the goal is low-cost operation. The reverse is true if the object is roadability, pretige, or comfort.

Product development and product image

Product development is a type of innovation, and most managers recognize that business must innovate or die.[6] Research and development expenditures tend to parallel the growth of sales in most companies. Thus, the importance of the effect of innovation and change on consumer attitudes can hardly be questioned. Generally, product development affects product image in two ways: (1) It causes people to reevaluate present images toward products that are threatened by innovation; and (2) it results in individuals forming new images toward products developed.

Attitudes favoring innovation. There has been a great deal of argument as to whether new products result from consumer pressures for change or from business pressures for sales. This argument has been adequately discussed elsewhere, and it need not concern us here. What does concern us is that there are some consumers who favor product innovation and some who do not.[7]

There are three reasons why people prefer product change. First, it leads to improved products. Improved products raise the consumer's level of living and provide greater satisfaction. Many of the products made obsolete serve a useful purpose in that they are the basis for a secondhand market. Second, innovation leads to different types of products, increasing consumer choice. Of course, it is possible that innovation can lead to improved products and more products of the same generic type without different products. Third, there is considerable psychic satisfaction in product development that affects product image. Types of psychic satisfaction derived from product innovation include: "keeping up with the Joneses," status and prestige arising out of ownership, and social acceptance or leadership. The plastics industry is an example of an industry that has expanded its uses of a basic product. The furniture, mobile home, and toy industries are good examples of innovation on the basis of multiplying and changing existing products. The chemical and petroleum industries exemplify innovation built on new and different products.

Consumer opposition to change. Not all consumers desire innovation. The Volkswagen demonstrates a case where consumers prefer less change in annual models. Other examples are found in bathroom fixtures and equipment and men's and women's underwear. The usual reasons given for desiring less change center around economy. First, the product may cost less, since the seller spends less on superficial features and style changes. Second, the seller can perfect the manufacturing of the product, thus reducing operating costs. Third, there is less depreciation, so a person can obtain full value for the product at resale. Fourth, it is argued that there is a kind of reverse psychology in owning standardized products. In a world where change is taken for granted, a person can be distinctive by failing to change.

Types of obsolescence

Product innovation invariably leads to product obsolescence. Since much innovation is planned by business, we must conclude that much obsolescence is also planned. Planned obsolescence is not necessarily bad, but it is a fact of the consumer's life that affects attitudes.

One source lists four types of planned obsolescence as follows:

1. *Technological obsolescence.* Here we have true innovation, and there has been some real and beneficial change in the product as measured by technical standards. The introduction of jet engines for piston engines on aircraft is an example of technological obsolescence.

2. *Postponed obsolescence.* This is putting off technological improvements until the market needs a stimulus. Technology results only from market pressure.

3. *Intentionally designed physical obsolescence.* Here the physical life of the product is purposefully shortened. The purpose is to create a larger replacement market.

4. *Style obsolescence or fashion obsolescence.* This type of obsolescence occurs where minor or superficial changes are made in the

product in order to make people feel out of style. High-style clothing, automobiles, and appliances fall into this category.

Consumers who favor change also favor obsolescence, although the individual does not necessarily recognize this fact. Technological and style obsolescence are most sought by American consumers, and physical obsolescence is not far behind. Consumers opposed to change favor postponed obsolescence, but these consumers appear to be in a minority at the present time.

STYLE OR FASHION OBSOLESCENCE

Style or fashion obsolescence is one of the more important types of obsolescence in our society. Since fashion plays such an important part in shaping consumer product images and consumer behavior, it is necessary to delve into this aspect of product development in more detail. Style and fashion are often used interchangeably, but there is a difference in the meaning of the terms. Paul Nystrom defined style as, "a characteristic or distinctive mode or method of expression, presentation or conception in the field of some art."[8] A fashion is any style that is popularly accepted over, at least, one normal season. Fashion depends on imitation. People want to be different, but not too different, and adherence to fashion satisfies both these needs. There are several reasons why people respond to fashion. Imitation reduces the risk of making a wrong purchase. Adherence to fashion saves time in deciding on merchandise. Purchases based on fashion gain approval for us because the purchase conforms to social norms. Imitation of others also satisfies our need for belonging to the group.

Vertical diffusion of fashion

A style does not become a fashion overnight nor does the same fashion necessarily exist at the same time in all strata of the society and for all geographic locations. The speed with which attitudes change and style is accepted, if indeed it is accepted, varies. Nevertheless, a successful style does follow increasing waves of popularity as it appeals to successive types of consumers. Thus, the understanding of vertical diffusion of fashion depends on knowledge of the fashion cycle.[9]

The fashion cycle has four stages, as follows:

1. *Distinctive stage.* The product is available in very small supply, is often even handmade. The price is very high. The style has just been introduced or reintroduced. Innovators who are willing to pay

extra to be different and people who just like the style are purchasers at this stage.

2. *Emulation stage.* The quantity of the product increases and price declines, but supply is still short and price high. The style has caught on with fashion leaders. These fashion leaders are early adopters.

3. *Economic emulation stage.* This is the stage where the style has become popular with the masses. The style has become fashion. The style is mass produced, price is low, and merchandise is available in all expected outlets. By this stage the innovators and early adopters are losing interest in the style.

4. *Decline stage.* In the decline stage, production has slowed or stopped. Retailers are working off inventories, and the already low price is further reduced. Laggards purchase at this stage.

Horizontal diffusion of fashion

The acceptance of fashion must move horizontally within groups of people as well as vertically between social groups. Actually, vertical and horizontal diffusion occur simultaneously.[10] Even as fashion moves from, say, the emulation stage to the economic emulation stage, it must become acceptable to the majority of people in each of those stages. If the majority of consumers at one stage fails to accept the fashion, it is not likely to have much success at the next stage. The horizontal diffusion of fashion is greatly influenced by the social group, group leadership, personal association, and mass media. Within the group, each member may at one time or another function as a leader because of unique experience with mass media or other groups not shared by the members of his or her own group.[11] Thus, group leaders and followers exchange roles from time to time. Leaders may be barely ahead of the other members in those qualities that makes them leaders. Influence tends to follow the paths of casual everyday contact between people. One couple gets a new color television set, and color sets begin to crop up among this couple's dinner group, downstairs neighbors, the bridge club, and coffee group at work. To this extent, even physical location has an important effect on diffusion.

Fashion leadership

Product change is not altogether acceptable to the average consumer. Average people do frequently bring about product change, but the accomplishment is often by accident. The average consumer is not very venturesome or innovative, and is more likely to follow fashion trends than to lead. A fashion leader causes things to happen, and although the fashion leader may be ordinary in most respects, he or she does possess certain characteristics that influence others where a particular fashion is concerned. One study of campus fashion leaders found them likely to be a freshman or sophomore, socially active, narcissitic, highly appearance-conscious, and strongly attuned to the rock culture.[12] The leader is strongly motivated toward possessing student power.

Fashion leaders typically possess one or more of the following qualifications.

First, there is the individual dissatisfied with the product status quo. Although, not necessarily a leader, this person actively fosters change because he or she doesn't like things the way they are. The person who could not stand horses, and ventured on the street in the first automobile was a fashion leader. That person was initially ridiculed, but followed because of the ultimate soundness of the position.

Second, there are people who set fashion because they are in a position of leadership. These people are imitated because of their status, occupation, social position, or wealth. Leaders may be followed because the average person either looks up to them or down upon them. President's wives are imitated only a little more often than the movie star who may be immoral according to some standards. Thus, the fashion leader may point the way and leave it to others to devise the techniques and methods of change.

Third, there is the person of unusual ability. This person may not be dissatisfied, but he or she is inquisitive. Some people want to find out about things, and in the course of their research they develop better things, techniques, and methods. This type person is a fashion leader because he or she is out in front of the group in ideas.

No consumer is necessarily immune to the desire to lead the fashion parade. People with status, people with special talent, and people of unusual ability may aspire to be fashion leaders.[13] There are many reasons why a consumer may want to be a fashion leader including the following:

1. To achieve status or prestige within the group.
2. Personal ambition.
3. For reasons of personal self-expression.
4. Because of a special interest in a particular style.
5. Curiosity about a style or fashion.
6. Occupation or social position may necessitate fashion leadership.

Other factors that may lead a person to seek a position of fashion leadership are envy, insecurity, and need for recognition.

Fashion leaders and opinion leaders

The relationship between fashion leaders and opinion leaders needs clarifying. Opinion leaders were introduced earlier as the communicators of ideas that affect consumer behavior over a broad spectrum of product, store, price, and service decisions. Fashion leadership is concerned most specifically with the consumer's choice of products or particular brands. Thus, a fashion leader is a type of opinion leader, but an opinion leader may be affecting consumers on a broader scale than just fashion. Both the fashion leader and the opinion leader operate through the individual's basic determinants. That is to say, they affect consumer needs and motives as well as the awareness factors of perception, attitudes, and learning. The difference is in what the effect is directed toward.

Fashion leaders may have little or no interest in where the individual shops, manner of travel to the store, how to treat salespersons, etc. The fashion leader's entire attention is directed at the impression made, based on the manner of dress or other product use. An opinion leader may be more concerned with women's lib as it affects consumption, protection of the environment, business ethics, morality in sales, and a wide range of similar activities. Both type of leaders are instruments of change, and both types are important to consumer behavior.

PACKAGING AND BRANDING

The product package and brand complement one another, and each has an important impact on product image.[14] Have you ever wondered why you selected a particular brand of product or what it was that attracted your attention to one product on the seller's shelf? Chances are the brand or the package had something to do with your choice.

The brand and package are becoming more important in the American market.[15] Several factors account for the new emphasis on these product features. The American consumer is becoming more affluent, and the level of living for most people is rising. Thus, people have more choice as to how they spend their money. Effective packaging and branding can swing the consumer from one product to another. Competition has increased over the years, and there is greater pressure for differentiated products, favorable shelf space, and increased promotion. Packaging and branding are the basis for these types of competition.

Another factor has been the increase in the number of products offered to consumers. Consumer choice is improved by the greater number of items, but there is often confusion about the merits of all these different products. Probably one of the more important factors increasing the emphasis on brand and package is the tendency toward self-service, self-selection, and automatic vending. All these sales techniques that decrease the importance of salesmen put greater emphasis on brand and package. In effect, the product must sell itself at the point of sale.

Brand and package influences

The package and brand affect consumer attitudes in a number of important ways. Package and brand gain attention for the product, identify the product, communicate information, generate psychological connotations, and specify product function.

Attention. Consumers must be aware of products before attitudes can be formed. Almost everything about a product can be a source of attention, but some of the more important factors are color, the brand name, slogans, and symbols. Consumers revealed in one study that they do often like the product package. The study shows, however, that customer likes differ from those of designers and management. Of course, the ability of the product to attract attention may be the deciding factor that causes an individual to select the product over another.

Identification. Package and brand help to identify the product. Product identification is paramount as a basis for associating attitudes toward use, quality, and price with a particular good. Kleenex, Hormel, Allstate, and Kodak are brands quickly associated with their product. Most people can recognize the Chevrolet, Mr. Clean, and Eastern Airlines symbols on sight. Identification is enhanced when the package and brand are integrated. Colors, symbols, and slogans must be clear and suited to the product. Most important, the package must be easily identified.

Content communication. Brand and package help consumers build images about the nature of the content or benefit of the product. Benefits may be suggested by the product name or by various elements of the package. Names like Soilex, Great Shakes, and Hotpoint speak eloquently about the product. A picture of beans on a can, the color combinations on cigarette packages, and a drawing of a green giant also speak well of the product or its benefits. The psychological characteristics of the package can also have considerable effect on the way that it is perceived.

Psychological connotations. This factor concerns the consumer's overall emotional response to the package or brand. The use of white space, formal lettering, and balance on the package convey impressions to consumers that cannot always be separated from the product. In one study, respondents were asked to rate different beers on selected characteristics with: (1) bottle unmarked, (2) only the brand known, and (3) the regular label used. Returns showed that the label made the most difference in consumer attitude.

Function. This factor refers primarily to the package. Function means what the package does that leaves an impression on people. The package should be easy to open and close. It should be sufficiently strong to protect the contents, and the package should store easily. Information contained on the package, labels, and slogans should be informative and accurate. Of course, license is given to portray information in symbolic terms.

Special brand and package attitudes

There are four special attitudes associated with brand and package that need to be mentioned at this point. First, there is the attitude consumers have toward manufacturer's and distributor's brands. Second, there is the fact that brand and package can create new products. Third, we must look into multiple packaging. Fourth, package size is changing some consumer images.

Attitude toward seller. Consumers do not view manufacturer's and distributor's brands alike.[16] Consumers consider manufacturer's brands to be superior to dealer (private) brands for the following reasons:

1. Manufacturers practice better quality control.
2. Manufacturers have a greater stake in the product because the seller is better known.
3. There is more prestige from owning manufacturer's products.
4. Because of better research, manufacturer's brands tend to improve in quality over time.
5. People feel they "know" the manufacturer's product.[17]

There is no consistent evidence that consumers are correct in their judgment of manufacturer's and private brands. True or not, consumers believe manufacturer's brands to be superior and purchase accordingly. Private brands do have significant advantages. Myers' study shows that housewives have greater acceptance of private brands than women working outside the home. Many people view private brands favorably for the following reasons:

1. Low product price.
2. Better suited to local needs.
3. Do not pay for unwanted extras.
4. Desire to support local products and merchants.
5. More product protection from known local dealers.[18]

Package and brand can create new products. There is no question but that brand and package can create new products. When the same product is put in a new or different package, it is perceived differently. For example, a private-brand washing machine does not have the same image as the manufacturer's brand, even when the consumer knows one producer made both machines.[19] Any change in product attributes can change the image and create a new product in the consumer's mind. A study of 50 successful and 50 unsuccessful brands had the following results. Of the successful brands, 44 had significantly better performance, higher prices, 24 had better performance, same price, and 16 had the same performance, same price. By contrast, 30 of the unsuccessful brands had the same performance, same price, and 30 had the same performance, higher price.[20] Furthermore, of the successful products, 20 were dramatically different and 48 were very different. The evidence suggests that brand success depends largely on having a marketable product.

The design of the package can, and often is, used for the purpose of creating a new product in the mind of the consumer.[21] Package design changes are frequently used for this purpose by toothpaste and food products manufacturers. The use of prizes and premiums can accomplish the same thing. Sometimes people become so obsessed with the premium that the contents of the package becomes secondary. Soap and cereal manufacturers frequently use premiums to change or maintain a product's image.

Multiple packaging. Multiple packaging, or the placing of several units of an item in a single package, can affect product image. The move to multiple packaging has been a long time coming in some industries, but where used, it has been successful. The technique recognizes that consumers use many products in small quantity. It further recognizes that consumers need to keep many products fresh even after the package is broken. Examples of products that have successfully used multiple packaging are crackers, soft drinks, beer, dog food, candy, handkerchiefs, shirts, flashlight batteries, and automobile tires. Multiple packages can also be used for complementary products such as razors and blades.

Package size. Package size can condition product attitudes. Package size allows the consumer to adjust cash outlay to only the amount of the item desired. The number of product sizes have tended to increase recently. Large-size packages have recently shown a tendency to be more successful than smaller packages. There is no question, however, that more product sizes give consumers more choice.

ATTITUDES TOWARD PRICE

Product price is another important factor in product image. The price of the merchandise influences consumer's product image in three ways. First, price is the measure of merchandise worth. Second, some prices are a convenience to customers. Finally, individuals have emotional responses to price. We shall look into each of these types of influence.

Price as an indicator of worth

Price is important in measuring the worth of products in two ways: it is used to indicate quality and it is used to specify a bargain or good buy.

Price indicates quality. Price, along with brand, is one of the most important ways used by consumers to estimate quality.[22] The use of price for this purpose differs when dealing with different socioeconomic classes, product types, and retail outlets.[23] Leavitt found that respondents selected higher-priced floor waxes, razor blades, moth flakes, and cooking sherry over lower-priced complements when asked to rate quality differences. There were more doubts about the lower-priced products selected. The use of unit pricing may reduce some of this effect in the future, but results on buyer behavior now are inconclusive.[24] It was concluded that a higher price may sometimes attract rather than repel consumers for particular brands. Studies indicate that products selling poorly at a lower price may sell better when the price is increased. Similarly a $400 value item acquired as a bargain may not be as attractive when offered at $200, as it would be if offered at $300, since the customer may associate the $200 priced item with a similar product of inferior quality regularly offered at $200.

Although price is an important indicator of quality, it can be overestimated as a purchase determinant. One researcher found that reliability of vendor, recommendations for best buy, and preselling of the line by the manufacturer were more important than price for determining purchase. Price is important, but just how important is difficult to say.

The good-buy price. Price is the factor that equalizes money and satisfaction in the consumer's mind. Any product is a good buy if the consumer feels he would rather have the satisfaction contained in the item than the money.[25] This type of attitude is always necessary in trade because a consumer will not willingly give up more than is received. A trade takes on an economy appeal when the consumer purchases primarily because of the lowness of price and not because of quality or other considerations. It is obvious that customers often do purchase because of price. One study investigated 60 frequently advertised and highly competitor-priced brand items. Seven thousand consumers were shown the goods and asked to recall the price of each item. The results varied greatly. For example, it was found that 86 percent of the respondents remembered the price of Coca-Cola six packs, and 91 percent could name the price within 5 percent of the correct amount. Only 2 percent of the respondents could recall the exact price of products such as shortening.[26] *Progressive Grocer* found that the factors of income, age, and sex seemed to make little difference in the amount of price awareness. In another study, using 640 English housewives, the fact that price consciousness for some products is quite high was demonstrated. This study shows a relationship between social class and price consciousness. Members of higher social classes were more willing to name prices of products, but those from lower social classes were more accurate in the prices named. These results tend to indicate that people in the lower social classes have more price awareness.

Price convenience

Some aspects of product pricing appeal to consumers from the standpoint of convenience. Three price policies make a convenience appeal: (1) the one-price policy, (2) price lining, and (3) full-line pricing. The American economy has generally adopted a one-price policy, in the sense that at any one offering, all customers are charged the same, and there is no haggling. A one-price policy saves time, presents the buyer a definite price, and may lower prices. The main advantage of a negotiated-price policy is the psychological satisfaction derived from haggling.

Price lining involves dividing merchandise into classes, establishing price points, and pricing at these points. Price lining is a convenience to consumers because it avoids the confusion of many prices, saves time, reduces confusion, and may reduce prices because of the seller's inventory savings.

Full-line pricing is simultaneously selling a high-priced line, a medium-priced line, and a low-priced line. Full-line pricing offers the customer a choice of quality and price considerations at one convenient location.

Psychological prices

People cannot help developing mental attitudes toward prices any more than they can avoid mental attitudes toward other product attributes. Price levels may be viewed as too high, too low, or just about right.[27] In short, customers are price sensitive, but there is evidence that there are degrees to this sensitivity. Research on consumer price sensitivity for coffee, toothpaste and green beans indicated significant differences.[28] Price recall was less accurate for coffee than for the other two.

Some people of low income resent all prices because of their inability to purchase. Other consumers are less interested in the product than in the status or prestige they can obtain from bragging about how much they paid for the product. Prices may also be considered for snob appeal. Schitovsky says:

> *Another basis for price discrimination is the premium some people put on certain goods and services merely for the sake of their expensiveness. A person may know that the more expensive model is no better than the cheaper one and yet prefer it for the mere fact that it is more expensive.*[29]

On the other hand, the reverse may be true. A person who can afford higher prices may stress publicly how little was paid for an item. Two price policies used by business are designed to take advantage of consumer price psychology: odd pricing and prestige pricing. Odd pricing refers to setting price just below psychological breaks in the dollar. Thus, a price is set at $0.49 or $0.98 rather than $0.50 or $1. It is psychologically wrong to price just above a break, because consumers will assume the product was marked up. "A given product may not move at $1.05 but a package containing only four-fifths as much, clearly labeled as to quantity, will readily sell at 98 cents."[30] Prestige pricing is taking high markups and/or pricing above the market. Many consumers are willing to pay more because (1) it is felt the product is of higher quality or possesses brand prestige, or (2) there is a snob value derived from owning high-priced products.

NOTES

1. William J. Stanton, *Fundamentals of Marketing* (New York: McGraw-Hill Book Co., 1975), p. 171.
2. Thomas S. Robertson, "The New Product Diffusion Process," *Marketing in a Changing World,* ed. Bernard A. Morin (Chicago: American Marketing Assn., 1969), pp. 80–86.
3. "Report of the Definitions Committee," *Journal of Marketing,* (October 1948), p. 205.
4. Edward M. Tauber, "Reduce New Product Failures: Measure Needs as Well as Purchase Interest," *Journal of Marketing,* vol. 37 (July 1973), pp. 61–70.
5. Sidney J. Levy, "Symbols by Which We Buy," *Advertising Marketing Efficiency,* ed. Lynn H. Stockman (Chicago: American Marketing Assn., December 1958), pp. 409–16.
6. William J. Constadse, "How to Launch New Products," *Business Topics,* (Winter 1971), pp. 29–34.
7. Laurence P. Feldman and Gary M. Armstrong, "Identifying Buyers of a Major Automotive Innovation," *Journal of Marketing,* vol. 39 (January 1975), pp. 47–53; Nancy C. Peat, James W. Gentry, and Thomas L.

Brown, "A Comment on Identifying Buyers of a Major Automotive Innovation," *Journal of Marketing,* vol. 39 (October 1975), pp. 61–62.

8. Paul H. Nystrom, *Economics of Fashion* (New York: Ronald Press Co., 1928), p. 3.
9. The fashion cycle is not a true cycle in that it has a definite rhythm or that it has predictive value. The fashion cycle does explain something of the adoptive process where fashion is concerned.
10. Claude R. Martin, Jr., "What Consumers of Fashion Want to Know," *Journal of Retailing,* vol. 47 (Winter 1971–72), pp. 65–71.
11. James H. Donnelly, Jr. and Michael J. Etzel, "Degrees of Product Newness and Early Trial," *Journal of Marketing Research,* vol. 10 (August 1973), pp. 295–300.
12. Steven A. Baumgarten, "The Innovative Communicator in the Diffusion Process," *Journal of Marketing Research,* vol. 12 (February 1975), pp. 12–18.
13. John O. Summers, "The Identity of Women's Clothing Fashion Opinion Leaders," *Journal of Marketing Research,* vol. 7 (May 1970), pp. 178–85.
14. Chem L. Narayana and Rom J. Markin, "Consumer Behavior and Product Performance: An Alternative Conceptualization," *Journal of Marketing,* vol. 39 (October 1975), pp. 1–6.
15. Thomas A. Staudt, "Higher Management Risks in Product Strategy," *Journal of Marketing,* vol. 37 (January 1973), pp. 4–9.
16. Barbara Davis Coe, "Private Versus National Preference Among Lower- and Middle-Income Consumers," *Journal of Retailing,* vol. 47 (Fall 1971), pp. 61–72.
17. John G. Myers, "Determinants of Private Brand Attitude," *Journal of Marketing Research,* vol. 4 (February 1967), pp. 73–81.
18. Ibid.
19. Philip C. Burger and Barbara Schott, "Can Private Brand Buyers Be Identified?" *Journal of Marketing Research,* vol. 9 (May 1972), pp. 219–22.
20. J. Hugh Davidson, "Why Most New Consumer Brands Fail," *Harvard Business Review,* (March–April 1976), pp. 117–122.
21. H. Paul Root, "Should Product Differentiation be Restricted?" *Journal of Marketing,* vol. 36 (July 1972), pp. 3–9.
22. Robert A. Peterson and Alain J. P. Jolibert, "A Cross-National Investigation of Price and Brand as Determinants of Perceived Product Quality," *Journal of Applied Psychology,* vol. 61 (1976), pp. 533–36; Arthur G. Bedeian, "Consumer Perception of Price as an Indicator of Product Quality," *Business Topics,* vol. 19 (Summer 1971), pp. 59–65; Benson P. Shapiro, "Price Reliance: Existence and Sources," *Journal of Marketing Research,* vol. 10 (August 1973), pp. 286–94.
23. Norman D. French, John J. Williams, and William A. Chance, "A Shopping Experiment on Price-Quality Relationships," *Journal of Retailing,* vol. 48 (Fall 1972), pp. 3–16.

24. Michael J. Houston, "The Effect of Unit-pricing on Choices of Brand and Size in Economic Shopping," *Journal of Marketing*, vol. 36 (July 1972), pp. 51–69.
25. John R. Nevin, "Laboratory Experiments for Estimating Consumer Demand: A Validation Study," *Journal of Marketing Research*, vol. 11 (August 1974), pp. 261–68.
26. B. P. Shapiro, "Psychology of Pricing," *Harvard Business Review*, vol. 46 (July–August 1968), pp. 14–16.
27. Evan E. Anderson, "The Effectiveness of Retail Price Reductions: A Comparison for Alternative Expressions of Price," *Journal of Marketing Research*, vol. 11 (August 1974), pp. 327–30; A. Oxenfeldt, D. Miller, A. Schuman, and C. Winick, *Insight into Pricing* (Belmont, Ca.: Wadsworth Publishing Co., 1969), Chap. 4.
28. Karl A. Shilliff, "Determinants of Consumer Price Sensitivity for Selected Supermarket Products: An Empirical Investigation," *Akron Business & Economic Review*, vol. 6 (September 1975), pp. 26–32.
29. Tibor Scitovsky, "Some Consequences of the Habit of Judging Quality by Price," *Review of Economic Studies*, vol. 12 (1944–45).
30. Chester R. Wasson, "The Psychological Aspect of Price," *The Economics of Managerial Decision: Profit Opportunity Analysis* (New York: Appleton-Century-Crofts, 1956), pp. 130–33.

QUESTIONS

1. What is a product? What is meant by product influence? Explain how the product motivates consumers to buy.
2. What is product design? How does design influence the consumer? In what ways do consumer attitudes toward the product differ?
3. Why do some consumers favor product change and some do not? Explain.
4. What is the effect of obsolescence on consumers? Define the types of obsolescence and discuss the importance of each on consumers.
5. Define style. Define fashion. Explain vertical and horizontal diffusion of fashion. Illustrate how each affects consumer behavior.
6. What is meant by fashion leadership? Contrast the fashion leader with the opinion leader. Why do consumers want to be fashion leaders?
7. Define package. Define brand. Discuss the manner of influence on consumers that results from package and brand.
8. Do consumers view manufacturer and dealer brands alike? Why or why not? Are the consumers right in their view? Explain. How can the package create a new product in the eyes of consumers?
9. What does price mean to the consumer? How does price indicate quality?
10. What is price convenience? What is psychological price? How do they affect consumer behavior? Explain and illustrate.

26

The consumer's store image

Store benefits offered to consumers
Adjust physical product
Make buying convenient
Psychic satisfaction
Company image not universally effective
Elements of store image identified
General consumer impressions
Consumer impressions affected by peer groups
Consumer image and consumer self-image
Other intangible emotional factors
Functional elements of company image
Location influences consumer image
Store design conveys company image
Product assortment affects company image
The service aspect of company image
Personnel affect store image
Differences between company images

The image the consumer holds of the firm may be as important in shopping behavior as the image the consumer has of the product. The decision of whether to trade with a given store is dependent as much on what the consumer conceives that store or firm to be as on any other environmental factor. Important store-related issues that affect consumer purchase decisions include the store's location, store design, product assortment, services offered, and store personnel. These and related subjects are discussed in this chapter.

STORE BENEFITS OFFERED TO CONSUMERS

The overriding purpose of all aspects of store operations is to influence consumers to be favorably disposed toward the company or company's products. Thus, the store image must convey the message that the store's operations offer desired benefits to consumers. Generally speaking, store operations can benefit consumers in three ways—by adjusting the physical product to customer wants, by making buying convenient, or by providing psychic satisfaction.

Adjust physical product

One important benefit of company operations is to adjust, in the mind of consumers, the physical product more nearly to consumer wants.[1] We have previously established that few physical products are tailor-made for the individual. Also, many people want more than the physical product. The consumer may want the product now but may be short of funds and will therefore need credit. The individual may not wish to handle the product physically, so delivery is necessary. The desire for protection of the product, and for privacy and convenience in handling it, creates a need for wrapping. Examples are legion where businesses with essentially similar brands of merchandise successfully adjust to specific target markets through variations in service. Classic examples are found in the differences in service philosophy between department stores and discount department stores and between chain grocery stores and mom-and-pop grocery stores.

The point is that no matter how similar the physical products offered by different firms may be, the total product of a firm can be made different through various combinations of services. It should be noted that the use of services is not the only method for adjusting physical product; actually, everything the firm does can be used as a basis for such adjustment. In one study, 4,500 women shoppers were asked why they preferred one store over another. The stores were classified as to (1) fashion appeal, (2) price appeal, and (3) broad appeals. The results are summarized as follows:

1. *Fashion appeal.* Has the strongest image. Style and quality of merchandise, service, reputation and reliability are mentioned more often than with the other two types. Layout and displays are considered better.

2. *Price appeal.* Little mention of fashion or quality merchandise or salesclerk service. More mention of low price and bargains. Discount stores fit this group as well as those offering a variety of services other than salesclerk services. These services are taken for granted by fashion-store patrons but not by price-appeal customers.

3. *Broad appeals.* Falls between previous two in image presented. Offers some degree of attraction in both fashions and bargains. Ranks equal to price-appeal store in reputation and reliability but ahead of them in clerk service, layout, and display.[2]

The fashion-appeal stores were favored by high-income women and women over 40 without children at home. Low-income women and women over 40 with children favored the price-appeal stores. The broad-appeal store fitted the needs of low-income women and women under 40 with children.

Make buying convenient

The factors of store personality make a substantial contribution to customer convenience. How much and what type of a contribution depends on what the customer wants made convenient. The rule is that every convenience offered by a firm has some cost connected with it. This cost may take the form of a *commodity cost* or a *convenience cost*. Commodity cost is the price of the merchandise; a particular convenience may result in the individual's paying more for the merchandise. Convenience cost is the monetary, physical, and mental expenditure necessary to overcome frictions of time and space in shopping.[3] Obtaining one satisfaction usually necessitates giving up something else.

A consumer who wants to shop and compare quality and prices may travel downtown rather than shop in a nearby shopping center. There are more stores and more products to compare downtown, but the shopper has to travel further and to incur costs associated with congestion and crowds. In order to obtain the satisfaction of lower prices, a person may be willing to incur the convenience costs from travel far out into the suburbs to trade with a discount house located in a low-rent district. A consumer who seeks the convenience of delivery service may visit a department store, even though the person knows the product can be purchased for less at a discount house.

The importance of convenience was shown in a study which investigated the relationship of price perceptions to supermarket patronage.

In this study, 1,000 consumers were interviewed in five states, and the number one reason the respondents gave for selecting a particular grocery store was convenience. This points up the importance of traffic patterns and location to store selection. The second reason given for patronage was price. Shoppers who patronized the lowest-priced stores were the most valid perceivers of price, whereas those patronizing the highest-priced stores were the least valid perceivers. However, additional costs were associated with shopping at the lowest-price stores in terms of travel, assortment, and convenience.[4]

Psychic satisfaction

Some effects of store operations on consumers cannot be explained by any specific actions taken by the company. One study demonstrated that the brand choice of housewives differed in different stores offering the same brands. This study covered paper, drugs, and food.[5] The shopper may just feel comfortable in the store, or there is an extra little sense of pride in owning merchandise from some particular store.[6] Even the consumer may not be sure why the feeling exists. We refer to this as psychic satisfaction. Probably everything the store does contributes some to this feeling. Psychic satisfaction may be summed up as resulting from all those aspects of store operations that makes shopping a pleasant experience.

Company image not universally effective

It is surprising how often business leaders are deluded by their belief in the mass market. The myth persists that an image based on a wide line of merchandise can successfully appeal to everyone. Pierre Martineau reports:

> *One Chicago retailer believes that his store does the largest volume in its product category in the market. I asked him about the character of his customer body. He did not hesitate to state that the entire market was his oyster–people from all income brackets, all surrounding areas, and all social groups.*[7]

Actually, a disproportionate number of the firm's customers came from the lowest economic group, and rather than drawing from the entire city, sales were centered around its southern part. This is not an isolated example. There is no such thing as a company image that appeals universally in the market.[8] A given store personality does not have equal impact on all races, ages, status groups, and income levels. Furthermore, a business may have appeal because of one type of product and not of another.[9] A firm may appeal differently depending on the time element—time of day, day of the week, and time the customer has available to shop.

ELEMENTS OF STORE IMAGE IDENTIFIED

Company, or store, image was defined in the previous chapter as the subjective attitude the consumer takes toward the business institution as a functioning entity. Meaningfully to discuss the manner of influence on customers resulting from store operations, we must first identify the elements of store image.[10] There are aspects of store image that relate to the consumer's interpretation of the firm's policies in specific functional areas of the business, and there are apects of store image that can only be explained by consumer's general impressions of the total business.[11] The latter may result from viewing all the functional elements simultaneously, or may have no necessary foundation in anything specific done by the organization. Thus, the elements of store image divide logically into specific functional elements and general impressions.

There are five specific functional elements of company image, and the consumer may form impressions of each individually. They are: (1) store location, (2) store design, (3) product assortment, (4) store services, and (5) store personnel.[12] *Location* is defined as the physical placement of the enterprise in its environment. *Store design* refers to aspects of exterior and interior architecture that give the physical facility its distinct character. *Product assortment* is defined as the number of different types of products carried by the firm, the variety of styles and models of each type, and the number of each item stocked. *Store services* are defined as intangibles that surround the product and are desired by customers only because the product is purchased. *Store personnel* refers to the employees of the store that come in contact with its customers.

In a manner of speaking, the store personality is the consumer's impression of the five specific elements described above.[13] However, we cannot account for all consumer attitudes toward the firm by these elements—a fact which brings us to the consumer's subjective attitude toward the business as a unit. These general impressions of store image are defined as overall impressions consumers hold toward the company that cannot be pinned down to specific factors of the store's operations.[14] General impressions may be based on intuition or on nothing at all. Who can pin a housewife down to anything concrete when she reports, "It's a nice store," or when a friend says, "You hear a lot about that store, so it must be a good place to trade." In the remainder of this chapter, we shall discuss the general consumer impressions and the functional elements that constitute store image. The discussion begins with the general consumer impressions.

GENERAL CONSUMER IMPRESSIONS

The functional elements play a large part in shaping store image as we shall see later, but that is only a part of the story. Consumers may react to individual parts of a store individually, but individuals also react to the store as a unit. Even the view of a store as a coordinated whole does not tell the full story. Some consumers just have a feeling for the store, and this impression is not based on anything concrete.

We now want to discuss several aspects of consumer store impressions: the attitude of peer groups, company image and consumer self-image, and other intangible emotional factors.

Consumer impressions affected by peer groups

The attitude of other members of one's peer group toward a store is extremely important to the formation of one's own attitude. The old saying is that the word gets around, and the word, correctly or incorrectly, gets around concerning what to expect from specific businesses. Individuals tend to trade with stores that are acceptable to their peer group. Some stores have a high-class image and some have a low-class image, and shoppers trade accordingly. The sophisticated group feels out of place in low-class stores, and lower-status shoppers feel out of place in high-status stores. One must remember that certain types of stores, notably department stores and grocery stores, are acceptable to all classes of people.[15] High-income and low-income shoppers can rub elbows in these stores without discomfort to either party. The stores themselves are neutral in any conflicts between the classes.

Company image and consumer self-image

It is a general rule that consumers trade in stores where they feel comfortable.[16] However, many types of consumers may feel comfortable in the same store. For example, society women, lawyer's wives, and the wives of business executives may shop the same stores, but they were unlikely to shop the same stores as maids and waitresses. Consumers in work clothes avoid prestige stores. Young married couples, mothers with children, and shoppers in a hurry feel more at home in suburban shopping centers. The reason is that the centers have an image of casual, relaxed, informality, and they are conveniently located. Lower-status shoppers tend to be interested in product function. These shoppers feel more comfortable in stores that reflect economy, use, and practical considerations. Higher-status consumers pay less attention to price. The shoppers look for businesses that appeal on the basis of quality and service. All customers, no matter what income or social class, have an idea of the type of stores that are compatible with their own life-styles.

Other intangible emotional factors

Sometimes the intangibles of store image are the most important factors of all in deciding consumer actions. Often, one look determines if the consumer likes or dislikes the store. There is no tangible reason for the reaction, but once formed it is difficult to change. The consumer may just like the color combinations used by the store, or it may be the smile of an employee. The reaction may have nothing to do with the business. The person may be in a good or a bad mood because of something that happened at home, or the store symbol may trigger the memory of some pleasant or unpleasant experience from childhood. Whatever the reason, the consumer views the store and immediately likes or dislikes it.

FUNCTIONAL ELEMENTS OF COMPANY IMAGE

Some companies are extremely successful in portraying a clear, consistent image to their market. General Motors, General Foods, Ford, Procter and Gamble, and Texaco have clear and well-known images. Other companies are not so successful in developing distinct images. There is often a parallel between the relatively unsuccessful business operation and the lack of a clear-cut image. People are likely to have either no opinion or unclear attitudes about a business *because* they don't know much about it. We encounter statements such as, "I don't hear much about them."

Some consumers may object strongly to a successful firm simply because the company portrays a clear image that does not appeal to their group. The firm is successful because it appeals to some other group. The unsuccessful firm, on the other hand, just doesn't appeal to anyone very clearly. Let us now investigate the five elements of company image with respect to how they influence consumer attitudes.

Location influences consumer image

The location of the seller's establishment influences the consumer's attitude toward the store.[17] Consumers do not always stop to evaluate the effect of locations, but the conscious or unconscious effect is there. The more important location considerations that affect consumer attitudes are: (1) consumer location preferences, (2) consumer site bias, and (3) accessibility of site.

Consumer location preferences. Consumers expect to find some types of stores operating in specified ways located in certain places. Rich and Portis concluded, in a study, that store images are weaker and less distinctive in the suburbs, as compared with those located in the central business district. The move to the suburbs has resulted in a high degree of "sameness" among suburban branches of different types of downtown stores.[18] Even so, stores that pull customers from a large market area—discount houses, department stores, high-fashion specialty shops, automobile dealers, and banks—tend to have fewer stores located in the central business district and larger shopping centers. Shoppers expect to travel further to trade with these stores.[19] Grocery stores, drugstores, and hardware stores are examples of businesses that tend to locate in, or adjacent to, their primary market.

Sellers take on the character of their surroundings in the minds of consumers. Thus, stores in neighborhood shopping centers may be visualized as small, friendly, and interested, whereas stores in a regional center may appear busy, exciting, and impersonal. Consumers are likely to associate a store with high-quality merchandise if it is located among stores that emphasize quality. The same is true for stores emphasizing price. We have all heard consumers refer to a trade center as "ritzy" or "high class," when perhaps only some of the stores deserved the name.

Consumer site bias. Consumers have often demonstrated clear biases against certain specific sites in a retail complex. Studies have indicated that consumers located midway between two shopping areas will tend to patronize the one located to their right.

We have all seen examples of gasoline service stations located across the street from each other but one succeeds and the other does not. Many factors enter into the shopper's decision on a store or station, but the location is important. People show a marked tendency to bear to the right when riding or walking probably because more people are right handed. Other things equal, shoppers favor the right side of the street. Each consumer prefers to continue what he or she is doing rather than go to the trouble to change.

Traffic moves more smoothly when only right-hand turns are made—in heavily trafficked areas, particularly on streets with median strips, a left-hand turn may be nearly impossible. Thus, people resist turning back to a store, and the preference for one service station over another may merely reflect a reluctance to change directions or to cross a crowded street.

Location accessibility. Accessibility is another factor that affects the consumer's attitude toward stores. A comparison of high-income and low-income areas found that their similarities were more important than their differences in many aspects of shopping. Both groups reported convenience as the most important reason for visiting a grocery store.[20] Another study of three stores indicated that over 56 percent of respondents traveled less than half a mile to shop at convenience stores.[21]

The primary factors involved with convenience are traffic flow and parking. One of the important appeals of suburban shopping centers is the fact that they are accessible, and once there, it is not difficult to find convenient parking. Therefore, shoppers tend to think of shopping centers as convenient places to shop as compared to downtown.

There are exceptions to all these points made about consumer attitudes toward location of businesses. The best location is the one with which some group of consumers can identify.[22] Nevertheless, not every business is blessed with a good location, and this fact can, and often does, lead to failure. It is generally conceded that no amount of advertising or other types of promotion can completely offset the effect of a poor location. Promotion can help to reduce the poor image, but that is all it can accomplish.

Store design conveys company image

The store design, as much as anything, also conveys to consumers the company's self-image.[23] The physical attributes of the store are readily in the consumer's view. The customer is likely to feel that whatever the store stands for is reflected in these facilities. If the store exterior and interior are old-fashioned, people tend to view the company as traditional and conservative. Modern facilities convey liberal images; modern stores are viewed as willing to change and adopt new methods. When management allows its facilities to become run down, consumers can receive a message of incompetent or stingy managers.

There is no way that the business can avoid having its facilities convey some image to consumers. The consumer may misread the intentions of management, but some message will be received from store design.

A change in the exterior or interior design of the building can change the company image. The changed image may result in increased sales or it may not. Of course, it may be desirable to change the company image in order to appeal more effectively to consumers. A national retailer selling primarily low-priced goods, and men's, women's, and children's clothing, had very traditional stores. The stores used a gridiron layout, and lighting and fixtures were old-fashioned. Management decided that the most feasible way to increase sales was to modernize layout and equipment and became an up-to-date department store. This retailer has also updated its buildings and product assortment. Product and price lines have been broadened to include those traditionally handled by department stores, and today the company enjoys a successful image as a quality department store.

Exterior design sets the mood. The shopper first comes into direct contact with the exterior facilities of the business.[24] First impressions are as important to shoppers as to people in other social situations. The architecture, signs, and windows and doors, as well as the general condition of the building, all speak to consumers. The architecture of the exterior sets the image theme. Materials such as steel and aluminum still tend to be viewed as modern but cold. Concrete and glass are seen as modern but warm building materials. Brick, gargoyles, ironwork, and combinations of brick and cement are considered traditional. The modern tendency in store fronts is toward fewer upper-story windows but massive glass at the ground floor. Simple functional lines are also the trend in modern store fronts.

The company sign is important because it identifies the store and attracts attention. Signs are also important to the creation of company image. The colors and symbols used in the sign affect consumer attitudes. Symbols in the form of circles or ovals tend to get the most positive reaction from more customers. Triangles and squares are much less favored. The use of block letters and formal borders on the sign creates the feeling of permanence and tends to convey a feeling of conservative, tradition-oriented management. The use of script letters and open design gives the feeling of a modern, progressive firm. Success can be built on either type of image.

Color attracts more attention than black and white, but moving color or multiple colors get more attention than still color. However, too much flashing or too many poorly coordinated colors tend to be taken as cheap or gaudy by consumers. They may serve for price-appeal stores but are not generally suited for service-type firms. People tend to react differently to various colors. Bright colors create a feeling of movement, excitement, and progress, while pastels cause serene, quiet, relaxed sensations. Dark or muddy colors may convey a feeling of dirtiness to consumers.

Interior design follows through. The store interior should be coordinated with the exterior to have the greatest overall customer impact. The interior must carry out the theme suggested by the exterior design. Very few stores can afford to present customers with two different personalities.

The interior design should focus on customer satisfactions by establishing pleasant surroundings, emphasizing the merchandise offering, and providing for customer convenience.[25] Walls and floors should be in keeping with the overall effect, but they must also be functional and pleasant to the eye. Some theme, in terms of design, color combinations, pictures, and so on, should be carried out. Where possible, different parts of the store can be related to the overall theme but with variations. Lighting can also aid in providing a friendly, cheerful store atmosphere. Fixtures need to be pleasant to observe and functional.[26] They should not draw attention to themselves, but should emphasize the products, and they should be employed in such a way as to make it easy for shoppers to get at the merchandise.[27]

Self-selection and self-service are increasing in importance, and this fact puts greater emphasis on the use of fixtures to help sell merchandise. The tendency is to remove all barriers between customers and the merchandise.

Product assortment affects company image

The product assortment offered by a business affects the consumer's attitude toward product completeness and personal attention. Generally, consumer images of wide-line sellers, such as department stores and chains, are as follows:

1. Greater width and variety of product lines.
2. More different brands.
3. Wider price ranges.
4. Greater variation in merchandise quality.
5. Less personal attention to customers.
6. Less competent employees.
7. Impersonal relationships.
8. Greater variety of services.

Sellers who carry narrow lines of merchandise, such as most specialty shops, are viewed as follows:

1. Greater depth of merchandise, including all sizes and most styles.
2. Most product knowledge by employees.
3. More interest in customers.
4. No credit sales.
5. Service emphasis except for credit.
6. More personal attention to customers.

Of course, consumers can be, and often are, wrong in their general assessment of types of businesses. The consumer is probably on safer ground when evaluating individual enterprises based on experience. In spite of this fact, many consumers consider diversified stores as good places for shopping around, for picking up bargains, for multiple-product shopping, and for relatively quick service. Specialized businesses have a better image for finding a particular desired product, for an atmosphere of friendliness and competence, and as places to make prestige purchases.

The service aspect of company image

The various types of service offered by a business play an important part in shaping consumer images toward it. Services often make it possible for firms offering similar merchandise to make a specialized appeal to consumers.[28] Customers tend to visualize stores as service or nonservice stores. Service stores can repel some customers just as nonservice stores repel others. The customer's attitude toward service depends on what the individual expects from the specific purchase situation.

Cost and importance of services. The consumer's choice is not whether to take service or not. Some services accompany nearly all products. Parking, buyer information, and wrapping are services offered by most stores, but if these services are not available some others probably are. Thus, for most consumers the question of service is relative. The question is, How much service do I want at what price? The consumer's desire for service varies with the expected satisfaction to be derived from the service. While there is no consensus in attitude toward service satisfaction, the following list can serve to point out differences in importance.

A. Services that increase product satisfaction
    1. Credit
    2. Alterations, installation, performance checks
    3. Shopper information
B. Services that increase convenience
    1. Delivery
    2. Wrapping
    3. Parking
    4. Check cashing
    5. Telephone orders
C. Special benefit services
    1. Baby-sitting pools
    2. Product returns
    3. Handling of complaints
    4. Gift wrapping
    5. Repairs

Every service accepted by consumers has a cost, and no matter how much the person wants the service, cost must be considered. Unless the service cost is offset by some other consideration, such as lower cost from quantity purchases or higher revenue from volume sales, more service means higher product prices. In shopping for specific items, each of us invariably arrives at a point where the extra service is not worth the extra price.

Consumers have been especially concerned recently about the cost of repair service. Many consumers consider products repair prone, and the feeling that the repairs themselves cost too much. It is reported in one study that consumers perceive less problem with repairs.[29] Table 26–1 indicates that there may be a more positive attitude toward the cost of repair service. These are very interesting findings for a period of rising prices.

Table 26–1
Attitudes toward repair service

	Percent of respondents regarding repair cost as too high	
Product	*1972*	*1975*
Automobile	61	25
Television	58	21
Stereo	47	16
Refrigerator	43	28
Vacuum cleaner	42	13
Stove	39	19
Toaster	33	13
Electric can opener	N/A	13
Typewriter	N/A	8
Pocket calculator	N/A	0

Source: Lee Adler and James D. Hlavacek, "The Relationship Between Price and Repair Service for Consumer Durables," *Journal of Marketing*, vol. 40 (April 1976), pp. 80–82.

Merchandise and store effects on service. More service is expected with some types of goods than with other types, and most consumers are aware of the differences. Consumers expect very little service when purchasing convenience or staple goods, but consumers expect considerable service when purchasing shopping goods. Individuals expect alterations when purchasing clothing, installation when buying major appliances, and credit when purchasing furniture. Installation and alterations are types of services that usually cannot be separated from the product, as they are necessary to complete the product.

The type of store is as important as the type of product in determining consumer attitude toward service. We are all aware that some stores emphasize service, while others make a price appeal by reducing services. Consumer images differ for these types of stores, but services differ even among service stores. Specialty shops—such as shoe stores, candy stores, men's and women's apparel stores, and variety stores—tend to be characterized as cash-and-carry operations. These stores may offer other services, such as telephone orders, parking, check cashing, and gift wrapping. Consumers view department stores as the most service-minded of all businesses. All types of services can be found in some department stores, although not in all. Most people do not expect to pay cash to automobile dealers, mobile home dealers, or furniture stores.

The amount of a good purchased and the number of different products purchased have a similar effect on our attitudes toward service. Generally speaking, consumers require more services as the number and quantity of products bought increases. Most hardware is considered staple merchandise, and hardware is not associated with delivery service. However, if a person purchases several large items of hardware, delivery may be wanted. Another consumer may make several purchases at a department store. Some of these items may be convenience goods, but the consumer may charge the entire group of purchases and have the items delivered.

Personnel affect store image

Store personnel are the living symbol of the company. All the good effects of product assortment, location, store design, and service offering can be destroyed by ineffective personnel.[30] The importance of store employees to the creation of company image cannot be overemphasized. Many consumers consider the attitude of employees as the best guide to the true personality of the business.[31] In a group survey of retail salespeople and consumers conducted to ascertain why consumers bought, postponed buying, or refused to buy, there was considerable agreement between salespeople and consumers on the cause. It was concluded that a high measure of the responsibility for failure to make the sale was attributed to the salesperson.[32] Facilities and merchandise are controllable, and these aspects of store personality can be manipulated to the firm's advantage. Consumers feel that human feelings are less controllable. Over time, the true philosophy of the company toward customers will show up in the attitude of its salespeople. It has been estimated that 70 percent of customers who quit patronizing a particular firm do so because of employee attitude.

Customers want salespeople to treat them fairly, to show interest and attention rather than just to push sales. Customers want to be catered to, and they expect the salesperson to be able to answer all questions about the product. The qualities they most desired in salespersons are friendliness, courteous manner, and helpfulness. This is not so important in self-service stores because the consumer expects to depend on personal judgment. In sales-oriented firms, the customer often has to rely, mostly or wholly, on the word of the employee. Any enterprise, whether self-service or using sales personnel, can benefit from a company image of friendly, courteous, helpful customer relations.

DIFFERENCES BETWEEN COMPANY IMAGES

If managers had their way, all consumers would view their company favorably. If this were not possible, then at least everyone in some social, economic, or status group would view the business favorably. Managers work toward accomplishing this goal. No managers deliberately alienate customers. The fact that firms do not appeal to everyone indicates that some consumers' attitudes toward the company personality are different from the company's attitude toward itself. Even if two stores contain the same functional elements, many consumers will not attribute the same image to each store. No doubt millions of dollars in advertising are wasted by business each year because of failure to understand this important fact. In the final analysis, a business is whatever most consumers view it to be, and a considerable part of the consumer's attitude is based on emotional factors.

The store layout is basic to customer pleasure and/or convenience. For example, a gridiron layout is easy to learn and highly functional but not too interesting. A free-flow layout is interesting and provides customer exposure, but it is difficult to learn. There is a direct correlation between sales and merchandise locations passed, and between time spent in the store and money spent.

The fixtures probably have as much to do with creating the store image and making merchandise convenient as anything. Fixtures can be used to create a conservative or liberal atmosphere, and they can be traditional or modern. Research shows that shelf height, display, shelf facings, and fixture placement all affect consumer attitudes and sales.

NOTES

1. Arun K. Jain and Michael Etgar, "Measuring Store Image Through Multidimensional Scaling of Free Response Date," *Journal of Retailing*, vol. 52 (Winter 1976–77), pp. 61–70.

2. Stuart U. Rich, *Shopping Behavior of Department Store Customers* (Boston: Division of Research, Graduate School of Business Administration, Harvard University, 1963).

3. Philip B. Schary, "Consumption and the Problem of Time," *Journal of Marketing,* vol. 35 (April 1971), pp. 50–55.
4. F. E. Brown, "Price Perception and Store Patronage," *Marketing and the New Science of Planning,* ed. Robert L. King (Chicago: American Marketing Assn., 1968), pp. 371–76.
5. Tanniru R. Rao, "Modeling Consumer Purchase Behavior as a Stochastic Process," *Marketing and the New Science of Planning,* ed. Robert L. King (Chicago: American Marketing Assn., 1968), p. 599.
6. Danny N. Bellenger, Earle Steinber, and Wilbur W. Stanton, "The Congruence of Store Image and Self Image," *Journal of Retailing,* vol. 52 (Spring 1976), pp. 17–32.
7. Pierre Martineau, "The Personality of the Retail Store," *Harvard Business Review,* vol. 36 (January–February 1958), pp. 47–55.
8. Burton H. Marcus, "Image Variation and the Multi-Unit Retail Establishment," *Journal of Retailing,* vol. 48 (Summer 1972), pp. 29–43.
9. Stewart A. Smith, "How Do Consumers Choose Between Brands of Durable Goods?" *Journal of Retailing,* vol. 46 (Summer 1970), pp. 18–26.
10. Ronald B. Marks, "Operationalizing the Concept of Store Image," *Journal of Retailing,* vol. 52 (Fall 1976), pp. 37–46.
11. Kent B. Monroe and Joseph P. Guiltinan, "A Path-Analytic Exploration of Retail Patronage Influences," *Journal of Consumer Research,* vol. 2 (June 1975), pp. 19–28.
12. See: Leonard L. Berry, "The Components of Department Store Image: A Theoretical and Empirical Analysis," *Journal of Retailing,* vol. 45 (Spring 1969), pp. 3–20.
13. Morris L. Mayer, Joseph Barry Mason, and Morris Gee, "A Reconceptualization of Store Classification as Related to Retail Strategy Formulation," *Journal of Retailing,* vol. 47 (Fall 1971), pp. 27–36.
14. Thomas W. Whipple and Lester A. Neidell, "Black and White Perceptions of Competing Stores," *Journal of Retailing,* vol. 47 (Winter 1971–72), pp. 5–20.
15. Acceptability should not be confused with appeal. A store may be acceptable to most people and still not appeal to everyone. We simply mean by acceptability that no taint is associated with anyone who does choose to trade in the store.
16. John H. Murphy and Kenneth A. Coney, "Comments on 'Consumer Store Images and Store Loyalties'," *Journal of Marketing,* vol. 39 (July 1975), pp. 64–66; Danny N. Bellenger, Earle Steinberg, and Wilbur W. Stanton, "The Congruence of Store Image and Self Image," *Journal of Retailing,* vol. 52 (Spring 1976), pp. 17–32.
17. William R. Davidson, Alton F. Doody, and Daniel J. Sweeney, *Retailing Management* 4th ed. (New York: The Ronald Press Co., 1975), Chap. 20.
18. Stuart U. Rich and Bernard D. Portis, "The Images of Department Stores," *Journal of Marketing,* vol. 28 (April 1964), pp. 10–15.
19. Raymond A. Marquardt, James C. Makens, and Robert G. Roe, *Retail*

Management: Satisfaction of Consumer Needs (Hinsdale, Ill.: The Dryden Press, 1975), pp. 116–21.

20. Daniel J. McLaughlin, "Consumer Reaction to Retail Food Newspaper Advertising in High and Low Income Areas," *Business Ideas & Facts*, vol. 7 (Fall 1974), pp. 21–24.
21. Robert Dietrich, "Who Shops Convenience Stores?" *Progressive Grocer*, vol. 55 (November 1976), pp. 67–71.
22. Rom J. Markin, Charles M. Lillis, and Chem L. Narayana, "Social-Psychological Significance of Store Space," *Journal of Retailing*, vol. 52 (Spring 1976), pp. 43–54.
23. Delbert J. Duncan, Charles F. Phillips, and Stanley C. Hollander, *Modern Retailing Management: Basic Concepts and Practices*, 8th ed. (Homewood, Ill.: Richard D. Irwin, Inc., 1972), Chaps. 5 & 6.
24. Ibid.
25. David B. Kronenfeld, John Kronenfeld, and Jerrold E. Kronenfeld, "Toward a Science of Design for Successful Food Service," *Institutions: Volume Feeding*, vol. 70 (June 1972), pp. 38–44.
26. Ronald C. Curhan, "Shelf Space Allocation and Profit Maximization in Mass Retailing," *Journal of Marketing*, vol. 37 (July 1973), pp. 54–60.
27. Robert A. Peterson and James W. Cagley, "The Effect of Shelf Space Upon Sales of Branded Products: An Appraisal," *Journal of Marketing Research*, vol. 10 (February 1973), pp. 103–04.
28. William R. Darden and Warren French, "Selected Personal Services: Consumer Reactions," *Journal of Retailing*, vol. 48 (Fall 1972), pp. 42–48.
29. Lee Adler and James D. Hlavacek, "The Relationship Between Price and Repair Service for Consumer Durables," *Journal of Marketing*, vol. 40 (April 1976), pp. 80–82.
30. Irving Burstiner, "Current Personnel Practices in Department Stores," *Journal of Retailing*, vol. 51 (Winter 1975–76), pp. 3–14.
31. Richard W. Olshavsky, "Customer—Salesman Interaction in Appliance Retailing," *Journal of Marketing Research*, vol. 10 (May 1973), pp. 208–12.
32. H. L. Munn and W. K. Opdyke, "Group Interviews Reveal Consumer Buying Behavior," *Journal of Retailing*, vol. 37 (Fall 1961), pp. 26–31, 56.

QUESTIONS

1. Discuss the manner in which the store can adjust the physical product for consumers. How does the store make buying convenient? How does it provide psychic satisfaction? What is the importance of these adjustments?
2. What types of factors affect the consumer's impressions of retail stores? Explain.

3. Explain how consumer location preferences and site bias affect consumer behavior. Is accessibility important?
4. What is store design? Explain the function of exterior design. Interior design. Can you give examples of how each has affected your purchase behavior?
5. Contrast the image consumers generally have of wide line sellers with that of narrow line sellers.
6. Is service important to store image? How does cost affect the image of service? How does the type of store affect the consumer's service image?
7. Explain the importance of personnel in building consumer store image.
8. Discuss the differences between customer store impressions.
9. Illustrate how location, store design and service have played a part in creating your image of a department store and a specialty store.
10. In what ways do the store and product images complement each other? Explain.

27

Effect of promotion on consumers

Why promotion is necessary

Promotion, product, and store

What promotion can accomplish

Manner of promotional influence

Principles of promotional influence

Learning principles

Principles of influence

Principles of presentation

How promotion influences consumers

Educate consumers to desired information

Make information significant to consumers

Utilize techniques that add emphasis

Specific inducements make special appeals

The use of propaganda on consumers

Customer loyalty: Payoff of consumer behavior

Brand and store switching by customers

Types of brand loyalty

Degrees of loyalty between brand types and stores

We made the point at the beginning of Part Five that business cannot leave its influence to chance. We have discussed the place of the product and store in influencing consumers. However, as important as the product and store are, each is basically a passive agent of influence taken by itself. The product and store images must be communicated to be most persuasive. This is where promotion enters the picture. Promotion turns the passive elements of product and store into persuasive communications designed to cause people to think or act in some manner favorable to the firm. Promotion, as a factor of market influence, is the subject of this chapter.

WHY PROMOTION IS NECESSARY

When left to their own impression, consumers may misinterpret information presented by the firm or may ignore the company's information. The following reasons account for most misinterpretations by consumers:

1. Failure of the consumer to perceive all the facts presented.
2. Failure of the consumer to weigh the facts properly.
3. Failure of the consumer to understand all, or part, of the information presented.
4. Failure of the consumer to understand what the firm expects.

There are several reasons why consumers may ignore the information presented by business. The business may have failed to gain the consumer's attention, convince the consumer of the soundness of the proposal, or to overcome inertia on the part of consumers.

The business gains little or nothing if it fails to get the consumer to take the desired action. Business persuasion is designed to overcome these failures by influencing consumers in a number of ways.[1] Persuasion educates the consumer to the meaning desired by the firm, emphasizes the significance of the facts presented, utilizes emotional techniques to gain desired results, and, finally, may offer specific inducements to obtain desired ends.[2] Thus promotion aids the business to obtain its goals, and benefits consumers by the information furnished.

PROMOTION, PRODUCT, AND STORE

For our purpose, promotion is defined as *any paid for communications whereby the company informs, persuades, or reminds potential customers about itself, its products, or its services.* Promotion may be mass as in media advertising or individual as in personal selling, but our definition does not include nonbusiness promotion. There is a very specific relationship between the product, store, and promotion. The product and store determine what the business is, and promotion communicates this information to consumers. All three provide consumer satisfaction, but the type of satisfaction differs. The product and store are the basis for all consumer satisfaction, since the attributes, features, and characteristics of the product and store are the means from which consumers derive pleasure. Promotion provides the necessary information, for often consumers would not know about the store's products without it.

Thus, nearly all external information about the product or store is based on advertising or personal selling, publicity, or sales promotion.[3] Said another way, the product and store are the basis for customer images, but it is up to promotion to communicate and help shape those images. How the consumer perceives the business is pretty much dependent on the promotion used by the business.

Different media are more or less effective for selling the business, dependent on the characteristics of the customer. As might be expected, media effectiveness varies with the educational level of the audience. The higher the educational level, the greater the reliance on print. The lower the educational level, the greater the reliance on radio and television. Klopper found a personal appeal more effective than radio, radio more effective than print, and TV fell somewhere between.

WHAT PROMOTION CAN ACCOMPLISH

Promotion is designed to guide consumers along a path from a state of unawareness to some action desired by the business.[4] The action desired may be the acceptance of some idea on the development of a favorable attitude; but promotion is usually designed to induce consumers to purchase the firm's products. Table 27–1 relates behavioral dimensions and the types of promotion that can be used.

Leavitt points out that the critical responses by consumers to promotion are (1) the initial discovery of the message, (2) the continual perusal of the message or the ability to hold, and (3) the comprehension of the message.[5]

Actually, a consumer may be in any one of five levels, or stages of persuasion.[6] First, there is unawareness. Consumers at this stage have not heard of the product. Second, there is awareness. The consumer may be vaguely conscious of the brand or company name, but is essentially unaware of the product itself or its benefits. Third, there is comprehension where promotion has exerted influence over the consumer to the extent that the customer is now informed about the product or company. On Table 27–1, this stage occurs between knowledge and

Table 27–1
Consumer movement toward purchase, related behavior and type of promotion

Related behavioral dimensions	*Movement toward purchase*	*Types of promotion relevant to the steps*
	PURCHASE ↑	
CONATIVE—The realm of motives. Ads stimulate or direct desires	CONVICTION ↑	Point of purchase; retail store ads; deals; "last chance" offers; price appeals; testimonials
AFFECTIVE—The realm of emotions. Ads change attitudes and feelings	PREFERENCE ↑ LIKING ↑	Competitive ads; argumentative copy; "image" ads; status, glamour appeals
COGNITIVE—The realm of thoughts. Ads provide information and facts	KNOWLEDGE ↑ AWARENESS	Announcements; descriptive copy; classified ads, slogans; singles, sky writers, teaser campaigns

Reprinted with permission from Robert J. Lavidge and Gary A. Steiner, "A Model for Predictive Measurements of Advertising Effectiveness," *Journal of Marketing,* vol. 25 (October 1961), p. 61. Published by the American Marketing Assn.

preference. The consumer is aware of features and benefits offered by the product, and he may experiment. Fourth, conviction has the characteristics of the comprehension stage plus the fact that the consumer now feels that the product is the best solution to his problem. The fifth stage is the action or purchase stage as shown on the table. At this stage, the consumer is fully persuaded and becomes an immediate consumer. Of course, it is not necessary for the individual to move through all five levels or to go through the stages in sequence. A consumer could go directly from unawareness to conviction in a case where to know the product is to be convinced.

Beliefs are based on feeling and emotions, as well as logic. Consumers acquire conviction through a logical reasoning process, but it is a process based on emotional responses to situations.[7] Even true statements are not believed if they are too far removed from the normal situation. People tend to believe what fits into their experiences, but if motivation is strong enough, they will believe what is obviously false. Furthermore, consumers tend to believe propositions that are socially reinforced—that is, what their friends believe, and what is accepted by members of their reference group. Finally, consumers believe what caters to deep psychological cravings. That is to say, individuals believe what they want to believe and what caters to basic needs.

MANNER OF PROMOTIONAL INFLUENCE

Promotion of all types affects the wants, motives, perceptions, and attitudes of consumers. Furthermore, individuals who have been affected by advertising in turn influence other individuals through reference groups.

First, although promotion does not create consumer wants, it does make consumers aware of their latent wants and modifies or reinforces present wants.[8] Advertising and personal selling continually present to customers new or modified products and services that emphasize the person's present deficiencies. Of course, it may also happen that the result of a comparison of products reinforces the consumer's preference for present products or stores.

Second, advertising and personal selling continually cause each consumer to reevaluate feelings and attitudes. For example, an individual may consider a store high priced because of a previous experience. If this store continually emphasizes its low prices and sales, the consumer may decide to give the business another chance. Examples of cases where promotion changed consumer resistance can be found in automobiles, vacuum cleaners, TV dinners, and cigarettes. Promotion may also reasure the consumer of the soundness of previous decisions.

Third, promotion affects consumer wants and attitudes by conditioning perception. Advertising and personal selling affect individual's perception of themselves, products, stores, other people, and the past and future. Of course, promotion has no magic power to cause people to perceive, or act, against their nature or wishes. For example, most women see topless attire as immodest, but find nothing wrong with miniskirts. Young men, who once perceived long hair as "sissified," now view it as acceptable. Advertisers have shown reluctance to use black models in newspaper ads because of a fear of adverse white perceptions. The evidence is that black models create greater visibility in the black community without alienating white consumers.[9]

Fourth, promotion motivates consumers to action. The fact that a consumer is in a motivated state is a culmination of influences on wants, attitudes, and perception that convince the consumer of possible satisfaction. By making the consumer aware of the consequences of not acting a negative type motivation can also result.

PRINCIPLES OF PROMOTIONAL INFLUENCE

The effect of promotion on consumer behavior has come under considerable study in recent years. Certain principles are beginning to emerge, which may be categorized as learning principles, principles of influence, and principles of presentation. These principles apply equally well to advertising and personal selling.

Learning principles

Our discussion evolves around eleven learning principles identified by Britt as being important to promotion in shaping consumer behavior.[10]

1. *Appeals that are understood are remembered better than appeals learned by rote.*
2. *Unpleasant appeals can be learned as readily as pleasant appeals.* Appeals based on fear or risk, such as the appeal of insurance, can be effective. Reminder advertising that so often grates on the nerves can also be effective, as this principle states.
3. *Appeals have more effect when made over a period of time.* The policy of repeat calls by salespersonnel and repeat advertising is sound. On a given budget, it is better to promote periodically than to depend on one big splash. There is a direct correlation between initial interest and the ability to recall material over time.
4. *Appeals to several senses are more effective than appeals made to one sense.* On this basis television rates higher than radio in its effect on consumers.
5. *Different, or unique messages are better remembered.* The message stands out in a person's mind.
6. *It is easier to recognize on appeal than to recall it.* It is this fact that makes brand such an important supplement to advertising. The advertising may get a message across that is recognized when the brand is observed in the store.
7. *Forgetting is rapid immediately after learning.* This is one reason why repeat promotion is so important.[11]
8. *Knowledge of results increases learning of a message.* It is human nature to be interested in the payoff.
9. *Repetition is more effective when related to belongingness and satisfaction.* Repetition alone is not enough to get the message across. The message must relate to the consumer in some meaningful way. Continued repetition of the same advertising may result in fewer rather than more sales.
10. *Messages are easier to learn when they do not interfere with earlier habits.* People resist changing their patterns of behavior. A sufficiently strong appeal can change the consumer, but it takes more effort.

11. *Learning a new pattern of behavior can interfere with remembering something else.* Thus, promotion may serve as a partial block on competitors once the consumer has been convinced of the soundness of your argument.

Principles of influence

Principles that relate to how the consumer is influenced by promotion may be described as follows:[12]

1. *People selectively perceive communications that are favorable or congenial to their predispositions.*
2. *General or undifferentiated appeals have less influence on the audience than appeals directed at some particular interest.* The lesson is to know your audience and appeal to it directly.
3. *Persons of high intelligence tend to be influenced more than people of low intelligence when exposed to persuasive communications that rely on logical arguments.* This is true because the higher intelligence allows the person to follow the argument and draw valid conclusions.
4. *Persons of low intelligence tend to be influenced more than people of high intelligence by communications that rely on emotion, generalizations, or false, illogical, or irrelevant arguments.*
5. *The individual responds to persuasion in accordance to personality; the more aggressive, hostile, or unsociable a person is, the less likely he or she is to be persuaded by the majority opinion.* Often these people must be appealed to individually or left to make up their own minds without influence.
6. *Group-oriented people resist communications contrary to the group standards.* These people tend to put acceptance and participation above other considerations.

Principles of presentation

Principles associated with how the promotion is presented that affect consumer attitudes are the following:

1. *Present a one-sided argument when the audience is friendly or when yours is the only position being presented, and present both sides when the opposite is true.*
2. *Strong appeals to fear are less effective than mild appeals to fear.* Strong fear appeals develop tensions in the consumer that can actually cause the person to discount the entire argument. It may have happened in the case of the Surgeon General's appeal to people to stop smoking.

3. *In persuasive communications, it is better to state the conclusion rather than allow the audience to draw its own conclusions*. The argument may be, "Why take chances?" Actually, people given identical information come to different conclusions because of selective perception and because all information is interpreted in the light of the individual's motives and desires.
4. *The more trustworthy or creditable communicators appear to be, the greater the tendency to accept their conclusions*.
5. *Communicators can affect greater change in an audience if they express some views in common with the group*. This promotes a community of interest. Besides, anyone we can agree with can't be all wrong.
6. *Since audience attention is self-selective, people tend to select for consideration the same type of communications in different media*. The things that appeal in one case are likely to appeal in another case.
7. *Individuals do not learn items in the middle of a list, such as a list of sales points, until they have learned the items that go before*.

HOW PROMOTION INFLUENCES CONSUMERS

Just as our definition indicates, promotion is designed to influence consumers by informing, reminding, or persuading them to take some action. It is our intent, at this time, to look into the matter of how promotion informs, reminds, or persuades. We also want to consider the propaganda effects of advertising and personal selling. We take up the subjects of educating consumers, making information significant, techniques of emphasis, urging to action, specific inducements, and propaganda.

Educate consumers to desired information

A primary function of any type of promotion is to inform people about the company and its products. All advertisers use this function as the justification for the existence of advertising. It is also true that most persuasion has its foundation on some type of information. Thus, nothing is more fundamental to the shaping of consumer behavior by business than information. A recent study found that brands bought frequently were nearly always those with heavy advertising. The heavily advertised brands were also the most familiar ones to the consumer.[13]

Information increases consumer knowledge, and even though the consumer is left to his or her own devices concerning what to do with the data, its mere possession is influential.[14] A consumer cannot completely ignore information, once the mind conceives of its existence. Facts also influence by pointing out logical relationships. A sign, "Joe's Diner," relates hunger, diner, and satisfaction.

The consumer is much more likely to act in a manner favorable to the firm if the message is understood. Not only must the facts presented in the message be understood, but the facts must be interpreted in the manner intended by the business. A message understood is more difficult to ignore than one that is not understood. Besides, there is greater likelihood that the consumer will agree with the firm's position when that position is made clear.

There are personal and nonpersonal means that can be used to get facts across to consumers more clearly and with less chance of misunderstanding the firm's intent.[15] There is really little excuse for the customer's not understanding the message in a person-to-person relationship, but it often happens. The salesperson can make a point as many times as necessary.

Advertising and sales promotion have one advantage over personal selling where customer education is concerned. These two sales devices can be planned in advance. Thus, clarity and precision of the written or spoken word should be an absolute minimum objective in developing an ad. In an advertisement, objections by the consumer can be anticipated to some degree.

Make information significant to consumers

It is not enough for the consumer to understand the message contained in the promotion. Influence can be greater when the consumer is made aware of the personal significance of the message.[16] That is, the consumer wants to know, "What have I got to gain from following your advice?" Significance is impressed on the individual by emphasizing the rewards from following the promoter's advice and by educating the consumer to the consequences of a failure to act. Salespeople can tell a client about the significance of various points throughout the presentation. The salesperson can also check, by questioning, to see if the points are getting across. Insurance salespeople are emphasizing the consequence of not acting when they paint the picture of a destitute family resulting from the death of the breadwinner.

The headlines and body of an advertisement are both important in explaining the significance of the information in it. Firestone's slogan, "the safe tire," tells us that the benefit of owning Firestone tires is safety and peace of mind when driving. A General Foods ad proclaims, "Now Cool Whip's worth cool cash." Here the benefit is clearly a cash savings. The headline often points to or suggests the benefit, and the body expands on the meaning. Often more than one benefit is included in an ad.

Utilize techniques that add emphasis

Various mechanical techniques can be included in promotion that add emphasis to the point made and/or appeal to the consumer's emotions. These techniques influence consumers in several ways. The techniques used can gain the consumer's attention, be used for emphasis, create a pleasant mood, gain consumer sympathy, break tension created by the sales situation, and aid in leading the consumer to take action. It is possible for a consumer to miss the message completely but to purchase the product because something about the technique employed in the presentation influenced behavior. The customer may have been influenced by the salesperson's manner. The color combinations used in an ad can be the factor causing a person to purchase. The techniques used in promotion, like the means used to educate, can be divided into personal and nonpersonal techniques.

Personal techniques that influence consumers. Some of the more important personal techniques of influence are jokes, soft sell, testimonials, choice of words, and voice inflection. The soft-sell technique is becoming increasingly important in selling. It is a technique that considers the customer's needs. The soft sell understates claims, benefits, and performance, and its use involves no high-pressure devices. Testimonials can be developed around people we admire, or envy. In recent years, the tendency has been to use fewer glamorous people in testimonials and more average people that the consumer can identify with. The choice of words is important because it is by use of language that the salesperson conveys meaning. The voice of a salesperson can do much to hold attention and make an emotional appeal to action. Everyone responds to an effective speaker.

Nonpersonal techniques. Nonpersonal techniques that affect the consumer include the following: use of color, illustrations, type, white space, and layout.[17]

Color. We were introduced earlier to the fact that color can create moods. Not everyone reacts the same way to colors, but some typical emotional responses for certain colors are as follows:

Yellow: Cheerfulness, dishonesty, youth, light, hate, cowardice, joyousness, optimism, spring, brightness.

Red: Action, life, blood, fire, heat, passion, danger, power, loyalty, bravery, anger, excitement.

Blue: Coldness, serenity, depression, melancholy, truth, purity, formality, depth, restraint.

Orange: Harvest, fall, middle life, tastiness, abundance, fire, attention, action.

Green: Immaturity, youth, spring, nature, envy, greed, jealousy, cheapness, ignorance.

Violet: Dignity, royalty, sorrow, despair, richness.

White: Cleanliness, fear, purity, sickness, virginity.

Black: Mystery, strength, mourning, heaviness.

The exact emotion created by a color depends on the person, the product, and the situation.[18] For instance, results from a limited study indicate that black on yellow, buff, or goldenrod has greater pulling power in direct mail than does black on white. Menthol cigarette makers have successfully combined green with motion pictures or still pictures of young people in a nature setting to convey the idea of cool, refreshing taste. Colors are always important in promoting food, automobiles, soft drinks, beer, and furniture.

Illustrations. The illustration helps establish the emotional atmosphere of the entire advertisement.[19] Illustrations may convey action, or serve as an emotional bond to pull the person into the ad. Action is denoted by the elements contained in the illustration, by moving pictures, or by a series of still pictures. The illustrations may be in the form of photographs, charts, drawings, or cartoons. Pictures of teenagers enjoying themselves may not only attract the attention of young people but may also provide a pleasant experience for all viewers. The illustrations may also convey such abstract concepts as prestige, beauty, and faith.

Typography. Type can be an important factor in influencing through the emotions. The type used can create interest, draw attention to important aspects of the ad, and convey emotional meaning. Generally, block type is thought to be more formal, masculine, and modern. Script is considered feminine and modern. Roman style type conveys tradition, formality, prestige, and permanence. Ornamental type may convey a variety of moods and backgrounds, historical and cultural. It is considered masculine.

White space. The use of white space is another factor having an emotional appeal for consumers.[20] White space is the blank part of an ad. It is important because it affects the proportions of the ad. An ad with more white space conveys feelings of freedom, dignity, elegance, unhurriedness, permanence, and good taste. Crowded ads tend to evoke bargain, low-class, crowded, hurried, and price-appeal types of emotions in the consumer.

Layout. Layout comprises all the elements mentioned and others.[21] Layout determines the total emotional impact of an advertisement on consumers. If anyone doubts this point, let them compare a newspaper grocery advertisement with a newspaper department store advertisement. The difference can also be seen between a service department store and a discount department store. The layout of an advertisement for television is just as important as for a newspaper or magazine.

Specific inducements make special appeals

Nothing is more important in persuading consumers than asking for the sale.[22] The urge to action usually comes at the end of the sales presentation or the end of the advertisement, but it may come anytime. There are many techniques for closing a sale. The important point for consumer influence is that some place in the presentation the consumer must be told what he or she is expected to do. Sometimes specific inducements in the form of stamps or premiums are offered to influence consumers.[23] The premium is something of value offered as a bonus or bribe to the customer for purchasing. Many customers who receive trading stamps value and save them.

In a package, premiums need no follow-up, since the bonus comes with the purchase. With self-liquidating premiums, the individual must send money and some part of the box such as the top or a coupon from the back. Stamps, tapes, box tops, and coupons are continuous premiums that are saved and cashed in some manner, usually for merchandise.

Premiums influence in several ways: (1) The consumer feels he or she gets something for nothing; (2) the desire to collect things is satisfied by premiums; (3) merchandise is obtained that would not otherwise be bought; and (4) the premium adds suspense and excitement to shopping. Influence is exerted on the shopper by other family members desiring to obtain the premium. Many premiums are directed at children, and these children pressure their parents into purchasing the product. Dry breakfast cereal is a good example.

THE USE OF PROPAGANDA ON CONSUMERS

There is some element of propaganda in nearly all advertising. Propaganda goes one step further than simple persuasion. Persuasive promotion attempts to *influence* by reasoning and the force and soundness of the argument. However, propaganda attempts to *condition* the consumer's thinking process by whatever means are available. Persuasive promotion deals with the truth, but "Propaganda, by definition, is biased, partial, and one-sided. It has an ax to grind, therefore it is always controversial. It is deliberately planned to make its readers and listeners take sides."[24]

Propaganda can be found in personal selling and advertising. Some of the techniques used by the propagandist are as follows:

1. *Name calling:* Getting consumers to reject the product or idea without a fair trial by associating it with a bad label.
2. *Testimonial:* Getting someone who is respected or hated to say the product or idea is good or bad.

3. *Card stacking:* Using facts, illustrations, logical and illogical statements presented in the best or worst possible way.
4. *Bandwagon: All* of *us* are doing it, so you should follow the crowd.[25]

Propaganda as such, is neither good nor bad; it can be used honestly or dishonestly. We can clarify this point by considering the methods of the propagandist. They are: (1) presenting one-sided arguments; (2) showing data in the best light; (3) selecting data to present; (4) using innuendo and implication; (5) modifying results; and (6) presenting false and/or untruthful information. Most people agree that there is nothing much wrong with items (1) and (2). These two methods are considered, by many, to be a part of any persuasion. The selection of data and use of innuendo cause marketers more trouble. Is an advertiser justified in reporting that 80 percent of the people tested use his product, when mainly users were tested? Bayer aspirin has been criticized for advertising that it is "the best aspirin," when there is only one kind. Shell oil has been under fire for suggesting that platformate gives better mileage than competing gasolines. Not everyone is in agreement as to the extent to which these types of propaganda are justified. Most marketers do agree that modifying results and false advertising are an improper use of propaganda.

CUSTOMER LOYALTY: PAYOFF OF CONSUMER BEHAVIOR

In a very real sense, customer loyalty is the payoff of all consumer behavior. Consumer behavior culminates in a purchase decision to which both the individual and the business are parties. When consumer behavior is successful, the normal result is that:

1. individuals obtain satisfactory products, and
2. business firms receive profit from service.

In any case, what is created is a loyal customer. The individual is as anxious to repeat the successful behavior as the store is anxious for repeat sales. Successful business operations are built on customer loy-

Figure 27–1

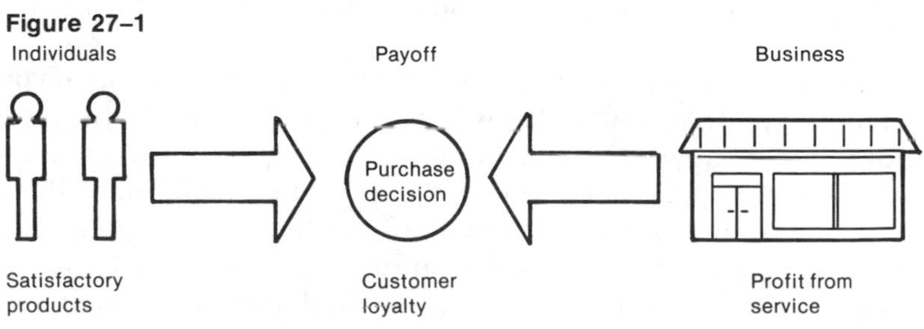

alty. Thus this discussion of customer loyalty brings the subject of consumer behavior full circle.

Consumers may be loyal to the brand, the store, or both. Consumer loyalty refers to a degree of unwillingness on the part of the consumer to switch brands or stores. Specifically, consumer loyalty is defined as:

> *the propensity of a customer to purchase the same brand or frequent the same store each time a purchase problem arises.*

Thus a customer who purchases a given product or brand eight times out of ten is more loyal than one who purchases four times out of ten. Very few, if any persons, are ever completely loyal to given products or stores.

Consumer loyalty is an important concept because it is a measure of the influence that businesses have on consumers. Loyal customers are those who have been convinced of the merit of the merchandise or the satisfaction derived from a specific enterprise. Loyalty implies that consumer experience has backed up the individual's faith in the store or product.[26] Consumer loyalty is still not fully understood. Evidence indicates that there is no particular type of personality that is more likely to be loyal. Socioeconomic factors such as age, sex, marital status, income, and occupation do not fully explain consumer loyalty. Customer loyalty appears to be oriented to individual product and store images held by consumers.

Brand and store switching by customers

Brand and store switching are as normal among consumers as loyalty.[27] Most consumers do some testing of competitive products and stores periodically, even though the consumer may remain essentially loyal to one brand or business for long periods. The principal reasons for switching are curiosity, disappointment, reassurance, chance, and inducement. Research suggests that a change in any market factor can cause consumers to re-evaluate their loyalty. This fact was demonstrated in a study of store loyalty toward an automobile dealership that was sold. The research shows different patterns of loyalty between the control group and the group that had previously favored the dealer that was sold.[28]

Curiosity is an important reason for switching. We live in a world of change, and people want to know about these changes. Consumers are curious about new products, different products, and competitive businesses, but spend more time gathering information than others.[29] A good example of switching can be found in the case of detergents and patent medicines. A substantial amount of curiosity switching is not permanent. Once curiosity has been satisfied, the consumer goes back to the favored brand. Also, consumers often switch out of disappointment. A person may be disappointed in a product that was previously considered satisfactory because the product may change. Perhaps the seller attempts to improve the product, but in the process creates a combination of features that no longer appeals to some consumers. It could be that the seller gradually allows quality standards to slip, thus alienating some consumers. The consumer may be the one to change. Individual taste and habits change over time, and this fact causes consumers to view former favored products in a new light.

It may sound odd, but many people change in order to remain the same. Consumers switch brands in order to reassure themselves that a favored product is still more satisfactory. Repeated purchasing of a brand reinforces the brand choice response. In an analysis of 600 Chicago families over a period of three years, Kuehn found that previous purchase patterns provided the foundation for predicting the probability of purchasing a particular brand on subsequent occasions.[30] Often consumers who switch for reassurance go back to their previous brands very quickly. These consumers may even select the new brand to try because they know or suspect in advance that it will prove unsatisfactory.

Brand switching may be the result of chance. The consumer tries a new brand at a neighbor's house, in a restaurant, or at a family party. It may be that the consumer was forced to try the new brand because the favored brand was not conveniently available. Switching from chance may, or may not, be permanent. The decision probably depends on the strength of the previous habit and the satisfaction found in the new brand.

Consumers switch products or stores because of inducement. This is one purpose of all promotion. Essentially, various competitive inducements can put doubt in the consumer's mind about previous product or store decisions.

Types of brand loyalty

The degree of loyalty exhibited by consumers differs among brands in part because of personal differences and differences in perception among consumers. A person who buys Arrow shirts 80 percent of the time is more loyal than a person who purchases Arrow shirts 60 percent of the time. In either case, if the majority of Arrow shirt buyers purchase this brand over 50 percent of the time, we can say that Arrow shirts have loyal customers. However, a more definitive identification of brand loyalty is desirable because it aids us in recognizing variations that exist among products.

Brand recognition. The consumers who are merely able to recognize brands are in the least loyal classification. While these consumers at least remember having heard or observed a brand name, they feel no particular devotion to the product. The consumer may purchase the product if other products in the market are even less recognized. If other products attract greater loyalty, the product will lose more sales than it gains.

Brand preference. A state of brand preference exists where the consumer has a definite bias toward the product, given a choice, but will accept a substitute before doing without the goods. This is the state of brand loyalty where many consumers purchase from habit and experience. The seller has an advantage so long as the product is generally available.

Brand insistence. Brand insistence is a loyalty state where the consumer will go without the good before accepting a substitute. A case of complete brand insistence is seldom found. There is usually some periodic brand switching, even by the most loyal customers. Where brand insistence does exist, consumers will go to considerable trouble to obtain the desired brand.

Degrees of loyalty between brand types and stores

Different brands of the same type product are able to command different degrees of loyalty.[31] Let's say that brands X and Y are types of soft drinks, and a majority of people who buy brand X are 70 percent loyal but a majority of people who purchase brand Y are only 55 percent loyal. It is clear that brand X has more loyal customers than brand Y. The same reasoning applies to different product types. We would expect different loyalty patterns to exist between chewing gum and vacuum cleaners or between vacuum cleaners and perfume.

The types of store loyalty parallel the types of brand loyalty. Consumers display store recognition, store preference, and store insistence tendencies.[32] The difference is that a given store may mean several things to the same consumer, who may be loyal to a store for all its products or for only one of its products. A person may buy clothes from a favorite department store and purchase shoes from a preferred specialty store. It is also true that a customer may display store insistence for one type of product but store preference for another type of product handled by the same store. The reader should recognize that there is considerable interdependence between product and store loyalty.

The discussion of customer loyalty brings to a close our presentation of consumer behavior. We began with an explanation of the consumer purchase decision, and we end with an individual who has successfully solved a problem. Of course, consumer behavior doesn't end there. Every loyal customer will, sooner or later, begin to question that loyalty. Furthermore, the loyal customer of one business is fair game for another. Attempts are continually being made to change the consumer's loyalty.

NOTES

1. Harper W. Boyd, Jr., Michael L. Ray, and Edward C. Strong, "An Attitudinal Framework for Advertising Strategy," *Journal of Marketing,* vol. 36 (April 1972), pp. 27–33.
2. Our purpose is to demonstrate how promotion influences, and not to discuss techniques of either advertising or personal selling. A thorough discussion of techniques can be found in the following: C. H. Sandage and Vernon Fryburger, *Advertising Theory and Practice,* 9th ed. (Homewood, Ill.: Richard D. Irwin, Inc., 1975); S. Watson Dunn and Arnold M. Barban, *Advertising: Its Role in Modern Marketing,* 3d ed. (Hinsdale, Ill.: The Dryden Press, 1974); David L. Kurtz, H. Robert Dodge, and Jay E. Klompmaker, *Professional Selling,* (Dallas, Texas: Business Publications, Inc., 1976).
3. Sidney J. Levy, *Promotional Behavior* (Glenview, Ill.: Scott, Foresman & Co., 1971); David L. Kurtz and Charles W. Hubbard, eds., *The Sales Function and Its Management* (Morristown, N.J.: General Learning Press, 1971).
4. Rachel Dardis and Clarita Anderson, "Newspaper Ads and Planned Purchases," *Journal of Advertising Research,* vol. 12 (June 1972), pp. 21–24; Patrick Dunne, "Some Demographic Characteristics of Direct Mail Purchasers," *Baylor Business Studies,* no. 104 (May, June, July 1975), pp. 67–72.
5. Edward M. Tauber, "Reduce New Product Failures: Measure Needs as Well as Purchase Interest," *Journal of Marketing,* vol. 37 (July 1973), pp. 61–70.
6. Terrence O'Brien, "Stages of Consumer Decision Making," *Journal of Marketing Research,* vol. 8 (August 1971), pp. 283–89; Fred D. Reynolds, "Problem Solving and Trial Use in the Adoption Process," *Journal of Marketing Research,* vol. 8 (February 1971), pp. 100–02.
7. Bent Stidsen, "Some Thoughts on the Advertising Process," *Journal of Marketing,* vol. 34 (January 1970), pp. 47–54.
8. Andrew S. C. Ehrenberg, "Repetitive Advertising and the Consumer," *Journal of Advertising Research,* vol. 14 (April 1974), pp. 25–33.
9. B. Stuart Tolley and John J. Goett, "Reactions to Blacks in Newspaper Ads," *Journal of Advertising Research,* vol. 11 (April 1971), pp. 11–16.
10. Steuart Henderson Britt, "How Advertising Can Use Psychology's Rules of Learning," *Printers' Ink,* vol. 252 (September 23, 1955), pp. 74, 77, 80.
11. Peter D. Bennett and Harold H. Kassarjian, *Consumer Behavior* (Englewood Cliffs, N.J.: Prentice-Hall, Inc., 1972), pp. 38–39.
12. James H. Myers and William H. Reynolds, *Consumer Behavior and Marketing Management* (Boston: Houghton Mifflin Co., 1967), pp. 267–98.
13. Leo Bogart and Charles Lehman, "What Makes a Brand Name Familiar?" *Journal of Marketing Research,* vol. 10 (February 1973), pp. 17–22.
14. Dennis H. Gensch, "Media Factors: A Review Article," *Journal of Marketing Research,* vol. 7 (May 1970), pp. 216–35.
15. A division by oral and written was not possible because advertising may

be written or oral, and this fact is also true, to some extent for personal selling, as when posters, charts, and other written material are used. The reader should be aware that some points made about a personal selling also apply to an oral advertisement.

16. Stanley E. Cohen, "Ads a 'Weak Signal' in Most Buying Decisions: Howard," *Advertising Age,* (June 1972).
17. These techniques can be used with equal effectiveness in newspapers, magazines, television, and billboards. Radio has some limitations in that none of the devices depending on sight can be utilized.
18. Sandage and Fryburger, *Advertising Theory and Practice,* pp. 344–50.
19. Dunn and Barban, *Advertising: Its Role in Modern Marketing,* p. 365.
20. Ibid., pp. 387–88.
21. Sandage and Fryburger, *Advertising Theory and Practice,* Chap. 17.
22. Charles A. Kirkpatrick, *Salesmanship,* 5th ed. (Cincinnati: South-Western Publishing Co., 1971), Chap. 17.
23. Ibid., pp. 100–01.
24. Edmund D. McGarry, "The Propaganda Function in Marketing," *Journal of Marketing,* vol. 23 (October 1958), pp. 131–39.
25. Alfred M. Lee and Elizabeth B. Lee, *The Fine Art of Propaganda* (New York: Harcourt, Brace, & Co., 1939), pp. 22–24.
26. P. Charlton and A. S. C. Ehrenberg, "An Experiment in Brand Choice." *Journal of Marketing Research,* vol. 13 (May 1976), pp. 152–60.
27. William A. Chance and Norman D. French, "An Exploratory Investigation of Brand Switching," *Journal of Marketing Research,* vol. 9 (May 1972), pp. 226–29.
28. Richard D. Nordstrom and John E. Swan, "Does a Change in Customer Loyalty Occur When a New Car Agency is Sold?" *Journal of Marketing,* vol. 13 (May 1976), pp. 173–77.
29. Ben Enis and Gordon W. Paul, "Store Loyalty: Characteristics of Shoppers and Switchers," *Southern Journal of Business* (July 1968), pp. 266–76.
30. Alfred A. Kuehn, "Consumer Brand Choice as a Learning Process," *Journal of Advertising Research,* vol. 2 (December, 1962), pp. 10–17.
31. Jacob Jacoby and David B. Kyner, "Brand Loyalty vs. Repeat Purchasing Behavior," *Journal of Marketing Research,* vol. 10 (February 1973), pp. 1–9.
32. Kenward L. Atkins, "Advertising and Store Patronage," *Journal of Advertising Research,* vol. 2 (December 1966), pp. 18–23.

QUESTIONS

1. What is promotion? What are the different types of promotion that affect consumers?
2. Discuss the relationship between promotion, product and store? Give examples of how the three operate together.

3. What are the steps in the buying process? Discuss the types of promotion that apply generally to each step.
4. Explain and provide examples from your own experience of how promotion influences consumers.
5. Discuss the learning principles of promotion.
6. Discuss the principles of influence.
7. Discuss the principles of presentation. Can you determine any relationship beween these principles? Can you give examples of how each affects consumer behavior?
8. How does promotion educate consumers? How does promotion make information significant? How does promotion add emphasis to information? Illustrate personal and nonpersonal techniques of emphasis.
9. What is customer loyalty? Why do customers switch bands? Explain and illustrate the types of brand loyalty.
10. Discuss the degrees of loyalty between brand types.

Indexes

Name index

A

B

C

M

N

T

U

V

W

Y

Z

Subject index

N

O

V

W

Y–Z

This book has been set in 10 and 9 point Caledonia, leaded 2 points. Part number and title and chapter title are 18 point Helvetica Semi-Bold, and chapter numbers are 48 point Caslon #540. The size of the type page is 27 by 45½ picas.